THE CHURCH OF ENGLAND IN THE TWENTIETH CENTURY

THE CHURCH COMMISSIONERS AND THE POLITICS OF REFORM 1948–1998

THE CHURCH OF ENGLAND IN THE TWENTIETH CENTURY

THE CHURCH COMMISSIONERS AND THE POLITICS OF REFORM 1948–1998

Andrew Chandler

THE BOYDELL PRESS

First published 2006
The Boydell Press, Woodbridge

ISBN 1 84383 165 1

The Boydell Press is an imprint of Boydell & Brewer Ltd
PO Box 9, Woodbridge, Suffolk IP12 3DF, UK
and of Boydell & Brewer Inc.
668 Mt Hope Avenue, Rochester, NY 14620, USA
website: www.boydellandbrewer.com

A catalogue record of this publication is available
from the British Library

This publication is printed on acid-free paper

Printed and bound in England by
Antony Rowe Ltd, Chippenham, Wiltshire

Contents

PART IV
THE INFLATIONARY SPIRAL AND THE NEW WISDOM:
THE PRIMACY OF ARCHBISHOP RUNCIE, 1979–1991

PART V
THE AGE OF DOUBT:
THE PRIMACY OF ARCHBISHOP CAREY, 1991–1998

There is a prosperity that a man findeth in misfortunes; and there is a gain that turneth to loss. There is a gift that shall not profit thee; and there is a gift whose recompense is double. There is an abasement because of glory; and there is that hath lifted up his head from a low estate. There is that buyeth much for a little, and payeth for it again sevenfold: *The Book of Ecclesiasticus xx*

Riches are for spending; And Spending for Honour and good Actions. Therefore Extraordinary Expence must be limited by the Worth of the Occasion: For Voluntary Undoing, may be aswell for a Mans Country, as for the Kingdome of Heaven. But Ordinary Expence ought to be limited by a Mans Estate; And governed with such regard, as it be within his Compasse: Francis Bacon, *Essayes or counsels civill and morall, 28: 'of Expence'*

For Eric and Janet Chandler
with a son's love and gratitude

Acknowledgements

The writing of a book incurs a great many debts, and a large book may well summon upon something of an army in its preliminary statement of acknowledgements. I am grateful to his Grace, archbishop Carey, for inviting me to attempt such a work and to Professor Owen Chadwick. This book rests upon the documents housed in the Church Commissioners' own archive and in Lambeth Palace Library and I am most grateful to the staff of both institutions for their generosity and kindness, particularly to Ed Pinsent for his great organisation of the materials in his care. While I have resisted the temptation to discuss the work of the Church Commissioners with many of its past and present officers, I am most grateful to those who have assisted me with particular enquiries and materials, including Patrick Locke CBE, Sir John Herbecq, Dame Betty Ridley, Howell Harris Hughes, Maureen Webb, Philip James and the Venerable Derek Hayward. I have also enjoyed the particular insights of David Hopkinson. I hope that many others will forgive me if I have seemed too intent on the archives to turn to them, much as I would, in so many ways, have liked to do so. I have discussed the book with many friends in academic life, and I should particularly wish to mention the kindness of Professor W. R. Ward, Professor David Jeremy, Professor Hugh McLeod and Dr Michael Snape. Any errors remaining are, of course, my own.

While working at 1 Millbank I was happily ensconced in the office of the Second Church Estates Commissioner, Stuart Bell, and I remain most grateful to the staff thereabouts, particularly to Maureen Webb, who has guided me in so many ways most generously, and to Bobbie Doerr and Julia Ward, who made me feel so welcome and so kindly helped a rather wayward presence through a working day there. I am also most grateful to Sue Jones, Stephen York and Michael Webster, who have saved me from many slips. My London jaunts have been made all the more agreeable by the generous hospitality of my aunt, Doreen Chandler, and of the Hon. Anne Lamb, widow of the former secretary to the Church Commissioners, Kenneth Lamb.

A book is written within a particular personal environment and during the last five years I have been fortunate in the company of the Fellows and Scholars of the George Bell Institute and that of the staff and students at the Queen's Foundation in Birmingham. I am particularly grateful to the librarians at the Foundation, Sheila Russell and Michael Gale. Meanwhile, the writer of any book owes much to the kindness and patience of friends and allies who have listened patiently to his or her developing reflections on the subject: I owe particular thanks to the Rt Revd Graham James, the Rt Revd John Austin, Melanie Barber, Andrew McCloskey and Eric Adams. Christine Linehan has been a splendidly wise, patient and sensitive copy-editor. Gary Windon has both listened to the ideas at work in the enterprise and turned the whole thing into what the publishing world now calls camera-ready-copy, I hardly have words with which to thank him adequately for all his great efforts. My wife, Fiona, has assumed a greater than usual domestic burden in my times of absence from Birmingham, and to her and to our two sons, Joel and Reuben, I also owe most of all – not least for teaching me so richly that even the government and finances of the Church of England should be held within a different kind of perspective.

Andrew Chandler

Abbreviations

AC	Assets Committee
ACUPA	Archbishops' Commission on Urban Priority Areas
CA	Church Assembly
CC	Church Commissioners
CEDIC	Church Estates Development and Improvement Company
CEIG	Christian Ethical Investment Group
CIO	Church Information Office
CSA	Central Stipends Authority
EFC	Estates and Finance Committee
EIWG	Ethical Investments Working Group
ELTSA	End Loans to South Africa
GPC	General Purposes Committee
GS	General Synod
HC	Houses Committee
ICC	Investment Co-ordination Committee
NAO	National Audit Office
PC	Pastoral Committee
RCC	Redundant Churches Committee

UPA   Urban Priority Area

WCC   World Council of Churches

Note on the Text

Unless otherwise stated all references to source material in the footnotes are to material held at the Church of England Record Centre, Bermondsey, London.

Introduction

The history of the Church of England in the twentieth century is a task barely begun by scholars. At the beginning of the twenty-first century the landscape of scholarship is indeed a somewhat odd one. On the one hand there have been careful forays into local realities in pursuit of 'secularisation', and a growing number of excellent studies of cathedrals. On the other there have been biographies and general surveys, often eloquent but resting insecurely on a rather narrow seam of already published material. Much is owed to historians like Owen Chadwick, Adrian Hastings and Alan Wilkinson, who have launched valuable ships onto an ocean which is still largely uncharted. Archbishops of Canterbury and York appear in a succession of biographies; some bishops too. There has been a good deal of journalism, most of it lively, some of it impressive. This haphazard situation will not be easy to remedy because the twentieth-century Church itself has bequeathed what is, at best, an irregular and unpredictable assortment of archival riches. There are the considerations of Convocation and of synodical government, to be sure, and a continuous church press. There are also the collected papers of the archbishops of Canterbury. But there are few collections of bishops' papers, and the dioceses have organised their administrative materials in many different ways. Seldom are parish leaflets preserved in the local record offices. Beside that, there is a colossal mountain of published primary material, theological, philosophical, ethical, under which sag the accommodating shelves of the SPCK bookshops of the nation.

In this general picture the work of the Church Commissioners has suffered a particularly ignominious fate. In his immense biography of archbishop Geoffrey Fisher, Edward Carpenter granted them only eight brief references; in his adroit study of archbishop Michael Ramsey, Owen Chadwick offered only three wry glimpses. None of the biographies of archbishop Robert Runcie say much about them: they intrude as a brief calamity, not as an ongoing dimension of the story. The autobiography of archbishop George Carey, meanwhile, looks at them more directly, but only as a precipitating factor in another tale. This reflects the fact that in the Church of England as a whole the Church Commissioners have rarely enjoyed much intelligent attention. Why? Perhaps it has been more enticing to talk of theology than practicalities, and of campaigns than structures. The remote, even slightly haughty, enterprises of church bureaucrats may well simply pass through the mind as a dull dimension of a livelier reality.

Yet the bulging archives of the Church Commissioners, presently in their unprepossessing home in Bermondsey, establish clearly how intricate and immense the responsibilities of the Commissioners were within the Church of England in the second half of the twentieth century, and to what extent they actually defined its patterns of activity and development. Here is a unique and essential key to the history of the Church. For the Commissioners and their agents and officers were utterly enmeshed in almost every aspect of its life and work, across the benefices, dioceses and provinces of the country. Their immersion was declared in the very property and revenues which had come to them from their august parents, the Ecclesiastical Commissioners and Queen Anne's Bounty; in benefices which were seen to merit amalgamation and whose boundaries needed adjustment; in churches which had faltered and were now confronting closure; in empty churches which faced conversion into other uses. Then again, clergy of all kinds must be paid stipends to keep them, as it was always pronounced, 'from want'; they must be paid pensions and housed satisfactorily. It was the Church Commissioners who not only produced grants and loans but also orchestrated the work of the forty-three dioceses in the payment of stipends, pensions and parsonage improvements; who saw to the expenses of the bishops and the furnishing and maintenance of their houses. Across the Church of England the Commissioners became the engine of uniformity and improvement in all these matters, as well as in the stipends and accommodation of the cathedral clergy and in the support of the cathedral buildings themselves. And even upon this there follows a succession of sundry other duties: financing chaplaincies, making contributions to chancel repairs, stoking up assorted foundations. The agenda of a Board meeting of the governors of the Church Commissioners in, say, the first decade of their history will take the reader from questions of national financial policy in one item to those of parochial life in the next. And it is in the papers prepared for these monthly meetings that one sees the Church of England as a whole in a state of steady, deliberate movement in all these parallel spheres at one particular moment. It is not easy to condense the workings of this prodigious administrative enterprise into a single sequential story. The history of the Commissioners sprawls, as does the history of the Church of England itself, across a jumbled accumulation of activities in many different spheres and at many different levels. Even where the Commissioners did not assume a new responsibility, they were integral to the discussions which established the new arrangements, bringing their influence to bear whenever invited – and they usually were, often because they were in some sense or other already involved. An historical study must place a subject within a context and show a contribution to the development of that wider picture. Yet when one confronts the history of the Church Commissioners, the clear perspectives of subject and context immediately blur into each other.

All of this demonstrates not simply the ubiquity of the Commissioners, but the need in the life of any Church for money, even in affairs which might appear to be governed only by the higher calls of theology or conscience. For when clergy threatened to resign over the ordination of women they expected to be compensated – and who should pay but the Commissioners? When the preface to *Crockford's directory* provoked controversy for complaining about an archbishop, as happened in 1986, who turned out to be its joint publishers but the General Synod and the Commissioners? One responsibility could be seen to bring others in its train and it became harder to draw lines between them: once the Church Commissioners had undertaken to pay bishops it appeared natural to pay for the suffragans. Once they paid for stipends it was natural to pay for pensions. Once they had pledged themselves to support parsonages it was natural that they should build new ones. Once they embraced pensions it was sensible to pay for retirement homes. Only a successful financial policy could make such things possible. Until 1989 that is exactly what the Church Commissioners appeared to have. Whether or not they exercised their discretionary powers effectively on behalf of their legal trusts and their financial resources must be one of the fundamental questions of this book.

What follows is, then, a story of the making, organising and spending of money, all in the name of the mission of the Church. Narrative histories are not much in fashion these days. Institutional histories certainly are not. This may be regretted, not least because life itself is experienced as a narrative, and most of us live and work in the context of institutions, often ones which we barely understand. In what follows I have sought to fashion a narrative which articulates an over-arching argument about this distinctive institution and its place in the Church it sought, often laboriously, even thanklessly, to serve. The *raison d'etre* of the Church Commissioners, a body which came to life in the context of the great Labour governments of 1945–51 and the new primacy of archbishop Fisher, was as a pragmatic liberal bureaucracy which existed not merely to maintain arrangements but actively to reform them. In this it was a characteristic twentieth-century British corporation. The special task of the Commissioners was to act as a force for improvement, confronting the ancient inequalities of the

Church with formulas devised by the administrative mind, fashioned by all the techniques and resources at its disposal and capable of carrying the support of the relevant political powers of the Church at large. What came to be widely regarded as their successes arose in the pursuit of this logic. Ultimately the judgement on their failures was pronounced by a new work of reform and improvement to which they themselves were attached in a new, over-arching authority.

It seems almost unarguable that without three bold decisions taken by the Church Commissioners the Church of England itself could not have become anything like the recognisable, self-respecting institution of the later twentieth century. These three decisions were to sell government bonds and to venture on to the Stock Exchange, a move which placed the Commissioners in the vanguard of the new, post-war financial policies of other public institutions; to reorganise the scattered properties held by the Commissioners in trust for the Church; and to combine this extraordinary wealth in property with a policy of development, in partnership with other companies suitably endowed with the necessary skills. Without these decisions, all taken quietly, without melodrama or much public attention, it is difficult to see how the Church of England could have built in these years an adequate system to provide for the income of its clergy and the 'cure of souls' across the parishes. For much as the powers of the dioceses prospered in these years, the Church as a whole possessed no other body with the financial power and administrative acumen to attack the inequalities of pay and conditions which abounded, or the resources to provide what British society was beginning to regard as a credible system of pensions. In such a way did the Church of England achieve, for a time, a more realistic relationship with its own inherited wealth. When the fortunes of the Commissioners appeared to crumble, dramatically, in the 1990s it could be seen just how fundamental a role they had assumed in the life of the Church. Even if, by that time, the dioceses saw themselves as the crucial providers of administration and finance, it was the Church Commissioners who had ensured that their ascendancy had been combined with a viable, coherent development of a national policy – and who still paid large sums to make that independence meaningful and effective.

Much of the money that the Commissioners spent fell into categories which lay – evidently – beyond dispute, for they were substantially governed by a trinity of trusts: to fund the clergy stipend, the clergy pension and the parsonage house. But another key to their fortunes lay in the discretionary power which they exercised over their 'General Fund'. The act by which the Ecclesiastical Commissioners became a permanent power in 1840 included Article 67 which charged them to apply this fund to 'the cure of souls' in a manner most conducive to the 'efficiency of the national Church'. The very phrase was a curious dialogue between two different, and rather distant, worlds: the 'cure of souls' can be traced back to an ancient source, deriving from the Fourth Lateran Council of 1215; the 'efficiency of the national Church', meanwhile, was something very characteristic of the reforming convictions of the British mid-nineteenth century. But what now did the cure of souls actually mean? And how could the efficiency of the national Church best be served? Over a period of fifty years this was not simply a dry administrative debate about powers and objects. It became the very index by which the condition and performance of the Church Commissioners could be measured. In an age of confidence the General Fund was exploited as the exchequer of bold improvement. In an age of doubt policies retreated to the indisputable bastions of Anglican life, back to the undisputed trinity itself. When controversy broke out it was often because it was feared that the Commissioners were in danger of exceeding their powers as they were properly understood. And yet it was exactly when they concentrated their efforts most intently within their undisputable spheres of activity that they descended into crisis.

The work of the Church Commissioners certainly involved a mass of detail and design. It is this very quality of intricacy and measured movement that the historian must accept and take seriously if their world is to be understood. It is through analysing the detail that a more sober and reasonable understanding may be reached of what it actually was to be part of the Church of England in the second half of the twentieth century. There can be found bishops shuffling with embarrassment over their stipends, or defending or deploring the inconveniences of their ancient houses; clergy agitating over their parsonages or differentials in their pensions; congregations in revolt against the closure or sale of their churches or the re-naming of their benefices; clergy relating to laity, bishops to clergy, and both of them to the bureaucrats, always laity, on whose expertise they were coming more and more to rely. All of this was played out within a greater continent of society and politics, a further dimension involving other authorities, priorities and institutions. The causes of change are so often found to be exceedingly small and deliberate; they are immensely hard to direct. It is when people understand this that they build enduring and successful institutions. It is when they pretend otherwise that institutional disasters occur.

This book is based especially upon the archives of two archbishops of Canterbury, Geoffrey Fisher and Michael Ramsey. Later collections are not as yet available to the scholar, but it is not likely that they offer very much, beyond the rigmaroles of appointments, for no archbishop took as great an interest in the Commissioners' work as Fisher. Then there are the proceedings of the Church Assembly and its successor, the General Synod. The function of these bodies was to legislate, but their debates also give a flavour of committed Anglican opinion. None of these collections carry us nearly so far as the material in the Commissioners' own archives. But they do offer points of reference, and at times they are valuable ones, not least in showing how the Church Commissioners had to attach themselves to other authorities in order to justify themselves. The affairs of the last decade in this history remain a lively aspect of the present and it may well surprise that the oral testimony of those who themselves participated in events is seldom used. It is no easy task to write history after so brief an interval, and it was felt that the archive sustained an essentially independent navigation of what remains a complicated map. There is no doubt that at various times in the history of the Commissioners participants have perceived, and judged, the frailty of the formal record. Where questions lingered they have been pursued elsewhere, carefully.

The book is organised by each successive primacy. As the archbishops had increasingly little to do with the life and work of the Commissioners this might well appear a questionable structure. Yet each of the five archbishops seemed to coincide with, and now and then even to symbolise, a distinctive climate and temper. Fisher saw in the Commissioners the engine which would drive the Church of England towards modernity; Ramsey blanched at its rather conspicuous cultivation of wealth and showed his dislike of corporate authorities (or at least secular ones); Coggan coincided with a period which saw a pursuit of improved living standards in an age of increasing inflation and economic uncertainty; Runcie with the Thatcher governments, the escalation of the Church's demands for improvement and the unfolding of a new financial policy; Carey picked up the pieces left by the Runcie period and brought the Commissioners, and the Church as a whole, to a dramatic new configuration of authorities.

1

The Foundations of an Institution

Westminster

The tidy little streets which lie at the heart of Westminster, to the west side of the abbey and parliament, running near to the bank of the Thames and along almost to Vauxhall bridge, are something of a world in themselves. They offer a glimpse of another dimension and another age, for in character they remain quietly domestic and undemonstrative and windows and doors look upon each other with a satisfactory intimacy, innocent, perhaps, of the possibility of intrusion. One house bears a plaque blessing those who pass by.

This neighbourhood was not at all a salubrious one in the nineteenth century. Here boot-makers, undertakers, various small businesses and shops were busily at work in a noisy, Cruikshankian bustle. But blue plaques now testify to the new fortunes of the area in the twentieth century and commemorate those whom the world might still know, a curious assortment. Here, in Cowley Street, Lord Reith lived when running the BBC; the writer Compton Mackenzie worked from his home in Lord North Street; around the corner in Barton Street lived, briefly, T. E. Lawrence, though he then called himself J. H. Ross. If this is still recognisably the world of the early eighteenth century, it is overlaid with others and they make a firm claim of their own. For here are the homes of venerable institutions: the political parties which govern from across the road; the Church of England, its bastion of synodical government, Church House, asserting itself rather dourly from Great Smith Street and glowering across Dean's Yard, and its greatest abbey towering over every corner; and Westminster School, one of the principal nurseries of the British 'establishment'.[1]

The quiet scale of the little streets is disrupted by further grandeur: St John's in Smith Square, whose purpose might be to subdue for it is a colossal and imposing statement; then, looking towards the Thames,

---

[1] See Stephen Hicks's splendid portrait *Around 1 Millbank: a history of the area,* London 1998.

a long terrace of the higher, grander buildings of Millbank, the first of
which settles in a conspicuous pile of red brick, high windows, many
floors and ornamentation, on the corner of one street and the main
thoroughfare. This is the home of the Church Commissioners and, in
fact, it was the building of this site which initiated the modern fortunes
of an area until then seen as ordinary, to say the least. And throughout
this small quarter is a scattering of offices, for lawyers and for business
and for the institutions of politics, religion and education. St Edward's
House, the austere home of an Anglican order, almost goes out of its
way to discourage further examination. At Number 3 Dean's Yard
could once be found Bounty House, the home of Queen Anne's
Bounty. Nearby, Mary Sumner House announces the headquarters of
the Mothers' Union. There are shops, too, in which the interests of
institutional existence and commerce coincide respectfully: the facade
of Wippells to this day maintains an august appearance, very Victorian
indeed. Here clergy buy vestments and their various necessities and, it
seems, huge menacing lecterns too. The bookshop at Faith House
stands only a stone's throw from the bookshop of Church House.

It is often said that the essential, defining reality of the Church of
England is to be found in an ordinary parish, perhaps in the centre of a
great city, a small town, a remote village. But what emerges clearly
from a traipse around these streets is a sense of the new self-
confidence which the world of national authority found, and built for
itself, in the early twentieth century.

Queen Anne's Bounty and the Ecclesiastical Commissioners

At the turn of the twentieth century the nationwide functions of the
Church of England were undergirded by two bodies, Queen Anne's
Bounty and the Ecclesiastical Commissioners. The Bounty made the
grander, or at least deeper, claim to history, for it had been founded in
1704 to receive the first fruits and tenths of land confiscated over two
centuries before by Henry VIII, for the express purpose of sustaining
poor clergy. It was a charity which gave grants to poorer benefices,
loans and disbursements for repair of clergy houses. At the beginning
of the new century it occupied offices in Dean's Yard, had a modest
staff and a handsome, though not imposing, account at Coutt's Bank.
Its trustees were already aware that the Bounty, for all its continuing
good works, was looking very like a noble relic in a Church which was
expanding, becoming more centralised, more professional. The very
name suggested an historical exhibit. Yet the Bounty did not continue
to exist by accident; it had its uses and its defenders and it commanded
the loyalties of people who viewed it with committed affection and

gave their time to it. The politics of institutional self-interest breathed through the Bounty still.

The Board of the Bounty expressed an early eighteenth-century logic, though its character and works had been adapted by an act of parliament in 1838 and by the Welsh Church Act in 1914. It comprised the two archbishops, the forty diocesan bishops, all the deans of the English cathedrals, the Speaker of the House of Commons, the Master of the Rolls, the privy councillors, the attorney-general, the solicitor-general, the lords-lieutenant of the counties of England and Wales, the chancellors and vice-chancellors of the universities of Oxford and Cambridge, the lord mayor and aldermen of the City of London, the lord mayor of York and all the mayors of the cities, the clerks in ordinary of the privy council, the King's Counsel and private benefactors as and when elected by the governors themselves. This, then, was by constitution not merely a church body: it was an argument, an instrument, of Church and State. By the dawning of the twentieth century the reality of it was a good deal less imposing than the theory. Certain offices had disappeared from the original list altogether. It had a Finance Committee and a Parsonages Committee. They met occasionally. The burden of daily business lay on the shoulders of the secretary, and treasurer and chairman of the Bounty committees.[2]

For their part, the Ecclesiastical Commissioners had been constituted as a corporation by an act of parliament in 1836 and then in 1840 and 1850. The Commissioners were charged with the management of the Church's existing estates and revenues, given the power to acquire more and to alter and redistribute ecclesiastical revenues. The Commissioners had no less of a fine constitution than the Bounty, and it pronounced much the same argument about the union of Church and State. There were ninety-five Commissioners, and the list, if tortuous, was significant for the calculations and choices which it displayed. It included the two archbishops, forty bishops, three deans (of Westminster, Canterbury and St Paul's), the Lord Chancellor, the Lord President of the Council, the First Lord of the Treasury, the Chancellor of the Exchequer, a secretary of state, the Lord Chief Justice, the Master of the Rolls, nine laymen, seven of them appointed by the crown and two by the archbishop, and three Church Estates Commissioners, two appointed by the crown and one by the archbishop of Canterbury. The three Church Estates Commissioners acted as treasurers. The secretary was responsible for the establishment as a whole. The administrative structure of the Ecclesiastical

[2] See Alan Savidge, *The foundations and early years of Queen Anne's Bounty*, London 1955, esp. pp. 26–30, 52–70.

Commissioners was more elaborate than that of its near neighbour in Dean's Yard.

On paper, none could doubt that of the two the Ecclesiastical Commissioners were the greater power. Their offices were also impressive, speaking clearly of more recent fortunes and a newer claim to eminence. The Millbank site had been acquired by the Ecclesiastical Commissioners from Westminster Abbey in 1869. In 1898 the London County Council began to redevelop the area, and from this the Commissioners took their cue, rebuilding Millbank and moving from offices in Whitehall Place to a new building, planned and built with room for expansion, their eyes already turned towards amalgamation with the Bounty. Strikingly, whereas the abbey had been built on rock, Millbank was built on sand. The new building was the work of the Commissioners' own architect, W. D. Caröe, who brought to the task a combination of the Franco-Flemish renaissance and what he had recently glimpsed himself on a visit to Barcelona. The front, facing the Thames, was decorative and suited the new facades of the London County Council's own Victoria Embankment extension scheme. The back conformed to the simpler brick of Great College Street, although there could be no denying the grandeur of the scale. The interior was equally grandiose but not, in contemporary eyes, elaborate. It took three years to build, had a steel frame to ensure against fire, speaking tubes and air-conditioning. On 21 and 22 September 1903 400,000 deeds and 80,000 files were moved inside, many with their shelves. Two days later the establishment was officially opened. Meanwhile, to a scattering of nearby addresses in Little College Street went the Commissioners' agents Cluttons and Smiths, Gore, Ingrams and Norton and their solicitors, Milles, Jennings, White and Foster.[3]

Perhaps this new site constituted the first of the many property developments for which the Church Commissioners would, at the end of the twentieth century, become widely known. According to those terms it was certainly a wise one. If the value of Millbank soared with the passing of each decade, time also changed perspectives and judgements on 1 Millbank itself. In the mid-1960s a senior member of the Church Assembly, invited to write a pamphlet on the Church Commissioners for a progressive Anglican journal, offered a more quizzical perspective, and in language that would presumably not have occurred to its architect and its founders. Number 1 now appeared 'unspectacular … a respectable, sober-faced building with dingy marble floors and worn staircases. The place', she wrote, 'is solid, immensely inconvenient, and faintly Forsytean (for that is its period) in

[3] Hicks, *Around 1 Millbank*, 22–3.

manner. That is to say that it has an authentic, embalmed middle-class C. of E. presence.'[4]

The arts of amalgamation

In 1900 many of those who bore practical responsibilities in the life of the Church of England were ready to argue that the Ecclesiastical Commissioners and Queen Anne's Bounty should sensibly be united. Yet fifty years were to pass before this happened. Why so long? The reason lay in an accumulation of factors, from institutional pride to political upheaval, economic disturbances and international conflict. It was also a story dogged by human frailty and mortality. What is inescapable, however, is that great and lasting alterations in the life of historic institutions are unavoidably tortuous: they take time.

The amalgamation of Queen Anne's Bounty and the Ecclesiastical Commissioners was a tale in four parts. The century began with the idea. In 1901 a joint committee drawn from members of both authorities submitted a report on the future of the two bodies. Then the ascendancy of the Commissioners was the driving force, and the vehicle itself was driven by the emerging powers of the new age. archbishop Frederick Temple led the charge; his successor Bishop Davidson, too, favoured union. But the pride of the Bounty was resistant, and it took a dogged and persistent stand. W. R. Le Fanu, secretary of the Bounty, did not favour union. The Board of the Bounty voted against amalgamation by nine to three. Three abstained. Such were the mathematics and the politics of the defeat.

When he wrote of this first skirmish, the historian Geoffrey Best viewed the refusal of the Bounty uncharitably: 'The case for amalgamation was indeed unanswerable. Yet amalgamation did not happen.' He added, 'What strings these men pulled, what prejudices and party interests they played on to frustrate the amalgamators, one can only guess.'[5] Certainly, there was now a pause. A bill was prepared based on the report of the joint committee. It was introduced in June 1902 and withdrawn in October. But it was not only the power of institutional obscurantism that sealed its fate. Forty-six years later, when he looked back on the failure of the joint committee, Sir James Brown attributed this defeat to quite different forces: to the Boer War, the death of Queen Victoria and the education crisis. At all events, for now the campaign was mired.[6]

[4] Valerie Pitt, *The Church Commissioners for England*, London n.d.

[5] G. F. A. Best, *Temporal pillars: Queen Anne's Bounty, the Ecclesiastical Commissioners and the Church of England*, Cambridge 1964, 463–4.

[6] James Brown, note on amalgamation, Archbishop Fisher papers, Lambeth Palace Library, London, vol. 42, fo. 215.

Twenty years passed. Best again suggested reasons for such an interval: post-war reconstruction and reform, the distraction caused by the disestablishment of the Church of Wales. The two bodies, too, had changed, for there had been a rearrangement and a redistribution of powers. In 1920 the Bounty had passed augmentations to the Commissioners, but was itself soon busy with dilapidations, pensions and tithes. A more vociferous campaign in the Church, for self-government, or something very like it, had yielded the Church Assembly in 1921. This had essentially recast the official legislative landscape in which any new change must make its way. Parliament was immersed in secular affairs; it had little time or inclination for church questions. But getting something through the Assembly was no simple matter. In its hands everything became politics. If the campaign of 1901 had quickly petered out, it was in a new context that something altogether more formidable emerged in 1924. This was the report of the Commission of Enquiry into Church Property and Revenues.[7] The commission, a weighty body, gave birth to a new committee, chaired by the archbishop of Canterbury. Its report was short and to the point. On 1 October 1924 it recommended that steps be taken by a new commission to explore again the reconstitution and amalgamation of the two bodies, and then to prepare a measure, or measures, with which to achieve it. But in the fabric of this difficulties could be seen increasingly clearly. They must attach the union to what was already an increasingly cluttered landscape of obligations and new rubrics, all of which tended not to diminish but increase the differences between the two authorities. Thus the committee ended up recommending amalgamation, but postponing it until all manner of entanglements had been ironed out. It did resolve that the Ecclesiastical Commissioners be empowered with a new shopping list of responsibilities: to supplement endowments of sees, take charge of bishops' estates, contribute to the repairs of certain episcopal houses and the maintenance of Lambeth Palace, pay the bishops' costs of legal proceedings (subject to safeguards), abolish first fruits and tenths and contribute to the pensions of bishops. But in also recommending an extension of the responsibilities of the Bounty, the committee may actually have ensured its continuing independent existence. Certainly, within a decade the Bounty had come to employ considerably more staff than the Ecclesiastical Commissioners.

It was clear to all that a separation which still appeared illogical should not last. There were persistent questions in the Church Assembly. Archbishop Cosmo Lang himself grew restive. 'This matter is always hanging over us and cannot of course be indefinitely

---

[7] *Report of the Commission of Enquiry into Church Property and Revenues*, London 1924.

postponed', he complained to Stanford Downing of the Commissioners in February 1932.[8]

Downing agreed, but both bodies were now thoroughly buried under the accumulating duties cast upon them by a succession of acts and measures, or by further piles of new special schemes. Even so, that was not reason enough to thwart union now: 'Indeed', remarked Downing, 'indefinite postponement seems no longer reasonable.' Somehow, they must try to frame that new course while maintaining their separate business.[9]

In May 1932 Lang met with a motley assortment of powers representing both interests. The session was conducted in, he observed, 'a quite informal manner', but from it was wrung a new and unanimous commitment that now was as good a time as any to proceed. Lord Selborne should move in the Assembly that there be a new commission to compose a new scheme embracing the governing body and for the 'future administrative relations' of the two. Lang added deliberately:

> the question of the actual constitution of the identical Governing Body should receive further consideration and not be bound by the Commission, and particular care must be taken that the Ecclesiastical Commissioners and Queen Anne's Bounty are not regarded as an Executive of the Church Assembly under its direction and control.[10]

The two archbishops set to work, drawing together the strands. In the following February they appointed a new commission under the chairmanship of Lord Selborne to report 'on the reconstitution of the Ecclesiastical Commission and Queen Anne's Bounty'. The secretary would be the energetic secretary to the former, James Brown.

The commission faced no easy task. It was said that the matter was 'delicate', that it deserved 'very full consideration'.[11] Neither made for speed. By October it was ready to offer a report to the Assembly. No debate was sought. The proposals of 1924 were substantially revived; what now needed discussion was their application 'in the altered circumstances of the present time'. The report noted that two decades earlier the two bodies were found to be distinct in purpose 'for the most part', though 'a still closer connection' between them might save some money. But now a good deal had altered, not in the life of the

---

[8] Archbishop Cosmo Lang to Sir Stanford Downing, 24 Feb. 1932, Archbishop Lang papers, Lambeth Palace Library, London, vol. 29, fo. 176.

[9] Downing to Lang, 25 Feb. 1932, ibid. fo. 177.

[10] Lang memorandum, 15 May 1932, ibid. fo. 188.

[11] Archbishop William Temple to Lang, 4 Oct. 1933, ibid. fo. 224; Sir George Middleton to Lang, n.d., fo. 227.

Commissioners, whose powers 'in the main' had been extended or varied only modestly, but in the work of the Bounty. This had been 'transformed'. While the augmentation of benefices was the sole concern of the Ecclesiastical Commissioners, and a steady one, the Bounty was now assisting poorer benefices with dilapidations and making loans for repairs and redeeming ecclesiastical tithe rent charges. This was a growing business. Furthermore, the commission found that the 'amount, complexity and importance' of its work had 'greatly increased', in the main in consequence of the Ecclesiastical Dilapidations Measure of the 1920s (1923–9) in the Church Assembly, of another Tithe Act of 1925 and of the Parsonages Measure of 1930: the effects of the latter were hard to judge 'in the abnormal financial conditions of the last two years'.

But if these changes expanded the significance of the Bounty it could be seen that they did so to such an extent that the work now demanded could not be done by that institution alone. Their officers had created new and necessary connections with the Commissioners. In particular, the Bounty simply lacked the financial weight that the Ecclesiastical Commissioners possessed. To exercise their duties they had continually to apply to the Church Assembly for the Commissioners' money. This did not make sense. The commission observed that it was also absurdly cumbersome:

> Each case of co-operation of this sort in administration requires the authority of a Measure so long as the Bodies remain separate entities, each with its separate powers, responsibilities and trusts. No reconstitution of the Boards would, of itself, altogether obviate the necessity for recurrent legislation, often quite petty in character.

While the care of the fabric of parsonage houses had now fallen into the hands of the Bounty, the Commissioners, meanwhile, made grants for sites, acquisitions, building or improvement. The parsonage houses issue showed the officers of both to be in alliance and working on the same lines. It might have been harmonious; it was certainly inconvenient. Both bodies saw that for some years they might even have held funds for the same benefices, but so many new applications had accumulated since the Bounty had taken charge of tithe rent charges that it was hard to take a clear view. Everybody could see that there were two offices in two institutions working on similar problems in the same spheres: 'the special qualifications required for the efficient conduct of the one office are also required for the efficient conduct of the other'. The commission granted that amalgamation must 'supersede' the Bounty's 'historic charter', but they looked to lawyers to preserve it while achieving union. After all, it was by amalgamation that the objects of the original charter could best be secured in the new age.

The commission now looked to a union of the two boards, something that was not in practice as difficult as it might sound, for in each case most members already sat on both boards. It was the theory which looked troublesome. On Queen Anne's Bounty the 200 governors required by the original constitution had multiplied by the middle of the twentieth century to a theoretical board of several hundreds. In 1850 the constitution of the Ecclesiastical Commission prescribed a board of no less than fifty-nine members, drawn variously from Church and State. The Selborne Commission had recommended that those who represented the crown, and the number of bishops, be reduced and that power be shifted to the Assembly, to 'a considerable proportion' of clerical and lay members. It had also recommended that the identical boards controlling both institutions should comprise thirty-nine members: the two archbishops, ten diocesan bishops, two deans, ten clergy, ten laymen, three Church Estates Commissioners and two ministers of state. With this, the new commission agreed 'in principle'. But now their logic bore more distinctly the mark of synodical authority. It seemed wise for the appointment of bishops, clergy and laity to be by direct election by their separate Houses or by the Church Assembly. 'Of course', they should all be members of the Assembly. Meanwhile, it was 'clearly desirable' to retain the Lord Chancellor: that was 'a valuable link with the Crown', and also the presence of a member of the court of aldermen of the City of London. This would recognise and sustain the history of the Bounty, and maintain a link which was 'real'. Then the archbishop of Canterbury might nominate two further lay members, this drawing upon a tradition from the Bounty charter which called for two KCs. These intricacies mattered.

The new constitution would accordingly produce a board of forty-one. They should all be members of the Church of England. A new institution must have a new name. The commission inevitably volunteered 'The Corporation of the Ecclesiastical Commission and Queen Anne's Bounty'.[12]

These quiet but purposeful manoeuvres did not go unobserved outside the Church. *The Times* welcomed what was afoot with an editorial bearing the title 'A wise fusion'. It praised greater representation on a united board, observing that the parochial clergy were given to complaining that their stipends were controlled by 'powerful bureaucracies over which they had no influence', and pointed at some anomalies, political and practical, which reinforced the

---

[12] *The Archbishops' Commission on the Reconstruction of the Ecclesiastical Commissioners and Queen Anne's Bounty*, London, 1933.

need for change (not least that the Queen Anne's Bounty had the 'surprising' total of seven hundred governors).[13]

The deliberations continue, 1933–46

If the 1933 report publicised the designs of the reformers, it also brought with it a principal reason for their continuing frustration. For Stanford Downing, the crucial presence in the commission's deliberations, had died suddenly, and when the report was published it began with a lamentation: 'It is not possible to exaggerate the value of the experience and ability which he put at our disposal with unfailing courtesy and kindness.' Now all this was lost, not simply to the commission, but to those who might hope to implement its recommendations. Downing had at least left those who sought reform with the momentum to carry it forward. In December 1933 the boards of the two bodies met. The upshot was the creation of a joint committee of both institutions, pulled together in February 1934 and soon busily at work. A Church Assembly committee was ready and waiting to receive its recommendations. But difficulties arose almost at once. While it was obvious that the numbers of *ex officio* seats on the Bounty, ordinarily vacant, were ludicrous, it was found that existing members, *ex officio* or not, were not necessarily eager to surrender their powers. It was said that the diocesan bishops feared disenfranchisement. Then, the mayors had come to be valued; so too the representatives of Oxford and Cambridge. There was also a question over whether the new authority of the institution should be established by charter or act of parliament. By April 1934 the joint secretary and treasurer to the Bounty, Sir George Middleton, was brandishing a theoretical council of the new corporation, which numbered 'perhaps over a hundred', owning the power to elect a board.[14] This board would comprise the two archbishops, three Church Estates Commissioners and eighteen others, of whom a third would be bishops, a third clergy and a third laity. It should have the power to co-opt four more, two of whom must be KCs. The board should have three committees: for estates, for tithes and for augmentations.

Archbishop Lang looked at this with an intelligent eye and approved. On 18 October 1934 he took the proposal to a general court meeting of the Bounty. In case any there wished to maintain the present arrangements, Lang himself inaugurated proceedings with unsparingly heavy irony:

---

[13] Editorial, *The Times*, preserved as cutting in the Lang papers, vol. 29, fo. 242.
[14] Middleton to Lang, 24 Apr. 1934, ibid, fo. 255.

I will merely say, first of all, that I am very glad to see some of the Governors who are not usually present at our ordinary business. They represent – what is it? – 700 other nominal Governors, and therefore I must take it that they represent not so much the quantity as the quality of the other Governors.

The 'first essential' now was that the two bodies should be brought together under one governing council. Lang pressed that there was 'great need for expedition'.[15] There were quibbles (the members of the court of the aldermen of the City of London still wished to be represented on the board of the new corporation) but the proposed resolutions were endorsed unanimously and representatives were appointed to carry the business forward. It was a vital step. The advocates of reform began to think that a bill for union could be drafted, that it could even be before parliament before the end of 1935 while there was still what they perceived as a sympathetic government in office. But when Lang met Middleton at the House of Lords on 20 November they were still unsure how to proceed: by charter, bill or measure? If it were simply a matter which concerned the Bounty the first might do, for it had been established by charter; but this would not do for the Commissioners, for they had been the creation of parliament. Moreover, with invested property of £146 million it was, thought Lang, 'too important a national concern'. Lang feared a new Labour government which might 'cast envious eye upon these accumulated funds and be unwilling to assist the Amalgamation as proposed'. He still preferred a parliamentary bill.[16]

The Church Assembly proposed alterations. These took some time to accommodate and proceedings began to drag. Quiet approaches to influential politicians were still in train. Lang had met the attorney-general, Sir Thomas Inskip, at Lambeth Palace on 23 October 1935. Inskip was a committed Anglican (perhaps too committed for some, for he had played a large part in sabotaging the new Prayer Book in the House of Commons in 1927). By 20 December Inskip had consulted his department at the Royal Courts of Justice. This, he wrote, must be 'a tremendous task'; had the commission and the committees quite realised what would be involved in a new work of legislation? Both institutions were mired in a 'vast mass of statute law'. The Bounty was affected by at least thirty acts of parliament; the Commissioners by more than a hundred. Inskip thought a new charter simply 'out of the

[15] Minutes of the special general court of the Queen Anne's Bounty, 18 Oct. 1934, ibid. fos 284–90.
[16] 'E.C. and Q.A.B', memorandum: record of a meeting between Lang and Middleton, 20 Nov. 1934, ibid. fo. 294.

question'. He also thought it a bad time to attempt a measure. It was doubtful whether the Assembly had the expertise to do something so complicated and he was a little fearful of what a new parliament might do. A new act would rely absolutely upon the co-operation of the government of the day, not least because the Commissioners were the largest owners of mining royalties in the country and the Church was embroiled in the question of tithes. Of course, Inskip added, this view was only his own.[17] For that, replied Lang, he was the more grateful. To Middleton he confessed that the weight of the verdict seemed irresistible. It was surely now time to sound out the prime minister himself.

The venture was now sunk not by the complexities of the law or the shifting fortunes of governments, but by what Inskip had also seen coming: the report of the Royal Commission on Tithes and, subsequently, the Tithe Bill and then the Coal Bill. The conviction of the moment was soon evaporating. By February 1938 Lang was finding that he was somewhat vaguer about the point they had reached before all this had broken ('I think I have already got somewhere the relevant documents', he wrote to Middleton).[18] If anybody asked about amalgamation in the Church Assembly, he added, the two bills should be raised by way of answer. Until tithe and coal were settled they could surely get no further.

But it was not even the landscape of national politics that destroyed the cause for change in the Church of England. In March 1938 German forces crossed the Austrian border. The peace of Europe was disintegrating. The amalgamation of two administrative institutions of the national Church was not now the matter weighing most heavily on responsible minds. The task which soon faced them was how best to maintain both Church and nation in a time of national emergency.

Between 1939 and 1942 nobody in authority could think the union of the Ecclesiastical Commissioners and Queen Anne's Bounty necessary to the survival of the British empire. But by 1943 the tide of the great conflict against the Axis powers had turned; it was reasonable to look forward and to plan. The agent of change now was Richard Denman, chairman of the committees of the Bounty. Just as his presence began to make itself felt fate again dealt a blow. Denman was struck by sudden deafness. The two boards, meanwhile, were beginning to grow more impatient for change. Must it be such a heavy task? Surely a greater union could simply occur by purely pragmatic administrative rearrangements? The idea, superficially, might well have appeared an attractive one, but a more profound understanding exposed an ocean of dangers. The secretary to the Commissioners,

---

[17] Thomas Inskip to Lang, 20 Dec. 1935, ibid. fo. 302; memorandum, fos 303–6.
[18] Lang to Middleton, 28 Feb. 1938, ibid. fo. 317.

James Brown, passed from irritation at this intrusion into office politics to exasperation – and then exploded. It was impossible; he could not be expected to oversee such a thing; he must offer his resignation. This went straight to the new archbishop of Canterbury, William Temple, at Lambeth. The amalgamation of administrative work, Brown explained, could only occur if it was managed not by two men but by one; a man who could declare to the staffs of both institutions, 'Here is the work: we are all in on it and must work in it and for it. You can trust me to see that everyone gets a fair deal. I want the loyalty of you all.' What he could not countenance was a division of loyalties: there would be an endless round of negotiations between superiors over the allocation of administrative tasks, and all in a deteriorating climate of suspicion and growing enmity. It was unworkable. Temple listened and decided, simply, 'I agree with him. He has convinced me that policy is wrong. If I were in his shoes, I should feel the same.'[19] There could be no amalgamation by degrees in the offices. Administrative pragmatism was not enough.

Peace brought new opportunities. By the summer of 1945 fresh documents were being produced to press the cause of change. In 1946 the politicians were hardly less strenuously at work, for the conclusion of the war had brought a landslide victory for the Labour party and a new period of almost frantic legislative bustle. But now the First Church Estates Commissioner, Sir Philip Baker Wilbraham, decided that in this new era parliament would surely 'be more ready to allow the Church to take the initiative in a matter so much concerning its own affairs. At any rate, the experiment was well worth trying'.[20] Now there was another loss: Sir George Middleton died suddenly. Baker Wilbraham would not be deterred. He superintended the drafting of a measure by the joint committee. In January 1946 the standing committee of the Church Assembly recommended that it pass to the Assembly. By degrees, it seemed, they were edging forward.

The new paradigm emerges

Details are seldom fascinating, but the life of institutions is governed by them and if the historian is to understand what would actually determine the course of the new body across five decades some intricate reckoning at the outset is a necessity. The ideas which framed this new body spoke of the understanding of authority and representation that governed the whole Church. They also

---

[19] Temple, notes of private conversation with Brown, 25 Oct. 1943, Archbishop Temple papers, Lambeth Palace Library, London, vol. 18, fo. 291.
[20] *Proceedings of the Church Assembly*, xxvi/1, London 1946, 23 (26 Feb. 1946).

demonstrate how that Church saw itself in the context of factors at work across society as a whole.

The Church Commissioners was emphatically a creation of a particular time and environment. But the proposed constitution of the new institution was also one which showed an almost assiduous respect for what had gone before. Much was owed to the Bounty, even if Baker Wilbraham referred to it in the Church Assembly as a 'relic'.[21] But reasons could be found to justify parts of its logic still. One of these was that of numbers. The ninety-odd Commissioners, retained from the 1935 scheme, might never attend, but they could be called upon and that was useful. Some had thought the modern universities might be represented. This was discounted. Oxford and Cambridge represented tradition, and the new constitution sought to value and express that. The term 'governors' belonged to the Bounty, too, and was adopted for the new body for that very reason.

The functions ascribed by the men of 1935 were now altered in important details. The annual general meeting would make resolutions on the reports and accounts presented to it, would appoint all the members of the Board (but not more than four to its Estates and Finance Committee) and consider how to spend surplus money. Trusts of whatever description would be maintained separately. The Commissioners would not want to be seen to be tampering with trust funds, at least not yet. Crucially, all income would be put in the General Fund. Surplus could be spent on anything relevant to either of the constituent funds. No longer would every Commissioner be free to propose business at the annual meeting as he wished on the day. It must be first cleared with the chairman. But a consortium of ten commissioners could ask the chairman to convene a special meeting. The Board would be chaired by the archbishop of Canterbury, and would comprise the two archbishops, the three Church Estates Commissioners and twenty-two other members. Of the twenty-two, six should be diocesan bishops, two deans, six other clerks in holy orders, and eight laymen, 'of whom six shall be chosen from those appointed by the Church Assembly'.

The niceties of language, however sensitively observed, were not always instructive. The new Estates and Finance Committee (EFC) was borrowed from the Estates Committee established for the Ecclesiastical Commissioners in 1850, and it retained the word 'finance' to declare its relationship with the Finance Committee of the Bounty. But in practice the Commissioners were its true parents. Then came a further, defining, aspect of the new order. The Ecclesiastical Commissioners had been served by three Church Estates Commissioners: the first a crown appointment, the second nominated by whichever party held a majority in parliament, the third appointed by the archbishop of Canterbury. The first and third were paid. This model was retained. Section 7 of the 1836 act had granted to the Treasury power to regulate the salaries of the officers of the Commissioners. The Bounty, meanwhile, had in this respect been independent, though it chose to follow Treasury examples. In 1946 Baker Wilbraham recognised the need to compete with the national Civil Service, with all its many and various prospects of enhancement. The best officers must be paid well and given the best conditions if they were to be attracted in the first place and retained thereafter. In this, then, the new institution followed the example of the state.[22]

The deliberations of the Church Assembly

How were these intricate proposals to be represented to the Church Assembly? If the new institution was to come to life as a legislative fact it must have a sponsor who knew the manners, the arts and the mind of that body. This was where Philip Baker Wilbraham excelled. He brought what was now called the Church Bounty Commissioners Measure to the Church Assembly on 26 February 1946. To do so, he said, was not merely a duty, but 'a pleasure', for he was now 'at last to be able to comply with the request of the Assembly, made over ten years ago, and to lay before it a Measure dealing with the merger of those two ancient bodies'.

Amalgamation, pronounced Baker Wilbraham, was 'inevitable and right'. It was not a question of 'serious abuse calling for remedy'. It was a matter of improvement. Then, at present there were, frankly, oddities. The constitution of the Bounty was, 'according to modern ideas, really rather fantastic'. Every governor was *ex officio*: all diocesan bishops, all deans, all privy councillors, all KCs, all mayors of cathedral cities ('and nobody knew whether the new cathedral cities counted'), all members of the Board of Green Cloth ('which had, he believed, disappeared') and 'various other people'. The clergy and laity were unrepresented, though a governorship might be secured by a modest benefaction. As for the Commissioners, they were 'more modern', but unrepresentative in the same way. Out of all this Baker Wilbraham hoped for 'the true path of progress':

> It was desirable to conserve all that had been good in the work of the two bodies, and to adapt them a little to modern conditions and democratic ideas without jeopardising any of their efficiency. If that could be done,

---

[22] See the *Church Commissioners Measure 1947* (CA 794).

they would go forward to increased usefulness in the service of God and His Church.

Baker Wilbraham might well have feared that his audience would struggle with what he now proposed. But the leading lights in the Assembly were not above manufacturing complexities of their own. From the moment he stopped speaking, the fate of the nascent Church Commissioners tumbled into the unpredictable, imponderable ocean of synodical deliberation. Almost immediately one of its foremost figures, Canon C. E. Douglas, moved an adjournment. He insisted that he did so in no state of opposition to the motion, but on 'purely constitutional' grounds. The whole procedure was 'unusual'. No Assembly committee had drafted the measure. The standing committee had not seen it. Members had received copies only a week previously (general approval required fifteen days, but there had been printing delays). The measure should have been introduced not by the Commissioners and the Bounty, but by the House of Bishops and through the standing committee. He invoked a history that had not been 'very creditable to the episcopacy of England', recalling the disputes of Blomfield, Peel and Sidney Smith in the 1830s. Now, he said, the bishops should assume responsibility for this 'vast' institution. Did they, he asked, 'really want this corporation to be a third glory in the government of the Church with the Assembly and Parliament?' The proffered explanatory pamphlet, *Number One, Millbank*, had looked to a future in which the new body would work 'in direct relation to the will of the Church as expressed in its deliberative assemblies'. Douglas was suspicious of this: it had not used the phrases 'under its control', or 'responsible to' it. This was 'a great change in the constitution of the Church'. Baker Wilbraham resisted gently, and tied questions of procedure up neatly in his own favour. After all, it was the Assembly itself which had asked the Bounty and the Commissioners to produce a measure. Relations of Church and State were not affected. If the motion for adjournment was passed amalgamation must be held up for another year.

A Liverpool priest then worried about the apparent relaxation of the requirement that all lay commissioners who were not so *ex officio* must declare their membership of the Church of England. A layman from Southwark was anxious about reports in church newspapers which had spoken of representation and even democracy. There should surely not be appointments from the Assembly, but elections. A prominent lay voice, Kenneth Grubb, asked if the annual report and accounts should be presented to parliament. It was 'a very important question of principle'. Baker Wilbraham replied in an almost kindly manner with a steady stream of reassurances, remarking to the layman of Southwark that it was for the Assembly itself to decide upon its processes of

appointment, but adding firmly that the constitution of the new body
was not representative, 'and was not intended to be'. It would simply
have a 'representative element'. This, surely, was a fair balance. In the
chair, the archbishop of Canterbury, Geoffrey Fisher, asked for the
consent of the Assembly that the motion be put, late though the
papers had been. That gained, the motion for general approval was
proposed. It was carried. After an adjournment the Assembly
proceeded to the Clergy Pensions (Supplementary Pensions) Measure,
a shape, if they had but known it, of things to come.[23]

When Baker Wilbraham returned on 17 June 1946, to move the
approval of certain revisions, he embarked on something more taxing.
After all the labours of the committees, the very name of the new
institution would turn out to be the decision of the Assembly. The
word 'Bounty' was out of favour; it was archaic and suggested an
offering of gifts, not a system of administration. The new institution
became the Church Commissioners. Baker Wilbraham accepted this
amiably.

There followed a tangle over new technicalities between Douglas,
who was looking indefatigable, and Baker Wilbraham, who still seemed
to take everything that was launched at him quite in his stride.[24] The
next day brought intricate discussions about the proper representation
of clergy members of different kinds and the significance of the words
'appointment' and 'election'. Should the phrase 'laymen' be replaced by
'lay people'? Baker Wilbraham replied that the phrase laymen
encompassed women under the Interpretation Act: 'He did not think
that the work was really women's work, but it was not desired to
exclude women.' This proposal was turned down.

What made some members nervous was not so much the
representation of church interests but the presence in this new
constitution of the state. 'Why', it was asked 'should it be said that all
the Commissioners except those in right of office should make a
declaration of their membership of the Church of England?' Where
did the three Church Estates Commissioners sit in this arrangement?
Did they hold their 'Commissionership' by right of office? They
should insist that loyal members of the Church of England, not
Catholics or agnostics, should manage its financial affairs. The act of
1836 had pronounced that a declaration was required of every layman.
A priest from Rochester reminded them that even if every *ex officio*
Commissioner was an outright atheist, that total would only constitute
about 25 per cent of the full body of ninety-five. A Liverpool priest
saw the relationship of Church and State to be 'delicate': 'The Church's
present relations with the Government were very happy, but it was a

[23] *Proceedings of the Church Assembly,* xxvi/1, 21–41 (26 Feb. 1946).
[24] Ibid. xxvi/2, 112–24 (17 June 1946).

great deal to expect that that condition would continue in an age which was altering as rapidly as this and in which there was continual economic and social pressure towards the subjugation to central planning of every phase of our social and national life.' A move towards 'totalitarianism' might bring confrontation, a divided Church and a political state which might seek to gain control. In such circumstances, 'a solid block of at least sixteen official members, who normally never attended the meetings of the Commission, might easily transfer the administration of the whole endowments of the Church to a section of the Church favourable to the Government of the day'. This evidently struck a chord. A colonel from Newcastle complained that this debate suggested a 'merely negative' definition of laymen. Baker Wilbraham smiled that this was all important. He offered two opinions, one pragmatic, the other one of principle. First, it was simply too late to wrangle. The officers of state who had been consulted had been told that it would not be necessary to be a member of the Church. It would be awkward to return now with a different requirement. It might affect the passage of the measure through parliament. He did not fear opposition there, but even a little debate would cost them time, and that would cost the bill. Then he unveiled a grander theme. Theirs was a national Church, proudly open to all, whatever their denomination: 'The door of the rectory or vicarage was open to all parishioners who were in trouble, no matter what their religious views might be.' Therefore, in a purely central administrative matter why should they not accept the help of men of goodwill who were prepared to be members of this body? It would be a sign of weakness and not of strength to say that they must be members of the Church of England.

It was enough. The Church Assembly finally voted the new Church Commissioners into existence.[25]

Institution-making, 1947–8

The Church Commissioners came into being in a Britain governed by the new Labour government of Clement Attlee and a Church led by archbishop Fisher. It bore the marks of this context. Its character was formed within the private conversations of oligarchies. In its methods it was, above all, a pragmatic liberal bureaucracy; a brisk but humane enterprise set in motion by experienced and committed executors who understood their tasks sensibly, rationally, without the show of politics. Men like James Brown and Philip Baker Wilbraham recognised that this world of organisation demanded its own necessary and distinct

<hr />

[25] Ibid. xxvi/2, 124–45 (18 June 1946). The 1947 Measure ultimately required membership of the Church of England. See paragraph 6 of Schedule I.

arts. Intricacy mattered, but it should not be fussed over. Nobody respected what was patently slipshod, not least because it could not be expected to work. Management did not justify itself; it was the servant of principle and duty. Paperwork was kept to a minimum. Meetings must be necessary if they were to happen at all.

However some members of the Church Assembly might tremble, the creation of the Church Commissioners showed both Church and State to be busy with their own affairs. This naturally made it difficult to attach them to each other. In time the Commissioners would be seen, and sometimes suspected, as one of the most establishment-orientated of the institutions of the Church of England. This might in part have been because the officers of the Commissioners had more to do with the unspectacular but insistently practical aspects of that world; questions of taxation, exemptions, legal guidance. At all events, what the establishment of the Church of England affirmed was that however self-confident the officers, oligarchies and synods of church life might be, they still inhabited a wider political society, and not some parallel universe of their own devising. Now and then the connection to the state let in a shaft of light which might not have otherwise appeared, and it could be the light of reality. It also exposed the mind of the Church to an insistence on different perspectives and priorities, and made clear the requirements of genuine institutional competence. The connection with the world of the state might not always be comfortable, but it could sometimes be a quiet advantage, glimpsed by rather few, far away from the campaigns about who should, or should not, appoint bishops.

On 14 March 1947 archbishop Fisher wrote to Attlee: 'As you may know, the Church Commissioners' Measure is now before Parliament.' If all went well, the measure would come into effect on 1 April 1948. The inaugural meeting must follow within ten days. It would be 'rather a historic event'. Both the former bodies had 'an honourable record'. The Commissioners had been, 'of course', established by parliament. He reminded the prime minister that 'certain officers of the State' were still to have a place in the new institution, 'though of course there is no need for them normally to attend, and it is our hope that some of them will be present at the Inaugural Meeting. In particular, I hope that you, the Lord Chancellor and the Speaker will be there'.[26] Attlee replied two days later that he would be very glad to attend.

The Church Commissioners Measure made its way quietly through a parliament absorbed in other affairs, almost unobserved. It received the Royal Assent on 2 April 1947. At a stroke this also set the timetable: amalgamation must take place within the next twelve months.

---

[26] Archbishop Fisher to Clement Attlee, 14 Mar. 1947, Fisher papers, vol. 42, fo. 1.

The Church Commissioners looked to the crown for their most important appointment, the First Church Estates Commissioner. Here at least there was one outstanding candidate: Philip Baker Wilbraham. As for the other four crown appointments, the hunt was conducted in the same discreet manner that produced new bishops for the Church. The dual expertise of an appointments secretary at 10 Downing Street could be seen to compensate for prime ministers who certainly lacked knowledge of ecclesiastical matters or the personal inclination to acquire it. Though he viewed church affairs with some wisdom and feeling, Attlee was not himself a Christian, and though he took his ecclesiastical appointments seriously, he never pressed a point when he felt he had one. In 1947 Attlee's appointments secretary was Anthony Bevir, a sensitive diplomat, who knew his way around both State and Church. Left largely to his own devices now, Bevir proved indecisive. He was receptive to suggestions.

The world of authority in 1947 thought naturally in terms of military or public service in wartime, and both of these in the continuing context of empire. Financial acumen was seldom mentioned in itself. In December 1947 James Brown sent a list of possible candidates to Fisher. They grew not out of 'personal reasons'; they were variously qualified; some were stronger than others. He added, significantly, 'What a pity Malcolm Eve is above our weight!'[27] Fisher also had his eye on Eve. Events would show why.

Brown's list was simultaneously, and characteristically, catholic and conservative; the Rt Hon. Ralph Assheton, aged forty-six, a businessman, but one who might be precluded by business interests, and who might yet entertain political ambitions; N. P. Birley, aged fifty-seven, formerly headmaster of the Merchant Taylor's School and King's School, Canterbury, a 'good churchman and son of the parsonage', an experienced administrator, 'not a fluent speaker, I believe, but clear and logical'; Lt Col. Henry Cator, aged fifty, 'considerable landowner (agriculture and urban), distinguished service with staff airborne division', Brown thought he should be known to the bishop of Norwich or to the king, who stayed with him when shooting; and Lt Gen. Sir W. G. Lindsell, an outstandingly successful organiser of transport in the North African campaign, who had subsequently worked for the diocese of Salisbury, whose bishop could offer a view.[28]

They also needed a Third Church Estates Commissioner, a position in the gift of the Church itself. Fisher wrote to Wil Spens, Master of Corpus Christi, Cambridge, describing the duties somewhat cursorily and adding that a new Third Church Estates Commissioner might

[27] Brown to Fisher, 5 Dec. 1947, ibid. fo. 6.
[28] Ibid. fos 7–10.

easily find in London other opportunities of a more cultural kind to fill the other half of his week.[29] Spens was not moved. He did not think that he was sufficiently a man of business. But another name put forward was that of Lord Bridgeman. Again Baker Wilbraham wrote to Fisher, 'I have had further information about Bridgeman from a cousin of mine by marriage, Paul Emrys Evans, who was under-secretary for the Dominions under the last Government.' He told him that Bridgeman was highly regarded – potentially a governor. Evans had seen Bridgeman, when a staff officer, report to 'those in authority' on the evacuation from Dunkirk, and do so 'brilliantly'. Come to that, Evans himself was 'the kind of man who would do the job of Third Commissioner quite well, probably: only there is no reason in the world why he should be thought of for it'.[30]

By the New Year, 1948, Brown had dispatched his ninth amalgamation report to Lambeth. Now he was thinking of the management of staff. 'In any modern organisation', he wrote, 'a machinery for consultation is essential. The little tin God is out of date. You want everybody to feel that he is part of a team working out problems and discussing difficulties together and then loyally accepting the reasoned decisions come to in the light of that joint-examination.' The workings of the new staff had now to be defined, a 'machinery for consultation' devised.

What Brown envisaged was a new joint consultative council, with every grade of employment represented, 'irrespective of trades union affiliation'. This must naturally be provisional; a permanent constitution could be set down after amalgamation, 'But I want to get the machinery for consultation established at once. We are now beginning to make decisions that interest the staffs pretty deeply, and we want to let them know and get their co-operation.' More than that, Brown and his ally at 1 Millbank, Mortimer Warren, possessed formal status and power only within the process of amalgamation, and not in the Queen Anne's Bounty and the Ecclesiastical Commissioners themselves, as separately constituted bodies. They needed authority 'to speak and to listen'. Arrangements now entered into must not be forgotten, and retrieved as grievances at a later time. It was agreed that Brown's Provisional Joint Consultation Council should continue for six months after amalgamation. On the 'official' side there should be only Brown and Warren; on the staff side, four individuals representing the four grades of employment. Goodwill secured co-

---

[29] Fisher to William Spens, n.d., ibid. fo. 12r–v.
[30] Philip Baker Wilbraham to Fisher, 6 Jan. 1948, ibid. fo. 24r–v.

operation, and that produced well-being, collaboration, efficiency.[31] To this Fisher offered his 'entire approval'.[32]

There was still no Third Church Estates Commissioner. For his part, Baker Wilbraham thought that Lord Bridgeman looked 'the most likely one to approach': 'he is very well spoken of as an administrator and it is useful to have somebody in the House of Lords who can speak on Church measures. I still have some hesitations about him but perhaps they are outweighed by the altogether admirable qualities of his mother'. As it happened, Bishop Wand of London had already asked her about Bridgeman's inclinations to work on 'something' recently. She had thought he would be unwilling to do more than he was already, something he duly confirmed for himself later.[33]

Brown stressed time and again that 'amalgamation will really be a process to be gradually completed over a year at least, and not an act of union'. Accordingly, provisional procedures should be given a year of life and 'drastic disturbance' avoided during that time. The Commissioners might well arrive on a representational basis, but they must recognise that they would be 'taking over the wheel of a vehicle which is already proceeding at full speed and not delaying the m.p.h. In that connection, the *desideratum*, etc. is executive rather than deliberative and regularity of attendance becomes essential'.[34] But Brown also delighted in his task, and he wrote of it with a growing pride:

> If one were to liken our work to that of engineers surveying for a new railway, the territory has been prospected, the line mapped and levels taken and some of the rails and equipment ordered: what remains is connected with gradients, tunnels, signals, tracks and engines, signal men, drivers and guards. The analogy illustrates the size, if not the nature, of the task: much remains to be accomplished before the first train can run.

The new offices had been planned to be economical and efficient, and every meticulous detail must now be worked out in consultation with the staff, 'upon whose understanding everything in the long run depends'. The executive level must be new, but it was accordingly all the more important that lower administrative levels should only be disturbed in the face of the 'absolutely necessary'. Brown remarked

---

[31] Brown to Fisher, 2 Jan. 1948, ibid. fos 16–17.
[32] Fisher to Brown, 7 Jan. 1948, ibid. fo. 25.
[33] Fisher to Bishop William Wand, 29 Jan. 1948, ibid. fo. 34.
[34] Brown to Fisher, 23 Jan. 1948, ibid. fos 32–3.

that elections to the consultative council had now been completed, 'not without some little flutter of misunderstanding'.[35]

By its founding measure, there would be ninety-five Church Commissioners. This, then, was both an ecclesiastical and a civil argument. The weight, theoretically, and potentially, lay with the bishops of the Church. The state was a presence to be reckoned with, on paper at least. There could be no doubting the constitutional grandeur of the enterprise. It must now lie with a future succession of archbishops and bishops, lay people, politicians, lawyers and civic dignitaries to play whatever role they saw fit within that splendid paradigm. The constitution of the new Church Commissioners announced that they worked at the heart of the Church of England, drawing into their affairs every diocesan bishop and representative voices of every other grade or shade of authority. Furthermore, that the Church itself stood at the heart of British society, as it could be understood in its political and civil offices.

The internal structure looked like this. The full body of Commissioners would meet once a year. Its work was essentially to be done by the Board, which comprised twenty-seven members, and might extend to three co-optees. This would meet monthly. It would mostly be made up of 'busy people', and its meetings should not be overlong. It would direct the Estates and Finance Committee, a general executive group of five, six or seven which would meet weekly. To the EFC, and to other committees, the Board could pass all agreed matters, for report or for execution. Bearing in mind that the Estates Committee of the Ecclesiastical Commissioners had met once a week, and over two days when it did, it was to be feared that the new EFC 'would quickly be submerged altogether'. Accordingly, there must be, at least for the first year, a second standing committee, an administrative committee, appointed by the Board and chaired by the Third Church Estates Commissioner, consisting of the three Church Estates Commissioners, not more than four commissioners, appointed by the Board, and then four others, not already on the EFC. To this the Board could pass business not sent on to the EFC. It would meet fortnightly. 'You can now see the shape of things to come', wrote Brown to Fisher. He reiterated: 'the Church Commissioners are an executive corporation, and ... all over the country we shall be looked to for quick answers to questions and speedy solutions to difficulties'.[36]

The job of the inaugural meeting of the Commissioners, then, must be to appoint a secretary. All other appointments would be made by the EFC. Beneath them, routine work in dioceses and cathedrals, benefices and parishes, architectural, legal and staffing, would 'flow to

[35] Ibid. fos 34–8.
[36] Brown, *aide-memoire* for Fisher, n.d., ibid., fos 39–52.

the committees by natural channels; it can be conveniently canalised or sectionalised'. Each department would work under a chief. 'The plan is to avoid by every means possible "third party" explanations and repetitions and bring the work directly from the officer actually responsible to the committee which is to reach decision or recommendation to the Board.' As for appointing the secretary in advance, Brown added modestly, 'I am only starting before the whistle because I must.'[37] Nobody in their right mind could deny that the essential architect of this new institution was the only proper candidate for the position.

Attlee wished one of his four crown appointments to be a woman. Evidently this had not occurred to anybody at 1 Millbank or Lambeth Palace. He proposed archbishop Temple's widow, Frances.[38] But for the inaugural meeting he had now to send his apologies.

The logic of the new institutional engineering might have looked clear at close quarters, but from the study of a bishop's house it could seem remote indeed. The business of nominations was also making some people nervous. There were hints that this new, representative body must surreptitiously be managed if advantage were not to be sought on behalf of one interest at the expense of another. For their part the bishops had been asked to nominate four of their number to the Board. The bishop of Winchester, Mervyn Haigh, wrote to Fisher on 1 March 1948:

> I have been doing my best to fill up the nomination papers to the Board of Governors, but I find it very difficult to know whom it would be best to nominate as additional members of the EFC ... there may be some little danger of the difficult little group of the Clergy Commissioners acting in a pre-arranged and united way and getting some difficult persons, including at least one or two of themselves, added to the EFC. Is it possible that Your Grace has some guidance to give the bishops as to which clerical and which lay Commissioners might be really useful and welcome members of the EFC?[39]

This balancing of interests was difficult within a limited number of places. Brown told Fisher that if they worked to avoid a contest between bishops and clergy on the new EFC the clergy as a whole might still find themselves in competition with the laity. It would be better to leave the committee to sort itself out.[40]

---

[37] Ibid. fo. 45.
[38] Attlee to Fisher, 10 Feb. 1948, ibid. fo. 72.
[39] Bishop Mervyn Haigh to Fisher, 1 Mar. 1948, ibid. fo. 94.
[40] Brown to Fisher, 8 Mar. 1948, ibid. fo. 109r–v.

On 9 March 1948 Brown reported to Fisher that he had met Lord Tovey, 'a very charming man', and found him 'anxious to serve', in whatever way seemed necessary. What about Tovey as a Third Church Estates Commissioner?[41] Fisher was persevering, fruitlessly, with another candidate. Meanwhile, all was not peaceful in the offices of the two, still divided, institutions. Brown had reported to Fisher on 11 March 1948 that 'The question of holidays has become rather a burning one.' Since 1939 staff at the Ecclesiastical Commissioners had worked a five-day week of forty hours. Before then, they had worked six days a week, for approximately thirty-eight hours. 'During the war nobody bothered about holidays.' Now, the staff wanted a five-day week.[42]

But the task was almost accomplished. The old era was passing. The final meetings of the Ecclesiastical Commissioners and of the Queen Anne's Bounty took place on 11 March. Both were charged with emotion. Almost at the last moment, the Treasury made a problem out of the incomes of the First and Third Church Estates Commissioners. On 17 March Brown reported to Fisher: 'They are very insistent that a salaried basis is only appropriate for full-time employment.' If a position were part-time, only a small honorarium, fees and reimbursements should be offered. 'But they tell me quite frankly that what they are afraid of is the appointment of "big business" with an outside substantially remunerated occupation to this office also as a salary. They are no doubt looking to their vulnerability in Parliament.' Brown was sure that an Estates Commissioner must work at least three days a week 'to fulfil his essential obligations'. He did not think the Treasury 'sticky'. The difficulty lay in the principle.[43] But Fisher saw something more than bureaucracy at stake in this. He complained:

> They connive at Heads of Boards of Nationalised Industries getting £8,000 a year for a full-time job. They cannot think it unreasonable if a really able man such as we want for an Estates Commissioner should get something like £5,000 a year for a whole-time job. It does not seem to me unreasonable that for that half-time job we should pay £1,500 a year. If they compel us to look for men who are content to do our half-time job and not take any other work, they are really precluding us from looking for men of outstanding ability who in many other openings could command a much higher salary. If there is a genuine

[41] Brown to Fisher, 9 Mar. 1948, ibid. fo. 123.
[42] Note for the general court of the Queen Anne's Bounty, 11 Mar. 1948, ibid. fos 117–18.
[43] Brown to Fisher, 17 Mar. 1948, ibid. fo. 149.

difficulty on the Treasury side I think they create a genuine difficulty on ours as well.[44]

Brown sought to be constructive: 'I think the right solution is to seek freedom from the Treasury control in connection with early consolidation of Acts and Measures relating to the Church Estates Commissioners generally.'[45]

On the penultimate day of the last financial year of the old order Brown sent his fifteenth and final amalgamation report. He wrote to Fisher, 'The train is laid, and the 1st of April will set the match to it.' And to Fisher himself he paid warm tribute: 'The speed and care of your guidance and decisions upon our many questions were the key to success … I cannot recall our being held up for an answer. The Church Commissioners will start deep in your debt.'[46] Indeed, if the Treasury had been difficult about stipends it was helpful in other matters. Licences had now been obtained to reopen the office canteen: in such matters they had been advised by Miss Tyson, the head of the Treasury's own catering division.

To the last there was a wrangle with the unions. A new consultative council, composed along the lines of a Whitley Council, had been established in something of a rush. The men and women of the Ecclesiastical Commissioners were, by and large, members of one of three unions: the Society of Civil Servants, the Civil Service Clerical Association or the Civil Service Union. The staff of the Bounty did not belong to unions. They could not be required to join one. At the same time, a council that was representative must embrace their wishes. How, then, should it be constituted? What was created in response to this seemed to many on the Ecclesiastical Commissioners' side to be 'an attack on trade unionism'. Brown found the atmosphere 'antithetic (almost antagonistic)'. The confidence which yields informality had evidently evaporated. But now the great task was almost done. Brown himself could take a benign view of it all: 'Things will find their own level.'[47]

The intricacies of amalgamation all but lay behind them. In the construction of the Church Commissioners lay more than the roots of the institution. The cast had been appointed that must now take to the stage and fashion its fortunes.

[44] Ibid.
[45] Fisher to Brown, 20 Mar. 1948, ibid. fo. 156.
[46] Brown to Fisher, 30 Mar. 1948, fos 170–1.
[47] Brown, appendix to the fifteenth amalgamation report, ibid. fos 193–203.

PART I

THE AGE OF IMPROVEMENT:
THE PRIMACY OF ARCHBISHOP FISHER, 1948–1961

2

The Age of Speculation

Of men, manners and methods

On 1 April 1948 the Church Commissioners began life as a new
ecclesiastical institution. Though hardly considered as a great event
across the Church of England as a whole, the architects of
amalgamation had carried this burden for years, and now viewed their
creation with exhilarated pride and a sense that this was a historic
moment. archbishop Fisher wrote privately to James Brown, 'It is a
real joy to see a great task like this carried through so finely.'[1] On the
same day he wrote to the staff at Millbank:

> This great human machine will, of course, have to settle
> down and find itself but all the members of it will bring with
> them the long and honourable traditions of the bodies to
> which they formerly belonged. The admirable spirit in which
> they have approached the amalgamation is itself a guarantee
> that they will give to the new body the full contribution of
> their loyalty and service and will make it a fine instrument
> for the service of the Church.[2]

Appointments: the politics of oligarchy

Yet not everything in the affairs of the Church Commissioners was
settled at the outset, and some absences were hardly negligible. At its
very apex, the new institution still lacked a Third Church Estates
Commissioner, for Lord Daryngton was staying on from the old
Ecclesiastical Commissioners only until a new candidate could be
found. In April 1948 the name of General Sir Bernard Paget was in the
air; 'a true Paget', remarked Brown, with 'straight blue eyes, energy,
high moral purpose, faith in the common man'. Paget would accept no

---

[1] Fisher to Brown, 1 Apr. 1948, Fisher papers, vol. 42, fo. 209.
[2] Fisher to the staff of the Church Commissioners, 1 Apr. 1948, ibid. fo. 210.

pay. But he also felt 'tied' to his responsibilities at home, at Ashridge, and doubted that he could do both.[3]

Fisher invited Paget to keep thinking about it, but when Sir Bernard let him down gently, cast his net more widely. He wrote to the chaplain-general asking for 'outstanding Senior Officers who were Churchwardens'. This brought a bigger catch: Sir Frederick Borenschen, a former Permanent Under Secretary of State for War, 'a keen churchman who was related in some way to archbishop Temple'; Field Marshall Lord Wilson, 'one of the most sagacious Commanders in the Army ... a man of great charm'; Sir Wilfred Lindsill, 'the master-brain of the administration of the whole Middle East, always a keen supporter of Chaplains and a regular worshipper at Cairo Cathedral'; Major-General A. J. K. Pigott, Director of Release and Demobilisation at the end of the war, found reading his Bible in English, Latin and Greek; Major-General J. H. L. Groves, director of Army Welfare, 'a man of conspicuous grace', whose family had long associations with the Church.[4]

A letter inquiring after General Sir Beauvoir de Lisle and Lord Dudley went off to Anthony Bevir, the prime minister's appointments secretary, at Downing Street. Fisher offered what he knew himself: that de Lisle was chairman of the Rochester Board of Finance; that he was highly spoken of by the bishop; 'and I notice he has just been elected to Grillions'; 'among other things he is a V.C.'.[5] Bevir was amiable: 'I should be surprised if it were a mistake to put him on.'[6] This was all Fisher needed. But de Lisle replied that though he was very much honoured to be asked, he saw no possibility of taking the position, even part-time, in the midst of his existing political work and private duties.

Fisher went straight back to the drawing board. Had not Brown mentioned that Admiral of the Fleet Lord Tovey 'might possibly do', he asked Baker Wilbraham? Lord Tovey was a Church Commissioner already, and was likely to be asked to take responsibility for cathedral grants 'because he is getting restive at having nothing major to do'. Fisher remarked that 'There is no doubt of his keenness. Are we likely to get anybody more convincing? Indeed is he not entirely convincing in himself?'.[7] Tovey accepted promptly and modestly. He had a little assortment of other duties, but nothing to intrude.[8] Now Fisher had what he needed. Daryngton, in turn, offered his own endorsement: 'I

[3] Brown to Fisher, 1 Apr. 1948, ibid. fo. 211.
[4] Frederick Llewelyn Hughes to Fisher, 10 May 1948, ibid. fo. 233.
[5] Fisher to Brown, 3 May 1948, ibid. fo. 235.
[6] Brown to Fisher, 4 June 1948, ibid. fo. 234.
[7] Fisher to Baker Wilbraham, 19 June 1948, ibid. fo. 241.
[8] Lord John Tovey to Fisher, 30 June 1948, ibid. fo. 245.

am more than glad to hear that Lord Tovey has accepted. He is very *humble* about himself ... *Everyone* will like him.'[9] For Tovey the work proved ideal. 'The more I see of it, the more the work attracts me', he wrote to Fisher on 12 July.[10]

But the great acquisition of the Fisher years came not from the world of the armed services, of politics or of finance. It came from the world of cement. This was Sir Malcolm Trustram Eve – and Eve was something of a genius. He joined the Board in 1948, became Third Church Estates Commissioner in 1952 and First Estates Commissioner in 1955.

Hunting for Second Church Estates Commissioners was no easier, for MPs were hard to entice. When Fisher sounded out the Labour MP John Edwards, he tried not to make the work seem too onerous and then was left to wonder if it seemed too insubstantial to make the invitation flattering. At all events Edwards was busy on the Council of Europe and kept disappearing off to Paris or Strasbourg at short notice. He thought he had better turn it down. 'I wish he had been a little less conscientious and accepted', remarked Fisher to Eve.[11] When Fisher wrote, rather desperately, to Lord Aldenham he declared that the Commissioners had saved the clergy from destitution and that to work for them would be fascinating. This time he hit the mark.[12]

Fisher remained restive. If the position of Second Church Estates Commissioner could be a paid one, and Downing Street approached on that basis, perhaps 'we should have a claim upon a good man and they could not fob us off with a weary old gentleman'. The bishop of London, William Wand, agreed that the First Commissioner should be paid; about the Second he was not so sure: 'We are, I fear, gravitating more and more to a time when men will be entering Parliament for what they can get out of it, and this might easily become another of the "jobs for the boys".'[13]

On 12 April 1950 Sir Richard Acland became Second Church Estates Commissioner, taking over from Lord Burden. He joined the Board of governors for the first time on 4 May 1950. Acland was succeeded by Crowder, who was a failure; then Ashton, a conspicuous, assiduous success ('We ought not to be so hopeful with another Parliamentary Commissioner', remarked Brown once to Fisher).[14] On

---

[9] Lord Daryngton to Fisher, 3 July 1948, ibid. fo. 248.

[10] Tovey to Fisher, 12 June 1948, ibid. fo. 252.

[11] Fisher to Malcolm Trustram Eve, 5 Feb. 1948, ibid. vol. 201, fo. 188.

[12] Fisher to Lord Aldenham, 31 Mar. 1958, and Aldenham to Fisher, 2 Apr. 1958, ibid. fos 199–200.

[13] Fisher to Montgomery Campbell, 20 Mar. 1956, ibid. fo. 187.

[14] London to Fisher, 21 Mar. 1956, ibid. fo. 188.

ceasing to be Second Estates Commissioner, Ashton duly reappeared as Third Estates Commissioner.

What was emerging clearly through the life of the new institution was the fundamental importance of the Estates Commissioners. 'As a matter of fact', observed Baker Wilbraham in March 1950, most of the detailed work is done not by two Church Estates Commissioners but by one sitting alone, either Lord Tovey or myself. These decisions are subsequently confirmed at a meeting of the Committee at which a quorum is present but the confirmation is a pure formality. Yet I think this is the only reasonable way of getting through the work.'[15]

Accountability

The history of the Church Commissioners would bear the marks of many debates about accountability, launched by church people who thought that the body owed too much to the state; by politicians who argued that it owed too little; by parishioners in distant towns who thought that people in London could know little about them and care even less; by members of the Church Assembly (or later, General Synod) who thought that the officers of 1 Millbank were too little governed by the collective mind of the Church. The system itself was clear. The Church Commissioners were accountable to three interests: to parliament, to the annual general meeting of all the Church Commissioners and to the synodical government of the Church.

Every year the Church Commissioners must submit their accounts to parliament. But the interest of the politicians could also find assurance in the presence of the Second Estates Commissioner in the House of Commons. This could be said to offer the Church of England ongoing representation in parliament, where bishops were irregular and largely unpredictable attenders, and a lay presence when its affairs were in these secular days usually explained by clergy there. Questions could be put (the number of them would vary markedly during the history of the Church Commissioners) and conversations might be had. Like so much in the constitution of the Commissioners, accountability rested on legal requirements but, more than that, on a culture of concern which might fluctuate. It was difficult for church figures, burrowing away in their various enterprises day by day, to know how to value this. But the Commissioners certainly did – and, in itself, this would make their popularity still more precarious within a Church which was increasingly given to going its own way, assuming all too readily that parliament was wholly unconcerned with its affairs and paradoxically growing irritable when interest was manifested.

---

[15] Baker Wilbraham to Fisher, 28 Mar. 1950, ibid. fo. 352r–v.

The annual general meeting of the Church Commissioners gathered to hear the news from the appointed powers, to read the annual report, to approve – or otherwise – what the Board proposed to do with what was agreed to be the surplus in the General Fund for the year. This almost invariably went off smoothly: no proposal from the Board was ever defeated by a rebellion of Commissioners on the floor of Lambeth Palace (for that is where they met). Some asked whether, since the meeting existed to approve new and grand policies, they should not receive something more detailed than the annual report if they were to exercise a judgement intelligently? To this there was an answer: the question itself simply asked too much of an annual general meeting. If individual Commissioners had doubts about details, they should approach the secretary personally for clarification or explanation. They could all do that without making a fuss.

But under the surface there was some agitation. In the Fisher era the modernising oligarchy had its opponents. Many of the clergy saw the great issue of the day to be the level of their stipends. It did not seem to them that money being spent elsewhere was being used properly, while they themselves were living in near poverty. In the Parochial Clergy Association they found their mouthpiece, and specifically in the person of Edward Courtman. Courtman was an experienced church politician, a busy, bustling presence at the Church Assembly, loud and insistent at the annual general meetings of the Church Commissioners, for he was a Commissioner to boot. Between the men at Millbank and the Parochial Clergy Association there was no love lost. At the annual general meeting of the Commissioners in October 1953 Courtman was persistent. Brown was taxed and replied with some asperity. Afterwards Courtman wrote a smooth disclaimer to Fisher, 'I thought Sir James appeared to be a little too much concerned over my guileless and business-like questions. My view is that the Church Commissioners, at the Annual Meeting, should not be expected to take such vast figures "as read". There is an obligation on every Commissioner to understand them, otherwise why have them before the general body at all?' He wanted fuller accounts and attached a list of further questions. That done, he signed himself 'Yours obediently', which would have placated nobody, least of all archbishop Fisher.[16]

Fisher gave this short shrift. He was, he replied, always glad that there should be questions at the annual general meeting, but questions 'designed to clear up any questions which are obscure':

> The trouble about your questions is this: that they are so remote from the actual concern of the Annual Meeting that people get rather impatient with them: and they do show, if

[16] Edward Courtman to Fisher, 23 Oct. 1953, ibid. vol. 121, fos 234–5.

I may say so, a lack of understanding of the nature of the affair. Many of the questions amount in fact to this: are the Commissioners quite sure that their staff are being honest and efficient in managing their business.

That said, Fisher conceded, one question on his list was good, and was 'a question of general principle'. It was about the future commercial value of woodlands. But he did not answer it.[17]

Though they were not directly under the thumb of the Church Assembly, the Church Commissioners submitted their annual report to it, and it was to the Church Assembly that they must turn when their existing mandates were not absolutely beyond doubt. This raised a question that was not merely legal and diplomatic, but practical. At their first annual general meeting, the Commissioners felt it unreasonable to submit the full accounts. Instead, a special deposition was written which summarised the accounts section by section, comprising 'all the information likely to be of general interest'.[18] A copy was dispatched to every member of the Assembly. The Commissioners were concerned to do well in the eyes of the Assembly, and to maintain a presence there. In the autumn of 1955 Fisher announced to the Assembly that the Commissioners had 'taken possession' of room 129 in Church House for the duration of the sessions, and that anybody who had a question for them, 'within reason', need only look inside.[19]

These conversations almost at once exposed a defining problem. The world of the Church Commissioners was a complex one and to understand it required expertise. It was the experience of most modern public corporations that it was difficult to link expertise to representation. Those who work with details must find it hard to submit to the judgement of those who know little about the practical arts involved in the work itself. Who, after all, is qualified to judge the right path: the expert who has no political mandate or the politician in parliament or Church House whose view is simply that of an amateur? This was no abstraction. Over fifty years it would be seen to matter decisively, within the life of the Church Commissioners and beyond.

The new financial strategy

In 1948 the new Church Commissioners had a grand total of £1,146,946 in the bank. In September 1948 Mortimer Warren produced an extensive report for the Estates and Finance Committee.

---

[17] Fisher to Courtman, 26 Oct. 1953, ibid. fos 236–7.
[18] Fisher to Brown, draft report, 29 July 1948, ibid. vol. 42, fos 255–8.
[19] *Proceedings of the Church Assembly,* xxxv/3, London 1955, 349 (15 Nov. 1955).

This outlined the financial position of the Commissioners and the contents of the General and Trust Funds, and offered general conclusions. It also showed the position of Stock Exchange securities, and the nominal value of government securities.

Warren's report sought to provide a solid body of information for the new institution and also to suggest the direction that it should take. 'A review of income and expenditure is a sombre exercise at the present time', he reflected. Money had been lost as a result of the Tithe Act and the Coal Act, through war damage, through the nationalisation of railways and electricity, and continuous redemptions of stocks and mortgage loans which had been replaced at lower rates. But what commanded Warren's closest attention now was the Commissioners' General Fund. Most of its income in interest was committed, 'mortgaged in perpetuity', by virtue of schemes of payment to beneficiaries. But there was more and it was 'available for any purposes within the Commissioners' powers and discretion'. Some was committed to permanent payments (for archdeacons, cathedral chapters and suchlike), the rest for grants. The General Fund was shown every year in two parts – an income and expenditure account, and an appropriation account. At the end of the year, the balance from the first would be transferred to the second. In 1948 much of this was already committed to existing schemes. Warren remarked that 'How best to divide this amount is for the Commissioners to decide, but variations in the size and shape of the slices does not alter the total weight of the cake to be cut.'

As for real estate, the Commissioners were committed to putting all their houses thoroughly in order, repairing, modernising, improving, while charging the full appropriate rent. In such a way they could 'enjoy easy consciences' and bring maximum income to the General Fund. They should even become more 'aggressive' in pressing for higher rents for better properties: it 'could hardly fail to be a source of satisfaction, and might be spectacularly successful'.[20]

This might have sounded unabashedly acquisitive, but there were already expectations in the air that the Commissioners would now take on new commitments – for glebe, for the creation of a central register of benefice incomes, for new churches and sites, for stipends and pensions. Yet the combined gross revenue of the Bounty and the Commissioners had shrunk. It was time to grasp the nettle: 'What can be done to increase income, the life-blood of the Commissioners'

[20] Mortimer Warren memorandum, 'Church Commissioners', Sept. 1948, Board of the Church Commissioners, agendas and papers, Church of England Record Centre, Bermondsey, ser. 95083/1.

functions? This is perhaps the true test of the Commissioners' virility of management.'[21]

To this there was one essential answer. It was to sell gilt-edged bonds – which had guarantees, but were only modestly profitable – and to venture, by degrees, into the world of stocks and shares in the private market. It was a step which few other such institutions – if there were any that could be compared – had the confidence to take. It was a departure, an innovation. That the Church of England became in the second half of the twentieth century a credible financial institution, at least according to the terms established by other public corporations, was in fact a result of this early move.

The measure which established the Church Commissioners gave to the Estates and Finance Committee 'full and exclusive power to exercise and discharge in the name of the Commissioners all functions of the Commissioners in matters relating to the making, realisation and change of investments', within the general rules made by the Board itself.[22] The Commissioners presently had £100 million in holdings. The government broker offered a cautious encouragement for a new course: he thought that holding 59 per cent in government securities was 'not excessive' and that it should stay as it was. But 5 per cent could be invested in ordinary shares 'of the very best commercial and industrial companies with long histories of successful trading'. Then, they could make further investments in insurance companies, banks and first-class preference shares in investment trusts. The money for the last two areas could be raised by the sale of the 3 per cent electricity stock issued as compensation for nationalisation. With this Warren concurred, not least because first-class ordinary shares increased in capital value inversely with the progressive fall in the value of money.

This might have struck a controversial chord. It could be represented, not illogically, as gambling. But there is little evidence of much heart-searching or debate on the Board or on its committees; perhaps that possibility was diminished by the air of respectability and responsibility with which the Commissioners surrounded themselves as they set out on this road. They enjoyed the benefits of the weightiest advice from the most conspicuous, the most impressive authorities. Moreover, within four years this deliberate move onto the stock market was showing remarkable results. Between 1948 and 1952 the investments of the Church Commissioners looked like this:

---

[21] Ibid. p. 26.
[22] Church Commissioners Measure, 1948, Ss. 1–12 (*see* appendix 1).

Table 1. Book value securities held for the General Fund[23]

Class	£s as on 1 April 1948	£s as on 1 April 1952
Government securities	60,746,000	91,861,000
Colonial	6,405,000	6,656,000
Corporation	14,608,000	12,420,000
Railway	356,000	227,000
Public board	6,610,000	4,853,000
Electricity	5,351,000	-----------
Gas	4,286,000	-----------
Water	2,958,000	3,225,000
Industrial	318,000	15,236,000
Miscellaneous	1,068,000	2,582,000

These figures showed only too clearly that while government securities had risen, in percentage terms, by 8 per cent, industrial securities had grown by 10.75 per cent (from a book value of £0.3 million to £15.2 million). The real disparity between the two was far greater. If the Commissioners had not, under the Stabilisation of Benefices Measure, taken over government securities held by benefice trusts with a book value of £29.5 million, the value of government securities, even bearing in mind nationalisation, would hardly have changed at all.

By June 1952 the financial landscape was so much altered that the EFC was turning back to the Board for a validation of its strategy. For by now no less than 66 per cent of the General Fund was made up of Stock Exchange securities, and the EFC wanted to buy still more. In the context of these unarguable currents, it was almost impossible for a sensible, practical mind to disagree.

The arrival of the 'really big people'

Here was a tremendous motor for change. It also signalled a growing liability. Until now the EFC could hold a cash investment of 10 per cent of the Church Commissioners' total assets in industry. This meant £19 million. Against this was set a reserve fund, so that commitments could be met if the value of investments fell. Was this enough? Lord Tovey stirred anxiously. This new, noisy dynamism must be contained within a 'greater watchfulness'.[24] Soon the EFC was seeking new advice from outside. They found Lord Brand and, through him,

[23] Granville Tyser memorandum, 'The Church Commissioners' investments', Board papers, 26 June 1952, ser. 95083/7.
[24] Ibid. p. 4.

Granville Tyser. Tyser was certainly august: he had been a financial
partner in the firm of Lazard Brothers. He had also chaired two
investment trusts and worked in investments for a major insurance
company, and he was happy to advise the Church Commissioners on
all the relevant questions before them: how to balance the various
classes of securities, the system under which the investments were
managed and controlled, overall policy. Tyser wrote a report and spoke
to the EFC itself; all of it without charge.

Tyser himself was satisfied with what he found in the Church
Commissioners' affairs. But he did gently propose that in these
changing circumstances the constitution of the EFC itself needed
another look: 'This ... is not such as would inspire complete
confidence in the City if, for example, it were the Board of Directors
of an Insurance Company or Investment Trust Company.' It should
have one or more members who had the right experience in these
things. This, learned the committee, was called 'top control'. Junior
staff might be chosen for their education and experience in finances
and investments. An 'investment officer' would be wise, and if he had
an intelligence department run by someone trained in statistics and
economics, all the better. Tyser also wondered at the policy of
employing only two firms of brokers. Nothing was urgent; everything
was going along nicely, but a City institution would certainly want to
achieve greater independence for itself by having more staff in these
areas. If the Commissioners feared that by doing so they might lose a
little in their contact with issuing houses and brokers, they could be
placed on their business lists.

Tyser now turned to what were called 'Proportions' – between gilt-
edged and equities, between ordinary shares and preferences or
debenture shares. Here there were no firm rules, he observed, and few
examples, come to that. But he thought that the Commissioners could
go further. Expanding would introduce more speculative industries
and 'companies of second grade'. But over the last fifty years, gilt-
edged had been prone to severe fluctuations, and then two wars had
caused such depreciations of the currency that the Commissioners
might sense that their responsibility to secure a greater income
demanded measures to compensate.[25] The EFC stirred thoughtfully
and presented Tyser's findings to the Board in June.

Fisher now took the lead. On 28 October 1952 he wrote to the
Chancellor of the Exchequer, Rab Butler, for advice on these great
questions. Would he see Malcolm Trustram Eve? Butler did not reply
promptly, but by 30 January 1953 he had in fact talked to Eve and had
put him in touch with the governor of the Bank of England who had,
in his turn, 'made some very helpful suggestions'. Stock Exchange

25 Ibid. ser. 95083/8.

investments and real estate might be dealt with separately. An advisory panel might be appointed to review the present portfolio and to recommend accordingly. After that they might meet regularly to look over what was happening. 'I gather that it is also a frequent practice in arrangements of this sort', observed Butler, 'that the Permanent Staff should consult one or more members of the Panel before making purchases or sales over a certain figure. The Panel would also be able to give the E. Committee useful advice about the general management of their funds.' A list of names emerged: Sir Richard Hopkins, Sir Eric Gore-Browne, Mr Granville Tyser himself, Mr G. G. Beamish of the London Assurance. As for real estate, both the Chancellor and the governor had drawn up a list of ideas and would make definite proposals in due course.[26]

Fisher replied, 'May I say how grateful I am for the trouble that you have taken over this matter and for the steps which you have put in motion.' The Commissioners, confided an eager James Brown to one of his contacts, were going to assemble a 'panel of really big people who will voluntarily offer their services in advising on general policy'.[27]

The coming of Eve

This new and surprising world made Fisher all the more fascinated by what the Commissioners were up to. If it was not quite the natural world of an archbishop, it certainly was a place where Malcolm Eve felt at home. By the time that the Commissioners' new fortunes were becoming apparent, Eve represented everything that the Church Commmssioners needed. He had chaired the War Damage Commission. He had managed the Crown Estates. He was chairman of the Cement Makers Federation. The growing importance of stocks and shares in the life of the Church Commissioners made him all the more obviously the man of the moment. On 24 July 1952 Sir Malcolm Trustram Eve, Bart., GBE, MC, TD, QC, made his first appearance as secretary, at a Board meeting in the Guard Room at Lambeth Palace. He was now ready to dominate what he found before him.

It was still no easy thing to import the 'really big people' into the existing structures of the organisation. To change or enlarge the composition of the EFC would mean legislation; nobody wanted that. It was best that the 'really big men' form an advisory panel, meeting periodically, co-operating with the Commissioners' own staff, advising,

[26] Rab Butler to Fisher, 30 Jan. 1953, Fisher papers, vol. 121, fo. 181. David Jeremy, *Capitalists and Christians: business leaders and the Churches in Britain, 1900–1960*, Oxford 1990, argues the importance of being clear as to who exactly was on this panel, not least because of the difficulty of finding out.

[27] Fisher to Butler, 30 Jan. 1953, Fisher papers, vol. 121, fo. 182.

but in no way assuming responsibility for decisions. In October 1952 the Board simply approved of this. The minutes record no debate. In so undemonstrative a way did the Church Commissioners venture yet more purposefully onto the ocean of speculation.

With the dawning of the age of Eve the oligarchy was in a mood to think confidently and boldly. On 12 February 1953 Eve visited Lambeth for a long discussion. Fisher himself recorded it at some length. Of Eve he noted: 'He himself greatly enjoys the work and is keenly interested in it. But', he continued,

> he said to me that he was frankly a little alarmed: he told me, which I had not realised before, that the Church Commissioners are the second largest holders of investments in the country, only being exceeded by the Prudential ... Further than that, they are the biggest single land holders in the country. All this means an immense responsibility, and he is frankly just a little anxious as to whether, admirable though the management has been, it stands up to such a very heavy responsibility.

Together they explored visions of change. Eve did not hesitate to remind the archbishop of his statutory responsibilities: 'Malcolm [for the first time], pointed out that I am Chairman of the Church Commissioners and that it is right that I should know what is happening and should enquire into it and give my opinion.'[28]

The future of the Church Commissioners lay before them. Eve hoped that Baker Wilbraham would go on as First Estates Commissioner 'for a long time yet. He is slow but there is no harm in that because he is so wise and good although one or two people get impatient with him'. But when he did go, Fisher told Eve that he hoped Eve would himself succeed him and that he wished him to recognise it. Eve had foreseen this, though he could scarcely see himself in a place like the Church Assembly. That was very natural, conceded Fisher; after all, Baker Wilbraham was 'a Church Assembly man through and through'.[29] Of course, the position was in the gift of the crown.

While this was going on quietly across the Thames, Brown, for his part, was drafting a letter of invitation for the new investment advisers. Soon there was a statistical department at Millbank, and also two firms of brokers acting for the Commissioners without charge.

[28] Fisher memorandum, 12 Feb. 1953, ibid. fos 186–90.
[29] Ibid. fo. 190.

When Baker Wilbraham published the first history of the Church Commissioners Fisher wrote to him in terms that were both congratulatory and valedictory:

> It is a splendid story and nobody could record it as you could. I was very glad when the Dean of Hereford said at our last meeting that the clergy were becoming increasingly conscious of the debt which they owed to the Commissioners for all that had been done in these last five years. As Malcolm Eve said the present happy condition is only the outcome of all that has been done under your leadership before, during and after the amalgamation.

It was this very success, murmured Fisher, which led him to wonder if further reorganisation should not now occur at the top?[30]

The gentle prod was not, after all, necessary. Baker Wilbraham replied that he was actually ready to depart. They had come to the end of the first chapter, and now the Church Commissioners could be handed on as 'a going concern'. He would gladly continue to serve in the Church Assembly and would help the new Third Commissioner. They must hunt for younger men.[31] Now it fell to Fisher to ensure that the crown would do as they all wished. He wrote persuasively to Anthony Bevir at Downing Street: on 22 October Bevir communicated the queen's approval of the new arrangements.

Brown was now sixty-two. He had been secretary for almost twenty years. That he should become the next Third Estates Commissioner was natural, and Eve was determined that he should. His admiration for Brown, whose wealth of experience appeared indispensable, was unaffected by Fisher's own ambivalence. Mortimer Warren was seen to be ripe to become the new secretary.

This was a mature and extremely effective quartet; the central constellation around which the affairs of the Commissioners revolved. It was this coalition that set the work of the whole institution on a remarkably confident foundation. Each man appeared to possess what the others lacked. Fisher knew the politics of the Church thoroughly and pragmatically; he saw how new ideas might seem to the people who mattered and, sometimes, how to persuade those whose approval might be necessary in bringing new ventures to life. This also placed the work of the Church Commissioners at the heart of the life of the Church of England. Between 1948 and his retirement in 1961 the archbishop of Canterbury occupied the chair of the Board ninety-nine times. Eve was the vigorous businessman, who knew how to seek

[30] Fisher to Baker Wilbraham, 27 July 1953, ibid. fo. 196.
[31] Baker Wilbraham to Fisher, 4 Aug. 1953, ibid. fos 198–201.

opportunities and shape a broad, bold sweep of policy. Brown knew the Commissioners intimately and understood administration delicately and precisely. Warren understood the intricacies of the finances and new investments better than any other. What mattered decisively in this first decade was that these four worked intelligently, creatively and loyally together, and with a remarkable sense of shared purpose. They knew when to tell each other what to do and when to defer to each other. Now and then they even told each other off. None was a natural democrat; their language was oligarchic and their command of it was often superb. What now happened was essentially their triumph.

The ripening fruits of speculation

The Commissioners were learning to their satisfaction that after the post-war doldrums there was a new vitality in the British economy. International trade, too, was stirring with purposeful life.[32] The 1953–4 financial year brought unprecedented activity in the Church Commissioners' portfolio. The EFC minutes show energetic discussions of policy and, every month, new results.

In that year alone the Commissioners again increased their investments in commercial and industrial holdings, aiming towards £40 million, selling off more gilt-edged securities and instead investing selectively in new commercial debenture issues of the highest class, and in the ordinary shares of insurance companies. The Commissioners now had ordinary shares in the food industry (13.5 per cent), light engineering (13.5 per cent), electrical engineering (9.5 per cent), chemicals and oils (7.0 per cent), heavy engineering and building (6 per cent), textiles (4.5 per cent), tobacco (4 per cent), and a diminishing range of others, including boots and shoes, linoleum, glassware, soap, paper and printing, metallurgy, motors, cables, rubber, drugs, rayon, machine tools, paint and shipping. New methods brought new room for manoeuvre. Treasury bills of over £18 million were purchased for brief spells, and earned interest of £16,700.

Quite simply, over a period of six years, income had grown far beyond the bold hopes of the reasonable men of Millbank. 'The Commissioners', observed an annual Stock Exchange report, 'are now carried along on the full tide of the general prosperity.'[33] By the year 1954–5 the Commissioners were employing the services of not two but ten firms of brokers and eight of the main issuing houses. All of

---

[32] For the finest overview of the development of business in the context of international trade cycles see Leslie Hannah, *The rise of the corporate economy*, London 1983.
[33] 'Stock exchange investments: report for the year to 31 Mar. 1954', Board papers, 24 June 1954, ser. 95083/9.

these were working to increase holdings in preference shares to £5 million, to invest in the ordinary shares of selected investment trusts, to invest in ordinary shares of discount companies; to increase money invested in commercial and industrial ordinary shares from £40 million to £50 million, to double the small investment made in ordinary shares in shipping companies; to increase to £1 million the money invested in the ordinary shares of the six steel companies which had recently been de-nationalised. At the beginning of that year the Commissioners held an authorised maximum investment in 164 companies, and that maximum was raised to allow them to invest in them still more heavily, while adding another sixty-five companies to the maximum investment portfolio. In a single year the Commissioners investments in ordinary shares had increased from nearly £28.5 million to just over £40.5 million. The disparate fortunes of government securities and industrial stocks and shares were now as clear as they could possibly be. Sober Warren was still cautious. Broadly, the future appeared 'favourable'. They must, quite simply, benefit from growing industries and avoid declining ones. But, in fact, the following year again sustained this momentum. The advisory panel was briskly busy and now meeting quarterly. Investments in commercial ordinary shares increased from £50 million to £60 million. Meanwhile, gilt-edged securities had actually gone down, reaching a low point on 29 November 1956. At this few could have been surprised: the British government had sent forces into Egypt.[34] By 31 March 1957 the Church Commissioners had only £45 million invested in the gilt-edged index, realising growth of broadly the same 3 per cent, and now £65 million in the industrial index, realising almost 7 per cent. Besides this, they had moved modestly, to the tune of about £10 million, into investment and property trusts.[35]

The discreet art of investing in the age of oligarchy: Mr Backhouse and Mr Macmillan

What did this actually look like in practice? An exchange of letters from November 1957, between Warren and one of his regular contacts, J. Backhouse, offers a glimpse of the courtesies and considerations of the business, and also indicates the quiet morality which was at work in it all. It was Mr Backhouse who inaugurated the exchange:

[34] 'Stock exchange investments: report for the year to 31 Mar. 1955', Board papers, 20 May 1955, ser. 95083/10.
[35] 'Five year distribution of stock exchange investments', Board papers, 5 July 1957, ibid.

Mr P. J. Greaves, the Managing Director of North Central Wagon, had lunch with us here yesterday. His company was formed about a century ago to finance wagon purchases by collieries, but, since coal nationalisation, has developed into a general sales finance concern and probably ranks third in the field. Like their competitors, they are always seeking deposits and pay high rates, and they have in their favour a good Balance Sheet and a first-class management.

It just occurred to me that you might have substantial funds available from time to time for short-term investment, in which case the rate offered by North Central Wagon might be attractive to you. Naturally there may be many reasons why such an investment would not be possible for you, but if you think that the suggestion might be of interest, I would very much like to put Mr Greaves in touch with you.

To which Warren duly replied:

It was only a short time ago that we considered whether we could place short term money with advantage in this way. At that time I was visited by one of the directors of the biggest people in this field and the proposition he made for six months' loans was very attractive indeed. I discussed it with my Commissioners and they turned it down for two separate reasons.

The first was that the finance company was coming to us because, owing to the credit squeeze, they could not get the money in the normal way and my Commissioners thought they ought not to frustrate the squeeze in this way. Secondly the Commissioners thought that for political reasons they had better not enter this particular field.

I do hope you do not think this sounds priggish but we do sometimes have to consider political expediency and at times it runs in opposition to what we should like to do.[36]

Eve, moreover, enjoyed an almost insouciant acquaintance with the most august powers of the age, whose names he could simply drop, lightly but deliberately, into passing conversation. In June 1957 the 'really big men' were pressing the Commissioners to buy United States and Canadian securities. In particular, they looked across to the American oil industry. Eve wrote to the prime minister, Harold

[36] AC, J. Backhouse to Warren, 3 Nov. 1957; Warren to Backhouse, 4 Nov. 1957; Backhouse to Warren, 8 Nov. 1957, Secretary's papers, CC/SEC/INVP/1.

Macmillan, on 12 June 1957: 'My dear Prime Minister and Church Commissioner'. They had recently met at lunch at Sir Edwin Herbert's. There, Eve had raised the question of tax levied on Easter offerings, which was then causing some bother in the Church, and Macmillan had asked him to put it down on paper for him. Now Eve thought to mention the new proposal that the Commissioners invest in the United States: 'I hope you won't mind my writing a letter like this, and I am sure you will tell me if you are embarrassed. If, however, you can give us quite privately your advice, as a fellow Church Commissioner, we should all be so grateful.'

Three days later came the reply, 'as a Church Commissioner I feel strongly the force of the arguments of the financial advantage which you put forward'. This was, he added, 'frankly a nice point'. But he had given it 'very careful thought indeed' and now

> It seems to me that there might be some danger that such a step might not only bring criticism upon the Church Commissioners but might encourage a more general movement which in the present finely balanced state of our economy would not be to the national advantage. I am, therefore, the more sorry to see that you consider that investment in Canada is ruled out for tax reasons ... It would not, of course, be proper for me in my position to give you what could be called market tips but it is I think a fact generally recognized that Canadian investments are bound to appreciate. Might not this appreciation outweigh the tax disadvantage?

Eve in his turn replied that he was confident that the EFC would act on this advice 'although I can assure you that no mention will be made of its source outside the Committee'. The trouble with Canada was that the present yield 'is so very low even to a tax-payer, and that a non-tax payer simply cannot afford to stand a deduction of 15% non-resident tax while at the same time providing the funds for investment out of the sale of other stocks probably producing at least 5% more'. Perhaps this might be mentioned to the new prime minister of Canada when he visited him soon? 'It does seem rather a sad thing that with such a virile Church of Canada in communion with the Church of England there is every discouragement to the Church of England to invest its funds in Canada.' He added, 'It is such a comfort for me to know that if a question of national policy arises in the Church Commissioners I can come to you for advice.'[37]

[37] Eve to Harold Macmillan, 12 June 1957; Macmillan to Eve 15 June 1957; Eve to Macmillan 18 June 1957, CC/SEC/INVP/2. The promptness of the prime minister's reply is certainly striking.

Presenting a new face

In 1953–4 the gross income from the General Fund was £8.5 million.
That marked an increase of £0.5 million over the year before and of
more than £1.5 million over the figure of 1948. The world of 1
Millbank may well have been a discreet one, but these vast sums of
money were sure to attract public attention. It was, equally, natural if
the Commissioners themselves chose to parade what was undoubtedly
a triumph. At once this gave rise to subtler, more complicated
calculations of policy, some of them moral (even theological), some of
them practical. To shout too loudly of the wealth of the Church did
not sound well to those who identified the religion of Christ with
poverty and the repudiation of riches. At the least it would seem
unduly self-congratulatory; there were many who would grumble at it.
Furthermore, there was perhaps a growing expectation that if needs of
almost any kind arose within the Church the Commissioners might be
expected to pay for them. This new wealth, somebody added, might
give the impression that there was less reason for the laity to
contribute to the Sunday morning collection plate in church.

But Fisher was eager to celebrate success. Being archbishop of
Canterbury offered few decisive and uncontroversial successes, and £1
million looked very like just that. It vindicated them all. After the
annual general meeting of the Church Commissioners in October 1954
he decided to give a press conference. He sought to sweep away
suspicion and rumour and instead to introduce the Church to what the
Commissioners made, not for themselves, but on behalf of them all. It
became more than a bland explanation; it was a grand statement:

> Inside and outside the Church there are many
> misconceptions, sometimes amounting to abysmal
> ignorance. It is known that the Church Commissioners have
> a very large annual income. It should be known … that by
> wise management that income has greatly increased in the
> last year or two. It is true that so far as figures go the church
> Commissioners have a greater income, and are spending
> larger amounts, than at any other time in their history.

That being the case, why was the Church always asking for more?
Why, then, were the clergy underpaid? First, neither the Church nor
the Commissioners received money from the state: 'That
misconception is still widely held and persists in spite of constant
denials.' They might well have £8.5 million but that was 'far from
being sufficient for our needs' for the cure of souls and the living
ministry of the churches. The parishes were raising perhaps as much
again, in part to supplement what the Commissioners could do for
them 'and mostly to do for themselves what the Commissioners

cannot do'. The previous year more than £7 million had been spent on clergy stipends. And that was only 'the hard core', for the rest of the money had been found from endowments and parish giving. Then came pensions, which would now annually absorb some £850,000 of the Commissioners' income. Then there were rectories and vicarages – often large buildings to maintain, sell, build, recondition, subdivide: another £885,000 a year. Then there were the new towns and housing areas: £1.5 million had been set aside for them. There were bishops' stipends, see houses, small grants to cathedrals, endowing new parishes. 'The point is that … the income of the Commissioners is fully spent. But for the increase in that income over the last few years, the Church would now be in a parlous state indeed.'

Fisher was eager to place this beside what he regarded as 'something like a revolution in the attitude of the laity' towards financial contributions over the last fifty years:

> They recognise as never before that the requirements of the Church for its maintenance and expansion rests squarely on their shoulders: and in diocese after diocese and parish after parish they take up the task. The Commissioners cannot now and never will be able to carry their burdens for them. No one would wish that they should. But it is an encouragement beyond price to them that the Church Commissioners under energetic and wise government can increasingly come to their aid, to the aid of the clergy and to the Church. In the strength of that partnership we go forward hopefully.[38]

To this Eve added some sage words of his own. He spoke of the Commissioners' assets and of how they were managed: 'There is no secret about it and it should be known.' 'We have', he said, 'an active financial policy in regard to our various investments which is something quite new.' Their investments had flourished. Then he introduced a new dimension: there was a gross income of almost £3 million from property 'of almost every conceivable kind'. As for urban properties, at times in the past it had been suggested that the Church was not the best of landlords ('I must be frank about this because we are very conscious of it') – they had even been called 'sham landlords', owners in some places of houses with 'an unsavoury reputation'. From such property they were determined the Church should not benefit. Their present policy would be to 'eliminate' all such property by improving it 'to decent modern standards': 'Bad estate management

---

[38] Fisher's speech at press conference, 12 Oct. 1954, Fisher papers, vol. 137, fos 132–7.

produces dilapidated property, loss of goodwill and loss of revenue.' He showed himself to be personally pledged to ensure that the Commissioners should 'bear comparison with the best of private landlords. I shall not feel happy until all do'. Then, in magisterial conclusion, 'our assets are over £200 million ... our General Fund income is over £8 ½ million. Last year we spent £9 ¼ million. On these figures we are one of the very large financial concerns in England'.[39]

The effect of these two speeches at first appeared entirely satisfactory. On 25 October 1954 Eve sent over to Lambeth copies of the *Economist* and the *Financial Times*, both of them informative and respectful. An article by Frances Chadwick in the former carried the neatly ambiguous headline 'The Church's talents', and began with 'the excellent if rather incongruous news that the Church of England has been doing well on the Stock Exchange'. Before it had been growing as poor as its mice. Now, if the business-like efficiency of 1 Millbank could be applied to the whole Church what could not be achieved? The Church was being inadequately run by harassed clergy who had other things to do. 'The Church has for too long tried to run itself unskilfully, inefficiently and on the cheap.' Lay administrators might need to be paid, but they would bring economies too. There was even a side-swipe against parsons who 'cling' to 'that mystical affair', their freehold. The commitments of the Church were heavy and they could only be met by 'streamlining'; modernising organisation and methods, 'overthrowing the customs of centuries and cutting through the jungle of Church finance – just as it has modernised, with such conspicuous success, its investment on the Stock Exchange'.[40] The *Financial Times* even had a leading article beginning with Theodore of Tarsus (seventh archbishop of Canterbury and first primate of England, noted amiably).[41] 'I hope you will agree with me', Eve observed, 'that they dispose pretty conclusively of the rumour that in investment matters the Church Commissioners are "amateurs"!'[42]

News of the Commissioners' success did indeed spread. The Provincial Trusts' Board of the Church of the Province of South Africa wrote to 1 Millbank asking for 'legal and ethical' advice in November 1955.[43] The treasurer and receiver-general of Westminster

---

[39] Ibid. fos 138–41.

[40] Fisher was delighted, himself offering Chadwick only a little correction about the generosity of the laity: Fisher to Frances Chadwick, 25 Oct. 1954, ibid. fos 142–4. The article was published in the *Economist* on 23 Oct. 1954.

[41] A cutting may be found in Fisher papers, vol. 137, fo. 144. The article was published in the *Financial Times* on 13 Oct. 1954.

[42] Eve to Fisher, 25 Oct. 1954, Fisher papers, vol. 137, fo. 142.

[43] Sir Clarence Bird to M. H. McQueen, 7 Nov. 1955, CC/SEC/INVP/2.

Abbey made their way around the corner for advice on buying equities.[44] Warren himself now wrote a little book of guidance for the interested public entitled *Investment for the common man*.[45] In the midst of this there were also shadows of things to come, letters of a different kind, scattered across the correspondence folders; anxious letters from clergy and laity asking to be reassured that the standards by which the Church should live were not in danger. In July 1959 Warren wrote to one such correspondent that the Commissioners did have shares in steel and engineering, and that could be considered a potential part of the armaments trade. But then, 'No investor in anything (e.g. Food) could put his hand on his heart and say that in no circumstances will any of his shares ever be connected with the pursuit of warfare.'[46] Another priest wrote that he had been leading a course on the Church's teaching on gambling, and had found himself asked to talk about the Church Commissioners' 'gambling on the Stock Exchange'.[47] Another observed the Church's criticisms of premium bonds and its simultaneous speculation on the Stock Exchange. 'I wonder', he wrote, 'whether you could give me a little help over this question as I know little or nothing about financial speculation.'[48] A vicar wrote that he had hidden all copies of the annual review of the Commissioners' activities, which were sent out to the parishes, because when he had distributed them as he should they caused more problems than they solved. For his part Warren drew some neat distinctions for such as these. There were, he said, two types of speculation in ordinary shares: the speculator who bought shares in the hope that the price would rise and a profit could then be made by selling them; and the 'true investor who buys them in the hope that the income from those shares will increase year by year'.[49] It could always be added, and often it was, that the income was, after all, to pay the clergy.

The estates of the Church

In 1948 the estates of the Church were widely scattered, sometimes almost idiosyncratically. There were large swathes of land in the great farms of the north, little patches of obscure land across parishes up and down the country, some of it fertile and profitable, some of it barren and without evident purpose. Tithe, too, remained a minor

[44] Receiver-general, Westminster Abbey, to Warren, 8 May 1959, ibid.
[45] Mortimer Warren, *Investment for the common man,* London 1958.
[46] Warren to P. W. Woodman, 30 July 1959, CC/SEC/INVP/2.
[47] J. C. Boyes to Church Commissioners, 11 Nov. 1959, CC/SEC/INVP/2.
[48] Ernest Gregson to Warren, n.d., ibid.
[49] Warren to H. K. R. Twinn, 10 Jan. 1961, ibid.

financial reality. The 1925 Tithe Act and the Measure which established the Church Commissioners in 1947 combined to make the Commissioners trustees and collectors of corn rents for 466 incumbents. In thirty other parishes corn rents were collected for the General Fund. The new age of rationalisation demanded that this portfolio be reformed, sensitively, over time. If the move onto the Stock Market was the first great financial revolution which the Church Commissioners had forged, the second was this immense work of rationalisation.

The countryside

The success of the investments on the Stock Exchange in the early 1950s might well have overshadowed that steadier dimension of the Commissioners' affairs, the countryside. But when Fisher and Eve had met in February 1953 with the future in mind they had turned to these questions too. Eve remarked that he was not 'perfectly satisfied' with the way in which the estates were managed. Cluttons and Smith Gore, in the south and the north, were wellknown, but independent: 'they go their own way'. Brown had had his spats with them. Among surveyors, sensed Eve, the Commissioners were thought to be hard landlords, and open to criticism. The tenants were 'not particularly fond of them'. Both Eve and Brown worried about this. Baker Wilbraham had tried to visit tenants, but not more than ten or fifteen in a year. Eve himself could hope only to do as much himself: 'it is a mere flea bite of the whole problem'. Brown had wondered whether one or two lay Commissioners might help out: but this might bring its own dangers, for they might appear to come between the tenants and the agents themselves and might provoke trouble. Fisher and Eve agreed that there was a need for somebody inside the Commissioners' office to give their whole time to the estates. Warren was in charge of the money which came in from investments and land; 'admirable' at both but he could not do both. Perhaps this could become the task of a new, full-time, salaried Third Commissioner? 'A country gentleman of some kind', ruminated Eve. Both Fisher and Eve agreed that the situation would never be 'really right' until the agents' control was decentralised. The two companies, Cluttons and Smith Gore, were immense. The smaller, local firms knew their people and were trusted by them.[50]

The conversation was significant not so much because of what came of it, for little did, but because it showed some sharpness in the Commissioners' necessary relationships; a great deal certainly was being set in train in the countryside. The ideal here was 'a lively and

[50] Fisher memorandum, 12 Feb. 1953, Fisher papers, vol. 121, fos 186–90.

humane administration'.[51] But the Commisssioners sought to play a social role too, and they took their role as landowners seriously. The Third Church Estates Commissioner would now disappear more than ever into the countryside on pastoral tours. Traditions were maintained stoutly. Every year dinners were held for tenants, the bishop of the diocese presiding and an assortment of Commissioners present. On a parochial level, the fact that the Commissioners owned land meant that they could be approached to contribute to the maintenance of the churches there. So they contributed to a variety of unexpected things: occasional organ appeals, for example.

Already the realities of the market were beginning to press upon this commitment. It could be seen that the Commissioners must reconcile this sincere, pastoral presence in the life and work of the agricultural world with a recognition that land, where it was not profitable, must be sold. Rationalisation proceeded with an unglamorous but steadfast purpose. At the end of the 1953–4 year, the Commissioners owned 213,095 acres (excluding woods and moors), significantly less than the 221,923 of the year before. There were acquisitions, but what was now bought must show clear evidence of its profitability. In 1955–6 rents were increased. The Commissioners also learnt how to save money on the management of estates. In 1956–7 they opened their own office on the newly acquired Halsall Estate in Lancashire, employing Lord Derby's former agent as their own full-time man, with a staff of two, to oversee the three estates of Fylde, Alston and Halsall, altogether almost 15,000 acres. This saved £2,000 on employing an independent firm of professional agents.[52] Altogether, by July 1957, the Church Commissioners employed 282 people outside Millbank to manage their estates; 124 of them on the agricultural estates, in woods, as general workers, labourers or gamekeepers.

In January 1960 a meeting of the EFC and the Commissioners' agents decided to divide all agricultural property into separate estate units, thirty-seven in the north, and eighteen in the south. But more than this, the Commissioners made it clear that if they were to continue to invest more than £11 million in agriculture they must see an improvement in what it yielded. Targets were now set down for each unit to produce a net yield of 4.10 per cent by the end of 1963, and 5 per cent by the end of 1967. The agents were, for the most part, confident that this could be achieved. By 1960 the Church Commissioners owned 9,241 acres of woodland, 6,548 acres of which were dedicated under arrangements with the Forestry Commission.

[51] Warren report, 'Rental accounts', 1, Board papers, 20 May 1955, ser. 95083/10.
[52] Warren, 'Report on the Commissioners' estates, and the rental accounts, for the year ended 31 Mar. 1957', Board papers, ibid. pt 15, sent out to members 5 July 1957.

Here, too, the weighing of advantage and liability swung back and forth. Dedication schemes brought £6,666 in grants, but then a rise or fall in the sales of timber made the income on woods vulnerable.[53]

Urban property

There was nothing new in the knowledge that the ownership of urban property, especially in London, made the Church Commissioners a serious amount of money.[54] The new oligarchy was determined to make money where money could properly be made. But it also knew from bitter experience that if urban property brought a higher return, residential property there was not without its dangers. Before the war scandal had broken out over the Paddington estates in London where, it was alleged, the Church effectively owned brothels. This left a mark on the Church Commissioners which would not disappear, but would linger, distastefully, even destructively, and for decades. Here, too, a certain amount of circumspect tidying up began. Odd allotments were swept away; there was much busy consolidation. But in the towns and cities the Commissioners also held commercial property: offices, shops, flats, showrooms, factories, workrooms. Most of it was in London. As the 1950s advanced, the capital was beginning again to flourish. It was time to reorder what was owned, and to take advantage of the new climate.

The rationalisation and development of the Commissioners' affairs here could be seen in details. During the financial year to 31 March 1954 they owned 5,155 properties, most of them houses, rented out on short lease, and 39,143 on long lease. These numbers were significantly lower than those for the previous year (6,525 and 40,060 respectively). But 'investment properties' had gone up markedly, from 88 at the end of 1952–3, to 120 at the close of 1953–4.[55] As the Commissioners were careful in what they now discarded they were also careful in choosing what to take on. In the year 1954–5 they were offered by their agents 376 properties, but chose to reject 333. They now adopted a general policy that they should own only 'well-defined' estates. The exceptions were large single investment properties and those situated, for example, in cathedral precincts. In November 1954 alone, 450 dispersed properties in London or around it were sold or auctioned off. Altogether, they realised around 50 per cent more than their

[53] Investments report for the year to 31 Mar. 1960, Board papers, 17 May 1960, ibid. pt 21, pp. 7–11.
[54] See Peter Scott's intensive study *Financial institutions and the British property investment market, 1850–1980*, Oxford 1992.
[55] Real estate and mortgages report for the year to 31 Mar. 1954, Board papers, 20 May 1954, ser. 95083/10–11.

reserve prices. This might have raised a question as to whether they might be worth keeping on, but then the money could be reinvested still more profitably elsewhere. Meanwhile, the glebe estate of St Mary Abbot, Kensington, was acquired for £374,000. The demand for first-class investments in commercial buildings was seen to be 'very keen'. In one year the Commissioners' gross rental income had yielded £362,000 more than the year before. This had been transferred straight into the General Fund.[56]

The housing estates in London, the fruits of the collaboration fifty years before with Octavia Hill, brought in a steady income; as social projects to benefit 'low income' groups, they were not, of course, meant to do more than that. In the year 1954–5 more than two-thirds of the income from the so-called Paddington estate was spent on improvements or maintenance. Now the portion in the south-east, financially the most lucrative area of the estate, was given a new title, the Hyde Park estate, and a new firm of agents was appointed to look after it. This marked a decisive shift in thinking, for the Commissioners now began to convert and even to redevelop this into 'one of the best residential areas in London'. To the north of London lay what was now called the Maida Vale estate. This, too, was reorganised and new agents appointed. The remainder became the Lancaster Gate estate. Much of this, the parts which could not be 'improved to a reasonable standard', the Commissioners sought to auction off, often to London County Council and Paddington Borough Council, for public housing.[57] By mid-1956 only one block at Lancaster Gate remained directly in the Commissioners' hands, and that would soon be sold. What was not sold was taken on by new agents.

The revolution in property development: the Church Estates Development and Improvement Company

It was within this great rationalisation that a still grander revolution of policy occurred in the financial affairs of the Church Commissioners. It unfolded within the property portfolio. As London and the cities of Britain stirred back into life after the onslaught of war the urban landscape was viewed again, with new and sharper eyes. Much of the capital, the docks of Southwark, the yawning terraces, the little high streets, the civic buildings of the boroughs, the businesses and factories and docks, had been destroyed. The new landscape was not without the power to inspire poetic fascination, not least in the British

[56] Purchases of urban properties, for the investments report for the year to 31 Mar. 1955, ibid.
[57] Ibid. p. 3.

film industry in films like *Hue and Cry* and *Passport to Pimlico*. But it also carried the lure of profit, for when conditions altered a great work of reconstruction must begin.

In the rebuilding of the cities, Malcolm Eve knew that there were opportunities to grasp, and the Church Commissioners were ideally placed to exploit them. Soon, as rental values soared, property was making millionaires. But Eve heard from friends that far more money was being made by businessmen involved in development. One of these was Sir Edward Gillett, senior partner of a prestigious Whitehall company of estate agents and chartered surveyors and a valuable ally to the Church Commissioners once they decided to sell their Paddington estate. It was this connection, and this sale, which brought Eve into the company of a young entrepreneur, Max Rayne. Rayne had little but the force of his own perceptions and ambition to recommend him. If the Church Commissioners wished to become wealthier still, he argued, they too must move into development. They must build, literally, on their greatest strength. They might begin with Eastbourne Terrace in Paddington. Furthermore, they could go into partnership with him. According to the journalist Terry Lovell, Rayne offered to put up £1,000. The Church Commissioners were invited to put up £1.75 million to finance the whole development.[58]

It was the beginning of a vast shift in the financial world of 1 Millbank. What they now needed was the freedom to set up partnerships with companies which had the expertise actually to contribute the practical work of development.

On 26 January 1956 a brief proposal from the EFC, to form a 'private limited company', came before the Board:

> In order to participate in the development of properties in collaboration with developers who have the necessary technical knowledge, the Committee has decided to form a private company to be called 'Church Estates Development and Improvement Company Limited'.

> The capital of the Company will be £100,000 in £1 shares. The three Church Estates Commissioners will sign the Memorandum of Association, and will hold one share each. The remaining £99,997 shares will be held by the Church Commissioners, who will therefore have complete control.

> Each property development is likely to be undertaken by a separate small company formed by the particular developer, in which company the 'Church Estates Development and

[58] Terry Lovell, *Number One Millbank: the financial downfall of the Church of England*, London 1997, 13–15.

Improvement Co. Ltd' will be a substantial shareholder with the right of nominating to a seat(s) on the board of directors. In this way 'C.E.D.I.C.' will be a holding company, and receive a share of the profits of each of a number of subsidiary companies. These profits will be passed on to the Commissioners in the form of dividends paid by 'C.E.D.I.C.'

The Committee reports for the information of the Board.[59]

For information, *not* resolution.

The minutes of the Board itself record no discussion. On 26 January a special general meeting was held at Lambeth Palace. CEDIC was on that agenda, too. This time there was some discussion: the archdeacon of Northampton, Cecil Grimes, asked about the capital of the company; the bishop of Sheffield, Leslie Hunter, expressed concern whether the EFC had the power to do such a thing without consultation with the Board or the Commissioners at large; Commander Agnew agitated about ultimate responsibility for the assets of the company; Mr Winckworth about the presence and powers of shareholders; and Edward Courtman on the extent of its operations. All of this Fisher dealt with briskly from the chair.[60]

If CEDIC was born discreetly, it was at once the heart of the urban property portfolio and of the affairs of the Church Commissioners. The 1956–7 financial year marked the start of a headlong campaign of sales, acquisitions and works of 'modernisation'. CEDIC soon held one half of the issued shares in two development companies, one of them soon busily at work on Eastbourne Terrace, the other on the west side of Tottenham Court Road. Meanwhile, the Commissioners sought larger shares in increasing rental values by granting shorter leases or putting rent revision clauses in long leases. Going 'up-market' seemed to make sense both financially and in steering clear of particular liabilities. Immoral use remained a persistent hazard, and the Commissioners were nervous of it. It was also a tangle. The lessee might be to blame, or the occupier, or both. At Hyde Park and Maida Vale the welfare officer interviewed all lessees and housekeepers of apartment blocks to make sure that their characters were good and that they recognised the risks involved in letting rooms to shady individuals or enterprises. Domestic decoration on the housing estates had now been transferred to the tenants themselves. What could not be 'modernised' was disposed of.[61] The Commissioners were also

[59] Board minutes, minute books, The Church Commissioners, 1 Millbank, London, 26 Jan. 1956, 2.
[60] Minutes of the special general meeting, 26 Jan. 1956, ser. 95083/13–14, p. 2.
[61] Urban property report, 1955–56, Board papers, 31 May 1956, ibid. pt 14, pp. 2–

viewing the Westminster Housing Estate, which included property in Hide Place and Esterbrooke Street, as 'ripe for modernization'.[62]

The determination to develop pressed forward and past any brief impediments. The architect Anthony Minoprio unveiled a 'master plan' for the Hyde Park estate, which was approved by the Board of the Commissioners. The second part of the Lancaster Gate estate was sold for £960,000 to one buyer who, in his turn, viewed it as an investment property. Chestertons continued to manage a small rump, but the Commissioners' office at Westbourne Terrace, which had opened in 1906, was now closed. It was decided to reduce their urban residential property to six, more profitable, estates in London: Hyde Park, Maida Vale, Westminster, Hampstead, Chelsea and St Mary Abbots. To do so would involve selling more than 40,000 properties, most of them ground rents, over a period of three years. When the pace of acquisition slowed, and then stopped, it was only because selling government securities could only be done at a heavy loss – and only after the Commissioners had snapped up the underleasehold interest in the Adelphi, of which they already owned the freehold.[63] In 1956–7 gross income from the Commissioners' estates for the first time exceeded £4 million. Within this the significance of the London estates was clear:[64]

Table 2. Income from the Commissioners' London estates, 1956–7

Estate	Capital value £	Net income £	Yield
Chelsea	452,000	30,000	6.7%
Hampstead	735,000	40,000	5.4%
Hyde Park	4,195,000	188,000	4.5%
Kensington	509,000	31,000	6.2%
Lancaster Gate	506,000	26,000	5.2%
Maida Vale	1,073,000	41,000	3.8%
Total	**7,470,000**	**356,000**	

7.

[62] Report on the Commissioners' estates, and the rental accounts, for the year to 31 Mar. 1957, pp. 3–5, Board papers, sent out 5 July 1957, ibid. pt 15.

[63] Ibid.

[64] Report on estates and mortgages to 31 Mar. 1958, Board papers, sent out 10 June 1958, ibid. pts 17–18.

Nineteen fifty seven saw the passage of the new Rent Act. This was entirely beneficial to the Commissioners, for, with the lifting of controls, rents could now be raised more freely, and they promptly were. At the same time, the men of Millbank were determined to show that they did not pursue profit at the cost of principle. In April 1958 Eve thought it helpful to offer a picture of how they were working under the act to Henry Brooke, minister for housing and local government. On the Commissioners' estates, he reported, there were no evictions, but a large number of new negotiated tenancies and leases. The process of negotiation was evidently handled with some sensitivity. In areas like Chelsea, rents were raised to market value, though even here allowances were made for good sitting tenants. In 'hard cases' – elderly invalids, for example – 'we are naturally taking the humane view'. To those who simply could not afford a rise (Eve thought 50 out of 800) alternative accommodation was offered. Some tenants were unreasonable: 'It is impossible always to be sympathetic.' In all, he believed that these increases must bring in about £50,000 a year. But it could not always be done. On the whole, they did well to trust to honesty and goodwill.[65]

In 1957–8 London County Council finally approved the 'masterplan' for Hyde Park, and the Commissioners began to set up the Hyde Park Estate Development Company Ltd. In this company the shares were owned by CEDIC and by Wates, the civil and building engineering contractors. If not all was well at Maida Vale, where multiple lettings were causing overcrowding, it was observed that 'There are signs that the estate is attracting a better class of tenant, and therefore improving in value, especially the southern portion.'[66] Again, the success of the broad strategy could be picked out in the details. In 1959–60 the Commissioners built four houses in Maida Vale and nine on the Hyde Park estate. The first group cost £21,075, but were soon sold for £31,500, in addition to which ground rents of £220 a year were reserved for ninety-nine years The nine in Hyde Park made £17,750, and ground rents totalling £1,350 a year were reserved, again for ninety-nine years. Added together, such activities promised the best of all worlds.

CEDIC had now become an immense enterprise in its own right. The accumulating consortia listed on its books showed the extent to which the Church Commissioners were not only providing the property for development but the financial weight to push every project forward. Naturally, their gains were the greater. In all, the

[65] Eve to Henry Brooke (copy), 8 Apr. 1958, sent to Fisher by Warren, 8 Apr. 1958, Fisher papers, vol. 201, fos 202–3.
[66] Report on investments, estates and mortgages, Board papers, sent out 10 June 1958, ser. 95083/17.

CEDIC now held shares in six joint development companies, five in London, a sixth in Croydon. Then there was the area surrounding St Paul's Cathedral. The Commissioners had received planning permission to develop into offices the site adjacent to the cathedral and bounded by Newgate Street, St Paul's Churchyard and Warwick Lane along with their new partners, Trollope and Colls, George Wimpey and Co., and John Laing and Son Ltd.[67]

Where did all this leave the Church Commissioners? Where did it leave the Church of England? In May 1960 Eve wrote to Fisher: 'As you will see, the figures available for distribution are vastly larger than ever before. Those of us who have been directly responsible naturally feel very delighted but, at the same time, the responsibility of running this great business is not, to say the least of it, reduced.' When he reported now on the money available for surplus allocations, Eve spoke glowingly of 'the first £1,000,000 (this is the first time I have ever used such a phrase!)'. It opened a world of opportunities for improvement. The sums were so considerable that the Estates Commissioners even wondered if they should go not simply to their annual meeting but to the Church Assembly with any new proposals. 'The embarrassment of riches', remarked Eve to Fisher, 'makes for difficulties, and I should be very grateful if there is anything you can help on to be told as soon as possible.'[68] Fisher replied, 'It is really very difficult to take in these vast sums. What a magnificent thing that under your guidance these vast sums are available, and the benefit to the Church cannot be told.' He would be utterly happy, and greatly relieved if it could be done without turning to the Assembly, and he entirely approved of doing so.[69]

[67] Report on investments, estates and mortgages to the end of 31 Mar. 1960, Board papers, sent out 17 May 1960, ibid. pt 21.
[68] Eve to Fisher, 9 May 1960, Fisher papers, vol. 238, fo. 164.
[69] Fisher to Eve, 11 May 1960, ibid. fo. 170.

3

The Cure of Souls and the Politics of Expenditure

Geoffrey Fisher arguably became archbishop of Canterbury because he was seen to be the man to put the Church in order.[1] Inordinate amounts of time were soon being committed to the revision of canon law, a campaign which seemed increasingly arid and irrelevant to those eager to pursue new responsibilities in an altered society. W. R. Matthews, dean of St Paul's, complained that a bishop now became like 'a man who occupied himself in rearranging the furniture when the house was on fire'.[2] This onslaught would not end until 1969. Then there were the church courts, and a good deal more huffing and puffing. But the age of Fisher was also one which brought a new earnestness in the organisational life of the dioceses. As Arthur Burns has shown, the dioceses had by 1870 reached a pitch of organisation. Bishops were more often to be found there; clergy discipline was effectively enforced; archdeacons and rural deans had come into their own; there were diocesan societies and conferences, missions and retreats.[3] Every diocese had from 1914 possessed a board of finance which connected with the Central Board of Finance in London. Other instruments had soon proliferated: dilapidations boards, pastoral committees, reorganisation committees. All of them answered to diocesan conferences, generally evenly divided between clergy and laity, over which the bishop himself presided. For his part, Fisher believed in the value of diocesan synods and encouraged them firmly. It was in this context of improvement that the practical work of the Church Commissioners largely came to rest, and it played an essential part in informing and sustaining it. The potential for tension between an administrative centre and these other forms was obvious, and the

[1] Paul Welsby gives the title 'Putting the house in order' to a chapter on these changes in his *A history of the Church of England, 1945–80,* Oxford 1984, 28–52.
[2] Ibid. 42.
[3] Arthur Burns, *The diocesan revival in the Church of England,* c. 1800–1870, Oxford 1999.

Commissioners were always wary of it. But in many ways it could also be seen that far from appropriating as much power as they could they framed the grammar by which power could be devolved to the dioceses themselves.

If the Church Commissioners had in 1948 inherited property and money from their two predecessors, they had also inherited a plethora of schemes for expenditure. By the so-called Scheme K the Commissioners augmented the stipends of benefices by half of whatever sum was necessary, so long as the parochial church council found the other half, with or without the help of the diocese. There were grants for first incumbencies, clergy pensions, block grants to curates, grants to conventual districts (new areas often moving towards parish status), then capital endowments in bequests and benefactions for new districts. But on 31 March 1954 most of the temporary schemes to which the Church Commissioners were committed would end. Thus it was not only in the making of money that new thought was needed, but equally in the framing of policy. Fisher, Eve, Brown and Warren were not satisfied simply to inherit old duties. They wished to modernise, to reform, to identify new needs and frame new purposes. They sought to build an efficient national Church in this modern, post-war society. In their discussions the flourishing General Fund increasingly commanded their attention.

In March 1951 Fisher received a quizzical letter from the current Second Church Estates Commissioner, Richard Acland. Now that the Commissioners were more and more deciding 'the major financial policy of the Church after 1954', should they look again at their primary trusts? As he understood them, they were 'to dispose of their resources so as best to sustain the work of existing incumbents, and so as to support the establishment and endowment of new parishes in developing areas'. He wondered if such terms were wide enough to enable them to commit themselves 'as best to serve the cause of God in the next half century?' He had seen the work of Canon Wickham in Sheffield and admired it. How could there be more Wickhams in the Church? He heard that the Commissioners had pronounced that such enterprises lay beyond their powers.[4] Fisher responded:

> The sole trust, I think of the Church Commissioners is to promote the cure of souls and if fresh needs, not already within its terms, arise, the Commissioners can always get authority from the Church Assembly but in the matter which you have in mind the element of cure of souls is certainly there. If the Commissioners wanted to there would, I think, be nothing to prevent them paying stipends

[4] Sir Richard Acland to Fisher, 5 Mar. 1951, Fisher papers, vol. 79, fos 4–5.

to Industrial Chaplains or to any other kind of special
ministry; but I think hitherto the point has been that neither
the Commissioners nor the Diocesan bodies behind them
wished them to extend in this way the use of their funds.

Much, continued Fisher, would be clarified by the terms of the new
stipends measure: who could be paid out of it and who not. The
Church Commissioners' trusts need not be changed, but they must be
sure which categories they encompassed.[5]

The Church Commissioners inherited two main trusts, one from the
Queen Anne's Bounty, for the benefit of poor clergy, and one from
the Ecclesiastical Commissioners, for 'the making of additional
provision for the cure of souls' (interpreted now as 'the relief of
spiritual destitution'). Now that the two old bodies had been welded
together, the two trusts should be weighed together.[6] The Church
Commissioners had one clear long-term commitment and that was for
the maintenance of living agents. Beyond this, inherited schemes could
be altered, or replaced altogether. So the EFC buried its head in
papers, and found that the exploration of such possibilities was lengthy
and complex. In the meantime, the dioceses received reassuring letters
lest they feared losses from new policies.

None of the Church Commissioners were evidently in any doubt
that the settling of a stable minimum income for the clergy must be a
'foundation' of future policy. Then there were the diocesan bishops
and the cathedral chapters; they had a claim, too. The cathedrals had
last received a substantial sum as long ago as 1934. There were soon
new proposals to consider too. Acland was not alone in looking to the
industrial north. Bishop Hunter of Sheffield wanted to create a new
force of industrial 'missioners', but he had no money and could get
none from his own diocese. Some of the Commissioners wanted to
support this new idea, some very much so. If the money for this were
raised at the cost of other enterprises, how should they compare their
virtues?

If the Board of the Church Commissioners itself was none too
certain of what properly lay within their mandate, it was not surprising
that the perimeters of these assorted schemes were not altogether clear
across the rest of the Church of England. It was inevitable that a
succession of appeals should arise from the dioceses and parishes,
particularly once the news of growing fortunes got about. In April
1953 Baker Wilbraham had written to Fisher: 'The Church
Commissioners are asked, or going to be asked, for substantial
contributions towards Church objects outside their usual trusts – for

[5] Fisher to Acland, 14 Mar. 1951, ibid. fos 9–10.
[6] EFC report for the Board, Board papers, 26 Apr. 1951, ser. 95083/5, p. 3.

example Westminster Abbey, St Paul's and Historic Churches.' As landlords the Commissioners had often been asked to contribute towards the repair of church towers and suchlike. Added to this, there had been a recent, 'fairly large', contribution to Canterbury Cathedral, 'justifying it on the ground that we are big landowners in that neighbourhood'. But they could expect more of this now and it would be as well to construct some kind of general rule. The simple truth was that the Commissioners were the only central body to which people turned.[7]

Fisher favoured something more pragmatic and piecemeal. He could see that the cathedrals did present a problem. But it was not a uniform problem. As the bishop of London, William Wand, observed to him, given that there was such a disparity between the financial resources of the ancient and modern cathedrals, how should that be recognised in the making of grants?[8] When, in September 1953, the Board discussed 'Contributions for Extra-Statutory Ecclesiastical Purposes' it was said that 'historic' churches needed to be preserved but had few allies. The Welsh Representative Body had asked for £500,000 to maintain its ministry. St David's College, Lampeter, sought new endowment, arguing that its theological hall housed students who were ordained not in Wales but in England and who were themselves English (over a third of 'ex-Lampeter clergymen' now worked in the provinces of Canterbury and York). Then Westminster Abbey was appealing for £1 million, and it did so happen that the Commissioners had just taken over all its estates.[9] Both the Welsh requests were turned down, but by eight votes to three a grant of £10,000 to Westminster Abbey was approved. Meanwhile, £2,000 was approved for the needs of historic churches. Fisher emphasised the 'quite exceptional' character of these grants; no future application would be approved, unless the Board itself voted for it.[10]

These were cautious stirrings. But the new ideas of this new age had yet to dawn, and as the new investments policy matured and bore fruit, such debates were to grow bolder.

The clergy stipend

Of the central importance of the clergy stipend nobody was in any doubt. The purpose of the stipend was to keep a priest in parochial ministry from want. For years everybody had agreed that it must be increased. Most now saw the Church Commissioners as the body most

[7] Baker Wilbraham to Fisher, 15 Apr. 1953, Fisher papers, vol. 121, fo. 222r–v.
[8] Fisher to Baker Wilbraham, 21 Apr. 1953, ibid. fo. 223.
[9] Board agenda, 24 Sept. 1953, ser. 95083/8–9.
[10] Board minutes, 24 Sept. 1953, p. 1.

able to raise it. But the trouble lay with the financial realities of the stipend itself: it was almost impossible to establish a clear formula. To find a practical basis for improvement, let alone a method for achieving it, was a daunting task.

'The doctor is paid by the State and by his private patients. A solicitor looks to his clients for fees. But the payment of the clergy', wrote Guy Mayfield, the archdeacon of Hastings, 'is not so simple.'[11] There was no paymaster-general, and no single source of stipend. Originally, much of a single stipend was drawn from the endowments or the glebe of the benefice itself; it might also derive from the Easter offerings, or various fees. As the financial structures of the benefices themselves varied, so too did their relationships with the dioceses in which they were situated. The only clergy who received anything from public funds were those attached to hospitals, gaols or service units: chaplains to the armed forces and the hospitals were paid entirely by the state.

By 1935 the Ecclesiastical Commissioners had augmented or endowed 9,300 of the 14,000 benefices of the Church of England in perpetuity, costing them £1,828,000 annually. This massive contribution was, it seemed, rarely acknowledged or praised. At the same time, the Church's ability to pay stipends had received a succession of blows. It had, for example, lost much in relinquishing coal royalties in 1938. Glebe land was a controversy in its own right. The Tithe Act of 1936 was, in effect, a bald work of state expropriation which meant surrendering the tithe for only £70,000,000 of government stock. It affected around 7,000 benefices, and caused an average loss in income of no less than 18.5 per cent. By it Queen Anne's Bounty had lost about £50,000 a year, and the cathedrals about £15,000. In 1958 it was reckoned that the ultimate capital loss to the Church was in the region of £18 million.[12] Even if that loss were evenly distributed across the benefices, such a figure could not be ignored. If, at first, the stipends of the clergy were not affected, those of their successors certainly would be, and some acutely.

When the money earned from glebe, capital, fees and Easter offerings was added up it was simply not enough to pay the clergy adequately or acceptably. During the 1939–45 war the Ecclesiastical Commissioners had resorted to temporary grants in urgent cases until a systematic response could be effected. By the time of the establishment of the Church Commissioners there was a new mood in the Church, which called not upon the endowments of the dead, but the commitment of the living. The laity must give more. There had been the 'Archbishop's Challenge' to the laity of the Church, which

[11] Guy Mayfield, *The Church of England: its members and its business*, Oxford 1958, 85.
[12] Ibid.

had aimed for a stipend of at least £500 a year for every beneficed clergyman. To this, the old Queen Anne's Bounty and the Ecclesiastical Commissioners had added, modestly. By 1948 the minimum stipend was set at £350, a figure still disturbingly low, not least when deductions were made for pensions, rates and the dilapidations of parsonages.

The payment of the clergy was, then, a matter of concern to a number of interlinked parties: the Church Commissioners, the diocese and the land and congregation of the parish itself. The Church Commissioners decided to grasp the issue with both hands. For some years the policy of the Church had been to separate the clergy stipend from the local politics of land ownership – in the Tithe Acts of 1925 and 1936, the Reorganisation of Areas Measure, the Pastoral Reorganisation Measure, the Church Commissioners Measure itself. Now it was possible to conceive of a national model for the stipend. But first a central register of benefice income was needed.

The crucial mechanism in the Commissioners' thinking now was not the benefice itself, but the diocese and its stipends fund. For in the modern diocese lay the means of national distribution, and only its officers could measure the realities of clergy stipends satisfactorily. At 1 Millbank it was seen to be better if the 'executive field' were claimed not by the Commissioners themselves but by the dioceses, the Commissioners confining themselves to the statement of general principles and basic conditions, giving grants to encourage local benefactions, keeping respectfully in the background. It was decided that all dioceses should be invited to join with them to 'evolve a new common policy' on the basis not of specific schemes, but diocesan block grants for purposes generally agreed and sanctioned.[13] It was not only with the intricacies of the clergy stipend that the Commissioners would have to contend. To attach the powerful, centralising motor to the arts of 'discussion and partnership' with what were, in effect, forty-three different bodies was almost to concoct a model of nationalisation without abolishing the old models of private management.

The origins of the diocesan stipends funds lay in the fabric of the Reorganisation Areas Measure of 1944, but they came into being five years later, after the Pastoral Reorganisation Measure of 1949. In every diocese in which a reorganisations scheme came into effect, the Commissioners opened a stipends account of which they became custodians. Into this went all money directed by any reorganisation scheme and all donations, legacies and other contributions made out to the bishop or to the fund itself. It was determined that a diocesan stipends fund would be used as the bishop and his board together

[13] 'Post-1954 policy: the methods of the Church Commissioners' assistance', pp. 8–13, Board papers, 26 Apr. 1951, ser. 95083/5–6.

decided, for purposes connected with the cure of souls within the diocese.

But what did the cure of souls mean? The EFC took legal advice and learned that it could embrace almost anything and anybody.[14] In October 1950 the Commissioners made the first of a series of annual block grants of £100,000 to the diocesan stipends funds, this over three and half years. These specified explicitly that the money was to be committed to clerical stipends. In November 1951 a new measure came before the Church Assembly. Philip Baker Wilbraham observed that the diocesan stipends funds existed 'for the benefit of the clergy – and for a few other people who were engaged in the cure of souls – and, for their part, the Commissioners were endeavouring to fulfil their trust'. There was a flurry of debate.[15] When a revised draft measure was returned to the Church Assembly in June 1952 it provoked a veritable parade of consecutive logical constructions. That a bishop alone might define who exercised the cure of souls still troubled some. What, it was asked, happened if the bishop was on holiday? Should he authorise somebody else to make decisions about such things? Would this not mean a transferral of episcopal authority to somebody else? 'That' said one, 'sounds rather frightening.' If it was indeed so, put in another, how should such a substitute bishop be chosen? Some clergy wanted to be sure that this money went only to the clergy. A layman from Chichester saw an amendment as a device to keep money from licensed lay readers or missioners. Somebody asked where had the Commissioners got all this money from, anyway? From bishops, deans and chapters, replied Baker Wilbraham – and they had a good claim on it too. This was not what the clergy wanted to hear. Archbishop Fisher volunteered from the chair that there was room within this measure for the diocesan board of finance to disagree with the bishop about who had the cure of souls. But then, it was asked, if the boards disagreed, by what right did they pronounce who had the cure of souls? On it went.[16] It was in November 1952 that the new diocesan stipends funds measure received final approval from the Church Assembly.

The vital task of establishing a central register of benefice incomes had by 1952 been completed. This and the new measure together offered a firm foundation for the new campaign to raise the clergy stipend. In the spring session of 1953 a motion was moved in the Church Assembly actually to thank the Commissioners for what they had done to improve the financial position of the clergy. In replying,

---

[14] See the joint opinion by J. N. Gray and W. S. Wigglesworth, 15 Dec. 1949, Board papers, 23 Mar. 1950, ibid. pts 3–4.

[15] *Proceedings of the Church Assembly*, xxxi/3, London 1951, 286–99 (13 Nov. 1951).

[16] Ibid. xxxii/2, London 1952, 10–49 (16 June 1952).

Baker Wilbraham remarked, graciously, they had worked to be just and faithful stewards. In the chair, Fisher recorded his own words of gratitude, remarking that few perhaps realised how the Commissioners did their work not merely as administrators but in a full consciousness of 'sharing in the enterprise of the Church'. To them they owed their 'deepest appreciation'.[17] It was, altogether, a felicitous note; the more so, perhaps for those who suspected the fragility of such affections.

The Church Commissioners had not waited for praise. The poverty of the clergy stipend was now attacked with force. The Commissioners were now looking to the dioceses to set down workable minima, something like £500. If that could be done, the Commissioners could raise it to £550, and do it without invoking the parishes at all. A diocese which could set down a figure of £550 could see it improved to the tune of £600. Some dioceses found it hard to reach the new minimum so soon. To them the Commissioners agreed further lump sum grants. Meanwhile, the minimum scales for curates were also raised. In general the new *modus operandi* was effective; there were few hiccoughs and the main features of the new campaign to raise the clergy stipend soon gathered momentum. By February 1953 the Board had already agreed that the incumbent of a united benefice, or benefices held in plurality, should have a minimum of £600, to be raised to £650 if the diocese judged that a car was necessary.

'The hopes of Eve'

By January 1954 Eve was looking to press still further. He told archbishop Fisher that he believed that the levels of payment were still 'derisory': 'I want to set myself and perhaps others a target to shoot at. Do you mind my doing this?' Some ideas were 'very radical' and the archbishop might not approve. He called the memorandum which followed 'The hopes of Eve'. They embraced all things: moving from the basic stipend to incremental stipends which would, as Fisher observed, introduce a salary scale for practically all. Added to this would be increments, marriage allowances, housing, exceptional responsibility stipends and pensions (at no less than two-thirds of the average stipend for the last three years of service). Then there might be a new system of grading parishes where stipends were grant-aided (Fisher was less sure about this). Fisher replied cheerily, '"The Hopes of Eve" are entirely along the right lines and directed towards the right goal'.[18]

On 27 October 1954 a conference took place at Millbank to which every diocese was invited to send two representatives. Eve set before

[17] Ibid. xxxiii/1, London 1953, 123–4 (12 Feb. 1953).
[18] Fisher to Eve, 25 Jan. 1954, Fisher papers, vol. 138, fo. 5.

them his broad ambitions and they found general favour. By November the Church Commissioners were giving £900,000 a year to the diocesan stipends funds. They could raise it to £1 million if the dioceses themselves observed three requirements specified by the Commissioners: that every diocese should meet the £550 net minimum stipend, unless its bishop made a case for exemption to that rule; that every assistant curate should have not less than the diocesan minimum; and that no grant from the diocese be reduced when any extra money was given as a contribution to an incumbent's stipends by his parochial church council or by private donors, again unless the bishop saw an exceptional case and took it up accordingly. This last condition had been framed because it was seen that an increase in parish giving was greeted by a corresponding reduction in the grant given by the diocese from its stipends fund.[19]

The campaign also received sporadic support through the letter box and even in the newspapers. In February 1956 a brigadier in Tunbridge Wells wrote that if the armed forces had seen their incomes raised should there not be a 'clarion call' to the nation to 'put an end to the deplorable financial condition of their parsons'? Could a covenant system be extended across the country? Fisher wrote to reassure him: 'The fact is that for several years we have been engaged on a gigantic operation.'[20] The director of religious education in the diocese of Norwich wrote to Fisher that unless the clergy were paid the same as the teachers there would be so few left that the parish system in the countryside would break down. It was simply impossible for a married man without private means and with a family to live on £550. Almost all the older clergy had some private money. But this was less and less true of the new generation. Fisher lamented in return:

> Part of the trouble is that every time we underline how far we have got from the point we started at, we are liable to be misunderstood as content with the progress made. The other trouble is that however far we get a great number of people take no notice of it and still think stipends are where they used to be.[21]

But by now 'practically every' diocese had a minimum of £600, in addition to a house free of rent, rates and dilapidations, with Easter offerings and, in many dioceses, allowances for those with families. Of the Commissioners Fisher was always deliberately lavish in his praise. He also saw that, 'steadily and faithfully' the laity was accepting that this matter fell to them and to nobody else.

[19] Warren to Fisher, 10 Nov. 1954, ibid. fo. 26.
[20] Fisher to Brigadier O. S. Cameron, 25 Feb. 1956, ibid. vol. 169, fo. 2.
[21] Fisher to Backhouse, 22 Sept. 1956, ibid. fo. 4.

If church authorities were now tempted to be complacent, there were still criticisms. In October 1958 Fisher spoke cheerfully in a television interview of what had been achieved. The following week he received letters of bitter complaint: one came from a clergy wife who thought he should have called the laity to their duty to pay the clergy more: 'We have the grimmest of struggles to maintain our position in the community, which is totally and wilfully unaware of the plight of their Parish Priest.' They had, she continued, the largest house in the village and did their best to present 'a tidy, if shabby, appearance to our parishioners'. But the house and grounds and mounting debts hung over them, though she had a full-time secretarial post, the whole family working together to wash, cook and clean, her husband employing a pensioner to help with the garden and perambulating a large and scattered parish on a bicycle. They rose at 7.00 and went to bed after midnight: 'I hope that my Daughters will not commit themselves to a similar life.'[22] To this, and to others, Fisher's chaplain asked Warren to draft a practical and solicitous reply.

Stipendiary controversies

The officers of the Church Commissioners knew that everything connected with the clergy stipend placed them on perilous ground – and that it always would. Conditions were constantly reviewed and altered. They may well have been borne aloft by the admiration of their archbishop and even a motion of approval from the Church Assembly, but there were also bitter questions in the dioceses when the annual allocations were not quite what had been hoped for, or expected.

If the creation of the Ecclesiastical Commissioners in the nineteenth century had affirmed a determination to overcome disparities across the whole Church, and if the Church Commissioners had inherited this purpose in a quite different age of nationalisation and centralisation, the Church itself was still divided into interests and insistent on remaining so. If anything, the evolution and the new confidence of the dioceses in the later twentieth century reinforced this. The diocese now was a political and financial power which looked to maintain itself. In this might well lie an ambivalence about a distribution of wealth which was seen to work against its own sharply drawn concerns. On 31 October 1956 Bishop Bardesley of Coventry wrote to Fisher that 'feeling is running very high in this Diocese as a result of the Commissioners' decision to augment the allocation for the Coventry Diocesan Stipends Fund by only £1,500, whereas other Dioceses are receiving considerably more'. Past methods of allocation would have

---

[22] Edith Warrington to Fisher, 17 Oct. 1958, ibid. vol. 201, fos 318–19.

yielded between £2,500 and £2,800. This drop was a 'serious discouragement' to further efforts to raise money in the diocese itself. In Coventry they had managed to raise £100,000 from industry and £100,000 from the Layman's Appeal and, in each year, £4,000 in the parishes for stipends, an 'immense effort'. The diocese of Coventry, he added, was not as wealthy as people appeared to think. There was one very wealthy city and two comparatively wealthy towns, but most of it was composed of small villages and few well-to-do families lived there. He warned that the archdeacon of Warwick, Malcom Parr, was also writing.[23]

The archdeacon's letter, copied to Eve, Warren and Fisher, was if anything harsher. Coventry had seen its allocation drop from £14,000 of the much paraded 'first million' to £1,500 of the 'second million'. This was 'very drastic'. The archbishop had urged the dioceses to take up the challenge of funding stipends, had even come to Coventry to promote the cause to industrialists there. Now they had done so they had been penalised. On this letter somebody, probably Warren, scribbled in the margin 'Very fortunate to have industrialists'. The policy, pressed the archdeacon, was 'misguided', 'short-sighted', 'regrettable', 'inequitable', 'calculated to encourage inertia and to subsidise inaction and to discourage self-help'. It would foster a spirit of "Wait and let the Church Commissioners do it'. ('Nonsense' scribbled again in the margin.) The archbishop had spoken publicly of a vast new general allocation of £250,000. Yet in Coventry they were receiving less than they had when less had been available.[24]

Fisher replied to the bishop that he found the archdeacon's attack 'rather a broadcast assault, and he should be warned against it .... you will tell him, I am sure, that while you cannot reveal all the methods adopted by the Church Commissioners, you are satisfied that their intentions are absolutely impartial and their results are the best they can do to meet all the needs of the clergy'.[25] To the archdeacon he then wrote, 'These matters are, as you know, full of difficulties and an Archangel cannot arrange them all to everybody's satisfaction.' The Commissioners worked with 'the most complete impartiality'. They were armed with the best statistics available and they sought 'a reasonable equality': 'Whether they succeed or fail is, so to speak, neither here nor there, because anybody might easily fail and nobody else would succeed so well as they do.'[26]

[23] Bishop Cuthbert Bardesley to Fisher, 31 Oct. 1956, ibid. vol. 169, fo. 7.
[24] Archdeacon of Warwick to Fisher, 9 Nov. 1956, ibid. fos 10–11.
[25] Fisher to Bardesley, 16 Nov. 1956, ibid. fo. 12.
[26] Fisher to the archdeacon of Warwick, 16 Nov. 1956, ibid. fo. 13.

Bishop Bardesley was then packed off to Eve, whom he found 'most helpful'. He promised 'some quiet words' with the archdeacon.[27] In such a way was this first rebellion against the allocations policy of the Church Commissioners subdued.

Wrestle as the Commissioners might, the struggle to standardise the stipend proved almost impossible, just as the computation of the minimum stipend was an ongoing drama, because the dioceses took a different view on how best to spend their quotas. They might be put towards the stipends of incumbents, or towards those of curates. Moreover, each diocese had its own methods of computing the stipends themselves. Some made allowances for clergy who had children, though these varied hugely. Some made car allowances. Some allowed that united benefices involved more work and wider responsibilities, for which augmentations should be made, but others did not on the grounds that every incumbent did a full-time job. Then came extra professional earnings, which the Commissioners permitted the dioceses to include 'to the extent to which the dioceses think proper'. Broadly, the Commissioners' own view was that they should be counted, but that a 'reasonable' part of them should be regarded not as income but as expenses.[28] But these complications did not rest merely on administrative abstractions. What governed the dioceses' methods was not philosophy but need. Some simply could not afford to exclude such earnings if they were to have a chance of reaching the minima. When Fisher took this to the bishops in search of a solution he learned that some dioceses counted none of these extra earnings. Some counted them only up to a level of 50 per cent. Some counted the lot and felt a grievance about it. The bishop of Ely argued that hospital boards would rebel if they knew that giving money to a chaplain must mean that he received proportionately less from the Church itself.

The general public was sure to be bemused by this. The clergy stipend was such an oddity that they evidently found it hard to know whether the clergy were well paid (with a free house) or badly paid (and still with expenses to find). When Fisher promoted the success of the Church in raising the 'net income' of its clergy, one vicar wrote to Fisher, 'We do not complain about our small clerical incomes. They are part of the privileges of our high calling. But we find it a bit hard when our "net" incomes are paraded publicly as being considerably larger than is in fact the case.'[29] A chaplain to the Royal Association in aid of the Deaf and Dumb had lost money year on year, had to move

[27] Bardesley to Fisher, 22 Nov. 1956, ibid. fo. 14.
[28] Memorandum, 'Clergy minimum stipend and extra earnings', 5 July 1954, ibid. vol. 138, fo. 21.
[29] Reginald Iliff to Fisher, 17 Oct. 1958, ibid. vol. 201, fo. 315.

house and had been without a family holiday for five years. His application to his diocese for £650 a year had been turned down time and again. Fisher had broadcast that a clergyman now received, on average, £717 with a free house. But he was paid £47 6s. 0d. per month and this still left him to pay for his self-employed National Health Stamp.[30]

At all events, by 1958 the minimum stipend of almost every benefice was £550 net. In some cases it had reached £600. The position of the clergy of the Church of England could be seen to compare favourably with that of the Church of Wales, the Church of Ireland, the Methodist Church or the Baptist Union.[31] By the later years of the Fisher era the question was clearly becoming the more comfortable one of how to secure justice for different responsibilities above the established minima.

If stipends were exhaustingly complicated, when it came to expenses a general rule was utterly beyond the power of anybody. Expenses varied from one benefice to another, from one individual to the next. The abridged annual report which the Church Commissioners published in 1959 took a closer look at them, and the closer they looked the worse it got. By now a committee of the House of Clergy had gathered to write down what they included, and came up with a list – postage, stationery, telephone bills, office equipment, secretarial help, a 'due share' of domestic costs – lighting, cleaning, maintenance, decoration, then transport, by bus or train, or by a car, motor-cycle or bicycle, all of which must be maintained, then robes, books and journals 'theological or essential', hospitality, *locum tenens* when ill or on holiday. Standing at the top of this great pile, the committee looked down and pronounced, 'these expenses are Church expenses and ought to be borne by the Church'. But they also saw that if they were met separately by the parish or the diocese, the quizzical private citizen would have a fairer picture of the real situation which the parish priest faced.

It was agreed that the way to deal with clergy expenses must be to raise stipends. But if there were to be a general improvement, was this a matter for the Church Commissioners, the diocese or the parishes? Parochial contributions might be encouraged, as they already were, for rates, dilapidations and mortgages. A questionnaire sent round the dioceses revealed that when they assessed stipendiary levels, sixteen of them ignored entirely parochial contributions to expenses, three ignored the first £50, twenty-four did take them into account, but not any increased contributions since 1 April 1955, in accordance with the rules of the Commissioners' own block grants. The great Central

[30] Stanley Barnett to Fisher, 17 Oct. 1958, ibid. fo. 316.
[31] See a report in *The Times*, 13 Feb. 1955.

Register now showed that in 3,996 out of the total 11,345 benefices the parish helped with expenses to the tune of around £35 a year. It was likely that expenses ran at an average of at least £100 a year. But the average did not much help: the realities by which a priest lived were not average but specific. At all events, it seemed unlikely that all parishes could manage to give more. Some dioceses feared that if they gave more in grants this would discourage the parishes from making more of an effort. The desire for change was mired in the complexities of the *status quo*.

For all this, the archbishop of Canterbury, the First Church Estates Commissioner and the secretary to the Commissioners still knew how to combine their forces successfully in the creation and direction of policy. Some campaigns lasted for years. For much of the 1950s the clergy were paid not monthly but quarterly. The oligarchy at Millbank, used to the ways of secular life, thought this altogether odd. The case against monthly payments rested largely on the fact that a new scheme would cost money to administer. Many clergy thought that if the money was there at all they would rather that it went not to some new scheme of administration, but to them directly. Some in the House of Clergy remarked loftily that if a vicar could not survive on quarterly payments he probably would fail to do so on monthly ones. A monthly payment looked like a salary, not a freeholder's stipend. In the summer of 1951 the House of Clergy of the Church Assembly had debated a proposal to change the arrangement and defeated a motion which proposed the adoption of monthly payments. It was referred to the ruridecanal conferences, which endorsed quarterly payments. The Commissioners now concocted an optional scheme whereby they could make monthly advances on account of quarterly payments at no cost to the incumbents themselves. In the spring of 1953 the House of Clergy threw this out as well. A year later it was back, but the result was exactly the same. The debate continued in the spring, summer and autumn sessions of 1954. At this last session, a motion to ask the Commissioners to prepare an optional scheme for monthly payments was only narrowly defeated (by forty-four votes to forty-one). The old consensus was being steadily worn away.

If the Commissioners were determined to persist it was partly because they saw support for a monthly system in the press and in their own correspondence. Many clergy lived on overdrafts. Tradesmen and suppliers refused to extend three months' credit. The younger clergy had too few savings to keep afloat. A curate on his first appointment had to wait three months before he was first paid. What grants were offered barely did more than enable them to scrape along. Some clergy approached the Commissioners directly with requests for advance payments. This presented a quandary: to meet their needs might interfere with the relationship between the clergy and their bishops. Warren, remarked Bishop Wand to Fisher, was 'not given to sentimentality', but he wanted the power to do what might be necessary for them at his own discretion.[32] He wanted change. So did Eve, and he was no genius at patience. Everybody on the Estates Committee favoured reform – except Canon Brierley, who spoke for the clergy. The advocates of change looked for room for manoeuvre. Now with so much more money in their hands it was perhaps a good time to try the House of Clergy once more.

Fisher took the matter to the bishops, who were set against any advance payments to struggling clergy. They even said that it would be 'fatal'. Moreover, he heard that the proposal had failed in the House of Clergy very largely 'because it was advocated by the wrong people, and in an offensive way', but also because the costs of setting up the new system would be deducted from the stipends.[33] Warren replied that he would simply look towards the day when opinion would change. For their part, Fisher and Eve discussed how to bring the House of Clergy round. They were also beginning to observe a division within the ranks of the clergy, between those who were older and more established, and had a strong voice in the Church Assembly, and those who were younger and poorer and were barely heard there. Could one really speak for the other? The young critics viewed their opponents in the Church Assembly as Victorians with private means, who thought it 'rather *infra dig*' to be paid monthly. For his part Fisher discounted the idea that a clergyman who could not manage on a quarterly stipend could not manage on a monthly one either: 'people who are not good with money sometimes look a month ahead, but find it baffling to look a quarter ahead'. If at least half the House of Clergy wanted it they should not allow themselves to be frustrated by what was now becoming a 'tiny majority'.[34]

Nobody knew as much about the clergy across the Church of England as the officers of the Church Commissioners. Warren now brought the arts of empiricism to bear on the politics of the Church. At Millbank they had found a handy new use for the Central Registry of Benefices:

> There are 344 members of the House and, if we deduct (say) 144 for archdeacons and deans, it still leaves 200 parochial clergy in the House. According to our central register of benefice incomes here only 14 of these 200 are on the minimum benefice income of £550. Therefore it is very

---

[32] Bishop of London to Fisher, 20 May 1954, Fisher papers, vol. 138, fo. 17.
[33] Fisher to Warren, n.d. [July 1954], ibid. fo. 22.
[34] Fisher to Eve, 24 Nov. 1954, ibid. fo. 33.

obvious that the members of the House of Clergy are not, generally speaking, those who feel the pinch from trying to live on £550 with quarterly payments.

Warren was now sure that the change must come. Its opponents could do no more. And it was better to set it in motion than wait and end up being pushed along by 'popular clamour'.[35] Fisher replied that this 'delighted' him.[36]

On 17 February 1957 Canon Brierley moved a compromise motion in the Church Assembly that, on request, an individual clergyman could apply to the Commissioners for an advance each month of approximately one-third of the net quarterly sum due to him as his stipend. He paid warm tribute to Malcolm Eve, 'a tremendous driving force in the Church's economic and financial position', blandly commended the measure and was followed by a respectful succession of advocates. There was modest resistance from Canon Hussey of Manchester; Major Monckton waved an amendment at them all but was asked firmly to put it down. The earl of Selborne observed that the debate would seem baffling to laity who dealt with business staffs. If the scheme would cost £15,000, it was only a fraction of the money spent by the Commissioners. A priest from York told the Assembly that poorer clergy owed much to the kindness of their bank managers: they should think of younger, poorer clergy with families at Christmas time. The House of Clergy did not speak for them. Fisher emphasised that this was a compromise, that the Commissioners themselves were divided. It seemed to him that the argument for monthly payments was a moral one, and opposition to it was a financial one. If £15,000 worried them, they should remember that the Commissioners spent £5 million on stipends altogether. He offered a few sums to reinforce the point and then blandly disclaimed a view of his own. Brierley measured his distance from the archbishop rather precisely and observed that he wanted an end to a business which he found sordid. There was a final flurry of confusion before the motion was carried; this time, Fisher observed, by a very large majority.[37] The campaign to introduce this modest reform had taken six years of hard labour and involved the attentions of almost every department and dimension of the Church's life. Within a generation it would be virtually forgotten.

[35] Warren to Fisher, 7 Dec. 1954, ibid. fo. 34.
[36] Fisher to Warren, 11 Dec. 1954, ibid. fo. 35.
[37] *Proceedings of the Church Assembly*, xxxvii/1, London 1957 (17 Feb. 1957).

The clergy pension

In earlier days the clergy had evidently not given much thought to retirement. But the pension was one of the defining social revolutions of the twentieth century, becoming a reality and then a general rule. But, even at the end of the century few, if any – from the politicians in parliaments and the civil servants of Whitehall to the actuaries and accountants of the life assurance companies and private companies – knew how to measure what this must involve, and what it must cost.

A compulsory pension scheme for the clergy had been established in 1927. A refining measure had passed through the Church Assembly in 1930. Soon an incumbent who retired at seventy having served forty years received £200 a year. By 1945 £50,000 of the annual budget of £145,000 of the Central Board of Finance was committed to clergy pensions. A further Clergy Pensions Measure, which tinkered with existing arrangements, followed in 1948. It was not enough. As the clergy stipend needed to be overhauled, so did the clergy pension.

In taking firm responsibility for retirement, however, the Commissioners had to deal with something more than the simple clergy pension. There were two other dimensions to the question. First, the position of clergy widows – and their plight was more severe still – and, second, the housing of retired clergy. If an incumbent lived in a house that was not his own, and which was attached to his job, he faced retirement without a home at all. If he died while working, his widow was homeless. For the first quarter of the twentieth century retirement was only possible if the incumbent simply took a quarter of the endowment income of his last parish. This was unsatisfactory, even destructive, for both the retiring incumbent and his successor. The Clergy Pensions Board of the Church Assembly had, in the 1950s, seventeen homes for 173 occupants, and also other houses, some of them bungalows. If he had nowhere to go, a clergyman must simply work until he died. Quite apart from anything else, the vision of a perpetually ageing clergy working with decreasing powers to the bitter end was not attractive, and not at all an image of a modern, vigorous Church. A suitable arrangement for retirement was absolutely necessary both for the clergy themselves and for their parishes.

Of all those who lobbied Lambeth in this new age, it was the advocates of improved pensions, for clergy, and for their widows, who shouted loudest and longest. There were letters from widows, letters from impoverished clergy, frustrated, indignant, lamenting. The push for improvement now came from the deans of the cathedrals who gathered in the summer of 1953 to issue a resolution calling for improvement. It was duly passed on to the Board of the Church Commissioners. By the end of 1953 momentum for a new measure had gathered. Stipends had reached a minimum of £550, and might rise to £600. But the present pension scale stood at only £210. A new paradigm was now sketched out. The Pensions Board had a fund of £8 million, which was not a great deal, and much of its income had to be used to support its capital, rather than extend their ongoing provision. This could be removed if the whole lot, minus the share relating to widows and dependants, passed into the General Fund of the Commissioners, where far more could be gained with it, and for it. The Commissioners might then guarantee the payment of all clergy pensions (excepting discretionary ones) and seek to raise the basic pension to £300 a year at the age of seventy, after forty years of service. The dioceses would no longer contribute; an annual contribution of £50,000 from the Church Assembly would end. All of this would do little to change the basic imprint of the 1948 Measure, 'but', it was added carefully, 'the Church Commissioners would, of course, have to control any financial commitment for which they might have to find the money'.

At Millbank they had inspected the figures. Of income they could be fairly sure when one put together the Commissioners' existing commitments (about £200,000), an additional allocation (about £330,000) and the Pensions Board's investments (about £320,000) there was something like £850,000 to bring to bear on the matter. 'On the side of outgoings, any precise calculation is extremely difficult. We must not promise more than we are able to perform.' All of this, Baker Wilbraham had owned to the Board, was complicated and would leave 'some loose ends': the next step would 'inevitably be a stop-gap Measure, to be replaced as soon as possible by a comprehensive Measure to consolidate and tidy up existing legislation'. But they must do something now.[38]

Whatever Baker Wilbraham's deprecations, this shot at a new measure marked a great step. For now, just as it was proposed that the assets of the Pensions Board move altogether into their hands, the Church Commissioners would assume full responsibility for the pensions of the clergy and their dependants, a responsibility not even shared by the clergy themselves, for this would be a non-contributory scheme. The Pensions Board had agreed to it unanimously, and would be a ready ally.

The new Clergy Pension Measure was now drafted surreptitiously, and with good reason for it was necessary to show that this work of administrative expertise stood above the politics of interests. Inevitably the pursuit of equity in one area often appeared simply to result in the creation of a new inequity in another. There was bound to be controversy. Nervously, they began to assess the mind of the Church

[38] Baker Wilbraham statement, 'Proposed new pensions scheme', Board papers, 10 Dec. 1953, ser. 95083/8–9.

Assembly. Now it fell not into the experienced hands of Baker Wilbraham, but of Eve. Eve still doubted himself. He had heard that 'a great many' would vote against it, preferring to relieve the diocesan funds *pro tanto*. A strong speech was called for. He asked Fisher whether he could 'be more than formal in the Chair or alternatively could you lay on somebody who could speak first and who would take a strong line?'[39]

This was, in fact, Eve's first appearance in the Church Assembly. His speech appeared, at least on the surface, brimful of confidence and purpose. He suggested that they need be 'a little careful about the Measure, because the fact that it was so good meant that it required careful probing to see whether there might not be some people who might not get quite as good treatment under it as others'. His other questions were bold and cheerful: 'How was all this possible?'; 'Would the scheme work?; Was it too good to be true?' His answers were yet bolder and happier. The actuary at the Clergy Pensions Board had approved every jot: these pensions were secure, as secure as were the stipends, and if there were troubles ahead they now had the Commissioners' reserves behind them. They foresaw a peak in the payment of pensions between 1958 and 1963, and then in the 1980s. All this had been taken into account. A contributory scheme would remain a heavy burden on assistant curates and curates with families. And so, in a sense, the new scheme was also an augmentation of stipends. It was not yet a perfect measure. It had been prepared at great speed and there were sure to be important revisions. But it was 'a very fine effort'.

There was something of a debate, but much of it wore a fortifying character. The motion was carried unanimously.[40] From there they simply raced ahead. Within just seven months of Baker Wilbraham's sketches to the Board of governors, the new measure had passed through all its stages in the Church Assembly, then through both houses of parliament and received the queen's consent. On 1 September 1954 the Pensions Board passed to the Commissioners fixed interest securities to the nominal value of £9,262,656, a book value on that day of £8,195,801, with an annual income of £289,040. The beginning of this new era was indeed a confident one. A steady succession of improvements, rationalisations and acts of consolidation followed. Almost at once the commitment began to increase.

---

[39] Eve to Fisher, 12 Feb. 1954, Fisher papers, vol. 138, fo. 43.
[40] *Proceedings of the Church Assembly*, xxxiv/1, London 1954, 2–18 (16 Feb. 1954).

A new tangle: differentials

If Eve and Warren struggled to understand the mind of the House of Clergy in stipendiary matters they found the going harder still when it came to the clergy pension. The stipend was worked out on a basis of differentials. Should the same apply to pensions? Logic and convention in secular life combined to commend it. The bishops already received higher pensions than the clergy. The rate of bishops' pensions had been fixed as long ago as 1926, and for suffragan bishops in 1945. But this was not enough to justify extension to other 'ranks' within the clergy.

The majority on the Pensions Board was known to be set against any attempt to introduce differentials in pensions for incumbents. The EFC felt that if differentials were to apply, pensions could be worked out roughly on the basis of half the minimum stipend (excluding, of course, the house). But the Board doubted that such an idea could pass easily through the House of Clergy. How could they persuade it? This was not work for Eve. Philip Baker Wilbraham was deployed cunningly at the Church Assembly, and on 18 June he addressed an informal meeting of around 150 members of the House of Clergy. He clearly sensed that the mood there was against attaching the pension to the level of stipend, and a resolution proposing it was defeated, by about two-thirds. Some contrary opinions were strong. Nobody spoke in favour of higher pensions for deans and provosts, and two spoke against them. But the clergy had not sponsored an alternative model either. The Church Commissioners were now in a difficulty. They had devised a new set of improvements for the clergy pension, and wished to press ahead with a new, general measure. But they must resolve this question of differentials first. Even Baker Wilbraham grew impatient. For his part, Eve was clear where the jurisdiction of the Assembly and Commissioners lay: 'All we can do is to ask the Assembly if they want some form of differential or *some* form of equality. The decision must then be that of the Commissioners and not of the Assembly.'[41] He was prepared to grasp the nettle. This quality of conviction might well have signalled a danger. Certainty is seldom amenable to contradiction.

A growing defensiveness began to breed muddle within the oligarchy itself. Fisher tried to take a lead on the Standing Committee of the Church Assembly and produced there a timetable quite at odds with that envisaged at Millbank. Eve was furious. He stated the power of the Commissioners firmly:

> I am very prepared, as you know, to seek the advice of the
> Assembly on general questions. I do feel, however, bound

[41] Eve to Fisher, 11 Jan. 1957, Fisher papers, vol. 191, fo. 15r–v.

to tell them that by statute it is the Church Commissioners
with the concurrence of the Pensions Board who have to
make the decisions, and we have arrived at the position that
the whole of the Pensions Board and the Estates and
Finance Committee of the Church Commissioners wish for
urgent advice on all the questions.[42]

Fisher offered his First Estates Commissioner a mollifying reply.
Surely they must not rush at this? But Eve was now riding a high horse
and was in no mood to get off it, even for the archbishop of
Canterbury. The Commissioners and the Pensions Board had given it
as their view that there must be a decision in February. To delay over
differentials must delay the other proposals. They could not hold back
simply for the sake of one house of the Assembly and one issue. Was
the General Fund of the Commissioners to be so determined? Such a
way of proceeding would establish a 'fatal' precedent.[43]

Eve's impatience was not winning allies. Brierley too had talked with
Eve and sensed that this meeting was, for Eve, irrelevant. At the
Church Assembly, the secretary John Guillam Scott remarked to
Fisher that Eve and the House of Clergy had 'got up against one
another'. The house had found him 'rather dictatorial': 'it will resist
anything which appears to be an attempt either to by-pass it or to
force it to accept the Commissioners' views'. Suspicion of the
Commissioners was growing.[44]

When the Board of the Church Commissioners met that month it
spent over an hour on pensions. Fisher himself was now stepping back
from the fray: 'I am not however prepared to die in the last ditch on
this issue. Malcolm and his supporters must fight it out with Gill and
his supporters. I shall vote with Malcolm but I doubt whether I shall
speak on the issue.'[45]

On 18 February 1957 Eve ventured into the House of Clergy and
saw there a motion proposing differentials trounced, by 104 votes to 6.
Exasperated, now he did not even want to pursue a debate in the
Assembly, not least since the official paper before the Assembly
declared that either differential or non-differential pensions could be
made to work. If Fisher still wanted a motion he must ask somebody
else to do it: 'It is quite clear that people, anyhow in the House of
Clergy, don't want differentials and, although I think they are
extremely foolish, I am not proposing myself to fight them.'[46]

[42] Eve to Fisher, 18 Jan. 1957, ibid. fo. 17r–v.
[43] Eve to Fisher, 21 Jan. 1957, ibid. fo. 19.
[44] Guillam Scott to Fisher, 21 Jan. 1957, ibid. fo. 23r–v.
[45] Fisher to Guillam Scott, 25 Jan. 1957, ibid. fo. 26.
[46] Eve to Fisher, 18 Feb. 1957, ibid. fo. 34.

The draft measure had grown bulky. By now the question of differentials was jostling for attention with the position of clergy widows, which was riddled with inconsistencies and called upon a sense of justice. A measure of 1936 had provided for obligatory contributions from every married clergyman ordained after June 1936 to ensure a capital sum of £200 on his death for an annuity for his widow. A later measure of 1948 provided for obligatory contributions from all clergy ordained after 1947, ensuring a pension of £50 a year for widows as of right and for fatherless children an allowance of £25 a year until they were 18. Then had dawned the age of state pensions, an age which had brought great improvements and, again, haunting anomalies. Clergy widows who fell foul of these systems must submit to the care of diocesan widows committees and their officers, all created by the 1936 measure, and a battery of ancient foundations: The Sons of the Clergy and the Clergy Orphans Corporations, amongst others. The Pensions Board also laid down a basic level which they should expect to receive from all sources together. If the various agencies failed to meet it, the Board would seek to ensure that the balance was met. The trouble with this was that the higher the standard became the less likely it was that the charities could reach it.

When the draft Pensions Measure reached the Church Assembly in February 1957 the bishop of Chichester, George Bell, moved that they make clergy widows their highest priority. It mattered far more than a pursuit of differentials. This won support and with each new speaker it gathered momentum.[47] It was in this context that Eve returned to press that in principle clergy pensions be determined as a proportion of the stipend received before retirement. He showed how this was indeed the way in which society itself was moving, looking at the views of both the main political parties. Furthermore, to attach a pension to the stipend in this way ensured that pensions, too, matched the increase in the cost of living. The Commissioners were, to be sure, neutral, but they and the Pensions Board did look for clear guidance. If they chose to repudiate differentials they must fix a floor and a ceiling, but he warned that this would very likely diminish pensions and also call forth a contribution from the clergy themselves. He had heard the House of Clergy appeal to principle. But where were these principles when they came to stipends? When he looked across the dioceses in search of a 'universally common stipend' he could not make one out. He simply asked the question, of course. It was not really for him to say. He was simply a servant of the Church trying to face facts.

Canon Gill replied for the clergy. Their sense of justice was outraged, he replied, by this scheme. The laity should try to understand the peculiarities of the clergy position. To begin with, they were self-

[47] *Proceedings of the Church Assembly*, xxxvii/1, 51–67 (18 Feb. 1957).

employed, not employed by the Church Commissioners. They could not differentiate between parishes; every one was different. The parochial clergy moved between jobs in a way quite different from what happened in the world of the laity, for quite different reasons and with different considerations in mind. Then it was difficult to quantify what clergy actually did, and how their work might be attached to money at all; 'surely it was wrong to import into a spiritual society conditions which obtained in the secular order'. This must create a kind of 'ecclesiastical *apartheid*'. Canon Youens then moved that all clergy, from bishops downwards, receive the same pensions. The bishops had told them to 'bear one another's burdens' in the wide differences in benefice incomes. They should apply this to pensions, then, as well. In the last session, he recalled, the bishop of Chichester had warned against the church being organised like a business. But differentials found advocates, too. The dean of Winchester, Edward Selwyn, stirred the pot by declaring that the House of Clergy had been motivated by 'the creed known as egalitarianism' ('Cries of dissent'). No other word, insisted the dean, was so right. As for all clergy being brothers, what about the laity? At no time in the New Testament did 'brethren' exclude them. Bishops and higher clergy had different needs from the parochial clergy. For one thing, they had more books (he thought bishops or deans had about 6,000), and in retirement they would want to house and read them. Another priest feared the intrusions of industry. One of the six clergy who had supported the new proposal remarked that the House of Clergy had not shown itself to be sufficiently practical. It was in vain. When the vote followed, the will of the Church Commissioners had been routed.[48]

When a new range of differential, non-contributory pensions for deans, provosts and archdeacons came before the Assembly they were approved. When it was the turn of the bishops a suggestion by Bishop Bell that they think of bishops another day suddenly became a motion. Eve now snarled that he was bewildered. The day was saved by two decisive interventions by laymen: Sir John Best-Shaw and the earl of Selborne. The motion to defer was defeated. All of a sudden the motion itself was carried.

Fisher thanked the Assembly and remarked how distressing he found any discussion about remuneration: 'They had to be on their guard, first, against a form of materialism which regarded justice as measured purely by whether one got no more and no less than somebody else, and, secondly, against the danger that one did not create group loyalties at the expense of the wider loyalties and wider fellowships.' The clergy were not a fellowship apart from everybody else: 'they were a part of the fellowship in which the laity had an equal

48 Ibid. xxxvii/1, 68–89.

place. This was a family matter, which they dealt with as equal members of a family, ready to recognize that each had got to bear his own burden and to help others in their burdens'.[49]

The archbishop's words were not kind to those who had taken the lead against the proposal. Gill later replied that he felt 'very sore' at Fisher's inferences. He had not himself initiated this debate. He had been deputed to oppose the motion. 'We did not start a "money wrangle".' If they were accused of materialism, the same could be levelled at the proponents of differentials: 'They seek to express differences of function and status in terms of money.' Fisher had observed a contemporary love of equality. This, responded Gill, was wrong. It was more the fashion to press for differentials. He added that the truth that he was paid on the level of his diocese's lowest stipend had exposed him to 'the obvious innuendo. I dreaded the debate'.[50] Fisher responded innocently that he could not think why he had so offended him. 'Nothing I said was aimed at you or anybody else. It was a modest contribution to a matter of public concern.' For good measure he added, 'Growing loyalty to Union, to firm, to party or to "cloth" is a very dangerous argument and can easily become a tyranny.' It is doubtful that Gill found this helpful.[51] For Eve, meanwhile, the vagaries of synodical government had this time altogether proven too much. He had marched indignantly out of the Church Assembly never to return. No appeal – if such were made – to lure him back would ever succeed. The imperturbable Third Estates Commissioner, Hubert Ashton, was now left with the duty of representing the Commissioners in that unavoidable quarter as best he could.

Within three years the Church Assembly faced a third great Pensions Measure, one which sought above all to tidy up. It brought the bishops out from the cover of their own rubric and united them with the other clergy. Restrictions left by the measures of 1926, 1936 and 1948 were lifted or made less stringent. The holes in survivorship pensions were filled and extended to all clergy wives widowed after 1 April 1961, at a rate of a third of their husbands' pension, by right. The Commissioners had already found the money for that. More, those widowed after 1 April 1960 were also embraced, calculated on the lower rate of pension which the husband would in such cases have had. What was fundamental to this measure – and what would prove crucial in the history of the Church Commissioners themselves – was that the new power of discretion meant that if the Commissioners had money to devote to pensions they could now do so without referring

49 Ibid. xxxvii/1, 92–111.
50 John Gill to Fisher, 23 Feb. 1957, Fisher papers, vol. 191, fo. 35r–v.
51 Fisher to Gill, 2 Mar. 1957, ibid. fo. 36.

to the Assembly at all. This was considered a great contribution to the cause of efficiency, for by now the Assembly must surely have been sagging under the weight of successive, accumulating alterations and perhaps experience gave reason to doubt its capacity to handle such intricacies coherently.[52]

[52] Memorandum, 'Clergy Pensions Measure', 21 July 1960, Board papers, 15 Sept. 1960, ser. 95083/21–2.

4

The Ancient Church and Modern Society

When he wrote of the post-war English parish in his history of the Church of England in the twentieth century, Roger Lloyd found it to be a power in decline. The reason for this lay with the clergy: there were too few of them. Between 1938 and 1949 the number of curates working in Manchester had plunged from 141 to fifty-four; in Birmingham from 178 to thirty-eight. Under these circumstances it was as much as the clergy could do simply to maintain the services of the local church as best they could. More than this, it was perceived that for many years the drive and evangelistic power of the Church had been found not in the parishes, but in other forms of ministry altogether. The parish itself had lost status.[1]

If much of the energy of the Church Commissioners during the Fisher era had been committed to a solution of the problem of clergy numbers and income, it was also to the fate of the parish that they were most profoundly connected. There was much in the practical life of the parish which creaked with antiquity and yielded only frustration. Nobody was sure what to do about glebe land, though everybody agreed that something must surely be done. Then the parsonage house was often seen to be another difficult legacy left by a history which had been governed by quite different patterns. Beyond a necessary, dogged confrontation with the bequests of the past, the parochial system must be reformed, continually. It must be made to work in these altered times, in which the population of the country was continuing to migrate from old towns to new, and in which attendance at churches anywhere was soon beginning to show persistent decline. The methods which the Commissioners now used were not new: they were the well-worn tools of trade of the Ecclesiastical Commissioners before them. But in this dense fabric the power of innovation would be called upon too.

[1] Roger Lloyd, *The Church of England in the twentieth century, 1900–1965,* London 1966, 514–17.

Living with the past: glebe and the parsonage house

The sale of glebe had fallen to the Ecclesiastical Commissioners; the sale and acquisition of parsonage houses had been the province of Queen Anne's Bounty. Both matters were now the business of their single successor. A reforming mind in 1948 might well have proposed that both be entirely incorporated within some national scheme. The fact that this did not happen revealed much about the Church of England and the context in which the Church Commissioners sought to operate.

Some dioceses had glebe agencies. But glebe was something too weighty and demanding for the dioceses yet to contend with – the northern ones would be overwhelmed. They would need large loans from the Commissioners, and if the Commissioners were to oblige they would have to apply for new powers 'unless such action could be construed as making better provision for the cure of souls'. Then there had been political change. In 1947 parliament had passed the Town and Country Planning Act, which was already absorbing the energies of the Commissioners' agents, and the Agriculture Act. Because of the latter a poor benefice might now find that it was legally required to reach certain standards, but lacked the money to comply. In this case, they might well ask the Church Commissioners for a loan.

Few believed that the matter of the glebe should remain as it was. But who should take it on? In 1938 the Parochial Endowments Commission of the Church Assembly had proposed that the Ecclesiastical Commissioners take over all glebe land of ten acres or more as vacancies occurred in the incumbencies, in exchange for the amount of the valuation of the land, or an equivalent annuity. It was a question of both management and investment. The Commissioners were not at all eager, seeing what a colossal responsibility it must be, and how difficult to manage. The more they looked into it, the worse it appeared. Their own land agents were reluctant. There was hardly any solid information to be had, about the size, location or condition of glebe land. The returns of 1937 had been incomplete (only 74 per cent). This could hardly be a priority, when there were so many other issues competing for attention and resources. It would create a new type of claimant, the poor, glebe-owning benefice. In May 1939 the Commissioners had turned up at the Church Assembly to reject the proposal.

Even as the measures for the amalgamation of Queen Anne's Bounty and the Ecclesiastical Commissioners were shuddering through their final stages, the two issues, glebe and the parsonage, were hanging in the air. On 28 February 1948 archbishop Fisher asked Philip Baker Wilbraham if it would not be better for the Church Commissioners to take it on themselves, on their own terms and in their own time, rather than have the Church Assembly force it upon them, as they had so nearly done before and as another Church Assembly committee had nearly done again. Baker Wilbraham saw that it was the Commissioners who possessed the 'accumulated experience, competent advisers and large resources' necessary to take such a matter to the Assembly. And they, too, were best suited to draft legislation and then put it into effect with some prospect of success. But still he was not eager. To begin such a task would require a great many surveyor's reports, a 'Doomsday Book of glebes' even. They should then have to negotiate buying prices which did justice to the benefices and were 'not ruinous' to the Commissioners themselves. Many were in a poor state and would need investment, even to sustain existing rents: 'Development value these days is a very doubtful quality.'[2] He was certainly right about that. Glebe land had been neglected during the agricultural depression before the war, and ignored during the war itself. The Commissioners were already being asked to approve sales at severely diminished prices, just to get rid of it.

Perhaps the dioceses could encourage the incumbents themselves to sell what seemed a burden? The Commissioners could be generous in their approval, and they would gain much valuable information this way, even helping where the greater interest of the Church was perceived to be at issue. If they saw that it was wiser in a particular case to hold on to land, rather than sell it, they might even be tempted to buy it themselves, or transfer it to the diocese, lending money for mortgages or guarantees. The Church Assembly tamely approved this proposal.

Here the matter rested until the autumn of 1956, and a bold document by Mortimer Warren. The passage of seven years had much altered the character of the Church Commissioners; nor was the Warren of 1956 quite the Warren of 1948. Both had grown in financial power and moral conviction. Now they were also clearer about the facts about glebe land because by now most – though not all – incumbents had filled in their returns to the Central Register of Benefices. At present 5,601 benefices turned in £377,226 in glebe income a year. If one guessed at the income as a whole it might be somewhere in the region of £400,000 a year. It would have been difficult for the Warren of 1957 not to have smiled at the thought of what such a figure might yield if set free and invested. In short, he looked upon glebe with a more favourable eye, and he encouraged the Commissioners to do the same.[3] Fisher supported this. Then there was

[2] Baker Wilbraham memorandum, 'Parsonage houses and glebe', 2 Mar. 1948, Fisher papers, vol. 42, fos 100–7.
[3] Warren memorandum: 'Proposal for transfer of all glebe to the ownership of the

an unexpected hitch. By January 1957 it was clear that the standing committee of the Church Assembly was opposed to this course. Eve complained to Fisher that he simply did not understand why. Again, the clergy were heard to be anxious. Some had muttered that it would amount to nationalisation. The House of Clergy saw its rights in danger. Glebe was mired in politics.

One result of the debate was a growth in information. By now it appeared that only a dozen incumbents actually farmed their own glebe land. But what was becoming clear was the new confidence of the dioceses. Glebe was often managed now either by a diocesan committee, by agents working on behalf of the diocesan dilapidations boards, by local agents employed directly by incumbents or by the incumbent himself. The first two seemed adequate, the second two less so. If Eve and Warren bristled with exasperation, they might still glimpse indications of a final resolution of the question.

In no way were the parochial clergy more obviously living and working within the bequests, the fashions and even the whims of history than in their housing. The parsonage house came with the benefice. A vicarage might be splendid to look upon but dreadful to inhabit; if it was large it was likely to be cold; if it was antiquated it was probably inconvenient and distressingly difficult to preserve, let alone maintain. A solitary bachelor might rattle around in a rectory with five bedrooms. A large clergy family could grow up in a home that was so poorly heated that they could only inhabit the odd room here or there.

The parson's freehold mattered here. His consent was necessary if work were to be undertaken at the house. But beyond this the world of the parsonage dissolved into complexity. It was enmeshed in successive Ecclesiastical Dilapidations Measures between 1923 and 1951 (which addressed maintenance); the Parsonages Measures of 1938 and 1947, the Gilbert Acts (which were refinements, or expansions, of the venerable 1776 Clergy Residences Repair Act), and a number of assorted grant or loan-making powers inherited from both Queen Anne's Bounty and the Ecclesiastical Commissioners under a Benefice Property Maintenance Scheme. If the incumbent were the legal owner, and if he or the bishop (in an interregnum) had the power to buy or sell, it was only once permission had been obtained from the diocesan dilapidations board and once Queen Anne's Bounty, the parochial church council and the patron had been notified.

In 1948 parsonage houses were seldom seen as investments, for they brought no income, but they were certainly liabilities. Now and then it was whispered that the Commissioners might take them all over and maintain them as they did bishops' houses. But managing forty

Church Commissioners', n.d. [27 Sept. 1956], ibid. vol. 187, fos 191–7.

bishops' houses was a very different matter from looking after 12,000 parsonages, and, besides, as Baker Wilbraham once laconically observed, 'we dock the Bishop of anything from one-third to one-half of his income, and then charge him a substantial rent, usually about £400 a year. To do anything of the same kind for incumbents would be out of the question'. Moreover, he went on, central ownership would remove from the parishes a degree of involvement and contribution which now were 'readily forthcoming'; 'Central funds should be used, whenever possible, to elicit local help and interest; never to supersede the necessity for them.'[4]

When the Church Commissioners became involved the incumbent paid for dilapidations himself by means of an annual charge assessed every five years by the diocesan surveyor. In many cases the parish paid that charge for him. If the parish were poor, Queen Anne's Bounty had made a grant to the level of two-thirds, a sensible arrangement but one strangely prone to dangers. To anticipate costs over a five-year period might work well in an economy of low inflation. This was not what the inter-war period brought and the war brought worse. Prices had rocketed. Work was postponed. Insurance costs rose. By 1948 it was reckoned that at least 6,831 parsonage inspections were overdue and that there were as many as 6,700 arrears, where inspections had taken place but work not undertaken or completed. Dilapidations were increasingly suspect: regarded as a means whereby poor buildings might be given a slightly longer lease of life when they should be altogether replaced.

Some had suggested that the cost of repairs might be spread among the clergy by, perhaps, a charge on benefice incomes. This Baker Wilbraham thought impractical. As for improvements, the Ecclesiastical Commissioners assisted with these, usually to the level of half the costs, the other half being produced locally. Perhaps, Baker Wilbraham mused, the legal estate in the houses might be vested in the Church Commissioners, especially if they became owners of the glebe? But even if advantages could be seen in a measure of centralisation, how could a central power step into such an intricate and thoroughly local arrangement?[5]

As early as December 1948 the EFC was reporting to the Board that the parsonage house was 'a problem', an 'extremely difficult one' too:

> The aim is clear. It is to have a reasonable house of residence in every place where effective discharge of the cure of souls requires a resident priest. To be reasonable, a house must be situated conveniently for the work, provide

---

[4] Baker Wilbraham memorandum, 'Parsonages and glebe', fos 100–7.
[5] Ibid. fos 103–7.

adequate accommodation (which with a married clergy includes accommodation for a wife and family) and be capable of being maintained without undue strain upon the available income, using 'maintained' in the widest sense to cover both run domestically as a home as well as kept in repair and decoration.

'The ideal', it added succinctly and devastatingly, 'will never be achieved in practice.' One man's needs could never match those of his predecessor or successor, new cures were always being formed and rearranged, houses were built to different standards; some wore out altogether. What must now be sought instead was 'a generally applicable method of dealing with each house on its own merits', maintaining it, altering it or replacing it. Maintenance was 'a universal and perpetual difficulty' and their first priority.[6] This, too, was a great deal to ask.

For twenty years the Church Assembly had been looking at the question of parsonage houses. There had been committees and commissions, there had been bishops' committees, departmental committees of Queens Anne's Bounty and departmental committees of the Ecclesiastical Commissioners. All this had come to next to nothing, and sometimes for the most eccentric reasons. One committee had advocated diocesan ownership, but a motion to the Assembly was proposed late one afternoon when at least a third of the members were having afternoon tea. The vote turned on one vote in one house.

It was clear to the Church Commissioners that there must be a new scheme, a new measure, for the parsonage house, and that this time it must embrace decorations and minor improvements as well as repairs, and it should embrace the houses of curates and other church workers, too:

> It is necessary to shift the final responsibility from the incumbent to an administrative authority; to separate parsonage houses from glebes and other property; to give the authority the power to plan and control the work; and to attract new money in association and not competition with other appeals.[7]

This would take time and trouble, debates in the Church Assembly, a campaign for approval, which could not be done, at least before April

---

[6] EFC report, 'Parsonage houses', 1 Dec. 1948, Board papers, 16 Dec. 1948; second report, [9] Feb. 1949, Board papers, 17 Feb. 1949, ser. 95083/1–2.
[7] EFC report, 1 Dec. 1948, ibid. p. 4.

1952. Yet the need was now, not later: 'Something must be done at once.'

There was a battery of interim schemes and allocations. One valuable effect of these was in a maturing entente with the dioceses. Arguments also crystallised. Parsonages should be separated utterly and finally from glebe and other benefice property and brought under one scheme. Responsibility for their maintenance should pass to the diocesan dilapidations boards, and any sums currently in credit in each benefice should be transferred to a diocesan pool. A conference with the dioceses confirmed the sense that something along these lines must be done. The Parsonage Houses Committee of the Church Assembly appeared to be broadly in agreement.

The Commissioners stepped into the Assembly gingerly. In the summer session of 1949 they declared a preparedness to frame a new, general scheme.[8] They then produced an interim and an ultimate scheme, the first giving more power to the diocesan dilapidations boards and maintaining them with block grants. In November 1950 Sir Philip Williams presented a further report, proposing a single, unified scheme to embrace the maintenance of parsonage houses and glebe buildings.[9] He prefaced his proposal by wondering how many sons had been put off the ordained ministry by the experience of growing up in a parsonage and declared that what the Commissioners now offered was a 'dynamic' solution. It made the incumbent a tenant of the diocese. If a house were sold, the money could be used again on behalf of the diocese. The weight of debate favoured the Commissioners now. If the clergy trembled for their freehold, it was pointed out, they must see that they were not truly freeholders. They could not pass their houses on to their families; they were obliged to see them maintained to a certain standard. A canon from Durham feared centralisation and its costs: 'In the locality from which he came, there were ancient castles occupied by hordes of officials running some of the industries which had been centralized.' But then the secretary of the dilapidations board of London told them that the rise in building costs had been such that, had it not been for the Commissioners' interim scheme, many dioceses would have broken down altogether. Edward Courtman asked if the 13,000 incumbents had been consulted about the plans. All benefice property and glebe was vested in the incumbent. These changes must not wear the aspect of confiscation. The bishop of St Edmundsbury and Ipswich, Richard Brook, argued that the Commissioners should explore the issue further with the

[8] CA 929.
[9] CA 970.

dioceses and with freedom to do so without an Assembly directive. This was accepted by the Assembly.[10]

By 1952 the dioceses had assumed a position of dominance. At the same time the Church Commissioners found themselves a party to almost every matter involving the parsonage. They held the balances of these individual benefice accounts and grant and loans funds, administered them and advised when invited to do so. They were present for the sale, the purchase, for any alteration. The EFC continued to monitor progress made by the dioceses in providing new parsonage houses where there were none at all and replacing old and unsuitable ones. A succession of conferences in the autumn of 1952 showed that the need was still palpable. Building costs had risen. House prices had declined. Replacement came at a deficit, sometimes a severe one. The EFC and the Board continued to ruminate on the complexities before them. The financial commitments of the Commissioners showed a steady increase.

By 1960 much had been paid out and much had certainly been done. For his part, Fisher was clear to those close to him that he hoped each parsonage house would simply pass into the hands either of the Commissioners or of the diocese. Warren agreed: 'I have always thought this myself but have despaired of general opinion changing in this matter.' It would come, but only when 'reactionary forces' had subsided.[11]

Confronting modern society: the new housing estates

The greatest social fact which challenged the parochial system of the Church of England after 1945 was that of migration. To some extent this was the consequence of what was now an established political consensus: the determination to extinguish the Victorian slum. Between 1945 and 1967 this gathered momentum: two-thirds of a million houses were demolished. Two million people were displaced. The cleared sites were then redeveloped. Furthermore, there was also a genuine shortage of housing, of any kind. During the war half a million houses had been destroyed or had become uninhabitable. A quarter of a million were severely damaged, and three and a quarter million damaged in some measure. On top of these colossal realities something else happened, and something which had not been foreseen. The population rose, and sharply.

Public housing became more than a pressing issue: it was the light by which public authority itself must be judged. Local authorities were

---

[10] *Proceedings of the Church Assembly*, vol. xxx/3, London 1950, 273–303 (14 Nov. 1950).

[11] Warren to Fisher, 26 Apr. 1960, Fisher papers, vol. 238, fo. 163.

offered heavy subsidies to build as quickly as they could. But the Labour governments of 1945–51 struggled to match their pledges. When the Conservative party returned to power it promised to produce no less than 300,000 dwellings a year. (It managed this only once, in 1954.) But the Conservatives brought a new dimension to the campaign which the Labour governments, for all their strenuous exertions, had disavowed: they encouraged the growth of private development firms. During the 1950s these overtook local authorities as the building powers of the country, almost doubling their achievements in 1961. Inevitably, this created two kinds of estates, a new form of explicit social separation in an old society which seemed oddly devoted to such distinctions.

As old towns and cities changed, so new towns were coming to life. The New Towns Act of 1946 granted the powers to designate any area of land as the site of a new town, and for the appointment of powerful development corporations to plan them. But the responsibility to provide education and health services remained in the hands of the local authorities. In 1946 Stevenage was designated under the act. Within three years, eight new towns had been created in the south-east alone, where the population was most densely located. After the Town Development Act of 1952 there followed a succession of town expansion schemes. By the mid-1960s there had been over fifty, half of them in London, the rest in Birmingham, Bristol, Liverpool, Manchester, Newcastle-upon-Tyne, Salford and Wolverhampton. Most, though not all, mirrored the patterns of new industries. There was also a growth of new developments, thrown up on the fringes of towns. In Manchester and London the new developments of Wythenshawe and Becontree housed 100,000 people, and were almost towns in themselves.

New planning policies in Whitehall stressed the importance not merely of rehousing but of creating new communities. Communities are not easy to create. They reappeared erratically and sometimes not at all. Often the new estates had their own schools, but few other resources – a collection of shops: a newsagent, perhaps a post office. Sometimes there were lending libraries, but not often. There were few cinemas. Bus services were variable and car ownership, though increasing, was not yet widespread. The new social and architectural consensus was the semi-detached house, with its clean lines, front and back garden and gently curving roads. Children who had once played together in back-streets were now peering over garden fences at each other, as strangers. Most of those on the council housing lists were young families, living in what Canon Roger Lloyd unhappily called 'great concentrations of immaturity, with every box-like house entered by the family on the day the last window was filled with glass'. For him, these were not houses but dwellings; not neighbourhoods but districts.[12]

And this was a secular landscape. There were no churches. This stirred in many Christian minds an old fear. In Sheffield, Canon Wickham could deplore that the Church of England had in the nineteenth century failed to baptise the emerging industrial society, but had left the great and swelling conurbations of the north and the Midlands without churches and without priests. Now, a figure like archbishop Fisher, who was hardly a model of Christian socialist anxiety, could see clearly that a great task lay ahead. It was natural for Christians of all kinds now to ask: what must a modern Church look like in this new, modern society? If there were new estates and new towns, there must be new churches, new parishes, new parsonages. How was that to be?

Much had already been done. Between the wars the Ecclesiastical Commissioners had offered to endow new districts where there were no churches to the tune of £200 a year, with a pledge that a further £50 a year would be added once a new church was consecrated. Under the New Parishes Measure of 1943, and then the Reorganization of Areas Measure of 1944, it had fallen to the Ecclesiastical Commissioners to approve buildings that were to become parish churches. Until that had happened it was only 'a separate district for spiritual purposes' with a 'minister' who was something less than a parochial incumbent, and whose population did not quite enjoy the rights of parishioners. A conventual district was then a kind of proto-parish, awaiting conversion into the real thing. For a few years yet this was the basic rubric which expressed the Church's commitment to the new estates.

Under the 1943 and 1944 measures, the official architect, and then the Administrative Committee of the Commissioners must approve new churches, and approve the plans of any new church, to be built by a diocesan board of finance under a reorganisation scheme. Aesthetic issues might be raised, but the basis of any objection was not to be on grounds of beauty, but purely practical matters of structure and accommodation. Immediately after the war it was impossible to think in terms of building new churches, but by June 1945 the Ecclesiastical Commissioners had set up an advisory panel on post-war church building, which included five architects and three clergy. In July 1946 it published a report:

> In settling our broad principles it was in our mind and has been in our mind throughout, that the Church has now a great opportunity to play a leading part in post-war moral

---

[12] Lloyd, *The Church of England*, 522.

re-establishment and that, indeed, if the Church is to
flourish as a living body, it must aim now to take its place *at
the centre of community life*. We are fully aware of the difficulties
of national reconstruction; but we are certain that national
reconstruction in the full sense of the term cannot be
properly planned, even if it can be planned at all, without
the Church having ample opportunity of a lead in moral
reconstruction.

Parochial and diocesan authorities should begin to plan as soon as they
could. Permanent buildings should be constructed to a high standard,
and embrace local materials and traditions. The public expected certain
things of a church; some parishes would insist on the Gothic. If so, it
should be, clearly, a modern Gothic. Building in stages was not
desirable and should happen only as a last resort: 'An uncompleted
Chancel remaining for forty or fifty years is not encouraging.'
Permanent halls which now served as churches would become halls
for social affairs once the church itself was built. Until then, they
should be used for worship, and social activities must take place in a
neighbouring temporary hall. If a temporary hall was impossible, the
sanctuary should be screened, with the latest methods of sound-
proofing, and a space for private worship and quiet maintained.[13]

In 1939 the cost of building had been lower than for twenty years. A
church to seat 350–500 could be built for anything between £8,000
and £15,000 (a figure which included fees, but not the site). Now
churches were more expensive to build. By 1948 the figure of £15,000
had risen to about £40,000. Naturally, this provoked a long debate
about how much money should be given to such a cause, and what
kind of church buildings should be put up. By 1949 the Church
Commissioners were offering generous, twenty-year interest-free loans
for the provision of buildings for public worship in new towns or new
developments. This did not spark a rush of applications: by July of that
year only eight had been received. Yet nobody could deny the reality of
these new housing areas. There was another discussion. Were the
terms of the offer 'unduly restrictive', or was demand less than they
had imagined? By June 1950 the Church Commissioners had decided
that grants should be made not only to post-war developments;
projects originating between the wars should be included.[14]

If the loans scheme was slow to attract interest at first, it was very
likely because the dioceses were still picking themselves up after the
war. At all events, it soon gathered momentum. This became apparent

---

[13] Report of the advisory panel on post-war church building: new churches report,
July 1946, Board papers, 23 Nov. 1950, ser. 95083/4.
[14] Board agenda, 15 June 1950, ibid. p. 3

at the annual general meetings of the Church Commissioners in July 1951 when three bishops raised questions about conventual districts, loans for curates in new areas and further forms of support for the dioceses in establishing church life in new towns. By now a total of almost £150,000 had been spent on thirty-nine applications. A further £100,000 was allocated in that financial year. Soon the Commissioners were worrying over the formation of new parishes with 'dual-purpose' buildings.[15] Should it be required that all or part of such buildings be consecrated? Here, as elsewhere, pragmatic considerations prevailed. The same mood translated the 'ministers' of these districts into 'vicars' in name, style and practice, and the districts themselves into 'perpetual curacies', if the building had a licence from the bishop for marriages.

The 1952 report

One point of significance was that this issue brought the Church Commissioners into the foreground as far as the Church Assembly was concerned. It also showed them to be in the *avant-garde* of the modernisation of the Church, for they spoke of it with commitment – and offered resources. They again proved themselves to be the engine of improvement, quite as Fisher believed they should.

In June 1952 a committee chaired by the bishop of Warrington, Charles Claxton, presented a new report to the Church Assembly.[16] This, began the bishop, was now an urgent situation. It was a 'staggering' fact that within a single generation a third of the people of the country had been re-housed. Soon they might see 1,000 families moving every day. These new estates, he observed, had become 'colossal dormitories with no life or soul of their own'. He knew of one estate of 17,000, blighted by juvenile delinquency, which had only two schools, six shops, one café and one small place of worship. The Church must now frame a clear strategy. In the new estates there was one priest to 10,000 people, and yet in one diocese there were 100 parishes with populations of 500 or less, each with its own incumbent. Clergy should be more mobile, and more of them were needed. Then, what should they build: temporary structures or permanent ones? How expensive should they allow these things to be?

Philip Baker Wilbraham assured the Assembly that, for their part, the Commissioners wished to make as large a financial provision as possible. Furthermore, they wished to host regular conferences at which the question might be widely discussed. A colonel from Salisbury remarked that he was surprised that there had evidently been no ecumenical consideration given to the business of church-building,

[15] AC report, 1 Apr. 1952, Board papers, 21 May 1952, ibid. pt 6.
[16] CA 1024.

as had occurred overseas. But, if the bishop of Warrington had seen an open door to mission, Bishop Jones of St Albans struck a damper note. In estates known to him the clergy had not arrived late in the day, but had arrived first and greeted the new families as they came. Yet here only a few 'faithful families' had gathered around them. The bishop of Warrington himself had observed an estate of 6,000 people, with only six families on whom the priest could rely. They would need to work hard for their conversions. A lieutenant-colonel from Exeter suggested that if they were short of priests they might appeal for lay-readers. A generation ago in the Canadian mid-West, the bishop of Brandon had sent twenty women volunteers as 'bishop's messengers' to a new community that was settling in a quite new area. They were still there. In closing the debate the bishop of Warrington again thanked the Commissioners for what they were doing. He returned to the Assembly in November to observe that the pace of resettlement had accelerated. They must 'build up the Body of Christ in places now destitute of Church Life'. In this second debate a priest in Oxford feared that they must also create evangelising cells of the faithful to endure in the rural communities and to feed the new towns. As it was, they were simply closing the churches and 'paganising' the countryside.[17]

That year the EFC recommended that once the Commissioners' pledges were fulfilled, all the excess left in balance in the appropriation account be transferred to a new reserve fund for new housing areas. This turned out to be £530,000 – no mean figure. By July 1953 the Board received a new report recommending the immediate distribution of £1.33 million for new buildings. Here the dioceses would receive the sum and distribute it at their own discretion. All of this was promptly agreed. By now, two conferences with diocesan representatives had taken place, gathering estimates of future needs and costs. The money to be committed rose to £3 million over the next ten years.

The New Housing Areas Measure, 1954

This burgeoning commitment was beginning to beg fundamental questions as to the nature and extent of the work of the Church Commissioners. If they wished to do more for the new estates, as undoubtedly they did, had they the legal powers to oblige? When the New Housing Areas Measure appeared before the Church Assembly it was partly in search of justification. That the Commissioners' money had been employed to increase the remuneration of the clergy and other living agents of the cure of souls was a matter of history. But

[17] *Proceedings of the Church Assembly*, xxxii/2, 171–80 (20 June 1952).

they would be changing their brief if they now committed capital to buildings. Men mattered more to the Church Commissioners than buildings. But, quite simply, asked Philip Baker Wilbraham, 'how could the man work effectively without what he might call the tools of his trade? He must have a house, and he must have some room in which the parishioners could meet and worship'. If they feared that their stipends might now be in competition with bricks and mortar he sought to reassure them.

For some this was not enough. Canon Douglas replied that the Commissioners could not make up their own minds 'on a side wind, so to speak'. He declared that 'all the money that the Church Commissioners had belonged to the clergy. The clergy had first call upon it, and they should have been consulted before more of their money had been handed over to a purpose for which it was not originally intended'. But these fears were not characteristic of the Assembly as a whole that day. Instead it was asked more keenly: should they distinguish between the claims of the inter-war estates and those built since 1945, which were, for the bishop of Warrington, the priority? Baker Wilbraham watched, listened and bided his time. But when he returned to speak he could not let Douglas's words pass. That most of the Commissioners' money had originally come from the clergy was true, but it had been greatly increased since then by the Commissioners' own stewardship. What mattered was the trust which governed the Commissioners, and here he offered a vital definition of the words of 1840: 'the Act said that the cure of souls was the ultimate objective of the church, and it was through the clergy that almost all the cure of souls took place'. The motion was put and carried.

It might well have seemed a satisfactory conclusion to a good day's work at the Church Assembly. In fact, many of the clergy were more or less up in arms. At the next session of the Assembly, in June 1953, a canon of Sheffield moved that any further consideration of the New Housing Areas Measure be delayed until the views of the parochial clergy had been elicited. He had talked of it with other clergy within his own diocese, and beyond, and found that that it evoked a rare, 'widespread disapproval'. This money was being 'alienated' from its proper purposes at a time of need. The clergy were still in dire straits, and deaconesses and lay workers too. Canon McGill, of Durham, suspected that 'Someone at the centre had a bright idea and therefore brought in a measure, and they had to deal with it at once.' Baker Wilbraham simply restated the urgency of the question itself. To say that this money belonged to the clergy was true only of what came from Queen Anne's Bounty; such a statement misinterpreted and misunderstood the foundation, the history and the basis of the common fund. Here, the beneficiaries were 'not the clergy but the souls to whom they ministered'. In 1840 there had been Church Building Acts and the state was 'pouring' money into church buildings. The hole, then, lay in the matter of stipends. That was the sole root of the tradition of giving to stipends. Now the hole lay in the matter of buildings. And if the sum of £1 million looked a great deal, they should see that it was 'not much' in reality. Only last January they had committed ten times as much to diocesan stipends funds.

Dogged resistance on the part of some of the clergy appeared to have been overcome by, as Fisher remarked emphatically from the chair, 'a considerable majority'. Baker Wilbraham moved that the measure proceed to revision; this was approved. But Douglas persisted: the Assembly had been presented with a *fait accompli*. This, as Baker Wilbraham replied, was illogical, for the Commissioners were simply giving effect to a policy adopted by the Assembly itself. There must be hundreds of cases in which the Commissioners must exercise their own powers under the measure. Must they all be reported? He asked the Assembly simply to trust them. But Douglas was now harrying the measure at every turn. He did not want the Assembly to give the Commissioners 'a blank cheque for ever'. But the money, Baker Wilbraham demurred, did not belong to the Assembly. The Commissioners themselves were its trustees and they were altering only the administration of their trust for the cure of souls. He repeated that he did not himself think that they need even have come to the Assembly in the first place. When the measure returned to the November session there was still resistance from members of the House of Clergy. The bishop of Warrington insisted that in supporting the cure of souls a distinction could not be drawn between the agent and the place in which he worked. The Assembly itself had asked the Commissioners to help. They could hardly turn against them for doing so. Baker Wilbraham concluded that 'he was sure (and he believed that most members would agree) that nothing could be more in line with the original trust to provide for the cure of souls than this provision to enable the people in these unchurched areas to worship together and meet for social purposes'.[18]

The 1954 measure was a landmark. Thirty-eight dioceses now became beneficiaries. For a new parish the Church Commissioners themselves usually provided a permanent annual grant of half the initial net stipend fixed by the diocese, which should not fall below the diocesan minimum or be above a maximum of £400 a year. This usually came from the diocesan stipends fund, or local contributions, or, usually, both. The new allocations were intended to cover a period of five years. But by March 1955 some dioceses were already looking certain to exhaust that allocation long before their five years were over.

[18] Ibid. xxxiii/1, 5–15 (10 Feb. 1953).

Five were asking for more. A special general meeting on 20 January 1955 approved a further transfer of unused allocations for stipends in previous years, now suspended – to the reserve for church buildings. By the end of the financial year a total of £929,000 would be in the New Housing Areas reserve. A 'second bite' for those who asked should be agreed; a 'third bite' for them all might well follow.[19] Accordingly, a further £500,000 went to twenty-eight of the original thirty-eight. Far from diminishing, demand accelerated. They had thought to review the situation in the spring of 1956. Now it looked as though this would be too late. The EFC wanted the freedom to make new grants and interest-free loans out of the fund as they now saw fit, referring periodically to the Board. It wished to make immediate grants totalling £10,000 to Hereford, Norwich and Truro, hitherto not considered deserving cases.[20] Thereafter the Commissioners issued a pamphlet which offered advice. A permanent record of new buildings was kept, and could be inspected by 'interested persons' at any time.

As consultations with the dioceses deepened, the financial relationships between the Commissioners and their beneficiaries altered. Now the original idea that grants should be matched by the dioceses was being questioned. When, in December 1956, a further allocation of £210,000 was agreed by the Board, it was also agreed that, with four exceptions, the total contribution required from each diocese be now raised, not lowered, to three-quarters of its total allocation. Definitions, however tidy in themselves, were still liable to break up in the hurly-burly of experience. What did the phrase 'church building' mean, after all? Not everybody had the same view.[21]

Between 1954 and 1959 the Church Commissioners had launched £3,200,404 at the new estates, and around £4 million was provided in addition to this by diocesan and local sources. But the EFC was still struck by the magnitude of the problem and the diocesan representatives themselves reckoned that £8 million more would have to be raised in the near future. By now it could be seen that, on average, since 1948, nineteen new districts or parishes had been created per year.

Unions and redundancies

If the idea of a national Church were to be a meaningful reality, every individual must find himself to be living in one of its parishes, able to receive the ministry and the services of the parish church. This was a bold principle which assumed a great deal, not least of a population

---

[19] See EFC report, 22 Feb. 1955, Board papers, 3 Mar. 1955, ser. 95083/11–12.
[20] See EFC report, 7 June 1955, Board papers, 30 June 1955, ibid.
[21] See AC report, 2 Jan. 1957, Board papers, 24 Jan. 1957, ibid. pts 15–16.

which professed many different affiliations and loyalties. Nor were its practical realities easy to maintain. Into the first half of the nineteenth century the parochial system was still essentially medieval. Most churches were hundreds of years old and located in places where the population had gathered many generations ago. Two vast changes then overtook the Church: population explosion and people moving in their thousands into the new manufacturing cities of the industrial age. Mere dots on the map like Manchester or Birmingham suddenly became centres of factories, workshops, commercial businesses, became the vast and sprawling cities of a new age. This tremendous movement presented the Church with much the same challenge as now faced the state as a whole. The old political structures were becoming hideously obsolete. In 1832 there had been the first national attempt to redraw the lines of the constituencies. But at this time – and for another ten years – an act of parliament was still required to create a new parish.[22]

By 1948 the institutions of the Church of England as a whole had been hard at a great work of adaptation, a sustained redrawing of lines, for many decades. There were now new dioceses, of Newcastle, Birmingham, Sheffield and Liverpool, the fruits of the last years of the nineteenth century and the first of the twentieth. There were hundreds of new, industrial parishes with solid gothic churches, built in the expectation of immense congregations. Equally, there were old country parishes which only a hundred years before had held 10,000 people, and which now had only a few hundred. But it was not enough to redraw the diocesan and parochial map. It was a matter of where to place the clergy. The situation, and hence the allocation of clergy, was changing all the time. To superintend the parochial system of the Church of England was a colossal task; and it was determined by the detail.

All this the Church Commissioners inherited from the Ecclesiastical Commissioners. In the cities they constructed new parishes and oversaw the adjustment of boundaries; in the countryside they amalgamated parishes in pursuit of a reasonable ratio between priests and people. If a church were closed the old benefice was absorbed by another, or by more than one of its neighbours: the rights of the parishioners were accordingly upheld for they still had a church to attend – it was simply that they must worship in another building within a new parish. A new church meanwhile came to life by degrees: at first there would be a hall, not in a parish but in a conventual district, and then, if new life took root and prospered, a new church building would follow and a new parish boundary.

---

[22] For a detailed survey see K. D. M. Snell and Paul S. Ell, *Rival Jerusalems: the geography of Victorian religion,* Cambridge 2000.

Parish churches in the countryside seldom shut down altogether. This was because an effort was made to accommodate dispersed patterns of residence. Moreover, if few redundant rural churches were actually demolished, that was also because they tended to be medieval and could not be knocked down without committing an offence against history and beauty. Thus the people of rural England continued to live in parishes where services were offered to all, but now they might find themselves in a united benefice which contained four churches and was four times larger than before. They would still have a parish priest, but he might be attached not to one building, but to several, and not to one parochial church council, but to three or even four. The practicalities of running these parishes could be acrobatic. Now and then the finances could be controversial. When an old benefice was united with another, the surplus income from it was often 'diverted' to the diocese. People were left to grumble, sometimes suspiciously, that it was diverted to the bishop himself.

In a city, the fact that the late Victorian period had seen such a proliferation of new churches, many of them chapels-of-ease, posed quite different problems. Three churches might well exist within walking, or even shouting, distance of each other, and their congregations be a fraction of what was envisaged by their creators. This superabundance of buildings, many of which struggled to justify themselves in congregational numbers, was something the rational mind could not enjoy in an age of decline, the more so because clergy were in shorter supply, revenue was declining and because these fine Victorian buildings were horribly difficult to maintain without great expense. In towns and cities the relationship between unions of benefices and redundancies was far more acute.

Whatever the claims of rational institutional wisdom, disputes about what should close were inevitable. If fewer people now attended church, those who did still cared as much about their religion, and about the spaces to which they had come to worship. This could never be a matter simply of pragmatic calculation. A church had been set aside, consecrated, to speak of the sacred in the midst of the busy world. It involved, profoundly, an individual's self-understanding and the story of a community. It was hard to find a way to climb down from these realities of experience. What then happened once a church building was declared redundant? A medieval church was a listed monument and could not be knocked down. That created one kind of problem. A Victorian church often was not, and could be exposed to the full force of arguments for destruction. But that courted dangers of other kinds.

During the new era claimed by the Church Commissioners there were some striking trends. First, the decline of the villages, and the growth of new towns, was continuing. Second, in the countryside chapels of ease were seldom sustainable and many were closing down. Such closures bore witness not only to a decline in congregations but also said something about the end of an age of lay patronage, a pattern confirmed by the fact that the new or reordered benefices were now invariably passed to the patronage of bishops. This was interesting in terms of the balance of clergy and lay power in the Church. It also had a centralising effect, for the dioceses were more and more under the thumb of the bishop and the diocesan boards. With the decline of the Victorian chapel-of-ease a still more vulnerable reality could be glimpsed – the inexorable decline of Anglo-Catholicism.

Sometimes churches disappeared from the landscape with barely a flicker of resistance, in dull, sombre exercises of rational calculation as the old Victorian zeal petered out steadily in the midst of the quietened landscapes of the countryside and the noisy indifference of the new towns and cities. Sometimes there were dramas, in various degrees, characterised by shifting levels of acceptance, disinclination, opposition and resistance. When controversy did break, it was the Board of the Church Commissioners itself that passed judgement. Thus did the governors find themselves moving almost every month from questions of national significance – stipends or pensions policy, perhaps – to the protests of the people of a little country parish in the south of England or a beleaguered church in the heart of a northern city. The Church Commissioners were proud, like the Ecclesiastical Commissioners before them, of their power to adjudicate, and there was every reason to think that these things were well done. The papers which describe the discussions are often lengthy and intricate. But more than once were there complaints that a distant group of invisible church dignitaries was no proper power to deliver final judgements on intricate affairs arising on ground upon which they had never even set foot. Sometimes, a member of the Board might come from a diocese in which a dispute had broken out. If that were so, he usually abstained when it came to a vote. The effects of such business on the perspectives and methods of a central organisation could be valuable, not least because it rooted the work of the Board, and the authority of the Church Commissioners as a whole, in local questions. Perhaps here was something to save them from inhabiting merely a super-structural world of their own devising.

It was their commitment to these questions which defined the Church Commissioners as not merely an institution of maintenance but as, essentially, an instrument of reform. The Union of Benefices Measure of 1923 needed to be overhauled. When a Union of Benefices (Disused Churches) Measure came before the Church Assembly in the autumn of 1951, it made it perfectly clear that for almost three decades these matters had been addressed without an explicit sense of general direction as far as the whole Church was concerned. There was a sense, too, that the problem of closure and union had now become an urgent one. The 1923 measure had made provision for schemes of appropriation of disused churches. The ordinary powers which the Commissioners possessed allowed them to make provision for demolition, to sell the site or appropriate it in other ways suitable to the educational or charitable purposes of the Church of England. These powers was now crucially extended to allow other uses for a disused church, as might be specified in the individual scheme itself, subject to consultation with the Central Council for the Care of Churches, the diocesan pastoral committee and the patron, incumbent and parochial church council – and also the Minister of Works in the case of a building of historical, or artistic significance. The consequences of this would certainly prove to be diverse.

Church and State: the fate of historic churches

When they had first settled to discuss their aims, the Commissioners had done so in the context of a chorus of pleas not for stipends, parsonages and pensions only, but on behalf of church buildings. Cathedrals applied for grants to boost their own appeals. Churches large and small wrote to the Commissioners with the same things in mind. The deteriorating fabric of churches and historic buildings found strong advocates who persevered. Here Fisher was not so quick to move; evidently he was more eager to pursue the present than prop up the past. But in 1950 there had occurred a succession of public statements, urging the case for assistance and appearing in a pattern that suggested some deft scheme of overall co-ordination. During March 1950 *The Times* carried an editorial observing that 'There is to-day a very wide concern, by no means confined to churchmen, for the preservation and proper upkeep of English churches. They embody or enshrine a large part of the nation's artistic heritage.' It acknowledged the work of the diocesan advisory committees and the Central Council for the Care of Churches over thirty years, but observed that the cathedrals lay beyond their powers.[23] Since 1930 people had been able to turn to the generosity of the Pilgrim Trust, the great legacy of a New Yorker, Edward Harkness. Now the trust had announced that no longer would it help individual churches, except in cases in which 'first aid' was required, until a grander strategy emerged within the Church itself. It had asked the archbishop to convene a conference. Nothing had yet happened.

[23] See *The Times*, 13 Mar. 1950. A cutting is in the Fisher papers, vol. 68, fo. 382.

A week later the dean of Winchester, Edward Selwyn, preached at a service to celebrate the renovation of his cathedral roof. How long, he asked, could the cathedral itself be maintained on such endowments as it had, and by public donations? Legislation over the last fifteen years had eroded the former. He saw that some feared that state support might come with an increase in state control, but he did not himself believe that. Fifty years previously support from the French government had been accepted, without adverse consequences. What was needed in England was a larger Pilgrim Trust.[24]

The secretary to the Pilgrim Trust, Lord Kilmaine, wrote to Lambeth a week later. Since the dean of Winchester had spoken 'from his pulpit' in favour of state aid, was it now appropriate for the archbishop to pronounce his own view, 'as head of the Church'? 'That might further prepare the way for State aid without any unpleasant conditions attached. If you felt so inclined you know, of course, we would be prepared to support you to the uttermost.'[25] Fisher was rather stung by the accusation that he had not so far moved. He could, however, tell Kilmaine that the matter would now come before the Church Commissioners when they next met. He needed, he wrote, to know more of church opinion before he made a statement, or approached the government.[26]

The Board of the Commissioners was in no mood to rush, either. It ruminated on the matter at some length, content, it seemed, in Fisher's own assurance that he asked only for thoughts, not grants. Nothing came of what was now spoken. But even if the Church Commissioners felt that this concerned them only slightly, a new chapter in their own history was beginning.

Whatever was happening on the national level, there was movement at a local level. It showed in sharp relief how the pastoral and financial realities of the Church of England had found themselves enmeshed in a dense, even haphazard web of civic and national institutions. The Church Assembly requested that a committee be set up to recommend a course of action for unwanted historic churches, and one chaired by Bishop Herbert of Norwich duly met. In due course this had recommended that such churches should be passed on to the Ministry of Works and Planning 'for guardianship'. It was not enough. The ministry could not address specific cases until a general rule had been set down. It would cost a great deal to maintain the churches, and the State would surely expect the Church to contribute at least the purchase cost of the sites. Then the Ministry might 'pick and choose'. The ministry had approached the Treasury to ask for finance and the

[24] Fisher papers, vol. 68, fo. 382.
[25] Lord Kilmaine to Fisher, 20 Mar. 1950, ibid. fo. 383.
[26] Fisher to Kilmaine, 28 Mar. 1950, ibid. fo. 384.

Church itself for a list of churches likely to require this support. The Commissioners had, in their turn, passed this back to the dioceses. Most had answered.

If the government were to intervene, where should the line be drawn? It would be hard to distinguish between the maintenance of redundant churches and those still in use. The Church, too, must somehow weigh claims for the maintenance of churches still used against those of churches now redundant – and also against the cost of building new churches altogether. A Repair of Churches Commission launched an exhaustive enquiry. In June 1952 Sir Ivor Bulmer-Thomas told the Church Assembly that there were still in existence more than 300 churches in which there had been Christian life before the coming of the Normans; another 8,000 built between then and the end of the Middle Ages; 800 or so between the dissolution of the monasteries and the end of the Napoleonic wars; and many more 'of real distinction'. This was a richness unparalleled. Not even the French had such. They had weathered the blasts of time well, but between 1939 and 1949 there had been a moratorium on repairs, and many had suffered. Bulmer-Thomas was an imposing presence, and now he issued a stentorian call to action. Over ten years they would need £4 million to make good that neglect. He believed that it could be found. They could count on the goodwill of the society they inhabited – 'The parish churches of England had no enemies' – they could appeal as the most English of English institutions, politely, persuasively, firmly. He now asked the Assembly to invite the archbishops to set up a Trust for the Preservation of Historic Churches, modelled in some degree on a body called the Friends of Ancient English Churches, but not centralising unduly or duplicating what was already done locally. He turned to the world of government. In easing taxation they had the goodwill of most politicians and at least two Chancellors of the Exchequer. They should hope to benefit much as the National Trust did. This struck a chord. Canon Brierley felt sure that Bulmer–Thomas was right to judge the public temper as he did. In 1937 £12,000 had been raised in just two weeks to maintain the church of St Peter's in Wolverhampton – £2,000 above the announced target – raising a host of 6,000 subscribers and the kindness of the corporation, which offered to flood-light the church at nights. The usual congregation of the church was about 1,000. Only the bishop of Norwich was a little curmudgeonly, which was the more surprising given that the city of Norwich had more to gain from such a venture than almost any other city in England, except York. The motion sailed through, along with proposals that every church be inspected every five years. The Historic

Churches Preservation Trust came into being to the sound of applause.[27] It was duly registered as an official charity in 1953.

Uniting, preserving, closing and demolishing: the world of the Administrative Committee

Unions of benefices were the lot of the Administrative Committee of the Church Commissioners. By the mid-1950s the committee was turning over business with impressive speed, settling orders for plurality, approving schemes for union and disunion, creating new districts, altering boundaries, diverting income. A national template proved elusive, for many churches fell under different rubrics and any deliberations on their fate involved various assortments of concerned bodies. By 1958 a church could be taken out of use in five different ways: under the Reorganisation Areas Measure 1944, by a supplementary scheme and order of the Commissioners; under the Union of Benefices Measure, by scheme of the Commissioners ratified by Order in Council; pursuant to faculty granted by the Chancellor of the diocese; under Public General Acts of Parliament, by compulsory purchase by a government department, a local authority or statutory undertaker with the sanction of the minister appointed; or by private or local act of parliament.[28]

Once detached from their original purposes, these buildings took on unpredictable new lives. The little church of All Hallows-on-the-Wall in Exeter had been built around 1840, on the site of an ancient burial ground. In February 1939 the two benefices, All Hallows and St Olave's, were united. All Hallows became the property of the Ecclesiastical Commissioners; they sought to demolish it and to sell the site. But the site could not be sold: it remained, though closed, a burial ground maintained by the city corporation. Accordingly, the only possible bidder, the corporation itself, bought the church for £50 so that it could knock it down and begin a road-widening scheme. This did not happen. In 1940 All Hallows had begun a new career, adopted by the Royal London Society for Teaching and Training the Blind as a home for blind basket-makers who had been evacuated from the capital and had nowhere to work. The bishop and corporation gave their blessing. In 1944 the basket-makers moved out and the church became a repository for furniture collected from bombed-out homes. The corporation forgot the Commissioners, and granted a three-year tenancy to a new occupant: All Hallows-on-the-Wall now became a corset factory. In 1945 the rural dean noticed. He informed the Commissioners. When confronted with this breach of understanding,

[27] *Proceedings of the Church Assembly*, xxxii/2, 116–31 (19 June 1952). See CA 1032.
[28] Administrative Committee report, Board papers, 27 Mar. 1958, ser. 95083/16.

the corporation replied robustly that local industry, severely affected by the war, must be encouraged. The Commissioners acquiesced, though not happily, refusing to accept any of the rent paid to the corporation, agitating and muttering about legal action. Still nothing happened. Then, in August 1949 they found that the unwanted tenant had simply disappeared. Cluttons took possession.[29]

Sometimes the Administrative Committee found itself immersed in battles over parsonage houses and arguments about local roads. At other times it faced accusations that its schemes were an insult to history itself or virtually amounted to theft. In July 1954 the Board was asked to inspect a scheme in the diocese of Coventry, drafted to unite Arrow with Weethley and Alcester with Oversley. This would produce a surplus of the aggregate endowment incomes of the two benefices of more than £600 a year to the diocesan stipends fund. The parochial church council of Arrow with Weethley found this 'an affront to the dignity of their united parish, which has a named list of rectors going back to 1308, and a failure to stand by a sacred trust from the benefactors of the past'. But here the mother of the patron of both benefices, Lady Helen Seymour, favoured the new change and 'disapproved' of the protest. The objections were overruled.[30] Whatever claims were made for history, few could doubt the pace at which the recent past had wrought change. Sometimes the committee found itself breaking apart parishes which had already been united once but had already altered fundamentally.

The factors to be taken into account were not simply geographical or historical. The different traditions of worship within the churches themselves must be reckoned with. April 1955 brought a controversy over a new scheme to unite Snodland with Paddlesworth and Lower Birling and Christ Church, in the diocese of Rochester. The two parishes were, in the bishop's eyes, so close as to be inter-related. Together they comprised 5,000 people, many of them employed in the mills at Snodland. This provoked representations from the incumbent and council of the former, and, unanimously, the council of the latter. The parishioners of Lower Birling themselves had pledged a further £360 a year to relieve the diocese of the costs of their continued existence, and this was more than twice the amount previously given to them by the diocese itself. The church was of a 'definite evangelical' character, and it was perceived that there was an 'ever-growing desire' for that character of worship there. Moreover, new housing development was anticipated in the parish and Snodland was felt to be too far away. The protesting incumbent warned that the people would see union as retrogression. For their part the council of Snodland did

[29] EFC report, 7 Sept. 1949, Board papers, 27 Oct. 1949, ibid. pts 3–4.
[30] Board agenda, 22 July 1954, ibid. pts 10–11.

not want their incumbent ensconced in the parsonage house of Lower Birling. The bishop was not placated by this. The new pledges were not permanent, the prospective incumbent was suitably evangelical. Lower Birling church would remain open; with a union, the new parish would be able to have a curate or lay assistant. He could not think this religious retrogression. As for the parsonages, Lower Birling was 'modern, modest and convenient, and with a not overlarge garden'. Snodland, on the other hand, was too big: the vicar currently lived only on one of three floors, letting the other two; it lay at the end of a long drive which ran through a field and was uninviting after dark; and its garden was huge and neglected. This was enough to defeat the Administrative Committee at 1 Millbank altogether. The scheme was dropped.[31]

In January 1957 a scheme to unite the parishes of Bracknell and Easthampstead in the diocese of Oxford met trenchant opposition, but not on quite the grounds that even the Commissioners might by now have expected. Easthampstead was old and venerable; Bracknell was a new town. The Easthampstead council appealed to the Queen-in-Council. Their church had a strong commitment to the Book of Common Prayer. But now they found that their perpetual curate was adopting another order altogether for communion, published in the Anglican Missal. The words of introduction, the Commandments, the Preparation, the Comfortable Words, the prayer of Humble Access, all were gone. Now they faced the Roman Introit, Gradual, Tract, Secret, Communion Sentence, Post Communion and Last Gospel. Then the canon of the Roman Mass was added, and a prayer for 'Pius our Pope' was said silently by the priest, who also said quietly, with the server at the altar, the Roman Preparation and Intercessions to the Saints. No new scheme could come to pass under these circumstances. Evidently, if the perpetual curate of Easthampstead was likely to unite with anything, it was not with the parish of Bracknell.[32]

A story of the countryside: Akenham church

Quite apart from local congregational realities and questions of clergy deployment, unions, redundancies and demolitions were acted out within the further dimension of town and country planning. In October 1956 the Board considered the fate of Akenham church, situated on the outskirts of Ipswich, in the diocese of St Edmundsbury and Ipswich. In 1951 the population of Akenham was sixty-four. A union of the parish with that of Whitton with Thurleston, retaining

---

[31] Board agenda, 28 Apr. 1955, ibid.
[32] Report, 'Bracknell and Easthamptstead', Board papers, 24 Jan. 1957, ibid. pts 15–16.

Whitton church as the parish church, had been proposed. Akenham church would be demolished, its site left to 'merge in the surrounding churchyard'. But Akenham was listed under Section 30 of the 1947 Town and Country Planning Act. The ministry saw it as an ancient building, however much restored. A new housing estate was to be built 1,000 yards to the south of it. Should they not hesitate?

If the incumbent saw a reason to delay, it was only to ensure that the furniture inside be evacuated and installed in a new church in a new housing area in Whitton. The Central Council for the Care of Churches murmured that they would not 'oppose', but they would 'deplore'. They preferred that it be left as 'a reasonably stable ruin'. It passed back to the ministry, which passed it back again to the diocesan pastoral committee. Demolition, it was adamant, must proceed: 'It is not considered desirable to defer demolition so that the church can be used as a temporary store for its own furniture.'

The Commissioners' senior assistant architect arrived at Akenham. He rather took to it, finding evidence of all periods of its history inside and outside, back to the eleventh century. The register went back to 1538. The west end and the tower had been rebuilt in 1854; the pews were of this time, the pulpit and altar rails perhaps a hundred years older. The white stone font was probably fourteenth-century. There were half a dozen holes in the roof, the pews and furniture sodden and decaying. A local farmer told him that two land mines had blown out the windows and shaken the roof during the war. The incumbent volunteered that if Akenham could be saved, he would probably be able to ensure that a service could take place there every Sunday, with the help of a lay reader. The assistant architect meditated upon it all: it would cost a good £3,000 to put right.

Prospects for survival were now seen to rest on the distinctive procedural convolutions which Akenham presented to its critics. If the scheme for its destruction were upheld, objections could be allowed within a defined period, as usual. If any arose, the committee must consider them and the Board must again make another recommendation. If the objections were overruled, the objectors could still appeal to the privy council and the scheme would have to rest on the table of both the House of Commons and the House of Lords for two months before it could be affirmed by Order in Council. Then the archbishop himself must give his consent. The Administrative Committee stirred uneasily, and gingerly offered to the Board a rather fatigued recommendation that demolition, still, would be the 'proper course'.[33]

---

[33] AC report, 'Akenham Church', 3 Oct. 1956, Board papers, 18 Oct. 1956, ibid. pts 13–14.

The Board proposed a public enquiry in order to judge the state of local opinion more confidently. It was well attended. A representative of the Friends of Friendless Churches offered to adopt the church. There were assurances that money could be found locally, observations that Ipswich was growing, protests that destruction was vandalism and objections from relations of those actually buried in the churchyard. In London the Administrative Committee began to wonder if simply a part of the church could be knocked down, vesting Akenham Church as a shell, a 'sacred structure', in the care of the diocese. The diocese did not want to do this. It would prefer to spend money on other causes. There was a concession here. Akenham should be demolished, but now down to a height of four feet. They would accept the draft scheme as it stood only if the Commissioners themselves paid for it out of their General Fund. This the Commissioners could not do.

It was a dreary impasse. In September 1958 the Administrative Committee recommended to the Board that the draft scheme be withdrawn and that the Friends of Friendless Churches be put in touch with the diocese for further discussions.[34]

A story of the city: St Michael's, Derby

The spectacle of cavernous, empty Victorian city churches hung over the Administrative Committee. Of all the struggles that broke out in the age of archbishop Fisher the greatest, most bitter of these was fought over a number years, and to the last ditch, in the diocese of Derby. It arose over a proposal to unite Derby All Saints and Derby St Michael, and thereby to leave the church of St Michael redundant.

St Michael's was built in 1856, a work of Victorian Gothic, on an ancient site until then occupied by older ecclesiastical buildings. It stood only 120 yards from the cathedral. Its congregation was drawn from across the city. There were 140 on the electoral role: 'it is not by any means all elderly', observed the Administrative Committee. Its tradition of worship was Anglo-Catholic, with incense, vestments and reservation – the one church of that tradition in the centre of the city. The church had had only two priests in twenty years, and was now in interregnum, kept afloat for the last twenty-one months by an elderly retired priest. The bishop did not want to make a new diocesan appointment. The cathedral said that it had no need of St Michael's, but would gladly accept the house and hall.

St Michael's had at first been listed, but, encouraged by the diocesan advisory committee, the Ministry of Works had struck it off its list. The committee promptly proposed union and demolition. This plan

34 AC report, 6 Aug. 1958, Board papers, 18 Sept. 1958, ibid. pts 17–18.

was as suddenly superseded. St Michael's should survive and be given to the Serbian Orthodox Church.

To this the parochial council could not assent. Its objection was accompanied by a petition with 2,955 signatures attached, then by a second petition with 1,004 signatures of the city's inhabitants, Anglican or not, and twenty letters of objection. The petitions raged in deploring 'this grievous error ... a grave injustice on the ... congregation; a flouting of past benefactors' wishes ... a deplorable loss to the Church life of the Church of England in the town and the diocese of Derby'. Demolition would be seen by the people of the city as vandalism, and something done 'not on pastoral considerations, but solely on materialistic grounds'. This was a weighty, increasingly voluble local coalition, and it was determined and well organised. The Serbian Orthodox Church looked on haplessly. The dispute gathered momentum.

The Administrative Committee of the Church Commissioners sent a deputation to Derby and met the parochial council, the pastoral committee, the archdeacon and the bishop. This usually secured a result of some kind. In Derby it did not. The parochial council simply denied that St. Michael's was redundant. They had always paid their dues to the diocese and were listed tenth amongst twenty-four churches paying a deanery apportionment to the diocese. In the current year there had been an average Sunday attendance of thirty-five. When the Serbs had worshipped at other churches they had moved furnishings and left candle stains on carpets, sand on the ground and toffee papers in the pews. A Roman Catholic had been heard to say that his church was building new churches while the Church of England was closing its own down: 'What is wrong with the Church of England'? All St Michael's needed was a priest. 'You Gentlemen in London', one letter deplored, 'who deal out such a scheme have little notion of the depth of disillusionment in, and feelings of bitterness towards the Church, produced in us who are on the receiving end.' The Church was not behaving like a mystical body but a materialistic corporation. A neighbouring incumbent murmured that the closure spoke of 'party prejudice' against Anglo-Catholicism. There were smaller churches – could not one of those be closed and given to the Serbs instead? A letter from an 'evangelical Anglican' appeared in the *Derby Evening Telegraph*: 'If people are looking for an instance of dictatorship, they do not need to go as far as Russia.' A woman for whom the congregation of St Michael's prayed for three months during a time of illness wrote that her doctor had found her recovery a miracle. Another wrote of eviction, robbery: 'As the people of Hungary are persecuted bodily by an overruling power – so St. Michael's people feel they are literally persecuted spiritually.' Why turn out one congregation simply to let in another? During the war it had been 'blacked out', and became a venue for evening services for five parishes: what if war came again and St Michael's had gone?

The bishop replied that no impartial person could support these objections. The cathedral and St Michael's, and yet another church, St Alkmund's, were within a stone's throw of each other. Any 'reasonable' Anglo-Catholic could find a spiritual home at the cathedral, for they were much the same; if not, St Anne's was quite as High, and only about a mile away. If people travelled a distance to St Michael's, they might just as reasonably travel to St Anne's. The objectors were speaking not in terms of churchmanship, but congregationalism. 'Ruthless realism' may well have demolished St Michael's. To give it to the Serbs was 'a desirable act of Christian charity towards those of a sister communion'. He could show no sympathy for this display of 'selfish denominationalism'. It was very easy to stir up local opinion, and easier to sign a petition than make practical plans for the future of a diocese. Next stepped up the Derby Diocesan Pastoral Committee, lamenting local propaganda and suspicious of local manipulations. Derby had a shortage of clergy – one of the worst in the country (at a time when clergy numbers were falling by 100 per year). There was also a shortage of money to pay them. Against this the population was rising. In the county of Derby it was expected to go up from 662,000 in 1947 to 808,000 in 1971. In the same period, it was expected to fall in the borough, by at least 12,000.

As all of this accumulated for the Board, a letter arrived from the Revd Dr D. F. Najdanovic, minister of the Serbian Eastern Orthodox Church in the United Kingdom. They had been waiting, 'almost breathlessly', for an opportunity to explain their needs to responsible authority; had kept their silence in the midst of this 'journalist propaganda'. There were 300 Serbian Orthodox people in Derby and about the same number across the region. Another 300 lived in Stoke-on-Trent and came to Derby to worship. Serbs were 'religious "refugees" par excellence', and without a church which they could call their own, they remained an uprooted, depressed, stray people. They looked to the Church of England as their closest friends in the west, their 'sister church'. Then, the Anglicans seemed to enjoy countless beautiful churches in Derby itself. It would be an act of 'elementary charity' to give them St Michael's.

In July the Board of the Commissioners reflected upon all this once more. Ten spoke. The upshot was that the union of benefices and parishes was approved, but that a decision on the future of St Michael's was postponed.

The provost of Derby now proposed that the parishes should be united and that St Michael's would become a chapel of ease to the

cathedral. The name of the church would have to change. This seemed
to gain ground. In December the Administrative Committee submitted
a further report to the Board, recommending that this be accepted. It
was.[35] In fact, the issue simply did not go away. By March 1958 the
Board learned that the council of St Michael's, the Derby branch of
the Church Union and thirteen individuals had objected to the
omission of the name of their patron from the title of the united
benefice and to the union itself. The provost and the bishop now
stood their ground. The Administrative Committee agreed that these
new objections should be overruled, but offered some further, minor
concessions to the resistance.[36] For now, the church survived.

The escalating problem

The number of church closures mounted, and as they did so the best
efforts of the Administrative Committee did not seem adequate to
match the rise. In November 1960 a new archbishops' commission on
redundant churches duly came before the Church Assembly. In this
the issue which pressed most of all was what to do with those
churches which were closed but found to be too eloquent with history
to demolish. The dean of Gloucester, Seriol Evans, insisted that if the
Church of England did not find a way to deal with the question it
would solve itself, and badly. He knew of a beautiful medieval church,
filled with Jacobean furniture, which had been occupied by gypsies
who had made a bonfire of the pulpit and font cover; another church
which now lay beside a motorway, vandalised by hooligans and used,
he said, for 'orgies'; of two town churches where the congregation had
simply walked away, leaving their hymn books on the seats, the hymn
numbers on the noticeboards and the churches to fall to pieces. But
the Assembly debate soon lost itself in obscurities. There was a little
discussion of consecration and deconsecration, and Fisher himself
made it worse by asking what the difference was between consecration
and dedication? He had deconsecrated churches when bishop of
London, and now he was wondering if he had been performing some
kind of theological error.[37] The debate was deferred. Spring flowered
into summer.

In the interval the Church Commissioners had not been idle. If the
historic churches were to be protected the Church must attract the
support of the State. This could only be done if the Church of
England itself offered money of its own. There must be a Redundant

[35] AC report, 'Derby All Saints', 5 June 1957, and attached papers, Board papers,
25 July 1957, ibid.; Board minutes, 5 June 1957.
[36] Board minutes, 27 Mar. 1958.
[37] *Proceedings of the Church Assembly*, xl/3, London 1960, 378–402 (Nov. 1960).

Churches Fund. At the Assembly James Brown announced that the Church Commissioners would readily put 'a substantial sum' towards it, in so doing making a valuable contribution to the cure of souls. Now it was that the proposal for a new advisory board, appointed by the archbishops with reference to the prime minister, came to life, and this within a new web of procedure. It would still fall to the Commissioners to pronounce a church redundant. A period of between one and three years would follow during which the diocesan board of finance and the Commissioners – the latter acting through a Uses Committee – would seek to find a new use for the building. Then a decision would be made on whether, if no use had been found, the church would be preserved as a monument or demolished under a scheme prepared by the Commissioners after consultation with the advisory board. This was the essential logic which would guide the future, and the future beyond the age of archbishop Fisher. This done, there arose a further amendment, this one a fateful pronouncement in the history of the Church Commissioners: 'That the Assembly is of the opinion that there should be power to sell or lease redundant churches to other Christian bodies in appropriate cases.' There was little heat in the issue that day, and the Assembly settled happily for an assurance that there should only be sales which were accompanied by 'appropriate safeguards'.[38]

Pursuing the future: the schools

Archbishop Fisher and the Millbank oligarchy sought an efficient, a modern Church. The requirements of the past and the present must of course be reconciled without violence to either, but a Church which aimed to speak convincingly in this new society could not be governed completely by historic antecedent and convention; these things might be viewed pragmatically. Some – the clergy in particular – alleged that the pursuit of change came with an erosion of principle.

The culture within which the Church Commissioners began its work was resolute in a common determination to build the future. The future could be seen in schools. In the eyes of the Church of England the 1943 concordat with the state still defined much in the sphere of primary and secondary education. However, interest in the state of church schools had been growing steadily during the first half of the 1950s. A Church Assembly report on church schools in rural areas concentrated this interest and pressed for new policies.[39] When the Church Assembly gathered in the summer of 1955 a new sense of momentum could be felt in the air. A motion was passed asking that

[38] Ibid. xli/2, London 1961, 327–65 (6 July 1961).
[39] Church of England Council for Education, *Church schools in rural areas*, CA 1146.

the Church Commissioners, the Central Board of Finance and the Schools Council take note of the report and work to implement its recommendations 'at the earliest possible moment'. Soon there was a meeting of representatives from the various interested bodies. Almost at once it became clear that the discussion was not confined to the countryside, for in terms of finance it made no sense to detach the rural from the urban, or, indeed, the secondary from the primary. What funds already existed for the schools made no such distinctions.

Another dogged empiric exercise now found that across the country the dioceses of the Church of England wished to retain 2,500 aided schools and 3,150 controlled schools. The Church Assembly Report had seen that 1,200 aided schools and 1,350 controlled schools were facing closure. At present the assets of church schools stood at £5.75 million, with a further £77,000 in annual income from diocesan and parochial sources – though this second sum was swallowed up in servicing loans from the Ministry of Education. What would it cost to keep the schools alive?

An estimate of works needed over twenty-five years had settled at £14.75 million. Existing capital could provide for £330,000 each year and existing income could secure servicing loans of about £80,000 each year. But to undertake the full programme to maintain the church schools of England would involve £590,000 a year. The Schools Council now judged that a new sum of £1 million would ensure the future of the 5,650 schools. With a sum such as this some of the rural schools apparently destined for closure might well be saved.

The Church Commissioners simply replied that they did not have the power to spend their money in such an area. But, they added purposefully, they would support legislation giving them authority to do so, 'if the Assembly were to show a clear desire that money, otherwise available for the future augmentation of stipends or pensions, or for assisting in the provision of parsonage houses and church buildings in new housing areas, should be transferred to assist church schools'. This may have sounded cautious. In fact, it compared rather forcibly with the Central Board of Finance which, for its part, was far less forthcoming.

This entire issue was now moving noisily into the foreground of church life. Arguments were being noised abroad; lobbies were gathering. At Millbank the EFC itself was bustling with enquiries. In June 1956 a further paper for the Board declared:

> it is clearly the desire of the Church Assembly that the General Fund of the Church Commissioners should contribute a sum of £1 m. spread over the next 25 years towards the maintenance of Church schools. It is equally clear that the Assembly wished that the annual provisions

towards this sum should be found out of moneys available
for lump-sum grants and not from prior moneys available
for augmentation of clergy stipends or pensions.

The paper pronounced firmly that 'Both these wishes are financially
acceptable if the Board accepts the policy.' Moreover, they could not
hesitate for long: 'If Church schools are to receive the full benefit of
the grants, speed is of the essence.' A draft measure might be worked
out by the Commissioners for consideration by the Assembly in the
autumn of that year: 'The measure can be short and easy to draft.'
They must observe some necessary delicacies. The Board of the
Commissioners should not assume responsibility for allocations to
dioceses, for that must lie with the Assembly. The Commissioners also
needed to rearrange and trim their own commitments – and that
would require another general meeting. They must also assure the
ninety-five Church Commissioners then duly assembled that their first,
'absolute' priority would remain stipends and pensions, then
parsonages and new church buildings, and then schools.[40]

The minutes of the Board read coolly. Ten of its members,
including the archbishop and the First and Second Church Estates
Commissioners, spoke. The Board resolved to accept the EFC's
recommendations entirely as they were. No vote was recorded. But
much is hidden by this. Elsewhere debate would be voluble, even
bitter. In truth, a tremendous argument was breaking out everywhere.[41]

The new proposal came before the Church Assembly on 13
November 1956. Its proposer, the archdeacon of Totnes, Edgar Hall,
expounded the logic and the detail of the measure with precision and,
rather than appealing to ideals and principles, remarked that it seemed
to him the 'only practical solution to a schools problem that had
baffled the Assembly for nearly three years'. Quite simply, the schools
themselves were at stake. The dioceses could not provide enough
money for them. At most they could bring to the question £2 million,
and £3 million was needed. This measure was 'right, proper and
timely'; it would bring 'new hope and inspiration'. But Hall was
followed at once by a leading light on the standing committee, Captain
Douglas Doig. It was Doig's purpose to expose the frailties, even the
illogicalities, of the new measure. The £1 million offered by the
Commissioners over twenty-five years was, he thought, 'a rather
preposterous' calculation. It had no basis in the Education Act or
anything else for that matter. A brigadier from Salisbury found the
measure 'inopportune', a case where sentiment had outweighed sound

[40] EFC paper, 'Church schools', 26 June 1956, Board papers, 28 June 1956, ser.
95083/13–14.
[41] Board minutes, 26 June 1956.

judgement. Here they were anticipating £2 million raised in the dioceses and parishes when an appeal for it had not even been launched. The sum of £40,000 a year from the Commissioners could be better spent in the new housing areas. A canon from Coventry referred to stipends and said that his own chapter was unanimous that the measure should be rejected. It was said that more thought was needed: the Commissioners had never before done anything for schools. But a laywoman from Southwark spoke of schools as 'the nurseries of the congregations of the future. Without them they would not have much need for clergy'. She saw the future of the Church of England at stake. Indeed, as the debate progressed, feeling in support of the measure was growing stronger. Speaker after speaker reinforced arguments in favour. When this had gone on long enough it was time to bring back the archdeacon of Totnes, who offered a neat balance of reassurance and clarification and stressed again that this must be 'now or never'. He warned sharply: 'if they lost a secondary school now ... they could never get it back'.

The bishops voted for the grant to save the church schools by twenty-five to two; the House of Clergy by 158 to sixty-two; the House of Laity by 194 to forty-two.[42]

The Church Commissioners were now free to proceed to their special general meeting. In December 1956 the revised allocations for the year were approved. By February 1957 the measure was passing through Assembly again for final amendments and corrections, but little was said then. The battle seemed to have been won. In June 1957 the measure returned for final approval and encountered a solemn protest from another eminent critic, Ivor Bulmer-Thomas, who complained that the Commissioners' fund 'must now be regarded as a fund for general church purposes, into which anyone could dip who was sufficiently persuasive to get a majority in the Assembly'.[43] But these words already acknowledged that the decision had been made.

But was the day won? Edward Courtman was still busy. In September 1956 he had addressed the conference of the Parochial Clergy Association at St Peter's Hall in Oxford and his text resurfaced almost at once as a leaflet with the populist title 'A million pounds at stake'. He rattled away at the laity for not doing their best over the last nine years to pay their clergy adequately: 'Does it not reveal that the bulk of the laity are entirely out of touch with the struggle that the Clergy have in paying their way?' The money given to schools could have made countless cold and damp parsonages warm and dry. Every clergy widow might receive an extra £25 a year; every clergy son and

[42] *Proceedings of the Church Assembly*, xxxvi/3, London 1956, 327–49 (13 Nov. 1956).
[43] Ibid. xxxvii/2, 177–80 (17 June 1957).

daughter new clothes. 'The Laity', deplored Courtman, 'must not let the Clergy pay the Church's bills.'[44]

This leaflet mattered because although the question had been settled in the Church Assembly it had not yet been ratified by parliament. It was to parliament that Courtman appealed. On 21 November 1957 John Guillam Scott reported to archbishop Fisher that the Church Schools Measure had faced 'a rather sticky passage' when it had come before the Ecclesiastical Committee. There was evidence that Courtman was reaching his target. Lord Ammon had, he thought, 'clearly been influenced by the propaganda which Courtman has circulated to members of the Committee and took the line that this was a most improper use of money provided for the augmentation of the stipends of the clergy'. Lord Grey and Lord Hawke had done their best to fend off the critics, but lacked a clear authority to speak for the Commissioners themselves. Meanwhile, a Church Commissioner, Sir Peter Agnew, was entirely against it, declaring that he would work for its defeat or withdrawal. When Lord Burden had moved that the committee approve the new measure, an MP, John Edwards, intercepted it by proposing an amendment: the committee should call for a conference on the subject. This was defeated – but by a whisker: eight votes to seven. The motion was carried by the same slender majority. At this point another member of the committee, Godfrey Nicolson, remarked that such a slender majority must have 'a most damaging effect' when it came to the House of Commons. It might even be lost there. The committee must try to be at least 'virtually' unanimous. But the truth was that it was divided.

What saved the day was not persuasion but procedure. The vote, it was observed, had now actually been taken and it was too late to think again. The committee must prepare its report and send it to the Legislative Committee, and if that other committee wanted a conference it could ask for one. Even now Agnew persisted. However, the committee was quite simply worn down by it all. A draft report was passed without amendment, to be sent back to the Legislative Committee with a note of warning.

Guillam Scott decided to ask Fisher to attend the meeting of the Legislative Committee. For his part, he thought the situation 'extremely confused'. They had not got rid of Agnew, either: he was on the Legislative Committee too.[45] Scott wracked his brains for a way forward. Fisher, too, was looking into every possibility. He asked Warren at Millbank if they actually needed a measure at all? 'Let me say at once', was the reply, 'that the opposition is not free from doubt, and

---

[44] See Courtman statement, Fisher papers, vol. 169, fos 5–6.
[45] Guillam Scott to Fisher, ibid. vol. 202, fos 115–17.

that is why different views have been taken at different times.' And so he warmed to his theme:

> A Church school is not merely a place in which souls are cured; it is also a place used for general education. The incumbent has the right to teach there, but other things are also taught. That being so the Commissioners thought that it would be better to say boldly that there was no existing power, and that they would only use their money for schools if the Assembly clearly desired them to do so and procured the necessary legislation.

> I think he would be a bold man who gave a firm legal opinion that the Commissioners have no power to provide for schools. But for political reasons it was thought better to assume that the power was absent. It would have been extremely awkward to have provided the money for Church schools and for it to have been legally challenged afterwards. It seems to me therefore that, while there may be legal power, the ice is thin, and that it would be dangerous, both legally and politically, to proceed without a Measure. The Commissioners' guiding principle was therefore: 'When in doubt ask the Assembly'.

Warren had talked with Brown and found him quite of the same mind. They thought it significant that every parish had a parson, a place of worship, a parsonage. But not every parish had a school. This money would not be used everywhere. The measure's opponents had argued that the grant must 'affect prejudicially the constitutional rights of any of Her Majesty's subjects'. Warren could not see how.[46] The case for bringing the measure to the Assembly was clearly not legal but political, for the legal power was already in the Commissioners' possession. What it needed was authority.[47]

When the parliamentary Legislative Committee met on 11 December 1957 another earnest excavation of Section 67 of the 1840 Act ensued. Agnew conceded nothing and turned on its head the idea that because not every parish had a school they might well be reasonably funded by this measure. The fact in itself showed that they were not a part of the cure of souls in parishes. But this time some earnest homework had clearly taken place; the advocates of the measure appeared far more sure of themselves. The sense of the Legislative Committee was turning against Agnew. This was a proper use of the General Fund 'as the beneficiaries of the Fund were the

[46] Warren to Fisher, 11 Dec. 1957, ibid. fo. 123r–v.
[47] Memorandum, 11 Dec. 1957, ibid. fos. 124–7.

souls of the parishioners and not the clergy themselves, that there were a number of previous measures of this kind and that church schools, whether primary or secondary, were for the benefit of the cure of souls in parishes'. It was agreed that there should be a further conference with the Ecclesiastical Committee.[48] That conference followed promptly, on 18 December.

'The cure of souls': Fisher versus Courtman

Fisher and Warren were on to Courtman now. Lord Grey had received a lobbying letter from Courtman, which he had simply passed on to Fisher. In his turn Fisher sent it to Warren. Fisher still ruminated: it might be said that if the 1840 Act did not give them power to support schools, even a new measure in Assembly might appear as a bid effectively to overrule the act, not supplement it. But as to the argument that the General Fund was a charitable fund held in trust for the maintenance of the clergy, he gave that short shrift: 'This is devoid of all truth and calculated to cause great damage to the Church Commissioners.' And he grew sterner still: Courtman was a Commissioner – was there a legal process by which a member of the Commissioners could be restrained from distributing false statements about them? If his leaflet went out to MPs the Commissioners might consider it their duty to take legal action against him. What would Warren himself say to that?[49]

Warren was categorical. The General Fund was 'certainly not held in trust exclusively for the maintenance of the clergy'. About a third originated in Queen Anne's Bounty, which had clearly existed for that purpose. The remainder was for making better provision for the cure of souls; 'we believe here that this means providing for the spiritual destitution of the laity'. Better provision naturally embraced supporting the clergy, but it must include other duties: 'I believe it to be of the utmost importance that the difference between the spiritual welfare of all people in the country on the one hand, and the material welfare of the clergy on the other hand, should be emphasized.' A new measure on schools would not override the 1840 Act, merely 'define and clarify one particular aspect of a general duty imposed on the Commissioners by that Act'. And this was nothing new. In the past they had clarified the act in order to assist cathedrals, pay archdeacons and residentiary canons and put up buildings in new housing areas.

As for Courtman, it was better to keep the law out of it. They must instead promote their own view. New elections to the Commissioners were due in the Assembly and he would ask Scott about Courtman's

[48] Church Assembly legislative committee minutes, 11 Dec. 1957, ibid. fo. 127.
[49] Fisher to Warren, 12 Dec. 1957, ibid. fo. 129.

position. Moreover, they had found Courtman using confidential information about glebe, sent to him as a member of the Board, in a speech made in the House of Clergy against the proposal that it be taken over by the Commissioners. Eve himself was 'very angry' about this. There might be a vote of censure on the Board. Courtman might even be invited to resign. In these circumstances his campaign against the schools measure simply made his situation worse: 'I think he is preparing a noose for his own neck.'[50]

But Fisher had his own way with turbulent priests. On 19 December 1957 he wrote to Courtman himself:

> The 1840 Act ... does not mention clergy at all. The funds are to be used for the cure of souls (which means presumably the cure of the souls of the laity) in parishes where such assistance is most required in such a manner as the Commissioners think most conducive to the effectiveness of the Established Church. The Commissioners are thus free to make up their own mind as to how best to further the cure of souls. In fact, for very many years they discharged their duty almost entirely, as they still do almost entirely, by providing stipends for the clergy: but that is an application of their powers in a particular way: the Act itself does not direct or suggest directly such an application.

To pay the clergy helped the cure of souls. In the last century it was the only way in which parishes needed such help. New churches, church halls and suchlike were provided by the local squire or gentry and the people of the parishes themselves. But now, 'on the scale of modern enterprises the parish left to itself cannot provide for all the needs required for effective ministration: whole classes of problems arise, and it is clearly within the rights of the Church Commissioners to consider where it can help the cure of souls in meeting some of these modern demands'.

If the Church's long-established place in the educational system were to be maintained, this new money from the Commissioners must be 'entirely justifiable'.[51] The Church itself had pronounced its view and no one should frustrate it, however disappointed they might feel. Courtman had said that the views which he promoted were not simply his, but those of a committee. Very well, responded Fisher, the committee could come to see him at Lambeth on 8 January 1958.

---

[50] Warren to Fisher, 13 Dec. 1957, ibid. fo. 131.
[51] Fisher to Courtman, 19 Dec. 1957, ibid. fos 144–5.

Courtman came, but alone. Fisher asked him again to produce his committee. The reply came that the identity of its members was a secret. ('No comment on that is necessary!' observed Fisher to Warren.) They had what Fisher called a 'straight' talk. But if Courtman plural was not present, the archbishop found that Courtman singular was not easy to dismiss. Indeed, he had just been elected as one of the Church Assembly representatives on the new policy-making standing committee of the Assembly.[52] Fisher wondered if he and Eve together might meet Courtman to make him realise that his responsibilities to the Commissioners and now to the Assembly were greater than his 'prejudices and passions'.[53] He wrote another letter to him to tell him that a new document which Courtman intended to circulate to MPs was 'gravely inaccurate'. Furthermore, he accused him of discourtesy, for this anonymous committee seemed only to turn down, anonymously, his invitations to meet it. He wanted them to try again. This time Courtman must bring his committee with him. If he did not comply Fisher would put the whole matter before the Church Assembly.

Courtman was unbowed. He replied that he regretted the discourtesy. He could not name his committee because its member had been 'victimised' for belonging to it. But he could tell the archbishop that his committee had seen the archbishop's letter and still wished to press ahead in its campaign. As for errors, the document which was being sent to all MPs under the archbishop's own name had errors in it as well. Furthermore, some of them perceived that in promoting church schools Fisher had been guilty of compromising Standing Order 28 of the Church Assembly, which had been set down to 'guide and limit the powers of the Chairman'. He quoted Fisher's own words back to him. This was hardly likely to ingratiate. If, he added, Fisher still thought that any good might be served by meeting again he would come and try to bring 'one or two' of his colleagues with him. But their campaign would not wait for it. He signed himself, improbably, 'Yours obediently'.[54]

With his unyielding letter Courtman enclosed a new version of his appeal to the MPs. It was if anything sharper than what had come before: this measure affected the rights of the clergy as Her Majesty's subjects. The 'cure of souls' was being altered to 'quite a new meaning'. For 116 years it had applied to 'the living agent in his work of cure of souls'. Those past measures which Fisher and his allies cited simply showed how the money was increasingly being diverted from its 'original purpose'. How then could the clergy do other than abstain,

[52] Fisher to Warren, 7 Jan. 1958, ibid. fo. 152.
[53] Fisher to Courtman, 15 Jan. 1958, ibid. fo. 153r–v.
[54] Courtman to Fisher, 17 Jan. 1958, ibid. fos 154–5.

as 124 of them had, in the Church Assembly, particularly after the archbishop of Canterbury had spoken as he had?[55]

Fisher's chaplain drafted a reply. This time he accused Courtman of being cowardly, discourteous, inaccurate, and deplorable.[56] That letter was not sent. But Fisher himself now saw that the climate had grown more dangerous, more political. He wrote a desultory note to Scott, 'My efforts to restrain Courtman have completely failed.'[57]

Final victory

Early in February the measure came before the House of Lords. Agnew had been busy lobbying against it, but many of those he approached subsequently headed off to the Second Church Estates Commissioner, Ashton, to ascertain his views. This Ashton found a 'delicate' position, for the Commissioners were supposed to be neutral in such a matter. He referred them to a selection of papers and offered what he regarded as facts only. In the house Agnew did his best to derail the measure, Ashton all the while watching intently. As it unfolded before him Ashton realised that he was relaxing. The measure was going to win through. It did, without a division. For good measure he told Fisher that if there had been a division he would have voted in his private capacity for the measure: 'we are rather proud of the fact that we are building a new Church School in our small village of South Weald'. But when he went to the next meeting of the Administrative Committee at Millbank Ashton also told them that if the Commissioners were so clear that they had the power to support the schools to go to the Assembly did seem to show a contrary course. Their opponents, at least, had been quite consistent throughout.[58]

No matter, Fisher found it 'a most happy outcome'. It was a great virtue, he congratulated Ashton, to know when not to speak. He was struck by the fact that the debate had actually in no way treated whether or not the measure represented a departure from the terms of the 1840 Act with which both proponents and critics alike had been so immensely preoccupied. For himself, he was sure that the Commissioners had the proper power. What lay at stake, to his mind, was the Commissioners' relationship with the Church Assembly. Agnew he felt he understood ('I have known him ever since he was a pupil under me at Repton'); Courtman still irked him. But, he concluded majestically:

---

[55] Ibid. fos 156–9.
[56] Eric Jay draft, n.d., ibid. fo. 161–2.
[57] Fisher to Guillam Scott, 20 Jan. 1958, ibid. vol. 203, fo. 284.
[58] Hubert Ashton to Fisher, 5/6 Feb. 1958, ibid. fos 164–5.

I am not unduly worried. I think it is rather good, on the whole, that Parliament should have this experience, provided that they draw from it the right conclusion that they ought to trust the Church Assembly to do its own job and to do it well, and to ignore recalcitrant people who circulate to them obviously partisan documents. So all is well: thank you very much indeed.[59]

---

[59] Fisher to Ashton, 10 Feb. 1958, fo. 166r–v.

5

The Costs of the Episcopacy and the Cathedrals

At the beginning of the twentieth century the incomes of many bishops were still attached to their own dioceses. Naturally, this produced great variety in the financial and material conditions of bishops, and an age which sought general standards was sure to turn to such inequalities with a gutsy determination to reform. Since 1943 increasing numbers of diocesan bishops had fallen under the Episcopal Endowments and Stipends Measure. This vital act of co-ordination facilitated the drawing up of schemes by which the episcopal residences and endowments of an individual bishop might be made over to the Ecclesiastical Commissioners in return for the management of a stipend and the maintenance (or even replacement) of the house. The bishops saw every reason to move in this direction. The measure appealed to principle and, equally, to ease. To remove these practical burdens from the shoulders of a bishop was in no small measure to liberate him from anxiety and set him free to perform his necessary tasks. By 1951 thirty-one of the forty-three sees were on board, and eight of the remainder had discussed the scheme at some point.

Generally the Church Commissioners made nothing, or very little indeed, out of the schemes which brought the diocesan bishops, one by one, within their realm: the finances of taking over the endowments of a see in exchange for a stipend, a house and official expenses had matched almost neatly. The mathematics of these arrangements was simple, but to try to alter or improve them uncovered many hidden snares. A setting of standards still proved horribly elusive, and not only here. Bishops' pensions were established upon a different legislative foundation from those of the clergy. The rate for diocesan bishops had been fixed in the Episcopal Pensions Measure of 1926, and for suffragan bishops in 1945. From his stipend a bishop paid a pension contribution which amounted to 10 per cent of the pension which he would receive. In practice, the sum was used by the Commissioners to offset the cost of the provision of pensions for their widows. Furthermore, the administration of bishops' expenses brought another taxing dimension into view. The bishops of Chelmsford and

Southwark had stipends which included travel allowances. Most did not. All now needed motor cars. The 1943 measure gave to the Commissioners discretionary power to pay all or part of a bishop's office expenses. An annual limit was agreed, not least because the Inland Revenue required one. Once again, a broad balance could sometimes be hoped for in the long run. Those bishops whose expenses fell under the limits tended to compensate for those who went over. Still another question hung over the matter of entertainment. A bishop could not lock himself up in his see house and disregard clergy who would wish to see him and local dignitaries who thought that a bishop was a part of civil society. Hospitality involved certain expectations, and costs. For this there must, again, be a general system of some kind. Before 1943 the bishops had not generally claimed for hospitality expenses. Now they did.

The Church Commissioners were soon to find the bishops embarrassed by these material questions. This could be a surprising obstacle to reform. When it arose the pressure for improvement appeared to come not from the House of Bishops, nor from the Board of the Church Commissioners, but from the Estates and Finance Committee at 1 Millbank. In January 1952 the Board received a paper from the committee recommending that now might be the time to establish a standard stipend for all diocesan bishops to the tune of £2,500. This might well have looked sensible, and a method, albeit an elaborate one, could be found for it. But when they were asked about the proposal it was found that the bishops thought it 'premature and likely to be misunderstood'.[1] It was dropped, but with a warning: 'There is a real risk of certain Sees proving financially embarrassing.' The Commissioners asked the bishops as a body for the freedom to allow them to deal with individual cases as they saw fit. Even this would still require the consent of the Board and the standing committee of the Church Assembly. This the bishops allowed.

But in the world of the bishops the *status quo* was neither stable nor durable. By the summer of the following year it was growing clearer that the Commissioners would in future be far more likely to lose than gain money through their bishops' schemes. To begin with, the cost of maintaining the houses was rising. Expenses were rising. Either the bishops must be asked to pay higher rents for their houses, and even to make money from their gardens, or their expenses budgets must be reined in or met from other sources. This would affect the poorest bishops first and worst. There was still no pension scheme for those who worked on the bishops' staffs. A loss of 'staff or mobility' would

[1] EFC memorandum, 'Episcopal endowments and stipends measure, 1943', Board papers, 24 July 1952, ser. 95083/7–8.

damage the Church and the effectiveness of the episcopacy altogether.[2] The Commissioners could now move either by supporting the expenses of the bishops as such, or by improving their stipends so that they were in a stronger position to deal with certain of those expenses themselves without a further concoction of grants. Again the prospect of a public pay rise made some, though far from all, bishops nervous. The argument for change was framed more sharply. It could be seen that future bishops might need to be chosen only from those who had additional resources to allow them to accept appointments in which otherwise they would not be able to make ends meet.

The most effective way to deal with episcopal embarrassment was simply to assure the bishops that these questions really lay beyond their jurisdiction. They could hardly feel awkward about matters in which they had no standing. In February 1956 the Commissioners secured by an Order in Council the power to increase bishops' stipends as they saw fit, all excepting Canterbury, London, Durham, Winchester and Oxford (for these were governed by other, earlier, schemes, all of them intricate). Yet the awkwardness still did not disappear, even when bishops who sat on the Board of the Church Commissioners left the room to avoid any accusation of self-interest. In 1960 an attempt to raise their pensions was seen by Fisher himself to embarrass a campaign in the Church Assembly to raise widows' pensions.[3] This dimension of awkwardness in the Church Commissioners' work was, in fact, here to stay.

The rise of the suffragan bishop

The history of the Church Commissioners coincided with the rise of the suffragan bishop in the Church of England. It was a rise which, in their turn, the Commissioners themselves did much to facilitate. Their adoption of the diocesan bishop made the support of suffragan bishops logical. It also attached their policies to a growing demand for expenditure.

The roots of this great, if quiet, ecclesial movement are difficult to discern. In the nineteenth century suffragan bishops had not proved popular, and not least with the Ecclesiastical Commissioners.[4] Now the trend spoke of a pragmatic commitment to maintain the visibility of the episcopacy in more demanding times. It could also be said to show the power that bishops possessed to get what they wanted. But it was also the case that the post-war diocese was in part a pragmatic commitment to maintain the reality, and the visibility, of the

[2] Ibid.
[3] Fisher to Eve, 15 Mar. 1960, Fisher papers, vol. 238, fo. 144.
[4] Burns, *Diocesan revival*, 210–15.

episcopacy in more demanding times. Diocesan bishops were more and more stretched by their commitments. But it was also the case that the post-war diocese was increasingly the defining model of ecclesial organisation. It was becoming more and more complicated to administer.

Some now whispered that a suffragan bishop was simply a bishop's curate. Others found it hard to distinguish between a diocesan and a suffragan bishop. Some suffragan bishops were also archdeacons, which did not much help. Some were canons of cathedrals. They therefore inhabited these different ministerial dimensions simultaneously, borrowing from each as was necessary. Whatever the practicalities, the theology or the ecclesial quantum mechanics of such matters, it increasingly fell to the Church Commissioners to create new suffragan bishops and to foot the bill for them.

Before 1948 the Ecclesiastical Commissioners had taken an ambivalent view of the suffragan. In 1942 the Episcopal Endowments and Houses of Residence Committee of the Church Assembly had recommended that the Commissioners be empowered to take over the endowments or augmentations of the suffragan bishops, and to pay each one a stipend of £900 a year. This the Commissioners themselves did not accept. They did not have the money for it. But then, under the 1943 measure, it was left to the Commissioners to pay all, or part, of the stipend of a suffragan bishop, if the diocesan bishop himself fell under their scheme. This produced a system of grants by which the suffragan was paid out of see funds or by the bishop himself.

The schemes which incorporated the diocesan bishops may have been straightforward, but the affairs of the suffragan bishops were anything but simple. The emoluments of the suffragans were derived from a motley assortment of sources: annexed preferments, preferments that were not annexed (these by far the largest source), the resources of diocesan sees, diocesan boards of finance or other diocesan bodies, the Church Commissioners themselves, the City Parochial Charities Fund, a variety of trusts. The other preferments on which the suffragan bishops were floated, accounting for 62.5 per cent of the whole, comprised thirteen archdeaconries, eleven canonries and sixteen benefices. Eight suffragan bishops lived in the houses attached to the residentiary canonries held by them, and twelve in parsonage houses of benefices now amalgamated with the suffragan bishopric. Five rented houses from their diocesan boards of finance, three had houses provided rent-free by the diocese or somebody else. Thirteen had no official residence.

In all kinds of ways it could be seen that the central administration of the Church of England was struggling to keep on top of this mounting confusion. Sums were not adding up. By 1951 it was clear that a deficit was opening up in the Bishops' Pension Fund. By 1953 there were forty-one suffragan bishops. In June 1954 a report from the EFC at 1 Millbank complained that there was so much variation to be found in the payment of suffragan bishops that it was difficult to see how a 'logical and fair' way of proceeding might emerge.[5] But try they must. Diocesan bishops had minimum stipends, so too deans and provost, canons, incumbents and assistant curates. Without one the suffragan bishops risked becoming an anomaly. The Church Commissioners largely understood themselves to be in the business of clearing up anomalies, not perpetuating them.

Fisher saw that all the 'deviations and inequalities' in suffragan bishops' pay, conditions and circumstances favoured the argument that they be treated within a universal framework created and maintained by the Church Commissioners.[6] The bishops, though, were found to be divided on this. The basis of the objection was purely financial. If the Commissioners now gave money to the diocese to help pay the suffragans, it would at a stroke replace an existing, incoming grant to the dioceses themselves which they were reluctant to lose. In a little time this was overcome. A new augmentation scheme from 1 April 1956 set down a minimum stipend for all suffragan bishops and a standard grant to meet the costs of house rents, rates and repairs. This significant work of centralisation passed through the Church Assembly without so much as a murmur.

The frustration of convenience: the story of four houses

By the terms of the Episcopal Endowments and Stipends Measure of 1943, a new scheme drawn up between the bishops and the Church Commissioners made the latter the owners of see houses. But bishops did not wish to be treated merely as rent-payers, to be treated with bureaucratic indifference by a national landlord. They were surely something more than this. The Church Commissioners could not have been surprised to find that the issue of see houses was an exceedingly delicate one.

Most see houses were venerable. Many were huge. They cost the Commissioners a great deal in taxes and rates. Then there was maintenance, which varied widely. Between 1944 and 1954 the London house had cost, in maintenance alone, £17,752; York, between 1943 and 1954, £22,978. Manchester, on the other had, cost only £63 between 1948 and 1954. Recently, costs of repair or modernisation at Exeter, Carlisle and Hereford had risen uncomfortably, provoking deep concern amongst the Commissioners

[5] EFC report, 11 May 1954, Board papers, 24 June 1954, ser. 95083/10–11.
[6] Fisher to Eve, 18 May 1954, Fisher papers, vol. 43, fos 72–4.

themselves and questions in the Church Assembly. It was time to take matters in hand. In the autumn of 1954 an EFC document pronounced boldly:

> The difficulty is not primarily one of finance but of policy. Put shortly and perhaps crudely, the first question is whether as a matter of principle the Church wishes to preserve historic houses as places in which (or in part of which) bishops are to live. The second question is whether it is a correct use of Church funds to pay for this retention in a world of changing economic values. If the answer to these questions is Yes, then there will always be a contingent heavy liability on the Commissioners, and the fact must be faced so that it occasions no surprise when the contingency matures.[7]

See houses were now divided into four classes. In the first were five (Canterbury, York, London, Durham and Winchester) which were historic and beautiful, and which must certainly be retained. In the second were eight which were less ornamental and had proven costly. In the third there were nine houses, 'the hard core of the difficulty'. They belonged to newer dioceses, mostly northern, but they were old and even, in parts, rotten. In the last class were twenty obliging houses which evidently presented no problems.

The EFC felt that 'a regular and thorough system of examination by their professional staff' should be established so that they could maintain a watchful eye on the see houses instead of waiting to be called in like a fire engine when disasters broke out. But a plethora of questions followed. Should out-goings fall to a bishop? Should he, therefore, have to pay the cost of the Church's commitment to hold on to old buildings? How could a bishop without private means pay for the furnishing of state rooms? Should the diocese do so? If the Commissioners provided a house for a bishop, and his successor arrived saying that he could not afford to live in it, should the Commissioners build or buy another for him, or should his acceptance of the see involve his acceptance of the house that came with it?[8]

Some palaces became in the Fisher period more resistant to reform than others. Some simply seemed obstinate; no matter what was done, they remained a difficulty. The onward march of bureaucratic modernisation could be diverted into in a series of utterly unyielding confrontations.

[7] EFC report, 14 Sept. 1954, Board papers, 28 Oct. 1954, ser. 95083/10–11.
[8] Ibid. p. 10.

Lambeth Palace

Lambeth Palace was a case set apart. It was effectively the home of the archbishop of Canterbury in his national capacity, just as the Old Palace in Canterbury was his home in his diocesan capacity. He divided his time between the two as evenly as he could. The administrative realities of Lambeth were also divided. The diocesan surveyor to Canterbury looked after the modern part and the Commissioners cared for the ancient part. That the Commissioners also looked after the Old Palace at Canterbury was acknowledged to be odd.

Lambeth Palace had been the London home of archbishops for hundreds of years, but it was not particularly grand. There was its gatehouse with twin towers, an impressive, even stately, main building with its sweeping staircase and reception rooms, now largely used for offices, a garden made more beautiful in the days of archbishop Lang and an annexe, the hostel, a bolt-hole for visiting bishops. The palace had been hit hard by war. In 1945 parts of it were virtually derelict. The fourteenth-century chapel and the upper part of Lollard's Tower were completely gutted. Half of the hammer-beam roof of the Great Hall had tumbled in; a bomb had fallen into the middle of Blore's building demolishing the principal reception rooms and everything above and below them. The caretaker/butler had been bombed out of his cottage and he and his wife and daughter were living in one room in the basement of the palace. The chimney smoked in the archbishop's study. The drawing room was 'open to the four winds'; by 1948 it was clear that it would have to be pulled down altogether. The archbishop lived in a flat and paid what was considered a rather nominal rent. The Fishers had their meals served from the hostel and for this they paid.

In November 1945 Fisher did not think that Lambeth should belong to the Commissioners. They should instead be holding trustees on behalf of the archbishop of Canterbury, and Lambeth should be used, subject to his consent, for any purpose connected with the Church. The archbishop should not have to get too involved in such matters: there should be a committee to do that. Some parts of the palace were better than others. Lollards Tower was the best, but was noisy with trams passing by. ('This, he conceded, 'may some day disappear.') Then there was the library. How could it be expanded? They must make proper arrangements for the collections. An archivist should be established in the old Big Study to go through all the papers so far 'scattered about the place', uncatalogued and unshelved. Fisher had already taken on a priest, J. B. Dakin, to do something about the Davidson papers, 'which are in a filthy condition'. Could they make something practical out of Morton's Tower? They needed a first-class independent architect, and as this would be a long job it should be trusted to 'youngish hands'.[9] Fisher knew who he wanted for the job: the firm of Paget and Seeley. 'My dear Paul', wrote the archbishop to his new man, 'Things are in train.'[10] They were indeed. By July 1946 Paget had produced a report.[11]

Fisher watched events with a benign eye. In July 1947 the foreman of Concrete Limited, Bill Allen, was busy at work on the floors of the cottage in the grounds when he found himself confronting the spectacle of the archbishop himself, in 'full marching order' – gaiters, knee breeches and clerical hat with guy ropes. A brief dialogue, noted cheerfully by Paget, followed:

Archbishop:	'Who are you?'
Foreman:	'I am the foreman for Concrete Ltd. I am fixing Bison floors.'
Archbishop:	'Oh good. And are you going to get results?'
Foreman.	'Yes sir.'
Archbishop:	'That is more than I can get. Results is what I cannot get.'
Foreman:	'Well, sir, Concrete Ltd gets 'em.'[12]

What now happened to Lambeth Palace symbolised what was being attempted across the Church of England itself. The demands of modernity were met with as much grace and fluency as the legacies of the past would allow. Private life remained difficult to attach to public responsibility, not least in the settling of financial questions. But the library would soon flourish and over the years become more of a haunt for scholars than archbishops. For the archbishop himself there was now 'a private lodging equipped for ease of management by present day standards'.[13] The idea that the palace might be opened to the public foundered because the archbishop's staff was seen to be too modest in numbers to rise to the challenge. Eve would make eyes at the commercial possibilities of the hostel, but it remained for 'gaiters' and guests.

[9] Notes on Lambeth Palace, Oct. 1945, sent to Brown, 19 Nov. 1945, Fisher papers, vol. 104, fos 15–17.
[10] Fisher to Grant, 17 Nov. 1945, ibid. fo. 20.
[11] Ibid. fos 41–70.
[12] Ibid. A slightly altered presentation of the conversation reported to Fisher himself by Paget, 9 July 1947, ibid. fo. 72.
[13] 'Lambeth resurgens', ibid. fo. 106.

The saga of the London see house: a first instalment

When he became bishop of London in 1901 Arthur Foley Winnington Ingram had inherited not one but two residences: London House in St James's Square – a residence which could be used as a town house – and Fulham Palace – a country residence, built on a site linked with the see since the seventh century. This dual arrangement could not be afforded. Between 1923 and 1940 London House was let to the Caledonian Club, to whom the Ecclesiastical Commissioners then sold the building for £47,000, the proceeds to be accumulated or invested for whatever purposes were agreed with the bishop and sanctioned by parliament or the Church Assembly. By 1948 the house had become the home of the Ministry of Town and Country Planning.

Fulham Palace still lay in the hands of the diocese of London, and it was not an easy thing to be left with. It had a great hall, a library, eighty-two rooms and thirty acres of grounds. Parts were Tudor, parts Georgian; parts had been bombed during the war and were derelict. In 1936 a deputation from Fulham Borough Council approached the Ecclesiastical Commissioners, eager for public spaces, and asked if the council might buy it if it was offered for sale once the bishop had moved out. This meeting exposed a curiosity. Fulham Palace could not be sold without the assent of the Church Commissioners, but they did not themselves actually own it. It belonged to the see, which had not declared a wish to sell.

In 1943, when Fisher was bishop, a scheme had been concocted whereby the Church Commissioners would take over Fulham and the endowments of the see, and at the same time assume responsibility for housing the bishop under the Episcopal Endowments and Stipends Measure of that year. Discussions between the London Diocesan Fund and the Commissioners began to sort out what to do with the palace. It might become a proper home for the bishop. It might make a diocesan conference venue, or a retreat house. The architects Seeley and Paget sketched some plans. The diocese promised the Commissioners that it would not do anything unexpected; the Commissioners promised the diocese not to sell off the palace. In the meantime, they absorbed the proceeds of the sale of London House with a view to acquiring a new residence. New repairs to parts damaged by bombs now revealed that only with extensive structural alterations could the building be converted to institutional purposes. The costs of these could not be claimed as war damage. Meanwhile, maintenance costs grew.

It all boiled down to a choice: either Fulham Palace must be rebuilt, or a new house must be put up. In 1948 the new bishop, William Wand, felt that even what the 1943 measure had proposed might not prove practical. The EFC began to fear that the costs of conversion might become exorbitant. Perhaps, the bishop suggested, he and his successors should be somewhere else altogether? Now the whole of London was being replanned, could not the bishop of London return again to the City, near St Paul's Cathedral itself? The bishop was encouraged to approach the City Corporation, the London Diocesan Fund and the dean and chapter of St Paul's. The Corporation seemed to welcome the bishop back with open arms. The diocesan fund and the dean and chapter also welcomed it – so long, they added, as Fulham Palace was not abandoned to secular use.

The hunt yielded a new site, half an acre in size, in Gresham Street, next door to the Church of St Anne Zachary and with the Goldsmiths Hall to the south. It was only a stone's throw away from St Paul's Cathedral itself and the historic wall of London to the west. It was the property of the Goldsmiths' Company. This the diocese pursued eagerly. It was expensive, but the money left over from London House, together with capital savings made by no longer maintaining Fulham Palace, could pay for the site and for the new building. But what about Fulham Palace? It was already feared that it could not become a conference house. Could it be a retirement home for clergy? Land which was presently given over to allotments could certainly be sold off: Fulham Borough Council and the London County Council would be glad about that. The standing committee of the London Diocesan Fund now agreed, by an 'overwhelming majority', that the Commissioners could do with Fulham Palace as they saw fit, expressing a 'strong hope' that it would remain in ecclesiastical use. But what mattered above all was that it must be sold if the new house was to be built. When a confidential letter from the Ministry of Works expressed interest in purchasing the palace nobody asked if the ministry was sufficiently ecclesiastical to merit it.[14] Other expressions of interest and other plans for development simply dissolved. As time dragged, Fulham Palace began to find allies within the Church. Then, suddenly, there was a collapse. In November the Board voted by nine to six not to acquire the site from the Goldsmiths' Company. The council of St Gabriel's were to be told that the cautious negotiations could no longer proceed. The bishop was to stay at Fulham.

Nothing moved for seven years. In 1956 the EFC submitted another report to the Board of the Commissioners. London had a new bishop, and now seemed a sensible time to look again at Fulham Palace. By now the Tudor sections around the courtyard had become the home of various rent-paying church organisations. The bishop was in a small flat. There were still fourteen acres, employing three gardeners, three cottages and a number of garages; the other sixteen acres were still allotments. Now Seeley and Paget proposed something

---

14 Board minutes, 28 Apr. 1949.

new. Two state rooms and six bedrooms would be allotted to the bishop, with a flat for a chaplain. Central heating would be installed and plumbing overhauled. The Board agreed to proceed, but also wished still to ponder a reduction in the bishop's accommodation. Nobody could have seen in this a grand solution. Of Fulham there would be a great deal more to come.[15]

Wells

Wells presented a sublime union of historic beauty with practical impossibility. The palace there had been the bishop's residence since the thirteenth century. It had forty-seven rooms: a main block, built by Bishop Jocelin in about 1230, with an entrance hall, a substantial undercroft, four state rooms and a gallery, and a top storey, added by Bishop Law in the early nineteenth century. The chapel, built by Bishop Burnell in about 1280, was beautiful but unheated and so cold that it was now felt to be unusable between November and April. In the mid-fourteenth century a north wing had been added to the palace by Bishop Bekynton for the accommodation of servants. In 1954 the Commissioners' architect condemned the palace as 'badly planned, and inconvenient'. By then it was also in decay.

In 1950 the bishop, Harold Bradfield, had had enough. He lived in a perpetual huff, fulminating against the palace and the many ways in which it conspired against episcopal efficiency. Architects had been consulted, but had failed to produce solutions. The diocesan board of finance had been offered the kitchen wing, but instead had turned up in an unused part of the deanery nearby. If it did move to the palace to satisfy the bishop it would upset the dean, who found his house far too large.

It might make rational sense to pack bags, abandon the palace precincts and start all over again. But this was not possible, not least because local opinion in the county, city and diocese was set against it. Bishop Bradfield now wished to have a new house built in the grounds, and to lease the old palace to the theological college. As the theological college eyed up the palace for potential lecture rooms and residential accommodation, the bishop's imagination turned the south-west corner of his garden into a potential building site.

At Millbank the EFC did not much like any of this. The bishop tried to reassure them and gained some support, largely because it was quite impossible to conceive of an alternative. An architect, Dykes Bower, was commissioned to prepare plans. These simply confirmed the problem rather than providing an answer. The palace was too big to be

[15] EFC report, 6 Mar. 1956, Board papers, 22 Mar. 1956, ibid. ser. 95083, pts 13–14.

a feasible home for a bishop. To build in its grounds would be 'very expensive' and would provoke criticism. To build beyond the moat would also be unacceptable. Courageously Dykes Bower recommended that the bishop stay where he was, but that alterations should be made. The upper floor of the main block could be removed, losing six unnecessary bedrooms; the crypt could be taken over by the diocesan registry. The diocesan board of finance might be coaxed into the north wing. This was what the EFC recommended; the Board accepted it.[16]

By 1954, after being in residence for eight years, the bishop had mellowed. When the Commissioners' official architects proposed turning the north wing into a residence Bradfield thought it would make 'a quite admirable and efficient' one. But something else had altered at Wells. The bishop was no longer there alone: an army of deathwatch beetles had also taken up residence. It was also now realised that past work, which had taken place as long ago as 1921, had been poor and must be remedied. Bradfield ventured, with cheerful sympathy: 'The problem here is whether the Commissioners ought to regard themselves as responsible for maintaining in good order and repair an ancient and historic building which is part of the superb array of mediaeval architecture which is the glory of Wells, and which is indeed world famous?' Responsibility aside, he added consolingly, these things must surely prove an asset over time. Thousands came to Wells in summertime, and £55 had been taken in just one afternoon by tourists paying to see only the gardens. The state rooms could be flung open and their treasures displayed; 'I am satisfied that this can be so arranged in practice as to provide the minimum disturbance to the amenities of the Bishop and his household.'[17]

Hartlebury

In May 1956 the Estates and Finance Committee pronounced that it had 'now formed a definite opinion that Hartlebury Castle should not continue as the See House of the Bishops of Worcester and that we cannot concur in expenditure on the house'.[18] The bishop of Worcester inhabited what was perhaps the most difficult palace of all. Hartlebury had been the home of bishops of Worcester since at least 852 (some said even earlier). Much of what was still standing dated from the fifteenth century. In modern times the bishop had enjoyed three homes, Hartlebury, an imposing house in Worcester itself and another residence in the Bredon hills. Time had transformed the

---

[16] Board minutes, 24 Jan. 1952, p. 3.
[17] EFC report, 1 May 1954, Board papers, 20 June 1954, ser. 95083, pts 10–11.
[18] Board minutes, 31 May 1956.

diocese of Worcester and its geographical logic. The diocese itself had
been divided into the separate sees of Worcester, Gloucester, Bristol
and Birmingham. This raised many questions, and not just about
Hartlebury.

Hartlebury had become the preoccupation of myriad committees,
busy with opinions and various designs. In 1956 the senior clergy of
the diocese, the diocesan board of finance and the diocesan advisory
committee were also sure that the palace should remain in the Church,
anxious that it should not fall into 'the wrong hands'. They felt that the
bishop's accommodation should be modernised and reduced in size.
But how? Partial demolition would not be possible without spoiling
the exterior; the great hall could not be converted into a chapel
without spoiling it altogether. In London the EFC judged that
Hartlebury was fundamentally inconvenient and beyond remodelling:
'further investigation is a waste of money and time'. 'How far', the
EFC asked, throwing up its hands almost histrionically, 'ought this
principle (of accepting inconvenience and excess cost) to apply to any
of the houses of the 37 other Diocesan Bishops?' They positively
glared in the direction of Hartlebury. By now there had been countless
ideas and proposals. They had come to nothing. The library of the
eighteenth-century Bishop Hurd must stay where it was. The paintings
could not but be retained. What the Commissioners hoped now to do
was to build, or to buy.[19]

By now a new bishop, Lewis Charles-Edwards, and his wife were
living in a hotel while diocesan committees busily confused and
misunderstood each other. The local press had reported that he was
'homeless'. But even in this adversity, in May 1956, he sent a
confidential note to Warren at Millbank. Hartlebury could yet become,
in part at least, 'convenient'. The cost of adaptation was for him and,
he thought, the diocese, the key question. No complete survey had
ever taken place: 'no one has the slightest idea what would be
involved'. He had once wanted a quick decision. Now he wanted time
for thought and care, an indefinite period if necessary.[20]

Another three years passed. On 25 June 1959 the First Church
Estates Commissioner reported to the Board that planning permission
had now been secured for partial demolition and 'radical' alterations to
Hartlebury. The Ancient Monuments Board disapproved, but nobody
else. This was simply swept under the table. The Board bid that the
process begin. The following month it was confirmed that Hartlebury

[19] Ibid.
[20] Bishop of Worcester memorandum, 15 May 1956, sent to Warren, 22 May 1956,
ser. 95083/14.

was suitable for retention, 'subject to the execution of the works referred to in the report'.[21]

Definite words again. Yet the tenders would bring their own shocks. Costs seemed suddenly to spiral, up towards £100,000, and beyond. By 31 January 1961 the feet of the EFC had gone thoroughly cold; these costs could be justified 'in no circumstances whatever'. Conversion must be abandoned. By now the Society for the Protection of Ancient Buildings had submitted an alternative scheme, but it left the bishop with 50 per cent more of the castle than he needed. Now the EFC pressed again that Hartlebury be classified as unsuitable, and urged that another building be found, as quickly as possible. The First Church Estates Commissioner's report was withdrawn at the Board meeting of 16 February 1961: a fuller one was on its way. At the end of the Fisher era the fate of Hartlebury was left hanging in the balance. Few then would have ventured any hopes for it.

The See Houses Committee, 1960

The cumulative effect of such stories could be observed in a growing scepticism in the work of the Church Commissioners. By the end of the Fisher era they were viewing the bishops, their stipends, expenses and houses, with sharper eyes. In 1960 their official architect suggested that a 'once for all' payment over two years of at least £200,000 would bring all the see houses up to a standard which could then be sensibly maintained thereafter. For the following years the costs for them could reasonably be estimated at £25,000. But perennial questions still hovered. Should such money be spent on houses which might well be considered unsuitable for the bishops of the present, let alone the future? Would it be better to spend even more on 'modern, convenient houses of a character in which a Bishop receiving a stipend of about £3,000 a year could afford to live without the use of private means'? The EFC now proposed that the Board appoint a completely new committee, the See Houses Committee. By statute all members should be Commissioners, though not necessarily Board members; it should include the three Estates Commissioners and be chaired by the Second Church Estates Commissioner. Moreover, 'It is thought that a woman member would be a great advantage. Failing that, it should be possible for the Committee to seek advice from people who are not Commissioners.' A new body brought a new scheme. See houses should be classified into five new categories: (A) those that must be kept under any circumstances; (B) certain other 'palaces' or 'castles' which should be retained – not more than four, not less than three; (C) suitable see houses; (D) palaces and castles considered unsuitable for

[21] Board minutes, 25 July 1959, p. 2.

bishops but suitable still for continued church ownership and some other 'seemly' church use; (E) the fatal list, those too costly to maintain or convert.

The new committee was appointed in March 1960 and evidently set to work with a will. By June it had condemned four houses: Blackburn, Manchester, Sheffield and Wakefield, all of them, strikingly, purchased in the 1940s. The next month it approved the retention of Lichfield and Bishopscourt, Rochester. Fisher watched this with a restless eye, and for a time there were hopes in some quarters that radical measures about bishops and their houses might follow. By 16 February 1961, however, the Board had retreated to the position that every palace or castle should be viewed on its own terms, and that any limits on retention be set aside. Furthermore, the remit of the See Houses Committee should be extended. It was now asked to report to the Board on the size, standard and costs of new buildings, and it should explore whether or not such houses might be opened to the curious public.

The Cathedrals

The cathedrals of England encapsulated the monumental grandeur and the historical eloquence of the Church. Even centuries after their completion, and in a very different world, they could dominate their surroundings and define the cities which bustled around them. By the twentieth century cathedrals came in two kinds: the medieval foundations, which were the grandest, and the so-called parish church cathedrals of the newer dioceses of the nineteenth and twentieth centuries. The former were certainly wealthier; the parish churches, like Birmingham or Sheffield, were modest by comparison. It might be thought that the newer cathedrals would by the second half of the twentieth century be standing up more confidently. That was far from the truth; in fact, they proved, if anything, more fragile. Medieval engineering was formidable; Victorian stone was not always of a high quality. The ancient cathedrals were generally set beside a close of houses, where canons and sometimes other staff lived, and where offices could now be found. At Norwich and Salisbury these were great creations in their own right. The newer cathedrals had rather little of this and scrambled about to find a few nearby houses, appropriate to their particular needs. It was hard to deny that this was a class system of its kind.

In administrative, as in national, life the cathedrals seemed to occupy a category of their own. The Church Commissioners inherited their responsibilities for the cathedrals from the Ecclesiastical Commissioners, whose founding act set down their responsibility for a number of canonries. They also received their annual accounts. But there was also the question of maintenance, a thorny, taxing question, and a constant one. In 1948 the national Church in no way qualified for assistance from the state to support these venerable piles. Some thought that this priceless part of English history and identity should receive support from the nation's exchequer. However, though the idea that the cathedrals might receive the attentions of the state might be periodically revived within the Church, most feared the suggestion. A secular state would lay down terms.

When the Church Commissioners were established in 1948 the cathedrals were in deep trouble. When it came to fabric, the cost of maintenance was rising. The houses which dignified their closes were increasingly deemed completely unsuitable. Their clergy were poor. The new Church Commissioners were seen as the power to change all this.

Under Section 20 of the Cathedrals Measure of 1931, grants could be made to historic cathedrals in distress, in light of other competing claims, and subject to a resolution of the Church Assembly. Between 1934 and 1948, total grants in a single year could be made up to a ceiling fixed at £18,000. Parish church cathedrals were entitled to claim, normally, up to £300, but for living agents, not fabric or capital. Furthermore, modest grants were also frequently made to the cathedrals on the grounds that the Commissioners possessed the right to make grants wherever they owned land. With the coming of war, this existing pattern of grants was renewed annually.

As far as the Church Commissioners were concerned, the movement to reform the finances of the Church of England reached the cathedrals in the summer of 1949. The method was, again, empirical; the object once more to set down a new standard. Cathedral accounts were examined; a number of cathedral authorities were asked questions. Here the work was no more straightforward than anywhere else, for each cathedral had its own statutes and many related to the old practices in central funding in quite different ways. Canterbury, Ely, Manchester and Oxford did not qualify for support under the 1931 measure. As for the parish church cathedrals, they could not be dealt with until a commission of the Church Assembly had reported on them. To delay now could not be satisfactory. The Commissioners decided to encourage applications for exceptional grants which could be given without offending existing rubrics. In the following financial year, 1950–1, £9,731 was given in grants to eighteen ancient cathedrals, the smallest to Norwich (£105) and the largest to Chichester (£2,300). The sum of £5,791 was assigned to the parish church cathedrals, the smallest to Bradford (£150) and the largest to St Albans (£889).

A cathedral is the seat of the bishop, but it is largely run by a chapter of clergy, and at the heart of this is a college comprising the dean, or provost, and the canons; four in the older foundations, perhaps two in the newer ones. The canons had nominal positions which declared their medieval origins: a canon treasurer, a canon chancellor, a canon librarian, a canon precentor, who had his eyes on liturgy. The twentieth century had brought some new categories: one was a canon missioner. These titles could mean a great deal, or rather little. A new canon should possess the gifts to suit this distinctive environment: he should be more than usually thoughtful, perhaps scholarly in interests and temperament. A cathedral was held to be a source of quality in Anglican worship, music and culture, just as it was in architecture.

The financial support of fabric and of living agents might well appear very different budgetary categories. But austerity had driven them together. Legislation in 1934 had specified that Section 20 grants could also be used to increase remuneration for living agents. By 1951 many of the cathedrals were seeking to survive by juggling priorities, and also by pinpointing responsibilities which might be off-loaded onto other shoulders. Few, if any, at the Church Commissioners thought this could last. Firm action was now precipitated by three particular cases. The Ecclesiastical Commissioners had made a statutory contribution to the Regius Professor of Divinity at Cambridge, who was a canon of Ely. But, under a new act of 1940, the chair was detached from the cathedral and the canonry abolished. The grant, however, was not: £600 towards the stipend every year was charged on the capitular revenues, so long as the chair at the university remained Anglican. The cathedral was finding this increasingly difficult to sustain; the chapter wanted to disentangle itself from the arrangement. The Regius Chair, it maintained, was something for the whole Church to support, not just Ely. Could the 1940 Act be amended, or could they receive more money? The bishop agreed. If the Commissioners could not give money directly, could they not give something to the chapter in general, to ease its troubles?

The Board of the Commissioners responded briskly, resolving that 'it would greatly deplore any cessation of this payment by the Chapter'. It would bear Ely in mind when the support for cathedrals came up again next spring, under Section 20.[22] But by June 1952 Ely was all too clearly in a parlous state: over £50,000 was now needed for urgent fabric repairs. The Church Commissioners had to think again, and by now there were other claims to weigh. For four of the last five years Exeter Cathedral had been running in deficit. It had applied for help but had been turned down, the Commissioners resorting to a

[22] Board agenda, 13 Dec. 1951, ser. 95083/6.

suggestion that one of the residentiary canonries there be suspended until matters improved. But now wages were expected to increase, so too repairs. The Friends of the cathedral were providing £2,000 a year to assist, but only for three years. The mayor had launched an endowment appeal for £15,000. Then there was Truro Cathedral, which wanted to pay its canon treasurer £200 more than it already did, and where only the vacancy of two canonries over the last year had saved the accounts from a £400 deficit. Repairs loomed large at Truro, too. When the Board of the Commissioners responded with additional grants, they were not heroic ones.[23] Their whole policy was looking shaky and makeshift.

In November 1952 the movement to improve the lot of the cathedrals was gathering pace across the whole Church. The Church Assembly approved £50,000 in grants paid by the Commissioners under Section 20 of the 1931 Cathedrals Measure. It also resolved that from the beginning of the next financial year, the annual ceiling under which the Commissioners worked be raised to £50,000. It also asked the Commissioners to look into the financial affairs of residentiary canons receiving less than £700 a year. By July 1953 the EFC was warning that this was unlikely to be sufficient. When money to cover the existing renewals was taken away, and funds to establish a minimum standard stipend for deans (£1,400), provosts (£1,200) and canons (£80) subtracted, there would be £23,000 left. This would be evenly divided between the ancient cathedrals and the parish church cathedrals, to be used for any living agent as they themselves saw fit.

These sums may have looked simple enough. But within weeks the Administrative Committee of the Commissioners had uncovered new difficulties in the arrangement. Which agents should they support? If a dignitary had no official house, how much of his stipend should be computed for his rent, rates and repairs? What about canons who were also archdeacons and who received a stipend for being such? The term residentiary canonries had no uniform meaning. Some had endowments, or provision out of the cathedral revenues. Other residentiary canons – at Leicester, St Albans, Sheffield and Southwark – were not endowed and drew their stipends from benefices and other appointments. Then there were residentiary canons who received their stipends partly from chapter revenues and partly from different sources – Sheffield had an industrial missioner who only received £4 4s. from revenues and had £554 from the diocese; Wakefield had a canon missioner who received £380 from cathedral revenues and £404 from lectureships. The committee saw a difference between those who had a diocesan role, and the realm of the cathedral churches themselves. The former were judged ineligible. But there were yet

---

[23] Board agenda, 21 May 1952, ibid.

other kinds. Gloucester, an ancient cathedral, also had a canon missioner who was classified as a residentiary canon. He did not draw his stipend from cathedral revenues, but from a special endowment from the Church Commissioners themselves and from diocesan sources. He too, it was decided, should be ineligible.[24] At some of the parish church cathedrals, meanwhile, founding statutes allowed for a number of residentiary canonries but the positions had never actually been filled. The committee saw a genuine need for at least one in every cathedral. Most had only a provost and one or two assistant curates. This could serve only inadequately a foundation which must be the mother church of the diocese. It was agreed that the Church Commissioners should encourage change by assisting in the endowment of these positions.

The growth of the financial commitment borne by the Church Commissioners was considerable. In June 1954 the Church Assembly approved a further grant of £25,000 to be paid to the cathedrals by the Church Commissioners. In November 1955 this figure was increased to £100,000. But this was not yet a new age in the life of the cathedrals, rather, heavy maintenance for the old one.

The Church Commissioners in 1961

When he retired in 1961 Fisher felt that he left the Church of England in very much better heart than he had found it. If he was little loved by those who sought bold campaigns bright with luminous principles, Fisher's worth was better known by those who undertook the workaday task of institutional reform. It was no mean task, either. In the dealings of the Church Commissioners he had perhaps found his element; for their part, it was in the Fisher primacy that they had started upon their work, matured and even become august. In 1961 they looked as though they might well have existed, at the heart of the Church of England, for many venerable years, largely because the job of chairing the Board of governors became integral to the work of the archbishop of Canterbury. But the servants at Millbank could not assume that this age of high favour was set on solid foundations. In fact, they would not see the like of archbishop Fisher again, and they would be fortunate to see much at all of those who succeeded him.

---

[24] AC report, 19 Sept. 1953, Board papers, 24 Sept. 1953, ser. 95083/8–9.

PART II

THE AGE OF AMBIVALENCE:
THE PRIMACY OF ARCHBISHOP RAMSEY, 1961–1974

6

The Embarrassment of Riches

The ascetic and the tycoon

The arrival of Michael Ramsey at Lambeth Palace in 1961 marked a new departure for the Church of England, if not something of a reaction to the world of his predecessor. Ramsey saw principles of political justice with a sharper, readier eye than his predecessor, who could be complacently at ease with familiar names and forms. He was by nature a liberal in those public matters in which Fisher had been a conservative. Moreover, his understanding of the Church was arguably more intensely theological and intellectual than that of his predecessor, who had a stronger sense of it as a public corporation.[1] This would matter. For thirteen years the officials of 1 Millbank had enjoyed the constant interest and practical support of the archbishop across the river. Now things would be very different. The Church Commissioners did not attract Ramsey at all. He shied away from the worldliness of money, and when he moved to Lambeth Palace the Commissioners were making it – and more and more of it. At all events, Ramsey viewed the Board meetings at Millbank with distaste, as disconcertingly worldly. Five years after arriving at Lambeth, he would write to the bishop of London:

> One of the more godly laymen on the Board of the Church Commissioners has asked why the meetings do not begin with prayer. When I became Chairman I was informed that it was not their custom to have prayer and I followed the existing pattern. I must confess that at the time I sometimes used to feel the proceedings were so ungodly that the custom was just as well, but there is really no reason why

[1] For the standard biography of Ramsey see Owen Chadwick, *Michael Ramsey: a life*, Oxford 1990.

this should be the one ecclesiastical body which does not pray at its meetings.[2]

If the Church Commissioners were to do their job well, they must increase the resources of the Church and furnish it with resources for ministry. When that happened it was natural for Millbank to congratulate itself at least a little and expect approval, even celebration. At the same time the Commissioners faced grumbles amongst those it sought to serve who felt either that wealth was problematic or that making much of a show of it compromised important ideals. Such anxieties men like Fisher, Warren and Brown could take in their stride. Not so Ramsey. In this he may have symbolised a new, critical climate. Certainly, he was not alone.

The breezy confidence of the Church Commissioners themselves did not much help. The gentle age of Baker Wilbraham and Brown had given way to a new power at 1 Millbank, Malcolm Trustram Eve. By 1961 Eve was unassailable; he was the financial wizard, the supremo. In 1963 he became Lord Silsoe (Ramsey named his cat after him). Owen Chadwick once wrote of him as a 'tycoon' who was nearly always right and knew it;[3] hawkish, imperious, authoritarian. Silsoe was in his element in some brisk, business-like conversation with archbishop Fisher. He was the very last kind of person to commune successfully with Ramsey within some cavernous, mystic silence. For his part, if Ramsey observed that he was not prepared to join in what he found to be 'the rather popular game of sniping at the Commissioners!',[4] he did grin when he came across it. The communication cord which attached Lambeth to Millbank did not snap, but, south of the Thames, it was often held by different hands. Ramsey began to share the chairmanship of the Board with other bishops. In other, ongoing affairs he effectively handed over the Church Commissioners to his rather more institutionally-minded secretary, Robert Beloe. However capable Beloe was, and he was a man to make a virtue out of capability, this inevitably failed to make up for what had clearly been lost.

The archbishops' group on the needs and resources of the Church

It was time to think more deliberately about the work of the whole Church in light of the growing resources which were available to it.

[2] Archbishop Michael Ramsey to Robert Stopford, bishop of London, 19 May 1967, Archbishop Ramsey papers, vol. 112, fo. 77. The Commissioner was A. C. W. Kimpton and his exchange with Ramsey (20 April and 13 May 1967) may be found at fos 69 and 76.
[3] See Chadwick, *Ramsey,* 120.
[4] Ramsey to David Paton, 12 May 1966, Ramsey papers, vol. 94, fo. 63.

Ramsey wrote to Donald Coggan, the new archbishop of York, that he had been talking with Eve: 'There seems to be little doubt that, if the country does not run into a disastrous period, the income of the Church Commissioners will rise very considerably indeed during the next ten years.' So they must work out what to do with it, how it would fit in with Christian stewardship and their understanding of what it was to be a Church.[5] The Commissioners appeared to be eager to spread the moral load beyond their own board and committee rooms. When, in the Church Assembly, too, the standing committee of the House of Laity thought that a review of sorts might be beneficial, Eve and Warren were more than glad to oblige. In October 1961 they had actually pressed Ramsey to initiate a working party on the financial policy of the Church 'in the widest terms'. Eve proposed that it meet not at Millbank, but at Lambeth, so that it might be something more than one of the Commissioners' policy meetings. People rarely flock to join committees, but this new model of unification was one group which they were actually eager to join.

The first meeting of a new, weighty ensemble occurred on 31 January 1962. Present were the two archbishops, Robert Stopford, bishop of London, and a fair spread of Church Assembly and Church Commissioners' men. As Beloe (there to take notes) later observed, it was 'almost for the first time' that the First Church Estates Commissioner and the chairman of the Central Board of Finance met to discuss the finances of the whole Church of England. They were all, in their different ways, true to form. Ramsey inaugurated the proceedings by saying that he feared that this growth of money might give the impression of a Church enjoying undue riches or growing self-absorbed. They must think not only of those at home but of those abroad. Should they support overseas students in hostels or the church training colleges – for he perceived that these lay outside the 'primary trusts' of the Commissioners and the cure of souls in parishes. Eve had offered a paper of aspirations for the clergy stipend and pension and this was happily endorsed. He then revived the progressive agendas of the Fisher era, nominating the cause of the church schools and of churches and parsonages on housing estates. Archbishop Coggan thought that the Church would do better in the eyes of society if it did more for the needy. He also thought the suffragan bishops badly looked after; likewise the chaplaincies at the redbrick universities and, particularly, overseas students attending them. Bishop Stopford remarked that if the laity gave more to stipends funds the Commissioners could commit more to 'outside jobs'. But Brierley reminded them that clergy representatives were already disturbed by what the Commissioners did for church schools and new churches.

[5] Ramsey to Donald Coggan, 7 Nov. 1961, ibid. vol. 20, fo. 190.

Eve turned to Ramsey: it was up to him to say what fell within the rubric 'cure of souls'. Ramsey did not reply. Hilder supported Brierley and feared the views of the House of Clergy. Archbishop Coggan was anxious that they should embrace the needs of the Church abroad.

The needs of assistant clergy, industrial chaplains and chaplains to the modern universities were added to the list. The group agreed, too, that provision be made for ordinands in training and for education, for housing and for overseas students. To do all this would cost roughly an extra £5.5 million a year. They sketched out what this might look like and how the proportions of the contributions made by the Commissioners, the laity, the Church Assembly and the dioceses might be measured. And, evidently, they left in good heart. A flurry of correspondence followed. 'Nothing', wrote Brown later to Ramsey, 'could be more encouraging than the aims set out!'[6]

By the end of May Captain Doig had prepared a schedule on 'The financial needs of the Church and sources from which they are met'. It detailed what came from the Commissioners, the Church Assembly and the Central Board of Finance, the dioceses, the parishes and the various societies. A further meeting of officers took place, significantly this time at Millbank. They asked what was needed to provide and maintain the men, women and buildings 'essential as a basis before the Church of England can begin to meet the claims upon it as a National Church'? Then, what were 'the further needs recognized by the Church of England as claims upon its conscience both in England and beyond'?[7] But this manner of proceeding exposed a problem. Bishop Stopford complained that they really could not ask the officers now maintaining the discussion to pursue such huge questions as these alone. Something more formal, a small working party, was convened under the chairmanship of the bishop himself.

At Millbank they began to wonder what line the paper produced by the archbishops' group might take on once it was released into the public domain. What would Anglicans think of these growing stipends? What would Free Church ministers think of the Anglicans? A third draft statement was sketched. Beloe wrote a challenging paragraph declaring that the Commissioners had undertaken 'a great programme'; that the whole Church must play its part, must be alive to the needs of others, must be forward-looking. Coggan took a look at this and added: 'the reference to the "limited" funds of the Church Commissioners needs clarifying for the average reader who thinks that they are almost limitless!'[8]

[6] Robert Beloe, minutes of the meeting, ibid. fos 202–4.
[7] 'The financial needs of the Church and sources from which they are met', 23 May 1962, ibid. fos 225–7.
[8] Coggan to Ramsey, 27 Sept. 1962, ibid. fo. 279.

By November a final draft existed. But who, now, should see it? Nobody had actually quite asked for it, after all. As few as possible at the moment, thought Eve. And when should it go to the Assembly, given that the Assembly was in dire straits financially and might not quite enjoy this buoyant document? This was swept aside. *The financial requirements of the Church of England* duly appeared before the Assembly after a debate on Christian stewardship and a pause for prayer on 21 February. The statistics were carefully pruned and the argument sharply drawn. They must all acknowledge that the Church in England was a part of the international Church. At home their requirements amounted to about £36 million a year. This was substantially met by endowments managed by the Church Commissioners (£13.5 million) and by lay giving (£21.5 million). The Church must keep pace with inflation in stipends and look after the needs of the clergy; it must expand in both ordained and lay ministry, enlarge their witness in education, industrial and social work, build in the new housing areas; it must give more abroad. All this must be reviewed by a new body, established by the archbishops themselves to oversee the Church's needs and resources. This would offer a report to the Assembly every year.

In the autumn of 1963 the two archbishops appointed a new group of advisors. Eve was one of them. The Church Assembly was represented; so too overseas and missionary interests. Reports followed annually. By January 1965 it could be seen that the Church Commissioners now bore responsibility for a third of the Church's entire financial commitments, providing £11.25 million of the total £15 million required for clergy stipends, £0.75 million of the £1.5 million for their houses, the whole £1.5 million for their pensions. But one truth emerged all too clearly in all these calculations. The benefactions of the past were not sufficient for the Church of the present day, let alone the Church of the future, even assuming that the Church Commissioners continued to prove as successful as they unarguably had been. The conclusion was inescapable: 'It is the laity alone who can provide the further funds which will undoubtedly be required during the next ten years.'[9]

The press and publicity

Increasingly, the press was seen to matter to the Church Commissioners, not because tenants in Paddington might be found at improper work, for example, but because perfectly respectable tenants might be paying high rents to live or to work in prestigious high-rise

[9] 'The financial requirements of the Church of England', 21 Feb.1960, ibid. vol. 39, fos 100–2.

developments which were built with a view to bringing the Commissioners large sums of money. The public, churchgoing or not, learned of the Church Commissioners from newspapers, newspapers with wide circulations. In the early 1960s *The Times* had a circulation of 280,000, the *Daily Telegraph* 1.3 million, the *Manchester Guardian* 240,000, the *Daily Express* 4.5 million, the *Daily Herald* 1 million.[10] A report which appeared in one of them was likely to appear promptly in the others. The reputation of the Church of England itself could be enhanced or marred in a few columns and within a few hours. Like most public institutions in Britain that were unused to public attention, the Commissioners were coming to realise, often reluctantly, that they inhabited a new world in which a popular press, eager to expose scandals, hypocrisies and embarrassments at the heart of established order, was busily snooping at the door. Fisher had been largely oblivious of such matters. In the age of Ramsey church officials were more than ever aware of them.

At the dawn of the Ramsey era, in 1961, the Commissioners' efforts to inform the public still lacked professionalism. Bishop Askwith of Gloucester contributed a quarterly newsletter on the Church and its money, *The Church Commissioners' Investments*, in which he fired off a battery of questions: what were the Church Commissioners doing on the Stock Exchange? ('There has been no *gambling*, only wise and careful reinvestment such as is made by every body of trustees responsible for other people's money. And it is no crime to be provident.') Furthermore, 'Only people with no understanding of the scale of a nation-wide undertaking with local organisation and responsibilities everywhere, or who were quite ignorant of the facts, could speak of the "great wealth" of the Church.'[11] It was a document which no one could accuse of flattering its audience. The public, it seemed, was dull-witted and the critic a cynic or a mischief-maker.

Added to this, there was a persistent suspicion that the clergy were cynical about what went on at 1 Millbank and that churchgoers did not understand what the Commissioners did in their name. The arts of self-explanation and self-promotion were not, if they could even be distinguished, easily acquired. When David Collenette joined the staff at Millbank in 1953 the Commissioners had no public or press relations. Little was said to explain their responsibilities and purpose, or the figures in their statements, to enquirers. In 1954 Collenette told Eve that if the Commissioners wished to be a progressive institution this would no longer do. In the following year he had proposed the

---

[10] Circulation figures noted in cuttings from *The Times*, the *Daily Telegraph* and the *Guardian*, 17 Dec. 1963; David Collenette, memorandum, Ramsey papers, vol. 55, fo. 236.

[11] Ibid. vol. 6, fos 149–50.

annual publication of a popular review of the Commissioners' activities, taken from the annual report, 'a sort of child's guide to the work of the Commissioners'. Twenty copies were sent to every incumbent, on the evening of the Annual General Meeting. It was judged a success and was repeated every year. By the end of 1963 Collenette perceived that the 'thinking general public' knew what they were about, 'although the facts have to be continually repeated'. Because the press knew that they had access to the Commissioners, they held them in 'special and friendly' regard. He believed that the public image of the Commissioners 'is now that of a sensible commercial enterprise which is entrusted with large assets and makes the best of them'.[12]

The annual reports were as much a presentation of an institutional argument as a statement of bald facts. In these new days that might well mean understating success in order to spare feelings. October 1961 found Warren writing to Ramsey that 'There is no intention in the present document, or in any previous documents, to emphasise in any way the success achieved by the E.F.C. in increasing the Commissioners' income.'[13]

In truth, Eve and Warren must now have enjoyed the attentions of the press, even if Ramsey did not. On 20 October 1961 Rhona Churchill, in the *Daily Mail*, contributed a positively glowing report, with the headline 'The man who gambled the Church's money: yesterday the happy news – he has doubled its income'. She unfolded 'a fascinating story of massive Stock Exchange juggling over a period of seven years by two brilliant lay financiers' and went on:

> This miracle has been brought about entirely by wise investment ... With enormous courage and against some opposition, Sir Malcolm plunged the Church's millions into the great jungle of Ordinary-share Stock Exchange dealing. He gambled on Britain's prosperity growing ... Sir Malcolm, aged 67, operates from a lovely panelled room overlooking the river on the first floor of No. 1 Millbank. He devotes two days a week to the Church's affairs. He looks what he was trained to be – a prosperous, quiet-voiced, shrewd barrister ... For all routine investment advice he relies on Sir Mortimer Warren, the 58-year old bespectacled chartered accountant who is the Church Commissioners' senior full-time executive. But these two men have at hand a panel of top-ranking city financiers to advise them cost-free whenever they choose to consult them.

[12] Ibid.
[13] Warren to Ramsey, 12 Oct. 1961, ibid. fo. 83.

The Church now had an investment portfolio comprising shares in 284 industrial and commercial companies and 126 investment trusts, and an interest in 'a wide range of British-made goods from shipping, steel and electronics to tobacco, "undies" and frozen food'. The only investment officially banned was in breweries, 'But today, with so much of the Church's money now in investment trusts, it seems more than likely that at least a fragment of the parson's pay rise comes from the profits on our pints of wallop.'[14]

Ramsey's gloom seemed, by contrast, to be deepening. On 4 April 1962 Eve wrote to him that the development of the Paternoster site to the north of St Paul's Cathedral had begun. Beloe learned that the buildings were to be let to the Central Electricity Generating Board, which would then lease back the shop accommodation to the Commissioners who would, in turn, let it at rack rents. Warren asked if the archbishop would conduct some kind of service for all this? Ramsey did not like the idea; he thought such an act would be misunderstood. Warren agreed to drop the suggestion. When the opening ceremony took place at the beginning of 1964 Ramsey told the EFC that he preferred not to take part. All the people invited were laymen and women. The dean of St Paul's was firm that in no way should the cathedral be identified with what was going on. Neither he nor any member of the chapter attended.[15]

For Ramsey it was going to get worse still. It was, again, speculation in property which attracted attention. The day after a new press release by the Commissioners, on 20 September 1962, a cartoon appeared in the *Daily Herald* showing a lady in fur coat and hat, with a small dog, beside an archbishop in top hat and gaiters: 'of course I never listen to rumours – but have you heard of a property development consortium between Cotton, Clore and Cantuar?' On the same day the *Daily Express* paraded a headline 'Church's £24,000,000 sale aids charity' and reported the fact that so far that year the Commissioners had raised £3,000,000 on the sale of forty-four buildings in London and the provinces to finance, wholly or partly, over the next two years, twenty-seven development companies. *The Guardian* had another: 'Church reinvests £24 millions: More pay for clergy'; the *Daily Mail*: 'The Church does a Clore'; *The Times*: 'Church to sell £11m. property'. On it went.[16]

Ramsey wrote to Eve that all this had 'very much disappointed' him, and he assumed, rather improbably, that Eve had been disappointed too. He hoped to set out the Church's assets in the context of its

[14] Rhona Churchill, *Daily Mail*, 20 Oct. 1961, cutting ibid. fo. 93.
[15] Lord Silsoe to Ramsey, 17 Jan. 1964, ibid. vol. 55, fo. 242.
[16] Cuttings, ibid. vol. 17, fos 244–6.

whole 'needs and claims'.[17] Eve replied that he had not seen the cartoon in the *Daily Herald*, but knew of it and could see that it must be 'galling' to the archbishop himself. Then he added rather nobly, 'I am afraid we must try to continue to take these attacks on ourselves and keep them from you.'[18]

But Ramsey was not merely burying his head in the moral high ground. The rector of Woolwich, Nicholas Stacey, wrote to Lambeth Palace that while he would not criticise either the integrity or the wisdom of the Church Commissioners, the announcement that they were putting £24 million into the development of office blocks, shops and luxury housing needed 'very skilful and careful handling' when one worked in an area where homelessness was the greatest problem. One of his own staff, an industrial chaplain, had seen the Friday newspapers and remarked, 'Thank God I haven't got to go round a factory this morning.' Did the Commissioners have to make their transactions public beyond the statutory requirements? He recalled that they had also announced the rise in clergy stipends at the height of the Pay Pause. Ramsey's chaplain replied sympathetically that the Commissioners were bound to make their announcements at particular times, regardless of the awkwardness of circumstances.[19]

As far as 1 Millbank was concerned, this image of success was materially beneficial too: 'If the Church Commissioners are regarded as a shrewd financial institution, the right kind of safe and profitable investment is offered to them.' It was not pleasant to be connected with Mr Clore and Mr Cotton. But it was advantageous to be 'linked with success'. 'We must', wrote Collenette, 'be frank and forthcoming about all our affairs because we have nothing to hide … We must not be afraid to be linked with "big business", because we want to be respected where it matters … We must face the fact that the Church Commissioners' job is to increase the income of the Church of England by whatever honest and commercial means because our shareholders are the very deserving clergy.'[20] As far as Ramsey was concerned, Collenette's 'thinking general public' comprised those who read *The Times* and the *Guardian*, as well as 'some of those who read the *Daily Telegraph*'. These were people who understood business. 'Then', he continued, 'there are the clergy.' They wanted assurance of efficiency, but were also sometimes 'disturbed' at where the money to pay their stipends came from. Then there were those on the fringes of the Church, people who were 'ready to find reasons why they should *not* support it'. They were the most ready to speak of the 'wealth of the

[17] Ramsey to Eve, 22 Sept. 1962, ibid. fo. 247.
[18] Eve to Ramsey, 24 Sept. 1962, ibid. fo. 248.
[19] Nicholas Stacey to Ramsey, 29 Sept. 1962, ibid. vol. 17, fo. 251.
[20] Collenette memorandum, 'Press relations', 28 Sept. 1962, ibid. fos 256–9.

Church'. Fourthly, there were 'the people about whom I care most of all, those whom the message of the Church of England has not yet touched'. They could be suspicious or critical. They might feel that the Church was not being Christian. When he had revised a recent statement by the Commissioners about pensions Ramsey said he had introduced 'what is called "a slant"'. He added, 'I claim myself no sort of competence in those matters, but I am anxious that the Commissioners should give thought to these wider aspects of publicity which Collenette's account does not touch.'[21]

But there were other claims to be made, beyond those of investments and development companies. Mervyn Stockwood, the bishop of Southwark, had suggested to Warren that the Commissioners draw the attention of the press to the plight of the homeless of London. What were the Commissioners themselves doing? First, replied the EFC, they owned estates which were occupied by 1,700 families on 'lower incomes'. They were supervised by a staff of lady managers who collected weekly rents but also looked after the welfare of the tenants. In 1961 a new block of twenty flats had been completed at Vauxhall, at a cost of £65,000, to let at low rents. Then there was a large area in Brixton which they had offered to London County Council with the proposal that the council clear it, for the Commissioners could not do so themselves, and lease it back so that accommodation could be provided for 200 families, nominated by the council itself. Furthermore, since 1948 the Commissioners had sold about 300 acres to local authorities across Greater London to encourage housing – almost seventy acres in Paddington alone, and fifty-six in Southwark.[22]

The reverse side of this new determination to promote the work of the Commissioners was a sharp resolve to punish offenders. If the *Financial Times* had offered a model of what the Commissioners aspired to, the model of what they most feared could also be seen. If Collenette had thought the brothels of Paddington had died out, they could still be found in the back streets of the public mind. On 17 November 1962 the journal *Parade*, a subsidiary of the *News of the World*, published a pugnacious article by one Charles Gretton called 'The Reluctant Landlords': 'In the gathering dusk the earnest-looking young man had his coat-collar turned up, so at first you could not see he was wearing a clerical black vest and dog-collar. Only the flushing embarrassment of a newly-ordained curate gave him away.' The young curate had found himself walking along streets of brothels, 'each one a house owned by the Church Commissioners for England!' And there were more, in Portsmouth, Durham, Leeds, Nottingham, where

---

[21] Ramsey to Eve, 10 Oct. 1962, ibid. fos 260–1.
[22] Collenette to Beloe, 31 Dec. 1962, ibid. vol. 55, fos 109–10.

'sexual orgies, drug parties and homosexual congresses are held as part of the night's business'. Gretton had ventured to Millbank expecting, he said, 'high-handed evasion ... sermons'; instead he encountered 'startling frankness': 'These slums are awaiting clearance.'[23]

This was simply fiction. Warren wrote promptly to Ramsey of *Parade* itself ('It is very unlikely that you have ... ever heard of it').[24] Eve showed his paces, talking not only to the archbishop, but also to the prime minister, the Lord Chief Justice, the Master of Rolls, the Lord Chamberlain, the attorney-general and the solicitor-general. They chorused unanimously that the Church Commissioners must sue. *Parade* proffered an apology. Eve was in no mood to appease. The apology was put in much stronger terms and sent back to the editor. This version was duly published after Warren had specified how large the letters should be.[25]

Before long these cases could be seen to be accumulating. Ramsey found that he had to draw a firm line when the *Jewish Chronicle* was almost taken to court for publishing a letter which revived the old taunts about prostitution.[26] He reminded Warren that he was a Joint-President of the Council of Christians and Jews and had worked against antisemitism.[27] When the Commissioners sued the *Economist* and *New Society* too Robert Hornby at the Church Information Office began to grumble that things had gone too far. It was one thing to go after *Parade*, which was 'neo-pornographic', but quite another to pursue journals which had sound reputations and had published their libels accidentally rather than maliciously. If this went on the Church might lose the goodwill of Fleet Street. He was stung that the Commissioners did not consult his department much, if at all, treating it instead as a 'subsidiary information department'. Now he had heard that they were about to employ a public relations consultant to publicise a luxury block of flats at Hyde Park. Could a tactful word be said?[28]

In fact, their troubles had reached their peak. Defamations did not now stop, but they became fewer and further between.

[23] *Parade*, no. 117, 17 Nov. 1962, ibid. vol. 17, fo. 277.

[24] Warren to Ramsey, 20 Dec. 1962, ibid. fo. 285.

[25] Ibid.

[26] This soon became a complicated business. See Beloe memorandum 'Jewish Chronicle', 23 Aug. 1963, ibid. fos 146–7.

[27] Beloe note, 23 Aug. 1963, ibid. fo. 145.

[28] Robert Hornby to Ramsey, 10 Dec. 1963, ibid. vol. 55, fo. 226r–v.

Investing, booming

In 1961 the investments panel of the Church Commissioners numbered five: D. J. Robarts (the chairman), G. G. Beamish, Sir Edwin Herbert, Lord Latymer and Sir John Woods. But this body hid a modest army of allies who floated about in the background of the financial life of Millbank. Eve had never thought it polite simply to assume their kindness. They should be thanked properly. On 26 June 1961 he had written to Ramsey:

> The Church Commissioners owe a great deal of their success on the Stock Exchange and in properties to many hundreds of advisers and colleagues who work with us in many deals. This close contact – and I am glad to say that nearly all of these gentlemen are close friends of our staff, and many of myself – is immeasurable in terms of cash. It is, however, very large indeed.

Some years previously he had 'ventured with some trepidation' to ask archbishop Fisher if he would approve of an evening party, at the expense of the Commissioners, in the Great Hall at Lambeth. Three parties had taken place every second year. If Ramsey disapproved he would understand. But he would be 'very disappointed'. It was now 'a rather pleasant custom'.[29] What followed was not, evidently, recorded. But the parties continued.

For these various connections, discussions and courtesies there was certainly much to show. Policy at this time observed something of a law of proportions. In 1961 40 per cent of all 'new money' was invested in Stock Exchange equities, 30 per cent in fixed-interest securities and 30 per cent in property. If this looked like a calculation in pursuit of stability, it was increasingly difficult to deny that one area in particular was simply bursting with power. It was property. When Ramsey became archbishop the seeds of a colossal change in the fortunes of the Church Commissioners had already been planted and shoots were becoming visible. Property sales continued. Since 1957, when rationalisation had begun, 28,500 properties, which together had produced an annual income of £300,000, had been sold for £8 million. The Commissioners had continued to sell ground-rents and scattered properties. They now stuck fast to their five London estates and those run by their lady managers. All of them prospered. The Commissioners had escaped criticism in the press levelled at landlords who were pursuing high increases. They felt that they had entered into free negotiations with tenants founded on a fair measuring of market

---

[29] Eve to Ramsey, 26 June 1961, ibid. vol. 6, fo. 68.

realities, and that cases of difficulty had been handled 'on their merits'.[30]

The simple truth was that London itself was flourishing. While they were at the helm, Eve and Warren were not men to rest content or wait around. They had tasted success and they were eager to pursue it further. The CEDIC report for 1960–1 spoke of how much had occurred since the creation of the body. At the start of the year shares were held by the Commissioners in six companies. By the end, there were eleven more, with four more coming along and still more in prospect. The fact that the Church Commissioners had capital gave them an edge over other development consortia, and 'providing finance' was taking place 'on a profit-sharing basis'. The logic of these new partnerships was solid. In three companies, CEDIC made a profit on the interest on development finance paid to the Commissioners by way of rent under a lessee, where an equity income was also receivable through CEDIC itself, then by loan interest paid to the Commissioners and then again through equity income paid through CEDIC. It seemed to tie up very well.

The realities of this prodigious activity indeed lay in mountains of detail. In the capital, subsidiary companies exploded into life. Bow Lane Developments had been set up to pursue interests in that area of London and was soon appointing an architect to design a new office block with shops. Then there appeared the Commissioners' first wholly-owned company, Burwood Place Properties, in the north-east corner of the Hyde Park estate, building houses and blocks of flats and new plans hatched under the 'Minoprio Plan'. Another, Chancery-Fleet Properties, was busily at work where an old building had been demolished and a new office block planned; Croydon Centre Development was busy demolishing and planning, Dominion and Finsbury Developments was demolishing on the site of 29/32 Finsbury Square, for which the architect had almost completed plans for another office block, and was casting its eyes towards a site in Dominion Street which should soon fall into its hands. The Paternoster Development beside St Paul's Cathedral was busy with excavations, demolitions and plans, and a potential tenant was already in view. Town-planning approval had been obtained for a seventeen-storey block of flats at Maida Vale. There were improvements and redevelopments at Hampstead, new ventures with Messrs Warburg and Co. (commercial) and Mr Victor Behrens (small shops) in Brighton. The same lessons were being learnt elsewhere. And all of

[30] Report, 'Residential property', Board papers, 5 July 1961, ser. 95083/21–2, pp. 3–7.

this was for one year, set down in a few quiet pages and signed by Mortimer Warren on 20 June 1961.[31]

What Ramsey now confronted was the fact that the Church of England was becoming a multi-million-pound force in the world of real estate development. And however much he may have shifted uncomfortably in his chair as he read this at Lambeth, no more than anybody else did he hesitate to accept the dividends for the Church of England as a whole. For this new money, accumulating steadily, powerfully, impressively, had the power to change that landscape dramatically, to increase stipends, to improve provision for pensions, to support episcopal ministry, to sustain cathedrals and to maintain parsonages. In short, it existed to do all the material things that they had most wanted. When Eve began to agitate that the Commissioners should sell more and more agricultural land Bishop Stopford resisted: they must not disturb the Church's historic relationship with the land; moreover, 'I am sufficiently old-fashioned to believe that land will have value when the bottom falls out of everything else.'[32] But beyond this, if CEDIC and all its works presented the spectacle of an irresistible force it did not apparently meet any immovable objections. Harris inherited this and maintained it purposefully.

Ethical investments

When, in 1948, the Commissioners had ventured into the seas of the stock market they confronted squarely the question of what they should invest in, and also what they should avoid. Accordingly, they placed in 'banned categories' activities that would be thought 'objectionable by a majority or a substantial minority of Church members'. This had meant armaments firms, brewers and distillers, hire purchase finance companies, newspapers and publishing, tobacco (but not at first, and not for some time) and then, as a final category, 'amusements (subject to suitable exceptions)'. A company that was banned was banned entirely, including 'debentures and loan stock and the underwriting acceptance of any stock or security'.[33] About these categories there was little debate on the Board, and the withdrawal from tobacco was quiet enough, not even occasioning debate in that quarter. The Church Commissioners felt themselves to be ahead of the field in all this. The Central Board of Finance had no such policy,

---

[31] 'Church Estates Development and Improvement Company Ltd', report for the year to 31 Mar. 1961, ibid. pp. 1–8.
[32] Stopford to Eve, 13 July 1962, EFC papers, Board papers, 5 July 1961, ibid. pt 22.
[33] Silsoe report, 'Banned categories', CC (68) 1, Board papers, 25 Jan. 1968, ibid. pt 31.

simply ruling out breweries and distilleries and, in time, tobacco. Nobody, apparently, had raised a voice against them. Silsoe had heard that they had even considered embracing the brewers, distillers and tobacco companies, and might even have done so had not the Commissioners maintained their ban. In short, for the first half of the 1960s, this debate appeared a relaxed one. When, in July 1967, Silsoe found himself asked whether some things mattered more to the Church Commissioners than profit, he had remarked laconically, 'Oh yes, we're influenced by Christian considerations. It is, however, pleasant to record I think that very, very often doing the right thing that way is the best result financially.'[34]

This may well have looked tidy enough, but the most superficial encounter with the realities of the stock market showed them to be anything but. Companies that held subsidiary or minor interests in the 'banned categories' were not excluded from the Commissioners' considerations. The bigger firms diversified, amalgamated, were taken over. At what point should a measure of a company's dealings in banned areas rule it out altogether? This was hard to gauge because companies themselves altered. One might fall over the line in one year and under it in the next. Government stocks surely involved to some degree or other an investment in armaments. In January 1968 Silsoe and the Assets Committee thought that it was best to take each case on its own terms. They offered the Board an example. When GEC had been bought up by AE, GEC was involved in arms manufactures – one of its subsidiaries was said to be making electronic apparatus for nuclear warheads. At that time the following reply had been made:

> The Commissioners' funds are very large indeed, and it is vital that they should be invested in a wide range of the country's leading industrial and commercial firms in order to promote that steady growth of income which alone enables clergy pay and pensions to be kept abreast of inflation. No doubt some such firms, through the wide spread of their activities, may become involved from time to time, directly or indirectly, in processes of a kind which can be used for the manufacture of armaments. But such a degree of involvement cannot reasonably be deemed to require that the firm should be categorised as an armament firm and, therefore, as unsuitable for Church investment.[35]

Factories were no simple matter either. It was not easy even to define what a certain factory was or what it might make. At present it would

---

[34] Annex, ibid.: extract from *The Money Programme*, BBC 2, 27 July 1967.
[35] Ibid.

simply be listed as 'heavy' or 'light'. The ban also extended to companies that were not registered in the United Kingdom itself. The Commissioners withdrew from investing in companies registered in South Africa, or registered in the United Kingdom but trading 'wholly or mainly' in South Africa long before the debate about South Africa gathered momentum, though they did so on economic grounds and the ban also included the United States.

The complications of the real world, and the ways in which they conspired against hard and fast rules, were equally evident in the Commissioners' other dealings. In property there existed no formal bans, but 'uses' were forbidden by the Commissioners' leases: publicans or licensed victuallers, the sale or consumption on or off the premises of wines and spirits, places of entertainment, noisy or offensive trade (no fun-fairs or amusement arcades), gambling, things illegal and immoral – which basically meant prostitution. These, too, were pragmatic. The first two could be permitted if appropriately licensed, entertainment could occur occasionally in, say, a hotel '(if this can be regarded as a "place of entertainment")'. The Commissioners did own some hotels and public houses and they had caused no problems. Only leases granted since 1961 prohibited legal changes to properties to make them into betting offices. As for the rest, a property should not be let directly as a betting shop, which had become legal after the Betting and Gaming Act of 1960. But if a lessee wished to convert premises into one the Commissioners could not unreasonably resist. They might object to planning permission, but if it were given and a licence to boot, that was effectively that. Even so, the Assets Committee would not welcome casinos, bingo halls or amusement arcades. Residential properties prohibited any use for non-residential purposes and all had covenants to stop immoral use and gaming. The Commissioners' agents were not armed with instructions or guidelines, which might give rise to misunderstandings. These matters all fell within the compass of 'good estate management' and that seemed to do well enough. Then there was the newer area of property development. The Commissioners did not scrutinise their partners and nothing untoward had yet occurred.[36]

In 1968 Silsoe asked whether the idea of 'banned categories' was still valid and necessary? If they were 'too firmly established to be dispensable', he still found them 'shot through with illogicalities. But this probably only reflects the illogicality inherent in all human affairs'. Newspapers were political and the ban still made sense there. Publishing had liabilities; however innocuous a house might be, it could still publish something controversial. Tobacco should remain

---

[36] Ibid. pp. 2–4.

banned, though it might well be profitable.[37] The Board of the Commissioners ruminated on this at the end of its meeting in September 1968. They agreed that it would be a mistake to set an exact point at which a questionable minority concern within a company threatened the entire investment: 'each case should continue to be considered on its merits'. They agreed that hire purchase companies should be admitted, and felt that a time might come when they should review investing in companies registered abroad – something that in any case the government presently prohibited on grounds of financial distress.[38]

When in November Silsoe submitted to the Board a report from the General Purposes and Assets Committees, it transpired that the Commissioners held investments in seventeen companies over 5 per cent of whose turnover or profits were drawn from South Africa or the African continent. Rio-Tinto Zinc now made a 'substantial' percentage of its profits in South Africa. The Church Commissioners thus found that they held investments, through holding companies, in copper mining in Zambia, asbestos mines in Rhodesia and even a factory in the Soviet Union. Quite simply, observed Silsoe:

> it is no longer possible entirely to avoid investments through subsidiaries or shareholdings in any particular part of the world and certainly not throughout a whole continent. Such a policy of avoidance in, say, South Africa, might prevent holding or making investments in British companies concerned with oil, aircraft, chemical products (including British Oxygen), cement, engineering, the motor industry (exports and Dunlop), packaging, shipping, shipbuilding, metals, exporting textiles, chemists (drugs); and presumably banks.

It would also be 'quite impossible' to halt fully holdings in investment trusts. They must do their best to avoid compromising relationships. But they should not be 'forced to avoid or forced to sell investments merely because some trade is carried on in, say, copper mining in Russia, in Arab countries, in Israel, in South Africa, in Cuba or in Rhodesia'. For his part, Silsoe believed that they should remain with Rio-Tinto Zinc, and even add to their shares in it.[39]

The Board, in its turn, was asked to confirm the Commissioners' policy not to invest in 'objectionable' companies, not to invest in companies registered outside the United Kingdom, not to buy shares

[37] Ibid. pp. 4–5.
[38] Board minutes, 18 July 1968.
[39] Silsoe report, 'Stock exchange investment policy', CC (68) 49, Board papers, 21 Nov. 1968, ser. 95083/32.

with a view to sale for capital gain. There was no dissent to these last two. There was, however, to the first. There was also a new fear over breweries, distilleries and tobacco companies, for it was rumoured that Distillers would buy up Schweppes, and the Commissioners did have shares in Schweppes. The innocuous Butlin's holiday camps, in which they also held shares, faced a takeover bid from the less innocuous Phonographic Equipment. The Board gave the Assets Committee power to judge for itself on behalf of the Commissioners, though there was clearly a sense that this would be no easy responsibility. Could the committee think again about how it expressed its position on where, and where not, to invest; become 'less definite without materially altering the intention behind the policy'?[40]

This reconsideration took the Assets Committee a year. Eventually it decided that its current definition of the banned categories was still viable: it was not 'unduly restrictive', and it had the benefit of being known and accepted inside 1 Millbank and outside. There was also a significant new departure. The committee asked the Board for authority to invest abroad, making it clear that it was looking towards the United States.[41] Of this both the General Purposes Committee and the Board approved.

Elsewhere, the debate had begun to move more towards the positive moral possibilities offered by investments. That autumn a Church Assembly report on 'Christians and World Development' had inspired an amendment calling upon the Church Commissioners to increase their investments in developing countries. The Commissioners as an institution were eager to prove themselves here. But this time the Assets Committee and Board minutes record 'reservations' about supporting poorer economies: 'The Committee would only take this step if they were satisfied that the investment was financially sound and that it in no way prejudiced the Commissioners' statutory duties towards the clergy of this country.' The Assets Committee was authorised to explore and pursue (or not pursue, for it was hardly encouraged) the whole question of overseas investment as it chose in confirmation of the First Church Estates Commissioner's reply to the Church Assembly.[42] As this debate matured another difficulty arose. Most poor countries were governed by dictators: while it was virtuous to support development, should money be invested in tyranny?

As the fragility of these questions grew more obvious so the discussions looked more sharply and nervously at the precision of

[40] Board minutes, 21 Nov. 1968.
[41] Memorandum, 'Overseas investment and "banned categories"', CC (69) 41, Board papers, 11 Dec. 1969, ser. 95083/32.
[42] Board minutes, 11 Dec. 1968.

language itself. In February 1971 the committees wondered whether the Commissioners should declare that they refrained from 'direct investment in companies operating wholly or mainly *in the following trades*' in South Africa. But then what were these trades to be? 'Is the activity one in which it is wrong in principle for the Church to invest its funds?' Then, 'If not, are there nevertheless considerations (other than purely investment ones) which make Church investment undesirable?' A paper by the clerical member Bernard Pawley had observed that 'The question of deciding what considerations should be allowed to influence the Commissioners' selection of investments has almost passed outside the sphere of ethics altogether because of the immense diversification which now obtains.' On armaments firms they could still be clear. They might simply say 'armaments', rather than 'armaments firms'.[43]

There was in these debates a steady weakening of opposition to the breweries and distilleries. By 1972 a majority on the Assets Committee wanted to lift the ban altogether. Ashton agreed. To be sure, they must allow for a tradition of Temperance. In a period of Anglican–Methodist conversations they might observe that the Church of England may be coming nearer to the Free Churches, who now appeared to bear that inheritance more distinctly. Alcohol, observed Canon Pawley, had seemed to take up an over-preponderant amount of time and energy at the Anglican–Methodist discussions. Pawley felt that the issue raised 'the usual question of public relations' with a public that was sensitive, even unfriendly to the Commissioners themselves. He talked with Edwin Barker, secretary of the General Synod's Board of Social Responsibility, and returned to argue that 'heavy drinking, alcoholism and drunkenness have declined considerably since the turn of the century'. Perhaps this was because society had improved altogether? But since the Second World War drunkenness, consumption and associated diseases had steadily increased again. The General Purposes Committee was unanimous in recommending that the ban remain. Could it really be said that the investments of the Commissioners were severely handicapped by their ban? Could a distinction be made between the brewers and the distillers? Pawley thought that the public would not see one. Harris was beginning to change his mind. Alcoholism, he observed, was a progressive disease, often beginning with 'normal social drinking, to excess and then dependence, beginning often with beer and ending in spirits'. It was not possible therefore to distinguish between breweries and distilleries.[44] He would also come to argue that however these

---

[43] See 'Investment policy: "banned categories"', CC (72) 5, Board papers, 20 Jan. 1972, ser. 95083/35.

[44] Ibid. pp. 3–4.

companies might protest that they sought only to encourage moderation, they must, *ex priori*, pursue higher sales of their products. This line would hold for almost a further three decades.

The 1972 review nodded to the other categories and confirmed inherited practice. As for property, there was no reason to change anything. But they should observe that there were now eleven betting shops on estates owned by the Commissioners, all established without offending the terms of the leases. This done, the Commissioners looked across to the Central Board of Finance again. There was no change there. So far as they could see, the Board was still following the standard of the Commissioners.[45] A glimmer of all this found its way into the 1972 annual report and accounts of the Commissioners, in a section outlining the dilemmas of their investment policies. Here, the banned categories were restated.[46]

South Africa

The demise of the Church Assembly and its replacement by the General Synod in 1970 did little to complicate the Commissioners' relationship with the representative assembly of the Church. It was in this new, or at least altered, context that voices were increasingly raised asking that the Church Commissioners' annual report be not merely presented, but also debated. This occurred for the first time on 21 February 1973. Harris commented happily on the closeness of the two bodies which permitted the Commissioners, in this anniversary year, to present their report in a full session for debate. But though this proved to be a good day for the Church Commissioners, they heard the first shots fired in a campaign which would soon come to define their history almost as much as any other, and one which would cost them dearly: South Africa. Today their name shone in comparison with the Central Board of Finance, which had found itself criticised for having shares in Consolidated Gold Fields (which had 20 per cent of its operations in South Africa). They heard Sir John Lawrence declare that he wished to ensure that the Central Board of Finance maintained the standards set by the Commissioners. They saw Canon Paul Oestreicher also pointing at the Central Board of Finance, and owning that to the Commissioners he was entirely sympathetic. Harris responded that the Church Commissioners steered a middle course. But one speech showed that the climate was beginning to change. A priest from York, H. W. F Bishop, who had been in South Africa for some time, warned that a large and growing proportion of African

[45] Ibid. pp. 4–7.
[46] *Annual Report of the Church Commissioners*, London 1972, 12.

opinion was in favour of disinvestment: 'they may be right or they may be wrong, but they have a right to be heard'.[47]

If Harris could congratulate both himself and the Commissioners on a calm passage this time, it was not the shape of things to come. A parliamentary select committee on trade in South Africa was being assembled. The *Guardian* had published lengthy reports on migrant labour in South African industries, and in General Synod that November Paul Oestreicher moved that members of the Church who held shares in South Africa do what they could towards 'the closing of the gap between their white and black employees'; that 'no funds controlled by any part of the Church of England should be invested in any firm which disregards the social and economic interests of any of its South African employees'; that the Board for Social Responsibility keep its eyes on the subject and advise the Church accordingly. Another motion urged that the Church Commissioners and the World Council of Churches 'reconsider' their present policies, and that the entire question of 'investment ethics' should be re-examined. The dean of Norwich, Alan Webster, reinforced this, welcoming a proposal made by the British Council of Churches that a 'common instrument' be established for all Churches and missionary societies. Harris assured Synod that the Commissioners would review their present policy in light of what had been said.[48]

A Millbank report duly reflected on this debate. Oestreicher, it seemed, could be met, if not absolutely on his own terms, then sympathetically and substantially. The motions had also spoken of a 'general acceptance' amongst Synod members that complete disinvestment from South Africa was 'impractical and unhelpful'. If disinvestment was the policy of the WCC, it was symbolic, and the WCC itself had not called upon individual Churches to do the same. A suggestion that the Commissioners become more profoundly involved as a way of influencing what occurred in South Africa did not convince. There was a difference between accepting an inevitable degree of involvement and making the stipends of the clergy of the Church of England depend in some real measure on the profitability of companies that were based on racism. There was a case for relaxing the ban in favour of companies there that sought to improve their practices in these terms: 'It is, however, suggested that to try to make judgments [*sic*] on the social behaviour of individual companies is so fraught with practical difficulties that the present policy of not investing in companies "operating wholly or mainly in Southern Africa" should stand.' As to the dean of Norwich's 'common

[47] *Report of the proceedings of the General Synod*, iv/1, London 1973, 81–108 (21 Feb. 1973).
[48] Ibid. iv/3, 890–913, 914–17.

instrument', this should not be discouraged, but it looked a more doubtful enterprise in practical terms. The Commissioners did well in their established roles.[49] At the Board itself, the robust David Hopkinson argued that the concept of 'banned categories' was no longer tenable: the Commissioners should rely solely on their perception as to whether a company was 'well-managed'. But this view was answered again by the argument that it was the sensitivities of clergy and church members that mattered, and these were not unfounded. The earl of March argued that the ban on companies operating wholly or mainly in South Africa should remain. Investment might be made to bring change, but it unarguably bolstered the South African economy. At the WCC it was seen that this was not simply an issue of working conditions in South Africa, but one of the ending of apartheid. In short, the Board now maintained its policy on South Africa, but agreed to discuss it again if that was seen to be necessary.[50]

Although Ramsey certainly had views on such matters they were not much in evidence. It was beginning to be the case that questions would be referred to him if they seemed insoluble when discussed by board or committee and required a higher moral capacity or power. In August 1967 Harris had written that he had been asked by the Assets Committee to ask the archbishop for advice over whether or not they should acquire a holding in British Drug Houses Limited, 'which they regard as offering a sound investment with good growth prospects', but which had a substantial share ('believed to be about 20%') of the United Kingdom market in the contraceptive pill. The committee had heard that it might be a hazard to health'. Ramsey replied:

> It is very difficult indeed for me to give advice as I simply do not know what are the hazards to health. I do therefore wonder whether with so many possible fields of investment available the Commissioners would not do better to invest in some concern which does not involve putting to me a question which I am inadequate to answer.[51]

A Revision: the Monckton Report

The history of what became the Monckton Report may appear, at least superficially, to reveal merely a revision of arrangements in the corporate life of the Church Commissioners. But it deserves close scrutiny for a fundamental reason: it offers the historian a rare glimpse

[49] See A. I. McDonald, 'Review of investment policies', A (73) 158, 6 Dec. 1973, Board papers, 14 Feb. 1974, ser. 95083/38.
[50] Board minutes, 14 Feb. 1974, pp. 1–2.
[51] Ramsey to Harris, 1 Sept. 1967, Ramsey papers, vol. 112, fo. 125.

of the 'establishment' of the Church of England busily at work, hardly observed, in the offices of Church and State in the second half of the twentieth century.

In July 1962 Edward Courtman felt that the time had come to challenge the Church Commissioners again. He published an incendiary editorial in his journal *Parson and Parish*, arguing that control of the Commissioners had slipped out of the hands of the institutions of the Church and lay with the state and the laity. The Church, through the bishops, clergy and laity of the Church Assembly, should have power over them. The 1924 commission, a very proper church affair which had reported to the Assembly and been debated openly in that forum, had been superseded by a world of 'secret bargaining' and 'sumptuous' lunches every year at Lambeth Palace. Courtman knew of no rules regulating the conduct of the three Church Estates Commissioners, two of whom, he added purposefully, were state appointees. He complained that the annual general meetings were virtually powerless to prevent any decision made by the Estates Commissioners themselves, with the support of the actuary and 'a small body called the Estates and Finance Committee', not least because it had too little information at its disposal. He now issued his own plan for reform, proposing that the powers of the Church Estates Commissioners be curtailed and the EFC enlarged. 'I contend', pronounced Courtman, 'that the 1947 Measure permits the Three Church Estates Commissioners to be a law unto themselves.'[52]

Although at Millbank and at Lambeth Palace this generated little comment, it did coincide with a debate about the structures of the Church Commissioners which had been steadily gathering momentum. The institutional machinery of the Commissioners was duly reviewed every five years. Eve, however, was not a man to leave arrangements undisturbed if he found in them room for improvement. By the early 1960s he had become convinced that something more than a review was required. The structures and committees no longer accommodated all the decisions which had to be made, and where they failed to do so the Estates Commissioners themselves were assuming growing responsibilities. There was reason to feel uncomfortable about this. The fundamental question which interested Eve was whether the Board of governors had the right people on it and, beyond that, whether the highest levels – the Church Estates Commissioners themselves, the Estates and Finance Committee, the committees which answered to the Board – were suitably recruited and properly staffed. Beyond that he left it to Ramsey, but with a hint that he might wonder if the entire membership of the Commissioners was worth examining.

[52] Courtman statement: extract from *Parson and Parish*, July 1962, ibid. vol. 17, fos 317–20.

'I think myself', he added, 'that this is an odd set-up, and ought very likely to be looked into.'

It was Eve who proposed to Ramsey that the archbishop might appoint 'a small and very high-powered' committee to conjure something up. By March 1962 Ramsey had agreed. It should not be public ('very undesirable'); indeed, it should be secret until its findings were published. For his part Eve thought there could be 'no harm' in it being an entirely lay enterprise; that there could be about four members – somebody from the Treasury, a 'really first-class industrialist ... who had worked right through and come to the top', an experienced administrator, a member or former member of the Church Assembly, a senior chartered accountant. The Central Board of Finance ought to come into the picture.[53]

Lambeth Palace and Millbank began to think of names. Such a committee had to possess weight, and must therefore be composed of eminent men. But eminent men are busy, in demand and often travelling to somewhere else. Such a committee must also speak from experience. Experience comes with age: older men get ill more often, and for longer, and can be governed by their doctors. In short, a weighty committee must consist of older and frailer men who were also already busy and often on aeroplanes. None of this made life at all straightforward. Viscount Monckton of Brenchley was invited to chair the group; a man of consummate practical skill and wide experience; the distinguished scion of a good Anglican family (whose cousin was actually the taxing Major Monckton). Ramsey, for his part, passed the enterprise over to Robert Beloe.

There was a muddle, and a significant one. Eve asked whether, if they were exploring the constitution, all this should first be cleared by the crown? As they were already hunting for a permanent secretary in the civil service to join the committee, and as that required consultation with Sir Norman Brook at 10 Downing Street, they could ask him at the same time. Beloe asked Ramsey what he thought about this. Ramsey simply referred him back to Eve. Eve now had the undertaking well and truly in his sights and was already busy putting his connections to work. He telephoned Beloe not from Millbank but from Brook's own office. What, Eve asked, did Lambeth now think the terms of reference of this new committee should be? He also had a list of names to propose – would they be acceptable? Caught on the spot, Beloe thought that they would be. Then, Eve pressed, would it be all right if Brook mentioned these to the prime minister? Beloe agreed. Brook, in his turn, agreed to find a Permanent Secretary for them.[54]

[53] Eve to Ramsey, 15 Mar. 1962, ibid. fo. 288.
[54] Beloe note, 16 Apr. 1962, ibid. fos 293–4. See also 'Note of conversation with

But now wires between 10 Downing Street and the Treasury became crossed.[55] The difference between the two turned on one question: was this to be a committee or a commission? C. L. Hewitt, deputy secretary to the Treasury, was speaking of a commission, which was no light matter. More than this, he feared that the report of this new commission might be used in public to promote an amending measure in the Church Assembly which would affect, and controversially, the connection between Church and State. It would be better to avoid a commission and appoint instead a smaller, quieter creature, a private committee that would report privately to the archbishop.[56] If the committee found a need for a constitutional alteration, the archbishop could discuss it with the prime minister and see if there should then be a commission and a public report.

Beloe clearly felt that Hewitt had got in the way. He remarked to Ramsey that they had 'at last' gained the prime minister's agreement, implying that Beloe himself had straightened the matter out through Downing Street. The possibility that Brook, Hewitt and the prime minister had simply been looking at the enterprise more thoroughly than had Lambeth or Millbank, did not enter this reckoning. Meanwhile, Monckton replied that he was not quite clear what he was being asked to do, and he asked for a few minutes of conversation. For Monckton was no more confined to domestic affairs than were the prime minister and the archbishop: quite apart from the Midland Bank, he had the Iraq Petroleum Company to run.

Brook had counselled helpfully that only half a dozen meetings would be needed, but this was soon looking unduly ambitious. When a meeting did take place on 28 November, the group was at half strength. Eve had modestly offered his own questions for the group to consider and drafted no fewer than thirty-two. By the end of the first hour the committee had covered only six of them and decided that they must do something else.

After a second meeting of the group on 1 January 1963 Beloe produced a memorandum wringing out of the discussion a list of main issues. This did not flatter the ninety-five Commissioners, who were described as 'a cumbrous body serving no major executive purpose'. Beloe noted, however, that this body did 'represent an historical position of equilibrium between the various forces at work'. The annual meeting had the virtue of allowing some to let off steam and had the appearance of an annual meeting of shareholders of a company. It was, arguably, best left alone as 'an historical survival doing very little harm and serving … some useful purpose'. But there

Hewitt', and Hewitt to Beloe, 24 Apr. 1962, ibid. fos 295–6.
[55] Beloe note, 25 Apr. 1962, ibid. fo. 297.
[56] Beloe memorandum, 30 Apr. 1962, ibid. fos 298–9.

was, at the heart of this, a considerable problem; in Beloe's words, the group was discerning that 'the problems and responsibilities of the Commissioners now bear little relationship to the kind of administrative structure set up under the measure of 1947'. This anxiety was most of all explicit in the matter of investments:

> When the Commission was confronted with grave problems about investment policy (e.g. when it had to decide what to do about its large holdings of shares (a) in the British Aluminium Company and (b) in Courtaulds) answers could only be found to the very tricky problems involved by Trustram Eve and Warren acting in consultation with Edwin Herbert, disregarding the statutory organisation.[57]

A note by one of the group, Sir Maurice Dean, suggested a harsher view in the committee. Dean favoured abolition of the ninety-five Commissioners and the creation of something a good deal smaller. Furthermore, he saw that a failure to differentiate between functions led to time-wasting, confusion and even the danger of disputes. The Parliamentary Commissioner was an anomaly, for he was unpaid, given a variety of time-consuming tasks, and yet was unable to take charge of any measures not initiated by the Commissioners. It surely wasted time for every Estates Commissioner to be on every committee. The fact that they were joint treasurers was meaningless and 'a little embarrassing'. When it came to the Commissioners' assets, the archbishop should appoint experts properly, for expertise was something they needed a good deal of when it came to such questions.[58]

This was a committee of institutional pragmatists, and the question of the arrangements of the Church Commissioners was not a political but a practical one. Where there were problems the rational mind could devise solutions. It was agreed that the three Estates Commissioners should remain, and although the authority of the First Estates Commissioner might now appear conspicuously powerful, the responsibilities of all three were essentially undisturbed. The Board of governors seemed much as it should be. But when it came to the committee structure there was surely work to be done. A new structure was soon emerging more clearly. It was time to ask the interested parties for their views.

Eve had hoped for a Fourth Church Estates Commissioner, and waved the idea goodbye with some fondness and lamentation. He also

[57] Memorandum by Beloe, 'The Church Commissioners: Note on the problem as it appeared after the meeting of Lord Monckton's Committee on 1 January: A Preliminary Statement', ibid. fos. 176–80.
[58] Sir Maurice Dean to Beloe, 28 Feb. 1963, ibid. vol. 34, fos 196–201.

'put in a very strong plea' that the committee should resist the word 'experts'.[59] Warren wrote to Beloe that it appeared to overlook the position of the secretary entirely and did nothing to acknowledge his burden or to help strengthen his hand. But both supported the substance of the recommendations. So did the archbishop of York, who was concerned that there should be more women Commissioners. They also discussed whether or not the Commissioners should have an office in the north, but decided not. On 1 July 1963 Ramsey met the full committee. There were no problems there.

If anything, a careful scrutiny of the draft proposals came not from the Church but, again, from the State. Hewitt at the Treasury asked: if the EFC became, in effect, an investment trust which had no control over income and no real control over the distribution of income, while the new General Purposes Committee was, in effect, the spending body, and if the First Church Estates Commissioner chaired both, might he not come under pressure from one body against the other? To Hewitt it all suggested an analogy between the spending departments in Whitehall and the Treasury. Beloe replied that this had not occurred to anyone else. They had been thinking of complaints which might break out within the Church in quite different areas; for example, as to whether the Commissioners had too much power over the distribution of surplus income. When it came to the role of the First Church Estates Commissioner, Hewitt observed, a little casually, it was true that the First Church Estates Commissioner would 'in some ways become more of a dictator ... but he would lose some of his present freedom of action'. Hewitt and Beloe also discussed the suggestion that a bishop sit on the Assets Committee. He would be there, said Beloe, 'simply to consider moral issues, arising over such questions as investments in drink and tobacco, or in connection with takeover bids'. But Hewitt, too, viewed these things practically. He thought that what he read amounted to a matter of housekeeping arrangements, and as such unlikely to see a need for the state to intervene.[60] When Hewitt's qualms were explained to Dean he conceded that the First Church Estates Commissioner would now be in 'a position of immensely augmented authority', yet he no longer enjoyed powers in his own right for he but owed them to his chairmanship of a committee, and he could be checked at the Board or on the Commission itself. To Hewitt he added, dryly, 'We would rather you didn't speak of the First Church Estates Commissioner as being "more of a dictator".'[61]

[59] Eve memorandum, n.d., ibid. fos 334–41.
[60] Beloe memorandum, 'Hewitt', 16 July 1963, ibid. fos 363–4.
[61] Dean to C. L. Hewitt, 24 July 1963, ibid. vol. 36, fo. 1.

As a final document the Monckton Report made three key proposals. Firstly, the EFC was indeed dissolved and divided now into a General Purposes Committee, in effect a policy committee with a wider representative power, and an Assets Committee, possessing one clerical member and enjoying exclusive power to manage the Commissioners' assets and the duty of informing the Board of what was available to spend and what might be reinvested or put in the reserve. Both would be chaired by the First Church Estates Commissioner. Secondly, there would be a Houses Committee to oversee see houses and grounds (though not the gardeners themselves), cathedral houses and benefice property, the repair, maintenance and disposal of parsonage houses and glebe. Third, there would be a pastoral committee for all matters parochial. Beyond this, the roles of the Church Estates Commissioners were set down with a new clarity. The Board should possess new powers to co-opt three new members. There was a calculation in all these bodies of the balance between clergy and laity, and clergy would be present on every one.[62]

However much interest Ramsey took in it all, his predecessor was still watching beadily from a position of rather over-active retirement. Fisher wrote to Beloe:

> I have no doubt that this stage of growth to adult manhood had to take place ... In the recommendations I found nothing but good sense: so all is well. If I have a regret it is that a little bit of the domestic atmosphere of the Commissioners has suffered, but as the whole world knows, that is the price being paid for increased efficiency.[63]

Not everybody was content. Major Monckton deplored that the ninety-five Church Commissioners had not even known that this committee existed. Certainly they had not made any representations to it. The whole set-up was a calculated discourtesy to the crown and to the Assembly.[64] Even so, when the report was aired at the AGM in October there were few complaints. Kenneth Grubb, a lay Commissioner who was a power at the Assembly, made a helpful speech suggesting that the point of having ninety-five Church Commissioners was not that they take on active responsibilities but rather that they represent the life of and 'true facts' about the Commissioners to their own various circles. After a flurry of debate it

[62] *The administration of the Church Commissioners for England: report of the committee appointed by the Archbishop of Canterbury*, London 1963.
[63] Fisher to Beloe, 4 Oct. 1963, Ramsey papers, vol. 36, fo. 42.
[64] Monckton to Ramsey, 17 Oct. 1963, ibid. vol. 55, fo. 184.

was agreed that the matter must now pass to the Church Assembly. The motion was carried *nem. con.*[65]

The Monckton caravan duly turned up at the doors of the Church Assembly that autumn, on 6 November 1963. What followed was something of a rarity, for it gave that body an opportunity to discuss openly not simply what its members thought of the Monckton Report, but also to air its views on the Church Commissioners as a whole. Bishop Stopford, moving that it be received (even though, it might be said, the Assembly had not actually asked for it in the first place), set out on a laudatory note. He observed how few people really understood the powers or the responsibilities of the Church Commissioners, imagining perhaps that colossal sums were stashed away in deep vaults under Number 1 Millbank, and sat upon there by the misers who inhabited the offices above. What followed seemed to amount to something of a field day for archdeacons. The archdeacon of Croydon thought the Commissioners a Victorian outfit, a 'pseudo-government department, and in one sense a honeycomb of watertight compartments. Sometimes one felt it was almost sealed off from the rest of the Church'. Might they attempt a different model instead, creating offices to deal with all matters arising within a group of dioceses? The archdeacon of Aston sensed that criticism of the Commissioners was actually mounting within the Church. At the same time he observed a paradox: 'The clergy in criticism of the Church Commissioners would tell them what to spend the money on and even criticise them for their success on the Stock Exchange. But if, as a result of their criticisms and advice, the Commissioners had to reduce the personal cheques of the clergy by one half they would be startled and horrified.' The clergy, through the Assembly, should take complete control of the money themselves. But Bishop Reeve of Lichfield thought that the archdeacon of Aston had exaggerated criticism of the Commissioners. He did not think it was 'great and growing' ('Applause'), for they had removed a state of 'gnawing anxiety' from parsonage houses across the country ('Applause') and they had put churches on new housing estates which would have been too great a task for the local churches themselves. He saw that when the Commissioners were the target of 'slurs and innuendoes', these things were thrown at the Church itself. There was a brief discussion of the numbers of the Commissioners. Dr Wright Homes of Guildford said that he found that the list of Commissioners read like something out of Gilbert and Sullivan.[66]

[65] Minutes of the AGM of the Church Commissioners, 17 Oct. 1963, ibid. fos 203–5.
[66] *Proceedings of the Church Assembly*, xliii/3, London 1963, 565–89 (6 Nov. 1963).

Did the money that the Commissioners controlled truly belong to the clergy? Or did it belong to the whole Church of England. Ramsey, in the chair, simply deferred to the bishop of London. Rather caught off guard Stopford offered the best view that he could without ready access, he said, to 'the best advice': the monies derived from the endowments from

> past years of bishoprics, deans and chapters, benefices, and a number of private gifts made during the nineteenth century for the express purpose of making better provision for the cure of souls of the laity. He was also told that if one had to put it in a single sentence, the monies which the Church Commissioners administered belonged to the laity of the Church of England.

A motion to propose a reduction in the number of Commissioners was defeated. The report was received.[67]

The officers of the Commissioners turned the report into a legislative matter. Come the spring and the Church Assembly there was little more to be said about it. Major Monckton nobly did his best to joust with the new measure, but he looked a solitary figure. The measure sailed through on 6 February 1964, and on 9 July 1964 it secured final approval.

To construct a new arrangement was one task. But to find people to inhabit any arrangements was no easier than it ever had been. This had emerged clearly as a fundamental problem in the life and work of the Church Commissioners. Eve's peerage had not helped him to lure in recruits. He hoped, rather faintly, that Ramsey himself would give a lead. By the beginning of February 1964 he was worrying about gaps on the Board itself. He had a provost, but lacked a dean. They had three deans on the Commissioners, but one was 'not avid for office' and had been elected to the Board without quite knowing how. At all events Silsoe was less than sanguine about him: 'the only time he has played any part was at a General Meeting when he barked up the wrong tree for a long time'. Another wanted to be on the Houses Committee more than the Board and believed that he must speak on behalf of ancient buildings, while a third felt a similar obligation to any financial questions which involved deans and chapters.[68] There was still a vacant seat on the Assets Committee, and it must be filled by a clergyman. But the new committee would meet every fortnight and that would demand some commitment and assiduity. Then, they must find a candidate with some skill in the art of investment itself. That,

[67] Ibid. 613–19.
[68] Silsoe to Ramsey, 4 Feb. 1964, Ramsey papers, vol. 55, fo. 258.

thought Silsoe, ruled out all the diocesan bishops. What about a suffragan bishop, a dean, a provost or an archdeacon? None of the available parish priests seemed appropriate – one of them was Courtman.[69] More shuffling. They looked at deans and provosts again. On it went.

Nor did everything go well with the promotion of the report. The Commissioners fell out with the Church Information Office about publishing costs, which exceeded their expectations and their agreement. There were 400 copies left unsold and the publishing officer of the CIO saw no reason why it should pay for them. The dependable Beloe was asked to clear the matter up. The Church Commissioners Measure, 1964, received the royal assent on the last day of July 1964. For a moment Ramsey was happy. 'I think it must also be a record', he wrote to Sir Maurice Dean on 13 August, 'for a report to have been made and to have been enacted within 24 months of the appointment of the original committee.'[70] But only three days later Beloe reported to Ramsey that 'In their anxiety to get ahead … the Commissioners failed to spot two procedures which could not go into operation until the Standing orders are approved by the general meeting of the Commissioners. They are in a hole because they have not got any absolutely correct way of signing cheques for sums exceeding £10,000, and for sealing documents.' Would the archbishop, the new secretary of the Church Commissioners, Ronald Harris asked, be very upset about this? Ramsey must now sign a document to confirm what they were now doing. Ramsey was not at all upset. Beloe told Harris that the archbishop was delighted that 'these great administrators' had slipped up, and even more delighted to be their source of rescue.[71]

Parenthesis: comings and goings at 1 Millbank

A new era in the history of the Church Commissioners was beginning. Warren had formally retired from the secretary's position at the general meeting of 31 May 1963. His successor, Ronald Harris, then fifty years old, had a background in the India Office and the Cabinet Office. Since 1960 he had worked as third secretary in the Treasury. Here he had been particularly concerned with overseas development, defence, science and the arts. He had also been a churchwarden. In the government, Sir Laurence Helsby thought the position of secretary to the Church Commissioners a little beneath a man of Harris's abilities. But Helsby also had his eye on the more substantial vacancy which

[69] Silsoe to Ramsey, 8 June 1964, ibid. fos 313–16.
[70] Ramsey to Dean, 13 Aug. 1964, ibid. fo. 343.
[71] Beloe to Harris, 21 Aug. 1964, ibid. fo. 348.

would occur before too long – for the First Church Estates Commissioner. He had remarked on this to Ramsey at least a year before and when, in January 1964, Harris had accepted the secretary's post, Helsby pressed again. Harris, he wrote, was 'outstanding' and he might not rest content with the position of secretary for the rest of his career. Beloe replied that as the appointment of the First Commissioner lay with the crown, Helsby would have the initiative when the time came. Even so, responded Helsby nicely, it was usual for the prime minister to consult with the archbishop of Canterbury. He hoped that what he said now would be remembered when that time came.[72]

On 19 March 1964 Harris's appointment was confirmed at a special meeting of the Church Commissioners. Kenneth Ryle, the financial and administrative secretary, became his deputy, a new post recommended by the Monckton Report. Patrick Locke became Harris's private secretary.

In the early 1960s there was only one woman within the ranks of the Church Commissioners. This was Betty Ridley, daughter of a bishop of Southwell and the widow of a clergyman; she was set to do great things. But Harris and, on the state side, Hewitt decided that it was time that one of the new Commissioners appointed by the crown be a woman. Beloe remarked that 'I thought that the kind of person we ought to have was an intelligent, sensible wife of a clergyman with plenty of experience of parsonage houses who could sit on the Houses Committee.' He looked through a list of Church Assembly members for candidates and found one or two clergy wives on diocesan dilapidations committees. Justice to women was not a cause uppermost in Beloe's mind. He remarked to John Guillam Scott, 'It does seem to me that this is really an opportunity for an imaginative appointment which would help the attitude of the clergy towards the Church Commissioners.'[73]

They aired one or two names, but came up with nothing decisive: one said too little for herself, another too much. It was decided that a confidential circular should be sent out to five diocesan bishops to invite suggestions. Beloe wrote it and asked for 'a lady who has real knowledge of the problems of parsonage houses'; an incumbent's wife, able to travel to London once a month for meetings of the Houses Committee. The bishops' replies may have carried episcopal authority and sought to be helpful, but were neither eager nor well-informed. This was not a familiar language and they were not quite sure how to speak it. The bishop of Salisbury proposed 'a Mrs Eddlestone', the wife of the vicar of Shillingstone. He added that his own wife had

[72] Beloe memorandum, 23 Jan. 1964, ibid. fos 247–8.
[73] Beloe to Scott, 19 Apr. 1965, ibid. vol. 74, fo. 18.

done 'a marvellous job' on the see house at Salisbury and was very practical. But then she had 'no knowledge of £.s.d.': 'Still, she might conceivably be useful and would certainly be willing to learn.' Then, Honor Williams, daughter of Sir Philip and sister of Sir David, was on the diocesan dilapidations board, sat in the Church Assembly and had 'status, standing and leisure'. The bishop of Chester proposed Mrs Wilfred Garlick, 'a gay person and competent', the chairwoman of the committee which ran Girls Friendly Society hostels, and wife of a vicar in Stockport. The bishop of Leicester nominated Constance Cray, a former president of the Mother's Union, whose husband was frail and about to retire through ill-health. Recently he had appointed her a lay canon of the cathedral ('This was much welcomed'). The bishop of London proposed Sheila Gee of Towcester, a widow who ran her own farm and buildings and had considerable architectural experience. She was a churchwarden to boot, 'added to which she is a very sensible woman'. But, repeated Beloe, they wanted the wife of a clergyman.[74] Harris took the list to 10 Downing Street. There he heard the name of Rachel Moss, wife of a canon of Bristol, almost certainly from Hewitt.[75] Her name and that of Mrs Garlick went to the prime minister with Ramsey's blessing. Mrs Garlick it was to be.

In December 1972 the presence of women in the life of the Church Commissioners was more powerfully affirmed when Ramsey appointed Betty Ridley to succeed Hubert Ashton as Third Church Estates Commissioner.

---

[74] Replies from the bishops of Salisbury, Leicester, Norwich and Chester, ibid. vol. 74, fos 24–7; from bishop of London, fo. 32.
[75] Harris to Ramsey, 1 June 1965, ibid. fo. 35.

7

The Politics of Maintenance

Bishops and cathedrals

Ramsey was sharp on the privations of bishops. Since 1956 the Commissioners had abandoned an earlier commitment, expressed in the 1943 Episcopal Endowments and Stipends Measure, to pay a new bishop from the time when the see itself fell vacant. To Ramsey this seemed 'very hard indeed'. An incumbent could expect sequestration money to accumulate for him during a vacancy: 'Are you', he asked, 'expecting a new Bishop of Winchester to move into Wolverey without some accumulated income?'[1] Eve replied that the change had been made in 1956 to avoid hardship to bishops, for sequestration money had always been liable to tax and in that year they began to pay the removal expenses of new bishops. 'At the time, Bishops were very pleased with the change.' But he said he would look into it if the archbishop wished.[2] Ramsey, unusually, persisted:

> When I became Bishop of Durham I had to buy, besides all necessary robes etc., a motor car and a considerable quantity of furniture. I could not have done it without having about four months income of the See with, of course, tax deducted therefrom. I think the moving in process is a Bishop's biggest difficulty ... £200 removal expenses scarcely touches the problem at all.

He was 'really concerned' that in some cases he might have to advise the prime minister that a certain bishopric could only be held by a man with private means.[3] Eve would not be rushed. He promised, again, to look into it in the early autumn, after his holidays.

Almost a year later Ramsey was particularly anxious that a prospective bishop might struggle to find money to buy his robes of

[1] Ramsey to Eve, 12 July 1961, Ramsey papers, vol. 6, fo. 71.
[2] Eve to Ramsey, 18 July 1961, ibid. fo. 72.
[3] Ramsey to Eve, 20 July 1961, ibid. fo. 73.

investiture. Until now, new bishops had managed, but through the goodwill of friends. This was not adequate. He turned again to the Commissioners for the answer. In a new allocation agreed at the annual general meeting of May 1962 Ramsey got it. New bishops would receive grants towards 'episcopal clothing', support for furnishing, the full cost of removal expenses, money, if appropriate, to pay for the episcopal seal which would become the property of the see, cope, mitre, cutlery and crockery too, and also the legal costs of election and confirmation. 'I hope', wrote Eve, 'your grace will feel that these new arrangements are realistic and that there need be in future no fear that a suitable man would be unable, through lack of private resources, to accept a bishopric.'[4] Ramsey thought it would all be 'a big relief to the Bishops'.[5]

The diocesan bishop was doing more and more. Towards the end of 1964 the two archbishops sat down together to consider how they might best be supported 'on the basis of their present boundaries'. Now there were three kinds of bishops: diocesan, suffragan and assistant. Into the last category came retired bishops, or bishops newly returned from overseas, who were helping out in various ways, doing virtually the work of an 'episcopal assistant'. There was only one assistant bishop in the Church of England who had an income from the Church Commissioners. The others were paid for tasks as incumbents of smaller parishes or as members of a cathedral chapter. This vagueness could not go on. Ramsey believed that it was time for the bishops to decide what they needed. There were now forty-three suffragan bishops in twenty-eight dioceses (Ramsey thought they had been there for centuries). Nine were in London and the south-east. There were twenty-seven assistant bishops, 'active, or fairly active', in twenty-one dioceses. Ramsey and Coggan believed that the whole organisation needed to be formalised, and to be better financed. The Church Commissioners would provide the money.

In 1964 three dioceses needed new suffragan bishops 'now', three more wanted one in due course. As for assistant bishops, Ramsey proposed that a rate of grant should be set down. It appeared that nine more were needed. In four cases a grant would enable them to give up their incumbencies and become more useful. Ramsey wrote to Silsoe to this effect in January 1965. The contents of this letter were transferred by Silsoe into a General Purposes Committee paper for the attention of the Board. He observed that the situation had been 'rather haphazard' for, he thought, constitutional reasons. To create a new diocese required a measure in the Church Assembly. A new suffragan bishop did not even need the approval of an archbishop, and an

[4] Eve to Ramsey, 21 May 1962, ibid. vol. 17, fos 234–5.
[5] Ramsey to Eve, 24 May 1962, ibid. fo. 236.

assertive bishop in a state of less need might secure a suffragan where a more diffident one whose need was greater might not. Silsoe, too, saw a need for 'some more effective machinery' to encourage broader consultation – not least with the Commissioners themselves who would, he observed, foot the bill for the new episcopal creations.[6]

Ramsey himself had staked a claim and the General Purposes Committee wanted to be co-operative and constructive. It might also be that a more rigorous system might help them to restrict costs, or at least to measure them more successfully. Silsoe totted up some figures, and made up a bill:

Six suffragan bishops at £3,000 p.a. each	£18,000
Ten assistant bishops at £1,500	£15,000
	£33,000

They would have to watch pensions: 'it would hardly be equitable for a suffragan bishop to retire and then be re-employed as a paid assistant whilst in receipt of his full pension as a suffragan'. The dioceses themselves would deal with the houses.[7] The Board agreed upon a new plan to ensure full-time episcopal assistance for every diocesan bishop, and, in some dioceses, assistance from more than one full-time bishop. Where it was not felt that suffragan assistance was necessary a full-time assistant bishop could act in the capacity of suffragan.

In time, the Commissioners' financial contribution increased from one half to three-quarters of the amount paid towards a suffragan bishop's stipend and expenses. Assistant bishops, in turn, cost the Commissioners three-quarters as much as suffragans. The trouble with the assistant bishops was that, unlike the suffragans, they were a dying breed. It was also the case that the new suffragan bishoprics were being created in urban centres, and these required something more than the energies of septuagenarian colonial bishops. In fact, they might well require more than the energies of an existing diocesan bishop.

If the bishops were still easily embarrassed by material questions, this new decade was not likely to spare them. The progressive Christian journal *Prism* contained a letter critical of the bishops and their expenses by a well-known academic and Church Assembly member, Valerie Pitts, and another from an ally, David Webb, who suggested that the bishops were using what were apparently over-

---

[6] Ramsey to Silsoe, 'Episcopal help for diocesan bishops', CC (65) 1, Board papers, 28 Jan. 1965, ser. 95083/27.
[7] Ibid.

ample expenses allowances to improve their own living standards. This was a form of prelacy 'far removed from New Testament doctrine and quite out of keeping with the twentieth century. I doubt if the Methodists will accept it!' This incendiary missive stung the Commissioners, who moved promptly to defend their own systems and the bishops. Were the sums on which these accusations rested really correct? It was found that they were, but in offering averages the critics gave a distorted impression because they included a good deal of expenditure which lay over and above the bishops' stipends. This now created a difficulty: to reply in kind must give away material considered domestic and private – and might raise more questions than were answered. It was better to let the matter pass. At the same time, it had been agreed that bishops' expenses should be presented differently in future. There should be a column for stipends, and a new one for 'episcopal administration', detailing staff, salaries, travel, fees and other official expenditure specifically. This would be both more accurate and make the bishops themselves less vulnerable to criticism.

The suffragan bishops

In recent decades the policies and structures which accompanied the increase in the number of suffragan bishops were often makeshift and inconsistent. The Church Commissioners felt this keenly, not least because they were largely paying for them. In the Ramsey era they struggled to meld a variety of schemes and allocations into a more credible, coherent form. For their part, the Commissioners were increasingly querulous that they were, in effect, called upon to adjudicate applications which clearly begged important ecclesial questions involving the very nature of the Church of England. While these principles were being debated across the Church, should the Commissioners obstruct applications for new suffragan bishoprics which seemed reasonable in the pragmatic world which was acknowledged to be their own? Papers and memoranda mounted. In 1968 the Archbishops' Commission on the Organization of the Church by Dioceses in London and the South-East was set up.

The principle of episcopacy, like every other principle by which the Church of England was organised, immediately dissolved into details. Assistant bishops could not be 'created' in an institutional sense. There must first be bishops available who could serve as such. A suffragan see must, on the other hand, be formally constituted. The conversion of assistant bishops into suffragan bishops was accelerated by the fact that more and more of the former were retiring. In 1972 the bishop of Winchester revived an earlier application for a second suffragan see in his diocese. If approved, the new suffragan would also be a residentiary canon of Winchester Cathedral and would replace the full-time assistant bishop who worked with him at present and now wished to retire. Initially, in December 1971, the Board did not jump at this. The whole matter of episcopal jurisdiction was being discussed by the Church. They did not yet know what other requests might arrive. They hoped that he would seek another assistant bishop. They also saw that there were ten dioceses without a suffragan bishop (though of them seven had an assistant bishop). Including Winchester, there were sixteen dioceses with 'only' one suffragan bishop, and eight of those had larger populations than Winchester. Furthermore, Winchester had a smaller population than many dioceses which had one or two suffragan bishops, though it could be said that it was growing, and was spread out rather thinly. It included the Channel Islands.

The bishop of Winchester wrote to Harris for support 'from the financial angle'. That was clearly, to his mind, the Commissioners' role in the equation. The new see had been recommended by the Archbishop's Commission. He said simply that he already had the approval of the archbishop of Canterbury. A new bishop would have a house provided by the cathedral 'in return for fulfilling the minimal duties of a Residentiary Canon'.[8] The Board simply accepted the proposal.

By June 1972 there were forty-six suffragan bishops in forty-two dioceses. Nine were in posts created since 1965. There were also nine assistant bishops. Aware that questions about this issue rumbled away, rather ineffectually, in the General Synod, the Commissioners preferred to wait to see what it would decide before allowing more applications. But two cases, they found, would not wait. In July 1973 Ronald Harris forwarded to the General Purposes Committee a proposal for episcopal assistance in the dioceses of Salisbury and Worcester.

In Salisbury a campaign for a second suffragan had been going on since 1966. The diocesan synod was unanimous about the application. The whole diocese was being examined for needs and resources and this had turned up some unsettling realities. The average age of diocesan staff was over fifty-four. The present suffragan bishop of Sherborne was sixty-six, the assistant bishop was seventy-two and now wanted to retire, the archdeacons were seventy-one and sixty-nine respectively. The Vacancy in See Committee of the diocese also wanted a second suffragan, as did the diocesan secretary and the chairman of the diocesan board of finance. By the end of 1973 the bishop judged that the need was acute.

[8] GPC report, 'Episcopal assistance in the diocese of Winchester', GP (72) 36, Board papers, 20 July 1972, ibid. pt 36.

As matters stood, the see of Sherborne merged with the archdeaconry of Dorset. The proposal now was to add to this a suffragan bishopric of Ramsbury, merged with the archdeaconry of Wiltshire. It was not as though there would be too little for him to do. He would have the oversight of 110 parishes, 66 incumbents or priests-in-charge, nine curates, 100 church schools, five independent schools, fifteen hospitals (with one religious community), two women workers, fourteen retired clergy who had permission to officiate, five public preachers and ten 'others' and 207 Readers. He would have all archdiaconal responsibilities in Wiltshire at a time of change under the new Pastoral Measure. He would chair the Ministry Commission, the diocesan council of mission and unity, his own archdiaconal pastoral committee and parsonages board, the diocesan council of women's work. He would ordain, confirm and institute: 'It will be seen that there is a real full-time essentially episcopal job for a man to undertake.' They should not be asking an elderly assistant bishop to make long winter journeys around the diocese. The bishop attached a letter of support from the chairman of the diocesan board of finance, addressed to the episcopal secretary at Downing Street, which said that there was a need for leadership which, as the chairman of Wiltshire County Council he could well understand – and which he expected a government committed to the planning of health and social facilities to appreciate.[9]

As for Worcester, the bishop wanted a suffragan bishop to replace an assistant bishop. The northern part of the diocese included an expanding, urban Dudley, with a population of 250,000 people. Watching, still, the deliberations of Synod, the Board still deferred its decision. They realised that boundary changes in the dioceses of Worcester, Hereford and Lichfield, too, might alter the question. But by July the situation in Worcester had changed in a way they had not expected. The full-time assistant bishop, David Allenby, had accepted another post. In six months he would be gone.[10]

Because in Salisbury the suffragan bishopric would be combined with an archdeaconry, the Commissioners stood, in fact, to save money. Tired of waiting for the corporate mind of the Church to declare itself while they were doing their best to fend off applications, the Board gave up on Synod and decided that the General Purposes Committee should prepare a new paper on the issue. They also abandoned their resistance to the applications from Salisbury and Worcester.

[9] Harris paper, 'Episcopal assistance: dioceses of Salisbury and Worcester', CC (73) 52, Board papers, 19 July 1973, ibid. pt 37.
[10] Harris paper, 'Diocese of Worcester's proposed new suffragan see', CC (73) 28, Board papers, 15 Mar. 1973, ibid. See also Board minutes, 15 Mar. 1973, pp. 3–4.

Between 1965 and the end of 1973 the number of suffragan bishops rose by thirteen and the number of assistant bishops declined from ten to six. Beside this, three dioceses – Bradford, Leicester and Newcastle – still had no episcopal assistance paid for by the Commissioners. All were poor, industrial dioceses, two of them northern.

The see houses: suitable or unsuitable?

When the See Houses Committee was abolished by the Monckton Report the new Houses Committee took over responsibility for bishops' houses. They also supervised a mass of other duties: questions of acquisition or disposal, decoration, repair and maintenance, the furnishings and heirlooms, the grounds of see houses as well as of cathedral houses (these were new tasks) and also benefice property – parsonages and glebe (tasks bequeathed by the Administrative Committee). The Houses Committee reported to the Board when new legislation or general policy was involved or when a see house was to be acquired or disposed of, but in all other cases it possessed powers 'to do and complete'. In its first year it met eleven times and completed no less than 4,600 detailed matters, reporting to the board on five of them.[11]

By 1964 all but nine see houses had been classified as either 'suitable' or 'unsuitable', and for the remainder the new committee inherited opinions if not verdicts. It began life eager to improve matters but soon found difficulties. New building sites were 'virtually unobtainable'. Alternative houses 'scarcely any easier to find'. Building costs were high and rising.[12] By 1966/7, the committee was being forced to reconsider its early condemnations and to settle for improvements. The bishops and their dioceses seemed happy about this. Then there were the gardens. Gardens mattered to bishops. They were necessary for entertaining; they served a pastoral purpose. Full-time gardeners were felt to be essential. An age of austerity frowned at greenhouses, kitchen gardens, excessive manpower and large gardens altogether. By the end of 1967/8 it was biting deeper. At Chichester the bishop agreed to 'relinquish' his garden entirely: in future it would be managed by one gardener and additional help would be enlisted from contractors. Fulham had lost two of its three gardeners, and contractors were helping the head gardener until a second arrived (there would not be a third). Elsewhere contractors marched in, all of

---

[11] HC annual report to 31 Mar. 1965, CC (65) 19, Board papers, 3 June 1965, ser. 95083/28.
[12] HC annual report to 31 March 1967, Board papers, 20 Apr. 1967, ibid. pt 30.

them employed by the same firm. The garden at Southwark was now felt to be too small to justify even one full-time gardener.[13]

Silsoe was not a man to relish questions like these. In October 1968 his patience ran out. The Church must do something 'to reduce ostentation and expensive maintenance in clergy houses and, in particular, See houses'. In the course of the current century thirteen 'palaces' or 'castles' had been abandoned and replaced by houses, but twelve remained, or at least buildings which looked to him very much like palaces or castles. The Board, he complained, had been indecisive. The capitular houses of the ancient cathedrals were still mountainously expensive.[14] The General Purposes Committee flustered that there must be no further delay. The Board agreed that there must be a change.[15] The bishop of Manchester asked that the matter first be discussed by the diocesan bishops. Ramsey told the Board that they had already decided to do so at an early date.

The bishops were not intimidated; they stood their ground. Silsoe's campaign was soon entangled in discussion on one of the largest, one of the most historic, one of the most improbable of all the see houses, Auckland Castle. The residence of the bishops of Durham, Auckland, was a kingdom in itself, of 35,000 square feet (30,000 of them inhabited by the bishop), a large chapel, five state rooms, five further reception rooms and thirteen bedrooms. It had a wing called, ominously, Scotland. There were two flats rented out and four cottages for the chauffeur, the under-gardener and a retired butler. The fourth was let. The Commissioners had spent thousands of pounds on maintaining it, and expected to pay still more. No twentieth-century bishop could claim Auckland as a model for convenient and efficient episcopal living. But the current bishop, Ian Ramsey, proved strangely accepting of his lot. More to the point, he was sure that however costly and expensive it might be, to leave Auckland Castle would 'create dismay, and be a very severe shock to the whole diocese'. Undeniably, there was a great distance between the kitchen and rooms used for dining ('there is a great deal of unnecessary walking'), but that had become less of a nuisance, and an intercom-telephone helped. There was no diocesan house in Durham itself and Bishop's Auckland granted space for meetings, conferences, consultations, committees. The state rooms were in constant use, for fund-raising occasions, visits by parish parties and tenants' dinners. More: 'With respect, I can say that only those who have lived in Auckland Castle can know just how

[13] HC annual report to 31 March 1968, CC (68) 25, Board papers, 9 May 1968, ibid. pt 31.
[14] Silsoe memoranda, CC (68) 35, 36, Board papers, 17 Oct. 1968, ibid.
[15] Board minutes, 17 Oct. 1968.

convenient it is and how well suited to a Bishop's ministry.' He concluded:

> This building is a symbol of tradition which has been constantly worked out against contemporary needs. The rooms did more than provide a meeting place for Barrington's discussions on education or co-operative trading, or Westcott's industrial negotiations. It may be difficult in credit terms to evaluate an influence of this kind, and even easy to ignore it, but I hope that no-one who has a concern for the spirit of man will deny its existence.

True, it was costly. But they should have ideas. Ramsey himself proposed three.[16]

For all this, the See Houses Committee was evidently in no mood to indulge Auckland Castle, its poetry, its history or the local loyalties which it inspired. It agreed that it was unsuitable and should not be occupied by the next bishop of Durham. Its size made it inconvenient and costly. The committee made eyes instead at a space in a neighbouring park, presently leased to the local authority, but only until 1972.[17]

Meanwhile, the bishop of Peterborough had put up another resilient defence of the *status quo*. A move away from the cathedral would be 'greatly resented' in the city itself, for it was the bishop's ancient home and the significance of the cathedral as the mother church of the diocese would itself be undermined. It meant a great deal to be able to offer hospitality to meetings of clergy, industrialists, ordinands, fraternal and ecumenical gatherings, rather than lodging them in some hotel or hostel. The garden was constantly in use; it was 'the only open space in the middle of the City'. Its historical character was an 'added pleasure'. The real trouble with Peterborough, he maintained, was that the city itself was at the northernmost tip of the diocese. It would be easier to move the boundaries of the diocese itself than the bishop's house. He added, for good measure:

> I hope it will not be taken amiss if I offer some general observations on what a See House ought to be. It is to be seen in the context of the relationship of the Bishop to his clergy and people. He is not the General Manager of a large business concern, but he is the father of a large family, and meant to be recognised as such.[18]

---

[16] Letter from the bishop of Durham in 'Episcopal, capitular and incumbents' houses', CC (68) 52, Board papers, 21 Nov. 1968, ser. 95083/32.

[17] Board minutes, 22 July 1971, ibid. pt 34.

[18] Letter from the bishop of Peterborough, CC (68) 52, Board papers, 21 Nov.

By April 1969 the bishops had met together and held what Ramsey described as 'a considerable discussion'. They wanted more time to ponder upon the proper size and purposes of their houses. In the meantime they wished for no ruling against 'palaces'.[19]

Michael Ramsey himself was susceptible to the poetry of buildings. He viewed Lambeth Palace without affection ('a most inconvenient building'). Much of it was now given over to staff offices. But he would not change the Old Palace at Canterbury. He could not see that it presented a bad image: 'It interests people to know that what looks from the front like a modern house is in fact the house from which Thomas Becket walked to his martyrdom and contains features belonging to his time.'

Few things matter more to institutions and their inhabitants than the politics of space. Moreover, Ramsey may well have had his own reasons for viewing Silsoe's ambitions with a wary eye. Only four years previously Silsoe had pointed out to Ramsey that central London was changing around them. Sir Leslie Martin's plan for a national and government centre in Whitehall had only recently been published by the government. If adopted, it would see the demolition of Millbank and a new block of residential accommodation erected in its place. This being in prospect, volunteered Silsoe, it was better not to wait passively upon events but to take the initiative. The government might view with sympathy a proposal to move the inhabitants of 1 Millbank across the Thames to the land which lay between Lambeth Palace and the adjoining Archbishop's Park. It was only an idea, suggested Eve amiably, but might he look a little further into it? Ramsey replied that 'It would be entirely congenial to me and, I am sure, to my successors to have the Church Commissioners housed in proximity to the Palace.' But the Colonial Office would be vacating a considerable portion of Church House by the end of 1966. That might be a more natural relationship, for the Commissioners and Church House had grown so conspicuously and happily closer in recent years. Perhaps the land beside the palace would be more suited for the purposes of St Thomas's Hospital, to accommodate nurses? Silsoe could match this. The Colonial Office had too few square feet to meet their needs.[20] While Ramsey and Silsoe exchanged cunning missives across the Thames Beloe dashed off a discreet note to Guillam Scott at the Church Assembly, asking for pertinent information. Was there any other space for the Commissioners on that side of the river? Scott told

1968, ibid. pt 32.
[19] Ramsey to the Board of Governors, CC (69) 13, Board papers, 24 Apr. 1969, ibid.
[20] Silsoe to Ramsey, 28 July 1965; Ramsey to Silsoe 30 July 1965; Silsoe to Ramsey, 10 Aug. 1965, Ramsey papers, vol. 74, fos 45–63.

him that at present the Cowley Fathers, who were the Commissioners' tenants, were 'overhoused'. This the spiritual Ramsey could not believe.[21] In the event it all came to nothing because the Martin Plan, for all its bold grandeur, was simply put aside. None the less a succession of plans to alter both the house and the grounds at Lambeth followed.

In October 1969 a subcommittee of the Houses Committee visited Rose Castle, home of the bishop of Carlisle, to meet the bishop and sundry diocesan figures. The bishop reiterated that he wanted the castle to continue as the home of future bishops of Carlisle. He was asked, rather pointedly, what younger people thought? He replied that they did not seem to object to it, and the dean and the bishop of Penrith rejoined amiably that in the north they were not so worried about these things as people evidently were in the south. The committee could only accept this, and left with a parting warning about the condition of the tower of the building.[22]

Everywhere, it seemed, Silsoe's incendiaries were being politely but firmly extinguished. And this before any mention was made of Fulham Palace. In 1962 it had been deemed unsuitable, but ten years later the Commissioners found that they still owned it. It now housed a cluster of church organisations, while the bishop was ensconced in a flat in Westminster. This could not continue, and in October 1968 judgement seemed finally to fall on Fulham. Quite apart from its architectural liabilities it was badly located if the diocese were to remain within its present borders, and if they were changed, it would probably fall outside them. Fulham was once again classed as unsuitable and the bishop, the diocese and the Commissioners were united in the hope that a suitable replacement could be found.

The London question now took another turn. By December 1971 the Commissioners' Estates Department had its eye on 19 Cowley Street, Westminster, an elegant, five-storey Georgian house backing onto Great Peter Street. It could become a see house, but it was not big enough to contain the diocesan offices too. But then, after all, the Commissioners were not responsible for diocesan offices, simply for the bishop. The bishop and Mrs Stopford had a look around but were disappointed. It would be 'sub-standard as See houses go'. It was smaller than the old rectory which the bishop of Willesden was going to have (this was wrong).[23] The bishop looked at the plans and wondered whether he would be able to entertain 'in the manner the diocese expects'? But these were quibbles. In the end Bishop Stopford

---

[21] Beloe to Scott, 8 Sept. 1965, ibid. fo. 60.
[22] HC report, 'Rose Castle', CC (70) 6, Board papers, 15 Jan. 1970, ser. 95083/34.
[23] Mentioned later in HC report, 'London see house', CC (74) 15, Board papers, 25 Apr. 1974, ibid. pt 38.

approved 19 Cowley Street and the Houses Committee recommended to the Board that it be acquired.[24] The Board agreed.

Bishop Stopford thought that the future of Fulham Palace should be left to the Church Commissioners themselves to deal with. He himself should proceed to Cowley Street without further delay. At Millbank the General Purposes Committee agreed. But this was not the end. Indeed, it was about to get far worse.

The bishop of Chester, Gerald Ellison, who had been a member of the General Purposes Committee when 19 Cowley Street was approved, succeeded Stopford as bishop of London on 16 July 1973. Now that he had to live in the house himself, he completely changed his mind about it. He wrote to the Commissioners that it simply did not work; that it was unsuitable and another should be found. It was too small for entertaining, too small for meetings and conferences. The bedrooms were too few. The chapel was too small. It was their statutory duty, he warned, to provide a diocesan bishop with a suitable house and they were not complying with this responsibility. 'Eventually', he wrote, with more than a glimmer of menace, 'I shall be required to agree that the statutory obligations have been fulfilled.'

This was news to the Commissioners who knew of no such statutory obligation, 'technically'. They rifled through their papers and saw that the 1943 measure made no actual mention at all of suitability, though, naturally, they always hoped to provide such a thing. Suitability, muttered the Houses Committee, tartly, did not mean 'ideal', or 'suited to the ideas of any particular occupant of the See'. (Come to that, the measure pronounced that the Commissioners 'may' provide a house, but not 'must'.) To be sure, there was a licence which a bishop should sign, and in which the bishop accepted that his house was suitable, but this was custom. The only legal necessity was that if the Church Commissioners did provide a house they should 'let' it to the bishop.[25] In February the Houses Committee trooped around the corner to Cowley Street again. They wondered if 19 was simply so convenient that more people dropped in to be entertained than would otherwise be the case. Ellison stiffened. He wanted Cowley Street to be classified as 'unsuitable'; another house must be bought, at once. Even a return to Fulham Palace should not be ruled out. There was more muttering from the Houses Committee. Stubbornly it maintained that 19 Cowley Street was the best compromise in an imperfect world.

This soon developed into a dogged tussle between the bishop and the Houses Committee. Ellison was adamant that he was effectively prevented from carrying out his duties by his own house. But the

[24] HC report, 'London see house', CC (72) 4, Board papers, 21 Jan. 1972, ibid. pt 35.
[25] Ibid. pp. 5–6.

advocates of Cowley Street held firm. They would be held up to criticism if they spent a new and large sum on a new house. Perhaps the bishop's administrative staff could be lodged at the diocesan office?[26] It was agreed that the diocese of London itself should now be brought formally into the debate. A joint advisory subcommittee representing both the Commissioners and the diocese of London was convened, chaired by Betty Ridley. But then something unexpected happened. The Commissioners learned that they could buy in the lease of the adjourning house, 8 Barton Street, presently inhabited by a firm of solicitors. The two houses might be linked by new doorways and any surplus space re-let for offices. The bishop looked in at 8 Barton Street and was much taken with it. But when a vote was taken it was now found that five of the six members of the advisory subcommittee thought that it would not make a suitable see house. It was frankly depressing. There was no garden and no garage. If this bishop of London wanted it, another might well not.

Ellison disagreed with these objections. In almost no time, it seemed, there were four possible plans and they were all dispatched to the Board. It was not desirable to live and work in one and a quarter houses, which would spoil two perfectly good ones. Number 8 Barton Street should become the bishop's house and 19 Cowley Street a valuable asset.[27] Now there was real dissatisfaction on the Board. The cost of the works at Barton Street would be considerable and the bishop stood to gain only 1,000 square feet as a result. The Church was being criticised for the lifestyle of its bishops, and here would be grist to the mill. A great deal had already been spent on the conversion of Cowley Street, and in an unfavourable financial climate. It would be wasted. But others again expressed 'strong support' for the bishop. The bishop and his staff, it was said, were under strain. It was said that it was time for the House of Bishops to discuss the lifestyles of bishops in general, and as a matter of urgency. There was a vote. The Board was divided, eleven members supported the bishop of London, eight did not.[28] The battle of Cowley Street was over, but not the war over the London see house.

The simple truth was that in complicated battles like this Silsoe's grand strategy was ground into dust. However impatient he might be, and however the Houses Committee of the Church Commissioners might bristle and fulminate, this was a dimension of church life that could never achieve a definite resolution.

[26] Board minutes, 25 Apr. 1974, pp. 3–5.
[27] See Houses Committee report, 'London see house', CC (74) 73 and appendices, Board papers, 21 Nov. 1974, ser. 95083/39.
[28] Board minutes, 12 Nov. 1974.

The Cathedrals

In the age of archbishop Ramsey the relationship of the cathedrals with the Commissioners was a curious one, and still one that did not rest on solid foundations. Apart from Southwell Minster, for which the Commissioners had a statutory maintenance liability, responsibility for the upkeep of the fabric of the cathedrals was not explicitly expressed in the Commissioners' founding statutes. Section 53 of the Ecclesiastical Commissioners Act, 1840, allowed them to contribute to the fabric funds of the old foundations whose lands, rents or profits had passed to the Commissioners themselves. But this must be calculated in proportion to the rents. Section 20 of the 1931 Cathedrals Measure allowed for payments out of the General Fund, but only in conjunction with a resolution passed by the Church Assembly. Only in 1950 did a report uncover Section 6 of the New Parishes Act of 1843, under which they could give money to local appeals named in that section. But this was still difficult, even shaky, ground, and it had little to do with cathedrals themselves. In the same way donations had been made to agricultural shows and societies, schools repairs, a war memorial, concrete bollards on a village green, a fence on Burnhope Moor, a bus shelter at Stoke Canon in Devon, cleaning out a pond in Portsmouth and in 1953 coronation commemoration grants.[29]

It was time for a lengthy reconsideration. The eventual report of a new Cathedrals Commission, *The cathedrals in modern life*, in the preparation of which the Commissioners had been actively involved, was submitted to the Church Assembly in February 1961. Under its terms the Church Commissioners would now undertake to pay the full stipends of a dean and also of two canons at each cathedral, their being wholly committed to the work of the cathedral itself. Now the stipends of deans and canons were seen to be a matter of 'urgent' concern. By May 1962 the Commissioners were ready to undertake to pay the stipends of deans and two canons, and would have the power to fix the level of them. A number of deans had petitioned that they could not attract the best candidates because a canon was paid less than an incumbent. This would not do, the Board agreed. A canon should be paid as much as a better-paid incumbent. An interim scheme would augment their stipends until the new measure was passed.[30]

By the summer of 1962 the recommendations of the Cathedrals Commission had been condensed into a draft measure and on 3 July Bishop Williams of Leicester moved general approval in the Church

[29] EFC report, 'Voluntary donations by the Church Commissioners as landowners', Board papers, 19 Dec. 1961, ser. 95083/24.
[30] EFC report, 'Financial assistance for cathedrals', 17 Apr. 1962, Board papers, 24 May 1962, ibid.

Assembly. The debate exposed the new thinking to some sharp questions. Williams himself acknowledged the generosity of the Church Commissioners, observing that from them the cathedrals would also receive capital grants for the provision and improvement of houses, but then a rear-admiral from Durham alleged that the Commissioners themselves held 'large sums' which were not theirs, but belonged to the cathedral chapters themselves. The provost of St Edmundsbury, John Waddington, complained that the new system would not be equitable. They should look again at each cathedral on its own terms. At his own cathedral they fared worst of all, and the income from their benefice amounted to only £400 a year. As for the two minor canons there, they lived in 'rather poor villas' in the back streets of the town. Archdeacon Forder of York thought that the report might have gone further in encouraging the participation of the laity in the life of the cathedrals: 'he would hate to think that cathedrals should be the last ditch of clericalism'.[31] When the Assembly next gathered, in November, Williams observed that the new measure was inspiring few attacks or criticisms. But they stuck at one clause. Clause 20 required a cathedral to apply to the Commissioners before acquiring or disposing of property. The Commissioners withstood pressure to make loans from the cathedral capital which they held, determined instead to conserve it. For this, said the bishop, they could hardly be blamed, particularly since they had been criticised for their own treatment of cathedral capital over the past hundred years. But the dean of York, Alan Richardson, pronounced that when the cathedrals investments had been managed by accountants and stockbrokers known to them they had done well; when they had turned to the Commissioners they had lost heavily. The dean of Worcester, Robert Milburn, was fearful that in the block grants given annually by the Commissioners for living agents the Commissioners should not take from the living agents with one hand while giving to the deans and canons with the other. He wanted a guarantee. Bishop Williams reassured him that in areas of debate the Commissioners were always most mindful of the will of the Assembly.[32] As for Clause 20, this campaign of criticism duly secured from the Commissioners a quiet concession.

The decision to finance deans and two canons was a decisive one in the history of the cathedrals. It brought uniformity; it also secured a new stability in their affairs. Nor was it merely a question of finance. Largely because of the intricacies of the measure itself, the Commissioners had now ended up with a share of the responsibility for defining the pastoral duties of the residentiary canon whose

[31] *Proceedings of the Church Assembly*, xlii/2, London 1962, 296–309 (3 July 1962).
[32] Ibid. xlii/3, 606–33.

stipend they paid. To Bishop Bloomer of Carlisle this smacked of
'centralisation', and, in fact, nobody appeared to like it much. But the
bishop of Leicester observed that, as the Commissioners were laying
out at least £200,000 a year, it was appropriate that, in marginal cases,
they should be permitted to say whether or not the conditions of the
measure were being met. He did not see why the cathedrals should be
any different from the rest of the Church of England, whose work was
similarly supported by the Commissioners.[33]

The property pool

Meanwhile, as the Commissioners continued to make their modest
annual grants as landowners, the costs of appeals were rising
exponentially. In 1967 Hereford launched an appeal for £188,000 for
fabric repairs. In an undertaking on this scale, a grant of £2,000 did
not look quite heroic and was unlikely to raise many cheers or earn
much gratitude. By now, however, the cathedrals were proving
themselves to be increasingly inventive in raising their own funds. In
1965 the chapters agitated to increase their income by using the capital
held for them by the Church Commissioners to buy real property. The
Assets Committee advanced the idea that some of the chapters had
too little to buy anything worth having. But they improved the idea by
advancing that of a general property pool in which a number could
participate. By September 1965 these plans had grown impressively. By
November they had gone back to the deans' conference, which
responded with general approval.

A bold, broad plan was framed. The pool would be run by the
Assets Committee. A cathedral could invest in the pool by buying
shares in it, and the Commissioners would do the same, but not
beyond 50 per cent. The portfolio would comprise offices (50 per
cent), shops (25 per cent) and factories (25 per cent), all expected to
make an average yield of 7.1 per cent. The income would come from
rents and would be distributed quarterly.

At 1 Millbank a problem was detected. If the Commissioners were
to buy property for this project, existing assets held by them would
have to be released. That must affect adversely the General Fund
income and so, in turn, undermine their power to make grants to
cathedrals from it. (By now, grants to cathedrals were at a level of
about £175,000 a year.) Still further, a cathedral which had a finger in
the property pool pie would appear less eligible for grants.[34] Even so,
by October 1973 twenty-nine chapters had joined the pool. The effects

[33] Ibid. lxiii/1, London 1963, 71–9. The whole debate is at pp. 71–89.
[34] Board minutes, 18 Nov. 1965. See also Silsoe paper 'Creation of a property
pool', CC (65) 42, Board papers, 12 Nov. 1965, ser. 95083/28.

of the scheme proved increasingly beneficial. At the same time, it was seen that Canterbury and Manchester had substantial investments in property outside the pool and that York was prospering on the Stock Exchange. From now on, therefore, they would receive only minimum grants.[35]

Cathedral houses

Because the Church Commissioners now paid out money for buildings, an elementary sense of financial responsibility dictated that they should at least approve what was being purchased and maintained. This power to approve had seldom made them popular in the homes of the bishops. Now the Commissioners risked further unpopularity in the cathedrals.

In the life of the English cathedrals, the Ramsey era was one of steady development. Many deans and chapters were busy improving their closes – if they had them – and their buildings and facilities. There were plans to build completely new closes at Chelmsford and Southwark, though they looked, for now, only 'long-term ideals'.[36] Under the terms of the 1963 Cathedrals Measure, the Commissioners undertook to make grants to provide suitable houses for cathedral clergy, and to help with repairs. Now, ordinary building projects received from the Commissioners grants to the level of two-thirds of their net costs. In the year 1964/5, as much as £3,567 was spent helping twenty new deans, provosts and canons to move house. Between 1964 and 1972 £850,000 was allocated for cathedral houses, and 147 cathedral clergy were 'suitably' housed in consequence. If the financial aspects of this were met readily enough, these new burdens of approval were not welcomed by the architects' department of the Commissioners, which already felt over-taxed.

Deans and chapters were responsible for the upkeep of deaneries, but the 1963 measure had given to the Commissioners a number of responsibilities in this sphere too. Their consent was required if a deanery were to be sold or leased, or a new one acquired. Likewise the expenditure of chapter capital on a deanery. But propping up difficult deaneries and canons' houses could seem like a very poor investment. In 1969 it was decided that grants should be withheld until the Houses Committee had declared what was suitable and what was not. Current deliberations on particular properties were stopped in their tracks. A

[35] GPC report, 'Cathedrals Measure 1963: grants under Section 31', 9 Oct. 1973, CC (73) 80, Board papers, 18 Oct. 1973, ibid. pt 38. See also Board minutes, 18 Oct. 1973.
[36] HC report, 'Unsuitable deaneries', CC (69) 12, Board papers, 26 June 1969, ser. 95083/32.

discussion on the state of the deanery at Chichester, where Walter Hussey wished to knock down a Victorian wing and put in its place something very like a garage, but one to be inhabited, was deferred.[37]

A rational method of classification might look very well on paper. The trouble, at least in part, was that deans could not easily be moved. They lived close to their cathedrals, usually only a stone's throw away, so it was hard to find a new house and virtually impossible to find a site for one. Either the deanery must be made suitable or else another house, already owned by the chapter, should be adopted as a new deanery. But this depended upon suitability and availability, for if a canon were ensconced in a house which had excited the interest of a dean it seemed brusque to uproot him. At the same time, lay tenants would be protected by the terms of their leases. Furthermore, moving deans around like this might leave an assortment of vacated deaneries, which would probably be huge, costly to heat and in a poor state. New tenants, if they could be found, must be chosen carefully because they would be, after all, so close to the cathedral. They could only really be sold to a church organisation. Solutions, when they did arise, were sure to be costly. In 1966 the dean of Wells moved into one of the canon's houses and a small 'close' of new houses for canons was built. The old deanery was sold and the old canons' houses were leased to the cathedral school. Towards this the Commissioners put £40,000 and undertook to provide a number of loans to allow the dean and chapter to meet whatever balance was left over from the whole scheme at the end. The overall estimate was £90,000. By August 1968 the costs had risen to £99,006. By February 1970 they stood, finally, at £116,034. The Board muttered uneasily at these costs, but approved.[38]

By now there had been some notable ventures in deaneries almost everywhere. At Wells, again, the old deanery now housed the diocesan offices; at Ely the bishop had moved in; at Bristol the cathedral school. Offices were envisaged at Peterborough. At Ripon, property might be sold for development. Meanwhile, if rambling deaneries were increasingly expensive to maintain, then new, convenient deaneries were increasingly expensive to build. Since 1945 three new deaneries had appeared, at Rochester (1960), Guildford (1960) and Leicester (1968). Here emerged, rather quietly, new evidence of differentials. All had been built, broadly, to the same size (between 2,869 and 3,112 square feet), about half the size of a new bishop's house. Seven houses for residentiary canons, built since 1964, had, meanwhile, been an average of 2,293 square feet. The average house for an incumbent was 1,937 square feet. However fortifying such examples might be, there

[37] Board minutes 26 June 1969, p. 1.
[38] HC report, 'Wells Cathedral', CC (70) 9, Board papers, 19 Feb. 1970, ser. 95083/33.

was known to be a core of unrepentant hard cases, persistent offenders; deaneries which stood stoutly in the way of the modern age of convenience.

The conditions of the clergy

The economic conditions of the clergy remained a complicated tapestry of stipends, grants, loans and exemptions. During the Ramsey era the state of the stipend remained a point of some pressure in the Commissioners' calculations. But there was reason to be satisfied that the campaigns of the 1950s had borne valuable fruit. In June 1961 the Board saw that the cost of living between March 1955 and March 1961 had risen by 18.25 per cent, and that average benefice income had risen by 21.75 per cent. The material conditions of the clergy owed much to their liberation from various kinds of taxation. This, too, had improved of late. After the 1961 Finance Act the value of the parsonage house was untaxed (whereas before it had been taxable, minus the maintenance claim). Then, contributions towards dilapidations, mortgages, rates, heating, lighting and cleaning, furniture and garden maintenance remained beyond the reach of taxation. There were also tax allowances if other costs were borne by the incumbent: for dilapidations and repairs (a quarter allowance), for rates (ditto), for heating, lighting and cleaning, for study allowance. It was the Commissioners who held the line with the Inland Revenue, and who later in 1969 would secure tax-free reimbursements on a clergyman's expenditure on heating, lighting and cleaning.

The Paul Report

On 14 July 1960 Lt-Colonel H. E. Madge had proposed in the Church Assembly that the Central Advisory Council on Training for the Ministry (CACTM) be invited to review the deployment and pay of the clergy. The council, in its turn, decided to ask an individual authority, suitably furnished with relevant expertise, to write something substantial, with an eye to the appointment of a new commission once it was done. They chose a sociologist, Leslie Paul. He set to work at once, conjuring with sociological material, employment statistics, figures about population, housing, the community, the family, the village and transport. This was gathered together under the umbrella of 'fact-finding', but there was argument here, too. Paul wrote of 'the impersonal society' and when he turned to the clergy he depicted their 'isolation' in the midst of it. He then outlined the structure of the ordained ministry in detail, and how the clergy were paid. He balanced the arguments for and against a redeployment, and then proceeded to unfold a 'blueprint' for a reconstructed ministry, to which was attached a sprinkling of other proposals about the laity, the church overseas, houses and freehold. Paul concluded with no less than sixty-two principal recommendations.[39]

The report appeared in January 1964 and within a fortnight 11,000 copies had been sold. It became, almost at once, the spark which ignited a new campaign. Not least did students in the theological colleges take it to heart. The students of Westcott House, Cambridge, declared roundly that it should not be rejected; if it were they would regard their own future in the Church 'with considerable foreboding'. At Wells the students lobbied for something to be done at once. A debate was launched at the Assembly itself, and the chairman found no fewer than forty members pressing to speak.[40]

At least the storm did not break directly over the heads of the Church Commissioners themselves, though they were soon enmeshed in its consequences. Within six months work had begun on a new Pastoral Measure, drafts of which could from 1964 be heard rumbling like convoys of heavy lorries through the Assembly. The measure received general approval in the spring of 1965 and entered then a long, if not exhaustingly intricate, process of revision. This legislative leviathan was driven through the Assembly with remarkable resolution by Bishop Brown of Warrington.

In the background there was a good deal of murmuring. In September 1965 Bishop Allen of Derby wrote to Ramsey that the Pastoral Reorganisation Measure was causing 'a good deal of unrest' in the dioceses, which feared centralisation around the Church Commissioners. The dioceses wanted more power for themselves. With these fears the bishop himself had some sympathy. He asked whether the bishops as a body should discuss this?[41] At the same time another commission was meeting under the chairman of the Pensions Board, Canon W. Fenton Morley, to work out a response to the Paul Report. Silsoe had been a member of it (though he insisted that the recommendations of the report in no way committed the Commissioners as a body). The upshot was *Partners in ministry*, which came before the Church Assembly on 6 July 1967. The appeal to partnership looked amiable enough, though Madge was brutally candid in response, observing that if they were keen to vaunt the idea of partnership in ministry, they might observe that the clergy seemed to him none too able to work well with each other in teams – or with the laity, for that matter. He suspected that their training placed too great an emphasis on individuality. This aside, the debate showed some

[39] Leslie Paul, *The deployment and payment of the clergy*, London 1964, 210–14.
[40] *Proceedings of the Church Assembly*, xliv/1, London 1964, 2–45.
[41] Allen to Ramsey, 20 Sept. 1965, Ramsey papers, vol. 74, fo. 64.

impatience to get on with the business of root and branch change. It also showed how firmly old positions were still held.[42] There would be no great alteration.

When it was complete it could be seen that the Pastoral Measure of 1968 effectively ended, or altered, no less than twenty-nine acts or measures passed between 1838 and 1953. This was a consolidating measure on a vast scale. The Commissioners stood back to view the whole colossus. In general the measure largely confirmed their place in the scheme of things. In the area of redundant churches there was a significant move towards the dioceses, which could now set up their own church uses committees. Then, in the new arrangements for the formation of new parishes and the alteration of boundaries – substituting one parish church for another, changing parish names – there lay, as Ashton observed in the Assembly, a weakening of the Commissioners' role. It is unlikely, however, that the earlier advocates of the Paul Report now found many barricades to climb. As one of its critics, Canon Eric James, observed, most were defeated by the sheer complexity of the measure. He found it all '"obscurantically" Anglican, unnecessarily and wrongfully so'. The place of the Commissioners he found one of the 'added' complexities. Another speaker was delighted to see thirty-nine acts condensed into one, but confessed that he found it a 'nightmare' to administer. It was asked, and not for the first time, what the Methodists would make of it?[43]

The politics of inflation and the creation of the Central Stipends Authority

The upshot of *Partners in ministry* impinged directly and profoundly on the work of the Commissioners. To begin with, in practical matters the difficulty which these emerging proposals exposed was not a new one in the world of the Commissioners. It was, simply, very hard to attach the new debates to ongoing business and to established patterns of daily work. They could be shut out deliberately until they were actually introduced. But more often they tended to hang over what was happening, introducing an aspect of qualification.

The payment of the clergy had become increasingly not just a calculation of assets and methods of supply: it was more and more the subject of political debate across society itself. From this the Church of England could not pretend to be immune. By 1967 the British government was struggling to maintain a freeze on incomes as part of its campaign against inflation. The Church of England behaved well.

---

[42] *Proceedings of the Church Assembly*, xlvii/3, London 1967, 460–519 (Madge, pp. 479–80) (6 July 1967).
[43] Ibid. xlvi/1, London 1966, 58–90 (15 Dec. 1966). The speakers cited here were Canon Eric James (pp. 69–71) and A. G. K. Esdaile (pp. 71–2).

The clergy stipends were duly raised, after consultation with the Department of Economic Affairs, on 1 July 1967. In 1968 the government had adopted an incomes policy. How would it view a rise in clergy stipends to the tune of 3 per cent? Informal soundings were again taken at the Department of Economic Affairs. The department was reassuring, but made a condition that future increases should not occur at less than twelve-monthly intervals, except in exceptional individual cases. The Board accepted this, though the dean of Gloucester, Seriol Evans, was more concerned at the prospect of the parochial clergy outstripping the residentiary canons than the school teachers or civil servants of Britain. Silsoe agreed. The dignitaries, he said, should be looked at next.[44]

Arguably the most significant aspect of *Partners in ministry* lay in the proposal that there should be a central payment authority to fix stipends, to consult the dioceses and submit schemes to the General Synod. This authority should, in effect, be the Church Commissioners. Silsoe was rather coy about it. After a period of careful watching, in April 1972 the Board agreed to bring the new body to life. To be sure, many of the powers of such an authority were already in the possession of the Commissioners, but the new body demanded a new bureaucratic strength. Now the Commissioners must have all the information that they required from the dioceses; they must be able to direct the dioceses in accordance with the decisions of the General Synod; they must determine distribution of available funds and frame conditions as they saw fit; they must set down standard terms and common methods of computing income for augmentation purposes. The new authority would not determine deployment, but must have close relations with whatever authority decided these matters.

The proposal for a new central stipends authority was brought to the summer session of the General Synod and combined there with a response to the Commission's proposal about glebe: the Commissioners now proposed a new measure to pool benefice endowment income including glebe income, and to transfer to the dioceses the ownership of glebe. It all went down well and proved a quiet resolution to an age-worn debate. By December 1972 Harris reported to the Board that a new stipends department would begin life at Millbank on 1 January 1973. It would answer to the General Purposes Committee. Its first secretary was Patrick Locke. Policy, the Commissioners insisted, would evolve through collaboration with diocesan representatives at regular conferences. Even so, it could not be denied that a great deal of power did lie explicitly within their hands. Now that the Commissioners had become the Central Stipends Authority, it fell to them to judge the 'target ranges' for stipends. The

---

[44] Board minutes, 28 Mar. 1968, pp. 2–3.

GPC clearly saw in the new authority a vehicle for improvement and at once ventured an increase in incumbents' stipends, also proposing national pay scales for assistant curates, deaconesses and licensed lay workers.

Pensions: the revolt of the widows

Under the terms of the 1961 Pensions Measure, the Commissioners had five seats on the Church of England Pensions Board. This did something to bring the pensions interest more firmly into the ambit of the Commissioners' life and work; perhaps to expose the Commissioners more fully to the pressure of its perspectives and priorities. Time would tell. But the Church Assembly retained a powerful interest and in that forum the question of the clergy pension appeared often enough, not least because the members of the Pensions Board were adept at promoting it there.

In 1961 the first aim had been to improve the position of clergy widows. This was no simple matter. The situation now rested upon the 1948 Pensions Measure, which had marked the first attempt to provide a pension for widows. Every clergyman ordained after 1947 – married or not – had to pay an increased contribution for both his pension and one of £50 a year for his widow and fatherless children up to the age of eighteen. This did not appear to cause resentment among those who were not married. The new, general 1954 scheme had made the 1948 system non-contributory, but there were qualifications within in. Now the Clergy Pensions Measure of 1961 maintained this provision and provided a survivorship pension for the first time. The combination of this non-contributory scheme with what had become, by 1961, a required annual contribution of £50 was obviously anomalous. Now, furthermore, the unmarried clergy could see no reason why they should pay for the widows of married clergy. In actual fact, only about 50 per cent of the contributors left widows, for another 20 per cent were unmarried and the wives of the other 30 per cent, predeceased them.[45] The logic of these arrangements still left gaps, to be filled with grants which the Pensions Board made available, with the permission of the Commissioners and at their expense. By 1961 the Pensions Board was committing £89,000 a year.

When stipends were raised, with some jubilation, at the annual general meeting of 1961 archbishop Ramsey received a letter from Bessie Harding of Shenfield, Essex, whose husband had served as a parish priest for fifty years and lived only twenty months after his retirement, still taking services and dying while leading evening prayers:

[45] See L. J. Sillito to Kenneth Ryle, 22 Jan. 1965, Board papers, 11 Mar. 1965, ser. 95083/27.

'As I listened to our Rector in Church yesterday speaking of the generosity of the Church Commissioners in granting still greater increased stipends, I thought with pity of the disappointed pre-1960 widows of clergy, who are not even allowed the crumbs from the rich man's table.' Many of them, she continued, were not eligible for state pensions. They were referred instead to diocesan charities, 'and there is no sympathy for the indignity of this position'.[46] Ramsey wrote simply and kindly that it was not a matter of asking for charity: 'I do assure you of this with all sincerity'.[47] Bessie Harding was not alone in pleading the cause of the widows. Regularly, after publication of the Church Commissioners' annual report, letters arrived at Lambeth. Ramsey asked Warren whether something could not be done. It was not so easy, cautioned Warren:

> I am sure you will understand … that in terms of arithmetic the matter is not as cogent as it may be politically. Giving them a small pension as of right would not necessarily make them any better off than they presently were … In some cases, the giving of a pension as of right merely has the effect of adding to those who have sufficient private means already.[48]

Warren and Eve promised to bear the matter in mind. Robert Beloe remarked: 'I think what upsets widows and indeed the clergy is the indignity of a woman who had perhaps been an unpaid curate and every other kind of assistant in parishes for 30 or 40 years.'[49]

To this wave of protest there was a response. At the annual general meeting of September 1962 further assistance for clergy widows was announced. In January 1964 the Board received a proposal from the EFC that the fresh commitments in perpetuity should make a priority of the pensions of the parochial clergy and their widows. By now they stood at £400 a year for a seventy-year-old man who had done forty years' service, and half of that for his widow. If the clergyman retired before the age of seventy, or with less than forty years under his belt, both he and his widow received less. If he died while still in office, his widow would also, generally, receive less.

The art of the pension was still a new one, and hard to measure. By the beginning of 1964 the cost of the pensions commitment was composed partly of actual disbursements and partly of annual transfers of funds to the reserve, to meet the rising costs of future pensions. The Board of the Commissioners saw that if the present scales of

---

[46] Mrs Bessy Harding to Ramsey, 22 Oct. 1961, Ramsey papers, vol. 6, fo. 203r–v.
[47] Ramsey to Harding, 8 Nov. 1961, ibid. fo. 205.
[48] Warren to Ramsey, 14 Nov. 1961, ibid. fo. 206.
[49] Beloe to Warren, 22 Nov. 1961, ibid. fo. 207.

pensions and transfers to the reserve remained constant, the total charge to the income and expenditure account until 1973 would rise; in that same period the amount transferred to the reserve would decrease markedly. In the preceding year the costs of widows' pensions had risen sharply because their proportion had risen from a third to a half, from 1 April 1963. But then the number of widows to be covered by these arrangements would increase, too. More:

> It has been calculated by the Actuary to the Pensions Board that the number of clergy retiring on pension will show a sharp increase over the period 1980 to 1985 and this actuarial assumption was behind the original setting up of a Reserve so as to equalise the charge for the remainder of the century. The amount in the Reserve for this possible future liability will be £2.6m. at the 31st March, 1964. Experience has shown, however, that the actual cost of pensions is likely to be less than the cautious actuarial assumption, and it may well be that it is not necessary to set anything further aside to the Reserve after the current year.

If there were new increases to the pensions – from £400 to £500 and from £200 to £250 – 'The expense is considerable and the question is how it can be financed'. After 1966/7 an average of an extra £60,000 each year must be provided as perpetuity provision until stability occurred in 1972/3. Then, if the actuary was right about the 'hump' of 1980–5, the extra cost of that might be taken from the Reserve of £2.6 million. The Board approved all this and it was subsequently adopted by the general meeting.[50]

When to retire?

After the campaign for clergy widows, the issue of pensions settled down for the next four years. When it resurfaced it was in a new and more dangerous form. How much pension should be paid to a clergyman who had retired before the age of seventy? A retirement age of seventy had been set down in January 1927. Since 1948 clergy who chose to retire between the ages of sixty-five and seventy received a carefully calculated fraction of the full pension for forty years' service. This was amended and reduced in the measure of 1961. But it was this measure, too, which gave to the Assembly the power to resolve that the age of retirement be lowered. This was a crucial shift of power, though it was hardly noted as such at the time.

---

[50] Board minutes, 30 Jan. 1964; EFC report 'Finance and distribution policy', 21 Jan. 1964, pp. 2–6, Board papers, 30 Jan. 1964, ser. 95083/26.

Much of the working population was now retiring at sixty-five (and women at sixty). When the Church Assembly sat in the summer of 1966 Canon Barfett asked if it would be practical for the clergy to follow this pattern. The reply was noncommittal: it was for the House of Clergy to declare its own view. In November 1967 Barfett was back, and this time on behalf of the House of Clergy, arguing that the age of retirement after forty years' service be reduced to sixty-five. He asked now that the Pensions Board and the Church Commissioners accept the principle and make it a priority. The Commissioners replied cautiously. In the Assembly there was an amendment, supported by the Commissioners, that the age be sixty-eight, with a view to sixty-five when it was considered possible. This was accepted.[51]

By now the legislative history of pensions was so substantial that it was felt necessary to publish a handbook to set out what had been done. By February 1969 the Pensions Board was putting together a new working party to judge how well the present arrangements worked. The sheer complexity of pensions reform intensified. An improvement in one area simply produced new anomalies in another. A striking example occurred in January 1971, when the Pensions Board proposed a new manoeuvre to the General Purposes Committee. If the new General Synod voted to reduce the normal age of retirement to sixty-five, should those clergy who had retired voluntarily, on a reduced pension, between the ages of sixty-five and seventy have their pensions increased by recalculating them as if the normal retiring age had been sixty-five when they had retired? The Commissioners were not eager. The Pensions Board persisted: 'these older clergy should be assisted in this way, particularly as they had not received the advantages of present-day conditions of employment'. Often hardship was involved. If they feared the expenditure, surely early retirement must mean a net reduction in the number of clergy requiring augmentation through the diocesan stipends funds?

This did not work. It was realised increasingly that the campaign to raise pensions must compete with that to improve stipends. The first responsibility of the Commissioners was to the serving clergy. The Board of the Church Commissioners began to watch Synod rather closely. Eventually it agreed that retroactive payments to those who had retired early would be 'a dangerous precedent', particularly in a context in which both the Commissioners and the Pensions Board were being lobbied by an informal alliance of those who had retired before March 1967, led by a clergyman, Cyril Brundritt, to back-date lump-sum payments as well.[52] This time, the Pensions Board

[51] *Proceedings of the Church Assembly*, xlvii/3 (House of Clergy), 820–30 (6 Nov. 1967).
[52] GPC paper, 'Clergy Pensions Measure 1961': pt III, CC (72) 24, Board papers, 16

acquiesced in the Commissioners' judgement, but promised to raise the matter again.

A proposal to lower the age of clergy retirement to sixty-five appeared again in a new and thorough report on pensions which was submitted to Synod in February 1971. Sir Austin Strutt, the voice of the Pensions Board and the Church Commissioners on these matters, told his audience there that they could not know exactly what this must cost because they did not know how many clergy would choose then to retire. They did know that when the age was seventy fewer than half of those entitled to retire then did so. The option of retirement at sixty-eight had not been in place long enough to suggest any lessons, but not much had apparently changed. The Board thought an annual cost of £150,000 a likely estimate. The Commissioners had now agreed to set this much aside, but would give it instead to stipends from April 1972 if Synod turned the proposal down. The choice appeared again: pensions or stipends?

It would not be compulsory to retire at sixty-five, as it had not been compulsory to retire at sixty-eight or seventy. Dr H. M. Williams thought the cost of this reform a small one and observed that it would bring them into line with 'other employers of labour'. The chairman of the Pensions Board, Canon Fenton Morley, represented the temper of the Board itself in arguing that the measure was required by 'compassion, justice and realism'. They must consider both the clergy and their wives. Ronald Harris observed that if the Commissioners sometimes appeared to resist improvements on pensions it was because they had other commitments to balance. They did, he insisted, work closely with the Pensions Board. The Commissioners, for their part, had favoured a longer period of 'gestation'. If they now chose pensions over stipends, Harris added:

> I ought to warn the Synod – they will not be surprised to hear it – that the financial prospects for that date as far as we can see are not very encouraging. Inevitably the Commissioners are faced by rising costs, less buoyant income and wage inflation for beyond what the Church seems likely to be able to match for its clergy, even if present Government policies succeed in achieving their object.

£150,000 was not a negligible sum. It was important not to be 'blinded' by the figures of millions in income accruing to the Commissioners. If Synod were to take this step it must take fully into account the fact that for every £1 the Commissioners' had to spend,

Mar. 1972, ser. 95083/35.

16*s*. 9*d*. was used for stipends, pensions and parsonage houses, leaving only 3*s*. 3*d*. While the Commissioners would not wish to 'influence unduly' a decision by Synod on the age of retirement, he could not pretend that even a gradual approach would ease the effect on their funds. This Strutt swept aside as exaggerated fear. The motion was put and carried. A further amendment from none other than Robert Beloe, that the alteration be expanded to accommodate those who had retired since 1961, was voted down.[53]

There was more. On 18 October 1973 the Board agreed to propose to the annual meeting of the Commissioners that they accept responsibility for the provision of pension contributions due to the Church Workers Pension Fund for deaconesses and licensed lay readers from 1 January 1975. If they acknowledged that they had no specific powers to do so they discerned another way: with the help of diocesan bishops, payments could be made direct to the Pensions Board through the diocesan stipends funds if they could be directed accordingly from there. The hope was also aired that the dioceses should think of raising their own share of the 1974 contributions to assist the Pensions Board with the provision of retirement accommodation, primarily for retired deaconesses and licensed lay workers.[54]

Thus, as the Ramsey period ended, the priorities of the Church Commissioners were beginning to alter, and to alter in favour of a cause which was complicated, expensive and immensely difficult to judge. It was a decisive move away from the possibility of innovation and towards a new conservatism.

[53] Report of the Proceedings of the Church Assembly, ii/1, London 1971, 33–49 (16 Feb. 1971).
[54] Board minutes, 18 Oct. 1973.

8

Reforming the Parish

Pluralities, of one kind or another

The life of the English parish across the Ramsey era showed a busy and intricate history of sifting, amending and reforming. Little of this was exciting; much was intricate and even tedious. Yet it was no less significant. The trouble with these complex and dull matters is that few took pains to understand them. It mattered, for a heavy price could be paid for misunderstandings in the lives of parishes across the country. Where rights and responsibilities were murky, contention could spring up. Relationships could come to grief, between clergy and clergy, between clergy and laity, between one denomination and another.

Over the reorganisation of parishes there always hung the threat of confrontation and controversy. Diverting incomes had always been provocative. On 1 February 1962 the Board of the Church Commissioners resolved that only in exceptional cases should the diversion of benefice income to diocesan stipends funds be attempted. The dioceses themselves should be discouraged. But pastoral reorganisation was, in general, a smooth business, prompting objections in only one in ten cases and most objections were overruled. When necessary, members of the Pastoral Committee went on visits to see for themselves how matters really were. Quite often this worked very well for objections were subsequently withdrawn.

The restructuring of parish boundaries could still bring controversy. In March 1968 the Board received papers about the name of a new rural deanery in the Wakefield diocese. The rural deanery of Huddersfield, which embraced fifty parishes, was to be reconstituted, fairly evenly, into four new rural deaneries: Huddersfield, Almondbury, Blackmoorfoot and Kirkburton. But one of the parish church councils did not wish to be in a new rural deanery called Blackmoorfoot. They did not like the name, which was only the name of a reservoir. What point could there be in naming a rural deanery of twelve parishes and 56,636 people after a large stretch of uninhabited water? They wanted to be called West Agbrigg instead, after the ancient wapentake of

Agbrigg in the west of the new deanery. Back this went to the bishop and his pastoral committee. They remonstrated that Agbrigg was hardly known at all, even as a mere name, and Blackmoorfoot was already a necessary compromise accepted by every other parish concerned. The parochial church council was duly overruled.[1]

New thinking on the overall development of the parish required orchestration. The Commissioners again used their position to foster debate, and in that debate they proved careful partners. If the balance of power swung again towards the dioceses it could often be seen that the Commissioners themselves were giving it a gentle push. There were conferences every year at which diocesan representatives raised all kinds of questions for the officers of the Commissioners. How large should a new parish be? How much should a new incumbent be paid? The costs of new church buildings were daunting to most dioceses: could the Commissioners give more, and be more flexible? A movement across the Church of England to create groups of parishes had not always proved successful. Some dioceses were wary of it altogether. For their part the Commissioners also viewed the idea cautiously. Few could deny that there were benefits to be had in the rural areas where local identity appeared important, and the church buildings themselves were beautiful, or in towns and cities where people appeared to set store by their independence. There were worries about the numbers of clergy, and fears that curacies were sometimes too short or too weak in building experience. Could the Commissioners provide new funds for curates? Might the parochial clergy receive grants with which to buy motor cars?[2]

During the Ramsey era the Church Commissioners were becoming steadily sharper in their scrutiny of what was going on in the dioceses. If the dioceses were indeed shouldering a greater share of responsibility they must show clearly how they used the money that they received. If they did not present some kind of balance sheet how could a central body measure the needs of the local Church and work out their own budgets and policies? A rather venerable article of legislative furniture, the New Parishes Measure of 1943, still served adequately in these new days. Under this the Church Commissioners had to adjudicate on proposals for the legal establishment of a new parish, to ensure that such a parish had a suitable church in which to worship and to see that it was satisfactorily endowed. They then considered a permanent grant of one half of the initial net stipend

[1] PC report, 'Rural deaneries (diocese of Wakefield)', CC (68) 17, Board papers, 28 Mar. 1968, ser. 95083/31.
[2] These questions arose at the three regional conferences that took place in 1961: AC report, 'Conferences on the work of the parochial reorganization, July 1961', Board papers, 20 July 1961, ibid. pt 23.

decided upon by the diocese, up to the level of £800 *per annum*. In addition, the architectural designs of new churches had been approved – some traditional, some more 'contemporary'. Since 1958 the Church Assembly had asked the Commissioners to keep a record of all new church buildings for inspiration and inspection by those considering building projects. By 1962 this archive held the details of 300 buildings – 100 parish churches, 140 dual purpose buildings, twenty mission churches and forty church halls. Incomplete details existed for 250 more and work continued. This archive was rather seldom visited. Meanwhile, the momentum of the Commissioners' commitment to the new housing estates carried on steadily, though with less dramatic zeal. There were occasional glimpses of idealistic generosity on the new sites. One firm of contractors, busily developing a new estate at Mickleover on the fringe of Derby, provided the site for a new parsonage house and built it for less than £6,000. No professional fees were charged.

Between the passing of the New Housing Areas (Church Buildings) Measure of 1954 and March 1967 time and effort had brought the purchase of 159 sites, the building of 373 churches, 433 church halls or dual-purpose buildings and 239 clergy houses. Gone, now, was the requirement that the Commissioners approve the formation of new parishes and the availability of a suitable endowment. It would now be for the bishop simply to submit a proposal, accept, if he chose, amendments suggested by the Commissioners and prepare and issue the scheme. Henceforth, they were to be mechanics but not judges. No longer must a new parish, or an existing one, have a parish church or any place of worship that required the Commissioners' approval. Gone, too, was their power to decide upon the alteration of diocesan boundaries. But the new authority which they now shouldered in the creation of team and group ministries grew onerous. Meanwhile, the wheels of the Pastoral Committee were clogged with objections to, and representations about, schemes. In 1971–2 the staff of that department was increased. Dioceses were asked to send less information in support of their proposals. Still a wide gap remained between the arrival and completion of proposals. Already in 1973 there were rumbles in the General Synod that the Pastoral Measure needed to be amended.

The commitment to the new estates had by now become more than a matter of bricks and mortar, and more than a question for the Church of England alone. In 1965 Convocation suggested that the archbishops appoint a new commission to look into the matter of sharing churches with other denominations. The Leicester Commission (for it was chaired by Bishop R. R. Williams) duly submitted a report in January 1967 favouring this course. Convocation ruminated on it, the archbishops appointed an assortment of lawyers to consider legislation. Until now, the 1954 Measure had embraced buildings that were used 'wholly or mainly for purposes connected with the Church of England'. Did this allow the Church Commissioners enough latitude to embrace sharing with other denominations? The Commissioners themselves were doubtful. They had not really had this kind of thing in mind before, and felt that the word 'mainly' could allow the use of church halls for games or recreation, but not by Methodists and Congregationalists. Yet the simple truth was that by 1967 church buildings were already being shared between denominations. A number of dioceses were asking that their allocations from the Commissioners should allow for shared projects and they had been turned down because the Commissioners could not think that they had the power to allow it. In this state of uncertainty, faces were turned again towards the Church Assembly. The talk of the lawyers grew louder in the background. If the powers of the 1954 Measure were to be extended, should that be by parliamentary bill or a Church Assembly measure?

In terms of money, at least, the GPC did not think that executing such broad powers need necessarily cost more – in fact, it might well save money by sharing the burden – but they must mark a distinction between shared use and shared ownership. The Archbishops' Commission had clearly meant the sharing of buildings owned by the Church of England. It had proposed that an incumbent, a bishop and a parochial church council could make an agreement to share with a 'non-Anglican community' for a fixed term of years, and to bind their successors to that agreement. Joint ownership was something which they did not encourage. It might simply 'provide the country with yet one more denomination'. The members of the GPC foresaw a period of experimentation. A likely pattern seemed to be that the church building itself might be provided by the Church of England and the other 'church authority' might provide the hall and other ancillary buildings, 'or vice-versa'. If this happened, how should the Commissioners make grants? Should they be conditional upon a commitment made by the other church authority? This was something that other Churches must consider from their own side, too. Sharing would necessarily involve amending the marriage laws in parliament, and, that being so, it might be sensible simply to attach the practical matters which were the concern of the Commissioners to that bill.[3] All this was kept under wraps until the Church Assembly had spoken.

In October 1967 the archbishops sent a memorandum and a copy of a draft bill to Convocation. This went beyond the recommendations

---

[3] Silsoe report, 'New Housing Areas (Church Buildings) Measure, 1954', 14 Apr. 1967, CC (67) 15, Board papers, 20 Apr. 1967, ibid. pt 30.

of the commission, for it proposed the authorisation of joint ownership. These documents duly went forward to the Church Assembly which, in its turn, voted to set up a committee to work on new legislation with the Commissioners and representatives of other Churches. The contours of a new policy emerged. Shared buildings should be vested in bodies of trustees representing the Church involved. In the case of existing church buildings, this could be done by a scheme under the terms of the new Pastoral Measure, if its requirements for the better provision of the cure of souls in a diocese as a whole was better served by it, if the work of those engaged in the cure of souls was properly provided for and if the 'traditions, needs and characteristics' of the parish itself were provided for.[4] Eventually, by April 1968, the policy was before them.[5] Within the new framework the Board agreed that a further sum of £1 million should be allocated for church buildings in new housing areas in July 1969. Thereafter, the need, and the definition, of the new housing areas was regularly scrutinised. The relationship between the Commissioners and the dioceses was again tightened, and it was agreed now that future allocations should bear in mind their past records and progress with old grants.[6]

Team and group ministries

The great 1968 Pastoral Measure set down that teams and groups of clergy in large or demanding parishes be constituted by schemes prepared by the Commissioners in accordance with the proposals of a bishop and his pastoral committee. This was then submitted to the necessary procedure of consultation with incumbents, patrons, parochial church councils, archdeacons, rural deans and local planning authorities, all finally to be confirmed by Order in Council. Teams and groups could be altered by a pastoral order, which would also be the work of the Commissioners, in which case objections could not in this case be made to the Queen-in-Council.

The movement to create team and group ministries was gathering momentum. If the new Pastoral Measure had relieved the Church Commissioners of particular powers of approval, in this sphere the need for their advice was seen to have grown. Sometimes a team was created for an existing benefice, sometimes for a new benefice made up of perhaps seven or eight old ones. Team rectors were generally to be appointed by a patronage board, constituted to maintain existing

[4] Silsoe report, 'Sharing of churches legislation', 21 Feb. 1968, CC (68) 10, Board papers, 29 Feb. 1968, ibid. pt 31.
[5] Board minutes 14 Apr. 1968.
[6] Ibid. 26 June 1969.

interests, and most had fixed terms, usually between five and ten years. The same went for team vicars. At first about half the team rectors enjoyed freehold. The level of a team rector's stipend was also open to question. Patronage could prove a problem, especially where the crown was involved, for how could the queen reasonably be expected to sit and vote on a patronage board, or succumb to the approval of the diocesan bishop before exercising a right of presentation to a benefice now included in a group? All this brought a new assortment of complications. A group ministry did not much affect the question of houses. A team ministry did. There would be only one incumbent and one parsonage house. The vicars had status 'equal to that of an incumbent' but were not 'corporate sole' with their own official residences. Some team vicars' houses were owned by the diocese, the parish, the benefice or were in private hands. They were not subject to the Ecclesiastical Dilapidations Measures. The Commissioners had no say as to their acquisition, alteration or disposal.[7]

The dioceses themselves were feeling their way in this new territory. In 1970 no new scheme along these lines was completed. By the end of the following year, however, proposals had been made for the creation of twenty-eight team ministries and seven group ministries. In 1970–1 three team ministries were actually brought to life; in the following year twenty-three; in the year after thirty. By 1973 there were 125 priests employed in teams. In 1973–4 there were forty more, making a total of ninety-six in thirty-five dioceses employing 206 priests. The growth of group ministries, meanwhile, was more modest: three in 1970–1, none the following year, seven the year after, ten in 1973–4. These twenty included seventy-two benefices in seventeen dioceses.[8]

The parsonage house

In the administration of pastoral matters the Church Commissioners prided themselves on viewing the local affairs of the Church with a detached, rational mind. Yet the daily routines of the Church Commissioners were immersed in details. In this lay the possibility that the clear perspective, and the effective solution, might become as difficult for them to discern as it was for everybody else. At times they, too, must accept that they were an interest like any other and must submit to the adjudication of new authorities.

[7] PC annual report to 31 Mar. 1970, CC (70) 34, Board papers, 28 May 1970, ser. 95083/33, pp. 3–4.
[8] PC annual report to 31 Mar. 1973, CC (73) 46, Board papers, 21 June 1973, ibid. pt 37.

Despite the reforms of the Fisher era, the maintenance of the parsonage house was still a problem; one to which the Church Assembly returned time and again, and on each occasion with less success than the last. In 1956 the Commissioners had drawn a line between grants for capital purposes and those for maintenance purposes. But it all looked untidy, and part of the untidiness lay in the fact that dioceses were not always co-operative. They sent to London dilapidations assessments which could be, frankly, unrealistic about how much money they needed for improvements and how much they could realise on the sales of properties. Soon the officers of 1 Millbank were scheming to reduce their allocations unless they got more reasonable proposals, but this came to nothing. It was the question of dilapidations which proved the thorniest; the unlikely scene for a conflict of interests which threw up virtual barricades and clouds of vituperation.

The dilapidations regulations under which the dioceses laboured had been framed in 1923, and by the later 1950s they had become a source of generalised disquiet. A Church Assembly commission set to work in 1958 and took four years to conclude that the maintenance of parsonages lay more properly on the shoulders of the dioceses than on those of the incumbents. It proposed the creation of a parsonages fund in every diocese, into which the Commissioners would pay substantial grants, as they already did, while the laity was asked to find the balance in each particular situation. This automatically created a difficulty because the proposal might produce new ways of spending the Commissioners' money which were not entirely under their control. Furthermore, if the incumbent were no longer responsible, where did the legal security for the scheme lie? And how would the laity feel about the consequent increase in the diocesan quotas?

The debate rambled on. The Dilapidations Commission and the Commissioners were soon at loggerheads over the way in which budgets for such an arrangement should be prepared. Before long there were two proposals: one from the commission (with which the Church Commissioners did not agree) and another from the Commissioners (which the commission scorned). Time was slipping by and the commission grew restive; it had promised to report to the Assembly in the autumn of 1962. For their part, the Commissioners strained to avoid the embarrassment of a public contest between them. If the commission went to the Assembly now, then the division between them must become common knowledge. The only way to avoid this was to hold the commission back still further. That autumn Ramsey read a prepared statement to the Assembly from the chair, observing to those impatient for a result that it was in the interests of all if the present discussion went on a little longer.

A further meeting of the protagonists had been arranged for the second half of September. Beloe invited an eminent lawyer, Sir John Ashworth, to chair it and adjudicate ('Oh yes', remarked Ramsey, 'is that not the man with whom I was at school at Sandroyd?'[9]). Beloe found himself in the awkward position of handling a barrage of complaints about the Commissioners from the Venerable J. A. M. Clayson of the commission, who was also secretary of the Canterbury board of finance. Feeling, warned Clayson, was running high. Shrouding this dispute in mystery simply encouraged people to ask questions, many of them wrong ones. He pressed that the confrontation should be brought into the open in the Assembly itself; for who governed the Church – the Church Assembly or 'a dictatorship of Number 1 Millbank?'[10]

Meanwhile, the Commissioners in their turn grumbled about Clayson's commission. The meeting between them was delayed. Ashworth received a pile of submissions. Frankly, he observed to Beloe, he found it far from easy to boil down the differences between the commission and the Commissioners to 'a simple form'; 'though no doubt the difficulty is partly due to the fact that the authors of the papers are thoroughly familiar with the matters under discussion, whereas I am not'.[11] But he saw that if anything was to be achieved they must avoid becoming lost in the detail. This complicated church affair seemed to him to be about two things: houses and money. Liability for reimbursements to the parsonages fund should, he proposed, be placed upon the shoulders of the diocese. Then he simply reconfigured the disputed route made by the money from the parsonages fund to the diocesan stipends funds, and diocesan boards of finance to the Commissioners, in a way which was not utterly to the satisfaction of the commission, but substantially so, and eventually acceptable to the Commissioners too. The Commissioners were amenable. At another meeting it could be seen that the Ashworth solution worked. At the summer session of the Church Assembly in 1964 the Dilapidations Legislation Commission proposed a new measure, significant in that it could be seen largely to transfer financial and executive responsibility for the matter to the dioceses, but still to satisfy the Commissioners' requirements on finance and liability. Legislation was soon being prepared and it was duly passed without a murmur.

No longer would statutory outgoings on parsonage houses be met by grants made from diocesan stipends funds and no longer would an incumbent have to meet the statutory outgoings on his parsonage

---

[9] Beloe to Ashworth, 23 July 1963, Ramsey papers, vol. 37, fo. 278.
[10] J. A. M. Clayson to Beloe, 3 Oct. 1963, ibid. fo. 296.
[11] Ashworth to Beloe, 15 Oct. 1963, ibid. fo. 301.

house – rates, repairs, mortgages and, if appropriate, rent – out of his own pocket and without reimbursement. This new weighting towards the dioceses required a new layer of discussion between the Commissioners and the diocesan representatives. On 1 April 1965 a Parsonages Outgoings Fund was set up for every diocese, to be fortified with an extra £150,000 a year in total from the Commissioners. The fund soon found its feet. By the end of 1967 the Commissioners had managed to learn something of how the dioceses were managing their grants. Some operated a scale of grants while others were more individualistic, regarding each case on its own merits. On the suitability of houses, meanwhile, the dioceses showed 'a considerable degree of uniformity'.[12]

By January 1969 as many as one in seven parsonage houses was still considered 'overlarge and otherwise unsuitable'. Increasingly, it was said that there should be a major new campaign. There were new grants, new schemes, some of them to encourage lay giving, which, mercifully, flourished. The significance of what new thinking emerged now was that the Commissioners were moving steadily away from the issuing of block grants towards a new situation in which the dioceses themselves had to justify the financial and pastoral need in every case. The diocesan allocations would be reviewed every three years: in such a way would the Commissioners exercise firm control over the capital spent.

Over seven years, from 1961 to 1968, £17.4 million was spent on capital works to parsonage houses. Of this £7.1 million was produced through sale proceeds, £1.3 million came from the laity, £5.7 million from Commissioners' grants and £2.4 million from their loans. The remainder came from miscellaneous sources.[13] Here, too, the Commissioners were learning to tread increasingly carefully. In 1968 they decided to make a new grant not at one blow, but in two instalments, the second when the projects themselves were clearly underway. A third sum could be allocated in light of need. They noted that many of the dioceses did not spend all the money that they had received, and called them to account: if the money allocated earlier had not been required for their intended schemes, they should now revise their proposals and tell the Commissioners. Only then would the new grant be made.

However these things were judged, what was crucial here was the emphasis which the parsonage house received in the scale of priorities set by the Millbank establishment. By the end of the Ramsey era it

[12] James Shelley report, 'Capital expenditure on parsonage houses', CC (67) 44, Board papers, 14 Dec. 1967, ser. 95083/31.
[13] Letter to diocesan secretaries, 'Diocesan dilapidations boards', Board papers, 25 Jan. 1968, ibid.

could be seen how deeply and intricately enmeshed in the complicated fortunes of the parsonage house the Church Commissioners had become. This was no limited liability either. As Harris once observed, the perpetual rise in standards of living meant that this work must always go on. The standards of one day were an improvement on those of another.[14]

The politics of redundancy

Most of the churches that closed were still in the towns and cities. Urban benefices changed not simply because of the rise and decline of certain congregations but because the cities themselves changed, sometimes beyond recognition. The Church of St Matthew and St George, built in Leicester in 1823 with space for 800 people, found itself by 1970 a stray island in a vast area of commercial buildings with a resident population of fewer than twenty-five.[15]

If most churches shuffled sadly into redundancy without much of a contest, where controversy arose it could last for years. Small, dwindling, ageing congregations often complained that they would never have declined to such a level if the bishop had not for some time been running them down. The most tenacious opponent of schemes of redundancy came not in the shape of outraged parochial church councils or offended local residents, not in the form of campaign societies for the Protestant faith or for architectural merit, but in a single, isolated west-country character, B. J. Lloyd. Lloyd was a master stonemason and a director of Associated Monumental Masons Ltd. He first made his mark in the paperwork of the Church Commissioners in July 1971, when he registered an objection to the redundancy of the church of St Nicholas, a chapel-of-ease in the parish of Winterbourne Monckton and Berwick Bassett.

The country was divided, according to Lloyd, into scribes and masons. The former were the lower and included solicitors. The latter, higher, category was that of the creator of the carved image. The scribes were made blind by the very fact of writing. The scribes had not understood Christ. The carved ornament inspired people to do what was right. Civilisations flourished while they carved and died when they began to write. The Bible itself 'is simply the work of a scribe describing a series of pictures designed by the ancient mason. This is why it is so perfect'. 'The Church', meanwhile, 'is where the mason rules Britain with his carvings.' To close a church would mean that the realm of the carved ornament would be extinguished and that

[14] Board minutes, 25 Mar. 1971.
[15] PC report, 'Leicester St Matthew and St George', CC (70) 58, Board papers, 17 Dec. 1970, ser. 95083/34.

of the scribes and their writings would prevail. That could not work. They should respond to the decline of popular religion not by shutting down churches but by commissioning more carved ornaments than ever before.

This objection was patiently assessed. The bishop of Salisbury said he knew Lloyd and admired his work, but he confessed that he found his opinions 'quite incomprehensible'. The Board of governors of the Church Commissioners overruled Mr Lloyd.[16] But they had not heard the last of him. Moreover, he had his rights. In every case his representations would have to be copied, circulated and assessed rationally by that class of scribes which he so marvellously scorned.

Selling redundant churches

Under the terms of the 1952 Measure redundant churches could still be sold. At first it appeared that the beneficiaries were mostly in London, and they included the Greek Orthodox Church, the Serbian Orthodox Church and the London Russian Orthodox Parish Community. Between 1953 and 1965 five schemes had sold churches to the Orthodox Churches, and by the end of that year three more were in train. Meanwhile, the Open Spaces Act of 1906 allowed local authorities to take over disused burial grounds. But this had not embraced consecrated ground until comparatively recently. Sometimes roads were altered and this was approved by faculty – the ground itself was after all undisturbed. The Town and Country Planning Acts did apply to consecrated land, and provided for the removal of remains. The Minister of Health could close a churchyard, and had actually done so now and then.

Redundancy and the threat of dereliction struck down even the most imposing creations. It happened right on the Church Commissioners' own doorstep, or at least around the corner. In 1963 it was necessary to pass a bill by which the diocese of London could authorise the sale and reconstruction of St John's Smith Square in Westminster. The church had been built by Thomas Archer in 1728, had been seriously damaged by fire in 1742, substantially altered in 1825, severely bombed in 1941. After redundancy the diocese decided to use it as a repository for its records. But it did not restore St John's, and soon decided that it did not want it at all. A determined organisation, 'The Friends of St John's, Smith Square', was formed with a heady mixture of Right Honourables to acquire the church, restore and endow it by public subscription and convert it into a concert hall in which 'music of every epoch may be produced',

---

[16] PC report, 'Avebury with Winterbourne Monckton and Berwick Bassett', CC (71) 38, Board papers, 22 July 1971, ibid.

exhibitions of 'paintings and sculptures of all schools, whether ancient or modern', plays produced, religious addresses, services 'from time to time'. St John's enjoyed august patrons and every possibility of an impressive life beyond death.[17] Not so others: the Victorian churches of northern towns, the stray ancient churches of the countryside. In 1964 the Administrative Committee reported that unions of benefices had left fourteen churches redundant. Of these, nine – none of them listed – were demolished and three closed, with only two appropriated for another use. Sometimes architectural eminence ensured survival on the most surprising terms. The remains of the church of St Mary Aldermanbury, a Wren church bombed during the war, had been shipped off to Fulton University in the United States, there to be reconstructed as a memorial to Winston Churchill – not the kind of pastoral reorganisation that the measure of 1944 had quite foreseen.

Now and then the Commissioners were approached by various religious denominations that sought to buy a site and put up a building for worship, or perhaps a minister's house. These applications most often happened where new developments were appearing, and they provoked few anxieties, as long as the application was for land not too near the parish church itself and the denomination was not 'inimical' to the church's own interests. Beyond this there were no principles on which to draw. Every case was treated on its own terms. In 1960 an Archbishops' Commission on Redundant Churches, chaired by Lord Bridges, had pronounced that it could see no reason why redundant churches should not be leased or sold in ways that encouraged alternative uses. It did, however, step neatly around the dangerous questions which this prompted. Each case should be considered 'on its merits'. They might foresee 'serious difficulties', but these should be left to 'the Church'. This, then, stopped short of yielding a definite policy. The effect was to leave a body like the Church Commissioners with room for manoeuvre, something which they were inclined to favour. But it also left them without any justifying rubric which carried the weight and consent of a wider power.

As the 1960s unfolded some general patterns were becoming more distinct, and to some minds this seemed increasingly to require some setting of rules. In March 1963 the Board of the Commissioners inspected a new paper on the 'Sales of sites to other denominations for church purposes'. This arose now not as an abstract calculation of policy, for it offered a particular case for consideration. It was one thing to sell to other traditions – but what of faiths which the Church might not respect? What, in short, of the Mormons, who now wished to purchase one-and-a-half acres in Harton, South Shields, and to build a church there, about half a mile from the parish church itself? For their part the Commissioners had hoped to sell the plot for a while, and, for theirs, the Mormons had offered a good price. But the local authority was also showing signs of interest, and they might well appear a preferable candidate, not least because a sale to the Mormons might well excite complaints from local Anglicans, from the incumbent and 'probably' the bishop too. Again it was asked: was it time, then, for the Commissioners to frame a 'general policy'? Still the Board judged that any future problems should be referred to it as they arrived. But the Mormons of Harton should be denied.[18]

'The Reformation in reverse': St John's Aylesbury

Pressure against the pragmatists was beginning to mount. In January 1965 a union of benefices in the diocese of Bath and Wells brought before the Board a very different case from these, and a still sharper difficulty. The bishop had asked the Pastoral Committee that a scheme be prepared for Christ Church, Crewkerne, a chapel-of-ease, to be appropriated as a church by the Roman Catholics. This was something that had never happened to the Commissioners before.

To offer an Anglican church in the heart of England to Roman Catholics struck a resonant chord. By 1965 there was every reason to feel that popular animus against Romanism belonged to an earlier age, a once popular spirit of agitation whose respectability had been scrubbed away by the patient labours of at least two generations of ecumenical courtesies, liberal tolerance, benign agnostic civilities and secular indifference. And the Roman Catholics of Crewkerne looked very unlike a case of Papal Aggression. At present they worshipped in a modest wooden church in the town.

Christ Church itself had been consecrated in 1854, was a chapel-of-ease, not listed and had seating for 400 people. The churchyard was closed for burials. One evening service took place there every Sunday, with a mostly elderly congregation of between twenty and thirty people and a choir of twelve. In 1965 the diocese felt that such a situation showed that it was 'pastorally redundant'. It reflected that the parish church was a quarter of a mile away, was in 'reasonable' condition and had 800 seats. Under the 1952 Measure, the chapel would be vested in the diocesan board of finance and the diocese would be allowed to work out a scheme with the Roman Catholics, subject to terms and conditions – about repairs, insurance and suchlike. The Catholics would pay a nominal rent. Naturally, there must be consultation with all interested parties, from the patron (in the case of Christ Church, Crewkerne, the Lord Chancellor), the incumbent and the parochial

[18] EFC report, 'Sales of sites to other denominations for church purposes', 19 Mar. 1963, Board papers, 28 Mar. 1963, ser. 95083/25; Board minutes, 28 Mar. 1963.

church council, to the Ministry of Public Building and Works. The Ministry of Housing and local government must also be informed.

This deliberate procession of powers presented something of a challenge to the administrative authorities, but they carried it off dutifully. The parochial church council felt that it was better that the church remain a place of worship than that it be knocked down or made into a store of some kind. The incumbent, the bishop and the diocesan pastoral committee all nodded. They invited the Commissioners to nod, too. They were sympathetic, but pointed out a number of practical details. No service of reconsecration should take place. And what, it was asked, of faculties? The Catholics might wish to alter what they found, put in new ornaments, fittings or furnishings, the things that Catholic worshippers expected.[19]

All went well at Crewkerne, but there were soon two more chapels-of-ease to deal with: St John's, Aylesbury, in the diocese of Oxford, and Jesus Church, Oundle, in the Peterborough diocese. The second of these was unlikely to provoke controversy: it had been closed since December 1962 and its patron knew that it could not continue. Not so St John's.

St John's was High Church in tradition. Consecrated in 1883, it could seat 330 people but in 1964 had a congregation of no more than thirty. It could not support itself financially. It lay only five minutes' walk away from the parish church. The building itself was not listed and needed repairs. Aylesbury was a growing town, but it was not growing around St John's, and a new roundabout was about to be built in front of the church. Services had ceased a few months previously, though to this there had been vocal opposition and letters of protest sent to the *Bucks Herald*. But now the incumbent, who was also rural dean, felt the dispute had settled down as half the congregation of St John's grew familiar with their parish church and the others went to two other local churches, one in a neighbouring parish, one another chapel-of-ease in the same parish.

The incumbent supported the scheme to lease the church to the Roman Catholics, and his parochial council agreed (by twenty-two votes to one). There was a large Catholic population in Aylesbury and it had only a small church in which to worship. At first, all looked to be well. But a trickle of objections had begun to arrive. Then, somehow, the news reached the offices of the Protestant Truth Society in London which exploded into life, pouring scorn upon the plan, deploring 'this great affront to our National Protestantism', fearing a 'Reformation in reverse'. A protest meeting took place at the Alliance

[19] Ashton paper, 'Appropriation of churches to use by Roman Catholic authorities', 8 Dec. 1965, CC (65) 51, Board papers, 16 Dec. 1965, ser. 95083/29.

Hall in Westminster, resolving to dispatch a party of Wickliffe preachers to Aylesbury, armed with 10,000 leaflets.

The mayor was invited to attend a rally in Aylesbury town hall but did not go. The meeting, chaired by a councillor, who was also Clerk of Aylesbury, was, according to the society itself, attended by 400 people ('over thirty of whom claimed to be former worshippers of St. John's Church'). On the platform was a retired bishop (D. A. Thompson, of the Bible Christian Unity Fellowship), together with five vicars and five 'pastors'. A resolution of protest was passed, with only four in the hall not voting in favour. For while the Church of Rome maintained the doctrine of the sacrifice of the mass, the mediation of the Virgin Mary, the invocation of saints, absolution by a 'human priest', the doctrine of purgatory and the infallibility of the pope it should not lay hands on St John's, Aylesbury. It would be shameful, blasphemous, treason against the Protestant constitution, 'a betrayal of a sacred trust won for the people of England at the price of Martyrs' blood'.

Now the matter could not simply be viewed as a little local difficulty: there had also been an article in *The Times*. More correspondence arrived at 1 Millbank: from the Protestant Alliance, the Bible Christian Unity Fellowship, the Bethel Free Baptist Church at Resolven, Glamorganshire, the Beulah Faith Mission at Abedere, Glamorganshire; from a solicitor acting on behalf of a parishioner who intended a petition. The Commissioners were under no statutory obligation to consider all this – at least, not yet, because the draft scheme itself did not exist, but they were now finding that the business of drafting was itself raising other kinds of problems: of law, of terminology. For the time being the Aylesbury scheme was withdrawn, along with the scheme for the innocuous Jesus Church in Oundle. It was not a reprieve so much as a stay of execution. In July 1967 a new scheme was aired, then published and widely put about in Aylesbury itself. It specified that the church might be used for worship by the Roman Catholic Church and for no other purpose, and that the Roman Catholic authorities should repair, maintain and insure the church and its fittings to the satisfaction of the diocesan authority. The Catholics wanted more security. This, said the diocese, might well be theirs in time.

Thirteen formal objections arrived within the permitted twenty-one days, five from former members of the church itself. St John's had been solvent, the Commissioners read; the congregation had been happy there and now they were to be robbed of their own church. One added that it should not be passed over to 'aliens' whose first loyalty was not to the queen but to a foreign power. Another disavowed anti-Catholic views but thought that the Catholic Church could well afford to provide its own buildings. Another wondered if the Catholics were being as attentive to the needs of Anglicans as were the Anglicans to the Catholics? If the Church of England was not wealthy, they should sell St John's to the highest bidder: 'I believe it is the duty of the Church to win souls for Christ, and not to provide buildings in which to promote false doctrine.' One letter came from a member whose parents had taught in the Sunday school and given to the building fund, whose uncle was a Sunday school superintendent and sidesman who had given a lectern in memory of his wife. He himself had been baptised and confirmed there, had been in the Church Lads Brigade, had worshipped and worked there all his life.

The bishop was unmoved and offered his comments briefly. It all went to the Pastoral Committee and the bishop. They repeated the arguments, defining them a little more sharply, adding some new information. Back it went to the Board of the Commissioners. Here, suddenly, it stuck; the Board hesitated. Was this a good time to have such a battle, in light of the progress of the new Pastoral Measure, then rumbling through the Church Assembly? Safe passage of this measure would actually give the Commissioners the legal powers to transfer the actual ownership of the church. Why not simply shut the church for the moment and wait for a more propitious time to do a more thorough job? This suggestion was agreed. The bishop now proposed that a new scheme be drawn up, this time simply to close the church.

This time there were only two objections, both from parishioners. The Commissioners approved the scheme. The 'Protestant' societies with all their vehemence and outrage, their leaflets and fuss, fell silent; their flying corps of agitators packed their bags and disappeared. There were no more glorious, indignant resolutions passed by righteous committees; the assembly hall was empty. Now only a little handful of objectors remained – the bishop thought only two or three people – abandoned without a second thought by their short-term allies with their brittle ardour, hopelessly stranded by the verdicts of responsible authorities, left only to their own conversations, memories and silences. St John's Church was shut.[20]

At the Commissioners there was now a refinement of method, and further reflection. In October 1969 the Board discussed a paper drawn up by the newly created Redundant Churches Committee. A general policy was still resisted. But now some guidance for diocesan uses committees was ventured.[21]

[20] Ibid. See also PC report 'Aylesbury St Mary (diocese of Oxford)', 13 July 1967, CC (67) 35, Board papers, 20 July 1967, ibid. pt 30, and PC report, 'Objections to proposed closure of St John's Chapel-of-ease', CC (68) 8, 29 Feb. 1968, ibid. pt 31.
[21] Ridley paper, 'Proposed use of redundant churches by the Roman Catholics', 19

In time, such problems were greeted with a weary familiarity. When the final arrangements at Crewkerne were eventually passed to the Board for approval, the committee added a proposal that in future there would be no need to pass on such cases to the Board, unless there were objections or special circumstances. About this there was some debate. One Commissioner 'urged' that more efforts at revitalising the Church would diminish the current of redundancy; he could not approve of owning a church on a lease which was used by Roman Catholics. Selling them outright was a different matter. By twenty-three votes to one the Board ruled that it was acceptable that churches be made available to Roman Catholics for worship. However, the Board was not yet ready to leave the Redundant Churches Committee to its own devices.[22]

The fate of historic, redundant churches

In 1961 a sharp mind might well have found it difficult to see how the preservation of historic redundant churches fell within the remit of 'the cure of souls'. And in 1961, quite simply, it did not. It did not figure within the Commissioners' own rubrics. But no one could deny that the question needed something more than the efforts of diocesan boards. It was a matter of national concern, and something to which the Church nationally could not rightly be indifferent. The whole matter fell logically to the Church Commissioners because they possessed administrative expertise in the preparation of schemes, but also because it required, unavoidably, a considerable commitment of money.

Since its creation in 1952, the Historic Churches Preservation Trust had operated quietly and effectively. It was not a large body, and it existed to assist efforts that were already being made within parishes. The Church Commissioners had volunteered modest support in their own way, after September 1953 using the licence that they now enjoyed to give grants in their capacity as landowners to support the trust to the tune of £2,000 a year.

But by then this was only a part of a broader discussion between more powerful forces. In 1960 the Bridges Commission had recommended that a new fund be set up under a new Pastoral Measure to preserve churches of acknowledged historic or architectural worth. The Church, it pronounced, had still 'a partial and continuing responsibility' for churches of historic interest. The proceeds of any sales of such churches should be equally divided between the dioceses in which they lay and the new fund itself. The Commission had also

Oct. 1969, CC (69) 32, ibid. pt 32.
[22] Board minutes, 16 Oct. 1969.

argued that such a fund should be supported financially by the state and should elicit contributions from the public. By the end of the year the Board of the Church Commissioners had accepted this in principle and declared their readiness to find money to support the new fund. But they added that that they did not themselves have statutory power to make grants. If they were to do so, it must be with the approval of the Church Assembly. For its part, the government had proven amenable, even constructive. A commitment of £200,000 over five years was offered, as long as the Church matched it.

It was seen to be best not to make a single measure out of the conservation of historic churches, but to incorporate proposals within the revision of the Pastoral Measure. This showed wisdom, but that greater work was soon so immense that the prospect of a prompt solution evaporated almost at once. Time passed – and brought other changes. The financial pledge had been made by a Conservative government which had subsequently lost a general election. In the Church people were asking whether the new Labour government would honour the decision of its predecessor?

By June 1965 Silsoe sensed that it was time to give a lead, both to State and Church. He now saw that the money could be found, in non-perpetuity income, and assurances could be given that it would not prejudice the claims of the clergy or anything else if it was allocated in this way. If the government would renew its earlier pledge, the Commissioners could indeed underwrite the Church's side of the bargain. Silsoe carried the Board of the Commissioners with him.[23] But this was not enough. They must await the mind of a Church Assembly which was still much exercised by the coming Pastoral Measure. As this now stood in draft, it gave the Commissioners power to make grants to a Redundant Churches Fund to the tune of £200,000 for five years (it might be altered thereafter, as the Assembly directed). It had also adopted the proposal of the Archbishops' Commission that a half of the proceeds from a sale should be made out to the diocese concerned and a half to the new fund On this the Commissioners wished to insist. But it was becoming clear that the dioceses wanted more, and they dug in their heels. The upshot was that two-thirds of the net proceeds of sales of churches and of sites, or any premiums on the grant of a lease, would be paid to the diocesan pastoral account and one-third to the Redundant Churches Fund itself. On 21 October 1965 the Board of the Church Commissioners acquiesced in this, but with misgivings.[24] The obvious problem was that the less the new fund

[23] Board minutes, 3 June 1965. See also GPC paper, 'Draft Pastoral Measure: Redundant Churches Fund', CC (65) 21, 27 May 1965, Board papers, 3 June 1965, ser. 95083/28.
[24] Board minutes, 21 Oct. 1965.

received from the dioceses, the more it would need to be supported by somebody else: either by the Commissioners, by the state or by the Assembly. Discussions in the Assembly brought little reassurance. There were complaints that the new draft clauses were 'open-ended' and gave the Assembly itself no control over the sums passing in such a way to the Redundant Churches Fund. Then it was urged that if the Assembly had no need to find money during that first period of five years, it must surely be free to allocate extra sums as it saw fit. There were other critics: some perceived too great an insistence on 'museum pieces', where they should be maintaining churches that were still 'living'. Some dioceses observed that they had few historic churches to sell but many to maintain.[25] Inevitably, another committee was appointed. Meanwhile, the state agreed that its early offer remained unaltered. The passage of the Pastoral Measure in 1968 brought a final resolution. The framework within which Church and State would co-operate in the preservation of historic churches had been established. There were also three new instruments of authority with an interest in any closure of churches: the Advisory Board for Redundant Churches, the Redundant Churches Fund and the Redundant Churches Committee of the Church Commissioners.

The Redundant Churches Committee

The passage of the Pastoral Measure in 1968 did not merely enable the Church of England to enter into a new concordat with the state over the conservation of historic buildings. In some measure it created a new climate, and also a new atmosphere of expectation. The sale or lease of a church was thereby made not only easier, but more widely available for what might be deemed a 'suitable use'. The likelihood that more and more churches would become redundant and might be sold or leased had not been kept quiet – on the contrary, it had received increasing public attention. Applications had arrived at the doors of diocesan redundant churches uses committees, even at Millbank, and for uses not before anticipated or considered appropriate. Different bishops and committees might well have different views as to what might be acceptable.

The Redundant Churches Committee of the Church Commissioners met for the first time in March 1969. It began, patiently, to work out its practical character and tasks. The following twelve months proved difficult. The three bodies now at work in this sphere were soon treading on each other's toes. The chairman of the fund, Ivor Bulmer-Thomas, was querulous. There were disagreements and controversies almost at once.

[25] *Proceedings of the Church Assembly*, xlvii/2, 117–53 (14 Feb. 1967).

In the past, redundant churches had become places of worship for Greek, Russian and Serbian Orthodox congregations and for Danish, Latvian and Estonian Lutherans; they had become homes to special forms of ministry (for the deaf and dumb, for the Industrial Christian Fellowship). They had taken on new life as headquarters for church organisations, as university and college chapels or institutes, parish halls, Sunday schools, youth centres, museums, libraries, record offices, halls and warehouses, as a theatre, as the physiotherapy department of a hospital, a store for the contents of demolished churches. Commercial use might well be acceptable: leases might have restrictive covenants. But it was difficult to lay down a general rule: every locality had its own peculiarities. Some had agreed that churches in rural areas might become 'spiritual centres' for private prayer, quietness, study, listening to music. If such proposals made sense financially that was all very well. There had been an application to turn a church into a private residence, which the committee thought was 'probably unique', and it had been approved (partly in the expectation that it would prove unique).[26] But in the bustle of objections, protests and controversies, which was the lot of all bodies concerned with this difficult matter, the committee found not only that the Redundant Churches Fund was stepping on its toes, but that it could actually agitate and campaign against it. In February 1971 the committee reported to the Board on representations received against the proposed redundancy of Lightcliffe Old Church in the diocese of Wakefield. These had come from the Ancient Monuments Society, the Friends of Friendless Churches, the Yorkshire Archaeological Society, Mr John Smith, a former MP for Westminster, now 'prime mover and chief beneficiary' of the Landmark Trust – and also from the chairman of the Redundant Churches Fund, Ivor Bulmer-Thomas.[27]

There was a burgeoning public interest in the phenomenon in the local and national newspapers and on the television. The idea that as many as 700 churches might be available for sale inspired a fascinated response: in the summer of 1970 more than a hundred letters arrived from correspondents who wanted to live in them or ship them across the Atlantic and live in them in Canada. Redundancy also created situations which were notably odd, however well they were managed within rational administrative processes. In the year 1972–3 the committee had visited the church of St Paul, Penge, in the diocese of Rochester. The Advisory Board had counselled that this should not be demolished. It was a fine example of the work of the nineteenth-

---

[26] RCC report, 'Suitable uses for redundant churches', CC (70) 1, 6 Jan. 1970, Board papers, 22 Jan. 1970, ser. 95083/33.

[27] RCC report, 'Lightcliffe Old Church (diocese of Wakefield)', CC (71) 9, 18 Feb. 1971, Board papers, 25 Feb. 1971, ibid. pt 34.

century architect Bassett Keeling and had a striking decorative motif on the inside walls. But initial repairs would amount to at least £20,000. It was hard to imagine a future occupant. After three years it should surely pass into the hands of the Redundant Churches Fund. This looked sensible enough. But then it was realised that if the church were restored and preserved it would in fact be in very much better condition than the parish church itself, which was temporary and inadequate. And this, in a depressed south London parish, looked not simply curious but questionable. The committee reconsidered and now felt it wiser to demolish St Paul altogether to avoid embarrassment. This contradicted the advice of the Advisory Board for the first time. The Board agreed. The Victorian Society objected, but it was not enough.[28]

Redundancy in a nation of many faiths: St Mary, Savile Town

On the purchase of redundant church buildings by other Christian bodies (including what the committee called 'deviations') the Redundant Churches Committee soon reached 'a common mind': these Churches must be members, or associate members, or aspirant members, of the World Council of Churches if they were to be thought suitable. But here, too, each case should be viewed on its own terms. A new document should, it was agreed, be written. It should not be sent to the press, but the Church Information Office would have a copy and make it available to those who specifically asked for it.[29]

But what if a redundant church building were adopted for worship by non-Christian faiths? This was too much for the committee alone. In January 1970 the Board of the Church Commissioners examined not one but two papers framing a new set of dilemmas. The first began:

> There can be no argument in a democratic and plural society against the right of such a community, whether large or small, to worship and to advocate their way of life either in the open air or in *some* building – provided that the law of the land governing such assemblies is observed. Presumably, none of us at this stage in history would wish to take our stand on the maxim 'Error has no rights over against truth'.

There followed an exercise in logic, the logic of dialogue and the logic of charity. Dialogue between faiths should not be simply a matter of

[28] RCC annual report to 31 Mar. 1973, CC (73) 42, Board papers, 21 June 1973, ibid. pt 37.
[29] Ibid. pp. 3–4.

intellectual discussions: the transfer of redundant churches might well be a facet of it. They must ask themselves, how did church people view Moslems?

> Some of us undoubtedly see them as the fierce warriors of the Jehad, moving aggressively into more and more of Christian England. Others of us see depressed groups of melancholy men in shabby mackintoshes looking for somewhere to say their prayers amid the damps and fogs of the industrial West Riding. Probably, neither group is seeing the true picture. But, in any event, if human beings are somehow reaching out to God, are we to hinder this search on the grounds that we believe the route to be a wrong one? ... It is arguable that we shall communicate more of the God in whom we believe by an open-eyed offer than by a principled refusal.

To refuse the use of a redundant church 'for any socially legitimate purpose would be interpreted as discrimination on racial grounds'. The world was moving to embrace what Eric Abbott, dean of Westminster, had recently called 'the universal conscience of mankind'. The Church should identify with that too.

There followed the case against. When a church was consecrated it was solemnly set apart to be used by the Church of England alone. Strictly speaking, this must mean for ever, but few adhered to this now, and the Pastoral Measure of 1968 legitimised the view of the majority. But a line must still be drawn. It must not be used for criminal or immoral purposes, of course. What mattered was that any non-Christian faith, 'however high or noble it may be', and even if it was in part sympathetic to Christianity, was sure to be, still, 'in positive opposition' to it, must even have a 'substantial anti-Christian element' within it. To allow a church building to become the home of such opposition must, morally, be 'a breach of its trust in relation to that building'. Then there were pastoral and practical aspects. Converts to Christianity would feel hurt. It was quite different in the case of other Christian denominations, because they too sought to advance the Christian cause. Christians might well help people of other faiths to find resources and facilities, but they should not give them their churches.

The pragmatic method was still maintained. Both papers agreed, at least, that each case was best considered on its own merits.[30]

---

[30] RCC paper, 'Suitable uses for redundant churches', CC (70) 1, appendix A, Board papers, 16 Jan. 1970, ibid. pt 33.

Only a year later this was put to the test. In February 1971 the Board received a paper warning them of a redundant church whose fate seemed to be moving into this barely charted region. St Mary, Savile Town, had been built as a chapel-of-ease in the parish of Thornhill Lees, a suburb of Dewsbury, in 1900. There had evidently been no firm opposition to its closure: the parish church lay half-a-mile away and most of the congregation of St Mary's had decamped there. St Mary's was not listed and it was felt that nobody could rightly oppose its demolition on architectural grounds. But there were reasons to move with care, for the church had been redundant for only a few months, and some of its worshippers could remember it being built or could even recall their own parents helping to build it.

Within two decades the social environment around St Mary's had altered beyond recognition. A Muslim community of about 2,000 had settled in Wakefield, much of it near the church itself. Now the Muslim Welfare Society of Batley and Dewsbury had asked if they might convert it into a mosque. The proposal went before the Redundant Churches Uses Committee of Wakefield, which approved, but by a very narrow margin. The incumbent of the parish, the parochial church council and the congregation were opposed. They would rather see St Mary's demolished. The bishop agreed. The financial realities were odd: the value of the site itself was not felt to be greater than that of the building, for it was not an area that appeared to invite development. Meanwhile, local opinion was difficult to measure. The local press had been asked by the diocese to remain silent for the moment, and had done so, but this could not continue. When it was understood that the Muslims themselves would never allow a building that had been a mosque to be used for anything else it was suggested that this might make them understand more readily a mood against the proposal and a decision against them.

Betty Ridley (the Third Church Estates Commissioner and chair of the Redundant Churches Committee) had travelled to Wakefield to inspect the scene for herself. She met the secretary of the Diocesan Uses Committee, the incumbent, two former members of the congregation and the rural dean. She heard the views of the local planning officer, who supported the proposal. The church itself, she found, was subject to damp and had already been vandalised. Most of the windows were broken, the floor torn up, a gutter stolen. Meanwhile local Muslims worshipped in each other's homes and in a converted woollen mill in Dewsbury. They believed that they could summon a weekly congregation of 200–300, and courses of instruction for their children on five evenings a week. Ridley heard that the parochial church council felt that relations between people of different backgrounds in Wakefield were not much in danger, but they sensed their fragility and feared that giving the church to the Muslims might provoke something worse. It was remarked that 'one effect would be to drive out the remaining white population'. It looked safer to demolish and to build a new mosque, but then, it was remarked, the Muslims might be less interested if they had to build the mosque themselves.

The rural dean was in favour of the proposal, but could not be sure whether giving the building to the Muslims would prove a 'stabilizing factor in the community or a dangerous venture'. Then it was difficult to know what to plan for the future – it was an area dependent on the woollen industry, and the prospects for that were uncertain. It had been suggested that if the object of their policy was to benefit community relations, then perhaps it would be better served if the church was knocked down and a children's playground put on the site instead. But that would only happen if Dewsbury was designated by the council an 'improvement' area.[31] No one knew whether Dewsbury would improve.

In February 1971 the Board received a recommendation that the church be demolished and the site sold 'without restriction as to use'. It concurred, pronouncing that it would be 'most unfortunate' if 'the present racial balance should be disturbed, as seemed likely' if the building were converted.[32] The provost of Wakefield, meanwhile, sensed that the Muslims of Wakefield might already be looking elsewhere. But three months later the matter was reopened. A deputation from the Batley and Dewsbury Muslim Welfare Society had visited Ridley in London to present their case. If the church was demolished they could not buy the site and build a mosque on it, for that would cost a great deal. When the deputation was asked if it was true that a mosque could never be passed on to another use, its members confessed that they had never heard of such a thing happening. But they added that if the building became not a mosque but a 'place of prayer', they could dispose of it if necessary. It had been rumoured that the local authority had offered them buildings, but that they had turned them down. This they denied.

Three town clerks were consulted. The bishop, Eric Treacy, felt that a 'political motive' underlay the Muslims' application. He preferred to trust to the perceptions of local churchgoers. If the transaction took place he would do all he could to win over the parochial church council, but he would not disguise his own feelings when speaking to the press. One eighth of the population of the area was Pakistani, and one in four babies there was born to a Pakistani mother. 'Naturally', he said, 'the local people are worried about the prospects of the Pakistanis

[31] RCC report, 18 Dec. 1971, CC (71) 10, Board papers, 25 Feb. 1971, ibid. pt 34.
[32] Board minutes, 25 Feb. 1971.

taking over in the next ten years or so.' He judged that the representatives of the Muslim community were increasingly inclined to make demands, not requests. Moreover, he thought that the Church Commissioners should support a diocesan bishop in a matter like this.

Ridley was quizzical. How much weight, she wondered, should they actually be attaching to a bishop's views? And if local people knew most about what was happening in Wakefield itself, did they understand the broader issues involved? The Church's credibility in the field of race relations might be dented if they turned down the proposal. It was currently encouraging a movement to teach about 'other faiths' in schools. Were the Muslims asking for too much? Anglican missions abroad had begun on a modest scale, and here were Muslims in Dewsbury wanting a church building almost overnight. Was the Church being manipulated? Did the Muslims really seek a prestigious victory?

In one conversation in Wakefield, Ridley heard that it was contradictory to support the conversion of Muslims to Christianity abroad while providing them with mosques in Britain itself. This sent her to the General Secretary of the Church Missionary Society, who told her that most missionaries would be glad to see minorities in England accorded the same treatment that Christians hoped to encounter themselves in other countries. She then sounded out the Anglican assistant bishop of Jerusalem, Kenneth Cragg, who remarked that the affinity between Islam and Christianity was increasingly recognised: they worshipped the same God, Muslims acknowledged Christ to be a great prophet, if not the Son of God. He added that his own efforts to encourage dialogue between Muslims and Christians in Jerusalem might be influenced by what occurred in England.

At Millbank the Redundant Churches Committee was still divided. By three votes to two (with five absentees) it recommended to the Board that a new scheme be drafted for the appropriation of the church by the Muslims as a place of worship. This might well have appeared the worst of all worlds, but it had reduced the issue to one single point: the only real ground on which to decide against the Muslim proposal was that non-Christian worship was not a suitable use for what had been a Christian church. On this principle the Board must meditate, not least because other cases would very likely follow. It was now agreed that a local meeting of Christians and Muslims, and of those who supported the proposal and those who resisted it, would surely be beneficial and yield a greater understanding. The Board asked Ridley to encourage the bishop to hold such a meeting before returning to the Commissioners for a verdict.[33]

---

[33] Board minutes, 22 July 1971.

By October 1971 the Board of the Commissioners had their new paper, written by Canon Douglas Webster at the invitation of Archbishop Coggan. 'I believe', wrote Webster, 'that this issue has to be seen in the broad context of religious liberty and the universal mission of the Church.' The Gospel must stand on its own two feet, not be protected from competition. In many non-Christian lands the church had received land or buildings from non-Christian leaders. As for the church building, it must be remembered that the Church existed in the people of God, not in the buildings: 'It is a pagan or sub-Christian view to think that holiness inheres like some physical substance.' The Church showed itself in a better light by acting with generosity and kindness, and this situation too could be an act of witness, an act of missionary commitment even. Mean-spiritedness, on the other hand, might foster misunderstanding and even hostility. If local Christian opinion were wounded, they must face the 'harsh realities of life everywhere that buildings are for people and can survive only so long as people continue to use them'. But Webster added firmly that he did not know about the church in Wakefield and he too believed that all cases should be judged on their own terms. Perhaps somebody like the assistant bishop of Jerusalem could be invited to hand over the church at a social occasion at which members of the community could come to know each other?

In Wakefield Bishop Treacy had now arranged a meeting of diocesan and parochial representatives and local Muslims. Treacy himself told them that the decision would be that of 'the Church Commissioners in London'. He dwelled on the fact that Muslims would never allow a building that had once been a mosque to be used for any other purposes. For his part, the incumbent questioned whether the church was most suitably placed for the local Muslim population. He felt that local opposition came not only from elderly people who had known and worshipped in the church all their lives, but also from others who felt that the church was 'part of them'. It was true that it had closed because numbers were declining, but numbers were declining because more and more Muslims were moving in. He told the Muslims that the bishop himself had given him the responsibility for the people of Thornhill Lees, and he could not disregard the emotional dimension of the debate:

> Whatever is done is going to unleash the emotions here and far from being friendly, there is going to be hatred for your people ... not so much from the practising Christians around but from other members of the white community who may well use this as the reason for stirring up strife against the Pakistanis.

The bishop intervened to say that he preferred the word 'unhappiness' to 'hatred', and thought that unhappiness was bound to arise one way or the other. Somebody observed that the Muslims of Batley worshipped in an old Methodist church. This did not inspire a move to ask other Churches how they were dealing with such issues. Indeed, the Church of England appeared determined to confront the politics of redundancy alone.

When all this was done, Treacy concluded archly that the decision now rested with 'the people in London'. The archdeacon of Pontefract wondered why the Muslims so clearly wanted the church when so many mills were being closed down around them.

Another meeting followed, this one between members and officers of the Community Relations Commission. Here it was heard that there were many Nonconformist churches now used for worship by Muslims. If this new plan provoked resentment, the bishop of Wakefield had a liaison officer with immigrant communities to deal with that. Somebody proposed a compromise of time and space: could the church be transferred to the Muslims as a community centre, but one with a hall for prayer? The centre could also teach English (the 'Muslim priest' who led the Muslims at Savile Town had been persuaded to teach the faith in English). It was agreed that it seemed wrong to demolish a church purely to ensure that the Muslims did not get it. It was heard that if they feared political advantage they might remember that Islam placed great emphasis on humility.[34]

The proposal still stood before the Board. A statement from archbishop Ramsey pronounced: 'I should regret the making of a contrary decision, having regard to the whole missionary situation in this country and overseas.' But the Board itself had no common mind. There was a proposal that the church be demolished forthwith. This was defeated. Some members wanted outright sale. Others thought such a decision best left to the diocese. Others again pronounced that the church had been set aside for Christian worship forever, whatever the new Pastoral Measure said. The archdeacon of Lincoln proposed a service of de-consecration. What, the Board wondered, would this look like? It might bring comfort, even though it would be meaningless in law. Such services had happened during the war, in bombed churches.[35]

Bishop Treacy said he did not want to de-consecrate the church. Now discussion of the affair had broken out in the local press and there had been articles in the national newspapers and the church press too. There had been forty more letters to the Church Commissioners,

[34] RCC report, 'Savile Town St Mary (diocese of Wakefield)' and appendices, CC (71) 47, Board papers, 21 Oct. 1971, ser. 95083/35.
[35] Board minutes, 21 Oct. 1971, pp. 1–2.

mostly from local people, and a petition with a hundred names, all of them professing to have been worshippers at the church. They wanted St Mary's to be demolished. The St Mary's parochial church council came to London. Meanwhile, the committee had learned that two Methodist chapels had been sold to Muslim congregations, one at Purlwell, near Batley itself. There had been no controversy there.

As the debate intensified it became more exaggerated. The Muslims, it was said, required that a call to prayer be made outside the mosque. It was said that they sacrificed chickens, despite the efforts of the local council to stop them. Meanwhile, the local education authority was said to be unhappy that the children spent so much time being instructed in their faith that they fell asleep at school. There had been accusations that the Muslims behaved with contempt towards other local people: 'They delighted in appearing to outwit authority or the local residents.' It was in this context that the Dewsbury Deanery Synod voted by fifty-three votes to twenty-two against the scheme. The Redundant Churches Committee turned to a proposal that the new scheme be withdrawn and voted on it. There were five votes in favour and five against. They voted by six votes (but with four abstaining) that the Board defer a decision until the Wakefield synod had met.[36]

Bishop Treacy now repeated that he wanted demolition. But when it was pointed out that this would cost £1,000 and would mean that the pastoral account of his own diocese would lose as much as two-thirds of the net sale proceeds he changed his mind. He asked if the Commissioners could fund the demolition? The Commissioners blandly told him that they had not the money for that kind of thing. Treacy grew crosser by the day. He called upon the Commissioners to exercise their responsibilities, and complained plaintively that their indecision amounted to torture. Far from resolving anything, the diocesan synod of Wakefield issued a new list of proposals, one of them that the General Synod debate the issue, another that the Doctrinal Commission and the Board of Social Responsibility explore the theological and sociological significance of the affair. This did not work. When a debate did occur in General Synod it simply confirmed that Anglican opinion, in so far as the General Synod could be said to represent it, was utterly divided on the whole question, and ended up by simply noting the resolution of the Wakefield synod.[37]

The longer the delay the more the number of participants in the drama grew, and every one of them had a view to contribute. Responsible action demanded consultation. Consultation was at odds

[36] RCC report, 'Savile Town St Mary' CC (71) 47, Board papers, 16 Mar. 1972, ser. 95083.
[37] *Report of Proceedings of the General Synod*, iii/2, London 1972 (8 July 1972).

with prompt action. There was a clamour for both, usually by the same people. Meanwhile, vandals were knocking St Mary's to pieces.

The end was sudden. The Redundant Churches Committee clung to its recommendation that St Mary's be sold to the Muslims in Dewsbury, but when the Board of the Commissioners met in October 1972 it was clear that an alternative had emerged, and from a very distinct quarter. It was now proposed that the church be demolished and the site sold, no prior claim being accorded to the Muslims of Savile Town, and no prohibition against them either. This was carried unanimously.[38] The other authorities fell into line at once, either from conviction or exhaustion. A statement to the press was duly prepared. In such a way did St Mary's, Savile Town, Wakefield, perish, only seventy years after its birth.

Flux

As the Ramsey era drew to a close there were doubts and fears which refused somehow to depart. There were also great questions which needed answers. The Commissioners' relationship with the Redundant Churches Fund was still far from cordial, and at times was explosive. When Ramsey sought to mediate a second time Ivor Bulmer-Thomas reprimanded him: it was not at all proper for an archbishop of Canterbury to act 'merely as the instrument of the Church Commissioners'.[39] No sooner was this resolved (rather subtly) than trouble broke out at the Ancient Monuments Society. Of this Ivor Bulmer-Thomas turned out to be honorary secretary. Meanwhile, the state was not playing its part in the enterprise with much enthusiasm. When it did, it was wearyingly slow.

By December 1973 the Redundant Churches Fund believed that it would need a sum of £1,750,000 if it were to continue with its work for a second quinquennium. The Board of the Commissioners found this wholly reasonable. It was time to go back to the government, to the secretary of state for the Environment, and then, armed with the approval of the Treasury, to parliament itself – and this time it was hoped that the government would pledge more. But some saw a danger. The idea of state aid for churches and cathedrals was still being mooted, and appeared to be strengthening. The Commissioners agreed that no further requests should be made which might endanger what was clearly an important initiative. Furthermore, another debate in General Synod would be sure to rake over old ashes and rekindle arguments about the purpose of the Commissioners' money and the

---

[38] Board minutes, 19 Oct. 1972, pp. 5–6.
[39] Correspondence in paper, 'Redundant Churches Fund: third annual report', 11 May 1972, CC (72) 47, Board papers, 15 May 1972, ser. 95083/35.

commitment of the state.[40] In this sphere, then, the age of Ramsey drew to a close with matters very much in the air.

[40] Board minutes, 20 Dec. 1973.

PART III

'CATCHING UP':
THE PRIMACY OF ARCHBISHOP COGGAN,
1974–1979

9

The Struggle for the Stipend and the New Austerity

The stipend

Donald Coggan moved from the archbishopric of York to that of
Canterbury, and the Church Commissioners moved his belongings
from Bishopthorpe to Lambeth and to Canterbury Old Palace, at the
close of 1974. Coggan came to represent the 'short' 1970s much as
Ramsey had defined the 'long' 1960s. Some found him a less
memorable archbishop than his predecessors, but then his primacy
coincided with what might well appear a less significant period
altogether – and his stay was a short one.

Meanwhile, the Church Commissioners could now look from an
august height over a range of achievements. In 1977 they became a
part of a new ministry co-ordinating group and were attached by a
joint liaison committee to the Central Board of Finance. By the end of
the Coggan era the Church Commissioners and the Central Board of
Finance would both be chaired by Ronald Harris in his capacity as
First Church Estates Commissioner. This was no mean feat, and it
would not prove an easy task – either for the steady Harris or for his
successor.

The new constellation at the apex of the Church Commissioners
worked with a happy confidence. Coggan himself brought a quiet but
firm and consistent commitment to their work. From Ramsey he
inherited the art of rotating the chair of the Board, alternating where
necessary with the archbishop of York, Stuart Blanch, and the bishop
of London, Gerald Ellison. Harris, however generous to Ramsey,
noticed a difference, and one for the better. By now, Harris had made
the work of the First Church Estates Commissioner thoroughly his
own and had also established a close rapport with the Third Church
Estates Commissioner, Betty Ridley. Furthermore, he could feel with
satisfaction that the long years during which Silsoe had avoided
Church Assembly were more and more remote in the corporate

memory. Harris was a regular and unimpeachable presence in Synod, performing with poise, weight and affable self-assurance. He even found himself invited to give a series of Lenten lectures at Truro Cathedral, an undertaking which he carried off with aplomb, amiably juggling references to John Stuart Mill, C. F. Andrews, R. H. Tawney, Hans Kung and the Taizé community.[1] The general election of 1974, meanwhile, displaced the Second Church Estates Commissioner, Marcus Worsley, and brought a new name, the Labour MP for Kingswood, Bristol, Terrance Walker. In the art of appointment the Commissioners, even so, remained true to their traditions. In 1978 Worsley turned up once more as a Commissioner and deputy-chairman of the Assets Committee. Meanwhile, the secretary's office passed from Kenneth Ryle to a new figure at 1 Millbank, Paul Osmond.

Theologians might paint images of the Christian Church with rich colours and poetic eloquence, but the ongoing realities of money and bricks and mortar demand a less exciting vocabulary and are characterised by a more mundane pattern of affairs. Few in the Church could consider the Church Commissioners an essentially exciting enterprise. In many ways they were becoming less and less attractive because they were increasingly embroiled in thorny practical matters which offered few opportunities to the creative mind. More exciting was the politics of investment, for the endurance in South Africa of a system of racial apartheid was now inspiring not merely international disapproval but public campaigns, and campaigns which proposed a new instrument of opposition: economic withdrawal.

By 1979 the Commissioners understood their duties more than ever in terms of the conventional trinity: stipends, houses and pensions. Coggan had certainly proved himself to be a Christian with a liberal conscience, concerned for chaplaincies in universities, for foreign students and for the international mission of the Church. But as far as the Commissioners could see, the import of their trinity of commitments in a time of economic constraint was unarguable. This was not a time for adventures. In the 1970s the organisational life of the Church of England could be seen more than ever to conform to the general patterns of anxiety and self-interest which had come to characterise British corporate life. As the British economy was transfixed by the spectre of high inflation, the institutions of the Church watched the rising costs of living and the growth of salaries everywhere with gloom and sensed how easily all that they had achieved could suddenly be lost.

[1] See Ronald Harris, *Memory-soft the air: recollections of life with cabinet, crown and Church*, Edinburgh 1987, 221–37.

It was during the Coggan period that the clergy stipend assumed a massive presence in the deliberations of the Commissioners. Important in its own right, it influenced much else. It effectively led debates about the stipends of the bishops (of all kinds), the higher clergy, the deans, provosts and canons, the lay workers. In its train it brought pensions, for these, too, were measured against the stipend. The Commissioners also observed bleakly that their own costs mounted, relentlessly. These would prove taxing years.

The Central Stipends Authority

The great commission of the Central Stipends Authority was to set down what the ranges should be each year, to show what the cost to each diocese must be if they were to meet them and then to add the additional minimum allocation for stipends for the year made by the Commissioners. In such a way would the funds of the Commissioners ensure that every clergyman, whatever his benefice or diocese, and every deaconess or licensed lay worker, managed to clamber onto the agreed national scale. The CSA would bring a gentle pressure to bear on the dioceses to find as much money as they could, and the dioceses would do the same to their laity. This arrangement of parts was now linked more explicitly than ever into a clear mechanism. In return for an allocation from the Commissioners – ordinarily a quarter, or perhaps a third, of the overall figure, and this for every diocese – the dioceses would be asked to explain the terms on which their allocation was offered to the laity in the parishes, and would then seek to raise from them at least the balance of the new money required to meet that target. Moreover, the Commissioners recommended that from 1 April 1976 there be adopted a common, standard definition of income which would serve as the basis for future augmentation, something which would be put forward by the CSA for the approval of the General Synod. They should also seek a common method of computation – no mean feat, for there were immense variations. If they were able to do this, dioceses could still pay their clergy above the minimum target range as long as they raised the incomes of all their clergy, deaconesses and licensed lay workers as the adopted scales required.[2]

A deep-seated fear remained. It was suggested that dioceses which had done well so far in paying their clergy might be penalised, as they would not qualify for as much as those that had done poorly. It was also being said that those who would receive most would also have to do the most to help themselves. To attempt to formulate a scheme of grant-giving which actually took money-raising into account would be

[2] Board minutes, 20 Feb. 1975, pp. 1–2.

impossibly complex and time-consuming. The Church could not wait; what mattered was to act now. At the same time there was little inclination to pursue sanctions against dioceses which failed to meet national expectations. To withhold money from a diocese which figured way down on the income table would penalise not the diocese but its clergy. It was seen to be better to move quietly, to write to the dioceses which might be criticised for tardiness on stipends and to exploit personal contacts with them.

The world of the stipend was not simply concerned with the level of income. It also dealt with the deployment of clergy. To ensure that no diocese fell below an agreed number of clergy the Church Commissioners contrived a new mechanism and a new form of financial support. This was called 'pump-priming', or 'Sheffield pump-priming', for it bore the name of that diocese. Pump-priming had begun in 1977 with a modest sum of £140,000 to be spent over four years. Now the General Purposes Committee had become convinced not merely of the financial value of the policy, but of its political merit too. It had not penalised dioceses which were over-staffed. It was also not so grand as to inspire protests from dioceses which did not benefit from it. The pump-priming funds were allocated to twelve dioceses, all urban and northern, except Southwell.[3]

The danger of inflation

In the year in which Coggan became archbishop of Canterbury, inflation had begun to spiral upwards. The government responded promptly with a new White Paper: *The attack on inflation* which announced a battery of new counter-inflationary policies, chief among which was the control of incomes. At the onset of 1975 the GPC at 1 Millbank concurred that it was in the interests of the Church, too, to ensure 'the conquest of inflation'. They also reflected glumly that the laity, from whom the dioceses now expected more money than ever, would be caught up in this new period of constraint. The returns of 1975 were expected to reveal 'a repetition of the usual and discouraging situation', that about a third of all incumbents were returning incomes below the lower end of the approved range, and that more than ever were below the range altogether.[4]

The retail price index showed that the cost of living had risen between April 1974 and April 1975 by no less than 21.7 per cent. The trades unions agitated for wage increases to keep pace. At 1 Millbank

[3] GPC paper, 'Stipends ranges and scales in 1980', CC (79) 54, annex D, pp. 11–15, Board papers, 28 June 1979, ser. 95083/47.
[4] GPC report, 'Stipend levels and the Commissioners' allocations', CC (75) 68, Board papers, 1 Apr. 1975, ibid. pt 41.

such a figure turned the minds of the Commissioners again towards familiar questions. When all their exemptions and benefits were adumbrated, how could they measure the material conditions of the clergy as a breed? A letter was sent out to all diocesan bishops. The Commissioners were now set to propose that from 1 April 1976 the range for incumbents' stipends should increase from £2,100–£2,500 *per annum* to £2,400–£2,750 *per annum*, on the understanding that approved working expenses should be reimbursed in full. Archdeacons, assistant curates, deaconesses and lay workers would receive a comparable stipend, on the same terms. Bishops' stipends would be attended to in due course.

It was in this context that the figure of John Smallwood, from the diocese of Southwark, stepped into the foreground. By the mid-1970s Smallwood had established a defining, even heroic, presence in the stipendiary debates of the Church; in the papers of the Church Commissioners he appears again and again as a veritable Valiant-for-Truth in search of the right statistics, the proper interpretation and the just policy. Smallwood was tenacious in his quest for improvements. He was also something like a one-man civil service, working parallel to the Commissioners' own, turning out figures by the column and papers by the dozen. In July 1975 Smallwood was already pressing that incumbents be assured that whatever the government's restrictions on incomes, working expenses would still be fully reimbursed, and that no limit should be set upon them. But the Board was dubious. They must 'maintain the pressure on the parishes' to reimburse working expenses, and be quite explicit about this to the bishops. At the same time they must not seem to use this as a way of circumventing the government's incomes policy.[5] In such a way, and in one meeting, could the battle-lines of future campaigns be seen emerging with an awful clarity.

Church and State: National Insurance: employed or not?

It was not only the size of the stipend that troubled the Church Commissioners and the new CSA. As far as National Insurance was concerned, ministers of religion, unless clearly employed in a specifically salaried post, were classified as self-employed. This had by now been questioned by both Labour and Conservative governments. In November 1969 the Labour Government had even proposed to the Church Assembly that the classification be changed. This was voted down, largely because of cost. The ecumenical body which existed to represent the Churches' views on public policies, the Churches Main Committee, also threw the proposal out and soon the whole political

[5] Board minutes, 24 July 1975, pp. 3–4.

scheme, of which the proposal was a part, had in any case sunk without trace.

In July 1973 the Conservative government tested the mind of the Church again. This time a new social security paper sought to frame a new scheme in which all ministers of religion became 'employed earners', and the body responsible for paying the office-holder became the 'employer', and therefore liable for National Insurance contributions too. But then within a year the government had been defeated in a general election. The subsequent Labour government made broad changes to the Conservatives' scheme, but left those parts which touched the clergy as they found them. The Churches Main Committee issued a further challenge and a concession was won: a new regulation was contrived to allow ministers of religion to continue as 'self-employed', at least until 1 April 1977. During this time it was suggested that the Churches could work out their own views.

The debate itself, and the failure of the politicians to resolve it tidily, was no accident. It was a quagmire in which men of the sharpest intellect could sink; a morass of readjustments, new terminology, new ratios or percentages or guarantees. The fundamental question facing the Churches was one of simple material advantage. If the clergy were classified as 'employed', should they be contracted in or out of the state scheme? If they contracted out, the National Insurance contribution paid by the clergy themselves would decrease. But that would then leave the Church Commissioners with an employer's contribution to pay. The General Purposes Committee was inclined to feel that contracting out would enable 'a greater degree of control and integration with the State scheme' than the alternative. But then they also observed that if it meant that they should put aside large funds to meet future pensions, contracting out might actually prove almost as expensive as contracting in. While the committee held stoutly to the view that they should not be swayed by governments, or by other Churches for that matter, they might note that other Churches too were drawing this conclusion. In truth, the burdens of self-employment were growing and the clergy, too, appeared to favour change.

All things considered the committee recommended to the Board that the clergy should now become, officially, 'employed'. That the state pension was, after retirement, proofed against inflation seemed a 'major benefit', and there were other entitlements which might be noted and felt to be worth having: entitlement to unemployment and earnings-related sickness benefit, entitlement to sickness benefits if on holiday in the European Community. Harris warned the Board that it was by no means certain that the government would, at any event, accept that the clergy should remain self-employed.[6] The Board approved and so, in July 1976, did the General Synod.

A sudden change then occurred. On 22 July 1976 the Chancellor of the Exchequer, Denis Healey, announced an increase of 2 per cent in the employers' National Insurance contribution. This would mean another £700,000 for the Commissioners to find each year in addition to the £350,000 for which they had budgeted. The opinion of the Church, so laboriously determined, had rested on figures which had become, in a single day, obsolete. The General Purposes Committee agreed in a flurry that a letter should be sent to the Chancellor expressing 'extreme concern' and asking for exemption. After all, who actually did employ the clergy? The Church Commissioners were only partly responsible for paying the clergy, who still answered in important respects to the definition of 'self-employed'. Ronald Harris was not shy of pulling out all the stops. His letter to 11 Downing Street began, 'It is only rarely that the Commissioners venture to seek the assistance of the Chancellor in his joint capacity as Chancellor and a Commissioner.' These new costs could in no way be passed on by way of increased prices or charges, as might work in a commercial organisation. They must only serve to reduce the funds from which the clergy could be paid, and the clergy, who had 'probably been amongst the hardest hit of all in the lower-paid category of workers, would thus be doubly penalised', would also be more heavily taxed and would find prices rising around them as the commercial world sought to compensate for their own rising employment costs. In short, the Church may face 'grave and far-reaching' effects on its ministry, its churches; a nation which needed its ministry must feel the same. It could be stretched beyond its powers.

Church Commissioner or not, Healey stood firm. The new levy was necessary 'to encourage our national economy'. The public sector borrowing requirement must be reduced if the economy was to have an export-led and investment-based recovery from recession. Public expenditure must be cut; taxation must be raised. This new course might seem damaging, but it was less damaging than others. The economic future of the country rested on its counter-inflation policy. The Church would benefit from an improvement in the economy, after all. To make a special case of the Churches would be 'impossible'.[7]

This letter the General Purposes Committee dissected. They wanted national recovery too, but did not see why the Church and other charities should have to pay this much more for it. The Chancellor had argued that the burden must be spread 'evenly'. This was not at all

---

[6] GPC report, 'NI', CC (76) 30, Board papers, 22 Apr. 1976, ser. 95083/41.

[7] GPC report, 'NI', CC (76) 91, pp. 4–7, Board papers, 16 Sept. 1976, ibid. pt 42.

even. Healey had said that exemptions, 'however worthwhile and desirable in themselves' would amount to selectivity, and that would deflate the policy itself and make it more complicated to manage. This the committee found most disturbing of all. Who now had a voice to speak against it? Should the Commissioners write a new letter? Should they send a deputation? Should they report again to the General Synod in November? The committee was unanimous that an effort should be made to resist 'this new form of tax levy' upon the Churches. They agreed upon a deputation, but waited to see what view emerged from the collective mind of the Churches Main Committee.[8]

By the time the Board met in October 1976, the Churches Main Committee had proposed that a deputation be dispatched to 10 Downing Street on behalf of the Churches and the National Council of Social Service, 'to be led if possible by the archbishop of Canterbury on the one hand and Lord Allen of Abbeydale on the other'. For Allen, too, had protested and had received much the same treatment as the Church Commissioners. Until this had happened, a formal decision on the status of the clergy should be withheld from the state, and they should ask for the current exemption to be extended by a further year.[9] The new alliance gathered its powers and in January 1977 the joint deputation walked past 11 Downing Street to Number 10. The fruits of persistence fell justly upon them. Exemption from the surcharge was secured.

Catching up

By the summer of 1976 it could be seen that some clergy were paid stipends lower than the national minimum recommended by the CSA at least in part because of the government's incomes policy. In the following December the Board of the Church Commissioners agreed that further publicity must encourage the dioceses and the parishes to work harder to finance the clergy stipend. The Commissioners tried to manoeuvre within the government's incomes policy, but a deputation to the Department of Employment was told firmly that no compromise was possible and no concession could be made. The Second Estates Commissioner, Terence Walker, murmured that he had been told the same 'at Ministerial level'. This did nothing to temper fears within the Church itself. In April 1977 it said that at 1 Millbank they might soon face 'wide-ranging and inequitable differentials, comparable with those produced by differing endowments in the 19th century, and a consequent "freezing" of deployment and pastoral reorganisation … care must be taken to preserve the concept of a

[8] Ibid. pp. 1–3.
[9] Board minutes, 21 Oct. 1976, pp. 1–2.

national policy'. Now, when clergy stipends were being discussed, the word 'plight' began to appear again in the minutes.[10] There was another deputation. On 12 May 1977 the secretary, Paul Osmond, and Terence Walker visited the Department of Employment hoping that the clergy might be allowed rises above those permitted by the second stage of the government's pay policy. They were firmly turned down. The clergy were classed as 'employed persons', and from that certain things must follow. If the Commissioners did not like it they could take the matter to arbitration: 'that was up to them'.[11]

One consequence of the increasingly heavy emphasis on the stipend was that funding for it actually began to draw on money committed to other areas of the Commissioners' responsibilities. By the summer of 1977 it was argued that the increase in dignitaries' stipends could be achieved, in part, by reducing by £50,000 a year the additional grant previously proposed for cathedral chapters. Yet it could also be seen that if the minimum stipend for incumbents were achieved the Commissioners would lack the resources to achieve a basic pension rate of one half of the original stipend.[12] For the stipend was no easier to detach from other commitments than it ever had been.

Now the war against inflation took a new turn. In July 1977 the government announced the third phase of its incomes policy. Wage increases should be kept beneath 10 per cent. It was at once obvious that the Church Commissioners were hardly marching to its orders. In the same month the CSA had settled, but not yet announced, an increase in the clergy stipend that would amount to no less than 14.5 per cent. The Commissioners prepared to defend their ground. It was stressed that 14.5 per cent applied only to those who were presently receiving least. But if the mind of the CSA was set, soon the dioceses were coming back with different views. The Chichester board of finance had agreed to keep within the government's guidelines. In Southwark, by contrast, they wanted to raise the stipend even higher than did the CSA. When it met in January 1978 the Board of the Commissioners confirmed their July decision. All statistical material supported it – and now it was said that the dioceses could hardly feel other than disappointed if an intention which had been declared, albeit quietly, was now to be disclaimed. As for government fears, it was clear that if the proposed changes were put into effect, only about a third of incumbents would receive a rise of 14.5 per cent, and some would receive very little. As a 'national group', therefore, the increases for the clergy should not threaten the government's limit. The dignitaries, meanwhile – except the residentiary canons – would be

10 Ibid. 21 Apr. 1977, p. 2.
11 Ibid. 26 May 1977, p. 1.
12 Ibid. 28 July 1977, pp. 2–5.

spared embarrassment and receive 10 per cent exactly. Even this was risky: at least one voice was raised against this 'compression' of differentials.[13]

The structures and understandings upon which the entire work of the CSA rested were now looking increasingly fragile. It took only a single memorandum by one critic to show all too clearly how one complaint might lead at once to a battery of others. David Hopkinson of the Chichester diocese wrote that he was suspicious of centralisation and anything that smacked of 'corporatism'. It was not for the CSA to negotiate wages with the government. Granted, the clergy were underpaid. But so were many laymen. He did not accept the distinction between dignitaries and clergy at all: they should all be dealt with together. He even doubted that the CSA itself should exist. He perceived it as in conflict with the diocesan boards. Dioceses should not baldly receive allocations, but should share their resources amongst themselves as part of their Christian duty.[14] However the Church Commissioners represented what the CSA was doing, government policy was not being upheld. Soon Hopkinson was not alone. People across the Church were grumbling, and not quietly.

On that last point, at least, Paul Osmond could now reassure the Board. He had visited the Department of Employment again, and government had declared itself satisfied with what was afoot.[15] Betty Ridley now saw the need to justify the CSA itself before complaints against it gathered fatal momentum. Since 1972 it had, she observed, achieved much of what it had set out to do, above all in establishing and raising a minimum stipend. It had worked with care and in partnership with the dioceses, not least through the annual stipends conferences and the ongoing discussions which arose between their officers. Without the CSA the clergy would have struggled more in this age of inflation. Hopkinson was wrong to argue that it had undertaken negotiations with the government, for these exchanges could not be called negotiations 'strictly speaking'; they were only what had been necessary for a body which had to maintain a national policy of scales and ranges. Nor was the CSA remote from the dioceses and parishes – of its thirty members only one had not been a member of the General Synod and seventeen were 'Synod elected Commissioners'.[16] After

[13] Ibid. 26 Jan. 1978, pp. 2–5.
[14] Hopkinson note, annex C to GPC report, 'The future of the Central Stipends Authority', CC (78) 12, Board papers, 30 Mar. 1978, ser. 95083/46. See also Board minutes, 30 Mar. 1978.
[15] Board minutes, 20 July 1978, pp. 1–4.
[16] Ridley letter, annex D to GPC report, 'The future of the Central Stipends Authority', CC (78) 12, Board papers, 30 Mar. 1978, ser. 95083/46.

rather little debate, the Board endorsed the CSA and agreed that it should continue as it had until now.

The campaign for stipends now intensified. In July 1978 the Board had agreed that there must now be 'a major "catching up" operation' and that a new national minimum stipend for 1979 should be set at £3,300 *per annum,* an increase of 13.8 per cent with a new recommended range of £3,500 to £3,800. A statement was issued to the press, entitled firmly 'Clergy pay needs to catch up'. If the public consulted the retail price index of April 1978 it would be clear that clergy, deaconesses and lay workers were receiving at least £700– £1,000 less than they should. Between 1970 and 1975 they had fallen behind 'average (monthly paid) male salaries': these had increased by 95 per cent while theirs had grown only by 40 per cent. For three years the government's pay policy had prevented any effort to make up the 'lost ground' and the Church had been obedient. It was all the more important in this context to observe the role of the laity in raising this money; the Commissioners would provide only a quarter of it. The 'essential justice' of the new increases should surely be understood by government and employers and employed 'in other walks of life'.[17]

No sooner had this appeared than, on the very next day, the government published a new White Paper expressing the view that no increases in income should rise above 5 per cent. It did not take the Board of the Church Commissioners by surprise. But it was seen at once that this new government paper differed from its two predecessors in one important respect. It did not announce a statutory incomes policy; it appealed, but did not compel. As far as the Church of England was concerned, the appeal fell on stony ground. The CSA stuck to its guns. The dioceses were told that only something of 'quite unusual and unexpected importance' would alter the new recommendations.

To this the Department of Employment did not turn a blind eye. They invited representatives of the Commissioners to explain themselves. A dry letter from Harold Walker, Minister of State at the Department of Employment, observed that his department found the new announcement by the Church 'quite clearly in excess' of the government's guidelines and 'incompatible with the objectives of its pay policy'. He feared what would happen if the Church's example were followed elsewhere; the 'substantial improvement' so far achieved in the general economic situation might end; living standards would deteriorate and the lower paid would be affected most heavily. He had read their submission and still found it all 'singularly unfortunate in the circumstances'. They should reconsider.[18]

[17] Board minutes, 20 July 1978.
[18] S. P. Osmond note, 'Clergy stipends and government incomes policy', and

The Commissioners were unrepentant. The Church had behaved well, it had abided by the first stages of the government's policy and it was now a 'very firm view in the Church that, after a period of three years in which stipends have been "caught" at a particularly depressed level, steps must start to be taken at once towards achieving at least some part of the "catching-up" operation that we believe to be desirable and justified'. Moreover, nothing less than justice required that further increases should follow: this was only 'a modest first step'. Most of the funds were given voluntarily by the laity and were not strictly inflationary because they would otherwise have been spent on goods and services. The money was simply passing, in a sense, 'sideways'. The rise would produce no increase in prices: 'the general parochial ministrations of the clergy are available free to all who seek them'. These recommendations were the outcome of deliberate and careful discussions with all forty-three dioceses. The CSA did not feel that any modification could be justified.[19]

From the Department of Employment there came no reply.

Southwark's £4,000

At a time when British labour relations were being torn to shreds by strikes over pay, the Church of England was showing that its own internal affairs were similarly beset. The credibility of the CSA rested heavily on its ability to show consistency in its dealings with dioceses and consistency of policy over time. But pressure is a danger to consistency, and the authority faced mounting pressure on every joint, every sinew, of its work. In these circumstances it was more than ever difficult to build regular structures: the foundations were shifting constantly. It was all too easy to end up crying for uniformity where there was no uniformity.

The dioceses had accepted the new rise proposed by the CSA. But now Southwark broke ranks and proceeded to announce a higher minimum stipend of £4,000 for its incumbents for the year 1979. This suddenly called everything into question: immediately, the CSA received 'strong representations' from other dismayed dioceses. Was this in order? The men of Southwark pressed the Commissioners to support or repudiate them: their diocesan synod would meet on 26 October to confirm the figure and they must know the mind of the Commissioners first. Osmond was caught out; the question shot towards the General Purposes Committee. In something of a fluster it decided that Southwark's proposal was acceptable. It was not difficult to concede on a technicality: the world of clergy stipends was brimful

annexes, CC (78) 72, Board papers, 28 Sept. 1978, ser. 95083/46.
[19] Ibid. annex III.

of technical inconsistencies. The mind of the Board was not available to them: it did not meet again until 23 November which was too late. A new circular letter was dispatched to the dioceses on 13 October 1978. There would now be a modification of what had been agreed because of the 'strong representations' of one diocese. The minimum stipend would remain as it had been announced, but for a diocese which, like Southwark, had no 'internal differentials scheme for incumbents' the minimum could be considered to be £4,000:

> The reason for this change is, briefly, that where a diocese does not apply differentials for incumbents but nevertheless wishes to establish its general level of stipends as high as possible, it is not, by setting its standard at £3,800, able to achieve as high an *average* stipend as it would wish – and may indeed be able – to achieve, whereas this is possible, and is achieved, by dioceses which do in one form or another apply differential payments.

The CSA accepted what Southwark was doing: 'the £200 difference between £3,800 and £4,000 may be regarded as an "averaged-out" payment in lieu of differentials'. It added a promise that the ranges would be discussed fully at the next series of stipends conferences.[20]

This was a fatal mistake. The reaction was instant. The other dioceses tumbled over each other in rage. They heaped contumely upon Southwark and chastised those who had conceded. The bishop of Birmingham lamented that the purpose of the CSA was to promote a degree of uniformity, not more confusion. Moreover, 'I must make you aware that there is a grave feeling in some dioceses that policies are arranged to suit the convenience of the Diocese of Southwark, which is so heavily represented on the Church Commissioners.' Worse came from the bishop of Bradford, who observed that in his diocese they had had to make a great effort to reach £3,300 at all. If the CSA had sought to set a standard in stipends it had now made its own aspirations 'completely meaningless'. If this double standard between rich dioceses and poor continued then 'serious questions' would be asked about the Commissioners' policy in distributing its stipends funds. The bishop of Chelmsford added: 'I must say I was disturbed hearing the Bishop of Southwark speak on the subject when he casually threw out that, in justification for an increase to £4,000 a year, other dioceses have other (he suggested) undercover ways of augmenting stipends for their clergy.' Chelmsford had stuck strictly to the CSA's own scales and ranges, and so did 'a good many others'. If

[20] GPC report, 'Modification of the stipends policy for 1979/80', CC (78) 90, Board papers, 23 Nov. 1978, ibid.

more of this followed it would have a 'very grave effect' on the deployment of clergy. The bishop of Chichester wrote that nobody there understood the 'logic of the arithmetic' of the CSA's new justification. It made nonsense of all that had been agreed and seemed to 'throw the door wide open to those who want to push up stipends to a very high level'. The diocesan secretary of the Coventry diocese complained that the decision 'smacks of improper conduct' and undermined the very credibility of the CSA. The bishop of Durham, John Habgood, wrote of 'disquiet' that the CSA should be 'browbeaten' by Southwark. It was 'improper'; the credibility of the CSA must be restored. But he was also anxious that these rises, as a whole, contradicted the government's incomes policy:

> It is not that the clergy do not want increases; of course they do. As responsible citizens, though, we surely have an obligation to give a lead in supporting Government policy, however painful this may be. Our whole ability to speak in a disinterested way about the industrial and commercial life of the nation depends on being in an unassailable position.

Controversy mounted, horribly. There were letters from a surprised and concerned bishop of Jarrow, from the chair of the Durham diocesan board of finance; concern in Ely; 'bewilderment', 'bitter disappointment' and lamentations of 'calamity' in Gloucester ('everything has suddenly crumbled'); protest in Guildford; disturbance in Lichfield; dismay in Newcastle; complaints from a fuming Oxford and a resistant Truro; and even reports of 'chaos' in Peterborough (where the general secretary was not actually convinced that the clergy were underpaid in the first place). St Albans had been 'considerably taken aback'. All was indignation, uproar, consternation, accusation.[21]

This needed to be pulled back together, and quickly. Harris set to work, drafting an artful memorandum as chair of the General Purposes Committee. In June 1978, he noted carefully, the dioceses had all agreed that the Church should move towards a single national scale, subject to some phasing in. Southwark, he observed, had already had a scale somewhat above the average. Its more substantial rise could still be represented as a part of a steady long-term adjustment – downwards – towards a new national scale, though it must be conceded that, in the meantime, it perpetuated a discrepancy. And indeed it could be seen that Southwark was not alone, for Hereford, too, was agitating to pay more.[22]

---

[21] Ibid.
[22] GPC report, 'Proposed stipend scale for 1979 for curates', CC (78) 86, ibid.

John Smallwood had for some months warned the General Purposes Committee that Southwark would choose to enhance its scale for curates and he had encountered no resistance. But then Southwark had also decided to pay some 150 assistant staff £600 or more above the national levels, quite contrary to the CSA's recommendations. Early words of warning, complained Smallwood's critics on the committee, did not constitute a formal notification that the diocese of Southwark would not abide by new recommendations. Feeling was now running high. The credibility of the CSA was at stake. Southwark might inspire a destructive pattern. By seven votes to none (with two abstentions, one of them Smallwood) the committee resolved on 'the strongest possible action' against the diocese. But what should that be? It was hard to see how a penalty might be worked out without running into a mathematical mire or accidentally altering policies which had been widely accepted across the dioceses as a whole. Perhaps the Commissioners could simply express strong disapproval? This last course did not capture the mood of the committee. It had been too badly stung to mince words.[23]

In November 1978 the matter came before the Board, on this occasion chaired by archbishop Coggan. Harris tried to be amenable and was, again, subtle. He observed that a withdrawal of Southwark's new allocation should not be seen as 'punitive', but as a matter of redistribution. Smallwood resisted. Indignation across the dioceses was not because of what Southwark had done, but because the CSA had changed its rules to accommodate it. That was not Southwark's fault, for they had not themselves sought a change in the rules and had not thought it necessary. After all, the CSA was still in the business of recommending, not requiring. Oswald Clark, also of Southwark, agreed. Harris remonstrated that Smallwood was a member of the GPC and had been party both to Southwark's decision and the decision to change the policy of the CSA. The debate was robust. At last Smallwood asked the Board to consult the Holy Spirit for lessons, reading a passage from Scripture and speaking of love and peace – all of which might well suggest that something very like a riot had broken out. Next time, he added, they should meet at Lambeth Palace after a service of holy communion. Archbishop Coggan and 'several other members' sagely agreed that this would be a good thing. A decision was deferred. Southwark was invited to reconsider.[24]

When the Board next met in December, it was not at Lambeth, nor did it meet for holy communion. For Lambeth was found to be impractical, and people who had distances to travel could not arrive early. They could not conclude with holy communion either because

[23] Ibid. pp. 3–4.
[24] Board minutes, 23 Nov. 1974.

the First Church Estates Commissioner and others had to go on to a meeting of the Assets Committee. But the archbishop began with a reading and a prayer and it was wondered if a eucharist could be managed in July. At this unpropitious hour, it so happened that the draft of the Sixth Report of the CSA was being duly offered to the General Synod. Smallwood offered a new paper of statistics to show the deterioration of the clergy stipend since 1970 and asked if the CSA report should be submitted to Synod, not merely for information but for debate. But Harris observed drily that submission to Synod did not require a debate – that had never happened before – and that nobody had asked for it this time. Smallwood pressed on. The Church needed to know the situation with regard to stipends, not least to encourage those whose efforts to pay their clergy had, he thought, shown 'serious shortcomings'. They must not move only at the speed of the slowest dioceses.

In the hurly-burly one theme came to the fore. The men of Southwark were not simply seeking to question figures and methods. They were also attempting to wrest the whole debate about the clergy stipend from the hands of the bureaucrats and throw it into the courts of the synodical bodies of the Church. Now Paul Osmond received a missive from the bishop of Southwark, Mervyn Stockwood. Stockwood began as grandly as he could, as Episcopal Commissioner, diocesan bishop and member of the Board of governors. He had for years, he said, been concerned about the way the Church exploited its clergy 'at all levels and in every diocese'. 'We must', he said, 'listen to the General Synod voice, and not just to diocesan secretaries.' In Southwark they did not wish to undermine the CSA, but to negotiate and to persuade, not on the basis of 'levelling down' but 'levelling up'. As a declaration of good faith Southwark would propose a compromise. They would reduce their scales of pay for assistant staff by £200 and pay them from their own ministry fund. He also proposed that curates' stipends should be raised nationally by £200 at all points, 'and that this should be financed by Millbank'. Surely money could be found for this? Perhaps the Assets Committee could provide it.[25] Harris responded that this was all very unhelpful. Apart from anything else, Stockwood's compromise must involve yet another change of mind and policy by the CSA. There had been enough of that already.[26]

When the Board met again the diocese of Southwark was there in full strength, bristling, unrepentant. Southwark, deplored Smallwood, was being penalised simply for being open about its business. Its

[25] GPC report, 'Proposed stipend scale for 1979 for curates', annex 2, CC (78) 104, Board papers, 21 Dec. 1978, ser. 95083/46.
[26] Harris note ibid.

measures were true to the policy adopted by the General Synod after its discussion of a recent report, 'The Remuneration of the clergy'. He repeated that the CSA had not set down conditions. Clark urged that the feelings of the Southwark diocesan synod appeared more pressing to him than the 'constitutional' arguments now proffered by the CSA itself. Not much ground was being given by the other side, either. What mattered was the situation in all dioceses, most of which were neither 'pace-makers' nor 'laggards', and what was at stake was an agreed policy, 'common to all', which rested upon consultation and co-operation. Dioceses already possessed the power to vary as they saw fit, but they did so within the recommendations of the CSA.

Two motions now lay before them. The Board voted unanimously (the Southwark three abstaining) against a deduction of £90,000 *per annum* from the Commissioners' stipends allocation, but agreed by seventeen votes to one (the Southwark three again abstaining) to deny the bishop of Southwark his plea for assistant staff and also to withdraw the allocation of £37,000 of 'new' money for 1979. Smallwood moved in response that the same be done to every other diocese which did not comply 'fully and in detail' with the CSA's recommendations. This was lost by eighteen to twenty votes. One of the opponents was the bishop of Southwell. This would prove significant.[27]

The pursuit of peace with justice

What now of the government's incomes policy? In this quarter at least there was silence. Nobody in the Church evidently observed that though they might chastise the diocese of Southwark for breaking ranks, Southwark had only done to the Church of England what the Church itself had done to the government of the country.

Left to the diplomats, peace might now have been won. The months unfolded more gently; tempers were improved. Southwark attempted to be more amenable. After Christmas its representatives met some of the Commissioners and soon suggested that the diocese revise its scale for assistant staff downwards. Osmond conveyed the news to the Board with his strong endorsement. The Board accepted it, unanimously, at its January meeting. The bishop of Southwell then initiated a reconsideration of that earlier decision to withdraw the £37,000 from Southwark. That, it was agreed, should be restored only when Southwark's diocesan synod confirmed the new, lower levels for assistant staff. But this settlement was overthrown by a further meeting of the Southwark synod, which gathered in special session on 27 January, and for two-and-a-half hours. Osmond attended on behalf

[27] Board minutes, 21 Dec. 1978, pp. 1–7.

of the Commissioners and spoke there. There followed three motions. A vote took place on the compromise which the Board of the Commissioners had endorsed, moved by the archdeacon of Southwark. It was lost by seventy-five votes to sixty-seven. A motion that the synod should stand firm by its decision of October was firmly passed, by eighty-nine votes to fifty-eight. The bureaucrats and the diplomats were routed and sent scuttling back to their offices.[28]

The Board of the Commissioners simply 'took note' of all this and passed it all back to the General Purposes Committee before getting on with the next item on the agenda, a formidable national survey of the state of the clergy stipend by John Smallwood, which criticised both the laity and the dioceses for giving too little money to the cause. Smallwood did not mince his words: 'He believed that financial inertia, in some cases linked to dependence on such endowments, lay at the root of inadequate stipends.' This provoked a brief flurry of debate, some members suggesting instead that stipend allocations should relate to the 'potential' of a diocese, perhaps taking into account the average wage there. It was seen that poorer areas often gave more than wealthier ones. The debates of the Board were increasingly caught between Smallwood, who thought the Commissioners too mean, and Canon Marlow, of the diocese of Birmingham, who thought them too generous.[29]

The insurrection spreads

By March it was clear that Southwark was not alone. Chichester was falling out of line; Lincoln too. The former offered a compromise; the latter confessed that it had sinned innocently. The Board tried not to let its collective eyes wander, but looking again at the plea of Southwark they gave a little moral ground, agreeing unanimously that the allocation to Southwark should still be withheld, but for 1979 alone, and without prejudice to the decision that must be made about 1980. Lincoln's allocation was cut back firmly; the money that was saved was redistributed among those in particular need: Blackburn, Bristol, Chester and Wakefield. When Smallwood, who had left the room while the fate of Southwark was being discussed, heard this he complained that the Board was now adopting an altered definition of the term 'curates'. If this was so, Southwark should be informed, for if new changes were now occurring to suit Lincoln and Chichester their own calculations must be affected. Before pandemonium broke out again Smallwood and Oswald Clark were asked to withdraw from the

[28] GPC report, 'Proposed stipend scale for assistant staff: diocese of Southwark', CC (79) 15, Board papers, 25 Jan. 1979, ser. 95083/47.
[29] See Board minutes, 25 Feb. 1979, pp. 3–5.

meeting. The Board found its feet again. Smallwood and Clark were readmitted. Smallwood then observed tartly that if Lincoln and Chichester were having discussions with the CSA Southwark should be admitted to the party. This precipitated a debate on procedure. Then a further vote took place: that the judgement on Southwark be upheld 'except insofar as the consistency of the figures in regard to other dioceses was concerned'; that Lincoln and Chichester be referred back to the General Purposes Committee, along with no less than three motions by Smallwood himself about the definition of 'curates'.[30]

The revolt over stipends was no longer confined to the dioceses. It was a revolt not only of quantity but of quality, for it had surfaced in the House of Bishops too. In January 1979 Harris had spoken to the house about clergy stipends. This focused minds in that quarter. The bishop of Liverpool, David Sheppard, wrote to archbishop Coggan that it would be quite wrong in the present economic climate if the dignitaries received a rise of more than 5 per cent. To him it looked very much as though they were about to receive 17.5 per cent, to say nothing of the cathedral canons who were getting 25 per cent. This left him 'extremely distressed': 'This is at a time when lower-paid workers are being roundly condemned for taking damaging industrial action to obtain an increase of more than 9 per cent ... It cuts the ground from beneath the feet of any of us who have tried to say something in public about the national situation.' Every increase by one group created an inflationary pressure on others to keep their position in the 'league tables' of incomes. Coggan himself was equivocal: the issue might be more complicated than Sheppard alleged. Some dignitaries had heavy commitments to face. Harris himself had written to reassure Sheppard. This increase could not be construed as an act of selfishness on the part of the bishops, he remarked, because the bishops themselves had not voted for or against the proposals. Sheppard was not mollified by either of them. He thought at first to take the matter to the General Synod. Harris persuaded him not to; to write, instead, another letter to the First Commissioner himself which could be seen by 'appropriate bodies'. This the bishop did.[31]

Harris did not care for comparisons with wage disputes. He saw a fundamental distinction between what was occurring across society and what was taking place in the Church. These stipendiary rises had been proposed and accepted freely, they had not been demanded and there had been no negotiating, no campaigning: 'This ... the world at large will readily understand and accept.' Moreover, Sheppard's argument might suggest that each year they should look around to see

[30] Ibid. 22 Mar. 1979.
[31] GPC report, 'Stipend levels 1979–80: letter from the bishop of Liverpool', CC (79) 22, Board papers, 22 Mar. 1979, ser. 95084/47.

what the 'going rate' was before they decided what to do. They would not 'catch up' in the way – only 'fall back'. In fact, since 1970 the stipends of diocesan bishops had increased by 79 per cent. The average increase in the earnings of all workers had been 206 per cent.[32]

Sheppard was not expressing his views only to the bureaucrats. He had copied his letter to all bishops during General Synod, encouraging them to write to the Commissioners. Fifteen had agreed with him. Fourteen had disagreed, and disagreed 'rather more forcefully'. The Commissioners had been reminded that it was their own statutory responsibility to maintain the stipends of dignitaries. They must think of those with particular family responsibilities. If the press was critical they could not be led by that. They must do what was right and just. To their knowledge, only one other unnamed bishop had murmured anything along the same lines as Sheppard himself.

How was all this to be pulled together? The more the Southwark crisis dragged on the more the CSA was damaged, and the greater became the risk that still more anomalies might arise. Not for the first time the technicalities of the subject came to the rescue. There would indeed be a withdrawal of a portion of Southwark's quota for 1979, but it would be calculated by a different method, making use simply of the numbers of assistant staff actually involved in the three offending dioceses, to produce a new figure: a new, smaller figure. The bishop of Southwark's council smiled upon this. For good measure Smallwood promised that if this were adopted he would table no more supplementary motions. Yet what satisfied Southwark now did not win over Chichester. The beleaguered GPC proposed that it was perhaps safest to carry forward money which would not now be allocated.[33] Worse, by the time of the April Board meeting Hereford, too, was found to be in disgrace on stipends scales for assistant staff. Harris now found himself proposing that it should lose £2,000 of its allocation. In this Hereford acquiesced graciously. Archbishop Coggan concluded that they must all be clear that the CSA was not a court imposing penalties but 'a body seeking fairness within the Church'.[34]

The squabbles over the 1979 scales had lasted a year. No sooner had they ended than it was time to begin to agree the scales for 1980. A general election was in the offing now: the prospect of a new government might bring the lifting of wage restraints. Smallwood still had an appetite for reform. He observed, not lightly, that the clergy must catch up with the staff of the Church Commissioners themselves, who had seen their pay increase with the recent settlement of civil

[32] Board minutes, 22 Mar. 1979.
[33] GPC report, 'Withdrawal of part of allocation from certain dioceses', CC (79) 35, annex, and Hopkinson report, Board papers, 20 Apr. 1979, ser. 95083/47.
[34] Board minutes, 26 Apr. 1979, pp. 5–6.

service salaries. The Board lamely 'Took note'.[35] In July the protagonists were only silenced when Royle read a passage from the Book of Haggai and asked if the Church was putting its resources to the best use? They must, he said, seek the Lord's will; the archbishops should call the leaders of the Church to prayer and fasting. 'There was discussion', records the minutes soberly, 'as to how to proceed with this suggestion.' It was thought best to refer it to the bishops.[36]

Victory and defeat

The punishments, or redistributions, of the CSA might have given the Commissioners confidence that they had emerged from the battles of 1978 bloodied but victorious. If this was indeed so, the carpet on which they stood was yet again to be tugged from under their feet. It happened almost surreptitiously. After the Board meeting of July 1979, Oswald Clark had visited Ronald Harris. Clark remarked that he had asked the legal adviser to the General Synod how the CSA's decision against Southwark and the other offenders stood in law? He was advised that there was an arguable case that the CSA had exceeded its reasonable powers. If that was so, Clark pressed, it was time for it to pay up. It was not quite demanding money with menaces, but demanding money with lawyers might well have looked much the same.[37] Harris sought sympathetic counsel but found it less than sanguine about the Commissioners' defence.[38]

Quietly, doubt had been sown. This might go to the courts. Nobody, thought Harris, could want that. He discussed it with the other two Church Estates Commissioners and with other allies. They agreed with him that the money should be paid back to the errant dioceses forthwith. Archbishop Coggan concurred. Clark was found to be content. He pressed home the advantage and asked Harris to confirm that the ultimate legal responsibility for determining the level of the stipend lay with a diocese, and that the most the CSA could do was to offer 'direction'. Harris confirmed it.[39] All this reached the Board of the Commissioners in September, after the holiday season. Clark had sent his apologies: there was a general muttering against him. Bishop Stockwood observed that Mr Clark would always stand firmly against what he saw to be wrong, and this matter he had seen in that

[35] Ibid. 31 May 1979.
[36] Ibid. 27 July 1979, pp. 2–5.
[37] Harris note, 'Central Stipends Authority', CC (79) 74, Board papers, 27 Sept. 1979, ser. 95083/47, pp. 1–4.
[38] Board minutes, 27 Sept. 1979, pp. 3–5.
[39] Harris note, 'Central Stipends Authority', CC (79) 74, Board papers, 27 Sept. 1979, ser. 95083/47.

light. Others thought that a resolution of the business in this new manner might encourage a healing of divisions. Peace began to break out. Coggan spoke of his past unhappiness; Smallwood apologised if he had said anything hurtful to anybody. So the Board voted, fifteen in favour, one against and four necessarily abstaining, to pay the four dioceses the money that had been withheld.[40] Thus did the Church of England resolve its most dramatic stipendiary dispute.

Taking stock

This was where the matter stood at the end of the Coggan era. In the area of clergy stipend a common method and a shared language simply eluded the Church. It was no easier to contrive general rules now than it ever had been. They might well be resented by the dioceses as an act of centralisation. If some parties called for the whole arrangement to be turned over to independent advisers, they had to meet the objection that by now the CSA had years of experience behind it, and still found these matters complicated. Whatever was said there, the General Synod was of little help: it was attempting to respond to a fusion of intricate finance and politics and the best that it could manage was the platitude that a stipend must yield 'neither poverty nor riches'.[41]

After two years of 'catching up', the CSA owned frankly that they had not achieved as much as they had hoped, not least because inflation kept lurching upwards. They were still haunted by the oddities and complexities of their task, the embarrassments of statistics and the suspicions of their partners. Essential questions could not be answered. Should the CSA allow more flexibility between dioceses? Should allocations be adjusted with a view to historic assets in each diocese? At the end of 1979 this second idea split the Board in half.[42] The passage of time, however, would at least blow a new wind behind it.

Bishops and their houses in an age of austerity

It was not only clergy stipends that felt the impact of the economic dramas of the later 1970s. They also affected the financing of bishops. Between April 1973 and November 1975 the basic price of oil rose by 169.26 per cent, of electricity by approximately 94 per cent. Even when, in April 1974, the Commissioners began to reimburse not a

[40] Board minutes, 27 Sept. 1979, pp. 3–5.

[41] See D. J. Day (stipends secretary) note, 11 Dec. 1979 in 'Central Stipends Authority: stipends levels for 1981', CSA (80) 1, Board papers, 20 Dec. 1979, ser. 95083/47.

[42] Board minutes, 20 Dec. 1979, pp. 2–3.

quarter but a half of the bishops' heating, lighting and cleaning bills some of them were 'finding it difficult to maintain acceptable temperatures' in their own homes. The bishop of Chester, Hubert Whitsey, was almost freezing in a house in which necessary economies had led to a life of downright harshness. Meanwhile, austerity sharpened a sense of enduring anomalies. At Chester the bishop and his family occupied a third of the house but paid a half of its overall bills. He thought three-quarters official and one-quarter domestic would be nearer the mark. 'Would you – of your charity – please examine my request?'[43] The General Purposes Committee came up with a stunningly precise answer to this. A bishop might well be asked to pay 50 per cent of his costs, not for the whole house, but for 6,000 square feet of each house. When this formula was applied mathematically to the Chester see house, this would, in fact, leave the bishop of Chester with responsibility for 27.4 per cent of his bills.

There were new grants for domestic assistance too. Before long the Commissioners' bill appeared to be growing beyond their expectations. Soon it could be heard again on the committees of 1 Millbank that surely the bishops were proving more expensive than they should? There was concern about what expenditure of this kind must do to the General Fund.

This aside, the storm which had broken in the Ramsey era over the London see house ignited the fuse to a far bigger argument. The mood of the Houses Committee was verging on the vengeful. They clearly felt that they had run around after the bishops quite enough. The Board of the Church Commissioners now turned to the bishops as a whole. What did they all want from their see houses? At the beginning of 1975 a sharp memorandum, setting down the costs of maintaining the houses and expenses of the bishops, was being prepared.

Perhaps some at 1 Millbank believed that fundamental change might come of this. But others must surely have suspected otherwise. The trouble was in no small measure the bishops themselves: 'What suits one perfectly may be unacceptable to the next because he wants to live and work in a different way. What one bishop would regard as too large, his successor might regard as too small.'[44] Whatever the different themes and variations, the Commissioners must try to discern the 'general mind of the bishops'. There was another questionnaire. Would facilities for lunch or dinner parties of ten–twelve people still be needed? Would room for parties of between fifty to a hundred people, expecting a buffet or sherry, still be needed? Must there be a chapel? And a vestry? This did not assuage the appetite of the Board. Was it

---

[43] GPC report, 'Cost of heating and lighting see houses', CC (76) 1, Board papers, 15 Jan. 1976, ser. 95083/41, annex A.
[44] Ibid. p. 2.

time that bishops worked away from their houses and in offices elsewhere, and that they do the same when entertaining? Somebody even asked if it was quite necessary for bishops to be 'given to hospitality' at all?[45]

The bishop of Rochester, David Say, was sent to the House of Bishops with these stout demands in mind. He returned to Millbank with the news that the bishops would indeed reply, but one at a time. It would then be for the Commissioners to analyse the returns and report back to the bishops to tell them what they had all said. Hopkinson hoped waspishly that they would be quick about it; he observed 'considerable disquiet on the whole subject of bishops' needs being expressed in many quarters'. The Board 'Took note'.[46]

When they were collated it was seen that the bishops had shown 'a high degree of concurrence' in most answers. An overwhelming number believed that facilities for dinner or lunch parties for ten–twelve guests should be provided. Fourteen bishops said that space for entertaining between fifty and a hundred guests should be available, four that space for fifty would be nearer the mark, some put a lower number, ten said that this was not needed at all. Most thought a chapel necessary, though six thought not. Thirty-one bishops turned down a vestry; four wanted one. The answers to the question about gardens proved impossible to tabulate. 'Some Bishops would gladly see part of their grounds sold off.' A number hoped that they might find gardeners who could also drive them around, or drivers who could garden.[47] Altogether, the ideal bishop's house, built in the mind by the bricks of consensus and the mortar of compromise, looked very like the newer houses which had been built for the bishops of Gloucester, Norwich, Manchester and Truro. This clearly showed that in the affairs of the bishops the Church Commissioners, and the Ecclesiastical Commissioners before them, had got something important right.

But under the surface these interrogations were beginning to irritate the bishops. Discreet but severe criticisms were made. Harris stepped in to soothe ruffled feathers with gentle words, disclaiming any wish to offend on the part of the Commissioners, assuring that they sought only to give satisfaction. But all must surely concur that in the management of bishops the Houses Committee and the staff of the Commissioners faced 'an inherently difficult situation'; 'I say this not to excuse any failures, past or to come, but simply in order to achieve mutual recognition that rather more than goodwill and energy are

---

[45] Board minutes, 23 Jan. 1975, p. 1.
[46] Ibid. 20 Feb. 1975, p. 1.
[47] GPC and HC report, 'See houses and the needs of bishops', CC (75) 24, Board papers, 13 Mar. 1975, ser. 95083/40.

needed to get the best results.' If the bishops wished for more meetings with the First and Third Church Estates Commissioner and the secretary that would be most welcome. The Third Church Estates Commissioner was ready to meet the bishops' wives. The Commissioners' staff would try not to turn up at a see house unexpectedly.

Some bishops held an 'intractable' view that the dioceses should employ their own architects. They murmured that the Commissioners' insistence that their own architects be maintained was 'complacent and defensive'. For this the Commissioners were not yet ready. The alternative had indeed been tried, and had not been found very satisfactory – and it was more expensive too. The existing arrangement was also consistent with the financial responsibility that the Commissioners bore. Again, Harris was amiable and pragmatic. He did not wish to discourage flexibility or experiment. He wanted the bishops to be glad when they saw their staff at work for them. If a bishop's house was a very long way from London perhaps something could be tried, as long as the benefits and costs of the arrangement might be assessed.[48] Off the paper went to the House of Bishops. For now the grumbling on both sides subsided.

The Oxford and London see houses

In 1973 Fulham Palace began its new life as a museum. Meanwhile, in the spring of 1974, the Church Commissioners' official architect was busy in Barton Street. The bishop of London and his wife approved of what he now proposed, and there were more sketches, more tenders, more estimates, more negotiations with the City of Westminster. The bishop's council had now given its executive committee authority to state, if it saw fit, that Barton Street would be suitable as the see house not only for the present bishop but also for his successors. They had another look and then unanimously passed a resolution to that effect, and another that they hoped he would still have the garage that belonged to 19 Cowley Street. The bishop agreed. The Houses Committee did not much like this, and deferred a decision. The Board was none too happy, either. The costs of the new work were set to mount. The Board agreed that £100,000 was the most that should be spent.

In September 1975 the total cost of converting Barton Street was reckoned at £99,935.84. The work was due to be completed by the following August. It was not. There had been an outbreak of dry rot. The speed at which the workmen could make progress was also

---

[48] Osmond note, 'See houses and the office expenses of bishops', CC (75) 84, draft for the House of Bishops, Board papers, 16 Oct. 1975, ibid. pt 41.

sluggish: owners of adjourning properties required 'quiet working' practices. Soon the quantity surveyor estimated that the costs would be £101,000. Fulminating, no doubt, the Houses Committee agreed to go up by another £1,000.[49]

Where to house the bishop of Oxford had long been a matter for anxiety. In March 1977 the Houses Committee told the Board that a hunt was on for a new see house to replace Bishop's House, Cuddesdon, on condition that it would be self-financing. This unusual rejoinder was for a reason. In 1961–2 the house at Cuddesdon had been purpose-built on the very site occupied by the palace, which had burned down in 1958. But the bishop's own council now found that both the house and its grounds were too large and too expensive. Cuddesdon was also unsuitable because it was hard to reach by public transport and lacked, partly for that reason, enough domestic help, and because it was felt that a future bishop should live in a larger community. Deliberations dragged on. A new bishop arrived: Patrick Rodger. He did not want Cuddesdon either. There was now no public transport at all between the city and the see house. The official surveyer was despatched to find an acceptable temporary residence. Plans were made to put Cuddesdon and its two associated cottages on the market.

January 1979 found the bishop of Oxford living in a house at Woodstock, just outside Blenheim Palace, but a suitable house had been found in North Oxford, on sale for £50,000 and on a lease from one of the colleges. The bishop, Dame Betty Ridley, the official architect and the official surveyor had all seen it. The joint advisory committee approved. It was not ideal; it did not have room for a chapel or a secretary, but the secretary could work in the diocesan church house. At the Board meeting of the Commissioners the bishops of Worcester and Carlisle showed themselves to be protective of their brother bishop, agitating for action. They wanted this resolved as soon as possible. For its part the college clung onto its freehold. It was asked whether this need be a problem? For in twenty-eight years time, when the lease ran out, perhaps bishops would have quite different ideas about what a see house should be like. The price was agreed. Then, suddenly, the college, which was clearly not so genteel as to resist a little bold opportunism in its own interests, decided to raise the price to £75,000. There were more negotiations, then a compromise. Another year of temporary accommodation was found to be more than the bishop could tolerate.[50]

---

[49] HC report, 'London see house', CC (76) 73, Board papers, 22 July 1976, ibid. pt 42.

[50] HC report, 'Oxford see house', CC (78) 34, Board papers, 22 June 1978, ibid. pt 46.

A new suffragan bishop: Wolverhampton

In the Coggan era the number of suffragan bishops continued to rise. In September 1976 the Board discussed the creation of a third suffragan bishopric in the Lichfield diocese, 'of, say, Wolverhampton'. Lichfield was one of the largest dioceses in the country with more than 500 parishes and over 2 million people across 2,000 square miles. (Only eight dioceses were bigger and only four more populous; only two had more on their electoral roll.) The bishop, Kenneth Skelton, wrote that Lichfield was like Chelmsford, which, he observed drily, had three suffragans and lower confirmation numbers. In the boroughs of Wolverhampton and Walsall, Sandwell and Dudley there lived more than a million people with no episcopal presence in the area. The whole southern area of the diocese was to be reshaped by government reorganisation, redevelopment, shifting population, immigration; work in the area was 'an uphill struggle'. A bishop was 'a crying need'.

The bishop of Lichfield already had two suffragans – Stafford and Shrewsbury – and they appeared to have a brief for those areas. But Wolverhampton and the Black Country embraced a larger area still. Beyond this, however, the proposal was wreathed in complications. The bishop of Worcester had a suffragan bishop of Dudley. He had been serving, informally, in the Himley deanery of the diocese of Lichfield, which actually lay within the metropolitan borough of Dudley. In Skelton's eyes this showed that Himley had been favoured with 'a disproportionate share of episcopal time and attention, which has caused unfavourable comment in the remaining part of the Black Country'. The claims of Wolverhampton must surely be greater than those of Dudley.

Once it had been thought that the diocese of Worcester could relieve Lichfield of some of these industrial parishes. Nothing had happened. Moreover, Telford, a new town, lay partly in Lichfield and partly in the diocese of Hereford. A joint pastoral committee of the two dioceses had agreed, by a majority vote, that it should all belong to Lichfield. But the bishops decided not to proceed until a West Midlands Commission was set up to discuss diocesan boundaries. Progress had been sticky.[51]

Archbishop Coggan looked at this and concurred with Bishop Skelton. The Board took a broader view and reflected instead on the numbers of new suffragan and assistant bishops created in the last decade alone. They remembered that in December 1973 they had heard of expectations that Bradford, Leicester and Newcastle might in

---

[51] GPC report, 'Diocese of Lichfield: possible creation of a third suffragan bishopric', CC (76) 89, Board papers, 16 Sept. 1976, ibid. pt 42.

time have new suffragan bishops (presently they had none, though Newcastle now had an assistant bishop), and that the remaining assistant bishops would in due course be replaced by suffragans. How could they create a new bishopric in Lichfield before they were even sure of the diocesan borders? Might it simply be easier to redeploy the two existing suffragan bishops?[52]

The Commissioners had for some years felt themselves to be in a dubious position with regard to the creation of suffragan bishoprics. From these doubts, at least, they were to be finally delivered. In 1978 a new Dioceses Measure set down a procedure for the creation of new suffragan sees: the bishop should consult his archbishop; a proposal be approved by the standing committee of the General Synod and sent to the diocese commission; this, in turn, would consult with the Commissioners, not least in relation to its financial aspects. This done, the bishop should lay the proposal before his diocesan synod for approval and, if that was secured, it should go again to the General Synod. In short, a new bishopric could be accomplished in five steps and by a passage through seven bodies. At the end of the line the Commissioners would step in to take charge of the new bishop's financial armour, his stipend, his expenses allowances, two-thirds of his house, a half of his outgoings on the house thereafter. In financial terms, a new suffragan bishop was now an annual liability to the Church Commissioners of £5,710.

---

[52] Board minutes, 16 Sept. 1976, pp. 1–2.

10

The Perils of the Markets

While stipends were falling behind the rate of inflation the powers at Millbank saw that investment policy must concentrate on increasing current income. By the summer of 1975 it could be seen that the international economy was being hauled out of recession, principally by the United States and Japan. The Church Commissioners now held $23 million in US equities: 12 per cent of their whole portfolio and 5 per cent of their total income. Meanwhile, the significance of property was looming larger. It was obvious that for the last ten years property had out-performed Stock Exchange investments, and powerfully. Over the last ten years the average increase of the latter had been 3.6 per cent, and for the former 11.3 per cent. Within the property portfolio itself, income from offices and shops had increased by 250 per cent while income from industrial property had doubled and income from farms increased by more than 80 per cent. Little wonder that by the summer of 1975 41 per cent of the Church Commissioners' property portfolio was in offices.

During a single year, 1975–6, the value of the Commissioners' portfolio rose startlingly from £58.4 million to £246.6 million, most of that rise owed to the equity portfolio. But if it had been a good year in these terms, they had only to cast their eyes at the retail price index to grow sober. That had risen by 21 per cent. At every turn the Commissioners were haunted by the realities of inflation. The fortunes of the Church lay in the clutches of colossal economic movements which looked increasingly volatile.

The work of the Assets Committee itself was causing intermittent unease. By November 1977 one Commissioner appointed by the General Synod, H. S. Cranfield, was agitating that the Board of governors should know more of what it was up to. He even threatened a private member's motion at General Synod. At the Board itself Harris asked if members felt that they were sufficiently able to monitor what was happening. Should the minutes of all the committees be supplied to Board members on request? The verdict of the Board went against Cranfield. To maintain a distance between bodies was conducive to better decisions about policy. Harris observed coolly that the Commissioners' current practice was in keeping with the practice of Cabinet Office. Oswald Clark countered that some believed that government itself should be more open. Harris now became more resistant. If committee minutes were widely distributed confidentiality might be compromised. Administration would be undermined. Four voted for Clark's motion; fifteen against it. It did not rest there: another Synod appointee, T. L. F. Royle, now asked whether he were legally responsible for the decisions of the Commissioners, in the same way as the director of a public company? The official solicitor replied that this analogy was not appropriate. A Commissioner bore no personal liability. If that was so, replied Cranfield, could it be minuted?[1]

South Africa

Banking, as Ronald Harris once observed, was international 'in the widest sense'.[2] This made it not merely a vast and intricate subject, but a slippery one. An example of this could be seen in the view that the Commissioners took of credit companies. For decades they had avoided them purposefully. Now British exports were increasingly successful in no small measure because of a growing provision, by the banks, of sterling finance under short-term and longer-term export schemes. These were all guaranteed by the government's Export Credit Guarantee Department.

Historians of ecumenism have not paused much over the ecumenism of money. In fact, by the time of archbishop Coggan, the Church Commissioners' investments secretary was meeting a number of investors from other denominations twice a year, to seek a common mind on matters of mutual concern. These included the Central Board of Finance of the Church of England, its Pensions Board, the USPG, the Church of Scotland, various Methodist Church bodies, the Baptist Union and the Roman Catholic Church. The Commissioners were also placing their own financial decisions more deliberately in the public domain. At the same time they sought to show that in the world of investments they were prepared to refer to the views of other public authorities. The annual report of 1974 noted the CBI report 'The responsibilities of the British public company' and the fifth report of the House of Commons Select Committee on Expenditure on 'Wages

---

[1] Board minutes, 17 Nov. 1977, pp. 3–4.
[2] AC report, 'Bank loans to "undesirable regimes"', CC (77) 42, Board papers, 23 June 1977, ser. 95083/44.

and conditions of African workers employed by British firms in South Africa'.[3]

This last reference was suggestive. By the early 1970s South Africa had become the target of a wide international campaign of disapproval and protest. At first, the construction of a legal system of apartheid there had provoked little hostility abroad. But over time awareness sharpened and resistance began to be more vocal. In the United States the Civil Rights movement had repudiated racial segregation and a movement led by a Christian minister, Martin Luther King, had shown in no uncertain terms that the rightful place of Christians was in movements of resistance to racism. Meanwhile, in South Africa, the violence of apartheid, and the force used to maintain it, did not go uncontested. The massacre at Sharpeville in 1960 had given the world terrible images of the murder of defenceless men and women, assembling peacefully in the name of principles which every democratic society recognised and professed. When, in June 1976, school children in the black township of Soweto erupted into demonstrations of protest the army shot hundreds in the streets. In Britain Christian opinion was galvanised by Canon John Collins's International Defence and Aid Fund, which published material documenting, often meticulously, the barbarities of life in South Africa.[4] Groups and organisations dedicated to protest grew impressively. Some were Christian (like Christian Concern for Southern Africa); others were alliances which numbered many committed Christians among their members. Increasingly, particular British businesses known to have interests in South Africa were lobbied and boycotted.

It was still the policy of the Church Commissioners that they did not invest in companies operating wholly or substantially in South Africa. The qualification was recommended by the simple imperative of practicality, for it was seen to be almost impossible to avoid investments in huge companies which might have a very modest percentage of investments in South Africa somewhere in their portfolio. It was felt that to say this was quite enough. Such an approach would prove increasingly difficult to sustain.

The World Council of Churches was busily at work against apartheid. In the Church of England questions were now being raised in the General Synod. In November 1973 Paul Oestreicher had put forward a motion pressing the claims of South Africa upon the Anglican conscience again. Once Oestreicher had favoured the Commissioners. Now he argued that their policy 'hardly even begins to meet the problem'. They still made millions of pounds out of British

[3] Annual report of the Church Commissioners, London 1974, 15.
[4] See Diana Collins, Partners in protest: life with Canon Collins, London 1992, 222–7.

Leyland, ICI and General Electric, all of which had subsidiaries in South Africa. How much money did they put into the struggle against apartheid? The dean of Norwich, Alan Webster, proposed that there be some 'common instrument' by means of which the Church, together with other Churches, could judge these issues. Harris replied that none of the three companies to which Oestreicher had referred had interests above 7 per cent in South Africa. He added that, 'where the Commissioners do hold shares in a company operating to some extent in South Africa they will make whatever use they properly can of their position as a shareholder to try to influence the company's policy in relation to South Africa and indeed on any other moral or ethical issue'.[5] Harris must have sensed that the climate of opinion was altering around him.

Public campaigns seldom thrive on an acknowledgement of complexities. They require a particular target. In the early months of 1973 the National Council of Churches in the United States had been informed privately that the European-American Banking Corporation was sending money directly to the South African government. The corporation, some forty banks, American, Canadian, European and Japanese, included the Midland Bank in which the Church Commissioners held 600,000 shares.

Harris knew that at the annual general meeting of the Midland Bank, in April 1974, the chairman, Sir Archibald Forbes, had justified these loans by appealing to banking not political criteria. On 3 May 1974 Harris himself had written to Forbes to voice the concern of the Commissioners and to ask if these loans were to continue. Forbes assured Harris that these loans amounted to only 'a tiny fraction' of the business of the bank, and he invited Harris to talk it over with him. They met in July. What followed 'could not', in Harris's eyes, 'have been more frank'. Now Forbes was more specific: these loans altogether constituted only 0.3 per cent of the total figure loaned altogether by the Midland Bank. Investments generally involved questions of government only when the viability of commerce was at stake, so to withhold money from governments might undermine economies and that could not be in the true interests of its people. For his part, Forbes perceived that 'time was working slowly but surely against the continued effective maintenance of apartheid'. Harris persisted. What concerned the Commissioners was the fact that these loans were being made to the South African government itself.[6]

---

[5] *Report of the Proceedings of General Synod*, iv/3, 89–913 (9 Nov. 1972). Harris's speech is at pp. 909–10.
[6] See Harris note, 'Bank loans to the South African government', CC (76) 11, Board papers, 19 Feb. 1976, ser. 95083/41.

In August a resolution was passed by the Central Committee of the World Council of Churches, urging all member Churches, church organisations and Christians at large to press the Midland Bank to end its loans. There was a conversation between the Commissioners and the Board of Social Responsibility of the General Synod. The Commissioners promised to keep an eye on the situation. Even so, a Christian lobby group, 'End Loans to South Africa' (ELTSA), stepped up its campaign against them. Late in August 1 Millbank received a letter from its chairman, the Methodist minister David Haslam, asking them, as shareholders in the Midland, to demand the withdrawal of the loans. He was assured that the Commissioners were making their own enquiries, and that if they were dissatisfied, they 'would not hesitate' to make their views known to the management of the bank.[7]

Forbes and Harris exchanged further letters. But the time for quiet diplomacy was already passing. On 11 November 1974 ELTSA pressed for evidence of the Commissioners enquiries and asked for a meeting with their investments secretary. Harris replied that he needed frank discussions with the bank, and that frankness required confidentiality. In truth, he was beginning to resent this growing harassment. ELTSA had begun distributing fake GIRO forms in branches of the bank, with the words 'Deposit on Apartheid' printed over them. The Commissioners did not much like this. They could not turn their investments policies into political campaigns. There was no meeting. Another letter from ELTSA now expressed their disappointment that the Commissioners were not participating in this pressure campaign and assuming that they could not object to making this refusal to meet with them public. The Commissioners replied that they had no objection to publicity as long as the real basis of their case was presented.[8]

By now it was suspected that far from withdrawing from South Africa, the Midland Bank was actually increasing its loans. Haslam had argued that direct loans made by the Midland Bank represented 'immoral support for a racialist regime'. On 13 March 1975 Harris reported that a letter had been published in the *Guardian* two days before calling for all companies with connections with South Africa to end loans to that country: And in this the Commissioners had been challenged directly:

> Ordinary Christians are entitled to hear the full facts from those who administer their finances. The Church Commissioners are in theory a public body responsible not

[7] Ibid.
[8] Ibid. p. 2.

only to the Church but to the nation. They are however fond of hiding their light under a bushel.

> The Church of England has made its views on apartheid clear, but it continues to draw large amounts of income from companies and banks which profit from apartheid. It is essential that the Commissioners state publicly their position on matters like the Midland Bank loans, and their readiness eventually to sell their shares if no action is taken.[9]

This letter was the expression of a formidable coalition drawn from the coming generation: Trevor Beeson, vicar of Ware, Paul Oestreicher, Bishop Ambrose Reeves, Wilfred Wood, vicar of Catford, John Davies, Anglican chaplain at Keele University, and Bishop Colin Winter. The Church Commissioners rose to defend themselves. A reply, published on 15 March 1975, protested that their critics had been 'less than accurate', for the Commissioners were 'possibly unique' among investing institutions in publicly parading ethical criteria. There was nothing theoretical about their accountability to the General Synod of the Church of England and to parliament itself. They had been in 'constant touch' with the management of the Midland Bank during the past year to establish facts and voice 'genuine concern'. But they must maintain their confidentiality if they were to secure the fullest information and exploit their influence for good.[10] Here was the rub. Financial transactions required confidentiality. To convert the silent and unaccountable calculations of board rooms into public property and scrutiny amounted to an insistence that the essential method of the markets be altered.

By the end of the year Haslam had again written to the Commissioners to invite them to sponsor a shareholder resolution at the forthcoming annual general meeting of the Midland Bank that it 'make no further loans to the South African Government or its departments, agencies, or state corporations, and not to renew any existing loans'. By now ELTSA had grown in stature and influence. Its work was endorsed by a long list of luminaries, many of them prominent in the Churches. Haslam was confident that ELTSA had sufficient support to meet the requirement that such a resolution must be supported by 100 shareholders holding altogether 10,000 shares. He even enclosed a requisition form (postage paid).[11]

This time a memorandum drafted by Harris struck a firmer note. This was not simply a matter of South Africa, it was one about 'the proper role of the corporate investor'. The Assets Committee was

---

[9] Copy dated 15 Jan. 1975, ibid.
[10] Copy dated 15 Mar. 1975, ibid.
[11] 'The Midland Bank: some information for shareholders', ibid. pp. 15–16.

divided: a majority favoured a 'more non-committal "investment" line'; a minority something more committed. As chairman, Harris stated that he should propose this discussion from a position of neutrality, but he felt bound to add that he was reluctant to support the majority view. For his part he could see no reason why they should not make public the arguments which had been used to the bank privately. Were they to embrace the ELTSA resolution or not?

In Geneva the executive committee of the WCC had withdrawn its deposits with the Midland Bank, at the same time encouraging other parties to maintain 'continued pressure through consultation, shareholder action, and publicity culminating in the withdrawal of accounts if necessary'. At least one important change had occurred at the bank. Forbes had retired. Within a week of taking up his post, his successor, Lord Armstrong, faced a deputation from the World Council of Churches and the British Council of Churches, led by Lord March. Armstrong struck a less accommodating posture than his predecessor. The bank's policy should be guided by their responsibilities to their shareholders, customers and staff. They should follow 'normal banking practice' rather than be 'influenced either by our own personal opinions or by opinions expressed to us by others about the conduct of borrowers outside the commercial field'. The bank did business in 'virtually every country of the world' and in so doing benefited not only its shareholders but the British economy itself. To do this naturally involved governments and their agencies. None of this could influence banking policy or else it would become altogether 'impossible'. In this sense, indeed, the bank was acting with 'strict neutrality'; the idea that the banks should cease loans to South Africa was a political one. Those who sought economic withdrawal should press governments to change the law, and not hector the banks themselves. It was because the law had required the banks to pull out of Rhodesia that they had done so. The Midland Bank was immovable: rumours that although one loan had been paid off it had been replaced by a still larger one were confirmed.[12]

The Commissioners looked about them. The policy subcommittee of the Standing committee of the General Synod did not believe that the Church should become associated with the decisions at Geneva. On the other hand, the Central Board of Finance of the Methodist Church was 'reluctantly' in favour of the ELTSA resolution at the forthcoming AGM of the Midland Bank. The secretary of the Board remarked to Harris that the Methodists had generally followed the Commissioners, but now they felt that time had run out. 'More positive action' was necessary. In the background, ELTSA threatened

[12] Harris supplementary note, 'Midland Bank loans to the South African government', CC (76) 12, ibid. annex A.

that they would soon 'go public' in seeking support from the Church Commissioners.

It was time for Harris to meet Armstrong. On 8 January 1976 the two confronted each other for almost an hour. It did not go well. Harris restated the Commissioners' position. They had been talking now to the Bank for two years and it did not appear to be listening. Now they faced a 'crunch'. There was something else. Harris knew that if the Commissioners joined the ELTSA resolution one of the Church Commissioners, P. Shelbourne, would almost certainly resign, for he was on the board of the Midland Bank too. Out of this, Harris later reported to the Board, 'I got virtually no "change"'. Armstrong asked whether the socialists expected the bank to refuse to lend to Chile (he was right there), or the Jews press that they avoid Soviet Russia? 'The bank just could not set itself up as a judge of moral issues and attempt to apply moral criteria to commercial transactions.' Harris replied that the Confederation of British Industry had issued a report observing that the law only set 'minimum standards of conduct', and that these could not 'embody the whole duty of man', did not, in fact, necessarily make 'a good citizen or a good company'. Armstrong replied that he could not believe that this affair in South Africa was what the CBI had in mind. The bank was pursuing an 'open policy' in training black Africans in banking. They had also shown a willingness to give 'normal inter-banking facilities to a projected "Black Bank"'. If anything, observed Armstrong as 'a parting shot', it was time that some church body had the sense and courage to support the Midland Bank formally in its initiatives and criticise 'misplaced' agitation. If a resolution was got up against it at the AGM, it was sure to be defeated.[13]

This exchange hardened Harris. The Commissioners, he said, now faced a clear dilemma. 'I believe', he wrote to the Board in a lengthy memorandum setting out possible courses on 2 February 1976, 'that this matter raises such important issues of principle for the Commissioners that the full facts must be placed before the Board at its next meeting with a view to the Board deciding the matter.' They must decide whether or not to join the ELTSA resolution by 24 February. If they voted for the motion, they should be aware that this altered their habitual practice. But the outright rejection of their own discreet diplomacy altered the picture: they had brought their influence to bear on the bank and their efforts had come to nothing.

Whatever the Church Commissioners now decided would have far-reaching consequences. The Central Board of Finance had been kept in touch with the debate through the Commissioners' Investments Department, and it was clear that it would follow the Commissioners'

[13] Harris, 'Note for the record', 8 Jan. 1976, ibid.

example.[14] The Assets Committee assessed the problem with a sharp eye. Some favoured abstention on the grounds that they must be consistent with past policy. Involvement might yield influence; disinvestment could not. The involvement of the Midland Bank was too small to justify censure. What evidence was there that these loans actually bolstered the government of South Africa anyway? Others spoke of the Commissioners' own credibility. This was hardly a matter of bringing down the South African government or harming the black population of that country, but simply a matter of stopping the loans. In short, the committee was divided, though the majority favoured abstention from the ELTSA resolution. Harris abstained.[15] Sir John Arbuthnot complained to Harris that they were on a slippery slope. They should not, either as Commissioners or shareholders, now 'usurp' the powers that properly lay in the hands of the directors of the bank. The bank was acting responsibly and in line with the standards that should be expected of those who had a high position in the British banking system ('which is second to none'). A mass withdrawal of funds from South Africa might well disturb steady progress, even produce 'an Angolan situation'.[16]

The journal *Theology* published a thorough article by Ronald Preston criticising the Commissioners for adhering to 'an arbitrary and unsophisticated policy which smacks of an uninformed constituency and could easily give rise to the charges of humbug'.[17] This came up at the General Synod. The controversy was increasingly becoming one of the proper role of shareholders in ethical issues. Here Harris observed a difference between Armstrong and the Commissioners. Armstrong could not have regard to political factors. But the Commissioners had always maintained a responsibility to the interests of the wider community 'and that that wider community does not cease to exist at the Straits of Dover'. He did not believe that the Commissioners must lamely acquiesce in apartheid because it could be called 'political'. They must regard it instead as 'a highly privileged social system, with a high standard of living, based on elaborate racial discrimination'. Moreover, the Commissioners must not retreat publicly from what they had been seeking to achieve privately for two years now. That was, in effect, what Arbuthnot was proposing. Harris owned that he had strong views. At the same time he had increasingly come to feel that to sponsor the ELTSA resolution, or even to vote for it, 'might well

[14] Harris note, 'Midland Bank: loans to the South African government', A (76) 17, Board papers 19 Feb. 1976, ibid.
[15] AC minutes, annex B, in Board papers, ibid. p. 17.
[16] John Arbuthnot to Harris, 6 Feb. 1976, annex C, ibid. p. 19.
[17] See Ronald Preston, 'The ethics of investment', *Theology* lxxviii (1975), 507–18 at p. 511.

make infinitely harder their relations with company managements generally in the future'. He still wished to avoid a 'head-on' confrontation in public. They could vote at once in favour or against, they could abstain, or they could await the assurances of the bank and, if they were found inadequate, vote for the resolution after the debate.[18]

On the Assets Committee Arbuthnot held firmly to his line. They should not merely abstain, but actually vote against the resolution. But he did not carry the meeting with him. For the Commissioners to go back publicly on what they had been doing privately would be 'untenable and inconsistent'; it would seem as though the Commissioners 'lacked confidence in their own convictions'. There was a strong view against racialist or discriminatory governments in the Church and the Commissioners would do well to reflect that now. By nineteen votes to eight the Board agreed to desist from sponsoring the resolution but to vote in favour of it if they were not placated. More, they would ask the archbishop of Canterbury to approve the final form of the public statement.[19]

Coggan did so. Copies of their statement had been sent to the press, to the Midland Bank, to ELTSA, to all the Commissioners. ELTSA promptly invited the Commissioners to take part in a press conference, but Harris declined. The statement was enough. Betty Ridley had spoken to the General Synod and what she said appeared to go down well. Shelbourne, whose sympathies lay with his fellow directors of the Midland Bank, was spared the embarrassment of resignation as a Church Commissioner by the fact that his term was to end that very month. A personal letter from Harris to Armstrong had elicited an acknowledgement that this was 'an honest divergence of view'.[20]

Confronted by its shareholders on 7 April, the Midland Bank held its line. A special resolution was proposed with a statement from the Central Finance Board of the Methodist Church. Harris stepped in to make his statement to the meeting. The Church Commissioners regretted this 'open disagreement' with the management of the bank, 'particularly in view of their high regard for the British banking system and for the important place the Midland Bank occupies in it'. The Commissioners had acted with the greatest care and responsibility, for they saw that a substantial body of opinion would regard this not as a matters of politics, as did the management of the bank, but one of Christian conscience. Morality was something that went beyond the verdicts of the law or the government. These loans were made to a

[18] Harris, supplementary note, CC (76) 12, Board papers, 19 Feb. 1976, ser. 95083/41.
[19] Board minutes, 19 Feb. 1976, pp. 3–4.
[20] Ibid. 18 Mar. 1976, 1.

government which was viewed with 'abhorrence' by 'the great body of Church people', an abhorrence directed equally at any government which was racialist or oppressive.[21]

There was a long and orderly debate. Harris thought the tone lowered only when Armstrong remarked, 'I am sorry that so many Christian Churches have got themselves into this vengeful mood.' Then the vote: 3 million shares in favour of the resolution and 47 million shares against. The investment fund of the Central Board of Finance voted against it. The Church of Scotland abstained.[22] Much was made of it all by the press. There were letters to Millbank, most of them unhappy or critical. There was a public correspondence between Eldon Griffiths MP and the archbishop of Canterbury.

A new year brought a new annual general meeting of the Midland Bank, a new campaign by ELTSA and a new resolution against the loans. There was another invitation to join with ELTSA, another refusal from Harris: it was not the policy of the Commissioners to work in this way this year any more than it had been last year. But in the meantime ELTSA had been busy and its campaign had again gained ground, at least in popular support. This year the resolution was supported by Churches, religious organisations and secular organisations including local authorities: the Greater London Council, the London boroughs of Camden and Hounslow, the Methodist and United Reformed Churches, the Rowntree Social Service Trust and more than 100 others. On 13 January 1977 Harris and Osmond went to the Central Board of Finance, chaired by Sir Arnold France, to discuss the question and assist the debate on the position the Board should take. Four votes were taken and, while there were supporters for each of the proposals, the majority fell in behind abstention. The Commissioners and the Central Board of Finance were still divided.

At the Midland Lord Armstrong had not moved an inch. More, he cited a statement made by the parliamentary under-secretary of state for Foreign and Commonwealth Affairs to the House of Commons on 20 October 1976 that 'it is the Government's view that normal civil trade and investment should carry on in South Africa in the British national interest'. This year's motion, Armstrong added for good measure, would be moved by the deputy leader of the Greater London Council and would be 'decidedly' more political than that of the year before. In this, though, there was a quiet concession. Like other banks, observed Armstrong, the Midland was now 'pursuing a more detached policy' with regard to South Africa. He added that this could not be acknowledged publicly because it would give the bank's critics an

---

[21] Harris note, 'Midland Bank loans to South African government', CC (77) 19, annex B, Board papers, 24 Mar. 1977, ser. 95083/43.
[22] Ibid. p. 2.

opportunity to claim a victory and withdraw their resolution. That must 'gravely damage the Bank's future commercial freedom of judgement and action'. Armstrong, Harris found, was 'no less friendly ... but distinctly less abrasive'. Insofar as there had been change behind the scenes, Harris thought it might well be due more to considerations of commerce than anything else. Harris told him that on the basis of what he had heard he thought it likely that the Board of the Commissioners would choose again to vote for the resolution, but without drawing attention to themselves with another statement.[23]

The Assets Committee still shuffled uneasily. Had they made their point and, that done, was it enough? Should they now sell their holdings (a decision, to be sure, still in the province of the Assets Committee), even though they still did not offend their own policy, and even though it might suggest to the markets that the Church Commissioners were 'sellers'? Were the Commissioners making a credible stand or simply 'running away from an embarrassing situation? They recommended that the Board vote for the resolution.[24] This is what happened.

The logic unravels

In fact, the more the Commissioners examined the affairs of the Midland Bank, the more they began to question what they were doing elsewhere. There were rumours that another company, Hill Samuel, in which the Commissioners had 145,568 shares, had recently made a loan to the South African government. On the Board, Royle argued that if they were to avoid discriminating against the South African government they must adopt such an attitude towards other 'yet more oppressive regimes', in Eastern Europe and Latin America.[25] Cranfield was asking why South Africa was worse than the Soviet Union? Harris found himself asking Royle anxiously if he knew of other entanglements which might cause concern to the Commissioners? In reply he duly received a list naming nine banking companies, from Barclays to Schroder Wagg, and eleven countries, from Brazil to Yugoslavia.

For Harris South Africa was distinctive still: it maintained 'a particularly oppressive racialist regime based in law on colour of skin'. He also believed that here the Church Commissioners did possess the power to influence. Elsewhere he could observe a strict embargo on arms sales to many countries and clear rules by British and NATO defence committees over the export of armaments or 'sensitive

---

[23] 'Discussion with Lord Armstrong', 16 Mar. 1977, annex C, ibid.
[24] Ibid. p. 5.
[25] Board minutes, 24 Mar. 1977, pp. 2–3.

technology' to communist countries and others such as Uganda. Meanwhile, Brazil, Yugoslavia and Peru were viewed as developing countries, and the Commissioners had been asked to support international development. Harris observed that only about 20 per cent of the people of the world could be said to live in a 'free' country. But world trade itself required that banks work as they did, and trade must be supported if the masses of the world were not to become still poorer. He acknowledged that the Assets Committee, too, abhorred oppressive regimes wherever they may be, but would 'see little justification or practical value in endeavouring to oppose bank lending on a wider scale unless there was clear evidence of indefensible behaviour on the part of the bank involved in a particular case'.[26]

By now ethical enquiries were taking up so much time that A. I. McDonald, the investments secretary, was finding it hard to keep up with his work on the Commissioners' portfolio. It was time to set up a working party. With the agreement of archbishop Coggan, terms of reference were drafted and Osmond duly sent them out:

> In light of the relevant theological and ethical principles to consider the practical implications of the Commissioners holding interests in banks which, because of the international nature of the banking system, carry out part of their business with countries which, in varying degrees, restrict the religious, political and civil rights of their peoples, and to report to the Board.[27]

McDonald would be the assessor to the group; another assessor would come from the Board of Social Responsibility; Harris would chair it as First Church Estates Commissioner. This new group met three times and drew a number of expert witnesses from the academic and banking worlds to guide and reinforce their deliberations.

Could they frame a new set of rules? Overall, rigid guidelines were felt to be 'inappropriate and unhelpful'; better to follow a 'disaggregated approach', or judge each case on its own terms. This came naturally to the Commissioners, for it was their general attitude to most things. The principle 'to love one's neighbour as oneself' had been called (by C. F. Andrews) 'the accurate estimate and supply of someone else's need'. Then, more recently, the bishop of Lincoln, Simon Phipps, had written, 'We cannot make graven images – clear cut, rounded ethical models which will absolve us from the deep responsibility of ethical doubt and searching, trial and error'; this was seen to be helpful. And mistakes were inevitable. If the Commissioners

---

[26] Harris note, 'Bank loans to "Undesirable regimes"'.
[27] Board minutes, 23 June 1977, pp. 5–6.

were seen to be setting up some kind of 'moral court' their reputation in industrial and financial life would be damaged. Accordingly, the group pronounced that:

> Bank shares should not be sold on the single criterion that they make loans to countries with oppressive regimes, but that dialogue, research and study should be concentrated on determining the purposes for which loans are made; and that, providing loans can be identified as for legitimate trade or other social purposes, whether direct to a Government or not, objection should not be raised, but normal monitoring should continue and leverage exercised if appropriate.[28]

Some members of the Board did not feel that there was enough theology at work here, but the bishop of Worcester, Robert Wylmer, simply responded that it was not possible to frame a stronger theological view until the practical issues were themselves clearer. It was noted that in the 'Third World' the Church was often viewed sceptically as part of the established order. It was asked whether the new ecumenical twice-yearly meeting might include Jewish representatives? Hopkinson added that many in the City who shared their ethical concerns were not Christian.[29]

The passage of time and the arts of diplomacy brought some resolution. By the end of 1977 it was announced that the consortium of which the Midland Bank was a part would indeed no longer make loans to the South African government. Behind the scenes, pressure on the Midland Bank had mounted relentlessly, and in this the Commissioners' investments secretary had continued to play his undemonstrative part. Lord Armstrong now decided that the whole controversy had actually rested upon a misunderstanding. For two years the bank had not made any loans to the South African government for its own general purposes. In a statement to shareholders in 1978, he continued, 'Moreover, such new arrangements as we make for borrowers within South Africa are now confined to the finance of identifiable trade with the United Kingdom.'[30] The Assets Committee now perceived that the Commissioners' objections had finally been met. The Board was ready with its congratulations. This was a quiet victory, but a valuable vindication.

[28] Working group report, 'Investment in banking', CC (77) 78, Board papers, 17 Nov. 1977, ser. 95083/48.
[29] Board minutes, 17 Nov. 1977, pp. 1–3.
[30] Report by Osmond, 'Midland Bank: loans to South African government', CC (78) 22, Board papers, 27 Apr. 1978, ser. 95083/46.

The adventure brought a coda. Harris was now profoundly committed to the life and politics of South Africa and in January 1978 he went off to see what was happening for himself. When he returned it was with an altered perspective. There he had encountered 'very much to my surprise – complete unanimity of view against withdrawal of foreign investment as a means of bringing about change', and this included 'the great majority of responsible opponents and critics of the Government within South Africa'. More than this, the political opposition was hopelessly divided and ineffectual. This meant that only commercial agencies had the power to bring positive change. Now Harris proposed to the Assets Committee that a new section on 'investment aims and policies' be added to the annual report to mark out what he himself now called a 'shift in emphasis'.[31] The Assets Committee thought it better to leave things as they were, particularly as they now saw few constraints on what they did. Harris gave a speech about his visit to the General Synod in November 1979 and came close to publishing his report. But, evidently, he decided not to do so. Nobody, after all, could measure the consequences of such things confidently. What Harris's sustained exploration of South Africa had yielded was not a new clarity for the Church of England, but a deepening of the old ambiguity.

[31] Harris note, 'Investment in South Africa', CC (78) 56, Board papers, 20 July 1979, ibid. pt 47.

PART IV

THE INFLATIONARY SPIRAL AND THE
NEW WISDOM:
THE PRIMACY OF ARCHBISHOP RUNCIE, 1979–1991

11

Making and Amending: The Church under the Pastoral Measure

From the bishop's palace at St Albans Robert Runcie threaded his way somewhat diffidently towards Lambeth Palace. His appointment demonstrated that one did not have to have been archbishop of York, like four out of five of Runcie's immediate predecessors, in order to qualify for the great task. Runcie was keenly aware of the difficulties which beset the Church he was expected to lead, for it was awash with conflicts and competing claims, of people busily deploring that the Church was in crisis while making every effort to ensure that the crisis intensified. Runcie himself was a liberal Anglo-Catholic, subtle, humane and eloquent; an archbishop who wore his undoubted profundity rather lightly. At Lambeth he announced that he did not pretend to being an organiser, and when he looked across the Thames to Millbank he decided that there was not much that he could offer. It was not quite that Runcie disliked such worldliness, as had Ramsey. He simply assumed that in the Church Commissioners he found a successful 'establishment' institution which was founded upon the kind of expertise which he did not himself possess.[1] From the outset of his primacy he decided that he would chair the Board of the Commissioners, at most, three times a year.

On 22 May 1980, when he first took the chair, he was assured that the governors understood the reasons that he had given for attending only now and then. In his turn, the archbishop thanked the Commissioners' staff for helping him to move into the palace. On the next occasion, in December, the official photographer was alerted to make the most of the opportunity. Nor would Runcie always stay for the whole meeting. When, in May 1982, the secretary thanked him for having taken the chair, despite other and pressing preoccupations, not least a meeting shortly with the pope, Runcie thanked him and almost at once made for the door. That day he was replaced by David Say,

[1] See Humphrey Carpenter, *Robert Runcie: the reluctant archbishop,* London 1996, 200.

bishop of Rochester, upon whom the Commissioners were beginning to rely rather heavily. There was wisdom in Runcie's balancing of responsibilities. But his absence made the Commissioners more vulnerable to an old perception which had never really gone away: that essentially they were a secretive bureaucratic body making decisions of great moment largely on their own, only lightly attached to the two forms of authority which were acknowledged by the Anglican mind: the august world of archiepiscopal authority or the grand representative dimensions of Synod – duly present in appointed members though Synod was.

The debates of the 1970s had brought a focusing of the Commissioners' attentions. It was not that the General Purposes Committee, the Assets Committee, the Houses Committee and the others were not busy at their other habitual tasks. But something significant had altered, something in the psychological culture of the Commissioners. In their first decade they had owned the power to modernise the Church. If they had a characteristic fear, it was of straying beyond their trust to assist the cure of souls. But subsequently the Commissioners had moved from the new Jerusalem of the Attlee epoch and through the steadier ages of Macmillan and Wilson, in much the same way as every other British corporation. Now they were no longer pursuing a new ideal but immersed in maintaining unexciting necessities. Where British public life was deep in anxieties about salaries and standards of living the Church Commissioners were becoming obsessed with stipends, pensions, expenses and parsonages. Yet it was in these uncontroversial spheres that they were to court greater dangers than ever.

Runcie arrived at Lambeth Palace within months of the arrival of Margaret Thatcher in Downing Street. This was a new era. Life at 1 Millbank, too, was changing. In 1981 Betty Ridley stepped into an honourable retirement and was succeeded by Betsy Haworth, another clergy widow, a deaconess in the Manchester diocese and a member of the General Synod. Two years later Ronald Harris, too, was gone. The backstage manoeuvrings upon which the powers of Church and State relied to produce First Estates Commissioners now produced Sir Douglas Lovelock, a civil servant from the department of Customs and Excise, only a short walk from 1 Millbank itself. Nobody who was subsequently given to reflect upon the fortunes of the Church Commissioners in this new age found this to be anything less than a determining appointment. Lovelock's strength lay in his experience of the machinery of state, and to the Commissioners' dealings with these quarters he would bring a quality of self-assurance, even of ease. In later years Runcie thought this a 'Thatcherite' appointment, one which captured the new mood of the day.[2] This would hardly have been surprising: after all, Brown, Eve and Harris had all been very much men who spoke in their different ways of the general climate of their own age. But Lovelock was not a dogmatic adherent of financial politics of any particular description. While he had an administrator's predilection for institutional rationalities and consolidation, and a penchant for behind the scenes negotiations with government departments, he did not seem to be driven by any powerful vision or by a great fear. Meanwhile, in May 1980, Paul Osmond resigned as secretary and was succeeded by Kenneth Lamb, who had for twenty-five years held a succession of senior positions at the BBC. Perhaps this new constellation showed what Runcie meant when he spoke of the authorities of Millbank as the 'establishment'.[3] At all events, it declared that the Commissioners were still, more than anything else, an institution imbued with a particular culture of public service. It quietly demonstrated an impeccable sense of corporate responsibility. Its financial acumen would be more hotly debated.

The parish

The stark reality that underlay any discussions of the maintenance of the Anglican parish was that between 1959 and 1982 clergy numbers had fallen by 24 per cent. This decline had mostly been borne not by urban areas but by the countryside. Numbers had fallen by 41 per cent in the diocese of Ely, whereas they had actually risen by 1 per cent in Sheffield. Multi-parish benefices were, in general, rural. Now, in the 1980s, the decline slowed down. Many envisaged a further rapid decline in the 1990s, although they could also see that the growth of women's and lay ministry might compensate. Those who argued that women should be ordained had at last a powerful practical weapon in their armoury.

It was difficult to generalise about the current nature of the parish because each diocese had its own approach, and the Pastoral Measure leaned heavily upon the diocese as the decisive agent in pastoral reorganisation. Even comparing predominantly rural dioceses with each other showed up considerable divergences. In the dioceses of Salisbury and Exeter 15 per cent and 12 per cent respectively of benefices were team ministries. In Ely, Lincoln and Norwich they were just 1 per cent, 2 per cent and 3 per cent respectively.[4] By the end of 1980 a total of 267 team ministries and 64 group ministries affecting

---

[2] Ibid.
[3] Ibid.
[4] See the Commissioners' submission to the Archbishops' Commission on Rural Areas, CC (89) 28, p. 19, Board papers, 25 May 1989, ser. 95083/59.

258 benefices had been established across the country. In 104 cases the rector had freehold office, in 163 he served a term of years. Team and group schemes had established 556 team vicars' posts.[5] In all, this was a growing *modus operandi*. By the end of 1985 there were 355 schemes establishing team ministries and a further ninety-three group ministries.[6]

There were sometimes complaints that these industrious acts of amalgamation had gone a step too far. In January 1986 a representation was made against a scheme to rearrange five benefices in the north-east corner of the diocese of Norwich. The scheme intended the creation of nothing less than two six-parish benefices. A member of one wrote of her 'personal dismay' at the scale of these new units. It must reduce the incumbent merely to 'a travelling performer of ceremonies'; 'Miss Lewis', the report adds, 'says that, as someone who believes in the priesthood, she finds this disturbing.' The bishop replied that each parish had only about 200 members and that they were already in many ways linked together. It was difficult to think up an alternative, working, as they must, to their 'Sheffield' figures. Other reconfigurations had stumbled at the evident truth that some parishes did not 'get on' together or because the number so gathered would simply be too low to make sense. Even the new benefice would number only 1,200–1,300 people: the diocese tried to ensure that benefices across the board were no smaller. Benefices composed of five and six parishes were not now uncommon: 'Some benefices which are even larger than this are working well without any clerical help from the incumbent.'[7]

In the sphere of buildings, dealings with the government across the Runcie era often balanced advantages and disadvantages in a slightly haphazard way. By 1983 the state had, even in conditions of severe constraint on public expenditure, increased its contribution to the Redundant Churches Fund from 50 per cent to 60 per cent. If the government appeared generous here, the imposition of value-added tax on all restorative work cost the Church dearly. This also complicated in no small measure the search for alternative uses. By May 1988 the Commissioners faced the fifth quinquennium of the Redundant Churches Fund. The Church could complain that it had been hard hit by the effects of the new (and disastrous) Local Government Finance Bill. But because of this the Department of the Environment was found to be amenable to an increase in their support for the fund from 60 per cent to 70 per cent. With such a dominant

[5] PC, annual report to 31 Dec. 1980, Board papers, 21 May 1981, ibid. pt 50.
[6] PC, annual report to 31 Dec. 1985, 9, Board papers, 24 Apr. 1986, ibid. pt 57.
[7] PC report, Roughton with Felbrigg with Melton', CC (86) 5, Board papers, 27 Feb. 1986, ibid. pt 56.

share, some began to ask again if the government was beginning to acquire a greater power over the life of the Church of England than was acceptable to the Church itself.

In the matter of buildings, too, there were political scares over ecclesiastical exemption. Various conservation lobbies were persistently hankering after change and the government complained loudly that it was finding them hard to placate. Synod passed a stout motion to defend the rights of the Church; there were a few quiet, ongoing diplomatic sorties with a government which appeared not to have its heart on change and certainly had its mind on other affairs. In all this Lovelock and Locke were busy, and it brought out the best in the First Church Estates Commissioner, for in these quarters he was a self-assured performer who felt that he knew well how to judge matters. The upshot was only some strengthening of the hand of the secretary of state in disputed cases, while there was, at least, one result entirely in the Church's favour: that state aid for historic churches would involve a commitment of 'adequate resources' permanently.[8] Of this political success the Church Commissioners made much, and it was right that they should do so. It was a defining victory in a long-running saga.

Redundancy: trends, dilemmas and curiosities

The Church Commissioners had always been determined to present the closure of churches more as evidence of migration than anything smacking of decline. The whole question fell into two halves: redundancy and the growth of new housing areas. There had been an exhibition with a cunning title, 'The challenge of redundant churches: a measure of success', touring the country and ending up at Ipswich. Here it assisted in the announcement of a new scheme for the churches of the city centre, by which four medieval churches were conveyed to the council which, in turn, leased them to a new Ipswich Historic Churches Trust. Their future now lay in 'civic, public or educational' purposes. Within a year this exhibition had been incorporated within another, 'Just stewards?' In this, the Redundant Churches Committee noted, the press was certainly interested, particularly *Country Life*. Meanwhile, the Commissioners still received enquiries from private individuals who wished to buy and live in a church. There were articles in newspapers and television programmes,

---

[8] Bishop of Rochester note 'Ecclesiastical exemption', with papers, CC (86) 51, Board papers, 25 Sept. 1986, ibid. See also minutes of that meeting, pp. 3–4, and Shelley note, CC (86) 56, Board papers, 27 Nov. 1986, ser. 95083/56.

some positive and some not. One was called 'Discovering English Churches', another 'Heritage in Danger'.[9]

In the midst of this, the congregation of St Michael and All Angels in Derby fought on against their persistent adversaries. But now the battle to keep services going was all but lost. The Friends of St Michael's Church had been formed and in 1981 they organised a petition of 163 names against a new scheme to appropriate the church and convert it into offices to be leased by the Derby diocesan board of finance. The Friends preferred that the church become an ecclesiastical museum and cultural centre and worked to raise funds to support such a venture. Money did not come in; time ran out. The Friends asked for more of both. The plan to build offices loomed. A subcommittee of the Commissioners dutifully visited Derby and came down against the museum, for offices could be built at once and that was surely the best way to preserve the building. On September 1991 the Board overruled representations made against the scheme. This time it really was the end.[10]

Here and there a particular story showed the context in which the Commissioners worked to be an altered one. The debate over St Mary's, Savile Town, was part of the corporate memory at Millbank. The Commissioners were conscious that when it came to selling redundant churches to other faiths they were breaking new ground, and doing so without the cover of the General Synod. In short, until the mind of the Church had declared itself, the Commissioners themselves were exposed to dangers. But the caution, even the nervousness, which was the legacy of St Mary's was still no guarantee of a greater safety. It could even become a new danger in itself.

The Board of governors first discussed the redundant church of St Luke in Southampton in April 1982. The Redundant Churches Committee had proposed that it be taken over as a temple by local Sikhs. The Board was edgy and asked for reassurance about the state of local opinion. By May the diocesan secretary had carried out a thorough programme of consultation within the diocese. The result was overwhelmingly in favour of the scheme. The Board of the Commissioners declared itself satisfied, but also felt that they must preserve a judicial distance. They had had their fingers burned before. The bishop of Winchester, John Taylor, began to press for action. A diocesan deputation arrived. By 16 June 1982 the deanery synod was registering its concern at evidence of delay and urged that the Commissioners proceed, this time supporting their view with even heftier favourable majorities than before. The discrepancy between national and local church opinion began to attract curiosity. The

[9] RCC, annual report to 31 Dec. 1979, Board papers, 27 Mar. 1980, ibid. pt 49.
[10] Board minutes, 24 Sept. 1981, p. 6.

Sunday Times published an article: *Red faces in the Church of England.* By July the parochial church council and the deanery synod had again voted overwhelmingly for the scheme. Representatives from the city council had added their voices of support.

In September 1982 Bishop Taylor led valedictory services in a number of churches recently declared redundant in the centre of Southampton. He consulted the General Synod's Memorandum of Comment of 1973. All was done properly and well and with reference to every available authority, convention and expectation. The churches were, he pronounced, 'no longer set aside'. He then went around each one with members of the former church councils to make quite sure that all Christian symbols were removed. He found not only sadness, but 'a clear note of looking forward'. And they remembered that new churches had been built in other parts of the city to which people had moved in more recent years.[11]

Yet this was not the tone of the deliberations in London. When the Board returned to St Luke's church at the end of September, they inspected a collection of relevant papers and a little booklet on Sikhism in Southampton. The chairman of the Redundant Churches Committee at Millbank, Lord Sandford, observed that there was no real opposition to the scheme locally and that the bishop's submission was comprehensive and an exposition of theological principle. But Oswald Clark suspected that this weight of material and opinion from within the diocese might have undue influence on their own independent power.

At this point the Board of the Commissioners took what seemed to their critics a wrong turn. By the slenderest of margins (eleven to nine, with four abstaining) they decided to turn to the General Synod. Synod had not discussed the general issue since July 1973 when a motion that a redundant church should not be made over to another faith had been rejected.[12] When it met now, Synod made but a poor job of the question. The debate was inadequate and it was cut off abruptly. Most bishops favoured the motion that St Luke's be handed over to the Sikhs of Southampton (twenty-five to three); the House of Clergy was divided, but just in favour (101:92); and the House of Laity, almost equally divided, opposed (ninety to ninety-six). This meant that the motion was effectively 'negatived'. The problem was back with the Church Commissioners: would they approve the scheme and sell the church, or not?

By now it was February 1983. The last months had brought yet more representations in favour of the sale from Southampton itself.

[11] Shelley note, 'Southampton, St Luke', CC (83) 5, Board papers, 24 Feb. 1983, ser. 95083/53.
[12] Board minutes, 24 Feb. 1983, pp. 2–5.

The rural dean of Southampton emphasised the need to appear neighbourly and observed 'great disappointment' in the local area at the poverty and the brevity of the General Synod debate. The vicar of Andover remonstrated that local church people and civic authorities were unanimous. The chief executive of the City of Southampton observed that council members showed a 'very real and deep concern'. The honorary secretary of the Sikh Missionary Society wrote that surely it was better that it be used still for the worship of God than made into a warehouse or converted to sell liquor? The Sikhs preached tolerance and would never work against Christianity, indeed they had much in common with Christians. Even Ivor Bulmer-Thomas was in favour, this time in his capacity as chairman of the Friends of Friendless Churches (though he favoured a lease). Weighed against all this were just six local objectors.

But the harshest complaint of all came from Bishop Taylor, and he was furious. In Winchester, he thundered, they had had to wait for a decision on policy from the whole Church of England, yet there was no canon or ruling in existence to prohibit the sale of a redundant church to adherents to another faith. The General Synod had come up with rulings in February and July 1973 which were 'mutually contradictory'. As the Pastoral Measure clearly placed the power to adjudicate with the Commissioners they must take it on themselves to decide. Moreover, actually to defer a decision to the General Synod was in itself an exercise of power for which, under the Pastoral Measure, they had no authority. The hesitations of the Commissioners declared a public mistrust of his own judgement and of the diocesan submission. The local council was not only in favour, but had invited the Department of the Environment to make a grant of £100,000 out of the government's Urban Aid Fund to support the Sikhs. In their refusal to sell St Luke's to the Sikhs of Southampton the generosity of Christ himself was repudiated; his very image was distorted to become 'something self-regarding and ungenerous'.

Money, too, was involved. Two-thirds of the £80,000 that the Sikhs would pay once approval had been given would be paid into the diocesan pastoral account. And this account was used to support the work of five new worship centres in new areas, churches which needed money. If they lost that money Bishop Taylor wanted equivalent compensation, together with a grant to match the interest that they had lost because of the delay, and a third sum to cover maintenance of the church building.[13]

At Millbank they looked again at the proceedings of the General Synod to see what they could make of them. Kenneth Lamb observed

[13] Letters presented in RCC report, 'Use of redundant churches for worship by non-Christian faiths', CC (83) 66, Board papers, 24 Dec. 1983, ser. 95083/53.

that although the vote in Synod had been lost in houses, the overall majority was still in favour. Should they now proceed? Sandford remarked that Synod had discussed a general principle, not a specific case, and that was what the Commissioners had before them. He noted that in 1973 a majority in Synod had been opposed, and that now a majority was in favour (186:172; 216:191). Previously the laity had been two to one against; now it was evenly divided. In this light, the Redundant Churches Committee commended the case of St Luke's to the Board again with greater confidence. Clark continued to resist: the motion in Synod had been 'attractively couched' to win support, but it had only 40 per cent of the members behind it. It was said that even if Synod were divided, the bishops voted twenty-five to three in favour, and should they not be led by the bishops? To this came the reply that bishops might well be bishops, but they were only one house in a three-chamber synod. If the General Synod had voted against this motion how could one diocese appear to overrule the corporate mind of the Church? Relations between the Church Commissioners and Synod, observed the bishop of Southall, were delicate enough as it was. But, Sandford emphasised, a debate in Synod did not bind them.

It came to the vote. There were fourteen votes in favour of the sale and nine against. Bishop Say and Kenneth Lamb together warned the Board not to gossip to the press. Evidently there was the suspicion in the air that not everybody there had been acting quite well. The scheme came into effect on 16 March 1983. The sale of the building had been completed by August.[14]

The source and character of objections to schemes of redundancy could be exceedingly hard to predict. The stone mason, Ben Lloyd, who had written against the government of the scribes, opposed everything that the Salisbury diocese proposed, on the basis of numerical rhythms and schemes. In February 1984 the redundancy of St Mark's, Easton, in Bristol, provoked the representation of a woman who had not been a member of the congregation, was not a parishioner and had no connection with the church whatsoever. It was, she said simply, 'a beautiful old church in an oasis of green and peace in a truly awful inner city area'. Why could not the 'ugly' Baptist Church opposite be declared redundant instead, and its congregation transferred accordingly? To this the bishop of Bristol replied that the initiative for redundancy had come from the parochial church council of St Mark's itself. The church was full of dry rot, the organ had been removed for safety and the congregation, too, to St Anne's, Eastville, where they had settled in 'very successfully'. A high proportion of the local population belonged to other faiths and, among those neighbouring buildings, the church school had been sold two years

[14] Board minutes, 23 Dec. 1983, pp. 2–5.

before to an Islamic organisation.[15] In December 1989 a scheme to close the church of Holy Trinity in Scarborough excited an objection from a visitor to the town, a Miss T. L. Hill. Even small congregations, she wrote, should be encouraged. She wrote from her hotel, gave no other address and disappeared. Efforts to find her were unavailing. But, no matter, the Official Solicitor advised that the Commissioners must treat Miss Hill's letter in accordance with Section 6 of the Pastoral Measure. Holy Trinity, Scarborough disappeared along with its elusive protector.[16] And then a footnote to the great struggles of the Fisher period: in April 1984 the Board viewed a scheme for the dissolution of the benefice of Mildenhall and for its transfer into a neighbouring benefice, a team ministry. To this there were a number of voices of protest, one of them from Miss Patricia Courtman, its patron, and the daughter of its late incumbent, E. G. Courtman.[17]

Sometimes churches were left to nature itself. The church of East Hatley St Denis in the diocese of Ely, a building of thirteenth-century origin, had by 1985 been empty for almost twenty years, covered by creepers, occupied only by bats and owls and, in the crypt, a fox. But nature, too, brought its own qualities. Around the church of St Denis flourished a variety of unusual flora and fauna. The church was handed over to South Cambridgeshire District Council as a nature reserve and field study centre for natural history.[18] 1985, too, brought the first tale of what was called 'controlled ruination', a course framed in the new 1983 Pastoral Measure. The Church of St Mary, Levisham, in the York diocese, had been declared redundant in 1980. For a time it was occupied by the Society for the Promotion of the Preservation of English Parish Churches, whose efforts were increasingly dominated by its own self-preservation, and which then withdrew. A new body of friends rallied round the church, not however to save it but to allow it to die with dignity. The nave and tower roofs came off, the walls were capped; memorials were moved into the chancel and a wrought iron gate placed at the front of it. It all cost rather little and sufficient grants were raised.[19]

In the cities, meanwhile, the decade brought strains of a different kind. In February 1985 Lord Sandford observed that in London property developers were 'coming to regard as economic propositions the conversion of large but undistinguished Victorian churches, which might otherwise be demolished'. Indeed developers became more and more accomplished in their art, and as they did so they took on more

[15] Ibid. 23 Feb. 1984.
[16] Ibid. 14 Dec. 1989.
[17] Ibid. 26 Apr. 1984, p. 7.
[18] RCC, annual report to 31 Dec. 1984, Board papers, 28 Feb. 1985, ser. 95083/55.
[19] RCC, annual report to 31 Dec. 1985, Board papers, 22 May 1986, ibid. pt 56.

church buildings than ever before. Increasingly there was competition between rival bidders. At Holy Trinity, Paddington, the Commissioners had faced criticisms of worldliness, for they had appeared simply to off-load the site to the highest bidder. But they remonstrated in reply that 68 per cent of the sites sold so far had gone to community uses, and by July, of the money earned by the sale of that particular church, £200,000 was set aside to buy a youth work centre and a place for homeless families.[20]

For years the numbers of closures, sales, conversions and demolitions had been increasing. But now there was reason to think that the pace was slowing. When he submitted the report of the Redundant Churches Fund in February 1986, Sandford remarked that the demolition of churches had fallen to an 'all-time low'.[21] With the passage of time, the alternative uses to which some of these churches had first been put became redundant themselves. The church of St Margaret in Canterbury, only 150 yards from the cathedral precincts, had since 1958 served as a day centre for the deaf. Now the diocesan committee endorsed a proposal from the Canterbury Archaeological Trust Limited that it become the Canterbury Pilgrim Centre. Two million people a year visited the city. The church could bring in money for its own restoration. In 1989 the church of Covenham St Bartholomew was almost shipped off to California, bound for a parish which was in dispute with the Episcopal Church there. But the enterprise was thwarted by British conservation groups and by a flourish of higher politics within the Episcopal Church itself. The Redundant Churches Fund now held 200 church buildings, dating from the Saxon period through to the close of the nineteenth century.[22]

The dioceses were still responsible for the disposal of the contents of these churches, but the Commissioners held the central contents register. Now it was bulging. It had begun to receive Roman Catholic items too, gathered from churches and convents. Applicants for these items continued to lodge requests. Pews were most popular, but there was also a sustained interest in general sanctuary furniture, crosses, crucifixes, candlesticks, communion plate and thuribles, then wood panelling, stone flooring and masonry from walls. A church in Sri Lanka applied for a three-ton bell; St Mark's Episcopal cathedral in Salt Lake City, Utah, for a weathercock, 'to stare back', it was said, 'at the Mormons' Golden Angel'.[23]

---

[20] Board minutes, 28 Feb. 1985, pp. 4–5.
[21] Ibid. 27 Feb. 1986, p. 2.
[22] RCC, annual report to 31 Dec. 1985, Board papers, 22 May 1986, ser. 95083/56.
[23] RCC, annual report to 31 Dec. 1986, Board papers, 19 Feb. 1987, ibid. pt 57.

See houses

In the accommodation of bishops the Runcie years brought little change. In 1987–8 the old and often criticised system of maintaining a team of architects to watch over see houses, a system weakened by retirement and voluntary resignation, was finally altered. Supervision was devolved to the dioceses, and fifteen appointments of local architects and surveyors were made during the course of 1988 alone.

Nor was the saga of the London see house yet at an end. Indeed, it now came around once more, like a regularly revived gothic melodrama at a Victorian playhouse.

In 1981, after the retirement of Bishop Ellison, his successor, Graham Leonard, formerly of Truro, had moved into 8 Barton Street. Within a year he had written to the Commissioners that it would not do. Discussions dragged on for three years. In June 1984 the Houses Committee agreed that it was for the best to leave matters as they were, but a new search party set off on a new quest for a solution. Clearly they were expected to be some time, for no deadline was set down for their return.

For a while nothing turned up. But then one day two London archdeacons, one of them Derek Hayward of the diocesan board of finance, came up with the idea that an entirely new house might be built as a part of the redevelopment of the diocesan offices in Causton Street, a prestigious new enterprise which would also comprise an assembly hall and 40,000 square feet of office and other space. A flurry of meetings and reports followed. In May 1986 the archdeacons met Patrick Locke at Millbank. They believed that the new see house could be built for £1 million and Barton Street be sold for between £800,000 and £1 million. They were, furthermore, off to the bishop's council to propose that the diocese should share, equally with the Commissioners, costs beyond those realised by the sale of Barton Street. More figures, all of them notional, were tossed about. Locke replied coolly that he expected the Commissioners to be reluctant to pay out any extra money. The matter must go to the Board. The archdeacons asked if they could approach members of the Board themselves. That, said Locke, would not be unusual. The two archdeacons disappeared into the streets of Westminster.

In June Bishop Leonard read a statement about the London see house to his council, and then left it to consider the matter without him. He denied that this was, for him, a personal matter. He did not want to move, in fact he was too elderly to want such an upheaval, and by 1991 'at the latest' he would be gone anyway. He had observed the differing views of his diocese and had tried to hold them together as best he could without appearing to be himself biased in any way. He believed that even if the council pressed the Commissioners 'very strongly' to accept their responsibilities ('and I am very conscious of the way in which the assets of the See have been allowed to diminish over the years so that all we are left with is the present inadequate house') there would be criticism for such a use of money, even if it were no great sum, in the pursuit of adequacy. He believed that the whole matter should be put on one side, until it became a crisis, if that were to be the outcome. Until then, he would 'soldier on' in Barton Street.

By June 1986 the bishop's council had reaffirmed the inadequacy and unsuitability of 8 Barton Street; and affirmed that the Church Commissioners bore the responsibility to provide the diocese with a suitable and adequate house and, holding as they did the historic assets of the diocese, must do so while the present bishop was still with them. The council was convinced that it was necessary to develop the Causton Street site and believed that part of it 'could' be suitable for a new see house. The Commissioners should make this their 'first priority'. In his turn Patrick Locke had told Hayward and the other archdeacon that he expected the bishop's council to endorse their own rejection of Barton Street in 'letters of blood' ('or words to that effect'). To this the archdeacons replied cheerfully that no members of the council had offered a transfusion.[24] So now the diocese was not offering to put up any of its own money at all, over and above that raised by the sale of Barton Street. In July 1986 the Board saw these papers and agreed unanimously that Causton Street was no solution to the problem. That suggestion should be dropped. Nor were they sanguine about Barton Street. The Board might well accept that it had been a mistake from the beginning and start to look for another house. But then there had already been three years of that and nothing had appeared. They sent the matter back to the Houses Committee. There Ridley was sure that they had done what they could.[25]

[24] HC report, 'London see house', CC (86) 41 with annexes, Board papers, 24 July 1986, ibid. pt 56.
[25] Board minutes, 24 July 1986, pp. 2–3.

12

Four Campaigns

The insufficiency of enlightenment: the ethics of investment

The debates over the Midland Bank in the 1970s had demonstrated all too clearly that the more seriously such matters were taken, the more complicated and ambiguous they became. This experience was obviously at odds with the simplicities of public campaigns and rhetoric. The lobbies which generally defined open debate could be expected only too readily to convert qualifications into prevarications, assurances of private initiatives into acquiescence if not connivance, reiterations of complexities into lame excuses and deplorable failures of prophetic insight. This was observed, and lamented, often enough. Yet, at the same time, it was indeed the lobbies that could often see with a sharper eye that complicated matters should not inhibit the sensitive conscience, because they could be starkly clear and urgent on issues of justice. Moreover, these vocal groups could bring to their chosen controversies new insights and information from a wide variety of sources. This might well have compensated for a latent danger in the Commissioners' methods: it is possible to be too dependent upon 'official' material, or on the bland rationalism of conventional wisdom.

South Africa remained a crucial issue.[1] In 1981 the General Synod produced a new report, *Partners in mission*, in which could be found the words: 'The needs of the disadvantaged both in this country and in other countries (including, in particular, South Africa), should increasingly weigh with the Commissioners in shaping their investment policies and in exercising the influence which their investments make possible. The needs should be ascertained in consultation with the Church in the countries concerned.' In response the Church Commissioners dryly acknowledged their duties to beneficiaries and benefactors: that primary obligation to the clergy, deaconesses and

---

[1] It is interesting that it is the subject of South Africa which draws the Church Commissioners briefly into the foreground in Kenneth N. Medhurst and George H. Moyser, *Church and politics in a secular age,* Oxford 1988, 346–8.

licensed lay workers, and equal debt to those who had given money and land at the outset. This, they maintained, was the foundation of all their thinking. They must seek 'the best current income that is consistent with maintaining the real value of the Commissioners' assets'. But they also strove to be a model, conscious of their 'unique responsibility'. Now they could also assure Synod of regular meetings with the Central Board of Finance, the Board for Social Responsibility, with industrial chaplains, with the investing 'arms' of other church bodies.[2]

By the end of 1983 the Assets Committee submitted to the Board a new document on their 'ethical approach to investments', another of its periodic reappraisals of the situation, but the first on such a scale since 1972. This paper revealed an increasing determination to take moral responsibility for what the Commissioners actually did invest in, and to show concern and to exert influence for the purposes of enhancing the well-being of employees, of shareholders and of communities at large. Copious 'ethical' records were now maintained, discussions with company managements were constantly in train. The 1983 report offered recent examples of this: one was certainly curious enough. In June 1981 there had been allegations that the Falkland Islands Company, a subsidiary of Coalite – in which the Commissioners held shares – had 'collaborated' with Argentinian troops during the occupation of the islands, selling them wool and other goods and, after that, charging the British Ministry of Defence inordinately high rents for billeting British troops. In public the company was reluctant to say anything, and was not convincing. In private they proved 'much more forthcoming'. The Commissioners were entirely reassured. Such encounters appeared to vindicate the methods and the means whereby the Commissioners conducted their business. In the words of the memorandum, they did 'as much as anything can to bring the influence of the Church to bear on the world of business'. It was not public blandishment that produced results but respectful private manoeuvrings.

Any entanglement in the armaments industry still provoked the loudest opposition within the Church. Yet many manufacturing companies were to some degree involved in making armaments and it was not 'normally possible' to isolate particular companies exporting weapons to oppressive regimes. Gambling was easier: the Commissioners could still avoid it entirely. On breweries and distilleries there had been 'the greatest diversity' of opinions, particularly over breweries. Some feared that it signalled that members of the Church must be abstainers, and, solicitously, the Commissioners

---

[2] AC report, 'The Commissioners' ethical approach to investment', 9 Dec. 1983, CC (83) 72, appendix 1, Board papers, 15 Dec. 1983, ser. 95083/54.

wished to reassure those who were anxious on that account. Spirits
were more dangerous than beer, but beer still appeared to contribute
to alcoholism. In any case, many breweries were also involved in
distilling. Alcohol remained banned. On tobacco there could now be
no doubt; the same went for newspapers. As for publishing and
broadcasting, theatre and film, there was surely a case for 'modest
relaxation'. Would the Board now consider allowing investment in
companies concerned to 'encourage Christian endeavour and matters
of an educational nature'?[3]

But in the 1980s few searching eyes were looking at these matters.
They were still turned towards South Africa. It had to be
acknowledged that the mind of the Commissioners was not quite the
mind of Synod. By the spring of 1983 the view of the old
enlightenment was no longer in tune with the new times. When the
Board of Social Responsibility had produced the report, *Facing the facts*,[4]
Harris had spoken and then voted against its recommendations.
General Synod had passed a resolution that 'progressive
disengagement … is now the appropriate basic policy for this country
to adopt as a contribution to bringing about peaceful change in South
Africa'.[5] But recently the Commissioners had purchased mineral rights
in two areas of South Africa in order to perpetuate profitable sand and
gravel operations there. This was beginning to look ominous. A gulf
was opening up.

The Assets Committee wholly agreed with Harris. It felt that
Christians 'can properly and sincerely hold differing views as to how to
use whatever influence is available to them to help bring about the
objective which they all share'. Synod did recognise that 'total
disinvestment is impossible'. This made what was now being called
'constructive engagement' all the more important. The committee still
monitored carefully, 'a substantial operation involving a good deal of
correspondence and personal contact'. Since the synod resolution they
had adopted 'a slightly more questioning attitude'.[6] There were
frequent meetings with the Board of Social Responsibility and more
would follow. The Assets Committee did not want to look isolated in
this. It now looked to the Board to support them in maintaining the
present line.

In April 1985 Dean Webster suggested on the Board that mention
in the forthcoming report should be made of the unrest in South
Africa. This was prescient, for the situation in that country was

[3] Ibid.
[4] General Synod [GS] report 520.
[5] AC report, 'The Commissioners' ethical approach to investment', 9 Dec. 1983,
CC (83) 72, appendix 1, Board papers, 15 Dec. 1983, ser. 95083/54, 10–11.
[6] Ibid. p. 13.

deteriorating. Abroad, opinion was growing still more intense. It polarised. However sincerely and profoundly Harris, and Lovelock, held to a belief that an enlightened policy must be a mix of abstention and involvement, in this new context the Commissioners were seen to be backing the wrong horse – or, at least, the horse most often favoured not by the energetic campaigning forces of reform, but by the sullen, often unduly acquiescent forces of conservatism. At some times, and on some issues, it could often be said that it was enough for Christians to have their different views and to respect and accept each other for that. But now the public mood was becoming more restless, more critical, more insistent. Most critically, black opinion in South Africa itself was changing. Where this led the protesting world must surely follow.[7]

In September 1985 Runcie received a letter from Frank Field MP, questioning the practices of a number of companies operating in South Africa, in which the Church Commissioners had shares. The letter duly made its way to Millbank.[8] Lovelock contested much of the information on which Field based his letter and offered a robust defence. There was, he insisted, clear evidence that the business community in South Africa was pressing for reform in that country. This was something the Commissioners could reinforce:

> We believe that our policy of constructive engagement is the only practicable policy for a major Fund with our particular financial responsibilities and that it is the right policy. By encouraging British companies to pursue enlightened employment policies in South Africa, we believe we are making a contribution, however small, to the eventual dismemberment of the system of apartheid that we all abhor.[9]

In October 1985 Lovelock reported to the Board that he and Kenneth Lamb had recently met Bishop Tutu. 'He feared it had not been a meeting of minds.' Tutu had conceded, 'belatedly', that industry in South Africa was pressing President Botha to relax the apartheid system. But Tutu believed that industry must do more; that it should give Botha a year to dismantle apartheid and disinvest if he did not. The deputy chairman of the Assets Committee, Brian Howard, had also been to South Africa, to visit the senior management there of Barclays, Shell and Bowthorpe. He had met the archbishop of

---

[7] Board minutes, 25 Apr. 1985, p. 3.
[8] Frank Field's letter of 5 Sept. 1985 duly ended up in the papers for the Board papers of 19 Dec. 1985, as an appendix to the AC report, 'The Church Commissioners' investment policies', CC (85) 48, ser. 95083/55.
[9] Sir Douglas Lovelock to 16 Sept. 1985, ibid. appendix 3.

Capetown, who seemed, he thought, to have appreciated the Commissioners' line. Howard, believed that 'enlightened' business could train black employees and improve their situation, and that of their communities too. The country must benefit from new capital and new skills for these brought higher living standards. Sanctions, for their part, must deepen recession. Howard had returned 'even more convinced' that investment there was right. The bishop of Birmingham, Hugh Montefiore, had told the Commissioners that it would be a 'helpful gesture' if they could sell off one of their large holdings in a company like Barclays. But then Barclays had, it was felt, a good record in South Africa. Some black employees were in management positions. Any gesture could only be 'capricious'.[10]

The pressure of the debate was soon opening up fissures within the Church Commissioners. Frank Field had written to members of the Board pressing them to summon a special general meeting on the issue. Lovelock thought that to do so would circumvent the 'machinery' that already existed for the discussion of such questions. The Assets Committee would report to the Board as soon as it could. But Lovelock now found that the Board did not wish to be led by the Assets Committee. It was heard that the phrase 'constructive engagement' was unhelpful; it had been adopted as a policy of the American government and was hence 'discredited' as an independent term. Webster argued that they could not see their obligation to the clergy, the deaconesses and lay workers as being absolutely 'paramount'; 'the general welfare of mankind should come first'. Indeed, if finance were paramount, why did the Commissioners have any ethical criteria at all? In the midst of this tension there was a determination to present a 'powerful and positive' front to Synod.[11]

In South Africa itself the economic and social situation deteriorated sharply. Pressure outside the country had grown. The United States, the European Community and the Commonwealth were now all operating limited sanctions. The South African Council of Churches had called for disinvestment, and its general secretary, Beyers Naude, had addressed the General Synod of the Church of England and called upon the Church Commissioners to disinvest immediately 'from any institution which directly or indirectly supports the apartheid regime'. It was said that of their holdings worth over £1 million cited in the 1983 annual report, the Commissioners were seen to have a heavier than average inclination towards UK companies with South African interests. They were at odds with the mind of the General Synod. They were investing in apartheid itself.

10 Board minutes, 24 Oct. 1985, pp. 2–4.
11 AC report, 'The Church Commissioners' investment policy and South Africa', CC (85) 48, Board papers, 19 Dec. 1985, ser. 95083/55.

Many of these criticisms the Assets Committee waved aside as irrelevant. To take only the larger holdings must be misleading. Of the 146 British companies in which the Commissioners held shares, sixty-seven had some stake in South Africa. Many of them did not publish in their annual reports and accounts the percentage of sales or profits made in South Africa, so that it was not at all easy to see what they were doing. None of these sixty-seven were seen to have interests in South Africa amounting to more than 15 per cent of their total holdings. In short, the Church Commissioners' involvement in that country amounted to less than 1 per cent of the income from all their assets spread over eighty-two companies. The terminology used by the Commissioners to justify themselves no longer looked adequate. The Assets Committee favoured discarding the term 'constructive engagement', 'without implying a change of policy'. Since the latest Synod debate, the staff in the Investment Department had 'done a lot' to tighten up still further their monitoring, calling on the Department of Trade and Industry for company reports and drawing up an annual review of the affairs of each one. If a company were ever given the benefit of the doubt in one year they were scrutinised the more searchingly the next. At present there were four that they were not happy with and these were being 'actively pursued'. To sell shares in any company remained the last resort. When it came to South Africa, the Assets Committee was sure that they must pursue peaceful change. Economic growth and prosperity were essential to that. A black community that prospered was better able to pursue its own interests. Companies which supported social schemes also played their part in that way. Such initiatives 'eroded' apartheid. This was the 'enlightened' path of progress.

As the controversy became more political, it also grew more legalistic, and more complicated. In April 1984 a High Court judgement by Sir Robert Megarry, which resolved a dispute over the management of the Mineworkers Pension Fund, produced the verdict that the 'law on the duties of trustees was that they should exercise their powers in the best interests of the present and future beneficiaries of the trust ... when the purpose was to provide financial benefits for beneficiaries, their best interests were normally the best financial interests'. At the Church Commissioners this was soon being cited by advocates of continued, if limited, engagement with South Africa.

When a paper by the Assets Committee on South African investments came again before the Board, Lovelock remarked that he had only recently met representatives of the Urban Foundation, a liberal, multi-racial charity in South Africa, which had found British companies a force for good. A prominent black trade unionist, Mr

Xulu, opposed disinvestment, saying that many black workers saw
such investment as, in part, theirs too. The criticisms which Dr Naude
had made of them at Synod were ill-informed. Now Stanley Booth-
Clibborn, bishop of Manchester, had asked Lovelock to write to all
companies with interests there asking them to disinvest. He could not
think this wise. If they did so they would cause unemployment. At less
than 1 per cent the Commissioners' involvement was as slender as it
really could be. In this Lovelock was supported by the Second
Commissioner, Michael Alison. Did the Anglican Church in South
Africa support Dr Naude's views? What did the archbishop of
Capetown think? What did the archbishop of York, who had recently
been to the WCC meeting in Harare, think?

   This time there were critics. Bishop Westwood of Peterborough
asked whether the Assets Committee was equipped to deal with ethical
matters? They had no moral theologian among them. That being so
the Board must attach more weight to the views of the General Synod
and of church leaders in South Africa itself. The Assets Committee's
paper was not an adequate response to a situation which was
'potentially revolutionary'. The bishop was supported in these words.
It was said that the present policy could still represent 'implicit'
support for apartheid. To support the *status quo* might prejudice the
position of the Anglican Church in South Africa. It might even put at
risk the lives of its members. To disinvest, though, might strengthen
the position of moderate men like Bishop Tutu. Then the legal aspect
was not invulnerable. If the Megarry judgement were accepted as a
basis for investments, they might abolish all banned categories which
did not offend against Charity Law. Those governors appointed by the
General Synod feared more public dispute and hoped that the
Commissioners' policy would be modified at the next session of
Synod. To this Lovelock simply repeated the statutory responsibilities
of the Commissioners. To sell what amounted to two-thirds in value
of their portfolio was simply inconsistent with their obligations. These
companies were large and brought the assurance of impressive growth,
which smaller companies could not offer. The Assets Committee did
not lack an explicit element of moral guidance: it had a clerical
member, John Lewis, archdeacon of Cheltenham.[12]

   By February 1986 there were letters from the archbishop of York
and the archbishop of Capetown. The former found himself 'slightly
anxious about being set up as an expert on South Africa on the basis
of a 48 hour Conference in Harare', but he would do his best.
Sanctions had been much in the air there, but not disinvestment. He
observed confusion between symbolic, economic and political

[12] Board minutes, 19 Dec. 1985, pp. 1–6. Again, the unusual number of pages here
shows how protracted the discussion was.

expectations: the arguments and their counter-arguments rarely met on the same level, but moved between them. At the Foreign Office he had been told that the world of business was always, at the end of the day, going to run itself, and not be governed by political judgements. He himself doubted that Tutu's position would be enhanced by anything new done by the Commissioners in London. Further withdrawal would be minimal, and what was minimal could hardly be visible at that distance. They should await the outcome of a new initiative by the Commonwealth and support the British Council of Churches in their endorsement of targeted sanctions.[13] Meanwhile, the archbishop of Capetown felt himself unable to reply satisfactorily. The Churches in South Africa, he said, were themselves divided on the question. Tutu favoured disinvestment and sanctions; the Zulu leader Buthelezi did not. The white community was just as divided. There was no firm 'official' view.[14]

The difficulty which the Church Commissioners faced in these matters was partly that markets changed all the time. Shares moved around, directed by policy or not. This was not only a complication. At Millbank some were beginning to see how it might pave the way towards a solution of their troubles. General disinvestment and 'adverse economic factors' had begun to depress the 'proportionate stake' in South Africa held by a number of the companies in which the Commissioners had shares. This trend was gathering momentum. The wish of Synod in 1982 appeared 'in a practical way' to be fulfilled.[15] It looked to be enough. When he went to the Board Lovelock was keen to stress that because the clergy was unrepresented on the Assets Committee this did not necessarily mean that every other member of the committee was driven purely by financial values; 'they sought to combine Christian insights with business acumen'. This time a sense of 'general satisfaction' prevailed.[16]

It was brief. In July 1986 Synod passed a stiffer resolution, pledging itself to 'a new South Africa' as defined by Bishop Tutu, urging the government to adopt sanctions and urging all banking and commercial companies to increase pressure on the South African economy, by disengagement if necessary.[17] Another debate followed in November. Lovelock worked hard behind the scenes to take the sting out of a new

---

[13] Archbishop Habgood letter, 8 Jan. 1986, in AC report, 'The Church Commissioners' investment policies', CC (86) 9, Board papers, 27 Feb. 1986, ser. 95083/55.

[14] Philip Russell, Archbishop of Capetown, to Shelley, 7 Jan. 1986, ibid.

[15] Archbishop Habgood letter, in CC (86) 9.

[16] Board minutes, Jan. 1986, pp. 2–3.

[17] *Report of the Proceedings of the General Synod*, xvii/2, London 1986, 504–55 (7 July 1986).

motion calling for disengagement. His subtle politicking worked well
on the day, and he had every reason to feel pleased with himself.
Disengagement, however it might occur, was now being presented as a
decision of policy and a response to the mind of Synod, not as an
accident of economics. Such manoeuvring, arguably a sleight of hand,
did not go unnoticed, or unchallenged, on the Board itself.

The lawyers arrive

So far Synod had been the natural home for debate on South Africa.
But there was about to be another. At this point the arguments came
out of the committee rooms and the halls of the General Synod and
into the barristers' chambers and the courts. Accordingly, when it next
met, the Board faced four lawyers in succession. Instead of clarifying
the terms on which the Commissioners could properly invest their
funds, they now began to question the very purposes for which they
could be used. Mr Phillips at the Old Bailey (13 October 1986) advised
that to cling to the Megarry judgement would not do. This was not a
charity law case. If the Commissioners took that judgement so much
to heart 'it goes a long way to explaining how and why in my view they
are misdirecting themselves as to the nature of their discretion with
regard to their investment policy'. The National Union of Miners fund
was one to which the members themselves paid money for their own
benefit. A charitable trust was one to which individuals paid money
that would in turn be used not for their direct benefit but for
charitable purposes. The first was run merely by executors. The second
by trustees who must interpret and possess the power of discretion:
'they are the mind of the charity and interpreters of its purposes'.
Then:

> As regards the Church Commissioners, those purposes are
> not as I perceive it for the benefit of the clergy and their
> dependants etc. as such (though the Report talks about their
> 'statutory responsibilities to (our) beneficiaries') but to
> promote 'the cure of souls' (as it is quaintly called). That
> phrase, I believe, means in this context the advancement of
> Christianity by and through the Church of England, which
> in practical terms has traditionally and principally been
> interpreted as providing for the clergy – the spearhead of
> the 'cure'. The above distinction is significant in this debate.

For a religious charity the ends could not justify the means: 'the means
must be of a piece with Christian ends'. So this must affect choices of
investment, too. They must decide on things that would assist, not
undermine or be inconsistent with, those principal purposes.

A second opinion, by Mr Heath of Bates, Wells and Braithwaite, was sought by Alan Webster, the dean of St Paul's, and by the Revd William Whiffen. The very word 'beneficiaries' had, it was noted, arisen in the provisions of the Queen Anne's Bounty, and there the beneficiaries were 'the incumbent and other person or persons for the time being entitled to receive the emoluments of a benefice'. But now the beneficiaries must be understood 'in a loose metaphoric sense rather than as a precise description of any legal relationship'. A trust could not exist for the benefit of private individuals, but to promote a particular purpose. As for the Church Commissioners themselves, 'it is not easy to state or even to summarize' their objects; they 'must in my opinion be a matter of implication'. They were not expressly stated in the 1947 measure 'or (so far as I know) anywhere else'. He found their legal objects to be the promotion of the welfare and efficiency of the Church of England. There must be spiritual objects too, but they were not for him to measure.

The third opinion, from the Church Commissioners' own QC, Owen Swingland, stated that 'The Commissioners must apply and invest their funds as will best enable them to provide for the maintenance of the clergy (and achieve the other financial objects which statute has required them to do)'.

They were subject in their investments only to the ordinary rules of equity. Far from being irrelevant the Megarry judgement met the case entirely, and the notion that a pension fund was quite different from a charitable trust was 'misconceived'. The only question that mattered was whether or not deriving income directly or indirectly from a company with connections in South Africa defeated, or tended to defeat, its objects or duties, and since those duties are 'merely to provide the financial support which the clergy needs for its work' such investments would not necessarily be contrary to those duties or objects. In their investments the Commissioners went far beyond what might be understood as their duty, or even their proper concern. But they must not indulge political lobbies or take part in attempts to bring pressure for political purposes: 'That is certainly no part of their function, and would constitute a plain breach of duty.' If Mr Phillips and Mr Heath were right, and the Church Commissioners were charged not merely with the provision of maintenance but with the advancement of religion generally, 'all the additional powers conferred by various measures over the last forty years have been unnecessary'. That equally meant that his own view must carry the support of 'a long succession of Q.C. Commissioners' who had advised the Commissioners in such a way before him.[18]

[18] Lovelock note, 'The ethical aspects of investment', CC (87) 17, Board papers, 26 Mar. 1987, ser. 95083/57.

What was the Board of the Commissioners to make of this? Advocates of both points of view had turned to lawyers for a single shaft of brilliant, steady light and had instead found themselves peering through the lenses of a kaleidoscope. Lovelock said that he found Swingland persuasive. The law protected them from being, if they felt so tempted, capricious in their exercise of discretion. The discussion began to waver uncertainly. Perhaps a few shares could be sold to show that they were willing? But then, what difference could that be expected to make, one way or the other? There was a 'general feeling' that the Commissioners had gone as far as they could. For now, they decided, simply, to 'take note'.[19]

Peace did not prevail. Instead it was soon being suggested that Swingland's opinion should be tested in court. Lovelock opposed this course. It would not be a proper use of church money to appeal against the Commissioners' own legal advice. Whatever the lawyers were saying, the general debate was growing still fiercer, and it was spreading. Now archbishop Runcie made an appearance. He had been at the Anglican Consultative Conference in Singapore, which had discussed South Africa at length. A resolution had been passed calling for all Churches with financial resources in that country to disinvest; a resolution specifically calling upon the Church Commissioners to do so had been artfully intercepted by John Smallwood. (The Board thanked Smallwood, rather eagerly.) But the archbishop's report left a challenge. Were the Church Commissioners out of step, not only with a growing body of opinion at home and in South Africa, but across the Anglican communion at large?[20]

In October 1988 a letter from the bishop of Oxford, Richard Harries was sent to all governors. It enclosed a further legal opinion, this time from Mr Timothy Lloyd QC, of Bates, Wells and Braithwaite.[21] The Board was advised by the official solicitor, Edward Wills, that they would do well to stand their ground. They did so.[22] Yet the silence was a short one. By the beginning of 1990 it was clear that a new lobby, the Christian Ethical Investment Group (CEIG), was also pressing for a judicial review of the legal interpretation of the Commissioners duties and powers in matters in investments. The bishop of Oxford persisted. On 5 February Harries wrote to Lovelock: 'What is abundantly clear is that there is honest but fundamental confusion and disagreement concerning both the ultimate purposes of the Church Commissioners on the one hand, and their powers with

---

[19] Board minutes, 26 Mar. 1987, pp. 3–4.
[20] Ibid. 27 May 1987, 1–2.
[21] Shelley report, 'Investment and South Africa: letter from the bishop of Oxford', CC (88) 47, Board papers, 27 Oct. 1988, ser. 95083/59.
[22] Board minutes, 27 Oct. 1988, p. 3.

regard to investments on the other.' These things were of 'the greatest importance', and not only to the Church, for other charities might well watch. Such proceedings would bring 'significant expense', and whoever lost 'may well' have to bear them. On one side the bishop observed 'daunting personal risks' and 'uncertainty'; on the other he saw the Commissioners' assets. He asked if the Commissioners would pay 'reasonable costs', whatever the upshot. There was, he added, no 'personal animosity' involved in this, still less a 'desire to be difficult'. But there must be clarification.[23]

At the Assets Committee Lovelock fulminated. It was 'unacceptable', he remarked, that money which should be going to pay clergy stipends should be used instead to pay for a judicial review, the outcome of which might actually reduce the money available for their proper purposes still further.[24] Harries did not withdraw. When he next wrote, he did so 'as a fellow Church Commissioner', giving advance warning that he and two others would indeed be seeking a legal judgement. They feared 'damaging publicity' for the Church and sought to co-operate with the Commissioners to find resolution. It was not a hostile act; it was a friendly one. Lovelock was not in the least placated.

Lovelock asked Lambeth for a view and Runcie wrote that he respected this new move and the bishop of Oxford 'entirely'. But he found this course 'misguided':

> There will inevitably be occasions when individual Commissioners will disapprove of some particular investment with the Church's teachings. Such cases should of course be argued about and I could even understand someone bringing legal proceedings to stop a particular investment.
>
> But it seems to me unwise to bring proceedings on the very general basis proposed, not least because one must always allow for the possibility of the courts reaching a conclusion far removed from the one being sought. Moreover, even given what the CEIG would regard as a favourable result, I am not at all convinced that it would have the sweeping effect they expect.

Runcie did not think that it would be proper for the Commissioners to undertake to bear the costs. When it came to South Africa, he himself believed that the British government had been wrong to relax

---

[23] Lovelock report, 'The Commissioners' powers of investment', CC (90) 11, Board papers, 22 Mar. 1990, ser. 95084/61.
[24] AC minutes, 15 Mar. 1990.

sanctions before there was evidence that apartheid was actually being dismantled. Court action would only be 'an unnecessary diversion'. He hoped that the CEIG would think again.[25]

Harries had suggested that he and Lovelock should preside over a news conference to spell out why the action was being taken. Lovelock thought this inappropriate and so did the Assets Committee. The Board chorused regret. Unanimously they agreed not to meet the bishop's costs because this would prejudice the Commissioners seeking costs themselves.

On 26 July 1990 the Church Commissioners and the attorney-general were served with High Court summons from the bishop of Oxford, Michael Bourke, archdeacon of Bedford, and the Revd William Whiffen:

> That it may be determined on the true construction of Section 10 of the Church Commissioners Measure 1947 whether the above-named First Defendants (hereinafter called 'the Commissioners') in investing the assets from time to time comprised in their general fund and applying the same for the purposes mentioned in the said Section are obliged (or alternatively are at liberty) to have regard (a) to the object of promoting the Christian faith through the established Church of England; or (b) to some other (and if so what) object or objects.[26]

The mood of the Board was stiff. David Hopkinson and Bishop Westwood hoped that costs would be sought against the plaintiffs if they were upheld. Others agreed, for the clergy should be spared. But then they recognised that do to do so might look vindictive. The Official Solicitor suggested a neat middle course between vindictiveness and undue acquiescence. They should declare a will to pursue costs against the plaintiffs for the sake of the forms, but they need not yet decide to press any claim.

Bishop Booth-Clibborn had put down an order paper at the July Synod which seemed to suggest that the governors and the laymen of the Assets Committee were quite unaware of ethical considerations and needed to be advised by another source. Hopkinson looked to the bishops to defend the integrity of the laity. There was almost a vote of confidence in the morality of the members of the Assets Committee, but not quite, for the ethical policy of the Board and of the Assets Committee was, after all, 'one and the same'. Bishop Harries had asserted that some of the governors of the Commissioners themselves

[25] Runcie to Lovelock, 12 Apr. 1990, in A (90) 25, reproduced in CC (90) 11, Board papers, 26 Apr. 1990, ser. 95083/61.
[26] Board papers, 26 July 1990, ibid.

supported what he was doing. But neither now nor earlier had any governor spoken on his side. The more the Board ruminated, the fiercer the mood became. It 'deplored' this action against them. There must be 'a full and vigorous rebuttal'.[27]

Whatever Harries's wishes for co-operation the impression that he was creating was unarguable. A bishop had dragged his own Church off to the dock at the High Court. And there could be little doubt that they were indeed being dragged there. The Oxford hearing occurred not that summer but in the autumn: on 7–9 October 1991. Lovelock was now complaining that the action was serving to obscure other matters, not least the debate in Synod on the Commissioners' own annual report and a further report on the constitution of the Assets Committee. By September legal costs had risen to £60,000 and were expected to exceed £100,000. The 'notional' costs to staff lay in the region of £12,000. The governors worried about more than money; they feared 'the media aspect'.[28]

In the event, the position of the Church Commissioners was upheld in the High Court by Vice-Chancellor Nichols. The state offered other voices of reassurance. Lovelock could tell the Board that the attorney-general had commented to him that it was 'a firm endorsement' of their own ethical policy. Vice-Chancellor Nichols had made no further order for costs beyond the figure of £30,000, the sum in the bishop of Oxford's guarantee fund. It was again lamented at the Board that laymen were felt to be any less able to judge ethical questions than clergy, and that the plaintiffs had been unwilling to discuss the matter with the Assets Committee itself. These things must be said clearly in Synod.[29]

'Faith in the city'

The conservative world of the Church Commissioners was not entirely absorbed in mundane questions of church maintenance. Nor was it immune to the appeal of progressive campaigns. Indeed, the experience and acumen of the Commissioners remained vital to the success of any grand enterprise of improvement or reform. The Runcie era was not an age of confidence or expansion. But it yielded one defining statement of idealistic vision. This was the Archbishop's Commission on Urban Priority Areas (ACUPA) and its report *Faith in the city*.

[27] Board minutes, 26 July 1990, pp. 2–3.
[28] Ibid. 26 Sept. 1991, 1. For brief comment see Norman Doe, *The legal framework of the Church of England: a critical study in a comparative context*, Oxford 1996, 486.
[29] Board minutes, 7 Nov. 1991, p. 1.

The first two years of the first Thatcher government had seen the effective destruction of heavy industry in Britain and a precipitous rise in unemployment. Then, in the summer of 1982, a wave of riots broke out in inner city areas, most notably in Brixton in south London. Many blamed economic policies which could not support the structures and cultures of urban life and a government which was prepared to stand by as they disintegrated from within. But this controversy was at once overlaid with a no less intense debate on racial relations and about the character of a white police force and its engagement with black communities. What happened in Brixton crystallised the country's anxieties about its government, its economy and itself.

Archbishops' commissions were an irregular feature of Anglican life in the twentieth century. Most concerned the Church's own affairs. But the state of the inner cities provoked a new effort because a close friend of Runcie's, Canon Eric James, called for a new commission in a letter to the *The Times*. James had worked for many years in central London and was now in charge of John Collins's Christian Action. His letter struck a chord. Soon the Church of England was busy with new activities and initiatives. One of these was the Archbishops' Commission on Urban Priority Areas (ACUPA) based at Church House and soon stirring purposefully to life under Sir Richard O'Brien.

This new enterprise inevitably turned to the Church Commissioners. Early contacts were informal. First, O'Brien wished to ask about investment policies. Patrick Locke and a team went off to meet Bishop Sheppard of Liverpool to talk of the pastoral and administrative dimensions of the Commissioners' work. It all went off very well and O'Brien was impressed and grateful. The Archbishops' Commission was beginning to prepare its recommendations and he wrote formally to invite the Commissioners to give evidence. Recommendations would involve the Commissioners themselves, in matters of funding the ministry of the Church, in housing and in investment policies. For their part, the Commissioners were more than ready to oblige. It was an opportunity to show their virtues. They set down the 'vital' role which they played in maintaining across the nation, in areas both rich and poor, the ministry of the Church; the efficient management of its historic assets; the equitable distribution of its income; its administrative procedures. This involved an explanation of their duties to beneficiaries and a description of ethical and social themes (observing their investments in projects supporting small and new businesses in deprived areas, such as the Merseyside Enterprise Fund, on whose board the investments manager sat). But they were also establishing their limitations ('so many new projects, on any realistic assessment, offer little chance of success'). In social housing they had sought to expand, but could not because the government would not make available to them the assistance offered to Housing Associations ('we are driven to the regrettable conclusion that for the private sector to try and re-enter the field of low rent housing is no longer a realistic proposition'). There were matters of administration – of benefice and diocesan property, of pastoral reorganisation, of redundant churches, twenty-nine of which had been appropriated by African-Caribbean and other Pentecostal congregations. Finally, there were the grants for new towns and estates: £17.3 million spent since 1954 ('the pace has, however, slackened over the last five to ten years'). If anything, the support of the Commissioners had been pledged to those leaving the inner cities, not those remaining there. And in this lay a show of modest initiative on the Commissioners' part:

> From time to time, and as funds have been available, we have been authorised to help with the cure of souls in additional ways. Subject therefore to the priority which we must always give to the support of the 'living agents' of the Church, there would be precedents for, say, the reformulation of the New Housing Areas Measure 1954 to reflect more closely the likely needs of the 1980s and 1990s, including urban priority areas. We are ready sympathetically to consider that possibility.[30]

When the Board of the Church Commissioners discussed this submission, in March 1985, Lovelock thought it 'inevitable' that the ACUPA would ask them for funds. To this he wished to reply, gently but firmly, that theirs was a closed fund, with little new money, and any new commitments must be at the cost of old ones. He wished to be open to new ideas, of course. But they should be for projects that the Commissioners themselves would administer. Evidently, this represented the mood of the meeting.[31]

By April the Archbishops' Commission had offered a 'tentative' proposal that a new fund be set up for urban areas in need, that the Commissioners might contribute £1 million a year to it and that the Commissioners might also manage it. A public appeal would also be made. Although members of ACUPA found some of the Commissioners' more luxurious property developments an embarrassment to the Church, a deputation from the Commissioners was surprised not to be pressed by the commission to do more in development projects, like those already adopted in Liverpool and Plymouth. Lovelock cheerfully showed Robina Rafferty, assistant

---

[30] GPC report, 'Archbishop of Canterbury's Commission on Urban Priority Areas', CC (85) 15, Board papers, 21 Mar. 1985, ser. 95083/55.
[31] Board minutes, 28 Mar. 1985, pp. 1–2.

director of the Catholic Housing Association, around the Walworth and Lambeth estates.[32]

The final deliberations of ACUPA, published as *Faith in the city*,[33] provoked a sharp reaction from politicians. Controversial from the outset, it was eagerly promoted by a curious press that enjoyed the apparent spectacle of the Church of England launching a salvo of challenges against a powerful Conservative government. The report made specific proposals, some of which involved the work of the Commissioners themselves: that all church buildings be shared; that a local non-stipendiary ministry be extended; that dioceses do more to assist clergy in poor areas who struggled to find reimbursement for expenses; that there be structural changes to achieve a better integration of black Christians into the Church itself. The Commissioners' investments were sympathetically treated, and there was a proposal that a Council for Small Industries in Urban Areas be set up, something like the Council for Small Industries in Rural Areas. In matters of housing the ACUPA acknowledged the pressures which the Commissioners faced, but these sections wore an aspect of faint criticism and the Commissioners thought their good work somewhat undervalued. There was much for the dioceses to reflect upon, not least in the distribution of the historic resources of the Church. But towering over all was a financial proposal of weight, that a Church Urban Fund be created.[34]

By December 1985 the ACUPA had confirmed the suggestion that the Church Commissioners should themselves contribute to the new fund. The Church Estates Commissioners responded sympathetically. But if raising money was one thing there must also be a mechanism to direct funds and there must be power actually to do the things that were set down. In short, the Church Urban Fund must either become an institution itself, or else must work within the framework of an existing institution. The Commissioners had already declared that they would only provide funds which they could afterwards administer themselves. A method which might satisfy all the interested parties began to emerge: the General Synod must issue the mandate, the dioceses must concoct strategies and ways of implementing. The Commissioners would become the central grant-making authority, for the dioceses saw them as 'independent and fair'. From the new fund, projects would receive grants of 50 per cent of their costs, the dioceses finding the balance. In total, grants to the tune of £2 million a year

[32] Ibid. 25 Apr. 1985, p. 1.
[33] *Faith in the city: a call for action by Church and nation: the report of the Commission on Urban Priority Areas,* London 1991.
[34] See, in particular, ibid. 153–4. See also 'Summary of report as it affects the Commissioners', CC (86) 10, Board papers, 27 Feb. 1986, ser. 95083/56.

should be made, half of that sum coming from the Commissioners themselves, the balance being the interest on £10 million raised for capital in a national appeal.[35]

But one question of substance still hung in the air. What exactly was an urban priority area? The new secretary to the Church Commissioners, James Shelley, was invited onto a working group to supply a definition, setting down criteria for the dioceses. At first the Commission had thought broadly in terms of unemployment, old people who were living alone, single-parent families, ethnicity, overcrowding and homes lacking basic amenities. But guidance of a more sophisticated nature was soon sought from academic studies. The categories accumulated: they must also weigh up housing defects, low income levels, vandalism, physical or mental illness, high rates of crime. Soon twenty categories had been identified by the ACUPA itself. Once they knew to what kind of urban areas the money should go they must still work out on what it should be spent. It should not go on clergy stipends, to be sure, but certainly, and as a main priority, it should be used for the employment of lay workers, licensed or not, and local non-stipendiary ministers. Grants should be made for works to adapt churches to new forms of sharing with other traditions.

In February 1986 Synod gave the proposal for this new fund an eager, general approval, urging the standing committee to bring a measure forward 'as soon as possible'. In May 1986 archbishop Runcie expressed his gratitude to the Commissioners for what they were doing to get the new enterprise off the ground. On the Board itself Alan Webster observed how much interest was being shown in *Faith in the city* in the pages of the *Financial Times*.[36] By September it could be seen that legislation would be needed if the Commissioners were to provide their first £1 million. It could best be done by simply moving an amendment to the existing 1954 New Housing Areas Measure, widening those powers to meet new social or economic needs. The Commissioners would make grants or loans out of their General Fund to support 'innovatory, experimental and ecumenical projects involving the better use of church buildings and increased financial support for layworkers'. This did indeed lie within the Commissioners own remit to support the cure of souls. There was, moreover, a commitment to support understanding between people of different faiths.[37]

In November 1986 the legislation was proposed to the General Synod and caused barely a ripple there. But the new campaign had

[35] Ibid. note B.
[36] Board minutes, 22 May 1986, pp. 1–2.
[37] GPC report, 'The Church Urban Fund: enabling legislation', CC (86) 46, pp. 1–3, Board papers, 25 Sept. 1986, ser. 95083/56.

already thrown up an oddity in the matter of ethical investments. A parish had been offered a cheque from Imperial Tobacco and it had been returned to the donor because tobacco was listed in the Commissioners' own banned categories. Lovelock told the Board that he regretted this: 'there was an intellectual distinction to be drawn between owning shares in a company and accepting a donation from it'. He asked that governors might use their own influence to 'prevent such occurrences elsewhere'.[38] By now a board had been appointed to oversee the fund and the Commissioners had won a third seat on it after expressing their disquiet at the prospect of only two. The Church Commissioners (Assistance for Priority Areas) Measure was finally and unanimously passed by the General Synod in February 1988.

The public appeal was launched in April 1988. As for their own undertaking, on 26 May 1988 Lovelock informed the Board that the Church Commissioners had made their first payment of £1 million to the Church Urban Fund.

The failure of centralisation: the Millbank project

The politics of church government were always in flux. They could not settle now, any more than they could in the ages of Ramsey or Fisher. In the 1980s the administrative powers of Church House and General Synod decided to apply their energies to a reform of the central organs of the Church of England: to Synod and its administrative creatures, and to all the associated central bodies of the Church. It was time to concoct a new act of uniformity, this time for church bureaucrats. This meant thinking about bricks and mortar. It involved the site at Millbank itself and the accumulated properties owned by the Church of England along Great Smith Street. In particular, it involved Church House.

By the beginning of 1987 the General Synod had ventured a proposal, which had been accepted by the Corporation of Church House, to move the entire staff of Church House into completely new premises.[39] At Millbank the General Purposes Committee looked at this and decided to encourage the Board to approve. Lovelock was not excited. He assured the Board that this was purely a matter of moving chairs and desks: 'no organic merger of the various bodies was proposed'. But this was certainly to underestimate what was now afoot. The proposal that was being presented to the central bodies of the Church of England offered three potential initiatives, all of them bold: to redevelop Church House, to move everybody out of London, to move them around the corner and, actually, into Millbank, which

[38] Board minutes, 27 Nov. 1986, p. 1.
[39] GS 763.

would be refurbished to the tune of £5 million. Not everything could be moved into Millbank; some quite different place would have to be found for the archives, for example. The Board of the Commissioners felt that if Church House wanted to move their staff out of London altogether that was a matter for them. They did support the proposal that the Commissioners offer accommodation next to their own in Millbank for staff now busy in Church House, 'without pressurizing them to come'.[40]

If Lovelock seemed detached, the secretary to the Commissioners, James Shelley, appeared a good deal more enthusiastic about the plan. Fifteen months passed. A large, charmless warehouse in Bermondsey was acquired for the Commissioners' archives. In May 1988 Shelley reported to the Board that much had now been accomplished. After great exertions, vacant possession of a number of properties had been secured; Cluttons had moved from Great College Street to Berkeley Square; the legal department of the Commissioners was now perched on the Albert Embankment. Some tidy acts of amalgamation with Church House had been effected: litho-printing, messengers, post, telephones, receptionists. Management contractors had already been appointed. The air was thick with 'hard' planning and people 'hard' at work. Planning and listed building consents had been obtained. It was now envisaged that staff from Church House would occupy two floors of nearby Fielden House, 'in order to allow a little more elbow room in the main building'. On 4 July construction work would begin. It would take a year.

The project was soon unravelling before the Commissioners' eyes. In February 1987 the work had been expected to cost £4.7 million. Now, little over a year later, the capital cost stood at £9.3 million, because of inflation, because of the addition of further work, because West End rents and capital values had 'rocketed'. The rent to be paid by Synod for its new offices had soared from £11 to £23 per square foot; the value of Church House itself from £8.5 million to £20 million. This, Shelley reflected bleakly, 'could not have been foreseen'. Shelley himself was loyal to the enterprise and keen to justify it: 'The underlying principles set out above, however, remain even more secure than ever.' He added, somewhat vaguely, 'Although the actual cost is much higher than forecast, the overall financial target remains intact.' The basics of the scheme still looked robust: Church House would pay the Commissioners a commercial rent, which would be regularly reviewed. Likewise rent would be charged for letting Church House.[41]

[40] Board minutes, 19 Feb. 1987, pp. 3–4.
[41] Shelley note, 'Millbank project', A (88) 22, Board papers, 26 May 1988, ser. 95083/58.

But in the background the mood of Synod was growing frostier by the minute. It was even said that the grand enterprise should be abandoned altogether. By July 1988 Lovelock had given evidence to a review by a subcommittee of the standing committee, chaired by Christina Baxter. Here he was far more optimistic about this 'unique opportunity to draw the central Church bodies together under one roof'. By now, the Commissioners may well have sensed an interest in seeing the project through. They had spent several millions in altering the Millbank buildings themselves. Lovelock warned that Synod should be quite clear that if the plans came to nothing this money would be utterly lost.[42]

When it came, the review was devastating. The Millbank project was fundamentally flawed, riddled with failures of information and errors of judgement. It should be abandoned. The standing committee of Synod itself was embarrassed. Archbishop Runcie was defensive and apologetic. New motions for Synod were framed nervously.[43] For their part, the Commissioners offered a tight-lipped note: by now most of a sum of £9.3 million had been committed; £1.25 million of it could not be retrieved, for it had been spent on building work. They still believed that to combine forces must be valuable, an opportunity in fact. The Pensions Board, at least, would come whatever Synod decided. But they insisted that they meant to bring no pressure to bear. Synod must decide for itself what to do.[44] In November 1988 the Millbank project, a monumental, deliberate initiative in corporate progress, shuddered to a halt in the hall of Church House. An overwhelming silent embarrassment ensued; a bracing for accusations. This could not be confined to the standing committee of General Synod. The archdeacon of Halifax, Alan Chesters, who was on the committee, asked of Lovelock that the role of the Board of the Church Commissioners be considered too: 'Those of us who are elected Commissioners by the General Synod were clearly placed at a disadvantage by some of the evidence produced by the Baxter Report.' Lovelock replied that he, too, had received the report only a few hours before the archdeacon 'and much of the information in it was as new (and some as surprising) to me as it was to you'. Parts of it, too, were 'incorrect'. Nothing there, however, which referred to the Commissioners themselves had not been reported by him to the General Purposes Committee or to the Board, or to both.[45]

[42] *Report of the Proceedings of the General Synod*, xix/2, London 1988, 646–66 (6 July 1988).

[43] GPC report, 'The Millbank project', CC (88) 45 (with GS 845), Board papers, 27 Oct. 1988, ser. 95083/59.

[44] Ibid; GS MISC 307.

[45] GPC report, 'The Millbank project', CC (88) 56, Board papers, 15 Dec. 1988,

Synod had accepted that it must foot the bill for the *débâcle*. If it had been a straightforward commercial situation, they would have been obliged to do so. But the money would be lost to the Church as a whole, and if it were to be found elsewhere it must be in the dioceses. Come to that, could Synod actually come up with such a sum as this? The Board of the Commissioners decided 'that a formal bill for the abortive costs should not be submitted but that ways of drawing the Synod's attention to the matter should be discussed at the next meeting'. Accordingly, Synod was given a surreptitious prod by the posing of a Synod question and answer. Why had it not paid its debt of £1.25 million to the Church Commissioners? The answer: that there would be no formal request for it, but that it was really a matter for Synod and would no doubt come up when the budget was debated in July. Otherwise, the Commissioners left the matter to chase about through Synod itself, without stirring too noticeably.

In February 1989 James Shelley told the Board that there had been a sudden bid to salvage something from the wreckage; to look again at the area that had been set aside, to turn it instead into a 'completely self-contained space planned to a modern commercial standard on a cost effective basis in order to attract the best tenant willing to pay a substantial rent'. Aspects of the project remained alive. The Pensions Board was moving in as planned. The basement at Millbank could still offer catering facilities. The archives were still moving into the new site at Bermondsey. And if the future of the conference hall at 1 Millbank was in doubt it was already partly in existence (for it had begun in November, just before the decision of Synod). Shelley now offered a final figure for the loss: £1,215,000 in abortive building costs and fees. Even this did not allow for interest lost because of Synod's November decision.[46]

Although the Church Commissioners had stuck firmly to the line that they had simply responded to an initiative which originated elsewhere, the feeling hung in the air that the Commissioners, too, had played their part in the fiasco. Had there been a failure in the conveyance of accurate information? Archdeacon Chesters still wanted the Board to examine itself and its relations with its committees severely. To do so could not but help 'promote greater understanding' between the Commissioners and the Synod. Lovelock replied dryly that he had offered his own oral 'situation reports' to the Board, the General Purposes and the Assets Committees. These had always allowed for questions.[47] Shelley meanwhile proposed, 'Board minutes are already circulated to any Commissioner who asks for them; the

ser. 95083/59.
[46] Shelley note, 'The Millbank project', CC (89) 2, Board papers, 16 Feb. 1989, ibid.
[47] Lovelock note, 'The role of the Board and committees', CC (89) 8, ibid.

circulation of Committee minutes has, however, in the past been felt to be undesirable.' These structures were usually reviewed every five years. The General Purposes Committee had come close to agreeing to the wider circulation of minutes in 1986, but turned back, only because they were waiting for the publication of a Synod Infrastructure Review.[48] This debate at the Board of the Church Commissioners exposed some tensions at the heart of the institution. It was heard, insistently, that Synod members who sat there were not mandated to represent the Synod but had a prime duty to the Commissioners themselves, like directors of a company. To 'promote a wider understanding' of the work of the Board, and of the Commissioners' committees of the Commissioners at large, it was agreed that minutes should be made available to any Commissioner who asked for them. It was heard that within the Church the Commissioners were widely 'held in high regard', though mistrusted by a 'small minority' in the Synod and amongst the bishops. It was sufficient to deal with that not with constitutional reform but with 'individual contact … to correct misunderstandings'. It was suggested that when a vacancy next occurred on the Assets Committee it should be filled by an elected member of the General Synod, to reassure the fearful in Synod itself. But the committee already had two 'non-experts', the clerical members, to whom the committee looked to provide ethical guidance. Another non-expert might increase its representative power but weaken its expertise. Lovelock reminded them that the committee had exclusive responsibility for its work. The Board agreed not to act yet, but to watch and await events.

General Synod was not quick to acknowledge its debt to the Church Commissioners. There was a legislative log-jam there. Instead, archbishop Runcie expressed the gratitude of the standing committee. On 31 May the Central Board of Finance recorded a resolution of gratitude too. The Commissioners, they declared, had been 'wise, reasonable and kind'. Furthermore, they were 'happy' that suitable new tenants had been found for the spaces that had been vacated. And that was true, for even after they had snapped shut there was consolation to be drawn from the jaws of defeat. It came at 5 Great College Street which by then had been let to a tenant who would soon be paying a rent 'substantially in excess of £35 per square foot'.[49] Commercial property, it appeared, had saved the day once again.

---

[48] Shelley note, 'The role of the Board and committees', CC (89) 5, ibid.
[49] Board minutes, 23 Feb. 1989, pp. 2–4.

The struggle for unification: historic resources and the stipend

General systems of distribution must be seen to be universally fair if financial wars are not to break out between interests. To construct rules that are appropriate and practical when the beneficiaries are often quite different from one another cannot be a task for any but the doughtiest bureaucrat, the deftest diplomat, the most winning politician – and the most accommodating recipients. If the dioceses were not always admirers of the central agencies of the Church, they sometimes viewed each other sceptically, too. If a diocese found only modest donations coming in from its congregations was this because they were poor? Or might it be because the diocese itself made less effort to attract money, in the knowledge that the Church Commissioners would increase their own grants to make up the shortfall? In the offices of 1 Millbank there were constant adjustments, revisions, calculations and recalculations. Figures from the dioceses were not always forthcoming. When they were they could prove difficult to assess centrally because dioceses had different ways of computing the same things, or computed different things altogether. Allocation was, in short, an art which could never achieve a definitive form.

The matter of what were called 'historic resources' was a continual problem. They were the final obstacle which held out against the long-drawn-out onslaught on financial inequalities within the Church of England. Some dioceses were richer than others by virtue of their very origins and material development. From their point of view, the establishment of national stipend ranges meant that they were seeking to reach a particular, universal level, but from vastly different beginnings. This had always been acknowledged, but it was in the age of Runcie that an underlying unease about these disparities was being more openly expressed, becoming more pressing. In December 1979 the Board of the Commissioners endorsed what had become a general view at the General Purposes Committee, that some quantity of any new money which might be directed towards stipends might instead be used to 'adjust discrepancies as between "historic resources" available to dioceses'.[50]

Many of the dioceses themselves agreed with this and pressed for a new framework. But the view was not unanimous. In January 1980 a diocesan stipends conference aired the matter and then voted for some 'levelling up', but by a majority of only twenty-nine to ten with four abstaining. The turn which the debate took was also suggestive. When it came to how best to calculate such 'levelling up', it was said that diocesan 'actualities' might not be assessed as much as 'potential' – a

[50] Ibid. 20 Dec. 1979, pp. 2–3.

proposal, no doubt meant to pinpoint any dioceses that failed to pull their proper weight. But how could potential be assessed? It might mean a great many different things, and involve a great many arguments. Apprehensive of complexities, the General Purposes Committee set up a representative working group to produce a 'preliminary examination' of an already extant 'historic resources' league table which could be found in the Commissioners' offices. By the end of February it appeared that this body, at least, could agree on most aspects of the matter: that allocations already made in perpetuity should not be touched; that whatever was agreed be set only for one year; that potential be marked by average figures for regular membership in dioceses already adjusted for their relative prosperity.[51]

Broadly, diocesan representatives warmed to this. At the end of February 1980 a second working group was set up to press ahead. Once more, it carefully reflected a range of opinion, this time from Carlisle, Blackburn, St Albans, Chester, Bath and Wells, Southwell, Newcastle and Liverpool. It soon reached a common mind on new questions: that calculations of allocations should be made on a manpower basis comprising 50 per cent Sheffield target figures and 50 per cent actual manpower; that potential should be measured by a combination of the general level of income in an area and the figures for usual Sunday attendance, with an acknowledgement that the latter gave a firmer indication of regular givers. The General Purposes Committee looked at this and concurred that it all seemed, broadly, 'right'.[52] It must pass now to the Board and then to the next diocesan conference, in April.

This was steady, patient work. It was too much to expect the diocesan conference which followed to resolve all these matters – or the one after, or even the one after that. But progress was marked by little victories. A league table of historic resources had by now won general assent. At the wealthier end of the adjusted league table produced by the working group were, by and large, the older dioceses: Lincoln, Bath and Wells, Norwich, Peterborough, Oxford and Ely; at the bottom end were both old and new, but mostly new: Liverpool, Sheffield, Birmingham, Durham and Newcastle. In April thirty-three dioceses had supported the new recommended stipends range of £4,900–£5,400 and seven had voted against. On 1 May the Board of the Commissioners had agreed to recommend to the Annual General Meeting that an extra £1 million pounds should be available for stipends and it was decided that £400,000 of that was to be used to adjust allocations upwards or downwards in light of the historic

---

[51] GPC report, 'Stipends policy: 1981–82', CC (80) 21, Board papers, 27 Mar. 1990, ser. 95083/49.
[52] Ibid.

resources of each diocese. But formidable complexities still hung in the air. Even if the new method were agreed, some dioceses were eager that the whole approach should not be introduced before they had quite prepared themselves for it. If it was seen suddenly that the greater part of new allocations was being made only to a few dioceses, there might well be a movement of resentment in the others.

John Smallwood doubted the figures on which these new calculations were based. He still believed that the CSA should set a higher minimum stipend of £5,000. To this, Harris replied that they must not meddle with the consensus that had now emerged and unpick what had been already agreed ('The strong reaction to a similar proposal when it was adopted for 1979 must, I should have thought, whatever the argument in logic, have taught us all a lesson we should not forget').[53] When the next round of diocesan conferences took place in January and February 1981, there was little campaigning in the air. At least eight dioceses now found they could achieve a minimum stipend of £5,500 from their own resources. Now it was agreed that allocations which involved a consideration of historic resources should be decided by weighing both electoral roll and usual Sunday attendance figures equally.[54]

Even though they accumulated, these little victories were not enough. In truth, the attempt to frame a legislative paper on historic resources had become tortuous. It could not yield a formula acceptable to all forty-three dioceses. One draft came after another. Many alternative approaches existed and jostled with each other. It was easier by far to make criticisms than it was actually to construct something that worked administratively and politically. By the time the dioceses gathered again, in September 1981, there was a new points system by which need might be assessed. This provoked further controversy, on the Board of governors as elsewhere. Surely, argued John Smallwood, the more the Commissioners allocated selectively, the higher the wealthier dioceses should be allowed to aim? He had met clergy in Southwark who were sure that they were worse off now than before. He suggested a London weighting allowance, more comprehensive car loan schemes, some kind of child allowance, more structures. The laity, he pressed, had not been challenged enough.[55]

By November 1982 the stipends policy section of the Church Commissioners had produced an eighth draft of a Green Paper on historic resources. It was heard on the Board that this new version was over-long and rather short of definite conclusions. John Herbecq was

[53] Board minutes, 22 May 1980, pp. 1–4.
[54] GPC report, 'Stipends policy', CC (81) 22, Board papers, 26 Mar. 1981, ser. 95083/50.
[55] Board minutes, 27 May 1982, pp. 3–4.

at pains to observe that it was all interesting and instructive, but he questioned the value of calculations of 'average income' in seeking to determine potential levels of giving, for many in the congregations were elderly and had little income. David Hopkinson feared that 'to draw significant conclusions from unproven estimates of potential would be unfair'. This aside, the new draft was given a solicitous, general encouragement, before being sent back to the officers for further work.[56]

By March 1983 the Green Paper had reached its eleventh draft and was felt to be ready to stand up, unassisted, 'subject to such detailed editorial and updating work as still remained to be completed'. But the Board of the Commissioners was this time less indulgent. David Hopkinson was powerful against it. He doubted its accuracy 'and felt that misgivings about the apparently inequitable distribution of resources between dioceses were conceived in the spirit of envy'. This was 'a materialist, divisive and difficult document'. Howard Gracey of the Pensions Board agreed. Worse came with Bishop Leonard of London. The paper did not, he said, tackle the problems of the parochial system – the effectiveness of which might well be doubted in rural areas, inner cities or depopulated areas. He wanted a preface to chart these things. Somebody said that if they wished to have a preface it might do well to pay tribute to the work of the staff who had laboured on it.

Lovelock stood his ground. The Commissioners were committed to bringing a report to Synod, he said, and the dioceses themselves had a timetable in mind. It was too late to withdraw now. There was more discussion. The secretary, Kenneth Lamb, repeated that they must not renege on their undertakings. It was determined, by fourteen votes to eight, that a section of conclusions should be retained but renamed, but then that it should be published and should face the harsh world outside as best it could.[57]

The context in which the debate occurred was shifting perceptibly. In May 1983, when the allocations to diocesan stipends funds for 1984–5 were discussed, Harris could observe for the first time that the Commissioners now met less than 50 per cent of the cost of stipends. Apart from anything else, he saw that this must increase the weight given to the voices of the dioceses in setting stipendiary levels.

Administrative reform is both an intricate art in itself and a labour of monumental perseverance which often relies on the eventual exhaustion of its critics. By the end of 1983 the debates about historic resources finally looked as though they were beginning to bear fruit. In October Lovelock reported on a conference with the heads of the

[56] Ibid. 25 Nov. 1982, p. 5.
[57] Ibid. 23 Mar. 1983, pp. 1–3.

diocesan boards of finance; a 'good meeting', he observed, in which 'a substantial measure of consensus' had been found.[58] The simple fact was that however many criticisms were heard, everybody agreed that something must be done. Smallwood remarked that the richer dioceses might prefer to see some of their resources going to particular aspects of the Church's work rather than simply to other, poorer, dioceses. The Green Paper encountered no disasters as it made its way around the dioceses. In March 1984 the diocese of London offered a self-confident reply which was warmly appreciative of the Commissioners' grasp of details and as warmly critical of their investment policies.[59] By February 1985 Lovelock had written to all diocesan bishops that they should expect a visit from the officers of Millbank to encourage consultation. A consensus seemed to suggest that a 'measure of equalisation' was still necessary, and that it could best be done by 'levelling up' the grants made to dioceses with low historic endowments. If that was to be the way of proceeding, they must wait for the Assets Committee to tell them whether there was enough money to do it.

The Board of the Commissioners appeared more receptive to the draft White Paper in July 1985. There were still fears that the strategy, which Lovelock himself expected to cost at £20 million over five years, might clash with other priorities in the Church, with the urban priority areas, with pensions. Lovelock was reassuring: he did not think that they need worry. The obstacles were now looking less substantial, and the architects of reform were beginning to find solid answers more readily.[60]

At the Board meeting in April 1986 it was reckoned that it would cost the Commissioners an additional £10 million a year over a five-year period to reduce income disparities, and much of this would have to go to dioceses with low historic resources and high potential. A further £20 million over the same period would be spent on selective grants for clergy housing, to reduce capital disparities. Even the regular interrogations of John Smallwood had become something that the amiable Lovelock could now take in his stride. Complete equalisation, he concluded, was beyond them – and what was now planned was not designed to achieve it. If in some cases disparities had widened recently, in others they had narrowed. Bishop Say stressed that what now existed on paper was the work of many years. The draft White

58 Ibid. 27 Oct. 1983, 7. See also 'Note of conference with chairmen of DBFs', 17 Oct. 1983, Board papers, 27 Oct. 1983, ser. 95083/54.
59 J. D. R. Hayward, 'The historic resources of the Church of England: a report by the Church Commissioners: the diocese of London's reply' (Mar. 1994). (Copy in the author's possession, with thanks to Derek Hayward.)
60 Board minutes, 26 July 1985, pp. 2–4.

Paper was approved for publication by fifteen votes to none, with two abstentions.[61] When, in May 1984, the Board reviewed another proposal from the CSA, that the new national minimum stipend should be £7,000, and a maximum average £7,500, it was seen that no less than thirty-one dioceses had said that they could achieve this without further help from the Commissioners. Very few clergy were now paid the national minimum. If some dioceses had looked for a lower range this was in part because they wished to be seen to be higher up the table and to be paying better within the accepted range.

The historic resources paper was a miracle because it was there at all. In a history of bureaucratic reform, it marked one of the greatest achievements of the Church Commissioners. Yet the great effort which yielded this impressive consensus did not overturn a climate of disagreement and confrontation across a divided Church. Every year the CSA persevered doggedly in the face of chill winds of criticism and even suspicion. The dioceses were still divided amongst themselves; at times some could be found voting tactically as well as in tune with their own independent understandings. Meanwhile, at every level people continued to discuss whether the clergy were well paid or not, as they had for decades.[62]

[61] Ibid. 24 Apr. 1986, pp. 2–3.
[62] See, for example, ibid. 29 Nov. 1988, pp. 3–4.

13

The Inflationary Spiral

However they might seek to frame their own policies within the bounds of their statutes, the work of the Church Commissioners always continued within contexts over which they had only a tenuous control. One was political. In 1987 the Thatcher government had entered triumphantly into its third successive term with a determination to reform local rates. Their solution to this quintessential source of British resentment was the community charge. Soon known as the 'poll tax', it was almost as soon notorious. The Churches feared its coming more, if anything, than most of its stoutest critics. For the old system had allowed a variety of exemptions from which the Churches had benefited conspicuously. The rather civilised understandings of the past, the old order itself, stood under threat.

It was time for alliances. On 14 April 1988 the Assets Committee heard that a deputation from the Churches' Main Committee, led by the bishop of London and including the First and Second Church Estates Commissioners, had called on the secretary of state for the Environment to voice its concern about the new levy. No direct concessions had been granted, but the Churches were hoping for some 'countervailing benefits' to compensate them. By 15 September the government was quietly offering them three benefits: a wide range of church buildings, including all church halls, would be exempt from rates; state aid for historic churches would be increased; and the government's share of the cost of the Redundant Churches Fund would be increased to 70 per cent. For the Church of England it was a pragmatic victory. For the government it avoided another controversy at a time when it had more than enough to deal with. But for the Church Commissioners it represented a loss, for these concessions were to the Church as a whole and while the community charge remained it was the Commissioners who must pay for it.

A second new fear was not political but ecclesial. The prospect of the ordination of women concerned the Church Commissioners because it was said that clergy who opposed it would resign, retire early and need to be compensated. In July 1985 Lovelock had responded that the Church should not assume that compensation and early retirement was a matter of principle. When the standing committee of the Church Assembly convened an ordination of women legislative group that November, Lovelock was on it. The deputy secretary and the pastoral secretary were the group's assessors. When a further, informal, group was set up to contemplate the implications of the ordination of women, Lovelock was on that too.

The opponents of the ordination of women were unsparing in their promotion of a fear of mass desertion. Consciences, evidently, now had a price. In the seventeenth century non-jurors had simply left the Church; in the twentieth century they expected compensation. At Millbank estimates rested on an assumption that one priest in every hundred would leave the Church. In March 1988 the Board of the Church Commissioners undertook to accept the liability, along the lines of a scheme now sketched out by the General Purposes Committee. By April 1989 a basic package had been worked out. It was seen that the whole bill might be as high as £11 million over twenty years. It was money, the General Purposes Committee ruefully observed, which would be taken away from dioceses and parishes, from stipends and housing. Lovelock asked the Commissioners to accept this liability so long as the Commissioners retained the power to consider and accept whatever scheme was submitted by the General Synod to parliament. Some were fearful that this must endanger their support for the serving clergy. But they approved what was set before them; it was hard to do otherwise.[1]

Both were significant issues in the period, not least because they either cost the Church Commissioners a great deal of money or because they threatened to do so. But the crucial event in the Runcie era was the crisis with which it ended.

At 1 Millbank, the function of the Assets Committee was to get money, and the function of the General Purposes Committee was, in part at least, to propose ways of spending it. Mutual understanding between these two bodies rested substantially on the ability of the Estates Commissioners and the secretary to mediate between them. It also depended on the power of the Board of governors to unite their logic within a clear, cogent general policy. Such a policy must, in its turn, heed Synod and express the statutory responsibilities and discretionary powers which the Church Commissioners possessed. This was never going to be easy, particularly in an age of growing pressure and bustle in which the separate parts of that equation were more than ever likely to turn in upon themselves, concentrating on the tasks in hand without seeing what was happening beyond their own

---

[1] Board Minutes, 27 Apr. 1989, pp. 2–3.

330 The Church of England in the Twentieth Century

parapets. Such was the growing reality of life in virtually all institutions of the day. It could prove immensely dangerous.

As far as the Church Commissioners were concerned these matters assumed a fundamental significance because both the gaining and the spending of money had now come to involve two vital programmes. The character of income was increasingly influenced by the power of the property portfolio; that of expenditure was increasingly dominated by two decisive features: the clergy pension and the parsonage house.

To what extent did burgeoning expenditure interact with, and even lead, a new, dynamic drive for income? To what extent did the Commissioners' distinct discretionary powers crumble into a new consensus across the institutions of the Church; a consensus built not around solid financial calculations but new campaigns for improvement? Here and there the papers of the committees reveal doubts about the mathematics of the Commissioners affairs. A minute of November 1983 finds Kenneth Lamb observing 'apparently disproportionately large increases in the levels of expenditure proposed for 1984'. He hoped that a new General Synod committee, chaired by the indefatigable Oswald Clark, would provide 'a renewed opportunity for proper consultation as to future levels of expenditure by the Board'.[2] But this would not occur. Lamb's remark was made when the income of the Commissioners was beginning to grow prodigiously. Success rarely concentrates minds in the way that failures inevitably must. What must be understood here is the force of that context and the nature of the policies which fuelled it.

The labrynthine world of the pension

The state of the stipend defined the level of the pension, which was thought appropriately set at half of it. But the clergy pension, unlike the stipend, had its own institutional body: the Pensions Board. Since the 1961 Pensions Measure, the Commissioners had had power to appoint five members of the Pensions Board, one of them a diocesan bishop. In practice, they usually nominated those who were, in the first place, suggested by the Pensions Board itself, people with the appropriate expertise. But the Pensions Board was no mere fusion of powers, or simply an administrative reality. It answered to its own distinct call. It was a lobby and its members understood their work clearly in those terms. The cause of the pension they constantly pressed, even 'urged' upon the Church Commissioners.[3] The proponents of pensions were also vigorous in Synod, whose members

[2] Minutes of the General Purposes Committee minutes, vol. 5, 3 Nov. 1983.
[3] See, for example, Pensions Board minutes, 18 Jan. 1980, pp. 2–3.

had by now voted in support of a motion that the Church of England move to lower the age of retirement from seventy to sixty-five.

By May 1980 the Pensions Board was again agitating for a rise in pensions to above half the cash level of the stipend. To this the General Purposes Committee was not immediately responsive. Many there again saw the arguments for raising stipends and raising pensions to be in competition with each other. Moreover, there was, as ever, a host of attendant details to assess. For all this, the Board approved the committee's recommendation of a new allocation of £3.65 million a year for pensions from the following April. This would enable the basic pension to rise to £2,500 *per annum*, attended by comparable rises for clergy widows, deaconesses and licensed lay workers. The lump sum given for full service would also be increased to a substantial £4,000.[4]

In November 1980 the General Purposes Committee and the Pensions Board submitted to the General Synod a new report, 'The pensions of the full-time ministry'.[5] More than a cumulative statement of a long-drawn-out, steady onslaught against old anomalies and their assorted intricacies, the report stood out because it announced the pursuit of vital, new improvements across the board. Harris showed the draft to the Board in September 1980 and assured it that these proposals could be regarded as 'acceptable to the Commissioners from a financial viewpoint'. But the proposal was an ambitious one, to raise clergy pensions from a level of half the previous year's national minimum stipend to two-thirds, to increase the clergy widows' pension by the same amount and to increase the lump sum payment by three times the present amount. The archdeacon of Cheltenham, Thomas Evans, worried that too much money was being used for pensions, not because they could not afford it, but because it must be at the expense of stipends. A level of 50 per cent of the stipend was surely sufficient. This did not gain sympathisers. The Board approved the report by seventeen votes to one.[6] It was a quiet victory, but a decisive one. Harris now went off to the General Synod and offered the programme as something between a commitment and an aspiration. The debate there exposed anxieties, not about the costs but about the condition of widows and the intricacies of the dioceses. Three Commissioners offered views of their own on the minutiae of the paper, but not on the fundamental aspirations. One of them, Philip Lovegrove, thought the package even now too cautious.[7] Evidence of such individualism

[4] Board minutes, 1 May 1980, p. 105.
[5] The joint report submitted to General Synod was GS 464. The final report was published as GS 519.
[6] Board minutes, 25 Sept. 1980, pp. 1–2.
[7] *Report of the Proceedings of General Synod*, xi/3, London 1980, 955–92 (14 Nov.

on the part of certain Commissioners unsettled the Pensions Board. Its chairman, Howard Gracey, fulminated later that the voices of the Commissioners in Synod had 'undermined' the consensus constructed by the two bodies, had even 'belittled the role of the Pensions Board as advocate for the pensions'.[8] When the Pensions Board met on 21 April 1982 it was observed, rather trenchantly, that 'although it was the Commissioners who had the resources, it was the Board to whom the Synod had given the power and responsibilities to assist the retired ministry with their housing needs'.[9]

Once it was all adopted by Synod – as it promptly was – the programme gathered something of the power of a firm, even a binding, undertaking. Yet almost at once it could be seen by some of the Commissioners that the mathematics of these reforms was dangerously askew. In April 1981 David Hopkinson told the Board of his concern that a 'serious "gap"' had developed between the growth of the Commissioners' income and the steady increase in their liabilities, for pensions and stipends in particular, and this in a world of high inflation. He found that the new annual report, which the Board had gathered to discuss, voiced no warning of the dangers that were likely over the next five years. He pressed that 'serious consideration needed to be given to ways in which the dangers he foresaw could be assessed and met': 'It was agreed that these important questions should be considered by the appropriate committees and that their views should be brought before the Board.'[10] The annual report of 1981 even presented a graph showing how pensions had almost doubled as a proportion of the Commissioners' expenditure from investment income across the last decade, and were now marching towards 30 per cent.

A defining aspect of the world of the pension in the 1980s was the housing of retired clergy and their wives. The roots of this question lay in the preceding decade. By the later 1970s it was becoming more natural to attach the question of the pensions which were offered by the Church to the burgeoning issue of retirement accommodation. It looked increasingly anomalous that while a priest was in work he was paid a stipend and given a house, but that when he had ceased to work he had a pension but nowhere to live. The Pensions Board grew more and more determined about this; they were pushing the Commissioners to come up with an answer and also the money to pay for it. The mood of the Church at large, insofar as it could be found in the General Synod, was also more restless and more insistent.

1980).
[8] Pensions Board minutes, 19 Nov. 1980, pp. 4–5.
[9] Ibid. 21 Apr. 1982, pp. 5–6.
[10] Board minutes, 30 Apr. 1981, p. 2.

Housing the retired clergy was still an *ad hoc*, patchwork project. Even so, its economic character was determined by a will to be benign. The Pensions Board contributed up to two-thirds of the cost of a property when the diocese offered one-third, as long as it approved of the property itself. The property was then vested in the Pensions Board and the diocese had no share in the equity. The diocese had the right to nominate the occupant once general rules governing eligibility were satisfied, but they must do so within three months; if they did not do so the Board could select a candidate from its own list. The diocese might propose that the property be sold and the proceeds employed to purchase another. The Pensions Board was entirely amenable to this, claiming exactly the same rights as before.[11] The dioceses welcomed the scheme, particularly since it encouraged an incumbent who really should retire but did not because of a fear of getting into difficulties.

In the matter of retirement housing, too, relations between the Church Commissioners and the Pensions Board were vulnerable to ambiguity. The Commissioners did not actually possess the power to provide housing assistance or homes for retired clergy, but they were at liberty to invest their money as they wished and it was this fact that allowed them to make a succession of loans to the Pensions Board, as long as they earned a reasonably 'commercial' rate of interest. 'In practice', a General Purposes Committee memorandum of 1978 had noted flatly that 'the Commissioners have always endeavoured to interpret the term "commercial" as liberally as possible.' Loans were made either for the provision of mortgages for those who could not acquire a home or to the Pensions Board itself for the purchase of properties.[12] On 24 March 1977 the Board had approved a maximum further loan of £1.25 million to the Pensions Board over five years for the purchase of houses, flats and bungalows. From time to time terms and rates of interest were adjusted as the Commissioners saw fit and as circumstances demanded. In the 1970s not all of this was taken up, however. Some wondered if the scheme lay beneath the pride of the clergy.

The fact that the issue was coming into the forefront of the Commissioners' thinking was shown when in July 1978 the Board had found itself weighing up whether to direct the weight of new allocations to the improvement of pensions, stipends or retirement housing. In September 1979 a working party presented a barrage of proposals, not least affirming that the Church was under an obligation to all full-time clergy to provide housing, but not to all part-time clergy. The General Purposes Committee had by now discussed all this

---

[11] Ibid. 25 Sept. 1980, pp. 2–3.
[12] GPC report, 'Housing assistance for the retired clergy', CC (78) 24, Board papers, 27 Apr. 1978, ser. 95085/44.

twice. The Pensions Board approved it. The Board of the Commissioners now agreed that it be published forthwith.[13]

New allocations were now being made to the Pensions Board to acquire houses to be inhabited under licence by retired clergy and by licensed lay workers and clergy widows at a 'commercial' rate of interest, accompanied by augmentation grants to an equivalent amount to enable all of them to meet the charges. In February 1980 a further advance of £31.4 million had been made to the Pensions Board for this purpose. But the Pensions Board found the money disappearing far more quickly than they had anticipated, and went back to the General Purposes Committee for more. The committee, in turn, asked the Board for a further £1.5 million in July, and got it. The logic was circular. 'As with previous advances', it was duly noted, 'it was doubtful that the Board would be able to meet the customary 9 per cent p.a. interest charge unless they received an equivalent amount from the Commissioners in augmentation.'[14]

A unification too far

There was some pressure on the standing committee of the General Synod to see if the central organs of the Church were working as well as they might. A new commission under Oswald Clark was launched to explore the possibility of a unified financial and administrative structure for the Church of England. This bold enterprise was charged to ask a number of fundamental questions, not least whether the Pensions Board and the Commissioners should be amalgamated.

To Lovelock union appeared natural. Working practice recommended it. To the General Purposes Committee in 1983, he observed 'the very significant increases in the levels of the Commissioners' involvement and support of the Pensions Board in recent years'. In his turn, Howard Gracey, the chairman of the Pensions Board, acknowledged firmly the Board's 'great debt' to the Commissioners. But if Lovelock was affably positive about the proposal, Gracey was clearly demurring. He did not think that amalgamation would save money, he could not judge the effects of a move of offices but feared 'disturbance and pain'. There was some debate, some fearing over-centralisation and preferring to improve what they could within existing structures and others urging what must seem the best use of resources. Clark observed the uncertainty and reassured them that his group would tread sensitively.[15]

---

[13] Board minutes, 27 Sept. 1979, pp. 8–9.
[14] Ibid. 24 July 1980, p. 3.
[15] Ibid. 25 Nov. 1982, pp. 1–2.

In 1982 the close inter-relationship of the two bodies might well have seemed to open the gate to greater exposure of the Church Commissioners to the pressing agendas of the Pensions Board. Conversely, there is little evidence that the pressure for pensions which the Board made manifest was at this time firmly constrained by a clear financial strategy expounded and governed by the Commissioners. The dynamic between them is difficult to determine with confidence, not least because they were so close, and to search for conclusive evidence that one initiated and the other responded would miss the obvious point that their priorities, and their members, were often one and the same. Even so, the relentless assertiveness of the Pensions Board in pressing for improvement is explicit: in disability pensions, widows' pensions, pensions for those who had retired at certain times and escaped certain rules. The papers of the Church Commissioners imply it time and again: there is persistent mention of tensions, difficulty and unhappiness. It might well have been the responsibility of the Pensions Board to set down what was needed to maintain their claimants; and it was equally the responsibility of the Commissioners to say what could, or could not, be managed. But somehow the structures, and the very psychology of pressure which pervaded them, made such distinctions foggy, even unreal. Lovelock once observed that a union of the two bodies in 1984 might well have resolved this. It is equally possible that it would have made matters worse.

At all events, when the Clark Report was finally published in July 1984 it did indeed propose the merging of the Pensions Board and the Commissioners. The Pensions Board itself at once split, with a heavy majority against the union, for all Lovelock's efforts to reassure them that the Commissioners had no desire to 'swallow up' their partners.[16] Synod delivered the *coup de grâce*. 'The possibility of organic change', lamented Lovelock, greatly dashed, 'is dead.'[17] To him, the defeat left both bodies with problems, not least the lack of a firm distinction between policy and the executive aspects of the Pensions Board's work. There followed some reshuffling of the Commissioners' nominations list. Now it would be fortified by the addition of the First and Third Commissioners, and by Sir John Herbecq and John Smallwood. The General Purposes Committee also believed that there should be an improved budgetary system at the Board: 'The Commissioners need to be satisfied that a satisfactory system is in place and operating.' Relocation to Millbank remained, to all parties, desirable. But it must be done at the proper time, and with care: 'otherwise the inevitable physical upheaval may throw up points of

---

[16] Pensions Board minutes, 27 Feb. 1984, p. 1.
[17] Chairman of the GPC, 'Pensions Board', CC (84) 52, Board papers, 27 Sept. 1984, ser. 95083/54.

difficulty which reinforce on both sides the entrenched attitudes of the past which it is our common aim to put behind us'.[18]

Momentum I

Improvements to pensions of all kinds continued to follow fast: for widowers of a woman deacon and their dependent children, and also for the widowers and children of female lay workers under the Standard Service Pension Scheme ('The extra cost ... would be unlikely to be very large'); then, in May 1985, for clergy widows with dependent children ('The additional cost to the Commissioners, £200,000 per annum at present prices, could be safely accommodated').[19] In July 1986 there followed a new improvement, this time for the early retirement of clergymen who were not required to retire by permanent infirmity. (Curiously, in this the deaconesses and licensed lay workers were seen to be better served.) The upshot was a new standard early retirement scheme. It was estimated that for twelve years the costs to the Commissioners would grow, and for the Church as a whole would fall; thereafter they would fall for the Commissioners too. This established, the Board was asked for general approval, which it gave.[20]

Devolution, expense and the parsonage house

Parsonages also required another close link with the dioceses and here, too, power could be seen to be increasingly devolving from the Church Commissioners to the dioceses themselves. This went hand-in-hand with a simplification of methods. Full responsibility for the use of allocations now lay with the dioceses. No longer were working drawings and specifications sent off to London for approval; no longer must the dioceses submit to Millbank accounts of their interior decorations allocations. By the end of 1979 all this seemed to the Houses Committee 'a long stride in the direction of greater diocesan responsibility'.[21] But the impression of devolution was at least in part illusory. In truth, the financial fate of the Church Commissioners was becoming more than ever attached to the houses of the clergy, present and retired. Far from ensuring a reduction of central funding,

[18] Ibid. p. 3.
[19] GPC report, 'Pensions matters: definition of pensionable service', CC (85) 47, Board papers 19 Dec. 1985, ibid. pt 55.
[20] GPC report, 'Pensions matters: early retirement', CC (86) 40, Board papers, 24 July 1986, ibid.
[21] HC, annual report to 31 Dec. 1979, 6, Board papers, 27 Mar. 1980, ibid. pt 49.

devolution brought a new language of increased, and constantly growing, central expenditure.

In the 1970s 2,221 unsuitable houses had been sold by the dioceses and 1,651 new ones had been provided (925 built, 726 purchased). Now it was recorded that a further 2,000 parsonage houses should be regarded as unsuitable, mostly because of size or cost of maintenance, and new estimates ventured that at least another £19 million would be needed to meet the costs of replacement. Costs had risen and houses had become smaller, but the rise in property values favoured the sale of old houses, whose value had increased almost five-fold in the course of the 1970s. Where team benefices had been established a greater number of houses was owned by the diocesan boards of finance and classified as diocesan glebe. They were still, like the houses in benefice ownership, eligible for the Commissioners' grants and they got them.

At the end of 1980 the Houses Committee reported a steep increase of 26 per cent in the cost of building in that year alone. They were, they confessed, puzzled by the evident inability of the dioceses to 'obtain more satisfactory tenders at a time when the building industry might have been expected to be in a competitive mood'. There was now a Green Guide on the improvement and replacement of parsonage houses which even proposed the precise dimensions of such new properties (1,804 square feet of floor space – anything much smaller was, experience suggested, generally unsatisfactory). By and large the dioceses managed to conform to it. They could build more houses if they built poorer or smaller ones. Better, thought the Houses Committee, to build fewer and maintain standards.[22]

In such a context it was hardly surprising to hear the argument that it would be better if the clergy owned their own homes. By the end of 1981 a general mood of interest in the question returned, briefly, to life in General Synod and the Third Commissioner agreed that the Commissioners should take another look. The view was unaltered. To attempt such a change would seriously affect the deployment of clergy and, accordingly, pastoral care. The general financial position of the clergy would not be much changed, if at all. Then, whatever periodic grumblings there may be, there was no 'widespread desire' for that change – particularly as their new clergy schemes were all the time improving matters for them. A plethora of other objections to private ownership were then listed, to make quite sure that the idea was buried. It was clear that no radical overhaul of the system was likely.[23] The mind of the Commissioners was firmly set.

[22] HC, annual report to 31 Dec. 1980, 4–6, Board papers, 30 Apr. 1981, ibid. pt 50.
[23] HC report, 'The ownership of clergy houses: memorandum by the Church Commissioners', 23 Sept. 1982, ibid, pt 52. See also GS MISC 37, 1975, a Church

By now the financial and political commitment of the Commissioners was manifest. But a decisive solution was looking as remote as it always had. The Houses Committee report of 1983 estimated that as many as one in six parsonages were too large or in some other way unsuitable. In that single year £5.79 million was passed over to dioceses to spend on individual houses as they saw fit. Many of the dioceses still actually needed the Commissioners to help repay their own loans. By April 1986 the Commissioners were also helping to rehouse seven deserted clergy wives and their families. There were in that year four conferences with dioceses on housing matters. Now the Commissioners' role was effectively defined by consenting to diocesan initiatives and proposals, including ones providing finance, and offering general guidance and judgement in the case of disputes. The dioceses would ask for sums of money as they saw fit and would, within a basic understanding, arrange the terms on which houses were sold and the details of building, purchasing or altering and improving existing houses.

These movements were now to yield a clear and new form. In May 1986 it was proposed that the Commissioners should for the first time provide capital assistance to dioceses for the provision or the renewal of housing assistance for curates, deaconesses and licensed lay workers, again by a combination of grants and loans. The Board agreed. At the Annual General Meeting that year a new allocation of £3 million was made, the first instalment of a grander grant of £20 million which would be spread across the next five years, to enable the dioceses to tackle unsuitable housing. So was born one of the defining monuments of the decade: the Parsonages Renewal Fund, an enterprise whose essential, justifying roots lay in the historic resources report, which had by then seen light of day. The new fund included a mechanism to calculate a just bias towards the needier dioceses, which leaned heavily northwards, for twelve of the fifteen dioceses that received 100 per cent grants were in the north. Within months the dioceses were busily putting this new money to use. Then there was a further barrage of grants and equity-sharing loans to assist dioceses in the housing of assistant staff.

The Parsonages Renewal Fund was an immensely bold undertaking for two principal reasons. First, it declared a commitment to fundamental improvement in one area which had before shown an ability simply to gobble up money (for otherwise the fund would never have been needed in the first place). Then it showed how much momentum had gathered not behind a cold measuring of the distinct, discretionary power of the Commissioners but behind the claims of

Commissioners' document on the same subject, and Board minutes, 30 Sept. 1982, pp. 4–5.

the dioceses. The dioceses had become more independent than ever, but on the Commissioners' money. The Commissioners congratulated themselves that they were doing something which enjoyed popularity.

There was, it seemed, almost no limit to the number of schemes a diocese might submit to the Commissioners for assistance. By October 1987 it had become clear that a pattern of considerable commitment was emerging and for the first time the minutes of the Board seem to reflect a hesitation. There were suggestions that a ceiling be set as soon as possible on the number of grant-aided schemes which could be approved for each diocese receiving grants to the tune of 100 per cent. But then there was also talk of a further allocation of £7 million to parsonages; that the £20 million already agreed for them would be spent in three years rather than five, and might then be extended by another period of five years.[24] When the dioceses themselves were asked for more information about their housing problems and estimates of future costs, it was reported that even now at least 1,850 houses remained unsuitable or in some way in need of improvement. This could cost as much as another £32 million. But now they were evidently so far steeped in grants that there was no turning back. Without still more money, it was said, the whole enterprise might falter. Now, grants made to dioceses eligible for 100 per cent deficit assistance accounted for almost 80 per cent of the total grants approved. The dioceses wanted more. Meanwhile, tours of particular dioceses showed how very impressive the work was.

The committees at Millbank did not work in parallel universes. There were links between the Assets Committee and the General Purposes Committee. In fact, here and there tension could be discerned between the two. On the Assets Committee it was heard that the 'prime duty' of the Commissioners lay with stipends and pensions; that retirement housing was 'something of a diversion'. It was asked, were the clergy being 'over-provided for', 'dependent'? Should they be encouraged to save, to make provision for themselves? They should be encouraged to begin their own saving schemes.[25] The General Purposes Committee would still look fondly on the Parsonages Renewal Fund. Evidently the Assets Committee viewed it frostily.

By 1987 limits had been set on all dioceses, but the momentum was colossal and the need was still said to press. On 17 December 1987 the Board approved an extra £4 million to the Parsonages Renewal Fund. In October 1988 the Board agreed in principle that a further £5 million should be allocated to the fund as a matter of 'urgent need' before the end of the year, bringing the total amount now committed

---

[24] D. N. Goodwin, 'Analysis of the Parsonages Renewal Fund schemes across the dioceses', H (87) 41, Board papers, 29 Oct. 1987, ser. 95083/58.
[25] AC minutes, 15 Apr. 1982.

to £25 million. It had been a good year for investments, the secretary assured them, and the Assets Committee had agreed that such a sum could be made available for such a purpose.[26]

But now the very ground on which that assurance was based was slipping away beneath their feet.

The politics of the portfolios

The investments of the Church Commissioners now bore all too clearly the marks of uncertain times. The ideal balanced portfolio was constantly under pressure from economic cycles which could make some commitments appear not so much fragile as altogether counter-productive, while others were performing in spectacular fashion. As the Commissioners needed more and more money to spend so were they increasingly likely to wash their hands of anything that failed to justify itself commercially – and to pursue with every energy anything that brought gain.

In December 1979 the Commissioners' Stock Exchange portfolio was doing remarkably well. For thirteen years dividends had been restricted by various controls imposed by the government. Now, in August 1979, these had been cast aside. More than this, in the budget of June 1979 exchange controls which had been in place for forty years had also been discarded. Hitherto investment overseas had involved a premium payment. This had now disappeared. Meanwhile the Commissioners were quietly managing their affairs with some virtuosity. For two years they had been refinancing a modest US portfolio by taking out the premium at rates of 25–45 per cent and then repurchasing the same stocks with dollars which had been acquired under loan and current 'swap' arrangements, a cunning financial ploy which actually made money.[27] But the 1970s had shown how fragile the international economic order could be, and the early 1980s brought a new, biting depression; in it much of British industry was simply wiped out.

Beside this, when they turned to their agricultural property portfolio the Commissioners could only find growing cause for alarm. The world of agriculture introduced an element of eloquence into the character of the Commissioners. For here they faced a responsibility to the environment, to the rural communities themselves, to their tenants, who suffered in hard times, and to the Church in the countryside. Their relationship with those who worked on the land was sometimes described as familial. This poetry was something to which Silsoe might

[26] Board minutes, 27 Oct. 1988, pp. 3–4.
[27] AC, annual report to 31 Dec. 1979, sent out to Board members, 24 Apr. 1980, ser. 95083/49.

have been broadly impervious. Harris was certainly not.[28] The intention to remain, almost come what may, among the largest of rural landowners had been affirmed and reaffirmed; so too their commitment to the landlord–tenant system and the policy of re-letting farms to sons or daughters who were deemed to be suitably qualified to take them on. But this could be shaken, for in times of economic misfortune it was to the countryside that sceptical eyes were turned. The claims of history, in all their grandeur, must still demand the sympathies of minds busy with calculations of money. In March 1983 some on the Board were murmuring that the Assets Committee was not as committed to agriculture as it might be.

Everyone knew that agricultural land had never made as much money as urban property. But a virtue had often been made of its historic stability, its financial steadiness. In the 1960s and 1970s farm rents had increased and were, indeed, one of the few forms of investment to match the pace of inflation. Capital values increased accordingly. But in the 1980s the claims of agriculture were quite simply being devastated. There was the problem of overproduction; there were milk quotas; prices stood still. The pattern of rent increases provided further evidence of decline. In 1978 the average gross rent per acre was £27, an annual increase of 19 per cent on the year before. Within a year it had fallen to an increase of 11 per cent; in 1980 it recovered to 20 per cent, but then in 1981 it almost halved, to 11 per cent. By 1985 it was just 6 per cent; in 1987 only 1 per cent. This was stark enough to alter attitudes. Whenever vacant possession was obtained, the Commissioners were selling land, unless particular reasons intruded. Tenants were being encouraged to 'diversify'.[29]

If this was depressing (the word itself was used often on the Assets Committee) the capital picture looked something like a disaster. At the end of the financial year to March 1979 the value per acre had stood at £750, a 32 per cent increase in the year. But then in the following year the increase halved; in 1980 it was 13 per cent; in 1983 it was 5 per cent; in 1984 it actually showed a loss of 5 per cent; in the two following years a loss of 15 per cent; and then a loss of 5 per cent again in 1987. The Assets Committee remarked glumly that 'Any institution seeing nearly one third of the asset value of part of its portfolio disappear must have cause for concern and it will, of course, be a much higher proportion in real terms. We rely on steadily

---

[28] In February 1972 Harris had found himself presiding over a farewell dinner for tenant farmers and their wives on the Fylde estate in Lancashire, now up for sale on the strongest advice of the Assets Committee. The experience was hateful to him: Harris, *Memory-soft the air*, 213.

[29] AC report, 'Investment in agricultural land', CC (88) 13, Board papers, 28 Apr. 1988, ser. 95083/58.

increasing capital values if we are to meet our income needs in the future.' Between 1978 and 1987 the value of the agricultural portfolio as a percentage of total asset value had fallen from 12.7 per cent to 6 per cent.

If it was sometimes worth holding on to investments in the hope of future recovery, such a recovery looked out of the question for the foreseeable future. The prospects were 'wholly gloomy'. The problem of the EEC surpluses would not go away. To make matters worse, new legislation would make rent increases more difficult and the best they could hope for was mere maintenance of existing rental levels. There was seen to be a market for land offered with vacant possession. For tenanted land it was 'virtually non-existent'. It had to be seen that to cling to the land in such dire adversity compromised the freedom to invest which the Commissioners actually possessed and their very chances of realising growth to sustain the Church by moving into other areas which offered profit. In effect, loyalty to the land was becoming a form of self-denial, and self-denial meant 'permanent financial loss'.[30] For some years the Commissioners had been selling, often to maximise the sale of land for development (something that actually involved relatively few acres, but which yielded impressive profits, for often that land was near towns and was sought for new housing). From 1984 they had sold farms which had no such potential, whenever vacant possession could be had, and had done so more and more vigorously. Between 1984 and 1988 480 acres had been sold for development, realising £13.7 million, 8,200 acres of farmland for £13.9 million and a miscellaneous 74 acres for £5.4 million. Of that £33 million, £6 million had financed equity sharing loans for various clergy housing projects. The rest went into Stock Exchange investments, ordinary and fixed interest. By the end of the Runcie era, in 1989, the portfolio comprised 426 farms of over 50 acres, grouped into 47 estate 'units'.[31]

In the residential property portfolio the Church Commissioners still held three main London estates: Octavia Hill, the affordable housing areas; Hyde Park, now looking more 'up-market' than ever; and the Maida Vale estates, which in character lay somewhere between the two. That fact signalled a new vulnerability for Maida Vale, for it made neither one point, philanthropy, nor the other, profit, quite convincingly. That was not enough in these new, more hard-edged days. Nor were the Octavia Hill estates immune to criticism, sometimes from surprising quarters. In February 1980 the two clerical members of the Assets Committee, the dean of Windsor, Michael Mann and Canon McDermid argued that in the long term the

[30] Ibid. pp. 2–3.
[31] Board minutes, 26 Apr. 1984, p. 2.

Commissioners should divest themselves of all low-rented property 'on the grounds that although this was clearly a proper role for the Christian Church to undertake, the Church Commissioners were not the right body to undertake it'. But Harris disagreed: he spoke 'of the pride that the Commissioners had traditionally felt in making this contribution to the welfare of society'. The committee agreed that six out of the eight Octavia Hill estates be retained, losing the Church Manor estate in Brixton and the Regency Street part of the Westminster estate.[32]

The new wisdom

It was in this difficult financial world that the Church Commissioners were galvanised by a new vision. It was based on a premise which few, if any could deny: the economy was all too prone to being blown off course, by inflation, the fortunes of sterling, trades unions, the ungovernable, rampaging cycles of world trade. By contrast, in the preceding decade the demand for property had exceeded supply. The Assets Committee was quick to observe a striking shift away from the old manufacturing industries, which succumbed so rapidly to the depression, and towards service industries and the consumer society. What had been simply an element in their thinking began to assume more significant proportions. They began to measure their fortune more and more in millions of pounds and thousands of square feet.

The property speculation which CEDIC had authored in the 1960s and 1970s had become a cornerstone of their fortunes. Most of it remained in London and it had grown there. The Paternoster development at St Paul's had now been completed. St Paul's Churchyard was seen to be one of their most ambitious, and most successful, enterprises: £6 million had been paid out to modernise a large Victorian block south of the cathedral, 40,000 square feet had been converted into 'top quality, air-conditioned office space', 70,000 as warehouses and showrooms. (An American bank took 27,000 square feet to rent; another 13,000 went to a big firm of Japanese stockbrokers.) The Paternoster development was meant to be a thing of beauty too. Harris was a man of taste and Elisabeth Frink was commissioned to produce a sculpture. When Harris retired the Commissioners bought him a maquette of it, without realising that he had also decided to buy them one, too.

There had been another scheme nearby, in Bow Lane. A narrow street occupied by pleasant though not striking buildings, it had, even so, 'an atmosphere of character and intimacy'. The Commissioners decided that it could do better. They agreed to leave the frontages and

[32] AC minutes, 21 Feb. 1980.

shops and a restaurant intact but behind them to convert twelve separate buildings into three; no easy task: it cost £2.25 million. The decision was vindicated promptly; almost at once the rents had been taken and they soon showed a yield of 11.5 per cent. In north London, on the City Road, the sites of three late Victorian properties were being viewed coolly as a potential 20,000 square feet of offices (with a small shop on the ground floor). The lease was about to end at Monmouth House further along the road, with its 40,000 square feet of office space ripe for improvement. It would be re-let on five-yearly reviews. The space was taken even before the work began. In March 1979 Monmouth House was estimated to be worth £2.8 million. After spending £0.8 million it was said to be worth £5.5 million. There was more. Connaught Place at Marble Arch lay at the south-east corner of the Commissioners' Hyde Park estate. For ten years they had planned to improve the buildings and redevelop the land that lay behind them. Now they would do so. At The Angel, Islington, they had agreed to go into partnership with their old ally Lord Rayne to build a substantial office and shop development.[33]

In short, by the mid-1980s the Commissioners' London office portfolio was showing so much *joie-de-vivre* that the Commissioners had to make an effort to restrain it. Not always did they try. In December 1985 Lovelock informed the Board that the Commissioners and their partners had sold the major interest in the offices to the north of St Paul's Cathedral. Five smaller blocks had also been released for sale and an offer for a 250-year lease had been promptly accepted. The sale itself realised £50 million. The dean of St Paul's, Alan Webster, was anxious that Paternoster Square itself might disappear because of the sale, and feared that the churches in the area had not been properly consulted by the Commissioners. Lovelock replied that he was sure that the dean would agree that 'historic issues could not be allowed to be the primary factor in considering investment decisions'.[34]

Nobody was actually quite sure why property had done so well. When the question was asked at a conference of urban receivers, no clear answer was forthcoming, 'even', it was noted, 'from dedicated property men'.[35] At all events, in the offices of Millbank a new pursuit of property development was purposefully constructed and powerfully promoted. Would it work? Naturally, every investment policy had risks. In 1980 the Assets Committee simply perceived that the risks could be measured sensibly and that when they were compared with the advantages they were heavily outweighed. In this the powers at

[33] Ibid.
[34] Board minutes, 19 Dec. 1985, p. 2.
[35] A. R. Gibson note, 'Property and the medium term outlook', 14 Nov. 1979, UR (79) 5, in CC/SEC/INVP/8B.

Millbank were not alone. The dioceses, too, wanted to press further. The cathedrals were now taking to the world of development: a new project was built on land west of Liverpool Cathedral and the dean and chapter asked the Commissioners for financial assistance to acquire housing for cathedral clergy and staff within that site. A number approached the Commissioners with a view to setting up a property unit trust, a pool in which they could invest the proceeds of the sale of glebe which had passed into their hands since the 1976 Endowments and Glebe Measure. To leave such money in the diocesan stipends funds earned only 5 per cent in interest and no growth. It did not look very exciting there. Discussions followed: a combined property pool would, it was hoped, be set up on 1 January 1981.[36]

In 1981 the assets secretary, James Shelley, offered the Assets Committee the first of a series of annual reviews of the Commissioners' investment policy. What he saw first of all was the weight of the Commissioners' present expenditure. He also recognised that these burdens were growing relentlessly. What is crucial here is that the new mood at the Commissioners was not to meet these growing demands for expenditure with a show of political discretion, but with a policy of financial success. Shelley noted that in 1970/1 pensions had taken 13 per cent of their income from assets. Now it was likely to be 27 per cent, and it was rising. They could share the payment of stipends with the parishes, but pensions were their charge alone. 'This', wrote Shelley, 'stresses the importance of maintaining the quality of the portfolio so as to be able to guarantee steadily growing income to finance *future* pension increases which are certain to be required. In other words the importance of future growth in income in relation to present income is increasing all the time.'

Over the previous few years property had come to amount, in capital terms, to two-thirds of the Commissioners' portfolio. If it was so strong a presence it was not because funds had been transferred into it, but because it had grown so impressively. The spread of income between property and equities, though, was more balanced: 52 per cent and 42 per cent respectively. Granted, property came with its own peculiar anxieties. If capital and income both grew, yields were low. It was inflexible in altered circumstances and could be 'politically sensitive', embarrassing even. It was also costly, for buildings had to be maintained and improved. Yet against these dangers could be set its history of stability. Moreover, the Commissioners had the very best property: 'the best is in short supply and so always in demand'.[37]

---

[36] Ibid. 7.
[37] Assets Secretary report, 'Investment policy review', A (81) 54, in CC/SEC/INVP/8B.

It was partly because of property speculation that Silsoe had sought to recast the Commissioners committees in 1964. Would the Monckton system bear the force of this new movement? There is no evidence that anybody doubted that the system of deliberation which by then had settled successfully into deepening grooves at Millbank was adequate to bear the weight of the new, far more active, direction of the property portfolio. The Assets Committee met every month and listed all the relevant experts which Millbank had to offer: the secretary, the estates secretary, the assets secretary, the property secretary, the accountant, the investments secretary, the under-secretaries and, towards the end of the decade, a representative of their agents, Chestertons. It was never easy to get a clerical member, and, to judge by the minutes, those there in that capacity were if anything more inclined to participate in the general economic debate than to offer a distinctive moral dimension. Furthermore, every six months there was a joint meeting of the Assets Committee and the Stock Exchange Advisory Panel. When Shelley succeeded Kenneth Lamb as secretary to the Commissioners in 1986 the new movement had found its prophet. There were critics, but the strong impression left by the records is that the critics were not in power.

1980–1983: crossing the Atlantic

In the past the Commissioners had developed what they already owned. But now they were going in search of completely new projects – and not only in Britain. For some time they had looked to increase their investments in the United States, and then in Japan and Australia. Now they began to entertain ambitions to venture into the US property market.

Sailing across the Atlantic to the New World has ever been an adventure rich in idealistic hopes. Now the Assets Committee saw in it the appearance of good commercial wisdom too. The American economy was strong and resilient, it was often observed. If there were disincentives to venturing into these new climes – different systems of taxation, a different set of rules to learn – they could be outweighed by a place in the most dynamic economy in the world. In the United States property offered a high yield. If a high yield involved a high risk, they might remind themselves again that this was an economy of unique power and size. Moreover, to hold all one's assets in the United Kingdom meant that the fortunes of the Commissioners were mortgaged to national prosperity. Should they be? Was it more responsible to spread them further afield, particularly when those fields promised so much?

In November 1980 the Assets Committee invited Shelley to investigate and report on possibilities of investment in the property market in the United States through real estate investment trusts. He found against them. They had a 'patchy' history and 'too dubious a reputation'. But he found that the American property market itself still appealed. For him, the 'prime factor' for a new strategy lay in the 'protection' offered by property in an age of high inflation. There were difficulties: greater planning and building controls in the United States, and also a constant supply of new buildings which affected the value of existing 'stock'. 'Nevertheless', pronounced Shelley, 'the fact remains that, at least for a domestic investor, the outlook is favourable.' If they were to move in this direction they must invest a high level of commitment, their money, their management time; and they must find suitable partners.[38]

By 1981 the Commissioners had decided to sell the Maida Vale estate. It was expected to yield at least £70 million. It was this money that Shelley favoured investing overseas. He proposed that the Commissioners increase their assets in the United States from 6 per cent to 10 per cent. 'This', he remarked, 'would be an important new departure for the Commissioners and the Committee will wish to consider very carefully the advantages and disadvantages of such a course.' Lamb and Shelley together now proposed that the Assets Committee approve a first tranche of £12 million in US property, added to £8 million in US equities and £2.5 million in Japan and the Far East.[39] About this there was a deliberate debate. The Assets Committee approved the £8 million in equities, but deferred a decision on investment in US properties until they had seen a new paper by the Estates Secretary. Lord Remnant sought an assurance that there were sufficient resources at Millbank to take into account the increasing complexity of the current investment world. Lamb replied that he believed that there were, but said that he would seek the assurance of Shelley himself. The main thrust of the strategy, to reinvest overseas the profits realised by residential sales, was in effect approved. From now on investment policy would be reviewed annually. In itself, to transfer 10 per cent of their total assets overseas could not, it was felt, be criticised. It was 'very much in line with many other institutions such as Pension Funds'.[40] The great enterprise had begun.

This policy soon acquired a strong momentum. By June 1982 the Assets Committee faced a firm recommendation from Shelley that a start be made towards building up a $100 million property portfolio as

[38] Investments Secretary note, 'Stock exchange investments: indirect investments in property in the USA', A (81) 6, ibid.
[39] Assets Secretary report, 'Investment policy review', A (81) 54, ibid.
[40] AC minutes, 15 Oct. 1981; Shelley note, 8 Oct. 1981, ibid.

soon as their cash flow allowed them, if possible by the end of 1983. Again, this was debated earnestly. To every doubt was offered an assurance. If a high yield did mean a high risk 'it was explained that these high yields were expected to come down as and when interest rates were reduced'. It was important to take advantage of the present climate, which was favourable to investment. If they were to avoid liability for British Corporation tax, the decisions about investments must be taken in the US itself, by a company acting within policy guidelines laid down by the Assets Committee. In London they would exercise their control over the enterprise by virtue of the simple fact that no sale or purchase could be authorised without the consent of the shareholders, not to mention the fact that the Commissioners themselves held the power to release the capital. They could monitor overheads simply by reading the company accounts. There was now a structure in such thinking. There should be a board with two shareholder directors (the assets and estates secretaries) and three US citizens, 'all eminent in property, real estate law and the US financial markets ... and preferably well connected with the Episcopalic [sic] Church'. Might there be criticism? If so, they must meet it with 'a concerted response', for this would, after all, be a benefit to their beneficiaries. Mann simply suggested that they must ensure the goodwill of the Episcopalian Church ('itself a substantial property investor') and Shelley said that either he or the Assets Secretary would personally visit the presiding bishop and the bishop of Boston to explain what they were doing and to ensure that they approved of the American directors. There was the reassurance of continuity, too: their old agent, Chestertons, was appointed to recommend on the portfolio. The Assets Committee settled to a discussion of details.[41]

By 21 October the directors of the holding company had been appointed. In the same month the Church Commissioners acquired shares in three more companies in the United States and had another in view. Diebold, a company making automated bank teller machines, was considered 'appropriate'.[42] There was now a sense of change in the patterns and rhythms of Millbank itself: it was now not only the bishops and deans of the Church of England who were regularly disappearing on trips abroad. On 20 January 1983 Shelley and the estates secretary, James Beard, turned up at a meeting of the Assets Committee having only hours before stepped off an aeroplane from New York. They now reported on the first meeting of the board of Deansbank Incorporated. For the new company now existed. 'The way was now clear for the purchase of the first property.'[43]

[41] AC minutes, 16 June 1982, ibid.
[42] Ibid. 21 Oct. 1982.
[43] Ibid. 20 Jan. 1983.

The new venture brought the Commissioners' commercial properties secretary, Michael Hutchings, into the foreground. By March he had his eyes on office property in Anaheim, south of Los Angeles, costing $15.25 million and expecting to yield 8.5 per cent. Deansbank had already spent all the money it currently held in the US. Because sterling was so low it was unattractive to purchase dollars. Deansbank was instead furnished with the power to borrow up to half of the cash it needed to complete new purchases. April 1983 saw shares bought in a further four companies. By July 1983 the board of Deansbank had approved four projects costing $60 million, with a yield of 9.5 per cent. By October Mann had also attended a board meeting there and returned with evangelistic zeal to urge other members of the Assets Committee to do the same. Income began to flow in. By January 1984 Deansbank had properties in California, Texas, Florida, the north-east, the mid-west, North Carolina. But it was also seen to be encountering intense competition for prime real estate. This sounded only one minor chord in a movement of symphonic splendour. Perhaps it was hardly audible.

By the time of his third investment policy review, in May 1983, James Shelley was optimistic that the Commissioners' own prospects were beginning to flourish. By now the committee had its sights on 15 per cent of their total assets in overseas property and stock. When they compared the spread of their portfolio with pensions funds, the Commissioners observed that with 62 per cent in property they had as much as three times the proportion of the nearest of the others. 'It does seem essential', wrote Shelley, 'that the US portfolio should be operated essentially as a portfolio for growth.'[44]

1984: the first dreadnought

On 16 February 1984 the Assets Committee agreed to disclose the Commissioners' assets, those over £1 million, in the annual report for the first time.

In Britain itself the new economic spirit was captured by one word: retail. It was said that shopping was becoming the nation's favourite pastime, even its *ersatz* religion. Pundits began to call the new supermarkets the cathedrals of the day; liturgists found what went on inside them curiously ritualistic. If this was indeed so, the Church Commissioners were loudly, ebulliently, in tune with the theme and they saw that this great enthusiasm would require new and grand forms: shopping centres which were bigger than anything seen before. In March 1983 the Assets Committee agreed to invest up to £52

[44] Shelley, 'Investment policy review', A (83) 42, for the meeting of 19 May 1983, in SEC/CC/INVP/8B.

million in a new retail development, St Enoch's, occupying eight acres
of prime site in the centre of Glasgow. This was a vast enterprise.
There were 192,000 acres of retail space, an L-shaped two-storey
shopping mall, one large department store, an ice rink, a multi-storey
car-park, all enclosed in glass. Shelley promoted it as 'an excellent
opportunity'. Chestertons were enthusiastic. Lovelock asked, was this
not a depressed area, with high levels of unemployment and crime? He
was assured that, for all this, it was a prime site. There were 2.5 million
people coming to the centre of the city to shop, many of them well
paid in the growing electronics industries. St Enoch's was a high-
quality building; the project enjoyed a top-class management.
Moreover, the fortunes of Glasgow itself were improving, and quickly.
St Enoch's was likely to be the largest development of its kind in the
United Kingdom. If the building itself looked disconcertingly
'futuristic' and hard to maintain, the glass envelope which encased it
was 'a special self-cleaning type'. They might observe, too, that
Glasgow was also wet. Approval was given subject to finding a suitable
partner and Chestertons own satisfaction as to various technical
aspects of the plans.[45]

Into such enterprises the various fractions of the property portfolio
were seen to disappear. In May 1984 the Assets Committee learnt that
in the first three years of their sales programme about half of the
Maida Vale estate had been sold, realising some £60 million 'with no
serious criticism either of the Commissioners or of their agents'.[46] At
this point it was decided to reinforce the new policies and to place
funds with growing boldness. They looked again towards their
faltering agricultural portfolio. When the Assets Committee discussed
Shelley's next review, in July 1984, it approved a proposal to invest a
further £40 million overseas, this to be financed by £10 million from
the sale of farms and £30 million of UK equities, together with a
switch of a further £25 million from UK equities into gilts, presumably
to compensate. Three-quarters of the £40 million would now be
invested in Japan and the Far East, and a quarter in the United States.
But now there was unease on the committee. Was the sale of farms
too ambitious? A month before Canon Marlow had been hesitant and
doubtful, detecting a 'moral dilemma in how much the Church
Commissioners' for England should be seen to be investing historic
resources overseas'. But Marlow was isolated and Shelley pushed
forward as purposefully as ever. For his part Lord Remnant suspected
that UK equities were less safe than were those in the Far East and the
US. Hopkinson again remarked that he was 'perturbed' about the cost
of the pensions bill. Still, he repeated, there should be 'separate

[45] AC minutes, 15 Mar. 1984.
[46] Ibid. 17 May 1984.

investment approaches' for the Commissioners' different activities. He too was in favour of reducing the Commissioners' property holdings and in favour of the drift towards gilts overseas.[47]

The Assets Committee inspected the first annual valuation of the US portfolio on 20 December 1984. It showed a capital growth of more than 5 per cent and with income growth added they had a total return of 13 per cent. In the context of the American policy a new issue was beginning clearly to emerge. The Deansbank company was being built, increasingly, on loans. If that was necessary, thought the committee, there was nothing 'inherently wrong in it', provided that it was done selectively, watching the consequences for income, and ensuring that the total sum borrowed did not exceed 25 per cent of the value of the whole portfolio.[48]

Boom: 1985–6

The international economy flourished; profits on property of all kinds soared; the Church Commissioners saw their new programme covered in glory. By 1985 Shelley could observe that stock markets across the world were at new highs. 'Investors', he reported to the Assets Committee, 'are clearly in confident mood.' Everything was measured as it should be: the balance of the Commissioners' portfolio was regularly compared with that of private funds, pension funds and insurance companies. As so often before, such studies did more to identify the unusual nature of their own portfolio than anything else. They now had far fewer UK equities than most, broadly similar levels of overseas investment, more commercial property than most – though not by much – and then far more farms and residential property. If the City was 'sceptical' about property as a form of investment that only served to add conviction to the Commissioners' plan to diversify their holdings through the new US property portfolio. For this, remarked Shelley, would ensure that the Commissioners would enjoy 'a uniquely advantageous position to meet the unexpected fluctuations of economic life that it is so difficult and, at times, impossible to forecast'. He added, with some bravura, 'I hope, therefore, that we do not pay too much attention to the current prophets of doom regarding the prospects for property.'[49]

By the time of Shelley's next review for the Assets Committee nobody could doubt that the new policy had crystallised into a 'radical reorganisation' of the commercial property portfolio in the United Kingdom. The future did not lie in 'older, ex-growth' offices,

[47] Ibid. 21 June 1984.
[48] Ibid. 20 Dec. 1984.
[49] Shelley, 'Investment policy review', A (85) 36, in SEC/CC/INVP/8B.

particularly those in 'suspect locations'. It lay in a far higher proportion
of retail property and small, high-specification office buildings in the
best locations with the best long-term growth prospects. The future,
indeed, looked more and more like St Enoch's. The results of this were
increasingly impressive. Properties rolled noisily onto the
Commissioners' books and off again. In 1985 the Commissioners had
sold Clifton House, Euston Road (£8 million), one block of
Eastbourne Terrace (£11 million) and office and industrial properties
at Finsbury (£10.5 million). As far as agricultural land was concerned,
what was not marked for permanent retention should be clearly
assessed as a 'trading option'. The sales of Maida Vale proceeded
apace. Now the target was to invest $125 million in the property
market in the US, this again financed by the sale of residential property
in the United Kingdom and a 'modest' programme of farm sales. They
would allow the Deansbank board to 'gear up' by borrowing, but
within limits. Deansbank itself now had five properties; two more
would be added later that year. By then the Commissioners' total
investment in the United States would amount to $97 million.[50]

This radical initiative could not take place without provoking unease
and anxiety. In May 1985 David Hopkinson told the Assets
Committee that he had attended a tenants' dinner at Chester and there
had been struck by the number of those he met who seemed unsure of
their future 'with regard to what they mistakenly believed to be the
Commissioners' new policy of disinvesting in agriculture'.[51] Again,
when the Assets Committee met the next month, there was evidence
of disquiet, and unease about their investments in the United States.
But now there was a second dreadnought. This was the MetroCentre
in Gateshead. It would occupy a 100 acre site, ideally located for a
number of northern towns, 1.5 million people living within a half-hour
drive. The design was typically American, and, at 1.5 million square
feet, the centre would be the largest such of its type in Europe. The
Commissioners were negotiating for an 8 per cent yield. Chestertons
had 'total confidence' in it all. The Newcastle shopping centre
development, not far away, had shown itself to be most successful.
Despite high local unemployment, trading was strong. The committee
approved in principle that their investment in the development be
increased to £130 million. They should tell the bishop of Durham
what was going on.[52]

The Commissioners acquired the freehold of the site of the
MetroCentre on 30 September. Shelley told the Assets Committee in
October that the press release announcing the development had

[50] Shelley, 'Investment policy review', July 1986, ibid.
[51] AC minutes, 16 May 1985.
[52] Ibid. 18 July 1985.

'deliberately minimised' their role, but that, in time, they would enjoy entire control of an investment 'expected to produce a gross income of £8.5 million a year'.[53] If Lovelock had asked questions about St Enoch's, he now seemed to be caught up in the new enthusiasm. He announced to the Board that the Commissioners had made their largest ever single investment. It would involve up to £100 million over a number of years and would create in the region of 6,000 new jobs in an area blighted by depression and unemployment. It would open in a year's time.

The world of retail was not entirely without its own controversies, dilemmas, conflicts of interest. Parliament was being harassed by ardent lobbies pressing that legislation be changed to allow shops to open on Sundays. At General Synod it had been suggested that the Commissioners should convey to all store groups in which they held shares the Synod's own view that the existing laws should be left largely undisturbed. The right of people not to work on one day of the week must be maintained. This caught the Commissioners off guard. Before his retirement, in July 1985, Lamb had 'reminded the Committee that the retail sector was the spearhead of the Commissioners' investment policy in the years ahead'. But, on the Assets Committee, Bishop Westwood of Peterborough insisted that this must be 'a major ethical decision' for the committee. The Commissioners, he added, should do as Synod bid. Brian Howard was anxious that feelings might be aggravated if the Commissioners took to lobbying. The committee decided to await publication of the proposed legislation, the bishop dissenting.[54]

Such matters might by now have seemed minor distractions. As 1986 unfolded, the construction of the Gateshead dreadnought drew the Commissioners further and further into its vortex. In April the Assets Committee approved the investment of a further £55 million in a third phase of the development. Phases 1 and 2, approved in July 1985, had altogether cost £130 million. Again, at Millbank itself, the virtues of the enterprise were paraded with some ardour. It appeared that retail spending had not been affected by high unemployment (why not, it was asked? Was it the low cost of living, the strength of the 'black' economy, 'a marked tendency to spend rather than save'?). At all events, by now the Commissioners were utterly committed to the enterprise. In only a few months the MetroCentre was open for business, officially launched by the Minister of State for the Environment, Nicholas Ridley. Some members of the Assets Committee were present.[55]

[53] Ibid. 17 Oct. 1985.
[54] Ibid. p. 2.
[55] Ibid. 15 Apr. 1986.

By this stage £40 million had been invested in Japan, where activities were in the hands of three outside fund managers. In Britain itself property sales went on steadily and the sums coming in were often formidable. The Paternoster complex was now sold for £50 million, the remainder of Eastbourne Terrace for £13.5 million, Condor House to Coal Industries Nominees for £25 million. It was increasingly evident that property was being bought and sold with a new ease. By April 1986 one of the Commissioners' most recent acquisitions, 55 Bishopsgate, had been sold to the Kumagai Gumi Company for £35 million. The bulk of the proceeds was again moved straight into the retail sector. Sales at Maida Vale continued, but not without resistance. In July 1985 three hundred people from the estate had turned up at General Synod to deplore what was happening to them. This was not even recorded in the papers of the Board or the Assets Committee. Shelley simply observed that the 'rump' of the estate was harder and more sensitive to sell. Added to all this, £16 million was realised in farm sales to the end of 1985 and the proceeds were invested in commercial property in the United States. The proportion of the commercial property portfolio which was committed to the retail sector moved steadily towards 50 per cent.

Besides the MetroCentre and St Enoch's two further dreadnoughts were under construction: Tower Ramparts in Ipswich and a further project in Cheltenham. These substantial investments were balanced by the acquisition of smaller, 'ready-made retail units' in market towns and 'sub-regional' centres. Consumer spending was seen to be rising and was expected to rise still further. Property companies everywhere were busy; competition for prime sites was intense. 'All the current evidence', reported Shelley, 'suggests that our major schemes will be highly successful.'

In the United States Deansbank now had a ceiling of $125 million, with a facility to borrow up to 25 per cent of the value of its portfolio, an effective gross ceiling of $166 million. The company's portfolio was now almost fully leased. Shelley reiterated that 'direct investment in property in what is clearly a dynamic and powerful economy still looks absolutely right in the longer term and the target areas for investment, the west coast, sunbelt and east coast, are still correct'. They should do more. He now proposed that the Commissioners raise the ceiling at Deansbank to $160 million, with an allowance to borrow not more than 30 per cent of the total portfolio. The policy of improving performance by switching between stocks should continue.[56] The investment ceiling for Deansbank was soon raised again, this time to $230 million. But now there were doubts. For all his confidence and conviction Shelley had to acknowledge that progress in the United

[56] Shelley, 'Annual investment review 1986–87', A (87) 46, in SEC/CC/INVP/8B.

States was not quite what they had hoped. Indeed, it was slow. There was determined competition for quality investments from European and Japanese funds. A weak dollar was affecting performance in the short term, but, he insisted, long-term prospects for income and capital growth remained good. What the minutes and papers of the Assets Committee show is that there was a query over the Deansbank initiative that would not go away. All the self-confident assurance notwithstanding, something was awry.

The pressures of the policy were throwing the Commissioners' agricultural holdings into still sharper relief. Now they would retain only the high-quality estates or those with real prospects of development 'within a reasonable timescale'.[57] As for Maida Vale, the Commissioners could not get out fast enough. By now the leases of all 900 modern rented flats at Hyde Park had also been sold.

1987 – and doubts

Although Shelley continued to get his own way when it came to fundamental decisions, it would be wrong to suggest that there was no discussion on the Assets Committee. When it debated his 1987 review there were murmurings 'again' about property, and commercial property in particular, in a market which could be 'volatile' and where 'mistakes could be easily made'. But then 'good active management and the example of the Oxford Colleges were cited as arguments for the present balance'.[58]

It was not only the making of money that worried the committee. A set of pensions projections showed that 'unless economic conditions seriously worsened' the Commissioners' commitment would soon peak and then decline to manageable levels. This being so, the Commissioners would be saved from a fate as 'solely a pension fund'. Hopkinson found these projections 'over-sanguine'. The Assets Committee showed 'some sympathy' for this and asked that there should now be projections every three years.[59] It was not only the Assets Committee that trembled at the mounting commitment to pensions. On the General Purposes Committee on 8 October 1987 the chief accountant asked that it should be noted. The trouble with pensions remained their unpredictability. It was exceedingly difficult to be sure what the future held, to make the right allowances for future improvements, changing patterns of ministry, ecumenical activity, the number of ordinands, for the economy altogether.

[57] Ibid.
[58] Ibid.
[59] AC minutes, 18 June 1987. See also correspondence with David Hopkinson, June 1987, and also A (87) 55, in SEC/CC/INVP/8B.

One question which now persisted went to the root of the new wisdom. It concerned capital. Hopkinson had argued that pension funds and charities sometimes needed to pursue different investment policies in line with their needs for income in the short-term or capital growth in the long-term. Pension funds, he remarked, could spend capital. Charities could not. Therefore they should only create capital in line with inflation. Lovelock and Shelley gave this short shrift. Lovelock remarked to Shelley:

> I have never been able to see the maxim 'we mustn't spend capital' as much more than a slogan. Of course, one should not receive a capital gain and simply spend it as income. But if one, for policy reasons, exchanges a high capital growth/ low income asset for the reverse because one needs the higher income, it seems to me only technically true to say that one is not spending capital. After a few years you have less capital than you would otherwise have had, but you have more income.

Shelley agreed that Hopkinson's distinction was 'ludicrous'; it 'simply does not exist'. He replied, 'In the long run it is only *capital* growth that will create income growth & therefore the best capital we can achieve, while being fair to our present beneficiaries, must be right.'[60]

The hectic pace of the new policies and pressing business might well have cluttered minds. Deansbank, meanwhile, continued to cause concern. On 19 March 1987 the Assets Committee reflected glumly that it had not seen a full report on it for two years. But then the Commissioners' agent, William Wells, materialised, along with a slide-show, to tell them that their US investments had shown no less than a 12.35 per cent return at the end of the preceding year. They had more offices in their portfolio than was perhaps ideal, and it was time to move into retail. Somebody asked about risks, but Wells replied that property in the US should be thought of solely as 'a commodity to be traded like any other'. After all, the average lifespan of a new office block there was only twenty years.[61]

Barely a month later the Assets Committee received a proposal that the Commissioners buy out one of their partners at the MetroCentre for £36 million, payable as £26 million in October 1987 and £10 million in 1990. If they bought their share early they would possess full control and the entire percentage growth of the future. On the Assets Committee there was, again, a stirring of 'anxiety' but the advocates of the enterprise, again, had the measure of their critics. Troubles of any

[60] Correspondence between Lovelock and Shelley, Oct. 1987, ibid.
[61] AC minutes, 19 Mar. 1987.

kind were simply dismissed as 'teething problems'; they could hardly be surprised by them, 'given the wholly novel nature of the enterprise'. Again, the proposal was approved.[62]

The National Audit Office and the decision to borrow

These great movements did not concern only those who haunted the committee rooms of Millbank. After auditing the 1986 accounts, the National Audit office registered 'disquiet' and pointedly questioned the arrangements that the Commissioners had put in place for the provision of interim income during the construction of their biggest development projects. By now these involved a subsidiary company, CC Projects Ltd., which was covenanting its profits back to the Commissioners as income. So pragmatic a relationship between fees, capital and costs was certainly too much for the NAO. It was 'too patently a device for converting capital to income'; it was a practice 'against the provisions of the Commissioners' constitution'; there were doubts whether it had the necessary authority of the Commissioners behind it. The Office rapped the Church Commissioners on the knuckles. Things must change.

Shelley broke this to the Assets Committee rather demurely. The Commissioners had always seen the provision of an interim return on development finance as a legitimate use of capital. They simply could not sustain their present policy without it. He invited the Committee to endorse this 'as a principle'. They could then, he added, work out something with the NAO about the method whereby they implemented the principle. They did so.[63]

The NAO had also expressed doubts about the manner in which the Commissioners were paying from capital for developments which had not yet begun to produce rents. This 'interim' income could be seen as a loss, but only technically because it served the purpose of greater long-term gain. A certain amount of this could be allowed, as long as there was a note to explain. But the sums committed in such ways had burgeoned, from £3 million in 1986 to no less than £150 million currently. In short it had come to involve 8–9 per cent of the total income of the Church Commissioners. If they called a halt to their policy the loss in income altogether would actually compromise their responsibilities to their beneficiaries. Property development had become something more than an important element in a design. It was now seen to define the design itself.

Shelley was advised that the judgement of the NAO must surely be accepted. But if the Commissioners could not use their own money to

[62] Ibid. 23 Apr. 1987.
[63] Ibid. 21 May 1987.

fund new developments, could they use somebody else's? 'Any other property developer', observed Shelley dryly, would borrow. Interest rates were 'relatively reasonable', and interest could be presented as part of the cost of development. In fact, Shelley and his colleagues had already met staff at the National Westminster Bank and begun to negotiate for a loan of up to £150 million. The interest rates and charges appeared modest. If they rose unacceptably, 'some sort of back-to-back arrangement' could be made to effect an exit. To this the NAO had offered no objection.[64] Nor, evidently, did the members of the Assets Committee. Indeed, they were heartily in favour. It was, after all, the best of all worlds: it got the Commissioners off the hook with the NAO; it ensured that their great programme was maintained; it released income, their own income, for more lucrative medium-term business. By the end of December 1987 a facility for a loan of £140 million had been framed. When it next met in February 1988 the committee approved it formally and smiled upon the modesty of the commitment fee.[65] This had never been done before. Nobody, evidently, asked if the Commissioners were offending against their traditions or obligations.

In the spring of 1988 it could be seen clearly where the new wisdom had brought the financial policy of the Church Commissioners. Their portfolio was, as usual, heavily biased towards property; the property portfolio was heavily inclined towards commercial property; the commercial property portfolio leaned heavily towards colossal new developments and these had become, in their turn, heavily dependent upon loans. And these were not the kind of gentle, preferential loans which the Commissioners made to their beneficiaries, but hard-nosed commercial loans from banks which worked for their own profits. In short, the financial policy which upheld much of the Church of England was founded in no small measure upon debt. The essential calculation which defined this relationship with debt was that it could be paid off by the success of the development programme itself. If that calculation of success failed the whole chain would collapse, possibly almost at once. That demonstrated another, and decisive, element in the equation. The Church Commissioners must ensure that their policy succeed, not merely in its financial calculations, but in that old and haunting question of investment: how to take the right step at the best time in a changing, uncontrollable context. Not all the expertise in the world can master the rhythms of time and chance.

[64] Shelley note, 'Finance for property development schemes', A (87) 75 in SEC/CC/INVP/8B.
[65] AC minutes, 18 Feb. 1988, 1–2.

Momentum II

By now the entire development cost of St Enoch's was £82 million, the Commissioners' share exactly half of that. They began to buy out their partners: off went £9 million, £17 million, a further £20 million. Mr Wells of Chestertons was unstoppable, completely convinced that his strategy was sound; he assured the committee that St Enoch's would open on time and that when it did there would be three times as many visitors as at the MetroCentre. The Assets Committee did not seem convinced. It asked for a regular review.

By 20 April 1988 the MetroCentre was largely complete. In June the Assets Committee agreed to charter an aeroplane to visit it and on the same day to drop in at St Enoch's. Perhaps Shelley and Wells believed that the physical reality, the magnitude of the sites, would confirm their wisdom and move the doubtful to belief. Perhaps it did.

Just as doubts were surfacing, Shelley's strategy found itself powerfully justified. One of the principal arguments for his policy was that property was stable in a world in which stocks and shares were haphazard. By the time that Shelley had written his 1988 investment policy review for the Assets Committee, the Stock Exchange had suffered a colossal seizure and the British government had been forced, in almost melodramatic circumstances, to cut loose from the European exchange rate mechanism and to devalue sterling. This sent shock waves across society, from the grandest bank to the modest family living in a mortgaged house. Yet, by contrast, the property market had seen the greatest increases in rental and capital value 'for very many years'. If property 'booms' had proven fragile in the past, they might reasonably hope that this one would prove more 'soundly based' and enduring. Now, with the stock market so shaken, funds would 'surely' be tempted to put more of their money into property, and, in so doing, fuel new rises in values. Indeed, even after what was almost at once called Black Monday, the Church Commissioners had ended 1987 with an asset value that had grown by no less than £120 million. 'It also puts us', declared Shelley, 'in a uniquely good position to take full advantage of the continuing property boom.'

To do this they did not need to put more money in. Loans from NatWest still appeared flexible and compelling. Now they were running up to a ceiling of £140 million, £70 million of which had already been drawn and the limit would be reached by the end of 1988. Shelley was clear about its advantages:

> Effectively we are able to undertake a very considerably extended programme of development, which we are fully organised and well qualified by experience to undertake, without having to worry unduly how the scheme will

eventually be financed or to suffer any income penalties. Provided, and this is important, that we only undertake high quality schemes that we would be wholly happy to include in our permanent portfolio. I believe this involves us in minimal risk and great potential profit. It is a highly flexible arrangement since, when the development is completed, we are able to determine, in the light of market conditions at the time and our own financial position, whether to take the scheme into our portfolio, whether to dispose of it profitably or whether even to refinance in some other way … Although the loan interest will be a capital charge as part of the cost of the development scheme in each case, it is of course true that the lower interest rates fall, the more attractive the use of the loan is.

If this view were shared, the Commissioners should apply to increase the present loan to about £250 million in order to expand their development programme: 'We understand that this would be readily forthcoming I would hope on even better terms than the first tranche.' If the sum appeared a large one, 'it is relatively modest against the totality of our £2.5 billion of virtually uncharged assets'.[66] With this the Assets Committee evidently agreed. Certainly it approved. Only approval mattered.

Meanwhile, the agricultural portfolio was pressed harder and harder: 'Are we doing enough to reduce the number of farms or estates which only have purely agricultural value?' Might they begin to sell tenanted farmland, something they had never done before. And might they try to sell one estate – Dawsmere in Lincolnshire – to test the market? As for Hyde Park, they should sell long leases across the whole estate now and then sell off the remainder. 'So far we have agreed to sell 154 flats for £23 million – so much', noted Shelley cheerily, 'for Black Monday!'[67]

By now the great rationalisations of the commercial property portfolio were almost complete. Over 50 per cent of it was now in retail property and the other half divided between offices and warehouses. It looked 'highly successful' and 'soundly based'. If all of this showed an immense gathering of momentum, only Deansbank had not yet been retrieved from the doldrums. Here, Shelley was rather more measured: recession in the United States had bitten deep; the strength of sterling was another disadvantage. But what could be seen all too clearly was a simple fact: that too much space was available for

[66] Shelley, 'Investment policy review 1987–88', A (88) 34, p. 9, in CC/SEC/INVP/8B.
[67] Ibid.

rent in the United States. The word 'disappointing' recurs in the memoranda and the minutes of the Assets Committee; the encouraging news was repeatedly offered beside the poor; but the bad news was persistent.[68]

Shelley remained in almost boisterously good heart. When he presented his 1988 review to the Assets Committee, in June 1988, he told them that he was 'now even more confident concerning the economy than when he had written the paper'. Some suggested that the property boom might be reaching its peak. The 'weight of opinion', however, was that there was further mileage to be had from it, 'for instance in a modest way into the provinces', where rental values were still comparatively low. There was a full discussion about the practice of funding 50 per cent of property improvements from revenue. It was agreed that it would be better to return to the old practice of charging the whole sum to capital. For Lovelock this was a time of brilliance: 1987 and 1988 together should see an increase of no less than 11 per cent in their income. Shelley pressed that it was still important to reduce the number of farms or estates which had only 'pure agricultural value'. Lovelock was insistent: they should be governed in such things not by sentiment or historic traditions, but only 'the facts of the case'. The Receivers should be given 'some sort of acreage guideline' on which to base a reduction in the purely agricultural content of the portfolio.[69]

Ashford Great Park

By the autumn of 1988 there was still a sense that the development market was 'buoyant'. The Commissioners pressed ahead, approving a new investment of up to £91 million in Maidenhead Business Park. They also discussed what to do with BP House and Ashdown House, just around the corner on Victoria Street, deciding to sell a lease on the former, generating £88.26 million and leaving the Commissioners still with a freehold worth £23.85 million. Such choices may well have seemed to speak of the luxury of riches.

But now there was a new project before them. The Commissioners received the recommendation that they buy 50 per cent of a half share held by the company Imry Merchant in the development of a site of 2,000 acres in Kent. This was Ashford Great Park. To participate in the building of this new dreadnought would involve another £10 million invested in cash and procuring £22 million in loans on which the partnership itself would pay interest. Here again was Mr Wells of Chestertons to describe its virtues and opportunities. If they ventured

[68] Ibid. 13.
[69] AC minutes, 16 June 1988.

in early a greater share of the profits would be theirs. The location was good: it lay beside the main line to London and had 'excellent' access to the nearby M20 motorway. Land values were low and so the potential was greater. 'Because so much land was in one ownership, the conditions were ripe for the construction of a really high quality international standard development which, in turn, would attract good quality companies.' And beside all this, there was the prospect of the Channel tunnel, which would bring with it a new infrastructure; the park was adjacent to the inland clearance depot, where companies would 'destock' and 'depackage'. True, planning permission was not yet theirs, but 'Chesterton believed that planning permission would only be needed for 20 per cent of the development to cover this risk.'

About all this the Assets Committee had questions. Wells was almost magisterial. Ashford, he replied, would become a 'major distribution centre'. The location was superb, even if a tunnel were not built under the English Channel. They were fortunate, the committee now concurred, to enjoy this opportunity. But what, again, of the question mark which hung over planning permission? 'Mr Wells was confident that this was the best site for the proposed use and that consent would be obtained.' It was sufficient. The Assets Committee approved the proposal.[70]

The final scramble

The Ashford proposal came at a time when the pattern of property development was beginning to appear almost hectic. Mr Wells and the Commissioners' own commercial property manager, Michael Hutchings, were eloquent on behalf of their proposals. At the other end of the country the MetroCentre was proving a great success. In one year it had received 20 million visitors. But more money needed to be spent for its popularity had created the demand for more car-parking space and improved road access. In February 1989 the Assets Committee heard that £30 million would buy the land around it. The committee counselled 'extreme care' before they gave their blessing. That done, another proposal appeared: to invest £41.5 million in an office and retail development in the centre of Birmingham. Again, they should move now, for 'to get in at the bottom of the cycle', would exploit the need for demand all the more effectively, and they could sell before 'the next plateau' was reached. The committee agreed that this must be pursued until the time was ripe to deliver a formal judgement. Another item, another proposal: that £11.1 million be spent on the freehold of a recently completed office development in Newbury in Buckinghamshire, offering an immediate yield of 7.54 per

[70] Ibid. 20 Oct. 1988, pp. 4–5.

cent; and then a further £35.3 million to join a partnership to develop a business park outside Banbury in Oxfordshire.[71] There soon followed the Gracechurch Centre, another partnership with Imry Merchant, at £60.16 million. This would be no long-term investment, for the Commissioners should angle to sell it once a refurbishment had been completed and the main leases renewed. Again with Imry, the Assets Committee formally approved the purchase and development of 55–73 Colmore Row, in Birmingham, costing £40 million.

Now the full £250 million loan from NatWest had been used up, and the burden of the interest was clearly beginning to tell. To be sure, wrote Shelley, it would be better if short-term interest rates were lower, naturally, but a strong growth in property values and the new value created by development itself still made the whole programme 'satisfactory'. If high interest rates continued indefinitely they would have to reconsider, but 'most commentators' believed that they would be coming down by the end of the year. They should remember that a commercial loan worked for them more than against them: 'In essence, it increases (by £250 million in the case of the NatWest facility) the value of assets that are working for us to create new wealth and thereby, over the years, should have a material effect on our income growth.'

By now Hutchings was sending out a monthly report listing the schemes supported by the loan. The Assets Committee noted, too, how this tremendous drive was increasing their room for manoeuvre. The development at Birchin Lane, London, could be brought into their portfolio when fully let or, if the prospects for properties in the City remained unpromising, it could be sold. To sell would realise £65–70 million. Birchin Lane had, all told, cost them £55 million. They would have made £10–15 million without, in effect, 'spending a penny of our own money'. This was the world which the bank loan had made possible. The simple truth was that in 1988 commercial property had seen a return of no less than 25 per cent.

Nobody now could have accused the Church Commissioners of relaxing their watch on the consequences of their policies or the environment in which they worked so busily. Every twist and turn was watched minutely, searching for new opportunities and for signs that this great boom might be nearing its end. 'In this sort of market', observed Shelley, 'it is all too easy to buy on the basis of over-optimistic rental projections and, therefore, special vigilance is required.' He judged that the best way to contain the risk was simply to spend their loans on properties of the highest quality. But it is difficult not to sense that the sheer momentum of the policy had acquired an almost mesmeric power over its advocates. Shelley once again sounded

[71] Ibid. 16 Feb. 1989.

out the Assets Committee on a new extension of the borrowing limit: 'I do believe that there are still excellent opportunities to be taken up.' They had started so well, were so well suited to the task, 'it would in many ways be a pity to stop entirely'. One or two more schemes, financed by borrowing, could still be possible: 'would the Committee, in principle, be willing to entertain this?' Shelley said that he did not want from them a 'specific authority', merely a 'general indication'.[72]

What of Deansbank now? While the US was still struggling to extricate itself from recession they would not increase their cash investment there: 'All further investment is, therefore, being financed either from borrowing which, in the US, can at present be done at around 9½ per cent which is just about covered by the rents from most of our properties or from sales.' Shelley observed that they had succeeded where they had shared the risks of development – the McPherson Building in Washington, the offices at Raleigh – and they had fallen short when they had acquired existing investment properties, often bought early in the campaign, which had not grown and were now proving difficult to sell. 'Investment in property will always tend to be a long term operation', remarked Shelley a shade defensively, 'and it is probably right to persevere with the US operation for the time being.' They knew, at least, that they had more experience now, and they trusted their agents, Chestertons. When an up-turn eventually occurred in the market they would be in a strong position to benefit.[73]

It was now that Shelley asked the question: 'has the time ... come to cash in on the increased property values and switch into, say, U.K. equities?' Here, at once, lay the rub. They could not. The development programme was not finished and they could hardly change their policy until they had seen it through. No matter, at least for now. But in the future? Increasingly it was heard that the property market must soon falter. Was time already running out? It could be said, and it was being said, that they did not know that equities would do better for them; 'Indeed, there is a good deal of advice that property can hope for yet another reasonably good year.' The City, for its part, predicted a down-turn in property, but then it was always sceptical about it. The property companies, for their part, still showed 'cautious confidence'. 'Indeed, all the economic reasons for forecasting doom and destruction in the property market seem likely to affect equity markets just as severely, if not more so.' They must press on.[74]

[72] Shelley, 'Investment policy review 1988–89', A (CC) 46, esp. pp. 5–6, in SEC/CC/INVP/8B.
[73] See A (89) 46, ibid.
[74] Ibid.

If the period of growth must end, how should they see it coming? On 15 June 1989 Shelley acknowledged to the Assets Committee that the economic climate was now looking 'uncertain'; and even that 'he might have overdone the optimism'. When it came to the property investment programme, he was 'content', but he acknowledged that 'in practice it would be difficult to change course, other than slowly, in the middle of the programme'. Now the committee was openly divided: 'there was support for both the optimistic and pessimistic viewpoints'.[75] There was 'some concern' that the level of borrowing might 'get out of hand'. But the committee still agreed that the loan from the National Westminster Bank had been a success and that 'too rigid a limitation on the continuation of the development programme would be a mistake'. In principle it was ready to approve a further £50 million advance to fund perhaps two more schemes 'of the highest quality'. Should they bring in new partners who could, in effect, finance the schemes at a lower rate of interest? But then, came the reply, if interest rates began to drop that would prove exactly the wrong thing to do.[76]

At Ashford the Assets Committee found their principal officers racing ahead so quickly that they were struggling to attach their labours to the monthly meetings of the committee itself. Now Hutchings argued they had a chance to increase their interest beyond the first phase; that the planning outlook was promising. 'It was unfortunate that it had been necessary to complete the negotiations without the Committee's prior approval but it had become clear that unless the new Partnership was legally put into force by a date prior to the Committee, it would not have been possible to exercise one of the crucial options to buy land within Phase II.' The committee was not quite appeased, but this was acknowledged to be 'truly exceptional'; consultation would have been impossible. But they still did not have planning permission.[77]

It was the Deansbank enterprise which clearly seemed to be in danger. In November 1989 Shelley announced to the Assets Committee a strengthening of the board there, with the appointment of a further director, a vice-president of Chase Manhattan Bank, an expert in strategic planning and marketing. But there was one insuperable problem with all that they were attempting: the US had, Shelley owned, 'a vast oversupply of almost every sort of property'. This time Wells, too, was sounding cautious. For the first time questions were asked about continuing the enterprise: 'Could it be argued that the US property market should be left to those with

[75] AC minutes, 15 June 1989.
[76] Ibid.
[77] Ibid. 19 Oct. 1989, p. 3.

greater experience of such a highly specialised market'? But, in return, note the minutes, it was 'explained' that in Deansbank and in Chestertons they already possessed such experience. Almost all Chestertons staff in New York was American. The argument for Deansbank still rested heavily upon the appeal to diversification and faith in the long-term prospects. Meanwhile, in Japan, the Commissioners had invested £90 million, which it could now be seen clearly was earning virtually nothing.[78]

For the first time debates on the Assets Committee began to show fear of both income and expenditure. When in December 1989 the committee received budgets for 1990, Shelley observed, significantly, that the varying completion dates of property sales meant that the Church Commissioners had 'very little to carry forward'. The mood was now changing; the discussion was frankly anxious.[79]

The crash

The Church Commissioners had banked heavily on wringing every last possibility of profit out of the age of growth. James Shelley had believed that a down-turn in the property market would be evident well before it actually struck, and that in this interval they could move adroitly to meet the danger by selling their assets. This strategy assumed that their various property schemes would by then have been finished. But at the beginning of 1990 many of the stoutest dreadnoughts were still resting on their slipways, incomplete, costing money, making none. When the crash did come it was so sudden, and so severe, that it allowed almost no room for manoeuvre. Furthermore the loans which had once worked in the Commissioners' favour now tightened around them like a vice.

The fortunes of the MetroCentre had always assumed symbolic significance at the heart of the great venture. Now, in February 1990, the Assets Committee found itself facing a succinct new paper by Hutchings, owning that it had never commanded their complete confidence. It began baldly: 'The Committee has, from the very beginning, expressed concern at the size of the Commissioners' investment in the MetroCentre compared to the value of the commercial portfolio as a whole. We now believe that the time has come to sell part of our investment.' The Commissioners' total cash investment here was currently £76 million, a further £117 million remaining outstanding from a loan from the Royal Bank of Scotland. The current 'rent roll' was £13.9 million; by September 1991 it was expected to rise to about £18 million. Wells suggested that rather than

---

[78] Ibid. 16 Nov. 1989.
[79] Ibid. 21 Dec. 1989.

court publicity it would be better to deal privately with a small selected number of potential buyers. With this Lovelock agreed. At the same meeting the committee was asked to approve the sale of Birchin Court for over £66 million.[80] The bazaar was beginning.

A modest number of the smaller property companies had suddenly collapsed around them. By May 1990 the Assets Committee was becoming more assertive *vis-à-vis* the policy-makers. There must be a detailed review of property development and disposal programmes; of how both affected the Commissioners' financial position, their portfolio, their income. When, in June 1990, Shelley once again offered his annual investment policy review he found that the mood was indeed an altered one. Nerves were on edge. There were questions and even regrets. For the first time, Shelley seemed to be on the defensive. The new wisdom had required intricate measurements, situations, timetables, partners. But with economic disturbances, it was becoming more and more difficult to navigate a safe passage: 'Investments markets are more than usually baffling at the present time ... almost universally bad economic news ... the prospect of 10% cent inflation, awful trade figures ... first rise in unemployment for some time ... a sharply slowing economy, interest rates still upwards ... a property sector generally in dire trouble.'

The essential truth of their new situation was not positive but disastrous. Another liability in their strategy was now being brutally exposed. The commercial loans which the Commissioners had taken out had not been agreed at fixed rates. Five years ago borrowing rates had been 5 per cent. Now they had exactly doubled. Shelley saw that to finance the completion of their programme they needed a further £430 million. To this must be added a further £120 million which the property portfolio had 'borrowed' from the Stock Exchange portfolio.

Now the Commissioners found themselves pressing ahead with not one but two campaigns: the development programme, which, tottering under a mass of debts and in danger of running out of finance, was racing towards completion, and the sales programme, accelerating in the opposite direction, the two barely seizing a chance to nod to each other as they passed. The calculations which informed both appeared increasingly desperate. To make ends meet they must realise at least £300 million in sales by the end of 1991: 'Our advisers are confident that this can be done.' For its part, the Assets Committee exhorted Shelley that the Commissioners should not even worry too much about realising the book cost of the properties. At least, said Shelley, their properties were so impressive they would surely sell. But when, and for how much? Indeed, such properties as theirs were not always easy to sell: large sums could simply get stuck in the middle of

[80] Ibid. 8 Feb. 1990.

transactions for uncertain periods. Moreover, property was becoming harder to sell by the day. They could see that some £500 million remained locked up in potential development. Prices were shrinking. Shelley asked the committee now to agree 'to realise the development value wherever possible'. It was not simply that commercial developments only brought in money once they had been completed. Often they did not even do so then, for in these new and different times prospective tenants could only be attracted by offers of initial, rent-free periods, or periods during which rents were at least reduced. In the countryside they must encourage 'by every proper means' vacancies on farms and then sell. And now they could even see that the release of capital from the Hyde Park sales and from other residential estates was slowing down. In 1988 it had brought in £57.2 million; in 1989 £28.5 million; in 1990 it was expected to bring in £23.5 million. The depression was also making final sales at Maida Vale 'even more difficult than we knew it would be'. Some £20 million was 'locked up' there, too.

Now the sheer scale of the new dreadnoughts assumed a new and awful significance. 'The trouble', confessed Shelley, 'is that over 75% of our retail property investments are tied up in six major shopping centres.' The last of these to be taken on, in Hemel Hempstead, was still under construction. The sooner it was opened the better. They found that they could get away with doing so when only 60 per cent of it was let.

Salvation was not forthcoming from across the Atlantic. Austin, Texas and Minneapolis were now being called 'black spots'; the properties held there by Deansbank were now 'worth very little'.[81]

The Assets Committee furrowed its brows censoriously. There was 'anxiety' at the level of borrowing; 'with hindsight it was suggested that the extent of this had been a mistake', for what had once seemed to offer flexibility now looked very like a strait-jacket. Interest rates were now as high as 15 per cent. The minutes record, lamely: 'it was felt it would be helpful to know more about our future needs, notably on pensions'. There was a discussion about income targets: were they ambitious enough? Were they 'challenging' already?[82]

There was now a scramble for income. In September 1990 the Assets Committee agreed that the sales programme should be 'pursued aggressively, even if it meant selling at unpalatable prices'. Hutchings told them that a principal concern was to raise sufficient capital from the sales programme to repay the loan they had taken out on Hemel Hempstead, for this was now due for repayment by the end of March

[81] Shelley, 'Annual investment policy review', A (90) 50.
[82] AC minutes, 21 June 1990.

1991. It did not give them long.[83] By now the Assets Committee had also approved an attempt to raise £100 million from their Stock Exchange portfolio, at least in part in case they failed to reach the target in the property sales programme that had been approved in June, and to bring in income for the coming year. By October £63 million had been sold in UK equities, £11 million in US, £4 million in European and £40 million in Japan and the Far East – in total £118 million, with an overall yield of 3.7 per cent. But this, too, was haunted by difficulties and frustrations. Shelley observed bleakly that it was proving very difficult in the present market conditions to translate 'agreed terms' into 'cash received'. Estimates were difficult to fix: 'So much depends on the amount and timing of the sales programme and the timing of loan repayments to the NatWest bank'.[84]

For the first time the Assets Committee leaned towards the alarm bell. The Church as a whole should begin to realise what was coming; it should be discouraged from making 'unrealistic demands' upon the Commissioners. The Church, reflected Lovelock, had come to assume that a steady growth of income would finance new projects. But they must disappoint them.[85]

On 29 November 1990 it was announced to the Assets Committee that a Property Executive Committee would now be set up to implement the Commissioners' decisions on commercial property, particularly on sales, and to liaise with agents. At the same meeting the committee learned that the Commissioners' income for 1990 was expected to be £149.6 million, a little more than budgeted, and an increase of 13 per cent. That, observed Shelley, in difficult circumstances was 'satisfactory'. But then:

> the essential problem for 1991 is that our commitments for that year are already considerable and require quite a large increase in our income just at a time when our income is under the greatest pressure partly as a result of the general deterioration in economic prospects and partly for particular reasons associated with the property development programme ... We had been planning, during 1990, for an income in 1991 of around the £161 million mark. As a result of the detailed review of income which forms part of our autumn budgetary operation, it is now quite clear that this is

---

[83] Ibid. 20 Sept. 1990
[84] Shelley, 'Annual investment policy review', A (90) 50, p. 14, in SEC/CC/INVP/8B.
[85] AC minutes, 18 Oct. 1990.

a considerable overstatement of what can be achieved without additional measures.[86]

That last phrase, 'additional measures', would acquire a doleful resonance in the history of the Church Commissioners.

In extremis

Suddenly the Church Commissioners looked to be in secure control of neither their income nor their expenditure. The community charge and the parsonage schemes had, owned Shelley, proved 'considerably more expensive than we had expected'. In addition they had by now approved 'substantial' allocations for stipends and pensions in the next year: 'these must clearly be honoured'.

They must try, somehow, almost anyhow, to reach a new income figure of £161 million for 1991. There was a way. They could switch from equities into fixed interest gilts. ('In rough terms we gain £6 million a year for every £100 million switched and this gain is preserved for future years.') Over two years they might, if they could not avoid it, switch £200 million. If they did manage to sell the MetroCentre that would bring them £3.5 million extra income from that one source. There was another way. Ordinarily, loans were repaid when a development was complete and producing income. They had planned to repay the loan on Hemel Hempstead on 31 March 1991. But by this time the centre would be only 75 per cent complete and many of the businesses there would be enjoying their rent-free periods. This being the case, could they not insist that the period of development was still running and that it would be 'proper' to delay their repayment, even if by only three months. In itself that one deferment would boost their income for that financial year by £3 million. Then they would rifle through the portfolio to see what else could be done. Shelley thought at least a further £1–2 million would come of this.

There was one other way, and this the worst, the toughest and the most controversial. They could switch within the gilt edged portfolio in order to collect additional interest payments. To be sure, this was something which they could not, in ordinary circumstances, contemplate:

Although this process, in that it can be expected to result in a matching reduction in capital value, is, in effect, simply transferring capital to income, it is a widely used mechanism for generating income. As a short term measure, it certainly

[86] Shelley note, 'Financial policy', 21 Nov. 1990, ser. 96699/61.

seems to us to have clear commercial advantages over, for instance, switching equities into fixed interest. The capital loss on gilt switching is, in rough terms, limited to the amount of the income gained and no more while a switch from equities risks a long term and considerable loss of capital if equity markets rise sharply as many observers think they are likely to do. While, therefore, I am sure the Committee would not wish to take excessive advantage of this way forward, it may feel that, in a year when we are facing particular problems, greater use of it should be made than usual.

Accordingly, they might switch from equities into gilt-edged bonds to preserve the current rate of interest for the future. Shelley envisaged what a switch of £100 million equities would look like. It was, he admitted, 'on normal investment criteria ... not at all a satisfactory spread and can only be justified on grounds of expediency'. The investments secretary pointed out that to rely so heavily on cash and gilt-edged bonds would reduce the proportion of their assets which had potential to grow. They would also be in danger of losing out on any substantial rise in equity values, and that was what many commentators predicted would happen.[87]

In November 1990 Lovelock and Shelley reported to the Assets Committee on what they had witnessed at a board meeting of Deansbank in New York. Lovelock wrote, glumly that 'It is no exaggeration to say that the mood of our American directors was one of almost unrelieved gloom.' Mr Knab, 'probably the most knowledgeable of them all on the property side', was the glummest of them all. The day of revival, insisted Lovelock, would come. But it could not come in time. The fundamental difficulty which had beset the American venture was that there was simply too much property there; and now banks were no longer financing speculative new construction. Chestertons now recommended 'an active sales programme' to realise $65 million within the next fifteen months.[88]

There were fears for the Commissioners' capital, which faced the threat of erosion. There were fears about their expenditure, which continued to mount. 'Doubt' was voiced about gilt-switching now. It was agreed that they would not 'switch' out of equities and that any significant amount of switching gilts was 'undesirable', that the shortage for 1991 must be made clear to the General Purposes Committee. The Assets Committee approved the sale of a 50 per cent interest on the MetroCentre. This, it was hoped, would raise £135

[87] Ibid. 2–3.
[88] Lovelock memorandum, 'Visit to America', A (90) 83, ser. 96699/61.

million. Wells warned them that this would be such a complicated transaction that it would take months to complete. They faced another proposal to sell the Commissioners' interest in the Angel Centre to their partner, London Merchant Securities, their last collaboration with the fabled Lord Rayne. The deputy secretary, Patrick Locke confessed that he felt reluctant to sell at £24 million and would prefer to wait until better times. But they could not. The sale was approved, as long as it be for not less than £24 million.[89] Again the question: had all possible savings on expenditure been made?

But the passing of another month brought a further blow to their hopes. The sale of the MetroCentre had fallen through. Chestertons could not think why. Then the Commissioners' chief accountant, Ian Archer, told the Assets Committee that, as it stood, the Church Commissioners' portfolio simply could not provide sufficient sustainable income to meet their expenditure commitments. It was not enough to increase income by sacrificing the prospect of growth. They must cut expenditure. There were other, unforeseen costs. It was at this worst possible moment that the bishop of Oxford was taking the Commissioners to court over the ethics of their investments.

Now the Assets Committee clutched in their hands a draft statement to the dioceses, warning that future allocations were in danger. This offered circumstantial reasons: the recession, the Gulf War. This did not satisfy some on the committee. The statement must surely mention the Commissioners' own borrowings to finance the commercial property development programme. The committee paused to congratulate Shelley on his CBE. But it must have seemed like honouring an admiral whose fleet was sinking around him.[90]

Never before, in times of achievement and success, had the history of the Church Commissioners appeared to be so central to the broader history of the Church of England.

[89] AC minutes, 29 Nov. 1990.
[90] Ibid. 17 Jan. 1991.

PART V

THE AGE OF DOUBT:
THE PRIMACY OF ARCHBISHOP CAREY, 1991–1998

14

Managing Crisis

In the 1980s the conservative Evangelical movement within the Church of England was acknowledged to be in the ascendant. Few, equally, could doubt the decline of Anglo-Catholicism. But both traditions persisted within a Church where numbers everywhere were dropping – numbers of regular attenders, numbers of baptisms and confirmations, numbers of weddings even. If the decade of precipitous popular withdrawal had been the 1960s, by the 1980s nobody could be in any doubt about what was happening, even if they did not quite know why.[1] It affected the Church's sense of itself: it affected what Christians talked about, and their priorities. Decline also altered finances. For years church institutions had been exhorting the laity to give more and now the laity were fewer and older.

For some years there had been persistent and often less than pleasant mutterings about a comfortable liberal establishment at the episcopal centre of the Church. It was time for the pendulum to swing the other way, and so it did, towards the Evangelical side. When it reappeared the figure of the bishop of Bath and Wells was seen to be sitting on the weight at the end. Of the burgeoning Evangelical movement George Carey could be seen to be representative, and certainly those who professed that tradition now had high expectations of him. The new archbishop was installed in April 1991 and promptly became heavily associated with a new decade of evangelism.

Carey came from a modest background, and in this he was glad to be compared with John Major, soon to be prime minister. Suddenly, the leading figures of the British establishment were not the products

---

[1] The historiography on 'secularisation' has accumulated over the last twenty years. The most recent extensive study is Callum G. Brown, *The death of Christian Britain: understanding secularisation, 1800–2000,* London 2001, 170–98. Brown emphasises the significance of the 1960s. See, too, Grace Davey, *Religion in Britain since 1945: believing without belonging,* Oxford 1994, and Robin Gill, *The myth of the empty church,* London 1993, 186–223. For statistics see Robert Currie, Alan Gilbert and Lee Horsley, *Churches and church-goers: patterns of church growth in the British Isles since 1700,* Oxford 1977.

of middle-class hothouses, not scions of Oxford and Cambridge, but the sons, respectively, of a hospital porter and a circus performer. Neither Carey nor Major were what were rather loosely called 'insiders'; neither quite carried that indefinable but palpable aura of self-assurance. In fact, a popular culture that was all too ready to resent privilege was quick to remind them of their reasons for that lack of confidence.

Across the Thames from Lambeth, on the other hand, Millbank might never have looked so confidently like an establishment in its own right. There was even a feeling that it wore the aspect of a knowing, rather too sanguine authority. Sir Douglas Lovelock had now been First Church Estates Commissioner for eight years, and whatever was going on inside the building, he wore a cheerful smile outside. The Church Commissioners had enjoyed four decades of conspicuous success. But the attachment of the Church Commissioners to Lambeth Palace was now far less clear than once it had been. Runcie had largely left Millbank alone, and in so doing reinforced a pattern of declining patronage. Carey, on his arrival, decided to do the same. In May 1991 the Board of governors looked for a new acting chairman and the new archbishop commended to them the bishop of Chelmsford, John Waine. It was a wise choice; Waine would serve them well. Paradoxically, perhaps, it was just as Carey decided to leave the Commissioners largely alone that he began to think that they had taken rather too much upon themselves. He heard people grumbling that they were remote. He came across bishops who were offended at being told what to do in their own houses by officials who seemed to them quite junior in status. Of all of this he duly took note.

Thus far the Church Commissioners had played a defining role in the development of the Church of England. They had served a cause greater than themselves. But in the age of Carey the Commissioners were to find themselves becoming a story in their own right, and not at all one of their own choosing. For it was the crash in their own fortunes which now drew them into the foreground of the life and discussions of the whole Church and then precipitated a new adventure in church government altogether. This was a period of internal accusation, recrimination, turmoil. In the midst of it the authorities at Millbank would find themselves fighting several campaigns simultaneously: to retrieve their own financial fortunes, to maintain the mission of the Church, to defend all that they were and all that they did. A new body of critics rounded upon them protesting loudly, purposefully, that something should be done about the Church as a whole and about the Church Commissioners in particular.

A vindication: the Wilding Report

None of this could be regarded as 'normal'. But the everyday routine had to be maintained. In the early 1990s the Redundant Churches Committee remained busy, balancing, sometimes precariously, the pastoral and the historical. Those who were prepared to battle to save the nation's heritage were more powerful than ever. Now there was a 'Thirties Society' to contend with. There were still debates to settle and when they were referred to the Board, not always was it able to decide. The commercial calculations of the 1980s affected them too. Was it better to lease churches or sell them? Leases might harbour continuing liabilities, but they might be justified by a subsequent rise in value and prospects of future redevelopment. Meanwhile, the London Stained Glass Repository still occupied the basement of Glaziers Hall at London Bridge and had become a charitable trust. Glass removed from some thirty churches was stored there. More than forty windows had been sent abroad, as far afield as Australia, the Falkland Islands, South Africa and Mexico City. Two windows from a Plymouth church had been reset in the American School in St John's Wood, London, as a memorial to two pupils who had died when terrorists blew up a civilian flight to the United States over the little Scottish village of Lockerbie.[2]

In May 1990 the committee welcomed the Wilding Report, a work with no fewer than sixty-five recommendations submitted both to the Commissioners and to the Department of the Environment. Wilding confirmed that what had been set up under the 1968 Pastoral Measure and consolidated by the 1983 Measure still worked well. But he argued for a more 'pivotal' role for the Commissioners in the business of vesting churches in the Redundant Churches Fund and sponsoring it; that the fund be financed for three-year, rather than five-year cycles; and that there be more flexibility, more 'streamlining', of procedures, a stronger emphasis on presentation and more staff. The Advisory Board for Redundant Churches and the Redundant Churches Fund should remain distinct and separate. Wilding sought 'a focal point where policy, priorities and resources can be considered together'. He concluded:

> The Church Commissioners should remain at the centre of the decision-making process and should be given a clearer role in the determination of policy and the choice of priorities. That role should include a fuller responsibility for agreeing plans and policies with the Department of the Environment as the principal source of funding, and for

[2] RCC, annual report to 31 Dec. 1989, CC (90) 23, pp. 3–4, Board papers, 17 May 1990, ser. 95083/61.

satisfying the DoE that public money is being spent to good advantage under a system which is working well.

In short, the sponsorship of the fund should pass from the government to the Commissioners themselves. Wilding also recommended that the fund change its name.[3] Discussion produced the Churches Conservation Trust. The government sponsor was now the Department of National Heritage. To change a name cost money: £100 for each new notice board, and 200 churches now required them. In an age of depression the Commissioners resented sums like this.

But the Church Commissioners had been vindicated. Both Church and State had demonstrated their confidence in them. But this was to be the last time that the Church Commissioners were invited to assume the central power to orchestrate the affairs of the Church. The new Pastoral (Amendment) Measure came into force on 1 April 1994, though the Department of National Heritage was still struggling to place it on parliament's agenda. Now the government gave 70 per cent and the Commissioners 30 per cent. For the 1989–94 period this meant £8.7 million and £3.7 million. In 1994 only one church was vested in the Churches Conservation Trust, bringing the total so far to 290.[4]

By October 1995, of 1,400 redundant churches examined since 1968, 800 had been converted to new uses, 300 had been vested in the Redundant Churches Fund (and then the Churches Conservation Trust) and 300 demolished. Between 1965 and 1998 more than £23 million brought in by the sale of redundant churches had been paid to dioceses to sustain the 'living' Church. By now, more churches were being built than demolished. For half a century the Commissioners had struggled to manage the consequences of the Victorian boom in church building. By the end of that period it might well have been felt that this battle, which had defined so much of their own history, was largely over. In May 1998 the Board heard that the dioceses expected only a relatively modest number of redundancies over the medium-term future.[5]

The gathering storm

The Commissioners thought that their relations with the General Synod were broadly good and when their affairs were discussed there

[3] Richard Wilding, *The care of redundant churches,* London 1990. See also RCC secretary and deputy-secretary joint note, RC (90) 46, Board papers, 13 Dec. 1990, ser. 95083/61.
[4] RCC, annual report to 31 Dec. 1994, CC (95) 39, Board papers, 27 July 1995 (cancelled), ser. 95083/72.
[5] Board minutes, 28 May 1998, pp. 2–3.

the tone was respectful. This may have been rather wide of the mark. There were certainly questions about the activities of the Assets Committee now. At Synod in November 1989 a private members' motion had been proposed by the inexhaustible Oswald Clark. He invited the Church Commissioners to report to Synod as to 'the scope for assuring to Commissioners elected by the General Synod a greater share in major decisions of general policy governing the management of those assets of the Commissioners for which the Assets Committee are by statute exclusively responsible; and ... any legislative changes to give effect thereto which would be called for'. This, and a second, comparable, motion was soon withdrawn, but it indicated a pressure.[6]

The simple answer to both these statements was a single word: expertise. The Assets Committee in 1990 comprised the First Commissioner, one clergyman, no less than three and no more than five laymen appointed by the archbishop of Canterbury, and the Second Commissioner who had the right to attend meetings. Those with actual financial experience were two company chairmen, one deputy chairman, one senior partner, a farmer, an archdeacon who was also a qualified chartered accountant, a director and the First and Second Church Estates Commissioners themselves. The committee now managed an investment portfolio of more than £3,000 million, generating an income to the Church of almost £150 million a year. As it was often observed, this was a unique and complicated portfolio. The arts of investment were increasingly complex. Schemes of £50 million or more were regularly discussed; the committee oversaw business of perhaps £40 million every month.

Almost all the governors on the Board of the Commissioners were also members of Synod, including eight diocesan bishops and sixteen clerical and lay Commissioners elected by Synod. It could therefore be argued that the Board was already the 'natural link' between the Assets Committee and Synod itself.[7] Though the Assets Committee was not accountable to the Board it shared members with it, and the agendas of the meetings showed that in the last previous five years the Board had discussed thirty-six items drawn from the committee's business. These were often ethical questions, mostly about South Africa. There were also detailed annual reports to the Board. There had never been a disagreement over 'a major issue of general policy' between the two bodies.

A gentle adjustment was now made to accommodate the temper of the times: one of the lay elected Commissioners was invited to sit with

[6] *Report of the proceedings of the General Synod*, xx/3, London 1989, 1288–92 (6 Nov. 1989).
[7] See Shelley note, 'Assets Committee and other constitutional matters', CC (90) 10, Board papers, 26 Apr. 1990, ser. 95083/61.

the Assets Committee as an associate member. To go further ran against the very constitution of the Church Commissioners, but not only this. As a memorandum remarked, 'The Assets Committee is much less a deliberative Committee than one with executive responsibilities for what is a large business.' Ten members were felt to be quite enough. The memorandum continued:

> It is no disrespect to the Synod to say that these restrictions will set practical limits to greater representations of Synod-elected Commissioners on this Committee. Firstly, there will probably never be very many Synod lay members who have these qualifications and, of those who have, a still smaller number will be able to spare the extra time to serve as Commissioners and Assets Committee members and thus qualify for the archbishop's nomination (always supposing that they are successful in the election). In this connection, the Commissioners urge that the Standing Committee consider whether there is a case for reminding Synod members, when Commissioner elections take place, of the particular needs for people qualified in this way.[8]

For his part, Smallwood believed that the statutory committees should cease altogether to be statutory and be determined by the Board.

When the Carey era began the crisis at 1 Millbank was escalating, but behind closed doors. When the 1991 allocations were in the air it became clear that the Commissioners must face the Church. On 15 January Lovelock strode off to the House of Bishops 'to sound a warning note on finance'. On 29 January he issued a statement and circulated 'a formidable set of papers' to diocesan bishops and chairmen of diocesan boards of finance.

Lovelock's statement set the tone for a stalwart defence of the Commissioners' conduct. In the 1980s, he explained, they had made more money than ever before; had succeeded, for a time, brilliantly, astonishingly. But the demands upon income had mounted inexorably. Clergy pensions had increased by 65 per cent above inflation; between 1988 and 1991 alone the cost of clergy pensions had increased by 30 per cent 'on the back of clergy stipends and national insurance increases'. In 1980 the Commissioners' allocations to the diocesan stipends funds had been £18.4 million; in 1990 they were £48.9 million; £36 million had been provided for the renewal of parsonages; £8 million had gone to new housing; £4 million had gone to the Church Urban Fund. Almost £115 million had been invested in equity sharing loans, mostly for retirement housing. £16 million had been lent

---

[8] Ibid. pp. 7–8.

to clergy in an interest-free car loan scheme. Diplomatic successes had, to be sure, saved them money: the government was now supporting the Redundant Churches Fund to a higher level than before. Other significant concessions had been wrung from the government: on state aid for churches, on second homes for the clergy, on relief on clergy accommodation, on the community charge. But all of this did not nearly compensate mathematically. The disparity between income and expenditure was brutal. When the boom which had maintained this age of illusions came to a sudden halt, liabilities continued to grow regardless.

Now, continued Lovelock, the British economy had foundered. There was another crisis in the Middle East. The property market was in deep difficulty. Rental values were stagnant, if not actually falling. Properties had become hard to let and harder to sell. Companies were freezing or cutting dividends. The fortunes of the countryside had declined still further. High interest rates afflicted development programmes which were substantially financed by borrowed money, and the high cost of borrowing lessened the profits. All this must be set against what the Commissioners had spent. In the same period there had been 'unprecedentedly large' allocations for stipends and clergy housing. These together had absorbed all the Commissioners' income and all their reserves.

Lovelock had warned before that a recession affected 'all institutions like ours'. He gave a rather broad picture of what the Commissioners were now doing in response and then dropped the bombshell:

> even taking account of all these measures, our income prospects have deteriorated to such an extent that we can no longer sustain the existing level of our renewable allocations for stipends and houses outgoings as well as meeting our prior commitment for pensions, national insurance, the stipends of the senior clergy and other unavoidable items costing in all an *extra* £8 million at least every year.

The first priority would be to maintain clergy pensions at the present level of two-thirds of the previous year's national minimum stipend. Allocations for stipends and houses outgoings would be 'adjusted' for the year 1991/2. In 1992/3 there must be cuts, of at least £4 million, in allocations for stipends and houses outgoings. This was only an estimate: 'We will do our utmost to avoid any further cuts beyond that.' This would be hard, for the dioceses were already suffering for the same reasons that the Church Commissioners themselves were. It might be necessary to look again at the distribution of money to ensure that the more vulnerable dioceses did not suffer severely. Then the lean years must end and the fat ones, 'at least to some extent' would return once more. For now, 'there is a huge gap between the 5% of net income we call for and the 2% of the net income we get'.[9] Word spread. In January Lovelock faced nine questions in the General Synod and he used them to warn again that all was not well.

The Marlowes Centre, Hemel Hempstead

News from the Assets Committee brought no relief. The latest dreadnoughts were stranded in their docks, incomplete. By the time the committee met on 21 February 1991 it was clear that the Marlowes Centre at Hemel Hempstead was in deep trouble. Arrangements there had been characteristic of the Commissioners' approach. There were three partners: the Church Commissioners provided the finance (in one way or another), the Imry company development and project management and McAlpine's the actual building. When the Assets Committee had first approved the development in November 1987, costs had been estimated at £66 million. Costs had overrun substantially. The Commissioners were now exposed to the tune of £126 million.[10]

Amid the confusion James Shelley was fading out of the picture, and Patrick Locke, his deputy, emerging into the foreground. At Hemel Hempstead Locke had taken immediate steps to stabilise liabilities, but even so they could rise as high as £146 million, for further interest was 'rolled up' until the end of 1992, the time when their two partners were to buy out their respective 25 per cent shares in the completed development. It was not just a question of costs. Imrys had fallen short. The partnership had failed. In the face of an accumulation of unyielding legal understandings Locke struggled to renegotiate. He had only one strong card to play: he must capitalise on the transformation of the very realities on which those understandings had only recently rested. First, he went back to NatWest to renegotiate the terms of the Commissioners' own loan. There he won a revised facility allowing greater flexibility in their repayments. Then he sought ways to control costs on the site itself, and at others. In February 1991 the Assets Committee heard all this with 'grave concern'. Sharp questions shot back and forth, but it was too late, for Hemel Hempstead at least. Locke must extricate them as best he could. From now on the committee wanted regular reports on all major developments. It was emphasised how important it was to choose the right partners. On the

[9] Lovelock note, 'Financial situation', CC (91) 4, Board papers, 28 Feb. 1991, ser. 95083/62.
[10] AC minutes, 21 Feb. 1991.

same day the committee learnt that one of the major tenants at St Enoch's, the Lewis Group, had gone into receivership.[11]

New prognostications

The Church, it was repeated, must be told of the developing crisis. Lovelock went off to warn a new conference of the dioceses that they were set for hard times. Some of the representatives there complained that they should have been warned sooner. Lovelock replied simply that they had been told as soon as the situation had become clear. When the Board met on 28 February 1991 it viewed a paper bearing the bland title, 'Financial Situation', and beneath it the new line recommended to it by the General Purposes Committee. The Assets Committee, meanwhile, had defined a new target for income in the coming financial year, a sum of £157 million. This should meet the Commissioners' pensions and stipends commitments fully, but only if the Board reduced by £4 million a year their allocations to offset the costs brought to the dioceses by the community charge.

How were all these problems to be presented? Had the dioceses yet grasped the extent of the cuts that they now faced? Had even the Board of the Church Commissioners itself? The bishop of Sheffield, David Lunn, hoped that the church buildings and the Church Urban Fund would not suffer because of the determination to maintain the stipend. Others evidently concurred. Some pressed that if the situation improved later in the year the Board might vote new allocations if it enjoyed a delegated power from the General Meeting. Others were gloomier. The parish quotas must increase now, and if stipends were not maintained they must increase still further. Somebody observed that the parishes were more ready to give for local ministry than to support the costs of dioceses or of the General Synod. The bishop of Rochester, Michael Turnbull, favoured 'a clear, challenging and spiritual message' to the parishes. Howard Gracey, of the Pensions Board, observed glumly that if stipends decreased so too would pensions. The proposals of the General Purposes Committee were solemnly endorsed.[12]

Extracting themselves from doomed property developments was proving horribly difficult. By March 1991 the Assets Committee had learned that the Commissioners were legally obliged to continue to provide the loan to the Hemel Hempstead partnership even though it had fallen apart. This would soon amount to £98 million. In the meantime there would be no income from the development and their partners would be accumulating repayment responsibilities to the

[11] Ibid.
[12] Board minutes, 28 Feb. 1991, pp. 2–3.

Commissioners significantly beyond the value of their interests in the partnership. The committee asked whether they could be 'reasonably sure' that their partners would be able to pay by the end of the year? Locke answered: 'No'. A second question: was this a 'quality asset'? The answer: 'Yes'.

Locke, together with Wells of Chestertons, was pressing their partners as hard as they could. Negotiations were 'intense'. A new understanding emerged, a victory of sorts. The Commissioners would now 'stop the clock' and settle all major outstanding construction costs; they would obtain complete control and ownership of the project on 25 March 1991; Imry would have no further involvement in the enterprise, unless invited; the Commissioners would receive £3.6 million on 25 March 1991 as 'commuted income payment'. They also agreed a final building cost with McAlpine's for 'a rapid and final settlement without recourse to contractual litigation'. Thus would the Commissioners save about £1 million. The committee asked about other developments where they were in partnership with Imry, at Ashford and Sutton Coldfield? On those, came the ominous reply, there would be more to say later.

There was further, curious evidence of the new economies. In March it was agreed that the Commissioners should for the first time sell lordships of manors. This had last been looked at, and turned down, in 1986. Now the value of such sales seemed to be increasing. The policy might cause some local controversy, it was owned, but that was outweighed by financial considerations.[13]

The first dispute

However public spirited it may be, a commercial company exists to make money. When it finds itself in dire straits it prunes as it finds it must. Directors may grieve to lay off workers, but it is part of their job to do so if they cannot maintain employment. The Church Commissioners could not do this. They were hemmed in now by the simple fact that their commitments to the Church could not be shrugged off even if their finances were in disorder. When the Board assembled in May 1991 it found archbishop Carey in the chair. They now examined a report from the Assets Committee on money available for allocation:

> no money was available for specific allocations in 1991; and £3 million per annum for additional recurring allocations should be available from 1 April 1992 which could be raised to £7 million per annum if a further £4 million per

13 AC minutes, 13 Mar. 1991.

annum reduction in stipends allocations with effect from 1
April 1992 was agreed.

Lovelock declared that there might be as many as three or four lean
years ahead and even if they ended sooner, the 'effects would linger'.
'The Assets Committee', he added, 'had wanted to be more cheerful',
but he was not hopeful of improvement in the short term. Brian
Howard, the deputy chairman of the Assets Committee, remarked that
he was frankly 'pessimistic' about the prospects of recovery: 'caution
had become the watchword and the protection of the asset base had to
have a high priority'.

It was reported that administrative costs must be cut. They must
make good a deficit in the Parsonages Renewal Fund, for there they
had clearly overspent. Then, they must confront a choice: to cut
stipends or the Church Urban Fund. But now there was tension.
Bishop Lunn simply disagreed that this was the choice which lay
before them. Rather it lay between the Church Urban Fund and a
withdrawal from the Commissioners' own reserves. Furthermore, the
difficulties surely lay not in 1991 but further ahead, in 1992. They
should make their grants for the next year with a warning for the next.
To maintain their commitments for the year ahead must involve their
integrity, and it also defined the practical realities faced by fundraisers.
But the bishop was resisted and Lovelock's alternatives were
reaffirmed. How, again, could they present this to the Church? The
bishop of Derby, Peter Dawes, argued that a £0.5 million grant to the
Church Urban Fund be made in 1991 with a warning that it may well
be that no more would follow for two years: 'This would signal that all
was not well, but that the Commissioners had kept faith in hard times.'
Already, the Board was informed, no less than thirty diocesan bishops
had supported this view, fearing the 'adverse publicity' which would
arise if a grant was not made at all. Somebody replied that policy
should not be set by public relations. There were always pressures for
funding from all areas in the Church. For all that, these 'core
responsibilities' for clergy stipends and pensions 'could not be
abrogated nor relegated – they were intrinsic to the mission of the
Church generally'. From this there should be no diversion, 'however
worthy'. The Church Urban Fund had built up income-earning
reserves: let them now be used. A number agreed with the bishop of
Derby. Some pressed for the figure of £1 million to be retained.
Others suggested that these decisions be left to individual clergy who
could make donations if they so wished. Any cut into reserves held for
stipends 'was effectively a compulsory levy and that the whole of the
reserve was necessary in the light of the Assets Committee's advice'.
Again it was urged that they must still clear the deficit in the
Parsonages Renewal Fund.

By nine votes to six the Board agreed that the AGM approve a reduction of £4 million a year in the stipends allocation from 1 April 1992 and, as for other matters, that the Assets Committee and the General Purposes Committee review the situation later in the year and report back. By eleven votes to four it was agreed that a £0.5 million grant to the Church Urban Fund was in principle desirable; nine to six still preferred £1 million. This, too, was to be passed back to the two committees. One governor was fearful that the Assets Committee might be drawing too close to making decisions that should properly be made by the Board.[14]

This meeting showed that the crisis was beginning to split the Board. Well might Lovelock have told them that they must choose between clergy stipends and the Church Urban Fund. But they would not choose. They wanted, and expected, both. The Assets Committee, for its part, might repeat that it bore a legal responsibility to manage the Commissioners assets responsibly but the lines between the province of one body and the other now appeared foggier than ever. Stoutly, with no crusading rhetoric and no grand morality at their disposal, the Assets Committee held out. They were being asked to do something that they were sure they could not do.

Somebody now leaked this to the press. On 4 June the *Daily Telegraph* announced, 'Church row flares over blocked grant'. Church administrators, it reported, had 'refused' to award the usual grant to the Church Urban Fund. There had been 'stormy scenes' at the Board of governors. A Board member was quoted, 'We are furious. This is a constitutional crisis. We voted for the grant and the Church's civil servants say we can't.' Some bishops were already working to reverse this decision. A bishop had threatened to resign from the Board. It was a 'devastating blow' to the Church Urban Fund.

Lovelock protested. It gave a 'completely misleading impression'. If the Board had been 'unable' to recommend an immediate further grant to the CUF, it affirmed its continued support for the fund and still stood by its administrative support ('worth £300,000 a year'). The Board had asked that there be a review at the end of the year; it was hoped that there would be a further grant 'at the earliest opportunity'. At all events, this was not an annual commitment and never had been. It had always been explicit, and it should have been understood, that such grants would be made yearly, and if surplus funds were available. The fund itself remarked on the fact in its annual reports. The fact that at least somebody on the Board had leaked such a vivid picture of its deliberations to the press was not mentioned.[15]

[14] Board minutes, 23 May 1991, pp. 2–5.
[15] Cuttings submitted to the Board, 26 Sept. 1991, ser. 95083/63.

If the Board was divided, even violently, the mood of the AGM, held at Lambeth Palace on 27 June 1991, was more firmly set. Here the cause of the Church Urban Fund lost to that of clergy stipends by a vast majority of thirty-eight to two. A reassuring statement was thereupon released to the press. To this it was added, purposefully, that because of 'prudent management in difficult times', the last year had still seen a 17 per cent increase in investment income. Because the Commissioners' commitments to pensions were set to grow, however, there would be no new money for capital grants for parsonages or other housing, or for grants on church buildings in priority areas. Up to £4 million would be withdrawn selectively from the dioceses in order to increase clergy pensions in line with stipends and also to deal with a growing employer's national insurance liability 'as well as other commitments'. There followed three paragraphs on the Church Urban Fund, which would not have 'got off the ground' without the Commissioners, which had been sustained on a 'massive' scale by them, which could not be administered without the Commissioners, which had accumulated funds of over £18 million of its own and to which the Commissioners were utterly committed.

This did not quite work. The press had kept its ears open for a righteous reaction, and it heard one. 'Church axes £1m. city aid despite plea by bishops', reported the *Daily Telegraph* again, calling the annual meeting 'a private session at Lambeth Palace'. Furthermore, the article referred to a loss of £500 million in assets. But this time the advocates of the new austerity had run off to the journalists too: 'One Commissioner said that the Bishops of Liverpool and Southwark, both known for their Left-wing views, had received "quite a hammering" from the Bishops of Peterborough and Rochester, who strongly backed the Church's financial experts.' Furthermore, the meeting 'ignored a suggestion from one Commissioner that the bishops should donate their six per cent pay rise to the Church Urban Fund'.

Lovelock again found this imaginative. He duly wrote a patient reply, and found it published under the title 'Reason reigned': 'I write with the authority of the archbishop of Canterbury, who was chairman of the meeting, to comment on your report of our annual meeting ... No one "hammered" anybody. The discussion was reasonable and temperate throughout, because all those present recognised the nature of the dilemma which faces us.'[16]

---

[16] Ibid. *Daily Telegraph*, 27 June 1991. Lovelock's letter was published on 5 July 1991.

Patrick Locke and the discreet birth of the Investment Co-ordination Committee

At 1 Millbank the old regime was, in fact, already passing. On 18 April 1991 Lovelock announced his intention to retire in early 1993. The commercial property manager, Michael Hutchings, was leaving too, after serving the Commissioners for twenty years. The Assets Committee was assured that in the past year they had met their property sales target of £150 million and even exceeded it, by £2 million.

By mid-May there was at least some good news. Debenham's had bought Lewis's lease in the MetroCentre. When the committee settled to discuss general investment strategy Shelley showed only 'mild optimism'. The committee, usually represented by the minutes as something of a Greek chorus, was 'much more pessimistic'. When Hutchings presented his final report he told them that they had come through a 'difficult year as well as could be expected'. The fact remained that lettings had 'slowed down considerably; in the second half of 1990'. At least, reflected Howard, by choosing to diversify, to spread their developments outside London and the south-east, they had been spared the very worst of the crash.[17]

Questions about property management returned, unrelentingly. Had they too much? How well had they handled it? In these matters the Assets Committee referred to a Commercial Property Executive Committee. Patrick Locke now saw this to be the place to begin a greater work of reclamation and reformation. He proposed that the committee's terms be widened to include all the Commissioners' assets and that it produce a clear reckoning of their financial position and prospects. He would chair it himself; it would meet monthly. This would be, substantially, a new creation and it would enjoy a new name: the Investment Co-ordination Committee (ICC). Its work would be fed by three supporting groups overseeing the commercial property portfolio, the relationship between borrowing, short-term loans and cash needs, and financial forecasts. Its particular role now would be to orchestrate the work of all those involved in assets to achieve the targets set down by the Assets Committee.

This quiet but decisive step indicated a movement in authority. If Locke was moving steadily into the foreground, the ICC was his chosen instrument. Behind the ICC hovered the accountancy firm Coopers, Lybrand & Deloitte, ready to pass judgement on whatever figures and policies emerged from its new deliberations.

On 20 June 1991 the Assets Committee was warned that Simon Hughes MP would be tabling a question in parliament, at prime minister's question time, about the Church Urban Fund. It can only

---

[17] AC minutes, 16 May 1991.

have seemed an irritation. Locke now told the Assets Committee frankly that they still had too much property and that their level of short-term borrowing must be reduced. A further £100 million of property beyond their target of £150 million would be sold by the end of the year. The committee concurred. They should aim at 'a rather more dull and conventional policy'. There would be no new development scheme for some time to come.[18]

When the ICC first met on 20 May 1991 Locke ruled that its first task was 'to establish the facts'. But he himself also 'placed the highest priority on trying to ensure that no further cuts in stipend allocations became necessary'. They must ensure that there was enough income to meet their recurring allocations and as many of their other, specific obligations as possible.[19] Establishing the facts was easier said than done. Structural arrangements were again questioned. The eyes of the General Purposes Committee looked sharply across to the Assets Committee now. What mechanism existed to connect the two bodies? If the General Purposes Committee had known more about the work of the Assets Committee, they might have suggested to the Board smaller allocations for the coming year. Lovelock replied that he sat on both bodies and the secretary attended the meetings of both. He knew of no unhappiness on the Assets Committee, but would see to it.

Sir Douglas goes to Synod

Lovelock knew that his time as First Church Estates Commissioner was almost at an end. He was also determined that, whatever had befallen the Commissioners over the last two years, it must be seen in a wider context. That context undoubtedly flattered. When he went to the General Synod in July 1991 he did so as both First Church Estates Commissioner and chair of the Central Board of Finance. This, today, was to his advantage, for he offered the two reports together, and the report of the CBF did something to shield its difficult partner. Furthermore, the chairman of the session at which he appeared, anxious to press ahead, fixed a five-minute limit on speeches. That was even better, perhaps.

Lovelock offered Synod 'A decade of progress'. But in doing so he uttered words of warning: 'We are now starting to call it the "fat years" because it is increasingly apparent that the next two or three – not seven, I feel sure – are going to be comparatively lean.' He stated just how much the Commissioners had done over those ten years – investment income up by 88 per cent above inflation; pensions raised

---

[18] AC minutes, 20 June 1991.
[19] Minutes of the Investment Co-ordination committee, 20 May 1991, ICC papers, ser. E/D/M 254, pt 1.

by 120 per cent above inflation; stipends by 74 per cent above inflation; £82 million provided in equity-sharing loans for retirement housing; £38 million for the Parsonages Fund; and £35 million for curates' housing. The list unrolled imposingly. But now they had struck the rock of recession: ('whenever you hear of a trader going out of business it may well be that that trader is one of our tenants'). There must be a cut, of £4 million in 1992–3, to help fund the continuing increases in pensions and national insurance, and it must be 'made good by giving'. The Church had risen to such a challenge before and they must do it again. There would be no new money for parsonages, 'for the time being at least', nor for church buildings in urban priority areas, nor, with 'very great regret', for the Church Urban Fund, though this last would be reviewed and he wished to state their commitment to it again. As for their assets, even there it could be seen that their performance had been 'creditable'. On the various indices others had done worse. Now, 'our prospects are flat'. As for property developments, 'with hindsight' there might have been fewer. No one could have foreseen how long the high interest rates would have continued. The long-term value of their properties was beyond doubt. Borrowing was 'higher than we would like', but 'very comfortable' compared with most other institutions, and now it was decreasing.

This was a clever, deft performance, and when he sat down Lovelock found that there was no ground-swell of rage. There was a stray complaint that the 'pledge' that had been made by the Church Commissioners in response to *Faith in the city* should be honoured. John Smallwood warned that in ten years lay giving in the Church had only doubled before his speech was suddenly cut short by the chairman's bell. The archdeacon of Exeter, John Richards, returned them to the Church Urban Fund and how the local project he knew best, in Devonport, would be affected by the cuts. But he was entirely sympathetic. In church circles they spoke too much of demand and too little of how wealth came about.

But there was one strong protest in Synod that day, a portent of things to come. A layman from Coventry, Michael Tyrell, refused to acquiesce in the generally accepting mood. He thought the annual report should be bound, not in 'lurid purple' but 'penitential pink': 'I think that there is a certain amount of raging hangover after financial indulgence.' When it came to property developments he noticed that by their own figures, the Commissioners reported a loss here of £168 million: 'That is coyly called "Net decrease on revaluation".' Hindsight granted, 'I do think that there is a very serious question to be addressed by the Assets Committee and Synod: where is the line to be drawn between an imaginative investment policy and an imprudent, ill-advised speculation?' An associate member of the Assets Committee,

Philip Lovegrove, waggled a finger at this: he must talk to the previous speaker afterwards, 'at some length'. He would remind Synod that the Commissioners' was a closed fund. It did not compare in that sense with other pensions funds. Because it was closed they must borrow. He observed, for good measure, that of the ten property companies floated on the Stock Exchange in 1988 only one was left (he had put one into liquidation himself, only the week before): 'That is the extent of the disaster out there.' But the Commissioners' portfolio was good and in the long term would prove itself.[20] The two reports were duly received; Synod again fell silent.

The new consensus – and the first cracks

The ICC and its three subcommittees met many times in the summer of 1991. There was a new quality of defensiveness in the air. Procedures tightened, everywhere. The great question now was simply how to close the gap between expenditure and income? It was out of the question to cut £20 million from stipends. If they sold £500 million of stocks and shares into gilts and property recovered they might lose out in terms of both capital and income. The gap would grow, not diminish, and they should have to make yet more cuts. The best way forward was a combination of methods.

By September 1991 the first report of the ICC was in the hands of the Assets Committee. This had established beyond any shade of a doubt, set down in black and white, the truth that since 1988 a growing, and steadily more colossal, divergence of income and expenditure had opened up underneath their very feet. There was nothing else for it: they must move now to create income temporarily. The problem, insisted Lovelock, had been essentially expenditure, and within that, pensions. He held now that 'in retrospect' their provisions for the community charge and for parsonages had been 'overgenerous'. But then the Church had pressed for them.

This, it was pronounced, was not a crisis. But it was a deep hole, and now they must brace themselves for a long struggle to dig their way out. At the Assets Committee there were 'some misgivings' about the creation of temporary income through gilt and loan management, and about the effect of such methods on their capital. There was concern, too, about the long-term effect of switching Stock Exchange equities into gilts. It was suggested that additional property sales might be ploughed back into equities and gilts. Some of the income on gilts might be put back into capital. But now they were clear enough that in

[20] *Report of the Proceedings of the General Synod*, xxii/2, London 1991, 458–76 (15 July 1991).

one area their generosity must diminish. New equity-sharing loans should be offered to clergy at a higher interest rate.[21]

Even now the motors of expenditure were still running noisily. The Board approved a new report from the General Purposes Committee, 'The pension scheme for those in stipendiary ministry', soon to be submitted in the name of the Commissioners and the Pensions Board to Synod. Within this was a proposal that sixty-five be the pensionable age for all those entering the scheme on or after 1 January 1992. Lovelock himself admitted that this was not the best of times for such a move, but they needed to settle quickly a debate about pension equalisation. Gracey supported this. There were doubts. It was said that to link pension increases to increases in stipends rather than inflation might be 'overgenerous and too costly'. Projections were being prepared. As for ages of retirement, the proposal would mean women not receiving their pension until five years after they became eligible for a state pension. They should resist a more flexible provision for early retirement: it would 'create pressure for the clergy to retire'.[22] On 17 October the Assets Committee requested a projection of income, to show budgeted, targeted and actual shortfall figures. By now the first ICC report had been shown to Coopers, whose accountants thought its projections realistic, though they also murmured that the income projection appeared 'somewhat optimistic'.[23] Now the ICC must re-examine projections of expenditure with as much rigour. Its members set to work again.

The imperatives stood starkly before them. There must be no further switching from equities into gilts, except temporarily, for investment reasons. There must be no further temporary creation of income except to the minimum required to balance income with expenditure in any year. They must reduce borrowing, increase the yield on the Stock Exchange portfolio without greater risk, increase the interest charged on all new equity sharing loans, reduce borrowing and clear the present deficit in the Parsonages Renewal Fund a soon as possible. They must also sell particular properties if it appeared opportune to rebalance their Stock Exchange investments and property with opportunistic property sales. In such measures as these could a new consensus, nurtured by the industrious Locke, be seen to emerge. For now, the Church Commissioners were intent on managing their own crisis.

The ICC report on income was debated by the Assets Committee and the General Purposes Committee in September and October. Here opinions differed. David Hopkinson wrote that he was

[21] AC minutes, 19 Sept. 1991, 10.
[22] Board minutes, 26 Sept. 1991, pp. 2–3.
[23] AC minutes, 17 Oct. 1991.

'extremely unhappy' about the options which were now being aired. This was now a debate which properly belonged to both the Assets and General Purposes Committees: 'In addition we have to consider whether it should really be new policy to promote unemployment in the Clergy by getting stipends and pensions too high.' They should not, he continued, switch from equities to gilts in chasing for income: 'if anything we should be going the other way'. There should be no 'gilt management i.e. dividend stripping': only in a crisis could this be done, on investment or ethical grounds. They must not throw the weight of cuts onto the clergy stipend but look to their own administration, to the episcopal administration and to housing outgoings. The Church Commissioners were still living beyond their means. The committees looked at the advantages and dangers of 'front-loading' the cuts (making them earlier rather than later) and 'rear-end loading' (the reverse).[24]

But Coopers, Lybrand & Deloitte were not just judging what the Commissioners were doing now. They were beginning to set the agenda. When the ICC showed them a new set of income forecasts in the autumn it was clear that they did not see the future quite as Locke did. Even if Locke was prepared to stand by what he thought, it was Coopers who proposed that there must now be a detailed review of both short and long-term investment strategy; that the Commissioners set up a reserve or 'income buffer' so that future fluctuations could be absorbed 'without resorting to asset manipulation to generate the required level of income'; that there be an actuarial review of ongoing pensions commitments. They also advised that the Commissioners revise, or 'revamp', the model which they used to create their forecasts. This could not be done overnight.[25]

In the midst of crisis Lovelock struck a dauntless pose. The new work which must lie before them would, he declared earnestly, be the Commissioners' first contribution to the 'decade of evangelism': 'We must not underestimate the severity of the problem but it is manageable and we intend to manage it.' That did not mean that they had not made mistakes. They had. Everybody had. He himself had warned Synod time and again: 'It is not entirely our fault if people do not heed and if diocesan representatives do not pass on what they have heard.' Had they been over-generous? 'Probably, with the light of hindsight', they had been. But they had not seen the recession coming. Nobody had.[26]

[24] See Hopkinson to Lovelock, 1 Oct. 1991, ICC papers E/D/M254, pt 2.
[25] Ibid. 11 Oct. 1991, pt 3. Coopers, Lybrand & Deloitte became Coopers & Lybrand on 1 June 1992.
[26] Lovelock note, 24 Oct. 1991 (his speaking notes for the AC/GPC meeting, 31 Oct. 1991, ibid. pt 4).

These words were spoken at a joint meeting of the General Purposes and Assets Committees. Now they all saw clearly that the Commissioners' capital base must be protected 'against the accepted need to continue to create some temporary income until the trend lines of income and expenditure had converged'. In an ideal world the financial realities would prompt a cut in expenditure of as much as £50 million. But the 'real' world of the Church Commissioners would allow only a reduction by £17 million at most. How to present this to the Church? If the Commissioners were too sanguine the dioceses would not listen. If they were too gloomy they might retrench. A paper must be prepared for the chairmen of the diocesan boards of finance, who would be meeting on 28 November. It should be 'frank but also challenging': 'DBF Chairmen were our allies and should be taken into our confidence'. They should air the prospect of no more than a 3–4 per cent increase in the 1993 national minimum stipend. They must repeat once more that there must be more giving by congregations. The Commissioners must 'steer' the chairmen, and the chairmen must, in turn, 'steer' the Commissioners.[27]

'Steering' had become the order of the day. Now Lovelock sought a 'steer' from the Board. In November he told it that 'We would have to get across the essential facts that our income would hold up but not grow in real terms, but our commitments would steadily rise.' A protest from John Smallwood showed how the criticism of the Assets Committee was steadily beginning to cohere. The source of their problems now, he remarked, had been within their commercial property portfolio. Because of this there had been an 'undesirable degree of asset switching'. The Board should have been referred to more often – about the power that the committee enjoyed to borrow money, the increasing levels of temporarily created income and what that had done to the capital base and the 'consequences of the availabilities of past monies'. Against this others still stressed the value of the property portfolio in withstanding the shock of the stock market crash of 1987. Traditionally, property had proven a 'stable and growing' income, and for a closed fund that had been a powerful virtue. Moreover, borrowing was inevitable in the development sector, and most did more of it than the Commissioners. There was a general conviction that the Board, the Assets Committee and the General Purposes Committee must now learn to speak together and listen to each other.

[27] Lovelock note, 'The financial outlook', CC (91) 28, Board papers, 7 Nov. 1991, ser. 95083/63.

The new campaign

It was not just a matter of putting the finances right. Nor was it now simply a matter of settling the politics of presentation. There must also be a vast political programme, involving virtually every institution of the Church. That the people in the parishes must give more was strenuously endorsed. But if that appeal were to succeed, congregations must be assured that their quotas would be calculated fairly and the parishes and dioceses managed in ways that could claim their confidence. Diocesan bishops must become 'progressive and imaginative' in ensuring that the parochial ministry was structured to maximise giving. The idea of a flat rate increase in stipends for that year won some favour. Somebody observed that recurring allocations for stipends and pensions effectively discriminated against specific allocations, for such as the Church Urban Fund, 'and, in effect, pre-empted decisions'. At all events, the CUF grant would still be reviewed in December. The centre held: the Board stood by its committees and endorsed their recommendations.[28]

When he met the diocesan chairmen and told them that allocations must be cut, Lovelock found them 'calm and good-tempered', 'generally supportive' and determined to 'face the challenge positively'. There were awkward moments even so. Somebody asked if the Commissioners had too much property and related debt? Another said that church people would want to be reassured that the Commissioners had the best professional advice on their management of assets. Lovelock had his reassurances ready: they were becoming well worn. With the proposed cuts in stipends of £4–6 million in 1993 'nobody argued'. With further cuts thereafter, nobody disagreed.

What emerged clearly from this conference was that most favoured that the cuts be evenly spread across three to four years. An overwhelming majority voted against any proposals to make additional cuts in order to fund specific allocations. The ramifications of the proposal were sombrely assessed. How would allocations be measured? Would clergy become unemployed? Clergy numbers had in many dioceses already been cut. Lovelock commiserated. Somebody suggested that the Commissioners were 'rapidly becoming a pension fund'. The chairmen asked for more information to help them plan in their turn and off they went in their forty-three different directions again.

The new calculations began to spin round and round: percentages, sums, periods of time, projections, shortfalls. But around them the whole financial situation had grown not better but still worse. At Millbank another statement was drafted. Recurring commitments

[28] Board minutes, 7 Nov. 1991, pp. 2–3.

would be honoured. No specific allocations would be made. The
Church Urban Fund would receive nothing. The Commissioners
confirmed 'with regret' that they would not make a grant but this was
offered with a valuable rejoinder: that they 'earnestly' hoped to have
given the full £10 million allocation by the end of the century.[29]
Lovelock wrote a letter to Carey; a 'personal initiative' and not on
behalf of the Board ('Although you get our board papers, you cannot
possibly be expected to study them [although perhaps you do!] so, for
convenience, I enclose extracts … These are all you need glance at for
present purposes'). He stated the position succinctly and expressed
some fear that the dioceses now seemed more inclined to retrench
than to rise to a challenge. Then he added, significantly:

> What is actually happening is only a very partial fulfilment of
> what was predicted 10 years ago – that the Commissioners'
> income would be increasingly required for pensions, with
> the rest of the Church finding the bulk of stipends money.
> The buoyant investment climate of the 1980s prevented this
> prediction from coming about: the current recession, so
> slow to depart, makes it a reality now, though there will still
> be large allocations for stipends and parsonages.

Lovelock suggested that the archbishop might give the General Synod
another 'powerful message', and asked if the bishops might 'put their
collective authority' behind it. They should not think too much of
cutting clergy 'beyond what is required' and cultivating non-stipendiary
ministers might be self-defeating 'because all the evidence shows that
clergy promote more giving than they themselves cost'.[30] He received a
supportive letter in reply.

When the Board met again in December 1991 it could only confirm
the new line. It was agreed that a cut of not less than £5 million be set
for 1993. Most favoured the idea that the cuts amounting to £17
million be exacted over three years, proffered with assurances that the
utmost would be done to avoid more beyond. It appeared a
'reasonable but realistic balance that would close the gap between
recurrent expenditure and sustainable income without causing panic or
overreaction'.[31] This chimed with the views of the diocesan chairmen.
However the Board might wriggle, the economics of their position
were virtually unassailable. For the Church Urban Fund there would
be no grant. A statement was prepared with care.

[29] Note, 'The financial situation: latest position', CC (91) 32, Board papers, 12 Dec.
1991, ser. 95083/63.
[30] Lovelock to Archbishop George Carey, 28 Nov. 1991, ibid.
[31] Board minutes, 12 Dec. 1991, pp. 2–4.

Into 1992

Each new week brought new developments, none of them encouraging. Even the gains upon which the Commissioners had come to rely so heavily could in a moment look precarious. On 21 November 1991 it had been reported to the Assets Committee that their agents, Chestertons, had made accounting mistakes overstating income from the MetroCentre and St Enoch's by £1 million in 1990. And now it was heard that another dreadnought, Ashford, was disintegrating. When the ICC met again on 3 December 1991 they learned that a new paper on projected pensions was showing that they were higher than had been predicted four years before. It was at this meeting that Locke announced a new, decisive truth: the Commissioners were unlikely to be able to continue to bear the whole cost of pensions beyond the ending of present arrangements in 1992.

Another month, another retreat. By 16 January 1992 it had been decided to suspend immediately the availability of housing assistance loans to retired clergy below the age of sixty-two. By now the ICC had capped commercial property developments, sold £250 million of commercial property and reduced unsecured borrowing from the NatWest to below £200 million. It could be seen that when the current sales programme was completed the proportion of their portfolio devoted to commercial property would be reduced from 42 per cent to 34 per cent of their assets. If they sold a half-share in the MetroCentre alone it would, at one fell swoop, reduce that size of that sector to 30 per cent of the asset base – virtually where it had stood in 1986.

A leaflet was prepared for the parishes. In February 1992 Smallwood asked the Board the question that would soon be at the top of their agenda: should they create a pensions reserve? For now, it was felt that the reserve should remain as part of the General Fund, for that was a more flexible arrangement.

Ashford Great Park

If the crisis was now being brought under control, the Church Commissioners were still haunted by ongoing embarrassments. Ashford Great Park had been one of their last dreadnoughts. They had undertaken to finance the whole project until the end of 1992. Half of their overall investment lay in loans to partners who had now collapsed. The Commissioners themselves had borrowed £50 million from the Sumitomo Bank to finance the development.

Locke told the Assets Committee that they must decide where their priority lay: to secure the return of the bulk of their capital or to get full control of the project? If their partners could not pay, they must turn to the courts. How would all this be entered in the accounts? The answer exposed the worst of the plight: they must remove the prospect of any income from their estimates after the end of 1992 but at the same time set down their obligation to repay the £50 million which they themselves owed, or at least the interest owed on that sum.[32] The site now passed to the Commissioners almost in its entirety.

The structures and conventions of the Church Commissioners continued to tighten defensively around them. When the investment manager presented his annual report to the Assets Committee on 23 April 1992 Locke deliberately reminded them that this was one of the ways in which the committee reported to the Board. He asked if anybody had any other ideas as to how they might keep the Board informed without 'overburdening' it.[33] The idea of a joint meeting was broached. On 18 June 1992 Shelley attended his last meeting of the committee. Bishop Westwood also stood down. The committee heard that one of their principal land agents, Nigel Clutton, had been made a CBE. In these days the honours system seemed to clang like a tolling bell over the heads of the Church Commissioners.

The explosion

In the midst of discussions, the relentless quest for explanations, the new sharp figures and buzzing calculations, the basic facts of the Commissioners' situation were simple. Between 1985 and 1989 the value of the Church Commissioners' assets had risen, in millions, from about £1,944 to £3,081, a remarkable growth. But in 1990 it had dropped to £2,479, in 1991 to £2,362, and in 1992 to £2,161. This was unarguably dramatic. So far the Church Commissioners had escaped a powerful challenge, but now it would come, not at General Synod, not in a conference with the dioceses, not from the House of Bishops, but in the columns of a newspaper, and perhaps the most sober of them all.

On 11 July 1992 the first page of the *Financial Times* announced: 'Church sees £500 million wiped off value of property investments.' The headline was followed by two photographs, one of archbishop Carey, resolute in full robes, and the other of the First Church Estates Commissioner with a spade, evidently digging a large hole in the ground. The article, by John Plender, summed up the case for the prosecution in one sentence: 'Nearly £500 million has been wiped off the value of the Church of England's property investments after heavy borrowing to fund speculative developments in Britain and the US just before the market plunged.' It was, Plender wrote, a *'débâcle'*.

[32] AC minutes, 19 Mar. 1992.
[33] Ibid. 23 Apr. 1992.

The *Financial Times* had itself launched a detailed investigation. On the inside pages there was more: 'Unholy saga of the Church's missing millions'. 'The Church Commissioners', it began 'have some explaining to do'; 'How did this august body, which ranks a number of distinguished City figures on its assets committee, get into such a mess?' Furthermore, the Commissioners, and the archbishop, had not been quite frank with the parishioners who must now face the consequences. They had blamed 'forces outside their control'; the archbishop had said that they had been 'badly hit by inflation'. The *Financial Times* had found differently, and what they had uncovered raised 'serious questions about the management and accountability of this discreet but powerful institution'.

Plender considered the Commissioners' American enterprise 'idiosyncratic'. Michael Hutchings had been 'temperamentally disinclined to fly', and set off across the Atlantic on the QE2, crossed America by train, car and bus, sending his own cases of wine ahead of him at his own expense. The Commissioners' commitment to the world of agriculture was dismissed in one short, brutal paragraph. Then followed their 'speculative developments'. Borrowing money for developments had been recommended to the Church as 'normal commercial practice'. But 'leading fund managers' approached by the *Financial Times* found it far from normal. They found it 'bizarre': 'For a closed fund with no new money coming in, borrowing for a high-risk speculative development was, in their view, extremely unorthodox. Even for a contributory pension fund with a positive cash-flow, borrowing is usually regarded as a questionable practice.' More than this, 'In effect, the church had decided to go into debt just before real rates of interest, after adjusting for inflation, rose to their highest level since the depression of the 1930s.' The *Financial Times* had shown the Commissioners' annual report to an independent fund manager who ran property portfolios for large pension funds. He found a 'lack of clarity' about performance objectives, about the management structure, on the figures of investment returns: 'In the absence of any clear statement of long-term asset allocation policy … they appear to be judge and jury in their own case.' The same went for their advisors at Chestertons, who both advised on purchases and provided valuations of performance. Lovelock himself had assured the newspaper that these levels of borrowing were not high when compared with those of property companies. But, Plender, asked, was it not 'odd' to compare 'this arm of the Anglican church with a property company'? Now the Commissioners had been forced to sell property, some of its best property, when property values were at their lowest for many years. Why had there been no investigation into this?[34]

---

[34] *Financial Times*, 11 July 1992. See Patrick Locke note, 'The financial situation', CC

This was, quite simply, a brilliant and devastating *exposé*. It posed a question which would alter fundamentally the course of events. The article was published just as General Synod was just about to assemble in York.

Sir Douglas returns to Synod

Lovelock had never claimed to be an economist or a financier. He was a civil servant with something more than a penchant for politics. But he did not cut a popular figure in Synod, and Synod now needed to be persuaded. On 13 July Lovelock presented himself at York to speak in the debate 'The financial situation facing the Church of England'. The debate was a sombre measuring of an imperfect world. There were no fireworks. Before starting Lovelock genially reminded Synod of his two favourite phrases: 'there is only one pot of gold', and 'policy and finance must be taken together'. The House of Bishops had again affirmed their commitment to a nationwide parochial ministry: 'We all have to work together to safeguard this. We at least are confident that it can be done.' Then, 'we have not lost £500 million'. It was simply that every year their assets were valued; sometimes those valuations went up, sometimes down. Every institution and company of any size had seen a decline in their capital value. The Commissioners had borrowed a great deal, to be sure, and they were reducing it. If they looked back over ten years, their income had increased by 159 per cent, compared with an RPI of 79 per cent. 'In other words we have beaten inflation twice over.' Performance indexes placed them in favourable positions on their tables: 'we have comfortably beaten the average' – 'you would not have guessed this from the newspaper articles you have recently read'.

For his part Carey reminded Synod that he was 'a fairly new archbishop'. He assured Synod that the criticisms of the Commissioners would be 'examined closely'. But now he declared a wish to move the debate forward, into the future. What mattered fundamentally was not money but the framing of 'a common vision'. Money would follow. The previous week he had heard the Third Commissioner observe that more new churches had been opened in the previous year than old ones closed: 'But we do not see that on the front page of our newspapers.' They were called to grow, not to decline: 'We call for sacrificial giving in order to swell the stream of Christian generosity to the wider world.'

This approach did not quite prevail. David Webster of the diocese of Rochester, a former employee of the *Financial Times,* now changed the direction of the debate. The *Financial Times*, he remarked, was not

(92) 37, Board papers, 23 July 1992, ser. 95083/64.

'a paper normally associated with irresponsible journalism', and Lovelock himself had quoted it approvingly when it had been complimentary a year before. In one year, according to the indexes to which Lovelock himself had pointed, the Commissioners had slipped from thirteen in Stock Exchange investments and twenty-four in property to twenty and fifty respectively: 'so clearly in the past year things have gone very badly'. Webster added, pointedly, that he was grateful to the archbishop for the assurance that there would be an enquiry, and added that it might be 'helpful' if it had some independent aspect. If they did not face a financial crisis, they must beware a crisis of confidence. If the Church could not itself prove that it was a good steward, they might be hard put to ask the people for more money. Furthermore, it was, he found, at least 'sad – possibly a stronger word would be more appropriate – that the Church Commissioners have taken the decisions they have done over the past 18 months without seemingly any reference first to the Central Board of Finance, the dioceses, other Church agencies or anyone else as far as I am aware'. Lovelock was amiable about this and respectful to the mover: it was simply, he replied, that a year before the *Financial Times* had been right; now it had 'got it wrong'.[35]

This debate was far from being a disaster for the Church Commissioners. But it had yielded the prospect of an inquiry, and with this the debate on their record began for the first time to move beyond the doors of 1 Millbank itself and to enter the Church as a whole. The control which the Commissioners had exercised over their situation would now diminish inexorably, and in a landscape of hostile mutterings. Those who had never loved the Church Commissioners knew that their hour had come.

At the Board meeting which followed the debate in General Synod the discussion was intricate and intense. Again, Patrick Locke was in the forefront. He assured members that though the archbishop was absent he was taking 'a close personal, and friendly interest, in recognition of his own special connection with the affairs of the Commissioners as their Chairman'. Lovelock then reported on the General Synod ('The tone had been concerned but calm'). As for the *Financial Times* article, that had been a combination of the 'tacky' and the fair, but there had been omissions. Lovelock defended Hutchings, as a man of integrity who had done his job with 'dedication and enthusiasm'. Much was now in train; much must now be attempted. The Assets Committee were reviewing the management of the commercial property portfolio 'and the possible introduction of fresh blood'. There must be a 'factual response' to Plender's article.

[35] *Report of the Proceedings of the General Synod*, xxiii/2, London 1992, 397–436 (13 July 1992).

There was a stiffening of will against criticism. The *Financial Times* had 'obscured the financial facts' and that could make it harder to 'communicate with parishes'. The real cash losses that had occurred were unexceptional for such a portfolio as theirs: 'Some felt they should be in a position to assess the actual extent of such losses. Others believed that it would be wrong to focus only on the mistakes. It was suggested that the relationship between the Board, the Assets Committee and the Commissioners' staff should be 'close and more open'.[36]

When the *Financial Times* article had been set before the Assets Committee it 'considered that, although the article was selective and in places inaccurate, there were clearly recognisable elements in it and it needed to be taken seriously'. But the committee fell in behind Lovelock and his 'robust' defence of their policies at General Synod. It was vital to give full assistance to diocesan secretaries to ensure that the 'full story' got across. They welcomed the archbishop's assurance of a 'close examination', and that this should refer to 'external and independent' representation. At the same meeting the committee inspected the Deansbank annual review. However hard they had worked and however strenuously it had been led, the American dreadnought had, it appeared, been sunk by a 'terrible over-supply in the market'. Quietly, behind the scenes, some were already beginning to work out how to scrap it.[37]

Just as Shelley had become secretary because he appeared the man to superintend a policy of expansion, so Patrick Locke now succeeded him because he was the man to organise a policy of rescue. On 16 July 1992 Locke attended his first Assets Committee meeting in his new guise. His position was unambiguous: with the passing of Shelley and the waning of Lovelock, the new secretary had every reason to recognise the strength of his own position. For the moment it looked as though he had the power to press ahead as he proposed. Locke submitted to the Assets Committee a document outlining a course of action for the next six months, detailing an 'urgent review' of the Commissioners' affairs. Nothing was sacred. Deansbank must be scrutinised; they must now obtain independent valuations on their commercial property portfolio, they must improve 'the breadth and quality' of the advice which they received. As for their structures, they must construct 'a coherent and simple system in which each part functioned well and contributed clearly to the whole'. He proposed to discuss these questions with at least half-a-dozen other funds with varying property portfolios, to interview three or four 'pre-eminent' firms of chartered surveyors in addition to Cluttons and Chestertons,

[36] Board minutes, 23 July 1992, pp. 2–4.
[37] Ibid. 16 June 1992.

all by the middle of the autumn. It was 'essential'; it 'must be done'. Now it was decided that to capitalise additional income brought by gilt-switching would 'complicate' the picture and undermine the point of the exercise itself. They would switch up to £200 million of equities into gilts to switch back again when the right time came.[38]

By mid-September the team at Deansbank had changed. An 'enthusiastic and committed' group was led there by Mr Knab. Locke told the committee that he was charging their commercial property portfolio with 'new blood', a 'strong competitive element'. There would be more meetings with their agents. Fees would be led by performance, not transaction. They would retain Chestertons – though the question as to whether they should do so was now being asked. Meanwhile, the MetroCentre was now classified as a special fund. A joint meeting of members of the Assets Committee and the Board took place.[39]

Every night now Locke could be seen leaving 1 Millbank with two bulging briefcases of material to work on into the night. It seemed that 1 Millbank itself was full of people wracking their memories and rifling through their filing cabinets. How had it all gone wrong? And when? The accountant Ian Archer found himself reflecting on one of the principal areas in which the Church Commissioners were now seen by their critics to be vulnerable – gilt-switching:

> I was asked by Brian Howard at the buffet lunch last Thursday how long temporary income had been created in this way. I answered that only in recent years had the amounts been large. However you may be interested in the attached papers which show it was decided in January 1987 (to have effect from 1/1/86) that all gilts should be accounted for on a coupon basis. This opened the way for what was then described as 'flexibility' and the AC, led by Mr Hopkinson, decided against the advice of Deloittes, Mr Burnett-Stuart and us accountants.

Furthermore, he could not think that the decision had been reviewed after two years, as had been originally intended. Archer continued:

> We now know that the Commissioners, from these humble beginnings of wanting to slightly correct figures to bring them into line with budget, have now reached the situation where such temporarily created income is planned ahead and we are dependent on that income at least for the next few years. I see this rather like taking a drug for medicinal

[38] AC minutes, 16 July 1992.
[39] Ibid. 17 Sept. 1992.

purposes but moving on to an addiction when withdrawal symptoms are severe.[40]

Locke's rescue policy needed to command a steady consensus, but by November opinion on the Assets Committee was dividing. Some believed that there should now be a property subcommittee; others did not, for the measure which established the Commissioners did not allow for it.[41] Meanwhile, in the background, the Ashford dreadnought offered a bleak subtext. On 10 December 1992 the Assets Committee learned that their partner, Imry, would not pay back the Commissioners at all. The land and the interests of their partners were placed in receivership. And this time, as though to prove that the world of the Commissioners had changed not superficially but at root, the board of Deansbank came for the first time to Millbank. The discussion was terse. Nothing in their portfolio was to be regarded as a 'sacred cow'. Corporate expenses were still high and must be reduced. There would now be a flexible strategy and no 'open-ended' commitments.[42]

The archbishop's assurance and the Lambeth Group

The ICC was the last attempt made by the Church Commissioners to reform themselves from within. It was the first in a new sequence of events by means of which the fate of the Commissioners slipped from their own hands and into those of new powers over which they would have, at best, a limited influence.

Archbishop Carey had assured Synod that the Commissioners would learn lessons. The Commissioners strained to listen to the dioceses, but as yet heard little to frighten them. But the archbishop's speech had set down a new agenda; it required a new body and a new process. It must be seen to scrutinise the work of the Church Commissioners not merely from inside, but with a detached eye; it must be seen to express the mind and the concerns of the Church at large. It must be based at Lambeth.

Locke and Bishop Waine, deputy chairman of the Board, had met archbishop Carey in the autumn of 1992. Soon a review was taking shape. There should be a small, weighty group chaired by Waine himself, comprising three senior Commissioners (Canon John Stanley, Sir John Herbecq and Brian Howard) and 'five eminent, external, and independent people' ('an eminent property man', 'an eminent name with experience of fund management', 'an eminent actuary', 'two other

[40] Ian Archer to Locke, 30 Sept. 1992, CC/SEC/LG/1.
[41] AC minutes, 19 Nov. 1992.
[42] Ibid. 10 Dec. 1992.

eminent external names'). Locke approached the governor of the Bank of England, Robin Leigh-Pemberton, about possible names and found him 'supportive and most helpful'.[43] A draft constitution and terms of reference for the new group were submitted to the Board. The accountants Coopers & Lybrand were to be invited to examine and report on the Commissioners' borrowings and on 'the information flow required for the management of their assets'. The birth of what was at once called the Lambeth Group was announced to the press on 8 October 1992. There was, then, little excitement about it, but for this there was perhaps time.[44]

The accountants and the new group set to work in parallel through the autumn, winter and spring of 1992–3. It was inevitable that there should be some rumblings and a few scuffles in the General Synod about its membership. Locke sought to reassure discordant voices: the 'external' members were the majority in the group. As John Herbecq later observed to a doubtful Lady Brentford, the Church Commissioners who now took their places in the group had themselves, after all, demanded an enquiry.[45] To be drawn from outside the world of 1 Millbank brought no firm guarantees. One of the group, Maurice Stonefoot, was the chairman of an insurance company which was in some difficulty itself. Coopers & Lybrand, meanwhile, had been auditors to some of the property companies with which the Church Commissioners had dealt, and which had failed.

For all this, it is clear from the paper trail that it left behind that the new group was very much in earnest. The old debate about the Commissioners' structures grew more intense. Herbecq pressed the question of the accountability of the Assets Committee, something that he found ambiguous. The official solicitor wrote in response to Locke that the committee was certainly accountable to the annual general meeting: its activities were published in the annual report. In practice, he thought it unlikely that a crisis would ever get that far without being 'dealt with' first. If it did, a resolution by a majority of the Church Commissioners to sack the Assets Committee could be passed and those responsible for appointments to that committee be asked to appoint a new one. But he thought it 'quite extraordinary ... that the Committee should have thought it proper to incur £500 million of indebtedness without so much as informing the Board, much less seeking its views'.[46]

[43] See 'The archbishop's assurance', CC (92) 39, Board papers, 24 Sept. 1992, ser. 95083/64.
[44] Ibid. annex.
[45] Sir John Herbecq note, May 1995, Herbecq papers (in the possession of the author).
[46] Edward Wills to Locke, 1 Dec. 1992, CC/SEC/LG/1–6.

The discussion of structures yielded a larger question. At what point in its deliberations should the group draw a line? On 22 December 1992 the banker Peter Baring wrote to Patrick Locke:

> My worry is that the natural drift of the Group's conclusions may tend to pre-empt fundamental organisational issues for the Church generally (we touched on all this in our discussion). Whereas, clearly, one would not wish to obstruct the free exercise of the Group's judgement, I think you and the Bishop of Chelmsford should be very clear-eyed where we could end up.[47]

In this dense fabric a crucial new strain might not at once leap out and seize the attention. But on 15 January 1993 Locke received a letter from Richard Davis at Coopers & Lybrand which suddenly placed all their discussions on a new foundation. The pension 'liabilities' of the Church Commissioners were, it appeared, about equal to the Commissioners' assets. They could meet the claims of the past and the present, but almost certainly not the future. When this sank in Baring thought it 'momentous'.[48] The group pondered the revelation on 21 January and decided that it was so important that a formal actuarial valuation must be commissioned to confirm it. Already, though, the consequences were stark. Should pensions become more important even than stipends? The Commissioners put £80 million a year towards them – if they cut such a figure back, who else would find it? Should they reduce both stipends and pensions? Would the Church end up reducing numbers in the ordained ministry?

Here were matters for the General Synod, for the bishops, for the whole Church. A new memorandum pronounced: 'Any consideration of the issues is bound to call in question the viability of the Church's present system of financial and resource direction. In particular, the existing fragmentation of overall responsibility will seem, at best, unhelpful. At the least some early and significant strengthening of the Church's overall finance function is urgently required.' This was sent back to the archbishop. Should the Lambeth Group's mandate be strengthened or should such questions be considered by another body in another way?[49]

'We must be positive', Locke had written to Baring on 20 January 1993. 'This challenge, if we rise to it, could transform the Church's financial system and the commitment of the laity.' He saw the next seven years ('a good biblical number') as a period through which they

---

[47] Peter Baring to Locke, 22 Dec. 1992, CC/SEC/LG/1.
[48] Locke to Baring, 19 Jan. 1993, with the letter of 15 Jan. 1993 from Davis of Coopers, ibid.
[49] Locke note, 'Memorandum by King', 21 Jan. 1993, ibid.

must 'manage' their way. To do that required closer relations with the General Synod, the Pensions Board, the Central Board of Finance, the forty-three dioceses. They must 'correct' the balance of their allocations, review the scope of their pensions commitments to see that they rested on solid ground, look again at their responsibilities, strengthen their constitution and their committee structure, reflect on the direction of all central resources and finances. There might be change; there might be a form of 'unification'.[50] But under this brittle surface could be glimpsed a mass of anxious and controversial private conversations, over lunches and dinners, on the telephone, in quiet offices. Why were these new projections showing greater deterioration than those of only a year before? How were they to win over the diocesan chairmen?

By January 1993 only one of the Church Commissioners' partners at Ashford, Cedarvale, remained solvent. European Land was in liquidation. Imry was now wholly owned by Barclay's Bank. The Commissioners had at once appointed a receiver. It was pointless now to pursue litigation, and such a course might well throw up its own dangers. But the Commissioners must still pay £0.5 million to Imry in final settlement for their services. The chief accountant confirmed that the site was now valued at only £15 million. Little wonder, perhaps, that the committee should now play to its strengths and go back to the MetroCentre. It approved a sum of £400,000 for the building of a cinema auditorium there.

Yet, even as the Lambeth Group picked its way through the debris, their conversations were dominated by one great danger: pensions. Herbecq found it difficult to believe that they had so underestimated the costs involved: 'We should hear Howard Gracey on this subject.'[51] The ripples were spreading. Another member of the group, Derek Fellows, began to think that the chairman of the Pensions Board should be an *ex officio* member of the Board of the Church Commissioners. Gracey himself was looking defensive: he wrote to Waine that if the enquiry's brief were to be widened, 'I sincerely hope that this does not mean that your Group wishes to give consideration to the level of benefits payable under the pension scheme, or the way in which the Pensions Board itself operates – certainly, without full consultation with the Pensions Board and the General Synod.' If Coopers & Lybrand were now moving into the question of pensions liability he should know of it: 'I am sure you will wish to ensure that Clergy pensioners will not be the scape-goat to divert attention from the main thrust of your study into the Church Commissioners'

[50] Locke to Baring, 20 Jan. 1993, ibid.
[51] Herbecq note, 18 Jan. 1993, Herbecq papers.

investment strategy.'[52] 'There does seem to be a slight edge to what he has to say', Bishop Waine remarked privately to Locke, 'but perhaps that is inevitable!'[53]

Gracey's position was indeed ambiguous. He was an actuary. Why had he not warned the Commissioners of the magnitude of the pensions commitment as it accumulated? The Lambeth Group found him relevant to much of what they examined in the affairs of the Commissioners, and yet he belonged somewhere else. Gracey told Waine that the Commissioners were not alone in their methods, that they bore comparison with other historic charities. But in pensions they had most of all in common with the public sector: theirs was a 'pay-as-you-go' policy, rather than a trust fund. More funding for clergy pensions should have been set aside in the previous decades; failure to do this had been compounded by the higher levels of benefits of the 1980s and the assumption of full responsibility for deaconesses' pensions. Gracey thought that a sound investment strategy required an equal attention to the growth of capital and of income. The 'excursions' of the Assets Committee into property development were, from an actuarial point of view, 'a high-risk departure from the long term strategy of steady income growth'. The Church Commissioners must decide: would they now run their pensions schemes on a pay-as-you-go basis, or as a trust fund?[54]

The Lambeth Group was determined to maintain its secrecy. Locke, and Herbecq, worried that loose talk was actually dangerous. Locke found that he was hearing it. He sent a note to the Commissioners' official solicitor, Edward Wills, on 24 February, observing that those who glimpsed the drafts of the Coopers & Lybrand report seemed to think corruption and fraud had been involved. 'I know of no evidence for this and I believe the weaknesses that have been uncovered are entirely explicable by reference to the nature and psychology of those concerned.'[55] Pressure mounted now in parliament where Frank Field secured from the Second Commissioner, Michael Alison, an assurance that the report of the Lambeth Group would certainly be published.

Here matters stood on 25 February 1993 when Lovelock retired. To those of the Lambeth Group tussling with the complexities of the Commissioners' affairs he may well have seemed for some time an increasingly remote figure, one who was kept in the picture only when new developments occurred. On 15 March Waine wrote to Carey to ask if the archbishop could spare him, Peter Baring and Patrick Locke

[52] Howard Gracey to Bishop John Waine, 25 Feb. 1993, CC/SEC/LG/1.
[53] Waine to Locke, 26 Feb. 1993, ibid.
[54] Gracey to Waine 5 Apr. 1993, ibid.
[55] Locke to Wills, 24 Feb. 1993, ibid.

an hour of his time 'in the reasonably near future?'.[56] Herbecq pressed as firmly as he could that the group simply must take up a position on the pensions question, but he confessed to himself that it was proving a 'tremendous battle'.[57] In truth, the implications of the debate were now spreading beyond the group itself. Locke received a letter from the secretary-general of the General Synod, Philip Mawer:

> It seems to me inevitable that the Lambeth Group will not be able to look at the Church Commissioners without looking at other aspects of the central organisation of the Church of England. While, in Sir Douglas's famous phrase, 'there is only one pot of gold', the Group will I am sure have rapidly realised that our institutional arrangements do not facilitate the co-ordinated management of the Church's financial resources. Nor is there any central system of policy direction for the whole Church.[58]

Locke was not himself sure that the disaster had exposed a weakness of structure. Nor was he confident, evidently, that the new debate was leading in the right direction. He remarked to Baring: 'If the "failure" was people because, as you at one point remarked, "the structure ought to have worked"; then (a) changing the structure will not of itself cure the problem; and (b) ought not any structural change to build in more safeguards, rather than less?'[59]

[56] Waine to Carey, 15 Mar. 1993, ibid.
[57] Herbecq note, 23 Apr. 1993, ibid.
[58] Philip Mawer to Locke, 6 Apr. 1993, ibid.
[59] Locke to Baring, 20 Apr. 1993, ibid.

15

An Orderly Retreat

On 15 April 1993 the new First Estates Commissioner, Sir Michael Colman, became involved in the work of the Assets Committee for the first time. Unlike his two predecessors, Colman was a man born and bred to the world of business. Politics held virtually no appeal for him. He could appear almost dryly matter-of-fact, but his opinions could also be pungent. He made his presence felt at once. The committee had settled to a discussion of moneys available and investment policy. Colman cut straight to the essence of the issue, observing at once that he would be 'uncomfortable' if recommendations for allocations in 1994 were to go to the Board without 'the clearest indication that the accompanying forecast showed a level of allocation in future years which could not be sustained on the current forecasts of likely income'. From now on investment policy must be directed towards a long-term growth in income. They must say plainly that further cuts in stipends might follow those by now agreed for 1994 and 1995. This was promptly endorsed by members of the committee and was seen as 'further strengthening and defining a number of anxieties which they themselves expressed over recent months'. There was also a 'clear and unanimous' recognition that the Church Commissioners must take the Church into their confidence, consult widely and avoid 'precipitate changes of direction'.[1] A week later the Board welcomed Colman's firm line and approved, unanimously, the proposal that financial provision for the casualties of the ordination of women be passed on to the dioceses. (They, at least, would also save money by the resignations.) But they must do such things with a proper tact, a more delicate use of language and not in unseemly haste. At the same time the annual general meeting should allocate £4.1 million *per annum* from 1 April 1994, primarily for pensions, and largely because they must meet expectations and commitments, and, simultaneously, reduce stipends allocations by £5.5 million from that same time.[2]

[1] AC minutes, 15 Apr. 1993.
[2] Board minutes, 22 Apr. 1993, pp. 2–3. See also reports, 'Investment policy', CC

The press had not gone away. The *Sunday Times* had published an unpleasant article, 'Church sees roof fall in on its property deals'. It made much of the role of Michael Hutchings. But Hutchings had gone after them, winning an apology in open court, and damages to boot. Locke noted to his satisfaction that the *Sunday Times* had put no less than four journalists onto the story: 'It was certainly my information at the time', he remarked to Canon Stanley on 29 April 1993, 'that they trawled and dug about for several weeks. In these circumstances I regard the thinness of the article and the speed with which the *Sunday Times* apologised as significant and reassuring.'[3]

Which way forward?

A great debate was in train, the scale of which was clearly demonstrated at one Board meeting. In May 1993 Board members considered a new paper from the General Purposes Committee, bearing the title 'Strategic issues'. This time archbishop Carey was in the chair. They turned to a General Synod report on *The ordained ministry: numbers, cost and deployment* and reminded themselves of its proposal that 40 per cent of the cost of stipends remain with the Commissioners and 40 per cent of their funds at least be given over to pensions. This was now almost meaningless: it could not be made to work. There must be a new approach. In fact, the new age of doubt had already altered life in the dioceses themselves. Many were beginning to cut their numbers of full-time stipendiary clergy. There were early signs of clergy unemployment, caused not only by the cut in numbers but by long vacancies. It was becoming harder to find title posts for ordinands. Some dioceses were arguing that their priority must be 'full employment' rather than higher stipends – others the reverse. Many now held to the ambition to become financially self-sufficient in the longer run. But then some parishes resented having to subsidise poorer parishes or parishes whose churches they might think less 'successful'. That must place poorer parishes at a disadvantage. Many parishes demanded more influence over diocesan and even national expenditure. Meanwhile the dioceses were doing their best to encourage higher levels of giving, balancing an appeal to ideals with a measurement of what might be possible.

How many clergy did the Church now need, and how many could it afford? How could they steer a course between 'a fragmentation into gathered congregations' and 'unproductive diocesan and central superstructures of committees, specialisms and bureaucracy'. How

(93) 16, and 'Money available', CC (93) 17, Board papers, 22 Apr, 1993, ser. 95083/65.

[3] Locke to John Stanley, 29 Apr. 1993, CC/SEC/LG/1.

should the costs of stipends, housing and pensions be divided between the Commissioners and the parishes? What, after all, did the Church want of the Commissioners? Indeed, added Bishop Waine, what were the Commissioners actually for? Were they to be involved in the 'living church' ('through stipends, housing and pastoral reorganisation'), or should they be, in effect, a pension fund? If the latter, how would that affect the work of other bodies? What were 'the most appropriate management structures' for the Commissioners? 'Is the Civil Service model (and its ethos) still appropriate?'

There was on the Board a 'general consensus' that the established Church must minister to the whole nation and maintain a full-time stipendiary ministry. In the 'decade of evangelism', they must plan not for retrenchment or mere maintenance, but for growth. With growth lay the answer to the pressure on the parishes: more church members would give more money. To reduce clergy numbers was to 'budget for erosion'. It could be seen that the clergy were overworking as it was and their families were suffering for it.

Some governors were not 'unduly alarmed' that the Commissioners might become, primarily, a pension fund. Most believed that the Commissioners 'remained in the best position to reinforce the nation-wide ministry of the Church and that it was desirable that they should continue to help those dioceses in greatest need'. Perhaps there should be a contributory system for pensions in light of the prospect that their commitments could not be maintained without new income? This was difficult, but church people must realise that 'pensions were not free', and might well need to be supported in the same way as stipends. Cuts there must be, and across the board. But they must not be so severe as to endanger the capacity of the established Church, as it lived and worked through its bishops and clergy, its synods, dioceses and parishes, to maintain itself.[4]

Meanwhile, in the world of investments, the retreat continued. On 27 May 1993 the Assets Committee approved the sale of the Gracechurch Centre for £58.35 million. In July Colman told the committee that though they had earlier intended to sell 50 per cent of their interest in the MetroCentre he would prefer them to sell 100 per cent. The enterprise might make money, but it was too big, too wide an exposure. It was not only here that Colman was making his mark. When Howard Gracey wrote to Colman that he himself favoured a fully approved occupational pension scheme for the Church, Colman's reply – drafted by Derek Fellows – was blunt. They must ensure that, whatever they produced, the benefits were not decided by parties who left the Church Commissioners to foot the bill.[5]

[4] Board minutes, 19 May 1993, pp. 1–8.
[5] Gracey to Sir Michael Colman, 2 July 1993. Fellows and Locke drafted Colman's

Publication of the Lambeth Report

The prospect of publication altered the report of the Lambeth Group as it was prodded and tweaked through its various drafts. Indeed, John Herbecq grew anxious that the group itself had worried more about the press than it should – and less about the Church itself. On the eve of publication archbishop Carey sent a morale-sustaining letter to all the staff at 1 Millbank. 'I shall', he said, 'firmly discourage recrimination.' It cannot have been altogether reassuring. He thanked them generously for all their work and loyalty in difficult times and observed that these would be 'tested again in the coming months'.[6]

The two reports, by Coopers & Lybrand and by the Lambeth Group itself, were published together on 22 July 1993. It was arranged that the Board of the Commissioners see them in advance, but only briefly, on the morning they were released. The text was substantially the work of Peter Baring (an advantage, reflected Herbecq, insofar as it did not read like a 'Millbank document').[7] The Lambeth Group acknowledged first of all that the contribution currently made by the Commissioners to the cost of pensions, stipends and housing could not be sustained. The role of the Commissioners must be redefined. They must preserve their capital in real terms and avoid vulnerability and narrow margins for error. There should be a separate pension fund. Increases in pensions should be attached not to stipends, which were regularly augmented, but to investment results and, perhaps, potential price increases. The Board and the General Purposes Committee should set down new 'general rules' for the direction of the Assets Committee. Membership of both the Assets Committee and the Board should remain as it was. The Committee, though, must now make a formal report every quarter to the Board and also an account of their work in each annual report. The Board should appoint an Audit Committee, balancing members of the Commissioners with outsiders and furnished with knowledge of 'the best practice in financial management and organisational control'. Added to this an experienced, private commercial accountancy firm should now audit the Commissioners' accounts. As for reforming the present portfolio, they should avoid speculative property development, maintain a portfolio which showed the same balances and commitments as comparable bodies, be advised by external fund managers or other professionals, 'continue to have regard to their special character as a major investor acting for the Church of England', 'normally' avoid borrowing and no longer generate 'temporary income' through

---

reply. CC/SEC/LG/1.
[6] Carey to Church Commissioners' staff, 21 July 1993, CC/SEC/LG/2.
[7] Herbecq note, 28 June 1993, Herbecq papers.

'coupon trading'. As for the Assets Committee, it should set itself more rules and have more reviews, often in partnership with the new Audit Committee. It should advise the Board on borrowing limits ('which should be modest'). The property portfolio should be reduced and managed with greater rigour and independence. There should be a new finance director. With such a formidable array of checks and balances it was a veritable American Constitution of amendments. It brought, in short, the essential new furniture of the age of doubt, a battery of mechanisms, structures for accountability – all the elements that a late twentieth-century financial institution would come to recognise only too well.[8]

In the little time that it had, the Board turned this over. It read that the Assets Committee had been 'exclusive' in their dealing. There was 'general agreement' that communication between the Board, the Assets Committee and the General Purposes Committee had in some degree broken down. David Hopkinson remarked that if 'the system' had been working properly the Board would have been setting down 'an order of priorities for expenditure and ensuring that this was adhered to'. Colman made clear that accountability must now follow as a first priority. This would mean that future mistakes could at least be laid at one door or another. In this there lay a firm implication. If the Assets Committee had been to blame for the *débâcle*, why had no one resigned from it? Because of this the Church Commissioners as a whole had been blamed for what had happened. At this point Waine reminded them that it was the mind of the archbishop that there should not be recriminations. He had himself asked counsel if he should resign as acting chair but had been advised against it. The Board welcomed this unanimously. Smallwood queried a statement from Coopers & Lybrands that the Commissioners' income was 'driven by expenditure'. He had never known of the Assets Committee being asked to raise more income to fuel specific commitments. It had always been the other way round. At the same time the Pensions Board had never set a timetable for the realisation of its 'aspirations'. Targets had been met, and quickly, because the money was said to be available. It was observed that in the background the bishop of Rochester, Michael Turnbull, wanted a wider 'mechanism' to draw the centres of planning and decision-making together. The chairman reported that the archbishop was already thinking about this, that a meeting had already occurred and that another would follow.

It required little imagination or experience to see that this could become a new, elaborate playground for lawyers and accountants, with layers of new papers, reports, audits, committees accumulating by the

[8] Locke, summary of the Lambeth Group report, CC (93) 42, Board papers, 23 Sept. 1993, ser. 95083/66.

day. None of this, as Locke bleakly remarked in a note to the Board, would make their load any lighter over the coming months. All the committees, and the Board too, would now be hard at work in the business of self-scrutiny – in fact, Waine had even suggested that a steering group be appointed simply to watch the process unfold and see the recommendations implemented. There was already an Archbishop's Advisory Group and, almost, a consultative group with the diocesan boards of finance.[9]

The Lambeth Group may have recommended the creation of a separately constituted pension fund but the lawyers were less sure. What advantages could be glimpsed carried with them heavy penalties – a mass of intricacies and complications – and they must ask if a body like the Church Commissioners would truly find it worth the trouble? Meanwhile, if the clergy were made to contribute something of their present earnings to their own pensions that would simply diminish their stipends at a time when the Church was working hard simply to make good on them. The recommendations on auditing were soon creating as many difficulties as they were evidently meant to solve: they were found to involve the constitution, and possibly parliament itself.[10]

By the autumn a hole of £20 million still lay between the Commissioners' income and their expenditure. Of seven of their development projects, four had now been sold at a loss and three at a profit. The net loss to the Commissioners had been £18.8 million.[11]

The Church Commissioners faced the coming of Synod stoutly. They themselves had distributed around 1,800 copies of the Lambeth Report and had undertaken most solemnly their 'thorough and detailed consideration' of it. They had accepted all the criticisms made there. They had a new First Church Estates Commissioner, a new secretary. Committees were being strengthened, independent advisers commissioned, external managers selected. A new Audit Committee was almost a reality.[12] In October it was asked on the Board if some kind of corporate apology should be made to the whole Church? Most thought it should, but with positive trimmings, for they should not be too defensive: they had had the best intentions, and they had been working under pressure to maximise income. Hopkinson argued that it would be well to remind Synod of the simple truth that all investment bore risk. Mostly the Commissioners had done well. If they dwelled too much on what had been 'fundamentally bad decisions' they might well lower morale. What mattered, it was agreed, was unity before the

---

[9] Board minutes, 22 July 1993, pp. 1–3.

[10] Locke, summary of the Lambeth Group report, CC (93) 42.

[11] Board minutes, 23 Sept. 1993, pp. 1–4.

[12] See 'Lambeth Group report: follow-up', CC (93) 46, Board papers, 28 Oct. 1993, ser. 95083/66.

world between the national bodies of the Church. For the press dearly loved division.[13]

Parliament calls upon the Commissioners

In that October meeting, two governors had observed the importance of the Commissioners' accountability to parliament. In fact, the powers at Westminster had already moved to make that clear for themselves. For two years the House of Commons' Social Security Committee had been examining the workings of various pensions funds. Now they wished to turn their attentions to the affairs of the Church Commissioners. On 29 July the chairman of the committee, Frank Field, invited the Church Commissioners to answer questions. Locke moved adroitly, sending off a clever letter to the principal private secretary to the Home Secretary:

> The Commissioners have, of course, nothing to hide and we wish to do everything we can to provide the House of Commons with full information about our affairs. On the other hand, we are not expert in the jurisdiction of the Select Committee and we would not wish, through ignorance, to do something which might embarrass the Home Secretary.[14]

It altered nothing. Soon a date was set for an appearance by the Church Commissioners in parliament: 8 December, 'and there was a possibility that it would be televised'.[15]

This could not have been welcomed at 1 Millbank. There was something about it that was very like being hauled off to court, particularly as the Social Security Committee had only recently been picking over the remains of a great public scandal which had exposed the newspaper tycoon Robert Maxwell for robbing the pensions fund of his own employees. But the committee's new interest in the Church Commissioners would prove to be something more subtle – and, ultimately, more sympathetic – than a court of enquiry, not least because it established a quite new meeting ground between Church and State.

The principal difficulty that the Social Security Committee faced was quite simply that the criticisms which could be made against the Church Commissioners could not be made against the new men at the

[13] Board minutes, 28 Oct. 1993, pp. 1–2.
[14] Locke to principal private secretary to the Home Secretary, 11 Aug. 1993, annex IV to Locke summary of Lambeth Group report, CC (93) 42, Board papers, 23 Sept. 1993, ser. 95083/66.
[15] Board minutes, 23 Nov. 1993, p. 5.

top. Equally, the men who were responsible for the *débâcle* were no longer in control. Of this their guests did not hesitate gently to remind them. The first meeting between the committee and the Commissioners defined much of what would follow. In particular, it established the authority of Colman himself.

One MP, David Faber, ventured that the Commissioners had been shown to have broken their trust. Colman thought such an accusation 'perfectly understandable'. Field pressed: had he asked his predecessors for an apology? Colman replied blandly that he was old enough not to be concerned with the actions of those who had gone before him. If mistakes had been made, that was for others to judge. Colman's task now was to 'rebuild' the institution. When Field asked why the Lambeth Group had consisted of so many men who were already working for the Commissioners, and why the very accountants who had been, auditors to 'some, if not all' the companies which had failed, had been invited to undertake its research, Colman responded that the Lambeth Group was set up before he arrived. He had simply assured himself in conversations that they had 'a free hand'. As for Coopers & Lybrand, 'They have a considerable reputation. If they cannot undertake an objective and thorough investigation of this kind, then we are in real trouble.' Stephen Day asked: 'how did Colman himself understand the Commissioners' past preponderance' in property? Colman: 'I do not think I can because I do not think it was altogether easy to understand.' Field again: had he seen evidence that those who had worked for the Commissioners had in fact criticised the policy? He himself had been told of such, but that it was unrecorded – 'they found that the nature of the minutes was changing'. This Colman thought customary for a board or committee: 'it is not important to me whether my advice is included in the minutes. What is important to me is whether I am influencing the balance of the assets'. If he was not doing that he would consider whether or not he should remain there. Thurnham rejoined, 'The whole thing stinks. I feel very unhappy about the whole set-up.' 'So', replied Colman, 'you should be.' And what of the Church Commissioners themselves? Who were they, and were did they come from? 'A lot' replied Colman, were elected by Synod; bishops and *ex officio* Commissioners turned up 'on the doorstep'. This was not a normal board. One had to accept what was given and work with that 'as part of the apparatus'. Field asked whether they should have a board of directors? Colman liked that: 'If you can use your influence to enable that to happen, I think it would be a step in the right direction.' Thurnham asked who would be the shareholders if they had one. Parliament, observed Colman, was the 'ultimate shareholder'.

About pensions Colman was clear. He did not believe that the Church Commissioners should become simply a pensions fund; that would have 'the worst effect on the church'. Might the parochial clergy, asked Field, who were not powerful at Millbank, prefer to see their pensions secured? Might there be a conflict of interests in all this? That, said Colman, begged again the question of representation, and that was again something over which he had no control. Did that mean that he had no influence, then? Colman observed, 'I do attach a lot of importance to working closely with the archbishop of Canterbury.' As for himself, he had 'input', but no 'deciding voice'.

Jeremy Corbyn MP deplored the scheme at Ashford Great Park. Colman: 'I am not disagreeing with you.' Then why was it undertaken? 'I have no idea.' Field asked about the MetroCentre. Colman was detached: 'I can tell you that it has not been a bad investment but it certainly has not been a wild success.' But it was 'very big'. He was not opposed to developments altogether, but he confessed that he was 'just a bit wary of going out and looking for developments as a property company would do'. That was why the Commissioners now had a property subgroup. Field asked whether the Commissioners were sure that they had a legal power to borrow? Colman was sure that they had. Field pressed about the development companies to which the Church Commissioners had so busily transferred their funds. How many of these companies were there now? All of the ones which remained were consolidated, assured Colman, and the Commissioners had produced consolidated accounts since 1992. He thought it true that 'a misleading impression was being created of income which, in fact, was replicated by an obligation in the subsidiary company': 'In the world which I come from, that is illegal.' Field pressed: was this not also illegal because the Commissioners were a closed fund? Colman replied that it was not a question of illegality, but of good or bad practice. There was no suggestion of illegality, chimed in Locke. It had all been open and above board. What of dividend stripping?, asked Field. Gilt-stripping had its place, replied Colman, but it was right to criticise it when it became a way of translating capital into income that was available for distribution.

Thurnham moved on to the role of parliament. The position that Colman held, he observed, was a crown appointment. If he thought of parliament as a shareholder, should it take a greater interest in what the Church Commissioners were doing? That, responded Colman amiably, was for them to decide, not him. If parliament had done more in the past, would that have revealed these 'unhappy matters' earlier? Colman: 'It might have done.' As for the Church at large, it had not been very good at asking how it would pay for what it was undertaking. 'We are quite good at entering into these obligations which are very justifiable. We are not good at saying that they have to be paid for.' While the committee was quite right to hope that the Commissioners would improve their powers of communication with the Church, there was the *caveat* that 'bishops in the diocese do not thank me if I trample all over their diocese and say, "Look here, I want to get the attention of some of your clergy". They say, "You are from Millbank. You stay in Millbank. We are in the diocese. We are running the diocese"'.

Colman was able to conclude on a magisterial note:

> I have made it clear that I regard it as very important to try and meet the aspirations of the archbishop of Canterbury who is, after all, the Chairman of the Commissioners. I think he would be very regretful if he did not have the ability to exercise the discretion to direct a lot of funds to those areas where he feels the real need lies in the Established Church within this country ... I hold myself, if you like, available to pursue a policy like that if that is what the archbishop and the church as a whole wishes to have.[16]

£16 million or £8 million?

The Lambeth Report stressed the need to preserve capital in real terms. This, insisted Colman, was the heart of the matter. Assets had been eroded. Some in the Church wanted them further weakened by the maintenance of various grants which no sound business mind could countenance. Against this, the Church Commissioners must mark a firm boundary. Moreover, they must be clear about what their 'core responsibilities' were. Locke concurred, adding that 'the legal forces which lay behind the Commissioners' current responsibilities were complex'. He set off now to produce a 'digest' of the different measures which gave rise to payments out of the General Fund.[17]

By the time the Central Stipends Authority held its conference in Peterborough, in November 1993, it could be seen clearly that if the Church Commissioners were to survive with a bare reserve of £2 million they must shave another £16 million off their allocations in 1995. But this was a vast sum. If they cut back still further the dioceses might see 'serious and largely irreversible damage'. For some the new figure could not be right. The General Purposes Committee were

---

[16] *The operation of pensions funds: the Church Commissioners and Church of England pensions* (Second Report of the House of Commons Social Security Committee), London 1995, 1–13, session of 8 Dec. 1993.

[17] Board of governors steering group, 'Notes of meeting held on 8 Nov. 1993, BSG (3), Board papers, 23 Nov. 1993, ser. 95083/66.

ready to urge the Assets Committee to create more temporary income. A new bottom line was advanced: the cuts simply could not be less than £8 million.

Now the Board must decide: which of those two figures it was to be? It was asked whether the Commissioners could operate a deficit? (The answer was that they could not.) As for creating 'temporary income' through coupon trading, this was now judged to be, at best, dubious legally. There continued to be quibbles: was there actually a difference between 'coupon-stripping' and a 're-positioning of assets'? Could there be new legislation to allow 'a modest amount of income' to be spent, subject to later repayment? Some looked to the dioceses, but they had different ideas as to what to do. Many dioceses acknowledged that there must be cuts but believed that they should all be borne by the Commissioners themselves.[18]

It was in November, too, that the Assets Committee decided that the American venture must now be abandoned. The management of the US property portfolio would pass to a suitable real estate corporation there. An 'exit plan' to take three years was outlined and promptly approved. On 14 December the Assets Committee property group met independent property advisers to work out what they should do with Ashford. Now, it appeared, the site had 'poor prospects'. Ashford, like the United States, was 'over-supplied' with land suitable for development and there were better schemes to be had. In September 1994 application for planning permission had again been delayed: planning officers had simply failed to complete their reports on time.[19]

In December 1993 the Board found itself trying to agree a budget for 1994 without being in possession of a set of estimates of income for the period. Yet they must, for to begin a new year without even a budget must further diminish confidence. Meanwhile, it was observed that the Commissioners' own staff numbers had dropped from 375 in 1982 to 289 in 1992.[20]

1994

No new year in the history of the Church Commissioners could have dawned on a bleaker note. At another joint meeting of the Assets and General Purposes Committees, on 20 January, it was seen that expenditure was still exceeding income by £20 million. Pensions were hard to cut; statutory expenditure impossible. They must cut their allocations for stipends. The property secretary was sombre about the

[18] Locke note, 'Financial planning', CSA (93) 8, p. 2, ibid.
[19] AC minutes, 14 Dec. 1993.
[20] Board minutes, 16 Dec. 1993, p. 3.

prospects for property: income forecasts were worse now than they had been the previous May. The securities secretary was solemn. Answers were not to be found in either, it seemed. All lamented what this must do to the ministry of the Church. Parishes might go bankrupt. The Church of England might no longer be a national Church. If parishes could not pay their quotas, clergy might find themselves redundant. If that happened some form of compensation would be required, and that would mean spending more money. If clergy retired that might diminish the stipends bill but increase the pensions bill. Some thought that pensions should be frozen. Others murmured about cuts in administrative costs: 'the Commissioners should "share the misery" as it was their financial troubles that were "causing the pain"'. Could they make their way to parliament with a new measure to enable them to spend their capital? The General Purposes Committee was now looking restless and unhappy and not always convinced by what they heard from the Assets Committee. It was held that these cuts were 'unacceptable'. But the Assets Committee had worked solidly, carefully and thoroughly, and again its members stuck fast.[21]

It was all very well to observe now that the Church Commissioners had been over-generous and that they had not sufficiently worked out their own liabilities. But the grants and the loans of the 1980s had established a new *status quo*, a new range of expectations by which the dioceses themselves lived and worked. To dismantle this would not be an easy matter. The Commissioners were trapped, almost completely, within their legal responsibilities, their financial obligations and their political relationships. An answer to one was sure to offend another. It was impossible to devise entire solutions. It was exceedingly difficult even to construct compromises. They could only seek to orchestrate a score of careful movements which might, within the time that was available, produce a coherent and constructive effect. The dioceses, meanwhile, could not wait any longer for a sharper measurement of these things. They needed to know what their allocations would be if they were to make their own plans.

On 24 January 1994 Colman wrote another note for the General Purposes Committee and the Board which made for dreary reading. The Commissioners themselves were still over-distributing 'by at least £50m p.a.'. The situation was stark: 'Distributions in excess of the sustainable level of 4% to 5% are eroding the capital. We are also in a very precarious short-term position because of the imminent exhaustion of reserves.' They must have a 'much firmer grasp' of their long-term liabilities. Colman himself – and his senior colleagues – saw

---

[21] AC/GPC meeting, 20 Jan. 1994, A/GPC (94) 1, Board papers 27 Jan. 1994, ser. 95083/67.

that the 'reality' of the Commissioners' finances would not be met even by the much contested £16 million. They would do better to cut allocations by about £21.8 million. But, he acknowledged, 'that position does not, evidently, command the acceptance we need to go forward'. Accordingly, he proposed that they tell the dioceses that by a number of means the Commissioners would find savings and additional income of up to £10 million in 1995 in order to keep the cuts down to £12 million in that calendar year. It could not be guaranteed. They could not be sure where it would come from. They must make plans to arrange loans 'as a last resort': 'This does not change the underlying reality, but we hope that it will give dioceses the confidence to plan 1995 in a way which avoids desperate remedies.'[22] When this 'interim' proposal came to the Board, the governors flung themselves upon it, as they might upon a life-boat.

On 7 January representatives of the Commissioners had met with the Pensions Board and the Central Board of Finance to work out a new outline for pensions policy. The proposal mooted now would mean that the Commissioners would earmark a part of their assets to meet pensions costs arising from past service liabilities, while future service liabilities would be met by the parishes out of their quotas. Those contributions would be managed by the Pensions Board. If this was to be done, the value of the Commissioners' assets must not decline further. There had been other meetings. Colman, Locke and Hopgood had been to the House of Bishops and later had met a small contingent of bishops at Lambeth. The bishops were shaken by the scale of these new cuts, had 'expressed considerable concern', but agreed that once the Assets Committee had worked out 'firm figures' they should adhere to them.[23]

In the midst of all the new thinking some of the old debates acquired a new force. For years a number of Commissioners had been urging that the bishops of Durham and Winchester should receive the same stipend as other diocesan bishops, though they were by tradition considered senior to them and paid accordingly. Now the archbishop of Canterbury agreed that their stipends should be reduced. The archbishop of York wrote that he would not oppose the measure, but he would regret it. The differential scales were abolished.[24] Meanwhile, the new finance director, Christopher Daws, was steadily building an historical picture of the Commissioners' affairs, and this was proving constructive. Expenditure levels in the later 1960s had been set down with some caution to a formula of no more than 5 per cent of the asset

[22] Michael Colman note, 'Financial support in 1995', CC (94) 4, GPC (94) 5, p. 2, ibid.
[23] See Board of governors' stipends' group, BSC (94), minutes of 20 Jan. 1994, ibid.
[24] Board minutes, 24 Feb. 1994, p. 2.

base. In the 1970s the value of that base had fallen severely and the Commissioners had lowered their support to match. The 5 per cent rule had been observed until the mid-1980s. Then the asset base increased; expenditure soared. They must, he argued, now return to their 5 per cent rule. The board dutifully resolved to do so. It also appointed the accountants, Watson's, to be the Commissioners' new auditors.

Colman's 'interim' policy made headway in the dioceses. Some there even said that they could cope with a larger cut in allocations in 1995. Where they divided was over the prospect of a further cut of £15.6 million in the year following. On the Board of the Commissioners, Hopkinson warned that the Commissioners risked making important decisions on the basis of income at the bottom of the recession. Surely their affairs might improve? There was something in this. When the Board examined the first quarterly report submitted to it by the Assets Committee Colman himself could observe that market conditions in general were improving, even though rents were not increasing. Stock Exchange securities were also performing satisfactorily.[25] Perhaps even at this stage the Commissioners' fortunes were changing for the better?

The new ways

The corporate life, in which the Church Commissioners operated, was altering. Companies and institutions had begun to adopt what were now being called 'mission statements', declarations of identity and purpose to brandish before the enquiring world, firm formulations by which their deeds might be judged. On 23 March 1994 the Board approved a mission statement for the Church Commissioners. It offered a significant reformulation of the old understandings:

> Our primary responsibility is to manage the investments entrusted to us to maximise our financial support for the ministry of the Church of England, particularly in areas of greatest need.

> We also seek to provide such central services as may be required by the Church, in areas such as clergy housing, pastoral reorganisation, redundant churches and the stipends and pensions payroll.

> We intend to provide the Church, by the year 2000, with a diversified and prospering asset base; a clear set of priorities

[25] Ibid. pp. 2–4.

for consistent support for mission; and a flexible structure responsive to their needs.[26]

There were reviews everywhere. It was felt that the committee structure had grown too complex and was causing confusion. The work of the Commissioners must yield to the logic of a new corporatism. A document on public relations and communications appeared; it was ruthless in observing a need to conform to the overall policy of the Church, to present 'as far as possible, a positive and unified message'; to increase 'strategic liaison' with Church House and Lambeth; owning that the Commissioners were remote and not much loved in the parishes; identifying a 'target audience' (just about everybody, it seemed) and a 'key audience' (the clergy and laity). In this language there unfolded a new world; here were 'strategic planning systems' and 'primary objectives', there 'a cascade of information', new 'systems' to strengthen staff communications, consolidations; all of it 'proactively to utilise' the opportunities presented by other church bodies, 'reactively' ensuring access to facts, 'generally to present the Commissioners as a tool for the Church's mission, rather than as an obstacle to it'.[27] The press release announcing the end of year statistics bore the bold legend 'Reform and recovery'.

Whether all of this achieved anything fundamental beyond the generation of piles of new papers and an increasingly oppressive quality of self-absorption is debatable. It did not get the Church Commissioners out of their old binds. The Board now found itself having to arbitrate between committees, for the General Purposes Committee was recommending an increase of £3 million a year to fund an additional renewable allocation of 3.3 per cent for pensions while the Assets Committee was proposing instead to give funds to the level of, at most, 2.5 per cent. Gracey warned that these aspirations had been endorsed by Synod and to renege must affect the credibility of the Commissioners. The mood of the Board lay behind 3.3 per cent and a majority voted for it.[28]

Back to parliament

The House of Commons select committee had not gone away. Far from it. Field was still working to expose to the light of day the history of the institution which now held his attention, while his committee

---

[26] Statement subsequently integrated into AC report, 23 Mar. 1994, pt IV, Board papers, 28 Apr. 1994, ser. 95083/68.
[27] Dickens report, 'Public relations and communications', GPC (94) 30, pp. 3–4, Board papers, 26 May 1994, ibid.
[28] Board minutes, 26 May 1994, pp. 1–2.

tussled with diaries in an attempt to meet the archbishop of Canterbury. At last, on 26 April 1994, a second session took place. Beside Carey now was a new constellation of church powers: Howard Gracey, Bishop Waine, Philip Mawer of Church House, Andrew Purkis, the archbishop's secretary for public affairs, and Patrick Locke. Carey was determined to be brisk, open and forward-looking. For this he was promptly congratulated. He demurred that he and 'the old regime' were not 'completely separate', but admitted that the first that he had known of the seriousness of the financial crisis had, 'to some extent', been the article in the *Financial Times,* though, to be sure, he had known for 'a year or two' that 'we were overspending at a remarkable rate'.

Field asked, if they had over-spent on pensions, had there not been projections? Periodically, replied Gracey. But had the Commissioners a picture of the cumulative liability which they had assumed? Gracey said that the Pensions Board had supplied the Commissioners with their various estimates, 'from time to time'. There was no actuarial report? 'No, there was no actuarial assessment as though it were a fund; there was no valuation of liabilities on a traditional actuarial assessment, beyond back-of-envelope calculations which I have done myself to make sure there was not a silly situation.' David Shaw MP pressed the point: was he to understand that the assets and liabilities, and the income and expenditure, of the Church had 'not really been under control or understood'? Gracey demurred. Coopers & Lybrand had pursued one particular model of evaluation. Normal actuarial patterns were not quite helpful here. The Church worked rather as the public sector did, 'on a pay-as-you-go basis': 'that does require a rather more subtle actuarial assessment and approach if you are to continue with it'.

But Carey was now looking ahead again. The Church Commissioners had made their mistakes and their apologies. There was now a 'proper structure' to make sure that they did not get into such a state again. The Church had 'a very clumsy machinery'; a new archbishops' commission, chaired by the bishop of Rochester would propose 'a much more streamlined central body'. Bishop Waine added that the criticisms which had been made of them had been accepted: 'There is no doubt that with a strengthened Assets Committee, with an Audit Committee keeping watch, with regular reports of the Assets Committee to the Board of Governors, I cannot see how this kind of situation could possibly develop in the future.'

They turned to the size of the Board. How many, exactly, sat on it? Carey did not know; he turned to Waine who did not know; he turned to Locke who offered an explanation of the proportions of interests, but not numbers. Field asked the archbishop if he would prefer something smaller. Carey replied that he thought he would. Waine added that representation of interests was not an easy thing to attach to an economy of numbers. Peter Thurnham MP asked whether the archbishop agreed with Colman that the connection with parliament should be strengthened? Carey said that he was always looking for ways of doing that. There followed something of a meander around establishment and disestablishment, but then they were back on to finances with a bump. Carey admitted that Colman would have preferred a more 'savage' cut than the present £12 million. Presumably, observed Field, because he did not wish for more gilt-stripping? Carey said he could not comment on that 'from a professional point of view', but the House of Bishops had the pastoral care of the clergy and their churches in their mind. Field persisted; Carey simply insisted that all their decisions were made in partnership.[29]

By the time a third session of the Social Security Committee took place another half-year had passed. The new men in power at the Church Commissioners had grown yet more assured. Meanwhile, the old masters looked more and more remote. On 14 December it was the turn of Sir Douglas Lovelock and James Shelley to enter the lions' den.

Now Field was determined to focus minds on the precipitous rise in clergy pensions. Where, he asked, had this commitment to make the pension two-thirds of the stipend come from? These, replied Lovelock, had been the 'aspirations' presented to Synod in Harris's day. He himself thought it odd that there had been no estimates of cost then. It must have been a time of 'total confidence'. Field asked Shelley if he knew more. Shelley simply replied he was not secretary then, but assets secretary. Field pressed further: had there been no age profile of the clergy? Shelley reminded him that he had now been retired for three years: 'I do not think there were no calculations. I think there was an age profile, but I do not think it was looked at very carefully, and I do not think a full actuarial examination was put in hand.' This was a matter for the Pensions Board. Field, again, asked, 'Would it be unreasonable to think that the Chairman of the Pensions Board, himself the senior partner of Watsons, should be advising you on dangers and pitfalls, rather than you giving the advice to him?' Lovelock thought this a fair point. He had himself proposed the union of the two bodies to Synod, but it had been turned down. He was 'absolutely convinced' that a union would have saved them from what had indeed happened. As for Gracey's back-of-an-envelope, he suspected that this was poetic licence. Was it true, then, added Field, that these aspirations for the clergy pension were accepted as a

[29] *The operation of pensions funds*, 14–29, session of 26 Apr. 1994.

commitment, there were no calculations and the Commissioners were left to foot the bill? Lovelock replied, 'That is absolutely right, Chairman.' There had been pensions, then stipends, then houses, the Church Urban Fund, the Community Charge, 'on and on we go'. It was all done for the best interests of the Church, but it had been a miscalculation.

They came, inevitably, to the property speculations of the later 1980s. Was there not a difference between developing one's own land and creating property companies to speculate, joint companies which would mean that the Commissioners could preserve their charitable status? The Commissioners had long had joint companies, replied Shelley. It was simply a convenient way to do business with partners, 'a useful channel'. These partners, persisted Field, had brought very little to the Church and taken away a great deal. The Commissioners had paid them from capital and they had paid back in income, something which blurred the accounts and made the level of income appear 'rather good'. Shelley demurred: 'I do not think that is how we saw it at all.' Lovelock added, 'I am quite sure it was not, Chairman. We would scorn to do any such thing … It would not even occur to us to do it in order to conceal something.' A barb about Michael Hutchings and his cases of wine was thrown in. Lovelock at once defended him. The Commissioners had not paid for the transport of his wine. There must have been a time, persisted Field, when the total borrowing of the Commissioners had been 'about a quarter' of their assets. A property company, observed Lovelock, would have as much as 50 or 60 per cent. Shelley stepped in to admit that 'in the euphoria of the 1980s we got the terms wrong'.

They moved to the consolidation of accounts. All the new companies, stated Shelley, were duly registered at Companies House. Had their losses been concealed within the overall accounts of the Commissioners? That, said Shelley, was a question of accounting and was something he did not know about. Field asked whether the Commissioners had fallen prey to 'unscrupulous people'? They should remember, replied Lovelock, that some of the best companies had collapsed in the crash. Was that a reason not to become involved in such things? 'Well', said Lovelock, 'if you do not get involved with anyone, you do not do anything.' Gilt-stripping, maintained Lovelock, had occurred because it served the interests of the Church which made its claims upon the Commissioners, not for any mean or dubious reason. It began in a small way and was meant to be only for a limited period. Had these failures been the consequences of the Commissioners' 'archaic' constitution? Lovelock conceded that it was 'peculiar'; that the Assets Committee was not subordinate to the Board seemed to him, in his experience, 'unique'. He did not think it a decisive issue. Once he had hoped for a principal finance officer, but he had not pushed much for it. Now the Commissioners had one. If they could not be like a commercial organisation that was, if he might say so, parliament's fault, for their constitution was set down by statute. They all knew how long it took to change that.[30]

The significance of the pension

While the select committee was intent on exhuming the past, the report from Watson's finally arrived on the desks of 1 Millbank. Its general verdict could hardly come as a surprise, but its recommendation was a vital one:

> In our opinion, the current situation has been brought about by the unrecognised liabilities which have been building up over a long period. Investment policy itself has not caused these problems, although it has accelerated their impact. All our investigations show that the distinction between income and capital is artificial, inappropriate in relation to the Commissioners' real liabilities, and unnecessarily constraining to their ability to adopt the most suitable investment policies. We recommend that this distinction should be removed and the Commissioners' objectives should instead recognise the need to protect the real value of the assets and hence the real level of income available for distribution.[31]

This document confirmed that the Commissioners' pensions policy was not viable. As the Audit Committee blandly observed to the Board, the Commissioners had a legal liability to provide pensions, but no hypothecated assets. Accordingly, the new policy must be not merely financial, but political, involving the whole Church, and even parliament. Quite what part should be played in this by the Commissioners would need to be established, but what could now be seen, for the first time, was that they should be free to give funds from both their capital and their income.

Mr Wigley of Watson's grimly told the General Purposes Committee that the problems were greater than he had anticipated. On the basis of the evaluations of March 1994, by 2010 they would have no money for stipends at all. By 2005 their non-discretionary and discretionary allowances would be 'unaffordable'. Conditions might change, of course. But they would be foolish to bank on it. They

[30] Ibid. pp. 30–49, session of 14 Dec. 1994.
[31] See 'Summary of conclusions: Watsons' report', CC (94) 53, Board papers, 28 July 1994, ser. 95083/69.

should be realistic. Watson's were. In other, bolder, days the committee might have launched a few questions at Wigley, but today only one little one managed to get off the ground. Would the average age of ordination, or the number of candidates, affect the projections? Wigley cast the question aside as an irrelevance.

The difference between the old ways and the new was now in sharp focus. When the projections submitted to the Assets Committee in 1987 were retrieved and dusted off they were found to be flawed by optimism, inconsistency and a lack of independence. Old illusions of the Commissioners' largesse had evaporated altogether. If the clergy pension was to survive the dioceses and parishes must begin to contribute to it. The air was thick with talk of 'rebasing to RPI', of re-structuring, distinctions, persuasions, insistences, legal responsibilities, principles, presentations.[32]

If the past failures of the Church Commissioners had been not simply financial but political, Colman was now seizing the political end of their affairs with an equally firm hand. The work of the Commissioners needed both a foundation and a character. Both of these could be found in the strong insistence that the Commissioners were responsible for a trust and must measure their duties as would trustees. This was something more than a call for a new clarity. It also looked to establish a particular logic to the Commissioners' activities, something which might make them less vulnerable to the political pressures and priorities of the bodies to which they were attached. When, on 22 September, it was the turn of the Board to mull over Watson's reports, Colman set down one requirement. Whatever pressures they faced, the Church Commissioners must remain true to their responsibility to maintain selective allocations to the poorer dioceses. It was in these that the fundamental justification of the Church Commissioners as a trust lay. This was not negotiable; indeed his position rested upon it.

Now they could look about them more clearly. Cuts to the dioceses had already been agreed: a cumulative total of £12 million in 1995, £22 million in 1996 and £32 million in 1997. With each cut the space which the Commissioners occupied in the foreground of the financial life of the Church of England could be seen to diminish. Fundamental change was sure to occur with pensions. Already there were detailed long-term models which integrated a restructuring of their investment strategy; which assumed a sustainable expenditure level of 3.5 per cent of assets; which 'ring-fenced' capital to cover pensions liabilities; and which included contributions by dioceses and parishes. Nor should the wider Church be protected in the longer term from the full costs of employing the clergy. The Church Commissioners must keep faith

---

[32] Board minutes, 22 Sept. 1994, p. 3.

with earlier generations whose money was given for the active ministry and with future generations who should not have to pay tomorrow the bills of today. Then, they must look to the medium term. For pensions, they must put together a 'comprehensive legal package'. Now came a first hint that a measure must be passed.

This the Board welcomed. Smallwood pleaded that the price of the pensions be met by a partnership between the Commissioners, the dioceses and the parishes. But this, came the reply, could only endanger the Commissioners' capacity to make selective allocations. Gracey, too, endorsed Colman's strategy. It was time to be definite. The Pensions Board was collaborating with the Commissioners on a new paper, which the General Purposes Committee would view in October, and the dioceses in November. Colman was managing to turn his policy into a new consensus. It was no mean feat.[33] When Smallwood attempted to launch a Synod motion that the Commissioners be empowered to run their reserve fund into a temporary deficit in order to maintain their allocations to the diocesan stipends funds, he found support in eleven dioceses but was thwarted thereafter.[34] At the policy committee of the General Synod Colman was there to tell him firmly that this was 'unhelpful and unnecessary'.[35] On 3 November the Board confirmed sombrely that 'Unilateral proposals would not help the Church'.[36]

It began to be seen that, in essence, a new statutory pension fund would be entirely separate from the Commissioners' residual capital. The Commissioners' liability would be met by transfers from their capital. Pension contributions would be legally charged, like stipends and national insurance contributions, to the diocesan boards of finance or to the cathedral chapters. There would be actuarial reviews every three years. The Third Church Estates Commissioner, Margaret Laird, wrote a stiff letter to the Pensions Board on behalf of the General Purposes Committee, stating the case and showing clearly the way the winds were blowing. In reply, Gracey remarked that these points were 'generally accepted', though he reminded her that the Board of the Commissioners included some who would still contest changes on pensions. They must be sure to carry the dioceses with them.[37] This unenviable task fell to the Commissioners' indefatigable Richard Hopgood. When he brought together the diocesan secretaries many

[33] Ibid. pp. 3–7.
[34] PC report, 'Mr John Smallwood's proposal', PC (94) 18, Board papers, 3 Nov. 1994, ser. 95083/69.
[35] Extract from PC minutes, ibid. annex II.
[36] Board minutes, 3 Nov. 1994, p. 1.
[37] Gracey to Laird, 27 Sept. 1994, CC (94) 68, annex 3, Board papers, 3 Nov. 1994, ser. 95083/69.

expressed the view that the credibility of the Commissioners was now so badly damaged that they should not control the support fund. 'A few dioceses were keen to rake over the ashes and attribute personal blame.' In his subsequent report for the Board Hopgood coolly observed:

> This was never going to be an easy Conference, given the unpalatable choices being laid before the dioceses, and the undercurrent of hostility to the Commissioners was unsurprising (albeit more forceful than many of us have experienced at this level). With hindsight, the papers were too complex for some dioceses to handle, which probably added to their frustration and unease.[38]

The foundations of the new policy were not a matter for debate as they were unavoidable. Indeed, the policy was already in train. At the Board itself some perceived that there was more support for the Commissioners' plans in the parishes than there was on the diocesan boards: 'It was feared that the dioceses were losing the vision of mutual support and turning inwards.'[39]

If this was true, it was not only true of the dioceses. Assessment of committee structures at the Church Commissioners was trundling on. Little that was inherited could be maintained without revision, if indeed it should be retained at all. There was now seen to be a 'heavy overlap' between the General Purposes Committee and the Board in at least six defining areas ('In 1993, around two-thirds of the main agenda items considered by the Board were also considered by the General Purposes Committee'). Old committees might merge with each other, or disappear altogether. Minutes from one committee would pass this way and that. Once, the Commissioners had worked on a conservative, 'need to know', basis. Now, it seemed, everybody needed to know everything. New methods carried their own costs. Only two years before, much had been made of the fact that the Commissioners had cut their own staff numbers. But by December 1994 they were seen to be creeping up again.

Secret conversations and manoeuvres multiplied. Increasingly, Locke himself was looking besieged and vulnerable. If he survived now it was partly because his critics could not think who should replace him and because they feared that another change in staff must signal yet more trouble. The representatives of Synod agitated that the powers of Millbank must show a new openness. If Smallwood did not get his way with one individual work of legislation, he did on another.

---

[38] GPC report, 'Nov. conference with diocesan boards of finance', GPC (94) 4, Board papers, 3 Nov. 1993, ibid.
[39] Board minutes, 15 Dec. 1994, p. 4.

In November 1994 Synod voted for an amendment to the Miscellaneous Provisions Measure, that three additional elected members were to be appointed to the Assets Committee. This time procedure had been properly observed, for the chairman of the Revision Committee of the Synod had been circulated, the proposal put fairly by the chairman to his committee and an overwhelming majority gained. To the Ecclesiastical Committee in parliament it must duly go. Colman bristled. He was chairman of the Assets Committee. Nobody had asked him about this amendment. 'He had no wish to become a "political football" in an issue between the prerogatives of Synod on the one hand and Parliament on the other.' The Second Commissioner, Michael Alison, agreed.[40] In truth, the new amendment left its advocates with more of a practical problem than a philosophical one: who could they actually find in Synod who was qualified to play a constructive part in the work of the Commissioners? It was not a new question.

1995

The Church Commissioners entered the new year armed with a battery of aims and objectives. Meanwhile, the new policy was promoted by a good deal of steady diplomacy. On 9 January Colman, Locke and Hopgood again trooped off to the House of Bishops to explain it, and found it 'broadly supportive' but 'particularly anxious that the consultation process should be full and thorough'. Locke subsequently observed rather bleakly to the Board that 'The desirability of a united front between all interested parties in these difficult times of uncertainty and change is self-evident. This presents us with an exceptionally difficult six months.'[41] As though to confirm the diagnosis, archbishop Carey visited the offices of 1 Millbank solicitously.

Time mattered. That the Commissioners should try to submit a report on pensions to Synod in July seemed to Locke 'highly desirable'. But then how could they put together something comprehensive and detailed and discuss it fully with forty-three dioceses in such a time? Better, then, to stick for now to 'core principles' rather than details. By now those principles were distinct: pensions contributions for future service liability would come from the parishes and be legally charged on the diocesan stipends funds; transitional provisions for perhaps ten years would phase them in; the Commissioners would confirm that they would pay their existing legal responsibilities for past service

[40] Ibid. pp. 1–4.
[41] Colman note, 'Pensions: next round of consultations', CC (95) 3/GP (95) 3, Board papers, 26 Jan. 1995, ser. 95083/70.

pensions liability, combined with a 'moral sponsorship' – a nice phrase coined by Gracey – for the discretionary liability for pension increments on that past service liability; new legislation would be framed to give the Commissioners power to use capital for pensions.[42] For the next three years the Commissioners planned to survive by a combination of accumulated reserves, gilt management and the cutting of costs. The new round of cuts for the next year, 1996, would now amount to £10 million.

At the Assets Committee it could be seen that the Commissioners' net income in 1994 had been £5.1 million over budget (£136.4 million). This was because of additional income from gilt management designed to increase the reserves carried forward into 1995. Meanwhile, it turned out that total expenditure had been £2.2 million less than budgeted (and so, £148.1 million), in part because the ordination of women had provoked fewer early retirements than expected. But lest this foster quiet hopes, the future was still precarious. Already 274 priests had notified the Church that they would resign because of Synod's eventual decision that women should be ordained, a figure that was expected to peak at 350. It would cost the Church Commissioners £4 million. It was now possible to predict that by 1996 the Commissioners would be matching income and expenditure more or less exactly. This left precious little margin for error or unforeseen circumstance.[43]

The cuts went on. Efforts were made to shelter the poorer cathedrals from the worst of them and to end grants to wealthier cathedrals completely. Here, too, the Commissioners were constrained. To cut Section 31 grants still further might undermine the cathedrals' own responsibilities under the recommendations of the recent Cathedrals Commission to appoint lay administrators, quite apart from the Commissioners' own statutory obligations to support a dean or provost and two canons. The cathedrals had argued that if the Commissioners' obligations to the bishops had been 'ring-fenced', their responsibilities to the cathedrals themselves should be treated in the same way. The Commissioners admitted some correspondence between these two spheres and soon conceded. But they also observed that this begged many other questions of 'balance', none of them straightforward.

Now a little group had gathered around the deans of York and Wells and the provost of Chelmsford. The cathedrals, they insisted, could not easily pass on any cuts in their allocations. A 'significant number' already carried budget deficits. Their congregations already paid a diocesan quota, and could not easily accept a second burden.

---

42 Ibid. 1.
43 Farrell note, 'CSA structures of support 1996', CSA (95) 2, ibid.

Section 31 grants were for many parish church cathedrals their largest source of income. They reminded the Commissioners that they, like the bishops, had produced the Commissioners' historic endowments. That said, a bundle of proposals to cut various grants, but modestly, was taken back to a conference of deans and provosts and accepted there.[44]

The age of the dreadnoughts was all but concluded. In February 1995 the MetroCentre went onto the market to be greeted by more than forty enquiries on the very first day. On 16 February 1995 the Assets Committee agreed to recommend the sale of the Commissioners' 50 per cent share in St Enoch's as soon as contracts were exchanged on the MetroCentre. By April the Marlowes Centre in Hemel Hempstead had been sold for £45 million.

The Social Security Committee reports

Many in the Church of England had seen the interest taken in its affairs by the parliamentary committee as an intrusion. However, the upshot was a thorough and cogent analysis of the Commissioners' recent history, and few now could deny that it had been valuable. The verdict was sharp. The committee complained of 'a certain degree of complacency about the loss of up to £800 million of the Commissioners' capital base', a complacency made all the more astonishing by a heavy succession of other sins. For they had 'failed to comply with normal accounting practices that are a legal requirement in the commercial world, thereby creating a misleading impression of the Church's finances'; they had created and substantially financed development companies 'without due diligence'; they had 'foolishly speculated' without proper expertise and with borrowed money; they had 'irreparably damaged' the Church's incomes and jeopardised its future; they had misled in their annual reports; they had failed to take steps to meet the increased pensions burden; and, finally, 'in all likelihood done more than any other single act to destroy the parish system of the national church'. The committee saw with concern that there was no evidence of a formal decision by the Assets Committee to invest so heavily in property, finding that the real power lay with the First Church Estates Commissioner and the secretary. If the law had not been compromised, ethics had been. The report concluded with a call for 'a new parliamentary mandate', the creation of a specific pensions fund and the establishment of a single executive Board. If there were to be reforms they should be pursued not as a measure but

[44] Hopgood note, 'Support for cathedrals in 1996 and beyond', CC (95) 1/GP (95) 1, ibid. The deans of York and Wells were Raymond Furnell and Richard Lewis. The provost of Chelmsford was John Moses.

as an act in parliament. It was this last argument that signalled not simply a reflection on the Commissioners' affairs but a new proposal for the Church to consider.[45]

The House of Commons turned to this on 11 May. Field knew that people in the Church were complaining that his committee was over-reaching itself in examining these matters. But he would make clear why the committee was concerned, and, furthermore, affirm the right which any committee of the house possessed to 'set its own agenda'. This was, he pronounced, a dark tale, but it had its heroes. One was John Plender, the journalist on the *Financial Times*. Another was the archbishop of Canterbury, who had taken blame where he was blameless and who was determined to expose the old, secret *mores* of the Church Commissioners to the light of public scrutiny. He was a leader who would see the Church through this crisis. Then there was Sir Michael Colman whose honesty had won over the parliamentary committee. Field repeated the committee's conviction that change within the Church should now be by act, not measure, for the latter gave parliament the power only to approve or reject, not to amend. He recalled that the measure to ordain women had been saddled with the proviso that clergy who would not accept it must be compensated. Many MPs had wanted the first, but not the second.

The Second Church Estates Commissioner, Michael Alison, replied that the committee had produced 'a veritable encyclopaedia' of a report, which was 'timely', 'relevant', 'a splendid job'. If the committee had been 'trenchant and unsparing' they had also been 'positive and constructive'. But rather than engage too deeply in the general post-mortem, he merely observed that 'there are many different ways of looking at the figures' and he proceeded at once to the question which now stood before them: the future of pensions in the Church. As for the committee's recommendation that there be a bill, this he could not encourage. The historic resources of the Church came, in the main, not from the crown but the Church itself. Synod would see a bill as a deprivation of their right to their own 'parallel and proper' voice within the 1919 settlement. Furthermore, it would be contentious.

There followed a dutiful speech from the under-secretary of state for the Home Office, Nicholas Baker, outlining the government's position. The essential point was clear. The House was too busy with its other affairs to deal with 'the details of Church Measures'. The government, moreover, was strictly neutral in such matters as these. One of Field's colleagues on the committee, Bernard Jenkin, bridled at this. Accountability to parliament had broken down: the Church Commissioners had 'rather forfeited Parliament's trust'. Baker would

[45] *House of Commons Social Security Committee report*, 12 Jan. 1995, pp. v-xxxvi. The report was released on 20 Apr. 1995.

not be moved. What mistakes had been made by the Church had been acknowledged and were being made good. They would not wish to venture into some greater legislative enterprise, something which might even lead to a review of the status of all exempted charities. Any future pensions legislation must naturally conform to the requirements of current legislation. At all events, the Church of England faced 'a formidable challenge' and the government, for its part, wished it well. The speech was a model of kindness and detachment.

This drew the ire of another Labour MP, Alun Michael. He found the minister's response 'lightweight and dismissive of Government responsibility' when it was remembered that the 'catastrophe' which had occasioned the committee's enquiry had imperilled not only the parish work of the Church of England but the 'health of communities'. This was something more than 'just ecclesiastical business', and if it was not a party matter it was still right for the opposition to see that government ministers understood their responsibilities as they should. The bishop of Bradford had been heard to remark that given an opportunity to discuss the Church's affairs the House of Commons might simply commit all its energies to 'justified but repetitious criticism'. Yet Michael himself saw that there was 'a keen interest' in these matters in the House and that parliament needed to be reassured. He agreed with the committee: a new pensions policy for the Church should be brought forward not as a measure but as a bill. Baker intervened but was rather brutally crushed; a few members began to launch their own interruptions. The Speaker had to call them all to order.

The House of Commons appeared to welcome this debate and, in turn, debated it well. There was even a lively, and often sympathetic, cross-bench culture. Alison was warmly praised for his work for them all. What emerged distinctly was a commitment to the poorer dioceses and parishes of the Church and a still clearer belief that the pensions of the Church should be changed by bill. Bernard Jenkin remarked that if important matters simply went through 'on the nod', people would ask why they should have an established Church at all?[46]

The swinging of the scythe and a new wind

From the *minutiae* of discussion, Locke saw a new tension emerging: they must, if they could, make the cut in their support for stipends in 1997 the last. Thereafter their support should be stable at around £18 million a year. What was viable politically still committed the Commissioners to a higher level of distribution than the actuaries

---

[46] *Hansard*, Debates of the House of Commons, 11 May 1995, cols 910–61.

recommended. Their own financial stability must be delayed accordingly.

A further national conference of diocesan secretaries followed at the end of April. Now the diocesan chairmen and secretaries were won over, 'virtually unanimous', to the core principles of the new pensions programme.[47] The path was clear to Synod. By 17 May Locke had prepared a draft report on pensions, to be proposed at Synod on behalf of the Commissioners, the Pensions Board, the Central Board of Finance after consultation with the diocesan secretaries and chairmen and with the endorsement of the House of Bishops; a weighty conglomeration, not an easy one to line up, but one ordered with some precision in an intricate timetable.

Now it was the turn of the bishops to face the Commissioners' scythe. A report offered to the Board by an 'activity-based review group' on episcopal administration became the new basis of the Church Commissioners' understanding of bishops. It was seen that a significant amount of money could be saved by simply revising existing book-keeping arrangements. Then before the eyes of the Commissioners' staff came more than 104 cars in the episcopal fleet. Here, too, modest, sensible measures might save them almost £12,000 a year. It was not a heroic sum. Once the Church Commissioners would barely have noticed it. On it went.[48]

The world in which these hectic, internal revisions were taking place was indeed changing. The agricultural sphere, so battered by adversity, so vulnerable to the disparagements of the worldly, had not been deserted and now it brought quiet reassurance. The income from farms was now seen to be 'buoyant', while as regards arable farming there was confidence in the air. The Common Agricultural Policy had been reformed. The milk market had been deregulated and dairy farmers had profited from higher prices. Potatoes, it was whispered, had 'advanced strongly'. The land market itself had picked up – there was even talk of a 'boom' – and prices had returned to the levels of 1989, or even of 1982. Even so, sales of church land would continue: £137.5 million might be realised from them over ten years, and it was not difficult to see why: the sale of Winnall Down farm in Winchester alone had realised £2,100,000.[49] In the sphere of development, the pattern was still rather haphazard, but 1994 could now be seen to present a 'strong and heartening performance'. At Bowdon, in Chester, the sale of three lots raised £2.9 million; Little Stanney in the same

[47] Locke note, 'Funding pensions', CC (95) 38, Board papers, 24 May 1995, ser. 95083/71.
[48] Report of the activity-based review group on episcopal administration, CC (95) 36, Board papers, 16 May 1995, ibid.
[49] Annual report on investments to 31 Dec. 1994, section II, ibid.

estate was bringing in £7.65 million in the first stage of development, and another £8.5 million should accrue in 1996 or 1997. In the residential portfolio there were sales; in Maida Vale they went on as intended in 1981, and there were 'opportunistic' sales of freehold in Chelsea, Kensington, Hampstead and Westminster, long leasehold sales at Hyde Park. The Octavia Hill estates were not in danger, 'for so long as they continue to perform well in financial terms but also on the grounds that they provide a valuable source of much-needed affordable rented accommodation in inner London'.[50] So many of these matters rested on the unaccountable ways of the world.

A brief distraction occurred, and a significant one. The Commissioners found themselves taken to court over the ordination of women. Paul Williamson, an Anglican priest, argued that they had no legal powers to fund women clergy. In this, if there were any danger, the Commissioners were saved by nothing less than the establishment of the Church of England itself. The judge presiding found that the legislative sanction of the state was in such questions decisive, and the ordination of women had been sanctioned thus. Few critics of the establishment evidently observed the development, or saw in it anything to influence them.[51]

In July 1995 Synod approved the five principles on pensions. It was hoped that legislation would be introduced by February 1996, and the new arrangements take effect in 1998. It was crucial, Hopgood remarked, that they now maintain momentum. There must be partnership, flexibility and 'an immense task of communicating'. A news sheet for wide distribution was published: *Supporting the ministry: sharing the cost.* 'Why', it asked 'should parishioners contribute towards pensions?' (Because they already paid for stipends and pensions were simply 'deferred pay').[52] In July, too, contracts for the MetroCentre were exchanged at £324 million. Towards the end of the year, on 21 November, the sale of the Commissioners' share in St Enoch's was completed, realising £80 million. In the same month Daws presented to the Board a picture of the long-term financial outlook, revising that covering the next twenty years prepared by Watson's. Now there was firm evidence of improvement: 'While the present figures still show a gap to be bridged between the totality of the commitments and the money available from the investments, this gap is now relatively modest within the overall picture.' Measuring these realities with the guidance of respected institutions did not always bring guarantees of certainty – or even respectability. In October the Commissioners had

[50] Ibid. section III.
[51] See official solicitor note, 'Turnbull Commission', CC (95) 9, ibid. pt 70.
[52] Hopgood, pensions progress, '*Supporting the ministry: sharing the cost*', CC (95) 52, Board papers, 27 Sept. 1995, ibid. pt 72.

appointed Binder Hamlyn as their auditors. Two months later the High Court ruled that that firm must pay up to £100 million damages because of information it had given during a takeover.[53]

Continuity under pressure

Given that the Church Commissioners had always worried about the press, it was inevitable that the crisis would attract great attention from that quarter, and that an element of defensiveness at 1 Millbank would now provoke an increase in the work of those who monitored the Commissioners' relationship with the world beyond their doors. At the onset on the new year it was seen that in 1995 the Commissioners had received more than 200 press enquiries and issued twenty-one press releases. Meanwhile, the Second Commissioner had answered forty-six questions in the House of Commons and the First and Third Commissioners exactly half that number in Synod.[54]

The Board could now take stock of another hectic year. Once again there was encouragement in what they read. The Stock Exchange annual report for 1995 showed a year of 'strong growth in the asset bases, substantial increases in equity income and the successful re-investment of cash generated from sales of property, particularly in the final quarter from the sale of the MetroCentre'. Two new groups had been set up, on securities and on ethical investment. Meanwhile, the Commissioners' agents were working harder than once they had, not least against each other. The management of the Hyde Park and Maida Vale commercial properties passed from Cluttons to Chestertons.[55]

As for the cathedrals, the grants given under Section 31 of the 1963 Cathedrals Measure had not increased since 1991. In 1995 they amounted to £3.1 million, out of a total given to cathedrals of £5.5 million in that year. Since 1983 the cathedrals had been divided into three groups, judged by their level of dependence on Section 31 grants and the level of their own income from property investments. The wealthiest group received nothing; the other two shared in a ratio of 2:1. The deans and provosts were ready to play their part, but did not want to be hurt more than the bishops or the dioceses. The cathedrals enjoyed the benefits of tourism, but they were under more pressure than ever to preserve their fabric to a high standard. At a Board meeting in May 1996, some governors even asked if it was any longer appropriate for the Commissioners to be supporting the cathedrals at

[53] Hopgood note, 'Nov. 1995 diocesan conference: long range financial outlook', CSA (95) 10, p. 1, ibid. pt 73.
[54] '1995 news brief. Annual summary', Board papers, 25 Jan. 1996, ibid, pt 74.
[55] Stock Exchange annual report to 31 Dec. 1995, A (96) 51, Board papers, 30 May 1995, ibid. pt 75.

all. Were they 'over-protecting' their staffing levels? But the cathedrals had their advocates on the Board too.[56]

In this new climate the Commissioners' were viewing their assets with sharper eyes. At Auckland Castle there was a unique collection of paintings by the Spanish painter Zurbaran, valued at £1.8 million. Legally these belonged to the Commissioners themselves. If the Zurbarans were sold, might the proceeds endow a new trust to run the state rooms at the castle? When the paintings were valued again, this time at £4 million, speculation mounted. When somebody remarked that without the paintings the long dining room at the castle would look threadbare it was suggested that works by local artists might be displayed instead. People, evidently, wanted to see the pictures of the bishops there more than the Zurbarans after all. This might have suggested something about who was being let in.[57]

Meanwhile, in September 1995, the Board of governors approved the acquisition of a new see house for London. The new bishop, Richard Chartres, had a large, young family. Cowley Street would not do at all. This time there was a solution. A leasehold interest was acquired in the Old Deanery of St Paul's Cathedral, a seventeenth-century building, though not a deanery since 1978. It was now vacant. In January 1996 the Board agreed, in principle, that the Old Deanery should replace 8 Barton Street as the London see house. The dean and chapter supported the idea in principle, but when Cluttons approached them on behalf of the Commissioners they found them unwilling to sell. The intricacies attached to ownership of the property were labrynthine: there was a headlease, an underlease, even a sub-underlease. Eventually they yielded a result of proportions: the dean and chapter would own the property, the Local Authorities Mutual Investment Trust would hold the headlease and the Commissioners would became the underlessees.[58] This, the committee determined, would be the see house for the bishops of London for the foreseeable future. In 1997 an offer of £1.57 million was made for the house at Barton Street, almost double its valuation.

[56] Board minutes, 30 May 1996, pp. 6–7.
[57] HC report, 'Auckland Castle', CC (95) 45, Board papers, 27 July 1995, ser. 95083/72.
[58] Board minutes, 25 Jan. 1996, pp. 5–6.

16

The Commissioners and the Commission

While the busy work of reform continued at 1 Millbank everybody there knew that the very ground on which the Church Commissioners stood was about to change. The Church itself was to be reformed. This introduced a new climate of doubt into the conversations, routines and decisions of the Commissioners. People constantly murmured to each other that whatever they did now might be overtaken by events determined by other powers. Increasingly people spoke uncertainly of a coming force in the Church, the new archbishops' commission.

In the eyes of Fisher and the men of 1948 the new Church Commissioners had been the driving force of a new model Church of England. In 1993 it was widely judged across the Church that it had broken down. The Lambeth Group had worked hard to mend it. But for some it could not be enough. There was a movement that favoured complete change; the Commissioners as a decision-making and executive body should be replaced. It was widely held that the institutional arrangements which governed the Church of England lacked coherence, unity, direction. There must be a reckoning, and it must be a bold one.

The new archbishops' commission was appointed to 'review the central policy-making and resource direction machinery of the Church of England'. At its head was the bishop of Rochester, Michael Turnbull. Some suspected that the enterprise smacked too much of a contemporary fascination with management which appeared to hold many of the bishop's generation in thrall. Of this there had already been a warning. In 1993 the Archbishops' Commission on Cathedrals had spoken of the college of canons as a managerial board, and of the bishop as the *ex officio* chairman of that board.[1] Evidently, these new *mores* tended to polarise opinion rather sharply. Some thought them suitable, clever and persuasive, for they reacted against years of

---

[1] *Heritage and renewal: the report of the Archbishops' Commission on Cathedrals*, London 1994.

complacency and vagary and made, in their way, their own appeal to modern society. Others furrowed brows, hurled back angry retorts and quite often, in various ways, simply blew up with rage at the sheer inappropriateness of this new 'managerialism'.

If this was indeed so, Turnbull himself was an imperturbable, implacable presence. He looked very like a force for management. The task which he faced was no simple one. The corridors of Anglican power were crammed with people who argued that change must come. But they did not know what form it should take. The Church Commissioners, too, welcomed the new commission a little more vociferously than was quite necessary, for fear that they might be suspected of sullen disinclination. If Turnbull viewed the Commissioners as one of the vested interests that he must challenge, the officers of 1 Millbank were unlikely to mistake him for a sympathetic ally. They knew at once what was at stake. If this commission was here to take away their powers, which powers would go, and how many?

The Turnbull Commission was invited openly, insistently even, to be 'radical'. Once it began to meet, its members – a fair spread, including Colman and Gracey – agreed that they were even prepared to be 'very radical'.[2] Supported by a group of assessors (including the dutiful but unhappy Locke), a secretariat and what had become a customary attachment to all such endeavours, a theological adviser, they set to work with a will. It was just and necessary that the commission should embrace the leading lights of all the church bodies which must, after all, be affected by their recommendations. But the psychology of the whole enterprise must surely have been a curious one, not least for the First Church Estates Commissioner, who was bound to two bodies, one of which could be said to have active designs on the other. As a member of the archbishops' commission he must observe the confidentiality of its deliberations. He must keep what was said from the very institution which he was supposed to lead. Nobody could pretend that this was not an exceedingly delicate, even faintly ridiculous, business.

The commission now requested from the Church Commissioners a statement of their role in the life of the Church of England. This was natural, and quite without critical implication. It was what every such commission would do. But it was also an inescapable fact that this new commission had arisen in the context of a crisis which was seen to be of the Commissioners' making, and it was unavoidable that such a request would earn not simply a memorandum of self-explanation but one which merged, almost imperceptibly, into self-justification. It was

<hr />

[2] *Working as one body: the report of the Archbishops' Commission on the Organization of the Church of England*, London 1995, pp. ix–x.

necessary to show not merely what the Commissioners did, but how well they did it. If there was, as usual in the air at 1 Millbank, the anxious sense that the work of the Commissioners was poorly valued, even when it was understood, that anxiety was sure to sharpen. They began to worry not simply about what they should say, but how much they should say. Too many pages may appear too strenuous or overbearing; too few disdainful or peevish. Was there even a shade of ambivalence about the invitation itself? Already it appeared that the commission wished to mark a critical distance between its own, emerging thoughts and the world of self-understandings which defined the work of the Church Commissioners.

In April 1994 Colman sent out to the governors a note of the briefing material which the staff at Millbank had drafted for the commission. It was, broadly, an historical survey which ended with the mission statement which the Board had approved only the month before. But now Colman found himself asking the governors frankly if the development of the Commissioners' function over the last fifty years fell within the scope of the mission statement which was offered as its conclusion? Was each function part of their historic trust of providing financial assistance in parishes where need was greatest? Should some of these things be done by the dioceses? In the meantime, the draft did not lack a critical thrust:

> Through spreading funds over all clergy (particularly through pensions) whilst retaining a (consequently) limited ability to focus funds strategically on poor clergy and on mission areas (e.g. the unchurched etc.), it is arguable, in political terms, that the Commissioners turned from a reforming charity into an agency which offered universal benefits to parishes and clergy (through flat rate allocations and pensions), whilst still seeking to retain their original historic functions.[3]

This the Board welcomed. But the various departments of the Commissioners' life and work continued to fidget uncertainly. Locke himself could not think that the commission would want a 'bulky "apologia"' from them. On the General Purposes Committee members felt that any material sent to the commission should be less modest about their strengths and achievements, for they remained a real pressure for 'radical reform', within the Commission and without.[4]

---

[3] Colman note, 'Rochester Commission', CC (94) 29, p. 3, Board papers, 28 Apr. 1994, ser. 95083/68.
[4] Exchange between Locke, Lewis and Jones, CC (95) 9, Board papers, 23 Feb. 1995, ibid. pt 70.

For some time little appeared to happen. Michael Turnbull became bishop of Durham, a move that was seen to confirm his standing in the Church and to lend further weight to his activities. By now some of the Commissioners may well have felt that they had lost the thread altogether. On 26 January 1995 Provost Moses asked to be reminded what actually had been sent to the commission on the Commissioners' behalf. Another member of the Board, Stephen Lowe, archdeacon of Sheffield, was a member of the archbishops' commission. The House of Bishops, replied Lowe, had been sounded out by the commission earlier that month, and it had been agreed that the governors of the Church Commissioners should now be formally approached. If this seemed an indirect manner of proceeding, to say the least, Lowe said that he hoped for as much openness as a proper balance between consultation and confidentiality might allow.[5] Nobody asked whether members of the Board were bound by the same rules of confidentiality as were, evidently, members of the commission.

Bishop Waine then had a few words with Bishop Turnbull. Locke reported this to the Board; his note indicates tension. Turnbull and those of his colleagues who sat both on the commission and on the Commissioners were invited to 1 Millbank simply to share 'common perceptions as to the distinctive nature of the Commissioners' responsibilities'. There was now a note from the Commissioners' official solicitor on the establishment of the Church and a second on the Commissioners' 'trusts', making quite clear how firmly the two were related. The latter described what must happen if Synod passed a measure altering the purposes for which the Commissioners' income was to be applied, but without the approval of the Commissioners themselves.[6] What these memoranda also showed was how utterly in the dark the Church Commissioners were. They hardly knew what to say, how to say it and when to do so.

When Turnbull met the Board of governors on 8 March 1995 it was at a closed, private meeting. The minutes which were taken were circulated only within the Board itself. In these new days it was quite unthinkable that Carey should take the chair, whatever the statutes might say. He had become a power to mediate between interests, and if he was connected to any of them it was certainly not to the Church Commissioners. Waine again took the chair and Turnbull read from a prepared statement. He was, he said, grateful for the privacy of the occasion. Neither he, nor for that matter Colman, Gracey or Lowe, could be drawn on any provisional conclusions which the commission 'might have' so far reached. 'May I', he went on unsparingly, 'remind

[5] Locke note, 'Turnbull Commission: clergy pensions policy', Board papers, 28 July 1994, with GPC minutes, 14 July 1994, ibid. pt 68.
[6] Board minutes, 26 Jan. 1995, pp. 7–8.

you of the trigger which caused the archbishops of Canterbury and York to establish this Commission.' It had been one of the final recommendations of the Lambeth Report that a review should take place. The standing committee of Synod had said that such a review required 'special machinery', and that the commission answered to that. 'This really is', said Turnbull, 'a very large task.' They might look at the Commissioners, the Pensions Board, the Central Board of Finance, the General Synod, the offices of the archbishops themselves, the relationships between central and diocesan and parish institutions. It was now that Turnbull said something profoundly significant: 'I have to tell you that the archbishops have strongly urged us to be willing to be radical in our approach, and I am sure they are wise in that.' For firm opinions, once declared, were often watered down, but were never made 'more radical'. This quiet rejoinder indicated not only the foundation of this new enterprise, but the mentality which would define the conduct of its proponents. They pronounced a wish for consultation, but they feared its effects.

For now, the bishop found it sufficient to observe that the commission looked for coherence, a point at which the various strands were drawn together, and this meant 'a focus at the centre which is now lacking': 'we simply must not allow the situation to recur where decisions are made in one part of the structure which have financial consequences which are borne by other parts of the structures'. If it was determined to be radical, Turnbull continued, the commission was not iconoclastic. The Church of England was episcopal and synodical, and that already gave it 'a distinctive pattern of dispersed authority'. There was delicacy to be seen in this, and it should be cherished. When they now looked at each administrative function, they asked if it should be carried out centrally or locally? What, he asked, was truly 'essential and indispensable' in the centre? What did the Board believe to be essential and indispensable in what they did? For his part he could not answer questions about the work of the commission itself, but he deprecated any notion that the commission had 'an agenda of its own'. It had been formed by the archbishops and would submit its recommendations to all the institutions of the Church. 'If what we recommend to them is impractical or so controversial that it cannot realistically be implemented, we shall not have served them well.'

It was time for questions, and many of the Commissioners seized their opportunity. Moses insisted upon the need for consultation and emphasised that the models of theology and management to which the commission was working would be 'crucial', something that was endorsed by Ben Lewers, the provost of Derby. The endowments of the Church were held as trusts and could not simply be redeployed. Archdeacon Austin remarked sagely that the archbishops' commission should say what it thought, and not parade proposals with an eye to what they might become after a watering down. The money which the Commissioners held did not actually belong to Synod. Michael Alison said that parliament had a commitment to bear the 'negligible' demands made on it by the Church, but any talk of disestablishment would disturb this. There would surely be complications if there were calls for disendowment and claimants to the assets. Alan Chesters, the bishop of Blackburn, feared that the Commissioners had become a soft target, a scapegoat. This was not enough: an alternative must be seen to be better. The Commissioners, for their part, worked with some independence from church politics; they should not be replaced by 'politicking at the centre'. Moreover, the Commissioners' work was biased towards the poor. Would a new structure also ensure this? But if these were defensive voices, another Board member, Mrs Granger was evidently prepared to dismantle the Church Commissioners herself; they need not, she said, be preserved 'at all'. Smallwood agreed with Granger: what the Commissioners did could be done 'fully and expertly' by General Synod and the Central Board of Finance. Millbank could be placed in the service of a body established under Synod and so integrated into the life of the Church. David Lunn, the bishop of Sheffield, was another internal critic. He remarked that there was another side to the question of the establishment, and that it was hardly surprising that the Commissioners, who were something of an 'Erastian quango' should favour it. (But he added that, come to that, he did not much like congregational churches either.) Stanley thought the parochial clergy 'deeply appreciative of the Commissioners'. For all of this the bishop of Durham said that he was duly thankful.[7]

Another silence fell. On 19 September there came a further note from Patrick Locke. The Turnbull report would be published on 20 September.

Working as one body

The archbishops' commission had certainly felt under a weighty obligation to show the courage of its emerging convictions. It must somehow draw a world of regrets, complaints and frustrations into a new formula. This must involve a scheme which could balance successfully those most delicate and sensitive arts of power and authority, accountability and representation, centralisation and devolution. The commission was fully aware of the tenacity of at least some vested interests and did not fear to cross them. *Working as one body* was an attempt at revolution by commission, a sharp, determined,

[7] Record of discussion, 8 Mar. 1995, CC (95) third meeting: Turnbull Commission, Board papers, 23 Mar. 1995, ser. 95083/70.

rather waspish production. It would capitalise powerfully on the age of doubt and the demoralisation of the old, sagging authorities to frame that new future. It sought a Church of England cleared of institutional ambiguity and confusion and free to pursue a new, bold path of mission. Its vision was almost completely uninformed by historical perspectives; it evidently found it had nothing to learn from the experiences of other Churches. A transformation far greater than anything envisaged in the painstaking union of the Queen Anne's Bounty and the Ecclesiastical Commissioners almost fifty years before had been now crammed into no more than fifteen meetings and 151 pages. The text of the report itself was neatly drawn around the commission's essential concerns: a loose theological preamble about the gifts of God; a section on the mission of the Church; a third on 'why we must work as one body'; the 'basis' of the proposals and then the new model: a central council for the Church of England. This then introduced the old bodies within a new framework: the General Synod, the House of Bishops and the archbishops, the Church Commissioners, the Pensions Board and the dioceses.

The commission disavowed centralisation. It observed that the powers in the ascendant in the Church of England were the dioceses and the parishes: a new view of these too might be necessary, to assess how they might best be orchestrated. Indeed, the diocese was claimed as 'the fundamental unit of the church' (p. 50). But the simple truth within this ecclesial guise was more prosaic: 'the Church needs to sort out it finances'. Historic resources were of diminishing importance. The purpose and character of its fundamental proposal – for a new, national Archbishops' Council, a body of seventeen members – was amply endowed with weighty nouns: it would build on 'the distinctive Anglican ecclesiology of the Bishop-in-Synod' and would enhance both synodical and episcopal government; it would yield 'a stronger sense of corporate responsibility for its mission and wellbeing' and provide a 'forum' for those who led the other institutions, providing consistency and coherence; it would be a 'focus', a body capable of 'strategic thinking and planning'; it would ensure 'transparency' and 'efficiency'. It would be chaired by the archbishop of Canterbury with the archbishop of York as vice-chairman. 'Most of the existing central bodies would disappear or be overseen by the National Council.' As for the Church Commissioners, they would be 'restructured' but would remain 'managers and trustees of the central historic assets of the Church'. On the council there would be four part-time executive chairmen responsible for 'human resources', 'mission resources', 'heritage and legal services' and finance; they would need imagination, commitment and management and presentational skills; indeed, it was owned generously, that they might well look for the attributes found in a First Church Estates Commissioner. This would be a body corporate and a charity. As for its authority, that would 'derive from its effectiveness in undertaking the work entrusted to it'. There would be a 'network' of 'accountabilities and checks and balances'.

Let it be noted that the commission had thought of abolishing the Church Commissioners. But they saw that it could not be right to 'erode' or 'disperse' the central historic assets of the Church. They respected the judgement of history – without, it seemed, a smile. As a link between Church and State, too, the Commissioners were still to be valued. But in the past the Commissioners had only been able to respond 'piecemeal to unconnected demands'. Now, these would be mediated by the new council. Charged with the maintenance of the capital assets of the Church, the Commissioners would be unable to distribute as grandly as once they had.

It was impossible to be coy about the force of this, even if the commission had been so inclined. The Church Commissioners stood to lose most of their functions; their composition would be changed 'totally'; their staff merged into the new national office. 'Nevertheless', the commission insisted, 'we believe that a radical refocusing on the Church Commissioners' core function would restore them to their appropriate place in the central structures of the Church'. If the Commissioners would remain responsible for the management of assets, by moving the power of allocations out of the hands of Church Commissioners those allocations would be placed more explicitly in a greater scale of things, in the hands of mission, just as pastoral casework could be attached, on the level of details, more clearly to policy. The statutes which bound the Commissioners would bind the council. Each year the Commissioners would require from the council a certificate to show that whatever income had been made available to the council had been spent in line with the Commissioners' own trusts and commitments.

Quite apart from the arguable sense of the old constitution, which might well appear archaic, dusty and even improbable, it was natural to argue that if the Church Commissioners did less, there should be fewer of them. *Working as one body* proposed a reduction from 95 to 15: to two Church Estates Commissioners, three crown appointments, the two archbishops, two bishops elected from the House of Bishops, a dean or provost, two clergy elected by the House of Clergy and two lay members elected by the House of Laity of the General Synod. There would be no separate Board of governors. There would be no Third Church Estates Commissioner. The Commissioners would have power over the Assets Committee: 'What is important is to protect the body managing the assets from undue pressure to over-distribute.' There would be an Audit Committee. All this would be established not by bill, but by measure.[8]

At once a cacophony of debate broke out across the institutions of the Church of England.

The response of the Church Commissioners

At 1 Millbank it was time now to think what kind of consultation should follow on this. The archbishop had 'made space in his diary' to hear the views of the General Purposes Committee of the Church Commissioners on 13 October.[9] Synod would debate it in November. Meanwhile, Patrick Locke and his senior colleagues were preparing a 'note of comment' for the committee and for the Board to identify parts of specific relevance to the work of the Commissioners themselves.

Some thought this gave the General Purposes Committee too much of a presence. But, Locke replied, it was a statutory committee, much of what the commission might debate involved it directly, and it could speak without prejudice to the views of the Board. There were worries, too, about the staff, who had reason to be anxious and who did not wish simply to be managed without having any voice of their own. The Board purposefully set down a minute to affirm that as good employers they would respect their obligations to their employees.

Locke's initial note of comment was not short. It would become the basis of the Commissioners' position, and it would define that position as both a defence of the institution itself and an intricate critique of the commission's proposal. Locke was not convinced by the commission. He recognised that there was a need for greater co-ordination between bodies, though he thought the commission's charge of overlapping responsibilities overdone. The report had entirely overlooked the existence of earlier co-ordinating structures: the Archbishops' Advisers on Needs and Resources, the Joint Liaison Committee and the Ministry Co-ordinating Group. When it came to the construction of a national council, Locke and his collaborators became a good deal sharper. They did indeed assume that the Commissioners would support the premise that there was a need for greater co-ordination at the centre. Let it be clear that the Commissioners certainly would work constructively with a new national council. But they could not but express concern at the concentration of power in the hands of this council and its officials. Synod may fear it; the dioceses and the parishes may well fear it.

[8] Working as one body, particularly pp. 81–95 and summary at pp. 118–25.
[9] Locke note, 'The Turnbull Report', CC (95) 49, Board papers, 22 Sept. 1995, ser. 95083/71.

When the work of the Church Commissioners was discussed in the report Locke and his colleagues found that it concentrated on their financial assets and provisions, but not at all on their work in pastoral reorganisation. Nor did the report reckon with their ability to weigh carefully conflicting demands from archbishops, bishops in general, synod and dioceses. It did not see how closely the Commissioners were connected to the dioceses, through the CSA conferences, consultative groups and their own membership. Indeed, Locke remarked, 'The Report does not, however, provide any *structural* reason as to why the Commissioners' trusts would be better protected' by a council than they already were by the Commissioners' own Board. To divide these two functions – the acquiring and the spending of funds – between two different sets of trustees looked unusual, if not altogether unique in the world of charities. The talk of a certificate to assure the Commissioners that the money was being spent in accordance with their trusts was no guarantee that they would be, for the council had the power of distribution. Two bodies would surely complicate decision-making processes. The Commissioners might even find themselves under more pressure to make money available than they already were. Then, what would parliament, to which the Church Commissioners were accountable, make of this? If there should be fewer Commissioners, as few as fifteen – a number that must be subject to approval of the state – this would dispatch most diocesan bishops and all officers of the state. Nobody, it seemed, would answer questions for them in the House of Commons.

The cumulative weight behind Locke's criticism was that this campaign to change what already existed was simply hollow. There might be virtues in a 'plan-led' system when it came to the administration of the Pastoral Measure, but this would leave the dioceses trying to reorganise what they already did simply in order to fit in with a national policy framework. This must actually weaken the dioceses in exactly those local matters where there were sensitivities and strong feelings. Indeed, as far as many of the functions held by the Commissioners were concerned, the report offered no clear reason why they should be passed to the council, beyond the idea that it 'could and should' do them. The Redundant Churches Committee would still exist, but it would now be co-ordinated by a new body, the Church Heritage Board which, in turn, found itself part of 'Heritage and Legal Services'. It was not clear that a new body would help at all. The commission seemed to underestimate the value of the Commissioners' 'dual accountability' to Church and State in operating the Pastoral Measure, something which Locke believed helped the Commissioners to 'hold the ring' between the Church and the government, local planners, local communities and conservationists.

The report suggested that all these changes could bring savings of between £0.75 million and £1 million a year, but it was not clear how these sums were arrived at. More, there was no attempt to 'cost' ministry planning and standards, financial strategy and communications, the new bodies (such as the Mission Resources Committee and the Church Heritage Board) or the four new executive chairmanships. The report hoped to save money by putting all the staff in one building – Millbank, Church House or somewhere else. But then a little later, it had talked of relocating some staff outside London altogether.

And there would be a veritable world of legislation to unravel: early forays had already established that there were 'several hundred' sections embedded in existing legislation which must be resolved. It appeared that not even all the comments made to the commission by the Church Commissioners' own official solicitor had been considered.[10]

With this in the air, most of the General Purposes Committee turned to Lambeth for their meeting with the archbishop of Canterbury. The Commissioners, said Bishop Waine, wanted to be constructive. The commission had faced a huge task and completed it in short order; it was quite understood that it had not been able to consider fully the details of its own proposals. It was something of a Green Paper which needed to become a White Paper. For their part the Commissioners must ensure that the charitable trusts and responsibilities which remained in their hands would be effectively discharged and those which were 'surrendered (most of which were in areas of work where their record was good)' were given up for 'good reason' to be managed as well, or better.

This meeting brought into the foreground the archdeacon of Auckland, George Gibson, who confessed that he was puzzled that work for which the Commissioners had been widely praised, and which the dioceses appeared to want them to continue, should now be taken from them. The Commissioners had earned a reputation for impartiality and, as a Synod-elected Commissioner he felt that the Synod was a more 'political' body. Why change? Carey acknowledged that their work had been excellent. But he wondered why a transfer of responsibilities would diminish it, if the same officers would be doing the work? And what did 'independence' mean? The archdeacon persisted: the expertise would remain, but the power to adjudicate, and to do so with apparent independence, was valued in the parishes. This clearly carried the conviction of the committee. The archbishop simply

[10] See 'The Turnbull Report', CC (95) 54, annex 1: Locke, 'Initial note of comment', Board papers, 26 Oct. 1995, ibid. pt 72.

said that what mattered was a coherent structure. But he acknowledged that the new arrangement must be effective.

They moved on to matters of finance. Waine showed concern that their trustee obligations and responsibilities, primarily to maintain the ordained ministry and the cure of souls in parishes, must be protected. If they were altered, there must be legal safeguards to protect them against political pressure. Moreover, as the new council would determine increases in the clergy pension the money which the Commissioners had to support active ministry must feel the consequences. To this there was no reply.

The committee sought to mount a defence of the rights of the dioceses. There was some talk of cathedrals, some of pensions. They came to the timetable. Waine feared that the Church was about to rush into change. Carey replied that there was a need to be seen to be responding with purpose and urgency. A commitment could be made to a broad legislative framework at least; the details could then be worked out in a more measured way.

As the meeting concluded Carey asked Locke if he discerned any *via media*? Locke replied that his personal view had for some time been that there was no 'fundamental incompatibility' between the 'broad thrust' of the report and the Commissioners' concerns. Carey pressed him. Locke continued: they might well look for a clearer articulation of the Commissioners' continuing trusts and functions, but there remained concerns about the redundant churches and related work under the Pastoral Measure, especially the appellate function, and the work of the cathedrals. Waine observed that if the report were a document inviting constructive debate that was one thing. But if it was a blueprint which made anything less than acceptance 'disloyal' that was quite another. What, then, was it? The archbishop was reassuring. He wanted to listen. There would be genuine consultation. He welcomed the committee's contribution. He supported the basic view of the commission that there should be a national council and a reorganisation of central responsibilities, and was ready to discuss 'other options' within that. But again he insisted on the urgency of the situation. They now had an opportunity to reconsider 'longstanding ecclesiological weaknesses'. This Waine 'greatly welcomed'. The institutions of the Church would 'motor together'.[11]

The essential terms of the debate had now hardened. When the Board settled into another discussion in October 1995 little new argument emerged. But this time the bishop of Durham was among them. For his part the bishop spoke of theology. The new council would work to 'reshape the Church into what we want it to be'. Wide

---

[11] 'Agreed note of a meeting between the archbishop and the GPC of the Church Commissioners', 13 Oct. 1995, ibid.

consultations were establishing that most people were broadly in favour of the idea, but remained concerned about details. He conceded that on those the report was thin, but then this was a paper for discussion, not a legislative document. The Commission did not want to rush. But it also saw that delay must weaken the powers for change.

Colman was again present. He remarked that the Assets Committee was generally content with what seemed to be afoot, but it was anxious that a new body must have protection against over-distribution. The Third Church Estates Commissioner, Margaret Laird, added that the Bishoprics Committee had concurred that change was needed but had fears about committees and accountability. The bishop of Durham sought to reassure. The Commissioners had been 'exemplary' in matters of pastoral reorganisation. That was not in question. But they could not fashion a course, take an overview. That was what the national council could supply. 'There was no question of the Council imposing its will on the dioceses.'[12]

The fundamental problem with *Working as one body* was becoming all too clear. Everybody professed to agree with it in general, but almost everybody disagreed with it in detail. This pattern emerged time and again as the various committees of the Commissioners set to work on their replies. On the Pastoral Committee even Penny Granger confessed that she was disappointed. Yet at no point did criticism of detail mount to such a degree point that the whole proposal was pigeon-holed.[13]

A new world of deliberation and consultation

Whatever assurances had been given to the effect that the path of reform would allow for reflection and discussion, the pace of events was accelerating. The House of Bishops discussed *Working as one body* in October; so did the Central Board of Finance. Then there were the bishop's councils, the diocesan synods, the diocesan boards of finance. Archbishop Carey pronounced that he wanted consultation to be as wide as possible. He stood ready to receive 'considered views from national bodies and dioceses' at Lambeth itself, there to be advised by the Archbishops' Advisory Group. There were four regional conferences. Every incumbent received a package and an audio cassette with information. The bishop at Lambeth, Frank Sargeant, explained to Locke that 'There is no presumption that individuals or individual parishes will necessarily wish to express an opinion, but if

[12] Board minutes, 26 Oct. 1995.
[13] For example see 'Agreed note of a meeting', annex II, Board papers, 13 Oct. 1995, ser. 95083, pt 72, ibid.

they do they are being asked to channel it through their Bishop, Diocesan Secretary or General Synod representatives.'[14]

Synod debated the report in November. The Commissioners attracted little angry fire. Were attitudes towards them changing? When the Board met in December 1995 it was suggested that a programme be worked out to introduce those newly elected to Synod to the work of the Commissioners. They might reintroduce receptions while Synod was in session so that members might meet the Commissioners' staff. Penny Granger insisted that the Board must discuss these matters scrupulously. The minutes of the last meeting had not, she thought, done justice to those who were sympathetic to the report. For his part, Colman was clearly not quite in a position to give a lead. Instead he prodded the governors to agree on a response.[15]

Towards the end of 1995 a second, urgent, round of discussion began. A further, special Synod was arranged for February 1996. By then it was hoped that there would be a consensus around the 'broad legislative framework'. What was, however, clearly emerging now – and not only at 1 Millbank – was a stronger sense of what in the old order must be defended. But there could be no denying that the Commissioners were surrendering their discretion over allocations, and that the power of the new council would bring no 'absolute safeguard' for the relief of poor parishes.[16] By November 1995 the archbishop and the Board were ready to meet again. The bishop of Durham was in the United States and sent a 'note' to assist the discussion. Now the temper was altogether firmer: Turnbull himself wrote more sharply that 'It is paradoxical to claim to accept the "broad thrust" of this fundamental concern and then argue that one function after another should in fact be retained.' If the archbishops' commission were building a new house and filling it with other people's furniture, the previous owners seemed to be sneaking through the back door to reclaim what had been expropriated, and even getting away with it. Enough was enough. It was above all important, he emphasised, now to work more effectively 'as one body'.

The commission offered some concessions to the Church Commissioners, but not many. They would leave the management of Lambeth Palace as it stood, so too the management of assets by the Church Commissioners and, to some extent, existing patterns of support for the bishops. But they unanimously rejected every other

[14] Sargeant to Locke, 9 Aug. 1995, in CC (95) 49, annex 1, Board papers, 27 Sept. 1995, ibid.
[15] Board minutes, 12 Dec. 1995, pp. 4–5.
[16] See GP (95) 9 minutes, pp. 1–2; annex to CC (95) 54; annex IV, memorandum of advice to the Church Commissioners by Simmons and Simmons, 10 Oct. 1995; CC (95) 61, annex II, Board papers, 16 Nov. 1995, ser. 95083/73.

plea. As for the Commissioners' claims to impartiality in pastoral affairs, they got short shrift. Turnbull had written:

> But who is to judge what amounts to fairness? One person's fairness is another's unfairness. Notions of fairness imply some criteria by which to judge it. In assessing fairness the Commissioners are making policy. And the effects of their decisions (e.g. on numbers in ministry) profoundly affect other policies. There is no reason in practice why the proposed National Council should not equally be able to act fairly, with its criteria made explicit and related to a coherent overview of the needs and resources of the Church as a whole.

In fact, to decide such detailed matters was the council's *raison d'être*. If the Commissioners feared for their legal trusts, they simply misunderstood the nature of the proposal. Their existing legal liabilities would be transferred to the new council. Of course the council and the Commissioners must maintain 'close and regular dialogue', not least so that the council could be assured that the Commissioners' investment policies took into account the wider needs of the Church. Then, the council would be accountable to parliament, as its own report had suggested. The council would not be 'a creature of Synod', though accountable to it in specified ways, and not a 'political' body: 'It will be a body led by the archbishops with its own basis in law.' They must beware 'loose allegations about a proposed centralisation of power'. The council would not be a government or Board of a Corporation, for it would lack the powers of coercion and compulsion which those models possessed. It would rely on trust and consent, of the bishops, the dioceses, the General Synod. The autonomy enjoyed by dioceses and parishes would be untouched. 'Our model is an Anglican model of leadership operating through consultation and consent – but leadership which is no longer weakened by current divisions of responsibility and culture.'[17]

Everybody, it seemed, deplored a rush, even as they were chasing frantically about. The Archbishops' Advisory Group – which included Colman, Waine, Locke and Gracey – pressed ahead. In just two meetings the group produced a draft White Paper and off it went, early in January 1996, to Millbank, to the Central Board of Finance, the House of Bishops, the standing committee of General Synod. There was not time to pass it on to the Commissioners' committees; it passed straight to the Board with the assurance that it must be satisfied that appropriate consultations had occurred in sufficient time and that

---

[17] Bishop of Durham note, 7 Nov. 1995, ibid.

these changes now commanded their support. This White Paper did not require their commitment 'at this stage'. They should merely show that they were ready and willing to enter into negotiations about significant changes to their own constitution, upon the initiative of the Archbishops' Council.[18]

Momentum

At 1 Millbank it was not Michael Colman but the Third Estates Commissioner, Margaret Laird, and General Synod representative, Alan Cooper, who sought to orchestrate the response of the Church Commissioners. This would serve the Commissioners well; both were widely admired, and known and respected across the Church. When, on 25 January 1996, the Board faced the draft White Paper it had been seen by the General Purposes Committee only hours before. Turnbull was there again. Now he saw evidence of agreement; they had indeed found the way forward. Their discussions would combine to convince parliament too, and give the White Paper 'a foundation in draft legislation and not merely in ideology' – a striking admission. But Herbecq again pleaded that such changes as these required time and even Bishop Lunn, who had been no apologist for the *status quo,* was now far less sure of himself. Michael Alison worried still about parliament, as it was, perhaps, his job to do. If the Second Church Estates Commissioner were to answer questions on behalf of the council as well as the Commissioners, parliament might be drawn more into the life of the Church. But if he faced questions there only on behalf of the Commissioners, and the Commissioners were charged simply with the management of assets, this would diminish parliament's role in the government of the Church: 'The Commissioners might ultimately lose their slot.'

Turnbull offered his replies and his assurances. The Commission had consulted the Home Office, members of the House of Lords, senior civil servants. There had been an all-party meeting: 'He treasured the relationship between the Church and State as a fundamental part of the Church's mission and it was vital not to allow it to be eroded by accident.' Granger still wanted the Church Commissioners to move more quickly and reminded them that last month she had proposed that a group be set up to ensure that they did. The Board corporately reiterated its wish to 'engage constructively and co-operatively' with the ongoing discussions and preparations.[19]

[18] See Laird and Cooper note, 'Turnbull: steering and coordinating group', CC (96) 3, Board papers, 25 Jan. 1996, ibid. pt 74.
[19] Board minutes, 25 Jan. 1996, pp. 2–5.

Synod duly voted for legislation. On 14 February the archbishop of Canterbury announced the next steps. There would be a steering group, chaired by the chairman of the Central Board of Finance, Alan McLintock, assembled 'urgently' and supported by an 'implementation team' working under the aegis of the Archbishops' Advisory Group. He reassured the Church of the seriousness with which all consultation was viewed.[20]

The 'follow-up steering group' worked relentlessly to draft legislation for general approval in July 1996; to revise thereafter, to seek the final approval of draft legislation by Synod in July, to go to parliament in November and so to receive the royal assent. It was determined that by January 1998 the Archbishops' Council would be a reality. This proved impossible. In July Synod faced only a progress report. Summer faded into autumn; GS 1188 faded into GS 1209. In this headlong pursuit something significant had actually altered in the prospects of the Church Commissioners. A reduction in the membership of the Commissioners was now envisaged as to be largely, though not entirely, achieved by the exclusion of all but four or six of the diocesan bishops. Now the number of synodically-elected members was reduced too. The Third Church Estates Commissioner remained on the list of endangered species.

The unexpected return of the Social Security Committee

Parliament had not yet finished with the Church Commissioners. Indeed, the sights of the Select Committee on Social Security were now firmly trained not merely on the future of clergy pensions but on the new movement of reform in the Church of England. Moreover, if nobody in the Church itself was going to tax the First Church Estates Commissioner on the vulnerability of his position in these altered times, the select committee would do so. On 1 April 1996 Colman and Locke returned to the committee rooms of the Palace of Westminster to face Field and his six inquisitors again. This time, however, the Church Commissioners did not encounter an accusation of quite the same character. To begin with, Colman and Locke could wear an aspect of vindication for, absolved of the sins of their predecessors, they had set to work with a will and now looked increasingly justified by the results. If there was a brief skirmish over coupon-trading, Colman had always been perfectly candid that he did not like it and would stop it as soon as he was able.

Did the First Church Estates Commissioner quite agree with the proposal for this new national council? Colman responded that he was a member of that commission and had signed its report. He saw an

[20] See ibid. 29 Feb. 1996, pp. 1–2.

'absolute need' for a national council because the Commissioners had for long been too heavily burdened with tasks for which nobody else would take responsibility, like the CSA. Even so, he was not a robust advocate. The committee did not, he added, need any help from him in forming its own view. When it was suggested that it was ironic that the Turnbull Commission had been provoked to life by a financial crisis – but that its report had left the Commissioners in charge of exactly the tasks in which it had seemed to fail, Colman replied, simply, 'Yes.' And when all the powers which the Commissioners had assumed without criticism were handed over to the new council, was that not also ironic? Colman: 'It is ironic.' Field pressed: perhaps in leaving the capital with the Church Commissioners the new council was contriving a way of making changes without having to concoct an act for parliament's approval? Colman merely replied that this had not occurred to him: 'You are better able to discern what is going on than I am.' Bernard Jenkin persisted: was it 'sensible' for the investments of the Commissioners to be independent of the allocations? In a way, came the reply, that already occurred, but between the Assets Committee and the General Purposes Committee at the Commissioners. Locke observed that the Church Commissioners themselves had come into being not by act but by measure. But that, responded Field, had simply been the union of two funds and not a change of function. The Commission would make the Commissioners into 'capital eunuchs'. All of this, replied Locke, was still being discussed by the Church; he could not 'properly' offer a view.[21]

On 22 April it was the turn of Church House, the Pensions Board and their financial advisers to visit the committee. There was something of a wrangle over the 1919 Act which established the existence and the powers of the Church Assembly. It did not much help when Philip Mawer dryly observed that the fortunes of church legislation in parliament hardly suggested that it was 'high in the list of anybody's priorities in parliament apart from a few people who are properly and rightly interested in those matters'. Field was quick to repudiate this. No less than 500 MPs had voted on the ordination of women, and without so much as a prod from the Whips. Mawer was not very amenable to this. Within the Church the dioceses were saying that if they were to find money for the central authorities they must have confidence in them, and influence over them. In particular, they were not confident in the Church Commissioners. Jenkin retorted that this looked to him like the privatisation of the Church, at the expense of the Church Commissioners who were answerable to parliament, and, accordingly, at the expense of parliament itself. Mawer could not

---

[21] *Church of England pensions (Fifth report of the House of Commons Social Security Committee,* London 1996), 1–14, session of 1 Apr. 1996.

agree. The Church did not wish to present parliament with a *fait accompli*, but something which lay within the 1919 settlement. Jenkin, again, asked to whom the archbishop's council would be accountable? Mawer replied that it would be answerable to the Church Commissioners, to Synod and then parliament: 'we have no desire to change the fundamental relationships with Parliament in this kind of area'. The committee did not sound convinced. Moreover, Jenkin could not see how, if the Commissioners had failed to regulate the Church's demand for expenditure before, they were any more likely to do so once control over expenditure had been removed from them altogether.[22]

Momentum

A comprehensive report might inspire few reasonable objections and require little subsequent refinement. But a hasty report must be made good by subsequent discussion. The authorities of the Church of England had now got themselves into the worst of both worlds. It was hard to deny that the archbishops' commission had rushed at its task and published a report which was riddled with weaknesses. Because of this it must be scrutinised all the more carefully. But the advocates of change still found it hard to distinguish between what must be a proper period of critical reflection across the Church and what might invite that mounting defence of old interests, and that softening of perspectives, which was their greatest fear. Indeed, the pace at which the reformers pressed ahead accelerated still more. Designed to respond to a perceived crisis in church management, the archbishops' commission was soon in danger of manufacturing a crisis of its own.

Somebody had to call a halt. By the end of April 1996 the Board of the Church Commissioners was fretting that the timetable was simply not practicable. On 9 May Colman and Laird discussed the present pile of papers, now aimed at the Advisory Group (on 14 May) and the Standing Committee (the day after). They acknowledged that the secretary-general, the Synod's legal advisor and yet another body called the 'Implementation Unit' were coping as best they could with 'severe pressure'. The plan was still to see a measure actually placed before the General Synod, ready for its general approval in July. But what was now occurring around the First and Third Church Estates Commissioners appeared simply 'unacceptable'. A draft measure was being circulated to the Archbishops' Advisory Committee and the standing committee of Synod without having first been considered by the steering group itself or any of the institutions which must be affected by it. Hardly any time had been allowed for preparatory staff

[22] Ibid. 32–50, session of 22 Apr. 1996.

work – the deputy secretary of the Commissioners and his legal adviser had only two hours notice before the draft was circulated. Laird and Cooper had persuaded the Board to do something that it had never done before, to agree in principle that the two of them should have an order-making power to make significant changes to the number of Church Commissioners, and also to settle a transfer of their powers, so long as they undertook to the Board itself to protect the Commissioners' responsibilities. This was a serious step, by any stretch of the institutional imagination, and it placed a weighty moral burden on all the participants. It looked more like an act of faith than a wise political instrument, even if it were legal. Now they saw that the stance which the Board had taken was itself in danger: 'the Third Commissioner and Mr Cooper felt themselves exposed in the absence of reciprocal recognition from other key players'. The order-making clause was 'too sweeping'; there was no evidence that what was presently being proposed to the Commissioners was even practicable. What they saw elsewhere was simply incompatible with the principle of co-operation which had been vaunted so loudly. It was time to press the Commissioners' claims more assertively. It was now that Colman at last took the helm. He went off to alert the secretary-general of the General Synod and both archbishops.[23]

For the Commissioners some of the most important questions of all remained, even now, up in the air. At present around fifty of the ninety-five Church Commissioners served on the Board and committees of the institution. *Working as one body* had proposed that the Commissioners be led by a new body, small enough to be a working group, but one with a sufficient show of relevant expertise to provide members for its attendant committees. This body must also reflect an accountability to Church and State, while achieving a proper balance between elected, appointed and *ex officio* members, and while showing a proper representation of the General Synod. Yet it must comprise only fifteen people.

The steering committee had wrestled with this, admitted defeat and then come up with another number: twenty-nine. They could allow for thirty-three during the transitional period. This agreed, numbers were recalculated and juggled. Additions and subtractions followed each other around neurotically and circuitously, the claims of the various bodies which might wish for representation were considered and reconsidered and then considered again. There was a new proposal: both archbishops would now sit on the Board alongside two Church Estates Commissioners, six appointed members (three by the crown; three by both archbishops), two bishops (elected by the bishops as a

---

[23] GPC report, '*Working as one body*', CC (96) 36, and annexes I and II, Board papers, 25 July 1996, ser. 95083/75.

body), one dean or provost (elected likewise from among their peers), three clergy (ditto), four members of the laity (ditto). To this new list was suddenly added no less than nine officers of state, appointed *exofficio*: the First Lord of the Treasury, the Lord President of the Council, the Lord Chancellor, the Speaker of the House of Commons, the attorney-general, the secretary of state for the Home Office, representatives of the City of London and of York and of the universities of Oxford and Cambridge.

On 22 May Michael Alison wrote a lengthy personal note for the Board to suggest how parliament might respond both to the Pensions Measure and to a measure which applied the Turnbull report. The parliamentary Ecclesiastical Committee would certainly, he thought, be much influenced by the scepticism of the Social Security Committee. Parliament would want to see some clarification of trustee obligations and some protection for the poorer parishes. All this activity had generated no little heat. Colman remarked purposefully to the Board that 'the Commissioners will wish to avoid becoming a football in a dispute between Parliament and Synod and we are using our best endeavours to cool the temperature'. It was not easy to make a way through this, for they were in some ways accountable to both.[24]

Parliament and the great reform

When, on 4 July 1996, the Social Security Committee released its second report on Church of England pensions, fears of a clash between Church and State intensified. The report affirmed the responsibility of parliament over these matters; it questioned the model proposed to Synod by the joint committee on pensions and wondered if members had been consulted as they should, and with reference to other possible models. It pressed that a limit be set on coupon-trading and it concluded by calling for a new Church of England bill. For it was one thing to change the furniture of the Church, as much of the Turnbull Report proposed to do, but quite another when it came to arrangements which affected the Church's historic resources.

This was debated, as Michael Alison noted, in 'prime morning parliamentary time' in the House of Commons a fortnight later. It was the second time that the house had debated the Church's 'affairs' in fourteen months: 'That is a striking signal of Parliament's concern for its responsibilities.' Alison himself gave a stately performance and encouraged the House to concentrate on the new Pensions Measure rather than the Turnbull Commission. Field responded graciously. The committee had given the new First Church Estates Commissioner, the

24 CC (96) 36, p. 3, ibid.

secretary and their staff 'a clear vote of confidence'. What questions now came were offered 'in friendship to those drafting the measure, not in a hostile manner'. Field commended a different model for pensions, a personal pension scheme, as opposed to a company scheme, and thought that such a step might well initiate a greater debate about 'second-funded pension provision' for people in all walks of life. But he reserved his fire for the Turnbull Report: it was 'a deeply un-Anglican document'. This Archbishops' Council would be something like a Roman curia: 'it will not be sustainable because it is trying to graft something on to a body that will reject it'; it was a 'short cut that will flounder'. This, he owned, was a personal comment; the Church was free to reform itself as it chose.

The under-secretary of state for the Home Office, Tom Sackville, congratulated the Church Commissioners, who had 'pulled out all the stops to get the affairs of the Commission back in order'. He was sure that church pensions were in 'the best possible hands'. Future changes could surely be managed by a measure, but a radical proposal which involved the transfer of 'a substantial part of the funds of the Church Commissioners' might well be seen by the House to require a bill. Bernard Jenkin thought that the Church was in danger of over-reacting to controversy, and pronounced that the Social Security Committee was sure that the Commissioners had 'repaired themselves effectively' and could become again 'a firm financial anchor for the Church of England, to the benefit of the Church of England and the whole nation'. He endorsed Field's view that a personal pensions scheme would be a credible way forward: 'traditional occupational pension schemes' smacked of 'a more paternalist age'. It was a good day for Alison, who faced retirement and whose parliamentary colleagues now sought to show that they valued him.[25]

But it was not enough to put heart into the Board of governors at 1 Millbank. They still saw all too clearly that the pressure against them came not from the great agora of the state but from the institutions of the Church of England itself. When the Board met in July 1996 its members sensed that they were accused, audibly and persistently, even within their own corridors, of dragging their feet. In a new note Locke protested that the Commissioners had been co-operative – after all, they had provided staff for this enterprise and indeed paid for it, as they had paid for at least half of the commission itself. The most senior of the Commissioners' staff had devoted at least half of their time to the follow-up process while still maintaining their existing responsibilities. Detailed work was being undertaken by no less than fourteen 'issues groups'. The Commissioners had, Locke maintained, offered 'constructive engagement with an acknowledgement of the

[25] *Hansard*, Debates of the House of Lords, 17 July 1996, cols 1080–97.

Commissioners' responsibility to safeguard their work in the meantime and to evaluate the detail of alternative arrangements before agreeing to hand responsibilities away'. It was a balanced stance. It was appropriate.[26] Yet Locke was a known critic of the new reform, and at least some of the Commissioners continued to mutter that he should do more to promote it.

At this stage another fundamental question was in the air: how many of these new proposals would actually require legislation? Certainly much could be done without it, but what could not was the transfer of the Commissioners' functions under the Pastoral Measure. The report of the Social Security Committee had asked that Synod give parliament an answer to the question. This was seen by Patrick Locke and Philip Mawer at Church House not merely to raise questions of procedure, but to 'influence the parameters within which as well as the manner in which the reform process is pursued'. To pursue legislation only by measure might bring a clash with parliament. To follow the alternative course might appear to some in the Church to be an improper concession to parliament, even an erosion of the legislative rights of Synod. And on what basis should the new Archbishops' Council be established? As an unincorporated body by resolution of Synod? Under the Companies Act as a Company Limited by Guarantee? By Royal Charter?[27]

Parliament had sent up a warning flare that no one could fail to see. When the Board of the Commissioners met in September the bishop of Durham sent his apologies. This time he would be in Lesotho. But he sent instead a note, and not a pacific one. There was a danger. The report of the Social Security Committee showed that parliament might be unduly influenced by over-concerned individuals there to feel unhappiness with this new movement for change within the Church when they might otherwise see no need for doubt. If it came to legislation, there might even be a defeat. He stated his 'deep concern' that the Board move to take the initiative in the process and assume its responsibilities fully. He knew which wounds to probe:

> Many of us on the Board have uneasy consciences that we did not accept responsibility for the activities of the Commissioners in the late 80s and early 90s. We must not allow that to happen again, particularly as the Pensions and Turnbull debates have taken us into the heart of the

26 Board minutes, 25 July 1996, pp. 1–4.
27 Locke note, 'Working as one body: the Church Commissioners' stance', CC (96) 36, Board papers, 26 Sept. 1996, ser. 95083/75, and also annex II 'Turnbull: Proceeding with or without legislation', Board papers, 26 September 1996, ser. 95083/75.

Church/State arena. Whether we like it or not the Commissioners are central to those debates ...

Turnbull feared that since April 1996 the Board had been 'sidelined' by the pressure of the process, and that it relied too heavily on its representatives. 'This leads to a fundamental question about authority within the Commissioners.' The Board must be sure who was determining the Commissioners' policy and who was expressing it. Turnbull found Frank Field's statements in parliament questionable 'on factual, theological and constitutional grounds'. The Commissioners should challenge them. Yet in parliament the Second Church Estates Commissioner had not done so, or even brought the comment to the Board. Whatever the verdict of the select committee, Turnbull perceived that the debate in parliament had actually produced no clear direction as to whether they should proceed by bill or measure. No longer could the Board duck the issue. It was at the heart of a 'political minefield', 'a major constitutional debate'. It must speak clearly and firmly.[28]

The Board stirred to defend itself. It agreed that the report of the Social Security Committee was inaccurate and should be challenged. Some, indeed, felt that the committee had exceeded its brief. The record should be put straight, but in a measured way. This was perhaps best done by the bishops in the House of Lords. Colman reminded them that Field and his committee had supported the draft legislation on pensions, and that their support had been of great value to the Church. He thought that Field might shift his position on 'Turnbull', too. They would do better to keep his sympathy.[29]

A letter had been sent to all ninety-five Church Commissioners asking for their views on what was now in the air. Fifty per cent of them had replied. Two-thirds agreed that the steering group was on the right lines, the remaining third was evenly split between those who complained that the proposals were too radical and those who said that they were not radical enough. The Commissioners' staff, meanwhile, appeared more anxious about terms and conditions than they were about redundancy: they saw all too clearly that whoever employed them there was an immensity of work to be done. Speed, at every turn, was an issue in itself; the issue to push aside all others; the issue to undo all others. 'The Church', the minutes recorded plaintively, 'could not be transformed overnight.'[30]

Parliament saw that the choice before the Church was between reform by act or by measure. But within the Church it was seen to lie

[28] Bishop of Durham note, 27 Aug. 1996, ibid.
[29] Board minutes, 26 Sept. 1996, pp. 4–5.
[30] Ibid. p. 5.

between a measure or synodical regulation and other means. The steering group decided that legislation would 'enshrine' change. Most of the Board of the Church Commissioners agreed.[31] Meanwhile, by October, the 'minimum' number of Commissioners was set down at twenty-nine, 'with a mechanism in the Order-making power for consequential reductions upon a transfer of functions'. This made sense in itself, but it was found to be at odds with the consultative document which both the steering group and the Commissioners themselves had already approved.[32]

Locke had now been reassured that the revision stage of the measure would last until November 1997. At Church House Mawer was soothing, remarking that this would allow for full consultation in Church and in parliament. By October 1996 two-thirds of the Commissioners had replied to the letter about the new proposals. Of that number, two-thirds approved of the new structure. This looked more like a mandate.[33]

The National Institutions Measure

By November 1996 the governors of the Commissioners actually held a draft National Institutions Measure in their hands. Locke said that he found it 'broadly satisfactory' from the Commissioners' perspective. Even now the number of Commissioners still seemed to be wrong – twenty-nine, not thirty-three – and the notion of 'dual trusteeship' was 'inherently a source of confusion'. Mawer was there to reassure again.[34] With the new Pensions Measure all went well. It received its final approval in Synod that month. Amendments were passed in the revision debate, but these did not alter the basic purpose or nature of the measure itself and could be taken in its stride.[35] Now it must be seen through parliament.

As the reform moved from politics to legislation the lawyers grew busier. The Commissioners had now lost their official solicitor, John Guy, who had died in June. They brought back Edward Wills who proposed that the suggestion of thirty-three Commissioners, produced by the first progress report, be revived. He also proposed that the measure should contain 'a mechanism whereby the Audit Committee could warn the State representatives of any substantial matter causing that committee grave concern'. Representatives of the cities of London

[31] Ibid.
[32] See report 'Working as one body: draft national institutions measure', CC (96) 49, Board papers, 21 Nov. 1996, ser. 95083/76.
[33] Board minutes, 24 Oct. 1996.
[34] CC (96) 49, p. 1, Board papers, 21 Nov. 1996, ser. 95083/76.
[35] Board minutes, 21 Nov. 1996, pp. 1–2.

and York, Oxford and Cambridge, had been hauled back on board. Wills thought this helpful 'in view of the archbishop's responsibility for appointing members of the Assets Committee'. Bishop Turnbull, for his part, did not like it. For him, even twenty-nine Commissioners were too many. This was a 'significant shift' from the thinking of the archbishops' commission. It might well be felt that to retain these representatives was evidence of elitism and anachronism. But others supported the new design. Why close down such avenues of support for the Church, for these places offered pools of expertise, on which the Commissioners could draw. History commended it. Advantage commended it.[36]

In April and June 1997 the general meetings of the Church Commissioners agreed to the main provisions of the new measure. A new draft appeared before the Board in September 1997. Locke observed, 'At official level, we are now moving very fast – as we need to do.' There was much still to work out. The mind of Synod and the mind of parliament could not be assumed. The order-making facility still provoked controversy: Locke called it, blandly and not sympathetically, 'novel'. The substructure had still not settled; the costs of the changes had not been established; and the question as to who would actually pay for the entire upheaval had not been resolved.[37] So when the Board met in September 1997 it faced a great deal of detail and a far from simple task. Its powers must now be devolved both to the council and to the forty-three executive dioceses. Capital was to be sent out to the dioceses while an income account was set up for the council. It was still unclear who was to be seen as the employer of the clergy – a fundamental and historical question which was still, evidently, without an answer.

Parliament was said to be watching, intently. But if the Social Security Committee had involved itself in the affairs of the Church with some energy, the prime minister's office was evidently watching with a more cautious eye. When Locke himself wrote to 10 Downing Street on 17 February he had to wait until 10 November for a comprehensive reply. The preference of government now was that instead of seeing the Commissioners reel in the attorney-general to sit on the Board, the Commissioners should give the seat to the somewhat less imposing secretary of state for Culture, Media and Sport (though the attorney-general would still be available to assist them if they so wished). There was, too, a little question of terminology. The government would prefer that the Commissioners be called, formally, Custodian Trustees, to distinguish them from the 'working' members. They welcomed the proposal that there be an

[36] Ibid. 27 Feb. 1996, pp. 1–3.
[37] Ibid. 25 Sept. 1997, pp. 1–4.

Audit Committee. The prime minister had been 'in some ways disappointed' that the original proposal for fifteen Commissioners had not survived, 'though he understands the reasons for this'. His inclination towards fifteen was not explained.[38]

By February 1998 General Synod had given its final approval to the new draft measure. An attempt to get the new vehicle off the ground on 1 October 1998 was abandoned. Now the Archbishops' Council would come into being on 1 January 1999. The Board of governors turned to practicalities. The reconstituted Assets Committee would continue; the bishoprics/cathedrals committee was now acquiring its terms of reference; the pastoral/heritage and redundant churches committees would be left undisturbed, as Synod agreed, for the moment, but the Church Heritage Forum was busy at work already. The CSA would see its powers passed to the council by a regulation in Synod. The payment of the clergy now looked 'relatively straightforward, if complex'. There would be a common personnel department 'laying the ground for a unified staff capacity' and a joint Church House/Millbank 'communications department'. By 1 January 2000 some of the staff of the Commissioners, and others drawn from other departments, would move into the 35,000 square feet of Church House left behind by the Ombudsman. There was to be a new procedure for the appointment of the new secretary to the council and the senior staff of the council would be appointed in the spring. The General Purposes Committee declared itself satisfied. The Board was evidently satisfied.

What, now, of parliament? On 30 April 1998 the bishop of Blackburn, Alan Chesters, told the Board that the Ecclesiastical Committee had met for the first time to discuss the National Institutions Measure, that the Commissioners had been praised there for their own handling of pastoral reorganisation and redundant churches, and hopes had been expressed that they would continue to hold on to these duties. The measure, along with a new Cathedrals Measure, should be discussed in the House before the summer recess. The Board congratulated Philip Mawer and the staff at 1 Millbank and General Synod for their work in seeing the measure safely through this important stage. It congratulated Mawer a second time, on his recent appointment as secretary-general designate of the Archbishops' Council.[39]

Whether through disinclination to linger over what it was beyond their power to alter, or through lack of interest, parliament passed the National Institutions Measure with barely a murmur on the evening of 18 June 1998. Sir Patrick Cormack thought it better than the report

[38] Catto to Locke, 11 Nov. 1997, Board papers, 18 Dec. 1997, ser. 95083/79.
[39] Board minutes, 30 Apr. 1998, p. 1.

which had been its source; there was a humane speech from Peter Bottomley, who observed that if these changes carried the great weight of the Church of England parliament must have 'extremely strong reasons' for challenging them. The new Second Church Estates Commissioner, Stuart Bell, concluded that the measure showed the Church to be 'coming to terms with the modern age'.[40] The measure reached the House of Lords on 29 June 1998, where it was moved by Bishop Chesters. Lord Newby, whose wife had been ordained as a deacon a day before, commented on the effort that had gone into the measure and perceived that its merits earned their support. On the Ecclesiastical Committee Lord Pilkington had remarked that 'This is a classic Anglican measure and we ought to support it. It is because of measures like this that the Church of England survives at all.' He agreed with it and so did the House. It was not so much a debate as a benign and not too lengthy nod.[41]

A new chapter in the history of the Church of England, and with it the history of the Church Commissioners, had now begun.

Two ethical endings

Across the 1990s events in South Africa had gathered powerful momentum. The political and legal structure of apartheid had begun to buckle. In May 1992 the Assets Committee decided upon a modest relaxation of its bans in South Africa, agreeing that investment in a company which made up to 10 per cent of its profits there could be allowed. In June 1993 the South African Council of Churches met at Utrecht and invited the Churches to end their campaign. A year later the South African parliament passed legislation to establish a multi-racial transitional executive council. An interim constitution was framed and passed.

In February 1994 the Board of the Church Commissioners inspected a new report from the Assets Committee. It now recommended that the Board lift completely its ban on companies operating in South Africa. The Central Board of Finance had already done so. By now it was seen that the maintenance of a system of banned categories was being commended as 'pragmatic' rather than 'intellectual'.[42] Everyone – principled, pragmatic or both in varying degrees – could see that South Africa had changed, or was changing. A world that had associated apartheid with the imprisonment of Nelson Mandela had seen him released. The South African Council of

[40] *Hansard*, Debates of the House of Commons, 18 June 1998, cols 587–95.
[41] Ibid. Debates of the House of Lords, 29 June 1998, cols 493–9.
[42] See Hardy and Shaw note, 'Ethical investment policy', CC (94) 10, Board papers, 24 Feb. 1994, ser. 95083/67.

Churches and the Anglican bishops in South Africa agreed that investment must now be permitted. The Assets Committee decided that at first they should restrict investments to multi-nationals with interests in that country, and not South African companies. The situation was still 'volatile': they must continue to monitor social and employment policies. Accordingly, on 24 February 1994, the Board of the Church Commissioners agreed to lift its ban on South Africa.[43] On 27 April 1994 the first non-racial, multi-party democratic election took place in that country.

Those who insisted that ethical questions must be owned by the Church at large usually meant that they must find a home at the General Synod. In March 1996 a new Ethical Investment Working Group (EIWG) met for the first time. It sought to provide a discussion group for members of the Commissioners' Assets Committee, the Board of Social Responsibility (represented from July 1997 by Michael Bourke, then bishop of Wolverhampton), the Pensions Board and the Central Board of Finance. It was agreed that the group should report annually to Synod. The number and range of issues before them multiplied. There were exchanges with GEC over armaments (or what was now called 'defence equipment'); a recommendation to disinvest from BSkyB, which had just launched a Playboy Channel ('considered to be pornographic'); a protest at the sale of National Lottery tickets to minors; a questioning of the activities of Shell Petroleum in Nigeria.[44] By February 1998 the group had produced a new statement of its ethical investment policy and was commending it to all bodies in the Church of England. In July 1998 the First Church Estates Commissioner announced to a fringe meeting at Synod:

> We have moved beyond a banned sector approach in favour of a company by company analysis, although we will not lose sight of the need to maintain our strict observation of those areas we believe the Church wishes to avoid. Our restriction on investment in gambling, armaments, tobacco, alcohol, pornography and newspapers remains at the heart of this approach.

The group did not campaign. It favoured dialogue, mutual understanding and the exercise of influence. It believed in a new phenomenon of the day called 'best business practice'. In short, it cut a greater dash, was a little more energetic in the production of papers, a little better at striking poses, a little more in love with the jargon of the

[43] Board minutes, 24 Feb. 1994, p. 4.
[44] Stock Exchange annual report, 1995, A (96) 51, Board papers, 30 May 1996, ser. 95083/75.

moment. It was also one of the few organs of the Church of England to cultivate ecumenical identity, as well as a sprawling variety of associations and connections with other like-minded organisations.[45]

For all this, there was little to distinguish the methods and decisions of the new ethical consortium from what had occurred before within the offices of 1 Millbank. In fact, far from being more rigorous, in one sphere at least the new model was soon found to be more relaxed. For some years those who favoured investment in alcohol had been wearing down a dwindling opposition, and in the 1990s they pressed harder. In 1996 the Ethical Investment Working Group reviewed breweries and distillers. Attitudes towards them had, it noted, 'changed radically over the years'.[46] A report was presented to the House of Bishops in January 1996. The bishops sagely agreed that society had changed (they did not say in what way), observed that the drinks industry too had changed, but agreed that any relaxation of old restrictions in this area should be pursued on 'a rigorously selective basis'. Major manufacturers of alcoholic products were unlikely, it was agreed, ever to be suitable partners. But many companies diversified. There were those that had interests in hotels, restaurants, leisure, family activities; ones which professed 'a positive approach to social policy'. They, surely, might now be viewed benignly.[47]

In light of this the EIWG produced a new paper on the breweries. 'The era', it began, 'of the neighbourhood pub tied to a brewer as a means of shifting beer volumes has largely passed.' The 1989 Beer Order had forced companies to choose between brewing and retailing. Women were influencing 'leisure choices', drawing men from the old pubs and into cheerful restaurants with their children. On the other hand heavy drinking was often a factor in delinquent behaviour and in approximately 40 per cent of cases involving domestic violence. According to the police, 70 per cent of violent crime was related to alcohol. 'Drink-driving' accounted for one in seven road accidents, but society had turned against it, through advertising campaigns, penalties, breathalysers, prosecutions, intolerance. 'Only' 9.2 per cent of collisions produced positive breathalyser tests. Then there were Alcopops, which were widely regarded as a way of encouraging under-age drinking. The bishops did not like them. But they could be blamed on the Australians, and as they were largely promoted by Bass, that company should still be on the banned list. Whitbread produced two brands; 'only' one was in the top ten currently on sale; it had said that it had 'particular concerns' about them and, while continuing to produce them, it would not market them 'actively'. It had also

[45] EIWG, second report, CC (98) 22, Board papers, 28 May 1998, ibid. pt 80.
[46] A (96) 51, pt V, p. 10, ibid. pt 75.
[47] EIWG, second report, p. 10.

withdrawn them from 400 of its 'family pubs'. Forty-one per cent of young men and 25 per cent of women were believed to exceed the weekly alcohol limits advised by government. It was estimated that 84,000 children between the ages of twelve and fifteen consumed alcohol 'in excess of recommended limits'. (Evidently no one observed that there were no 'recommended limits' for those below the age of 18 because they were not meant to be drinking at all.) Yet, concluded the EIWG report, 'excessive consumption is however the experience of the minority with millions integrating a responsible enjoyment of alcohol into family life'.[48]

A majority of the laity evidently agreed that the ban should be lifted. Colman wrote to the archbishops that a modest revision was in the air. Archbishop Carey replied with two sentences: he fully agreed. So did archbishop Habgood, though he thought another paper might be put before the bishops setting out the case again.[49] Only one voice, that of Philip Lovegrove, held out bravely against the new consensus. Alcohol, he maintained, should inhabit the same category of risk as tobacco. Bishop Bourke, who had made so much of small fractions when it was a matter of South African investments, simply denied this. It was said that Whitbread's brewing interests were declining; Greenalls had moved out of brewing altogether in 1990. Both companies were good employers, had excellent safety records and training and employment practices second to none. They promoted impressive community and sponsorship programmes. Surely, this need not go back to the bishops. In December 1998 the Board of the Church Commissioners was informed that the EIWG now recommended lifting restrictions on the two companies.[50]

This decision exposed two realities: of method and of context. The pragmatic danger of constructive engagement with company managements remained an old one. Unless strong counter-arguments were constantly kept in mind, there was always the danger of succumbing to the rational arguments by which even the most questionable commercial enterprise might justify itself. And in 1998 there was no strong lobby on behalf of abstention in the Church of England. The old anxieties had faded, and been replaced by a glib consensus which appeared ignorant of the force they had exerted. Thus was Temperance, one of the great, radical reform movements of the nineteenth century, quietly and gently buried, like a rather quixotic elderly aunt who belonged to a distant era and whom the younger, more modish members of the family had for some years failed quite to

[48] Report by the Stock Exchange Investment Manager, 'Breweries', CC (98) 39, Board papers, 8 Dec. 1998, ser. 95083/81.
[49] Ibid.
[50] Ibid. 1–2.

understand. Evidently, there were too few remaining sympathisers or advocates to attend the funeral and observe, in this lonely demise, a tragedy of a kind.

Conclusion

From their beginnings the Church Commissioners were animated by the belief that they were a necessary institution and a force for good in the Church of England. Equally, there was a persistent element of discomfort: they felt that they were poorly valued, and even regarded with suspicion, by those whom they sought to serve. This should not have surprised them. Money embarrasses the Church. And if there is one thing that Christians evidently dislike more than the making of money it is appearing to lose it. In fifty years the Church Commissioners did both, prodigiously. More than this, the institutional logic, and the constitution which created the Commissioners, affirmed openly the civic and political establishment of the Church of England. Across fifty years this made them appear more and more like a stranded whale as the practices of secular authority moved further away from the world of the nineteenth century and as the institutional culture of the Church itself became more insistently denominational. None of this made for a very promising context in which to work.

Solid scholarship is often justified by the claim that it offers a broader perspective as well as a more sensitive assessment of its subject. In this sense the task of historical scholarship remains the exploration of a paradox. For the historian must get under the skin of the subject itself while retaining a sense of overarching critical distance and judgement. The historian of the Church Commissioners who has spent many hours buried under its mountainous papers is almost inevitably bound to emerge with a perception of the Church of England which derives primarily from the perspective of that institution. To look outwards from the windows of the Commissioners arguably concedes too much to them; to their various measures of self-justification and to their own sense of their place in a wider scheme of things. Those who viewed the life of the Church of England from the windows of a parsonage, from a pew in a parish church, from a diocesan office or a see house, would take a different view of the Church in which they worshipped, and many of them would feel equally sure that they stood at the heart of it. In a sense, they were all quite right. The importance of the Commissioners' archive is that it presents not merely the perspective of the church bureaucrat, but so much diverse material which tumbled through the doors of 1 Millbank on behalf of the processes which they maintained. It is because of this that we may actually see how the affairs of the Church did look from those many, very different quarters, and how they might actually fit together. The Church Commissioners were, uniquely, the lens through which so much of the Church could be seen living and moving: because it drew so heavily upon its inhabitants and because its influences were so pervasive.

But then historical context is never easy to grasp. Inevitably, the views that people across the Church of England took of the Commissioners were more often expressed in conversation – and even gossip – than in the written record. This is not quite lost to us; for such things historians have their methods. But it is never more than a shadow. Moreover, old attitudes are resilient and they endure. A bishop of the Church may even now be heard to remark that the Church Commissioners' money 'really' belongs to the bishops, just as a dean may suggest that it 'really' belongs to the cathedrals. It is reasonable to assume that such beliefs were in the air fifty years before. Nobody has had the courage to make anything more than conversation out of such arguments, perhaps because they so obviously would not bear the weight of a credible historical, legal or ecclesial construction. If they have a value to the student of history it is only in showing how the practical work of the Church always makes its way through a sea of mutterings.

The tension between an internal and an external perspective was certainly a persistent characteristic of the work of the Church Commissioners as an institution. Those who were not a part of its great designs could well struggle to gain an understanding of its purposes and workings; this was a feeling to which even some of the ninety-five Church Commissioners themselves might be prone. Those who have grown haughty in the assurance of their own worth and too familiar with the corridors of power so easily forget what it might be like to live outside them. The Commissioners' senior staff was often resented for being remote, almost untouchable. But then practical people rarely have much love for moralisers and campaigners; those whose expertise is vindicated by fortune can usually only force a smile at the amateur. If the Church Commissioners were repeatedly criticised for a quality of immovable self-satisfaction they were perhaps no more guilty than any other contemporary corporation, growing ever more busily enmeshed in its own priorities and plans. If it were said that the Commissioners were inward-looking and remote, they were, even so, often the channel by which the Church of England itself looked at the outward world of political and economic forms and movements. They were a part of a machinery which linked Christians to a still broader landscape of life. Indeed, they affirmed that this landscape was unavoidable.

The problem of running the Church

At 1 Millbank itself, much of the burden of practical responsibility for the Church Commissioners' work lay upon the shoulders of the First Church Estates Commissioner and the secretary. Though disclaimers may have been duly offered by those who held these positions during the fifty-year history of the Church Commissioners, they almost certainly knew it. As far as financial policy was concerned, the Board of governors might appear to work as a court of opinion but it was prevented by its representative charter from being a board of directors such as the commercial world would understand. The Assets Committee, meanwhile, remained accountable to its own expertise. Though sporadic efforts were made to link expertise to representation, of the clergy, or of Synod, time and again they encountered severe objections. Indeed, as the expertise of the administrators of 1 Millbank matured and grew more sophisticated the gap between administrative knowledge and church politics widened. In a wise letter written to the bishop of Rochester in May 1994 Sir John Herbecq remarked that 'A forceful First Commissioner backed by the staff and the Assets Committee will always take some stopping'.[1] Yet this was exactly what made the Church Commissioners work.

But more than this, it was not so much because of their constitutional designs or their principal actors, but in the fabric of their daily routines that the Commissioners as an institution often succeeded in their task. During these fifty years they managed to construct for themselves a deliberate practice of consultation with their partners and the recipients of their funding which was, if anything, so intricate that they were exposed to the criticism that they had become ponderous and intrusive. Bishops grew exasperated about their houses; diocesan boards of finance blustered about their stipends ranges. But the impressive truth is how well the Church Commissioners actually did bring this all together, with coherence and sense of direction. In many ways they managed their relations with the dioceses far more sensitively and carefully than did the Ecclesiastical Commissioners and Queen Anne's Bounty in their day. That they achieved so much was largely because their officers worked assiduously, patiently and effectively with the complexities and *minutiae* which the Church presented to them. Sometimes this received a flicker of

---

[1] Herbecq to Turnbull, 10 May 1994, Herbecq papers.

acknowledgement. When the historic resources debates rumbled across the dioceses even the Commissioners' critics confessed that nobody else had the experience and knowledge to attempt such a work. In their steady, routine, management of a creaking parochial system the dutiful personnel of the Commissioners made an inestimable contribution to the life of the Church of England.

The structures of the Church

The history of the Church Commissioners between 1948 and 1998 is to a great extent a tracing of the movements of formal structures. Quite simply, it presents a brief period of unity of function sandwiched between two periods of division. What began with the Queen Anne's Bounty and the Ecclesiastical Commissioners ended with the Church Commissioners and the Archbishops' Council. The blunt significance of this is that it speaks of a Church that continued to tussle with its own understandings of authority and governance. The character and work of the Church Commissioners crystallised this uniquely, and long before the reform of 1998.

How would the student of secular politics measure the world of the Church of England in this period? In the unsteady evolution of the British political state after the passage of the Great Reform Act of 1832, politicians struggled to reconcile the rights of numbers with those of interests. Was the art of representation anchored simply to 'quantities' or should it develop out of the presence of 'qualities'? Only towards the end of the twentieth century, as the government of the day struggled to reform the House of Lords, was the contest between the two logics of representation almost resolved.

For its part the Church of England played with both forms of representation and found that it could not bear to part with either. Essentially it was a fusion of two logics, one vertical and the other horizontal; the former a logic of quantity and the latter one of quality. For a vertical logic showed there to be forty-three diocesan tribes and the hundreds of parishes within them, and a horizontal one revealed that there were castes across them all: the bishops, the clergy and the laity. These different strains permeated to the heart of the Church Commissioners too. The constitution of 1948 showed the Church adhering stoutly to both logics. For the much-maligned figure of ninety-five Church Commissioners did not appear merely as a quixotic response to a remote history, but was chosen to express the Church's understanding of itself: it was a formidable, inoperable presentation of the two logics, combined with the formidable theoretical presence of officers of the state. The National Institutions Measure of 1998 affected the same rationale, different though the result certainly was.

The story of the Church of England in the twentieth century was not merely one in which authority was reinvented. Its forms multiplied. The age began with government by parliament (wherein could be found the laity in various states of religiosity) and episcopacy. This was soon found to be unsatisfactory. Many in the Church did not like to be thought to be in the pockets of the bishops, or in the hands of parliament. The power of nonconformity in the nineteenth century and the prevailing winds of liberalism and populism altered attitudes forcefully. The failure of parliament to govern the Church when it began to attempt more and more institutional reform brought a practical mandate for reform. 1921 saw the creation of the Church Assembly, a church parliament for bishops, clergy and laity, and its Central Board of Finance.[2] Seventy-seven years later, the reforms of 1998 saw yet another creation of authority, the Archbishops' Council. What matters here is that none of these were abolished. They had to find a way to work with each other. The more institutions there were, the harder that must be, not least in a culture which observed no very clear line between philosophy on the one hand and administration on the other. The language which expressed this, perhaps above all, was that of money. This meant two things for an institution like the Church Commissioners. First, they sat squarely in the middle of a landscape that was both complex and ambiguous, one which might or might not work according to the needs of all its constituents. To this they must bring some power for coherence. Second, they were also vulnerable to the influence of their constituents. Indeed, the Board of the Commissioners was made up of them.

The history of the Church Commissioners showed that the establishment of the Church of England remained important, and that it could prove valuable to the Church in many ongoing, practical matters. Certainly, the place that was given in the structures of the Church Commissioners to officers of the state was widely ridiculed within the Church. After all, where were they? Yet it was a question which might not only have been asked of the politicians. The problem of absenteeism was rife in the representation of the Church too, and with far less excuse. The first fifty years of the Commissioners' history suggested that this actually mattered. Is it a coincidence that the Church Commissioners achieved their apotheosis at a time when the archbishop of Canterbury was actually to be found in the chair, loyally and powerfully supporting them, between 1948 and 1961? For of all the archbishops of Canterbury of this period, Fisher alone understood the fundamental significance of the Church Commissioners to the

---

[2] For a comprehensive discussion of the world of the Church Assembly see Kenneth A. Thompson, *Bureacracy and church reform: the organizational response of the Church of England to social change 1800–1965*, Oxford 1970.

Church of England. This fact in itself gave the men of the 1950s undoubted confidence in their task: the assurance that they acted with authority and that their work did actually stand at the heart of the Church of England. It was on this foundation that they became the great co-ordinating power in the Church, centralising, reordering, integrating, standardising: stipends, pensions, bishoprics, properties. The Commissioners inherited a neglected landscape of inequalities and dangers and became the engine of improvement and unification, drawing in to themselves all manner of private concerns. Episcopacy was, effectively, nationalised. The clergy stipend was raised and made more nearly standard. A modern scheme of pensions, with all its hazards, came into being. An innovative and often brilliant investment policy was orchestrated, one that was truly pioneering in the manner in which it sought to combine ethical considerations with financial gain. That the Church of England was recognisable as a modern institutional reality in the eyes of corporate society as a whole was the achievement of the Church Commissioners far more than of any other institution of the Church.

After 1961 there was enough momentum here, and in the vision of their leaders, to carry the Church Commissioners forward for some time yet. But a significant shift was about to take place. When they no longer enjoyed committed patronage, and as the dioceses found their feet and their self-confidence, the Commissioners were the more vulnerable to accusations that they were simply one department among many in the Church, and one whose claims and airs appeared too bold, too grandiose, to command respect. When their commercial policies failed and this, in turn, demonstrated indisputably their failure to judge soundly their discretionary powers, the Church Commissioners were left with few supporters. The co-ordinating power in the Church was assumed by a new authority – and the very construction of that authority showed the Commissioners at the last to be one of the powers to be themselves converted. In 1998 the leaders of the Church of England sought to recast the Church once more. In this they showed that they were prepared to overhaul an institution which they had made little effort to engage with, even when its statutes actually invited them to lead it. With the creation of the Archbishops' Council the Church ended up with a body which was far less representative than the Board of the Church Commissioners (indeed, it could fairly be said to represent nothing except itself). Weak in its representation of both quantity and quality, it relied instead on presenting a passable construction of centrality. It was a body which only acquired administrative substance by appropriating it, almost wholesale, from elsewhere; and a body whose relationships with the House of Bishops and the General Synod appeared, to say the least, ambiguous. In the short term it is hard to judge whether the ongoing life of the Church was more severely complicated by the erosion of the capital base of the Commissioners' assets, which occurred as a part of the policy of financial rescue in the early 1990s, or by the creation of this new, and arguable, source of authority.

Upon the Archbishops' Council the dust has yet to settle. It is perhaps sufficient now for a historian to suggest a comparison between the story of its birth and that of the Church Commissioners fifty years previously. In one, practical experience drove politics; in the other, politics proved the motor. This pragmatic liberal bureaucracy of the twentieth century, resting self-assuredly on its own careful empiricism, its undemonstrative exercise of discretionary power and its avoidance of campaigns and slogans may well look to us more and more like a lost civilisation. At all events, few know better than the officers of the Church Commissioners the difficulty of attaching the language of self-justification to practical administration. To be sure, the tasks of the new Archbishops' Council are different from those of the Commissioners, as they are now constituted. But there is now yet another layer of authority to which the Commissioners must relate in the governance of the Church. One is left, at the last, to reflect on the fragility of the line which distinguishes between a central authority, possessing the power to orchestrate a broader ensemble of powers, and another which simply adds to their number, reinforces many of the old embarrassments and complications, and even invents more of its own.

Leave-taking

What was the legacy of the work that the Church Commissioners performed on behalf of the Church of England, between their steady, purposeful creation in 1948 and the hectic fabrication of the Archbishops' Council in 1998? Across fifty years much power had been concentrated in their hands, and although it attracted a particular quality of grumbling, there was seldom much sense that such power was to be found in the wrong place, or was poorly applied. The Commissioners devoted themselves to the maintenance of unexciting necessities and even showed that they could relish periodic campaigns, as long as they answered to the broad requirements upon which a rational, liberal bureaucracy must insist. If the Commissioners found an uneasy place in the affairs and affections of the Church it was because they had so great a presence in the private and domestic realities about which individuals cared so much: incomes, homes, personal security.

Indeed, for the most part, the Commissioners handled their relationships with other departments of the Church, particularly those ensconced in Church House, as well as could be expected, given that the currency of their relations must inevitably owe something to suspicion and rivalry. At the same time, the Church cannot be governed solely by expertise, on the one hand, or by representative power on the other. If the Commissioners' relations with the Church Assembly, and then the General Synod, were wary, and even frosty, expertise and representation are rarely found quite at home together, and where they are drawn to each other by institutional necessities their relationship cannot be expected to be cordial. Perhaps the best they can be is productive. At certain points in the later twentieth century the authorities of the Church were successful in pursuing enterprises which not only maintained or reformed the Church itself but showed that the Church could seek to influence a wider society and a broader set of issues. Archbishop Fisher's drive towards a modern Church which could inhabit the post-war world with credibility was at least partly realised. But by the later 1990s it could too easily be seen how the authorities of the Church might turn in upon themselves and almost consume their energies in a frantic pursuit of the claims of an interior corporatism.

However much the dioceses may have resented the Church Commissioners, whose fraught task was to hold them together within some explicit scheme of uniformity, they owed much of their burgeoning powers to the Commissioners' organisational and financial policies. By the last two decades of the century they were truly corporations in their own right. It is natural to wonder how long this will last in the new century. The politics of diocesan quotas have already grown brittle, even querulous. New visions of the old inequalities rise before the eyes; of richer parishes who see little reason to support poorer ones; of richer dioceses who see no obligation to maintain weaker ones. The debate will probably first concentrate on the number of suffragan bishops, which rose so strikingly in the second half of the twentieth century. There may be something more than murmurs against the money found for a sprawling number of non-parochial, so-called 'sector' ministries. Loyal subscribers may begin to ask, more testily, whether it is altogether necessary for church dignitaries to live in such large houses?

But much of what defined the fortunes of the Church Commissioners between 1948 and 1998 lay entirely beyond the internal fortunes of these denominational bodies. British society as a whole was caught up in a constant upheaval of migration, and in unaccountable economic cycles which combined to force an unforgiving march from a society that had employed millions of manufacturers to one that comprised still more millions of consumers. The task of the Church Commissioners was to interpret and respond, to manage these shifts and patterns adroitly and sensitively as best they could, without rhetoric or illusion. Their greatest successes were brilliant, if soon forgotten; their great disaster will surely be held against them for decades.

Meanwhile, as the Church Commissioners sought to steer a steady course, so much in British Christianity was losing its vital force. The confident, liberal, ecumenical visions of the earlier century were by the close of the age looking hesitant and even bewildered. So many of the great new themes brought the Churches not opportunities, but reasons for doubt. The decline in numbers of active adherents was irregular, but the cumulative picture of decline across fifty years is a relentless one. Although the first ecumenical church-sharing projects in which the Church of England had participated had been full of hope, by the 1980s the Free Churches were often surviving by virtue of a new kind of ecumenism: patching up local unions, often between Methodist and United Reformed congregations which were not sufficiently dogmatic to justify their occupation of different premises. These rarely embraced the Church of England, which clung tenaciously to the parallel logic of its own constructions and perhaps trusted to Christians from other traditions to come its way because they no longer enjoyed an alternative. In the rural world the decline of the Free Churches was startling: chapels simply died on their feet. Much as the Church Commissioners might insist that they were establishing more new parishes than closing redundant churches, by the late 1960s none could deny that the Church's presence within the lives of the people was weakening inexorably, and by the year. To maintain a national parish system in such a dispiriting context was no simple task. If the Church Commissioners committed themselves to one mission above all others, it was to preserve precisely that continuing national system that secularisation steadily undermined.

The historian of the last fifty years is left only to wonder what the next fifty years will bring. Unless the societal patterns which have gathered such force in the later twentieth century are superseded by new ones which combine to benefit the cause of corporate Christianity, at some point decline must bite through the sinews of the body and into the structures, the very bones, which give it solid form and movement. Arguably, it was the achievement of the Church Commissioners between 1948 and 1998 to maintain, by a steady, ongoing reform of particulars, the contours of an order and a method which might well have decayed and even collapsed in some areas without their efforts. Perhaps a future age will observe that their legacy was simply to hold back for a period of time a decline which was altogether something too formidable to be halted by the Churches alone. For how much longer can the Church of Christ preserve a pervasive presence in the patterns of individual life, and in the localities of every community, when the landscape which it inhabits shows such a relentless erosion of explicit public devotion and committed participation? Such a phenomenon, in a society which Christianity has for centuries formed, characterised and dignified, brings no clear assurances and no obvious prospects.

Appendix 1

Church Estates Commissioners and Secretaries to the Church Commissioners

First Church Estates Commissioners (Crown appointment)

Sir Philip Baker Wilbraham, 1939–1954
Sir Malcolm Trustram Eve (Lord Silsoe 1963), 1954–1969
Sir Ronald Harris, 1969–1983
Sir Douglas Lovelock, 1983–1993
Sir Michael Colman, 1993–1998

Second Church Estates Commissioners (Crown appointment)

T.W. Burden, 1948–1949
Sir Richard Acland, 1949–1952
Sir John Crowder, 1952–1958
Sir Hubert Ashton, 1958–1962
John Arbuthnot, 1962–1964
E.L. Mallalieu QC, 1965–1970
Marcus Worsley, 1970–1973
E.S. Bishop JP, 1974
T. W. Walker, 1975–1979
William van Straubenzee MBE, 1979–1987
Michael Alison, 1987–1997
Stuart Bell, 1998

Third Church Estates Commissioners (Appointed by the archbishop of Canterbury)

Lord Tovey, 1948–1952
Sir Malcom Trustram Eve, 1952–1954
Sir James Brown, 1954–1962
Sir Hubert Ashton KBE, MC, DL, 1962–1973

Mrs Betty Ridley (Dame 1975), 1973–1981
Mrs Betsy Howarth, 1981–1988
Mrs Margaret Laird, 1989–1998

Secretaries

Sir James Brown, 1948–1954
Sir Mortimer Warren, 1954–1964
Sir Ronald Harris, 1964–1969
Kenneth Ryle, 1969–1975
S.P. Osmond, 1975–1980
Kenneth Lamb, 1981–1985
James Shelley, 1986–1993
Patrick Locke, 1994–1998

Appendix 2

The Basic Structures of the Church Commissioners

1948–1964

BOARD OF GOVERNORS
Meeting monthly

ESTATES AND FINANCE COMMITTEE

COMMITTEES OF THE BOARD
Administrative Committee
See Houses Committee

ADVISORY
Stock market Investments Advisory Group

1964–1998

BOARD OF GOVERNORS

COMMITTEES OF THE BOARD
General Purposes Committee
Assets Committee
Houses Committee
Pastoral Committee
Redundant Churches Committee 1968–
Audit Committee 1994–
Bishoprics Committee 1994–

LIAISON
Church of England Pensions Board 1963–

Appendix 3

The Church Commissioners Measure, 1947

A MEASURE passed by the National Assembly of the Church of England

To promote the more efficient and economical administration of the resources of the Church of England by uniting the Corporation of the Governors of the Bounty of Queen Anne for the augmentation of the maintenance of the poor clergy, founded by charter under the Great Seal in the year 1704, and the Ecclesiastical Commissioners for England originally established in the year 1836 by the statute 6 and 7 William the Fourth, chapter 77.

[2nd April 1947]

Establishment of the Church Commissioners

1. (I) For the Purpose of uniting Queen Anne's Bounty with the Ecclesiastical Commissioners there shall be established, by the name of the Church Commissioners of England, a body corporate having perpetual succession and a common seal and power to acquire and hold land without licence in mortmain.

(2) The said body (hereafter in this Measure referred to as "the Commissioners") shall be constituted in accordance with the provisions of the First Schedule to this Measure, and may for all purposes be referred to as the "Church Commissioners".

Transfer of functions and property

2. On that appointed day Queen Anne's Bounty and the Ecclesiastical Commissioners (hereafter in this Measure referred to as "the constituent authorities") shall be dissolved and-

(a) all functions, rights and privileges of either of them shall be transferred to, and become functions, rights and privileges of, the Commissioners ;

(b) all property vested in either of them shall be transferred to and, shall by virtue of this section and without any conveyance, assignment, transfer or other assurance vest in the Commissioners : and

(c) all property held in trust for either of them shall be held in trust for the Commissioners :

Provided that a vesting of property by virtue of paragraph (b) of this section shall not affect any previously existing trust or mortgage or other charge affecting the property, or any previously existing lease or tenancy thereof.

Method of business

3. The business of the Commissioners, except the exercise of powers which, under this or any other Measure or any enactment, are required to be exercised at a general meeting of the Commissioners, shall be transacted in accordance with the provisions of this Measure by Board of Governors (hereafter in this Measure referred to as "the Board"), the Church Estates Commissioners appointed under the Ecclesiastical Commissioners Act, 1850, and an Estates and Finance Committee.

General Meetings of the Commissioners

4. (I) The archbishop of Canterbury shall be the chairman of the Commissioners and, if at any general meeting thereof, he is not present, such member as the members present may select will act as chairman.

(2) The Commissioners shall in every financial year hold an annual general meeting for the purpose of-

(a) considering, and, if thought fit, passing resolutions with respect to, the annual report and accounts of the Commissioners and any other matters which may be brought before the meeting by the Board, or which the chairman, upon a request submitted to the secretary by any member, may have authorised the secretary to include in the notices of business to be considered ;

(b) appointing in a year when any such appointment falls to be made, persons to serve as members of the Board ;

(c) appointing persons to serve as members of the Estates and Finance Committee ; and

(d) considering and, if thought fit, adopting the recommendations of the Board as to the allocation of such moneys as the Board may report to be available.

(3) The annual general meeting shall be called by the chairman as soon as conveniently may be after the audit of the Commissioners' accounts for the preceding financial year has been completed.

(4) The chairman may call such other general meetings of the Commissioners as he deems necessary and he shall, so soon as reasonably practicable, call a meeting if ten or more members give to the secretary notice in writing that they desire a meeting to be called to consider matters to be specified in the notice.

(5) Not less than twenty-eight days before any general meeting notice of the day, hour and place appointed therefore, and not less than ten days before any general meeting notice of the business to be considered thereat, shall be sent by post to every member.

Constitution and function of the Board of Governors

5. (I) The Board shall be constituted in accordance with the provisions of the Second Schedule to this Measure.

(2) The archbishop of Canterbury shall be the chairman of the Board and, if at any meeting thereof he is not present such member as the members present may elect shall act as chairman.

(3) Subject to the provisions of this Measure, all the functions and business of the Commissioners shall be exercised and transacted by the Board.

(4) The Board shall have power –

(a) to refer for consideration and report any matter within their jurisdiction to the Estates and Finance Committee, or to any other committee consisting of Commissioners which the Board may appoint for the purpose ;

(b) to authorise the Estates and Finance Committee, or any other such committee as aforesaid, to do and complete any matter on behalf of the Board:

(c) to make general rules for the direction and guidance of the Estates and Finance Committee or any committee appointed by the Board, as to the matters and acts to be considered and done by that committee and as to the general principles upon which that committee shall act in carrying out such functions as may from time to time be delegated to them by the Board.

(5) The like notice of the business to be considered at a meeting of the Board as is given to members of the Board shall be given also to diocesan bishops who are not members thereof.

Church Estates Commissioners and Estates Finance Committee. 13 & 14 Vict. c. 94

6. (I) The three Church Estates Commissioners appointed from time to time under section one of the Ecclesiastical Commissioners Act, 1850, shall, together, with the persons appointed under the next succeeding subsection constitute a committee, to be known as the Estates and Finance Committee. They shall, subject to the provisions of subsection (3) of this section, be joint Treasurers of the Commissioners and shall be ex officio members of any committee appointed by the Board.

(2) The Commissioners shall in every year at their annual general meeting appoint not less than two or more than four of their number to be additional members of the Estates and Finance Committee, one half of the persons so appointed being laymen who are Commissioners otherwise than in right of office.

(3) The Estates and Finance Committee shall have the same functions in relation to the property and business of the Commissioners as the Estates Committee constituted under section seven of the said Act of 1850 had in relation to the property and business of the Ecclesiastical Commissioners immediately before the appointed day, and, accordingly, sections eight and nine of that Act and section 2 of the Ecclesiastical Commissioners Act, 1866, as set out with consequential adaptations in the Third Schedule to this Measure, shall continue to have effect :

Provided that during a vacancy in the office of one of the Church Estate Commissioners or for any other cause which he may think sufficient, the archbishop of Canterbury may from time to time appoint one of the additional lay members of the Estates and Finance Committee to act as an additional joint Treasurer during such period as the said archbishop shall determine, and while such appointment is in force the person so appointed shall be entitled to exercise the powers of a Church Estates Commissioner for any purpose for which the presence or concurrence of two or more Church Estates Commissioners is required by the said Acts.

(4) In addition to any other powers conferred on them by this Measure, but subject to any general rules made by this Board, the Estates and Finance Committee

shall have full and exclusive power to exercise and discharge in the name of the Commissioners all functions of the Commissioners in matters relating to –

(a) the making realisation and change of investments; and

(b) the appointment, terms of service, dismissal and direction of the Commissioners' officers, solicitors and agents and control over the expenses of administration : provided that this paragraph shall not apply in relation to the secretary of the Commissioners.

It shall be the duty of the Committee to act on behalf of and in the name of the Commissioners in any matter which in their opinion is urgent, but they shall report any such action to the Board at the next meeting thereof.

(5) The receipt of any two of the joint Treasurers, or the receipt of any one of them countersigned by the accountant of the Commissioners, or by some other officer authorised in that behalf by the Estates and Finance Committee, shall be a good and sufficient discharge for any money due and payable to the Commissioners.

(6) The provisions of any enactment or Measure relating to the payment of salaries and pensions to Church Estates Commissioners shall continue to have the effect with the substitution of reference to the Board and to the general fund of the Commissioners for references to the Ecclesiastical Commissioners and to their common fund.

Procedure

7. (I) The provision of the Fourth Schedule to this Measure shall have the effect with regard to the meetings and procedure of the Commissioners and of the Board and of any committee constituted by or under this measure.

(2) Subject to the aforesaid and to any other provisions of this Measure

(a) the Commissioners may regulate their own procedure and may from time to time at any general meeting make, vary and revoke Standing Orders for the purpose ;

(b) the Board may from time to time make, vary and revoke Standing Orders for regulating the procedure of the Board or of any Committee of the Board and subject to any such Standing Orders the Board and any such committee may regulate their own procedure ;

(c) the Estates and Finance Committee may regulate their own procedure and may from time to time make, vary and revoke Standing Orders for the purpose.

Secretary, agents and other officers

8. (I) The Commissioners shall from time to time at any general meeting appoint a secretary upon such terms as they may think fit.

(2) The Estates and Finance Committee shall from time to time in exercise of their powers under section six of this Measure appoint such other officers and such solicitors and agents as they deem necessary for the proper discharge of the functions of the Commissioners.

6 & 7 Will. 4. c. 77

(3) The proviso to section 7 of the Ecclesiastical Commissioners Act, 1836 (which authorises the Treasury to regulate the amount of the salaries of the officers employed by the Ecclesiastical Commissioners) shall not apply in relation to the officers employed by the Commissioners.

Seal of the
Commissioners

9. (I) The common seal of the Commissioners shall be judicially noticed and shall be authenticated by the signature of the secretary, or of some other officer of the Commissioners authorised by the Board to act in that behalf.

(2) Every document purporting to be sealed with the said seal and to be authenticated by the signature of the secretary, or of a person so authorised to act in that behalf, shall be received in evidence and be deemed to be such an instrument without further proof, unless evidence to the contrary is given.

Finance

10. (I) The financial year of the Commissioners shall commence on the first day of April.

(2) The accounts of the constituent authorities current on the first day of October preceding the appointed day shall not be required to be closed on the days on which, but for this Measure, they would have been closed, but shall be kept open (or, if necessary, reopened) and continued until the day preceding the appointed day at the end of that preceding day shall be closed and made up.

(3) The said accounts shall be audited by the persons and in the manner by whom and in which annual accounts of the authority in question were required to be audited, but shall be laid by the Board before the Commissioners at their first annual general meeting (which shall be held as soon as conveniently may be after the audit has been completed) and section twelve of this Measure shall, with any necessary adaptations, apply in relation to those accounts (including the auditors' reports thereon).

(4) As from the appointed day, the Commissioners shall keep a general fund to which shall be transferred on the appointed day any balances on income account from the common fund of the Ecclesiastical Commissioners and from the corporate fund of Queen Anne's Bounty.

(5) Any trust or other fund previously maintained by either of the constituent authorities as a separate fund shall be continued and maintained as a separate fund by the Commissioners : provided that funds maintained by the two constituent authorities for the same objects or purposes may be amalgamated.

(6) Subject to the last preceding subsection, the Commissioners shall carry all income received in respect of property and funds held by them into their general fund, and shall discharge thereout all trusts and commitments to which that income or any part thereof is subject and all expenses and obligations falling upon the Commissioners in the due discharge of their functions, and the balance from time to time thereafter remaining in the said fund shall be available for any purpose for which, but for this Measure, any surplus of the common fund of the Ecclesiastical Commissioners or of the corporate fund of Queen Anne's Bounty would have been available.

Accounts and
audit

11. (I) The Commissioners shall cause such accounts to be kept as may be required for the due performance and discharge of their functions.

(2) The accounts of the Commissioners shall in every year be audited in such manner and by such person as the Treasury may direct, and the auditor's report thereon shall for the purposes of the nest succeeding section be deemed to form part of the accounts.

Annual report and

12. (I) So soon as may be after the close of every financial year the Board shall

accounts to be laid before Parliament and Church Assembly

prepare a report of the work and proceedings of the Commissioners during that year, and shall present the report and accounts for that year to the Commissioners at their annual general meeting.

(2) Within thirty days after such meeting the secretary shall transmit the report and accounts, together with a copy of any resolution passed by the Commissioners with reference thereto, to the Secretary of State for the Home Department, who shall lay copies of the report, accounts and resolution, if any, before both Houses of Parliament.

(3) Within the same period the secretary shall also send copies of the said documents to the secretary of the Church Assembly, who shall lay them before the Assembly.

Pending and existing proceedings and contracts, etc.

13. (I) No proceedings or cause of action pending or existing immediately before the appointed day by or against either of the constituent authorities shall abate, be discontinued or in any way prejudicially affected by this Measure, but any such proceedings may be continued and enforced by or against the Commissioners,

(2) All contracts, bonds, agreements and other instruments subsisting immediately before the appointed day and affecting either of the constituent authorities shall be of as full force and effect against, or in favour of, the Commissioners had been a party thereto instead of the constituent authority.

Transfer of stock

14. (I) Where any stock is standing in the books of a company in the name of either of the constituent authorities, a request by the secretary of the Commissioners and production of a copy of this Measure printed by or for the King's Printer of Acts of Parliament shall be a sufficient authority to the company to transfer the stock into the name of and pay dividends on the stock to, the Commissioners.

(2) In this section the expression –

"company" includes the Bank of England and any company or person keeping books in which any stock is registered or inscribed ; and

"stock" includes any share, annuity or other security.

Transfer of Officers

15. (I) On the appointed day every officer of either of the constituent authorities shall be transferred to, and become an officer of the Commissioners.

(2) The Commissioners may assign to any such officer (hereafter in this Measure referred to as a "transferred officer") such duties as they think fit ; but he shall not be in any worse position as respects tenure of office, conditions of service or salary than he would have been if this Measure had not been passed.

(3) If within two years after the appointed day a transferred officer expresses to the Estates and Finances Committee his desire to retire on special terms and the Committee are satisfied that is equitable to allow him so to do, they shall, upon his resignation, grant him compensation of not less value than the superannuation benefits which he would have received had he resigned on the grounds of infirmity, and, if he so elects, shall on such terms as they deem equitable allow him to surrender a part of such compensation for the benefit of his spouse or dependants.

Transitional arrangements and inaugural meeting

16. (I) The first appointed and nominated Commissioners may be appointed and nominated at any time after the passing of this measure.

(2) The archbishop of Canterbury, after consultation with the constituent

of the
Commissioners

authorities, shall –

(a) make before the appointed day such temporary appointments as he may deem necessary to enable the functions of the Commissioners to be discharged until permanent appointments and arrangements can be made : and

(b) by notice in writing sent by post to each of them not less than twenty-eight days before the appointed day, summon the Commissioners to attend the inaugural general meeting of the Commissioners either on the appointed day or on some later day within ten days therefrom.

(3) At their inaugural meeting the Commissioners shall –

(a) appoint a secretary ;

(b) appoint members to serve on the Board and on the Estates and Finance Committee ; and

(c) transact any other business on which ten days' notice has been given to members.

(4) The secretary shall summon members of the Board to attend the first meeting thereof on such day as the Chairman my direct.

(5) The Estates and Finance Committee shall, without any necessity for previous notice to members thereof, meet at the close of the inaugural general meeting of the Commissioners to make, or appoint a meeting for the purpose of making, such other appointments and such arrangements for the conduct of the Commissioners' business as they deem necessary.

52 & 53 Vict. c. 63

The mention of particular matters in this section shall not be held to prejudice or affect the general application of section thirty-seven of the Interpolation Act, 1889.

Provisions as to
superannuation

17. (I) The Estates and Finance Committee shall make rules regulating the grant of superannuation benefits to the officers of the Commissioners, and the allocation of superannuation benefits to their spouses or dependants, and the provisions of the Ecclesiastical Commissioners (Superannuation) Act, 1865, the Queen Anne's Bounty (Superannuation) Act 1870, the Superannuation (Ecclesiastical Commissioners and Queen Anne's Bounty) Acts, 1914 and 1933, and the Superannuation (Various Services) Act, 1938, shall not apply to the Commissioners or their officers :

Provided that in the case of any transferred officer –

(a) service under either of the constituent authorities and service under the Commissioners shall be aggregated and treated as continuous service under the Commissioners ; and

(b) the superannuation benefits to be granted to him on his retirement shall not be less than those which might have been awarded had the provisions of the said Acts applied at that date to him and to the Commissioners and the Commissioners shall have the like power to permit the allocation of such superannuation benefits to his spouse or dependants as they would have had under section one of the Superannuation (Various Services) Act, 1938.

(2) As from the appointed day the liability of either of the constituent authorities to make payments in respect of superannuation benefits to a person who had been employed by them, but had before the appointed day ceased to be so employed, or to his spouse or dependants, shall be transferred to, and become a liability of, the Commissioners and be a charge on their general fund.

Interpretation

18. (I) In this Measure, unless the context otherwise requires –

"the appointed day" means the first day in April in such year as the archbishop of Canterbury may appoint by a notice published in the London Gazette not later than the first day of December the preceding year ;

"dean" includes the dean or provost of any cathedral church in England, and the deans of Westminster and Windsor ;

"functions" includes powers and duties ;

"officer" includes servant;

"procedure" includes the fixing of a quorum ;

"property" includes a thing in action any interest in real or personal property ;

"superannuation benefits" has the same meaning as it has in the Superannuation (Various Services) Act, 1938

(2) References in any Act or Measure (other than this Measure) or in any other document (including any testamentary document) to either of the constituent authorities, or to the common or corporate fund of either of them, shall be construed as references to the Commissioners or, as the case may be, to their general fund.

Short title

19. This measure may be cited as the Church Commissioners Measure, 1947.

SCHEDULE I

Section 1 (2)

CONSTITUTION OF THE COMMISSIONERS

I. The Commissioners shall be –

the archbishops of Canterbury and York and the diocesan bishops of the provinces of Canterbury and York ;

the three church estates commissioners ;

five deans appointed by the Church Assembly, three from the Province of Canterbury and two from the province of York ;

ten other clerks in Holy Orders appointed by the Church Assembly ;

four laymen nominated by His Majesty, and four persons nominated by the archbishop of Canterbury : provided that at least two of the eight Commissioners so nominated shall be, or have been, of counsel to His Majesty ;

The Lord Chancellor, the Lord President of the Council, the First Lord of the Treasury, the Chancellor of the Exchequer and the Secretary of State for the Home Department ;

the Speaker of the House of Commons ;

the Lord Chief Justice, the Master of the Rolls, the Attorney-General and the Solicitor-General ;

The Lord Mayor and two aldermen of the City of London and the Lord Mayor of the City of York ; and

one representative from each of the universities of Oxford and Cambridge, being either the Vice-Chancellor or a person nominated by him to serve during his own term of office.

2. Commissioners appointed by the Church Assembly (who need not be members thereof) shall be appointed for five years in such manner as the Assembly may from time to time determine.

Commissioners nominated by the archbishop of Canterbury shall be nominated for such number of years as he may from time to time determine.

The two aldermen of the City of London shall be appointed by the court of aldermen thereof either for one year or for such number of years not exceeding five as the court may from time to time determine.

In this paragraph the expression "year" means a period of twelve months commencing on the first day of April.

Any such Commissioner as is referred to in this paragraph shall be eligible for re-appointment or re-nomination.

3. In the event of delay in the appointment or nomination of a successor or any such Commissioner as is referred to in the last preceding paragraph shall. Notwithstanding the expiration of the period for which he was appointed or nominated, continue to hold office until a successor is appointed or nominated.

4. A person shall be disqualified from being a Commissioner so long as he is a salaried official of any central or diocesan body in the Church of England.

5. If an appointed Commissioner who was qualified for appointment by virtue of being a dean, a clerk in Holy Orders, or a layman appointed by the Church Assembly ceases to be so qualified, he shall thereby vacate his membership.

6. Every lay Commissioner not being a Commissioner in right of office shall, before otherwise acting in connection with the business of the Commissioners, declare in writing before an officer of the Commissioners that he is a member of the Church of England.

SCHEDULE II

CONSTITUTION OF THE BOARD OF GOVERNORS

1. The Board shall consist of the following persons –

the archbishops of Canterbury and York ;
the three church estates commissioners ;
twenty-two other Commissioners appointed by the Commissioners, and
such other Commissioners, if any, as may be co-opted in accordance with the
provisions of this Schedule.

2. Of the twenty-two members to be appointed by the Commissioners six shall be diocesan bishops, two shall be deans, six shall be other clerks in Holy Orders and eight shall be laymen, of whom six shall be chosen from those appointed by the Church Assembly.

3. At the inaugural general meeting of the Commissioners twenty-two members shall be appointed in the proportions laid down in the preceding paragraph and of the members so appointed one-half shall hold office for six-years and the remainder for three years. Thereafter, in every third year eleven members shall be appointed at the annual general meeting of the Commissioners to fill the places of members retiring in that year.

4. The period of office of an appointed member shall run from the day following the annual general meeting at which he is appointed to the close of the day on which his successor is appointed.

A member appointed at the inaugural general meeting shall enter upon his office forthwith, but the date for his retirement shall be calculated as if he had been appointed at the first annual general meeting of the Commissioners.

5. The eleven original members to hold office for six years shall be three bishops, one dean, three other clerks, three of the laymen appointed by the Church Assembly and one of the laymen not so appointed.

6. As between members in any category, those to hold office for six years shall be those receiving most votes :

Provided that if –

(a) in any category there is no contest ; or

(b) in a category where there is a contest, a selection must be made between two or more members whose votes were equal;

any necessary selection shall be made by lot.

For the purposes of this paragraph, lots shall be drawn by such persons and in such manner as the Chairman may direct.

7. The Board may from time to time co-opt as additional members of the Board not more than three persons being Commissioners at the date of co-optation.

Such co-optation may be for any period not extending beyond the next triennial election of members of the Board.

8. If a member of the Board who was qualified for membership by virtue of being a diocesan bishop, a dean, a clerk in Holy Orders, or a layman appointed by the Church Assembly, ceases to be so qualified, he shall thereby vacate his membership.

SCHEDULE III

Section 6 (3)

THE ECCLESIASTICAL COMMISSIONERS ACT, 1850

Sections 8 & 9, as adapted.

Estates and Finance Committee to manage all Estates of the Commissioners

8. It shall be the duty of the Estates and Finance Committee, or any three of them, of whom two or more shall be Church Estates Commissioners, to consider all matters in any away relating or incident to the sale, purchase, exchange, letting or management, by or on behalf of the Commissioners, of any land, tithes or heriditaments, and to devise such measures touching the same as shall appear to such committee to be most expedient ; and such committee, or any three of them, of whom two or more shall be Church Estates Commissioners, shall have full power and authority subject to such general rules as shall have been made by the Board of Governors of the Commissioners, to do and execute any act, including the affixing of the common seal to any scheme or other instrument within the power of the Commissioners, in respect of the sale, purchase, exchange, letting, or management, of any lands, tithes or heriditaments :

Provided always, that no such act shall be done or executed by the Commissioners otherwise than by the said Estates and Finance Committee, nor by such committee unless with the concurrence of at least two of the Church Estates Commissioners.

Chairman of the Estates and Finance Committee

9. At all meetings of the Estates and Finance Committee the first Church Estates Commissioner shall preside, or, if he is absent, the other Church Estates Commissioner appointed by His Majesty or the Church Estates Commissioner appointed by the archbishop, shall be chairman at alternate meetings ; and in the case of an equality of votes the chairman shall have a second or casting vote.

THE ECCLESIASTICAL COMMISSIONERS ACT, 1886

Section 2, as adapted.

Application of Ecclesiastical Commissioners Act, 1866, s. 2

All acts which the Estates and Finance Committee of the Commissioners are authorised by law to do and execute or to complete may be done and executed or completed by any two members of such Committee being Church Estates Commissioners.

SCHEDULE IV

Section 7 (I)

GENERAL PROVISIONS RELATING TO THE COMMISSIONERS, THE BOARD AND COMMITTEES

I. The proceedings of the Commissioners, the Board or a committee shall not be invalidated by any vacancy in the membership thereof, or by any defect in the qualification, appointment or nomination of any member.

2. When an appointed or nominated Commissioner proposes to retire, his intention so to do shall be notified by him in writing to the secretary of the Commissioners, who shall forthwith give notice to the person or body by whom such Commissioner was appointed or nominated.

3. Casual vacancies among appointed or nominated Commissioners may be filled by the person or body by whom the Commissioner vacating office was appointed or nominated. Casual vacancies among members of the Board or a committee may be filled by the Board.

4. Any person appointed or nominated to fill a casual vacancy shall hold office for the remainder of the term (if any) for which his predecessor was appointed or nominated.

5. At any meeting of the Commissioners, the Board or a committee, every question shall be decided by a majority of the votes of members present and voting on that question and in the case of equality of votes, the member presiding shall have a second or casting vote :

Provided that, if at the inaugural or any general meeting the Commissioners so decide, the Commissioners who are to serve as Members of the Board or of the Estates and Finance Committee, may be chosen at that meeting by ballot, or (notwithstanding anything contained in this Measure) within fourteen days after that meeting by means of voting papers issued and returned by post.

6. Minutes of the proceedings of the Commissioners or of the Board signed at the same or the next meeting by a member describing himself, or appearing to be, the person presiding at the meeting at which the minutes are signed, shall be received in evidence without further proof, and, until the contrary is proved every meeting of the Commissioners or of the Board, in respect of the proceedings whereof minutes have been so signed shall be deemed to have been duly convened and held.

7. The provisions of this Schedule relating to Committees shall in their application to the Estates and Finance Committee have effect subject to any special provisions with respect thereto contained in this Measure.

Appendix 4

National Institutions Measure 1998

1998 No. 1

Arrangement of Sections.

SCHEDULES:

A Measure passed by the General Synod of the Church of England to make better provision for the establishment and functions of the national institutions of the Church of England and for the management of the assets thereof; and for purposes connected therewith.

[2 July 1998]

Archbishops' Council

Establishment of the Archbishops' Council

1. – (1) There shall be a body to be known as "the Archbishops' Council" whose objects shall be to co-ordinate, promote, aid and further the work and mission of the Church of England.

(2) It is hereby declared that the Council is established for charitable purposes.

(3) The provisions of Schedule 1 to this Measure shall have effect with respect to the Council and its members, to the appointment of its staff and to its proceedings and incidental powers.

(4) Part 1 of Schedule 1 to this Measure may at any time be amended by resolution of the General Synod.

(5) The Statutory Instruments Act 1946 shall apply to any resolution of the General Synod under subsection (4) above as if it were a statutory instrument and as if this Measure were an Act providing that any such resolution shall be subject to an annulment in pursuance of a resolution of either House of Parliament.

Application of funds

2. – (1) It shall be the duty of the Church Commissioners-

(a) from time to time in general meeting to determine the amount of income from their assets which is to be made available to the Council for application or distribution under subsection (3) below in the course of such period as may be specified in the determination, and

(b) to the extent that the Church Commissioners are satisfied that it is available for application or distribution, to pay that amount to the Council in equal monthly instalments or as otherwise agreed by them and the Council.

(2) Before determining the amount mentioned in subsection (1)(a) above the Church Commissioners shall consult the Council and in making the determination they shall have regard to any proposals made by the Council.

(3) The Council shall consider and determine how to apply or distribute such sums as have been made available by the Church Commissioners under subsection (1) above, but those sums shall not be applied or distributed by the Council for any purpose other than one for which the balance in the Church Commissioners' general fund was available immediately before the coming into force of this section and in applying or distributing those sums the Council shall have particular regard to the requirements of section 67 of the Ecclesiastical Commissioners Act 1840 relating to the making of additional provision for the cure of souls in parishes where such assistance is most required.

(4) Where a decision is taken by the Council of the Church Commissioners to the effect that a plan should be produced under this subsection, those bodies acting jointly shall after consultation with any body appearing to them to be significantly affected, produce a plan which-

(a) contains an estimate by the Church Commissioners, having regard to any recommendation made by the Assets Committee under section 6(3)(b) of the Church Commissioners Measure 1947, of the amount of income from their assets available for application or distribution under subsection (3) above during a period not exceeding three years, and

(b) identifies the purposes for which the sums mentioned in subsection (3) above are to be applied or distributed in the course of that period or part thereof and the proportion of those sums appropriate for each purpose.

Any such plan may be amended or replaced in the same manner.

(5) Where a plan is produced under subsection (4) above –

(a) the Church Commissioners, in complying with the requirements of subsection (2) above, shall have regard to the plan, and

(b) the Council, in complying with the requirements of subsection (3) above, shall act in accordance with the plan,

in so far as the plan relates to the period in question.

(6) As soon as practicable after the end of each year the Council shall cause a certificate to be issued to the Church Commissioners to the effect that the application and distribution of the sums made available by them as aforesaid has been in accordance with subsection (3) above.

Accounts and
audit

3. – (1) The following provisions of this section shall have effect without prejudice to the provisions of Part VI of the Charities Act 1993.

(2) The accounts of the Council for each year shall be audited by a person appointed by the Council with the approval of the General Synod, being a person eligible under subsection (2) of section 43 of that Act to carry out an audit under that subsection.

(3) The person so appointed shall be deemed, for the purposes of the said Part VI, to have been appointed in pursuance of the said section 43.

(4) The auditor's report for any year, together with the accounts for that year, shall be laid before the General Synod before the end of June in the following year.

Reports and
budgets

4. – (1) The Council shall cause a report of its work and proceedings during the year in question, including any decisions taken as to its future work, to be laid before the General Synod before the end of June in the following year.

(2) The Council shall also, at each group of sessions of the General Synod, cause an account of the matters discussed and the decisions taken by it at its meetings held since the previous group of sessions to be laid before the General Synod.

(3) In each year the Council shall prepare a budget indicating its expected income and expenditure for the following year and, before the end of June, cause it to be laid before the General Synod for its approval.

(4) In considering the annual budget it shall not be open to the General Synod to alter the amount of the sums to be made available to the Council by the Church Commissioners under Section 2 above or the proposed application or distribution of those sums.

(5) The General Synod may request reports from the Council of any matter relating to the functions of the Council.

Transfer of functions and officers

Transfer of
functions

5. – (1) Subject to the following provisions of this section the archbishops of Canterbury and York acting jointly may, after consultation with any body appearing to them to be significantly affected, by order transfer to the Council or such other body as may be specified in the order any function previously exercisable by-

(a) the Church Commissioners other than-

(i) a function relating to the management or ownership of the Commissioners' assets,

(ii) a function relating to bishops under any enactment specified in Part I of Schedule 2 to this Measure

(iii) a function relating to cathedrals under any enactment specified in Part II of that Schedule, and

(iv) a function under the Church of England (Pensions) Measures 1961 to 1997 or

(b) the Central Board of Finance, or

(c) the Standing Committee of the General Synod or any of its sub-committees.

(2) Any such order may contain such incidental, consequential and supplemental provisions as may be necessary or expedient for the purpose of giving full effect to the order, including provisions-

(a) amending paragraph 1 of Schedule 1 to the Church Commissioners Measure 1947 (as substituted by section 7 below) so as to reduce the number of Commissioners;

(b) for the carrying on and completion by or under the authority of the Council or other body so specified of anything commenced by or under the authority of the Commissioners, the Central Board of Finance or the Standing Committee before the date on which the order takes effect;

(c) for such adaptation of the statutory provisions relating to any such function transferred as may be necessary to enable it to be exercised by or on behalf of the Council or other body so specified;

(d) for the substitution of the Council or other body so specified for the Commissioners, the Central Board of Finance or the Standing Committee in any instrument, contract or legal proceedings made or commenced before the date on which the order takes effect.

(3) Before making any such order which relates to the functions of the Church Commissioners under the Dioceses Measure 1978 or the Pastoral Measure 1983 the archbishops shall consult with the Prime Minister and the Church Commissioners.

(4) An order under subsection (1) above may be varied by a subsequent order made thereunder.

(5) A draft of any order proposed to be made under subsection (1) above shall be laid before the General Synod and if it is approved by the General Synod, whether with or without amendment, the draft order as so approved shall be referred to the archbishops.

(6) Where a draft order is referred to the archbishops under subsection (5) above then-

(a) if it has been approved by the General Synod without any amendment, the archbishops shall make the order;

(b) if it has been approved by the General Synod with amendment, the archbishops may make the order but, in the case of any order which relates to the functions of the Church Commissioners under the Dioceses Measure 1978 or the Pastoral Measure 1983, shall not do so without further consultation as required by subsection (3) above.

(7) An order under subsection (1) above which relates to the functions of the Church Commissioners under the Dioceses Measure 1978 or the Pastoral Measure 1983 shall not come into operation unless and until it has been approved by resolution of each house of Parliament.

(8) The Statutory Instruments Act 1946 shall apply to any order under subsection

(1) above as if it were a statutory instrument and, in the case of an order which does not relate to a function to which subsection 7 above applies, as if this Measure were an Act providing that any such order shall be subject to annulment in pursuance of a resolution of either House of Parliament.

Transfer of
officers

6. – (1) Where a person or body to whom this section applies determines that all or any of the officers of that person or body should be transferred to any body or partnership of the kind mention in subsection (4) below as a common employer and the last mentioned body or partnership agrees to the transfer, the provisions of Schedule 3 to this Measure shall have effect in relation to each officer transferred.

(2) This section applies to the following bodies-

the Archbishop's Council

the Church Commissioners

the Central Board of Finance

the Pensions Board.

(3) This section also applies to such other bodies or persons as the archbishops of Canterbury and York acting jointly may by order determine after consultation with the bodies specified in subsection (2) above.

(4) Where two or more of the bodies or persons to whom this section applies enter into an agreement-

(a) which would be a partnership within the meaning of the Partnership Act 1890 if they were carrying on a business with a view to profit, and

(b) which provides for the employment of officers,

that agreement shall be deemed to be a partnership for the purposes of that Act, notwithstanding that they are not carrying on such a business.

(5) Any partnership agreement of the kind mentioned in subsection (4) above may provide for the admission to the partnership of one or more of the bodies mentioned in subsection (2) above as general partners and of one or more of the bodies or persons to whom this section applies as limited partners.

In this subsection "limited partners" and "general partner" have the same meanings as in the Limited Partnerships Act 1907.

Church Commissioners

Amendment of
Church
Commissioners
Measure 1947

7. – (1) The Church Commissioners Measure 1947 shall have effect subject to the amendments specified in Schedule 4 to this Measure.

(2) The Church Commissioners in office immediately before the date of the coming into force of paragraph 8 of the said Schedule 4, other than those who are to be Church Commissioners ex officio by virtue of that paragraph, shall cease to be such

on that date.

(3) Any rules made by the General Purposes Committee under section 17 of the Church Commissioners Measure 1947 and in force immediately before the coming into force of paragraph 7 of the said Schedule 4 shall continue to have effect as if made by the Board of Governors of the Church Commissioners.

Management of assets

8. The Church Commissioners shall continue to manage their assets for the advancement of any purpose for which they held those assets immediately before the coming into force of this section, and in so doing they shall have particular regard to the requirements of section 67 of the Ecclesiastical Commissioners Act 1840 relating to the making of additional provision for the cure of souls in parishes where such assistance is most required.

General Provisions

Standing Orders of the General Synod

9. – The Standing Orders regulating the procedure of the General Synod shall include the provision –

(a) permitting the Archbishop's Council or the Business Committee of the General Synod to introduce to the General Synod draft legislation proposed to be passed by the General Synod;

(b) affording the General Synod an opportunity at each group of sessions-

(i) to consider any report or budget laid before it in pursuance of section 3 or 4 above,

(ii) to consider such other matters as may be referred to it by the Council, and

(iii) to question representatives of the Council in connection with any such report, budget or other matter.

Committees

10. The General Synod shall, without prejudice to paragraph 10 of Schedule 2 to the Synodical Government Measure 1969, appoint or provide by it Standing Orders for the Appointment of-

(a) a committee to be known as "the appointments Committee of the Church of England", the membership of which shall consist of persons who are members of the General Synod, at least one third being members of the Council;

(b) a committee to be known as "the Business Committee of the General Synod", the membership of which shall consist of persons who are members of the General Synod.

Restriction on elected membership of certain bodies

11. – (1) Where a person is elected by the General Synod or one of its Houses as a member of any body to whom this section applies when he is a member of any other such body, he shall cease to be a member of that other body.

(2) It shall not be open to any person to stand for election as a member of more than one body at the same time.

(3) This section applies to-

the Archbishops' Council,

the Church Commissioners,

The Church of England Pensions Board

The Appointments Committee of the Church of England, and

The Business Committee of the General Synod.

Interpretation

12. – (1) In this Measure, unless the Context otherwise requires-

"the Council" means the Archbishops' Council established by Section 1 above;

"functions" include powers and duties;

"officer" includes servant;

"statutory provision" means any provision contained in an Act or Measure or in an instrument under and Act or Measure;

"year" means the financial year of the Church Commissioners.

(2) References in this measure to the House of Bishops, the House of Clergy or the House of Laity shall be construed as references to the relevant House of the General Synod.

Amendments and repeals

13. – (1) The enactments mentioned in Schedule 5 to this Measure shall have effect subject to the amendments specified in that Schedule.

(2) In the Church Commissioners Measure 1947 the following provisions are hereby repealed-

in section 10, subsections (2) and (3);

in section 13, subsection (1);

section 14;

Schedule II

(3) In the Church of England (Miscellaneous Provisions) Measure 1995 section 6 is hereby repealed.

Extent

14. This Measure shall extend to the whole of the Provinces of Canterbury and York.

Short title and commencement

15. This Measure may be cited as the National Institutions Measure 1998 and shall come into force on such a day as may be appointed by the archbishops of Canterbury and York acting jointly, and different days may be appointed for different provisions.

SCHEDULE 1

THE ARCHBISHOPS' COUNCIL

PART I

CONSTITUTION AND MEMBERSHIP

1. – (1) The Council shall consist of-

(a) the archbishops of Canterbury and York;

(b) the Prolocutors of the Convocations of Canterbury and York;

(c) the chairman and vice-chairman of the House of Laity;

(d) two bishops elected by the House of Bishops from among its members;

(e) two clerks in Holy Orders elected by the House of Clergy from among its members;

(f) two lay persons elected by the House of Laity from among its members;

(g) such persons as may be appointed under sub-paragraph (2) below;

(h) one of the Church Estates Commissioners appointed by the archbishops of Canterbury and York acting jointly.

(2) Subject to sub-paragraph (3) below, the archbishops of Canterbury and York, acting jointly, may appoint not more than six persons as members of the Council.

(3) No appointment under sub-paragraph (2) above shall be made without the approval of the General Synod; and in considering the making of any such appointment (except on the first occasion when the power to appoint is exercised) the archbishops of Canterbury and York shall consult the Council and the Appointments Committee of the Church of England.

2. The archbishops of Canterbury and York shall be joint presidents of the Council.

3. The archbishop of Canterbury shall preside at meetings of the Council unless he determines otherwise, in which case the archbishop of York or one of the other members of the Council appointed after consultation with the archbishops, either generally for the purposes of this paragraph or an particular occasion, shall preside.

4. – (1) Subject to the following provisions of this Schedule, a member of the Council shall hold and vacate office in accordance with the terms of his appointment.

(2) Members of the Council elected under paragraph 1(1)(d), (e) or (f) above or appointed under paragraph 1(2) above shall serve for such number of years, being not less than three and not more than five, as may be determined in each case by the General Synod.

(3) In this paragraph "year" means a period of twelve months.

5. – (1) A member of the Council may, by notice in writing addressed to the archbishop of Canterbury, resign his membership.

(2) Where a member of the Council fails throughout a period of six consecutive months from his last attendance to attend any meeting of the Council he shall be deemed to have resigned his membership unless the archbishop of Canterbury determines that he had reasonable cause for not attending.

6. A member of the Council who ceases to be a member shall be eligible for re-election or re-appointment: Provided that a member elected under paragraph 1(1)(d), (e) or (f) above or appointed under paragraph 1(2) above shall not be eligible for re-election of re-appointment as such if he has served as member for a period amounting in the aggregate to ten years unless an interval of five years has elapsed since he last ceased to be a member.

7. The quorum of the council shall be ten.

PART II

GENERAL PROVISIONS

8. The Council shall be a body corporate, with perpetual succession and a common seal.

9. (1) A member of the Council appointed under paragraph 1 (2) above who is an actual communicant (as defined in rule 54(1) of the Church Representation Rules) shall, if not otherwise a member of the General Synod, be an ex-officio member –

(a) in the case of a bishop, of the House of Bishops,

(b) in the case of any other clerk in Holy Orders, of the House of Clergy, and

(c) in the case of a lay person, of the House of Laity.

(2) A member of the Council appointed under paragraph (2) above who is not an actual communicant (as so defined) shall be entitled to attend a group of sessions of the General Synod and, subject to such restrictions as may be imposed by the Standing Orders of the General Synod, to speak in any debate.

10. The arrangements relating to meetings of the Council shall be such as the Council may determine and, subject to paragraph 7 above, the Council shall have power to regulate its own procedure.

11. The validity of any proceedings of the Council shall not be affected by any vacancy among the members or by any defect in the appointment of any member.

12. The application of the seal of the Council shall be authenticated by the signature of the Secretary-General or of some other person authorised by the Council, either generally or specifically, to act for that purpose.

13. Any document purporting to be a document duly executed under the seal of the Council, or to be signed on behalf of the Council, shall be received in evidence and shall, unless the

contrary is proved, be deemed to be so executed or, as the case may be, signed.

14. – (1) It shall be within the capacity of the Council as a statutory corporation, in so far as its objects permit to do all such things and enter into all such transactions as are incidental or conducive to the discharge of its functions.

(2) Without prejudice to the foregoing, the powers of the Council shall include the power to acquire or dispose of any property and to borrow money.

15. – (1) The Council may appoint such committees as it considers expedient and may delegate any of its functions to a committee.

(2) Persons who are not members of the Council may be appointed to a Committee.

16. The Council shall appoint a chief executive, to be known as "the Secretary-General", and may appoint such other officers as it may determine.

SCHEDULE 2

FUNCTIONS OF CHURCH COMMISSIONERS EXCLUDED FROM SECTION 5

PART I

FUNCTIONS RELATING TO BISHOPS

Ecclesiastical Commissioners Act 1866 (29 & 30 Vict c. 111)

Ecclesiastical Commissioners Measure 1926 (16 & 17 Geo 5 No.4)

Episcopal Endowments and Stipends Measure 1943 (6 & 7 Geo 6 No.2)

Section 58 of the Ecclesiastical Jurisdiction Measure 1963 (1963 No.1)

Church Commissioners (Miscellaneous Provisions) Measure 1975 (1975 No.1)

Diocese in Europe Measure 1980 (1980 No.2)

Bishops (Retirement) Measure 1986 (1986 No.1)

Section 8 of the Ecclesiastical Fees Measure 1986 (1986 No.2)

PART II

FUNCTIONS RELATING TO CATHEDRALS

Cathedrals Measure 1963 (1963 No.2)

Cathedrals Measure (1976 No.1)

Care of Cathedrals (Supplementary Provisions) Measure 1994 (1994 No.2)

SCHEDULE 3

TRANSFER OF OFFICERS

Effect of transfer on contracts of employment etc.

1. – (1) Except where objection is made under subsection (6) below a transfer shall not operate so as to terminate a contract of employment, but ant contract which would otherwise have been terminated by the transfer as if originally made between the transferred officer concerned and the common employer.

(2) Without prejudice to sub-paragraph (1) above, but subject ti sub-paragraphs (3) and (6) below, on the completion of a transfer –

    (a) all transfer body's rights, powers, duties and liabilities under or in connection with any such contract shall be transferred by virtue of this paragraph to the common employer, and

    (b) anything done before the transfer is completed by or in relation to the transferor body in respect of that contract shall be deemed to have been done by or in relation to the common employer.

(3) Any rights, powers, duties and liabilities of the transferor body in respect of the provision of old age, invalidity or survivors; benefits under a pension scheme shall be transferred only to the extent that those benefits relate to a period of employment of the transferred officer after the transfer or to any voluntary contribution to the scheme made by him after the transfer.

(4) Sub-paragraph (2) above shall not transfer or otherwise affect the liability of any person to be prosecuted for, convicted of and sentenced for any offence.

(5) In the case of an officer transferred from the Church Commissioners or the Pensions Board, sub-paragraph (2) above shall not operate to transfer rights and powers in connection with any loan made to that officer.

(6) Sub-paragraphs (1) and (2) above shall not operate to transfer a contract of employment and rights, powers, duties and liabilities under or in connection with it if the employee to whom it relates informs the

transferor body or the common employer that he objects to becoming employed by the common employer.

(7) Where an employee so objects this paragraph shall operate so as to terminate his contract of employment with the transferor body but he shall not be treated, for any purpose, as having been dismissed by that body.

(8) Sub-paragraphs (1) and (6) above are without prejudice to any right of an employee arising apart from this paragraph to terminate his contract of employment without notice if a substantial change is made in his working conditions to his detriment; but no such right shall arise by reason only that, by virtue of this paragraph, the identity if his employer changes unless the employee shows that, in all the circumstances, the change is a significant change and to his detriment.

Effect of transfer on collective agreement

2. Where at the time of the transfer of an officer there exists a collective agreement as defined in the Trade Union and Labour Relations (Consolidation) Act 1992 made by or on behalf of the transferor body with a trade union recognised by that body in respect of that officer, then without prejudice to sections 179 and 180 of that Act (collective agreements presumed to be enforceable in specified circumstances) that agreement, in its application in relation to that officer, shall, after the transfer, have effect as if made by or on behalf of the common employer with that trade union, and accordingly anything done under or in connection with it, in its application as aforesaid by or in relation to the transferor body before the transfer, shall, after the transfer, be deemed to have been done by or in relation to the common employer.

Dismissal of an officer because of transfer

3. (1) Where either before or after transfer, an officer of the transferor body or the common employer is dismissed, that officer shall be treated for the purpose of Part X of the Employment Rights Act 1996 (Unfair Dismissal) as unfairly dismiss if the transfer or a reason connected with it is the reason for the dismissal.

(2) Where an economic, technical or organisational reason entailing changes in the workforce of either the transferor body or the common employer before or after the transfer is the reason or principal reason for dismissing an officer-

(a) sub-paragraph (1) above shall not apply to the dismissal, but

(b) without prejudice to the application of section 98(4) of the said Act of 1996 (test of fair dismissal), the dismissal shall for the purpose of section 98 (1) of that Act (substantial reason for dismissal) be regarded as having been for a substantial reason of a kind such as to justify the dismissal of an officer holding the position which that officer held.

Continuity of employment

4. For the purpose of any enactment any period during which the transferred officer was employed by the transferor body before the transfer shall count as a period of employment with the common employer, and the change of employer shall not break the continuity of the period of employment.

Interpretation

5. In this Schedule-

"common employer" in relation to a transfer means the body to which the transfer is made;

"transfer" means a transfer of employment in pursuance of an agreement such as is mentioned in section 6 above;

"transferor body" in relation to an officer means the person or body by whom the officer was employed immediately before the transfer.

SCHEDULE 4

AMENDMENTS OF CHURCH COMMISSIONERS MEASURE 1947

1. The Church Commissioners Measure 1947 shall be amended as follows.

2. In section 4(2) paragraph (b) shall be omitted.

3. In section 5-

(a) for subsection (1) there shall be substituted-

"(1) The Board shall consist of the Commissioners mentioned in paragraph 1(b) of the Schedule 1 to this Measure.";

(b) in subsection (4)-

(i) for paragraph (a) there shall be substituted-

"(a) to refer for consideration and report any matter within their jurisdiction to the Assets Committee or the Audit Committee, or to any other committee which the Board may appoint for the purpose or which the Board and the Archbishop's Council acting jointly may appoint;";

(ii) in paragraph (b) and (c) the words the General Purposes Committee or" shall be omitted;

(c) after subsection (4) there shall be inserted-

"(4A) Commissioners shall constitute a majority of the members of any committee appointed under subsection (4)(a) above.";

(d) subsection (5) shall be omitted.

4. In section 6-

(a) for subsection (1) there shall be substituted-

"(1) There shall be two committees, one to be known as the Assets Committee and the other as the Audit Committee, which shall be constituted as follows-

(a) the Assets Committee shall compromise the First Church Estates Commissioner, two Commissioners being clerks in Holy Orders (at least one being a Commissioner elected by the House of Clergy of the General Synod) appointed for three years by the Board and not less than four nor more than six lay Commissioners appointed for three years by the archbishop of Canterbury (at least one being a Commissioner elected by the House of Laity of the General Synod) being persons who in his opinion are well qualified to assist in the management of the assets of the Commissioners;

(b) the First Church Estates Commissioner shall be the chairman of the Assets Committee and a deputy chairman shall be elected annually by that committee and shall act as chairman at any meeting at which the chairman is not present;

(c) if a member of the Assets Committee appointed by the Board ceases to have the qualifications by virtue of which he was qualified for his appointment, he shall vacate his appointment;

(d) the Audit Committee shall comprise not less than four nor more than six persons appointed by the Board for three years, of whom at least one shall be an elected Commissioner and at least two shall be persons who are not Commissioners;

(e) the Board, with the agreement of the archbishop of Canterbury, shall appoint a member of the Audit Committee to be the chairman of that committee;

(f) the Church Estates Commissioners, the chairman of the Board and acting chairman of the Board (elected under section 5(2) above to act as chairman, when required during the following period of twelve months) shall not be eligible to be members of the Audit Committee.";

(b) subsection (2) shall be omitted;

(c) after subsection (3A) there shall be inserted-

"(3B) The Audit Committee shall have the following functions-

(a) a duty to review the Commissioners' accounting policies and practices, their annual accounts and any reports made and advice given to the Commissioners by the auditor appointed under section 11(2) below;

(b) a duty to keep under review the effectiveness if of the Commissioners' internal control system;

(c) a duty to consider any representations made to them;

(d) a duty to advise on the appointment of an auditor under section 11(2) below and to discuss with the auditor the conduct of the audit;

(e) a duty to report to those Commissioners who are not members of the Board on any matter relating to the functions and business of the Commissioners which causes the committee grave concern and about which the Board has been unable to satisfy the committee.

(3C) The Commissoners' officers hall supply the Audit Committee with such information in their possession as the Committee may require to enable the Committee to exercise their functions.";

(d) in subsection (4) the words "of the General Purposes Committee or" shall be omitted.

5. In section 7(2) for the words from the beginning of paragraph (c) to "Assets Committee" there shall be substituted the words "the Assets Committee and the Audit Committee".

6. In section 10(1) at the end there shall be inserted the words "or on such other date as the Commissioners may in general meeting determine".

7. In section 17(1) for the words "General Purposes Committee" there shall be substituted the word "Board".

8. In Schedule I-

(a) for paragraph I there shall be substituted-

"1. The Commissioners shall be-

(a) the following office-holders-

the First Lord of the Treasury;

the Lord President of the Council;

the Secretary of State for the Home Department;

the Lord Chancellor;

the Speaker of the House of Commons;

the Secretary of State for the Department for Culture, Media and Sport;

(b) the following other person-

the archbishops of Canterbury and York;

the Church Estates Commissioners;

four bishops elected by the House of bishops of the General Synod from among their number;

two deans or provosts elected by all the deans and provosts;

three other clerks in Holy Orders elected by those members of the House of Clergy of the General Synod who are not deans or provosts;

four lay persons elected by the House of Laity of the General Synod;

nine persons nominated as follows-

(i) three persons by Her Majesty,

(ii) three persons by the archbishops of Canterbury and York acting jointly, and

(iii) three persons by the archbishops of Canterbury and York acting jointly after consultation with the Lord Mayors of the City of London and the City of York, the Vice-Chancellors of the Universities of Oxford and Cambridge and such other persons as appear to the archbishop to be appropriate;

at least one of those nine persons being or having been of Counsel to Her Majesty.";

(b) for paragraph 2 there shall be substituted-

"2. Elected Commissioners shall hold office for five years and shall be elected at such time and in such manner as the General Synod may from time to time determine, but if the Synod alters the time at which they are to be elected the period of office of those Commissioners who are then in office shall be extended or reduced accordingly, as the circumstances require.

Nominated Commissioners shall hold office for such number of years as the person or persons making the nomination may determine.

In this paragraph the expression "year" means a period of twelve months commencing on the first day of April.

Any such Commissioner as is referred to in this paragraph shall be eligible for re-election or re-nomination.";

(c) in paragraph 3-

(i) for the word "appointment" there shall be substituted the word "election";

(ii) for the word "appointed" in both places where it appears there shall be substituted in each case the word "elected";

(d) for paragraph 5 there shall be substituted-

"5. If an elected Commissioner who was qualified for election by virtue of being a bishop, a dean or a provost, a clerk in Holy Orders or a lay person ceases to be so qualified, he shall cease to be a Commissioner.";

(e) for paragraph 5A there shall be substituted-

"5A. – (1) Without prejudice to paragraph 5 above, if a Commissioner elected by members of a House of the General Synod ceases to be a member thereof, then subject to paragraph (2) below, he shall cease to be a Commissioner"

(2) If a Commissioner to whom sub-paragraph (1) above apples ceases to be a member of the General Synod by reason of the dissolution of that Synod he shall not cease to be a Commissioner by virtue of that sub-paragraph; but if he does not stand for re-election to the General Synod or is not re-elected an election to fill his place as a Commissioner shall be held at the first meeting of the new Synod and he shall thereupon cease to be a Commissioner.".

9. In Schedule IV-

(a) in paragraph 1 for the words from "appointment" to the end there shall be substituted the words "election or nomination of any member or, in relation to a committee, in the appointment of any m ember";

(b) in paragraph 2-

(i) for rhe words "an appointed" there shall be substituted the words "an elected";

(ii) for the word "appointed" there shall be substituted the word "elected";

(c) for paragraph 3 there shall be substituted-

"3. Casual vacancies among elected or nominated Commissioners may be filled by the person or body by whom the Commissioner vacating office was elected or nominated. Casual vacancies among appointed members of a committee may be filled by the person or body by whom the member vacating office was appointed.";

(d) in paragraph 4c before the word "appointed" in both places where it appears there shall in each case be inserted the word "elected";

(e) in paragraph 5 the proviso shall be omitted;

(f) in paragraph 7 for the words "General Purposes Committee and the Assets Committee" there shall be substituted the words "Assets Committee and the Audit Committee".

SCHEDULE 5

AMENDMENT OF ENACTMENTS

Diocesan Stipends Funds Measure 1953

1. In the Diocesan Stipends Funds Measure 1953–

(a) in section 4(1) after paragraph (b) there shall be inserted the following paragraphs-

"(ba) participation in any collective investment scheme operated for the purposes of this paragraph by the Commissioners;

(bb) investment in any investments fund or deposit fund constituted under the Church Funds Investment Measure 1958.

(bc) investment under the powers conferred on a trustee by the Trustee Investments Act 1961, as relaxed or extended by any order or regulations made under section 70 or 71 of the Charities Act 1993;";

(b) in section 5(1) after paragraph (aa) there shall be inserted the following paragraph-

"(ab) in paying secondary Class 1 contributions under section 6 of the Social Security Contributions and Benefits Act 1992 in respect of ministers of the Church of England who are not employed under a contract of service; and".

Church Representation Rules

2. In the Synodical Government Measure 1969 in Schedule 3 (Church Representation Rules)-

(a) in rule 40(1) for the words "Standing Committee" there shall be substituted the words "Business Committee of the General Synod";

(b) in rule 42 (1) at the end there shall be inserted-

"(g) the members of the Archbishops' Council who are actual communicants";

(c) in rule 44 for paragraph (8) there shall be substituted the following paragraph-

"(8) An appeal arising out of an election or choice of members of the House of Laity of the General Synod shall, within the period if fourteen days of the appeal being lodged, be referred to the Chairman and Vice-Chairman of that House unless within that period, the appellant withdraws the appeal in writing. Subject to paragraph (9) of this rule, the Chairman and Vice-Chairman acting jointly shall appoint three persons from an appeal panel consisting of the Dean of the Arches and Auditor, the Vicar General of the Province of Canterbury, the Vicar General of the Province of York and twelve members of the House of Laity of the General Synod nominated by the Appointments Committee of the Church of England to consider and decide the appeal.";

(d) in rule 44(9) for the words "Standing Committee" there shall be substituted the words "General Synod";

(e) in rules 54(8)(a) and (c) for the words "Standing Committee" there shall be substituted in each case the words "Business Committee of the General Synod".

Repair of Benefice Buildings Measure 1972

3. In the Repair of Benefice Buildings Measure 1972 in section 31 (1) in the definition of "team vicar's house" the words "as part of the diocesan glebe land of the diocese" shall be omitted.

Endowments and Glebe Measure 1976

4. In the Endowments and Glebe Measure 1976 after section 35 there shall be inserted the following section –

"Moneys arising from investments of the capital moneys in diocesan stipend funds"

35A. – (1) The proceeds of the capital moneys arising from, any sale, exchange or other dealing with investments made by a Diocesan Board of Finance under section 4(1) of the Diocesan Stipends Funds Measure 1953 less the costs, charges and expenses directly attributable to the transaction in question shall be paid by the Board to the Commissioners immediately after the completion of the transaction, and the amount so paid shall be allocated by the Commissioners to the capital account of the diocesan stipends fund of the diocese concerned.

(2) All dividends or other payments in the nature of income received by a Diocesan Board of Finance in respect of the investment of any moneys standing to the credit of the capital account of the diocesan stipends fund of the diocese concerned shall be paid by the Board to the Commissioners at such times and in such manner as the Commissioners may specify, and the sums so paid shall be allocated by the Commissioners to the income account of that fund.

(3) Any question whether any sum paid to the Commissioners under this section should be allocated to the capital account or income account of a diocesan stipends fund shall be conclusively determined by the Commissioners.".

Pastoral Measures 1983

5. In the Pastoral Measures 1983 in section 78(A)2–

(a) after the words "loan to the" there shall be inserted the words "care, insurance";

(b) for the words "a diocesan board of finance" to the end there shall be inserted the words-

"(a) the Commissioners or a diocesan board of finance pending the coming into operation of arrangements under a redundancy scheme;

(b) a diocesan board of finance pending the coming into operation of arrangements under a new amended redundancy scheme;

(c) the Commissioners or a diocesan board of finance pending
the coming into operation of arrangements under a pastoral
scheme to which section 46 or 47 applies.".

Bibliography

Unpublished primary sources

London, The Church Commissioners, 1 Millbank

Board of the Church Commissioners: minute books

London, The Church of England Record Centre, Bermondsey

Administrative Committee: agendas and papers, 1963–, ser. 95076, 95031

Advisory Board for Redundant Churches, 1969–96, ser. 96943

Agendas and papers of the Board of the Church Commissioners, 1948–98, ser. 95083

Assets Committee: agendas and papers, 1964–97, ser. 96699

Assets Committee: minutes

Diocesan Redundant Churches Uses Committee: papers, 1969–97, ser. 96947

Estates and Finance Committee: minutes, 1948–63

Estates and Finance Committee: agendas and papers, 1948–63, ser. 95055

General Purposes Committee: agendas and papers, 1964–97, ser. 96700

General Purposes Committee: minutes, 1963–98

Houses Committee: agendas and documents, 1964–95, ser. 96675

Pastoral Committee: agendas and documents, 1964–97, ser. 95076

Redundant Churches Committee: agendas and documents, 1969–97, ser. 96951

Redundant Churches Fund/Churches Conservation Trust, 1968–90, ser. 96944

Secretary to the Church Commissioners: papers 1948–98, CC/SEC/various.

See Houses Committee: agendas and documents, 1960–4, ser. 96675

London, The Church of England Pensions Board, Church House

Church of England Pensions Board: minute books

London, Lambeth Palace Library

The papers of archbishop Geoffrey Fisher

The papers of archbishop Cosmo Lang

The papers of archbishop Michael Ramsey

The papers of archbishop William Temple

Published primary sources

Annual reports of the Church Commissioners, London 1948–98

The Archbishops' Commission on the Reconstruction of the Ecclesiastical Commissioners and Queen Anne's Bounty, C.A. 440, London 1933

Canons of the Church of England: canons ecclesiastical promulgated by the convocations of Canterbury and York in 1964 and 1969 and by the General Synod of the Church of England from 1970, 6th edn, London 2000

Church acts and measures: being a reprint of the Title Ecclesiastical Law from Halsbury's Statutes of England, 3rd edn, London 1969

The Church Commissioners: a guide for staff, London 1962

Church of England pensions (Fourth report of the House of Commons Social Security Committee), London 1996

The Church's needs and resources, four reports, London, 1965–70

Faith in the city: the report of the archbishop of Canterbury's Commission on Urban Priority areas, London 1991

Hansard, Debates of the House of Commons, London 1948–98

Hansard, Debates of the House of Lords, London 1948–98

Heritage and renewal: the report of the Archbishops' Commission on Cathedrals, London 1994

Minutes of the Ecclesiastical Committee of Parliament, London, 1948–98

The operation of pensions funds: the Church Commissioners and Church of England pensions (Second Report of the House of Commons Social Security Committee), London 1995

Proceedings and reports of the Church Assembly, London 1920–70

Report of the proceedings of the General Synod, London 1970–98

Report of the Commission of Enquiry into Church Property and Revenues, London 1924

Smethurst, A. F., H. R. Wilson and H. Riley, *Acts of the convocations of Canterbury and York (together with certain other resolutions passed since the reform of the convocations in 1921)*, enlarged edn continued to the end of the year 1960, London 1961

Who's Who, London 1947–98

Working as one body: the report of the Archbishops' Commission on the Organisation of the Church of England, London 1995

Secondary sources

Atherton, Ian, Eric Fernie, Christopher Harper-Bill and A. Hassell Smith, *Norwich Cathedral: church, city and diocese, 1096–1996*, London 1996

Aylmer, Gerald and John Tiller, *Hereford Cathedral*, London 2000

Baker Wilbraham, Philip, *The first five years: the story of the Church Commissioners*, London 1953

Best, G. F. A., *Temporal pillars: Queen Anne's Bounty, the Ecclesiastical Commissioners and the Church of England*, Cambridge 1964

Booth, Alan, *The British economy in the twentieth century*, Basingstoke 2001

Briden, Tim and Brian Hanson, *Moore's introduction to English canon law*, 3rd ed, London 1992

Brown, Callum G., *The death of Christian Britain: understanding secularisation, 1800–2000*, London 2001

Burns, Arthur, *The diocesan revival in the Church of England, c. 1800–1870*, Oxford 1999

Carpenter, Edward, *Geoffrey Fisher, archbishop of Canterbury*, Norwich 1991

Carpenter, Humphrey, *Robert Runcie: the reluctant archbishop*, London 1996

Carr-Saunders, A. M., D. Caradog Jones and C. A. Moser, *A survey of social conditions in England and Wales*, Oxford 1958

Chadwick, Owen, *Michael Ramsey: a life*, Oxford 1990

—— *The spirit of the Oxford Movement: Tractarian essays*, Cambridge 1990

Church of England yearbook, London 1947–98

Collinson, P. and N. Ramsay (eds), *A history of Canterbury Cathedral*, Oxford 1995

Cryer, Mary, *A short history of Lambeth Palace*, London 1988

Currie, Robert, Alan Gilbert and Lee Horsley, *Churches and church-goers: patterns of church growth in the British Isles since 1700*, Oxford 1977

Dale, Sir William, *The law of the parish church*, 5th edn, London 1975

Davey, Grace, *Religion in Britain since 1945: believing without belonging*, Oxford 1996 edn

Doe, Norman, *The legal framework of the Church of England: a critical study in a comparative context*, Oxford 1996

Earle, Nick, *What's wrong with the Church of England?*, London 1961

Edwards, David L., *Ian Ramsey, bishop of Durham*, London 1973

Ferris, Paul, *The Church of England*, London 1962

Fisher, Geoffrey, *The archbishop speaks: addresses and speeches by the archbishop of Canterbury, the Most Revd Geoffrey Francis Fisher*, selected by Edward Carpenter, London 1958

Gill, Robin, *The myth of the empty church*, London 1993

Grubb, Kenneth, *Crypts of power*, London 1971

Halsey, A. H., *Change in British society*, 3rd edn, Oxford 1986

___ *Trends in British society since 1900: a guide to the changing social structure of Britain*, London 1972

Hammond, Peter, *Towards a church architecture*, London 1962

Hannah, Leslie, *The rise of the corporate economy*, London 1983

Harris, Ronald, *Memory-soft the air: recollections of life with cabinet, crown and Church*, Edinburgh 1987

Hastings, Adrian, *A history of English Christianity, 1920–1990*, London 2001

Hicks, Stephen, *Around 1 Millbank: a history of the area*, London 1998

Holtby, Robert, *Robert Wright Stopford*, London 1988

Jeremy, David, *Capitalists and Christians: business leaders and the Churches in Britain, 1900–1960*, Oxford 1990

Jones, Emrys, *Town and cities*, Oxford 1966

Lloyd, Roger, *The Church of England in the twentieth century, 1900–1965*, London 1966

Lovell, Terry, *Number One Millbank: the financial downfall of the Church of England*, London 1997

Machin, G. I. T., *The Churches and social issues in the twentieth century*, Oxford 1998

Mayfield, Guy, *The Church of England: its members and its business*, Oxford 1958

____ *Like nothing on earth*, London 1965

Meadows, Peter and Nigel Ramsay (eds), *A history of Ely Cathedral*, Woodbridge 2003

Medhurst, Kenneth N. and George H. Moyser, *Church and politics in a secular age*, Oxford 1988

Mills, Edward D., *The modern Church*, London 1956

Morgan, Devi, *The Church in transition: reform in the Church of England*, London 1970

Morris, Richard, *Churches in the landscape*, London 1989

New, Anthony, *A guide to the cathedrals of Britain*, London 1980

Paul, Leslie, *A church by daylight*, London 1973

____ *The deployment and payment of the clergy*, London 1964

Pawley, Margaret, *Donald Coggan, servant of Christ*, London 1987

Peart-Binns, J. S., *Eric Treacy*, London 1980

____ *Wand of London*, London 1987

Pitt, Valerie, *The Church Commissioners for England* (Prism pamphlet xxxvi, n.d.)

Pounds, N. J. G., *A history of the English parish*, Cambridge 2000

Purcell, William, *Fisher of Lambeth*, London 1969

Rodes Jr, Robert E., *Law and modernization in the Church of England: Charles II to the welfare state*, Notre Dame, Indiana 1991

Rosman, Doreen, *The evolution of the English churches, 1500–2000*, Cambridge 2003

Russell, Anthony, *The clerical profession*, London 1980

Savidge, Alan, *The foundations and early years of Queen Anne's Bounty*, London 1955

Scott, Peter, *Financial institutions and the British property investment market, 1850–1980*, Oxford 1992

Snell, K. D. M. and Paul S. Ell, *Rival Jerusalems: the geography of Victorian religion*, Cambridge 2000

Tatton-Brown, Tim, *The English Cathedral*, London 2002

____ *Lambeth Palace: A history of the archbishops of Canterbury and their houses*, London 1998

Thompson, Kenneth A., *Bureaucracy and church reform: the organizational response of the Church of England to social change, 1800–1965*, Oxford 1970

Warren, Mortimer, *Investment for the common man*, London 1958

Welsby, Paul A., *A history of the Church of England, 1945–80*, Oxford 1984

____ *How the Church of England works*, London 1960

Wilding, Richard, *The care of redundant churches*, London 1990

Yates, Nigel and Paul A. Welsby (eds), *Faith and fabric; a history of Rochester Cathedral, 604–1994*, Woodbridge 1996

Index